CW00549165

PIMLICO

189

GOODBYE DOLLY GRAY

After serving in the British Merchant Navy in the
Second World War, Rayne Kruger qualified as a solicitor
in South Africa. He has also worked as a scriptwriter,
actor, journalist and businessman. After settling in
England he became a full-time writer and is the author
of eight books. He lives in Gloucestershire with his wife,
the cookery expert Prue Leith.

GOODBYE DOLLY GRAY

The Story of the Boer War

———

RAYNE KRUGER

PIMLICO

PIMLICO

An imprint of Random House
20 Vauxhall Bridge Road, London SW1V 2SA

Random House Australia (Pty) Ltd
20 Alfred Street, Milsons Point, Sydney
New South Wales 2061, Australia

Random House New Zealand Ltd
18 Poland Road, Glenfield
Auckland 10, New Zealand

Random House South Africa (Pty) Ltd
PO Box 337, Bergvlei, South Africa

Random House UK Ltd Reg. No. 954009

First published by Cassell & Company Ltd, 1959
Pimlico edition 1996

1 3 5 7 9 10 8 6 4 2

Papers used by Random House UK Limited are natural, recyclable products
made from wood grown in sustainable forests. The manufacturing processes
conform to the environmental regulations of the country of origin

Printed and bound in Great Britain
by Mackays of Chatham PLC

ISBN 0 7126 6285 5

To the Teachers and Companions of
my youth at Jeppe High School,
Johannesburg; and to the memory of
those of them who died in
World War II

AUTHOR'S NOTE

ANYONE writing about South Africa soon has difficulties over nomenclature. Here the difficulty is greater because Dutch words used in the Boer War have a different form in modern Afrikaans. Except for one or two words like *kopje* (hill) which have such a strong Boer War association that to change them seemed a pity, I have followed the modern form. Thus Afrikander becomes Afrikaner (unless part of a title or directly quoted). The word means African but is usually intended to denote Afrikaans-speaking white South Africans, whereas the non-white native of the African continent increasingly calls *himself* an African. Sometimes he is called a Bantu, which seems to me pedagogic and in any event only means men; and the Boer War usage of Kaffir has become offensive. I have therefore taken refuge in Native, which I hope will distress no one, since we are all natives of somewhere or other.

Names of participants and places have been kept to a minimum, which means omissions some readers may deplore, but my object has been to avoid confusing the general reader, who may also find the index useful for identifying names previously mentioned. There is also a glossary at the back of abbreviations and Afrikaans/Dutch words.

I give thanks to many people who have helped me with this book. In South Africa, to a number of friends and relatives, to officials in museums and libraries, and to kindly strangers met on the veld during my tour of the battlefields. I am especially grateful to Mr. J. C. N. Humphreys of Johannesburg, whose wonderful collection of Africana is only matched by the generosity with which he and his family welcome the student of it; to Mr. Terence Spencer and his assistant Mr. D. Shirley of SkyFotos (Pty) Ltd. for many toiling hours spent on invaluable photographic work for me; and to Mrs. De la Rey Morkel, whose hospitality I enjoyed the more for my admiration of her father, 'the old lion of the west'. In England too I am beholden to many friends, to my unspared family, and to library officials. My work and spirit were vastly the better for Lord and Lady Armstrong's unstinted hospitality. Mr. Paul Scott of David Higham Associates, Ltd. is godfather to this book, as Mr. Ronald Gow, who gave me freely of his wit, knowledge and quantities of helpful literature, was the minister at the christening. And it is a pleasure to thank my publishers for their help at all levels.

The following have been good enough to give me permission to quote from copyright works:

Mrs. George Bambridge—the works of Rudyard Kipling, including 'Boots' from *The Five Nations* (Methuen & Co. Ltd.) and other poems from *The Definitive Edition of Rudyard Kipling's Verse* (Hodder & Stoughton Ltd.);

The Public Trustee and The Society of Authors—the works of G. B. Shaw;

The proprietors of *Punch*;

The Director of Publications, H.M. Stationery Office—*Hansard*;

Faber & Faber Ltd. and Curtis Brown Ltd.—Deneys Reitz's *Commando*;

A. P. Watt & Son, J. C. Smuts Estate and Cassell & Co. Ltd.—*J. C. Smuts* by J. C. Smuts, Jnr.

For the illustrations I am indebted to:

Dr. R. S. Schultze of London, who freely gave me access to his unique collection of Biograph films, from which the shot of the Red Cross wagons is taken;

The very helpful officials of the National Film Theatre whose archives supplied the illustration of the Highlanders;

The Pretoria Museum, for the photograph of Kruger in Holland;

The Times History of the War in South Africa, for the pictures of Kitchener, Roberts, Cronje, and De Wet;

The *Illustrated London News*, in which appeared the illustrations of the Uitlanders, Wauchope's Burial, Roberts, British Amazon, French meeting Rhodes, Sword-sharpening, Back from the battlefield, Return of the C.I.V., Grenadier Guards;

And many others.

R.K., 1959

CONTENTS

ix

CONTENTS

ILLUSTRATIONS

MAPS

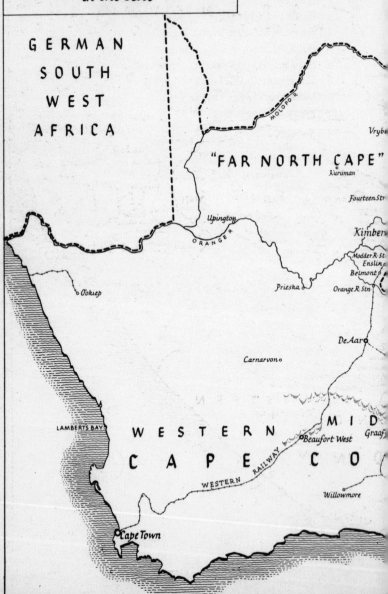

Map of
SOUTH AFRICA
showing Frontiers, Rivers,
Railways and Places mentioned
in the Text

BRITISH

BECHUANA

GERMAN

SOUTH

WEST

AFRICA

MOLOPO R

Vryb

"FAR NORTH CAPE"

Kuruman

Fourteen Str

Upington

ORANGE R

Kimber

Modder R. St
Enslin
Belmont

Priesha

Orange R. Stn

O'okiep

De Aar

Carnarvon

MID

WESTERN

Beaufort West

Graaf

CAPE

CO

WESTERN RAILWAY

LAMBERTS BAY

Willowmore

Cape Town

-MANN-

CHAPTER I

Victoria's England: High Noon

NEWSBOYS cried war through the streets of London and a great age had reached its climax. October 1899: outbreak of the Boer War, imminent turn of the century, end of a reign unparalleled: before those same cockney heralds of history cried peace again a new age would be upon England and the world.

Memories of what it was all like before then are now blurred. The closing decades of the nineteenth century lie remote behind whiskers and murky gaslight. For the Victorian they throbbed with achievement. We have inherited the achievement, without the throb.

On the oceans, wooden-clads had gone; refrigerated ships ferried more and cheaper food; liners were approaching 20,000 tons; a submarine had submerged for six hours; and this very year Parsons invented the turbine. On land, trains with corridor coaches and dining-cars made for Aberdeen from London at sixty-three m.p.h. (touching seventy-four on the way); the motor-car, released three years ago from the Red Flag Act, had arrived to disgust the respectable as a menace to horses and an affront to man; the new low bicycle with pneumatic tyres was used by everyone; there were trams powered by electricity from overhead, and London's first underground was ten years old. In the air, balloon journeys were commonplace and most of the research done to put the first aeroplane flight only four years in the future.

Other communications had even outpaced transport. Our Victorian, reaching his office by lift, could span half the world by telegram, or call the Midlands on the telephone, while the use of wireless at the latest naval manœuvres opened up undreamt-of possibilities. He could write his letters (the better informed for his use of statistics and market research) with a fountain-pen, or have them noted down by Sir Isaac

I

Pitman's shorthand system and typed. Photography was well established and 'moving pictures' flickered in dark and startled rooms, but by far the most potent medium of all had followed the abolition of stamp duty on newspapers—the launching of the popular Press.

Our Victorian could enjoy electric light, central heating, and plumbing recognizably ours. He could marvel at the revolution in medicine wrought by Pasteur's theory of bacteria, and at the vast meaning for tropical countries of proof that mosquitoes were the carriers of malaria. But he little guessed that the discovery of Röntgen Rays was to prove not only significant for medicine but a vital clue to the black magic of the atom.

Stimulating and stimulated by all this technological progress, and secured by England's maritime supremacy over the world's sea-routes, trade and industry had enormously expanded. There had been depressions; but the tendency, gathering speed during the final decade, had been upward: this very year, 1899, saw trade at its highest peak in a quarter of a century. Shipping, spinning, steel and chemicals were booming. Even agriculture, in the doldrums for so long, was reviving on scientific methods and the use of machinery. And if imports exceeded exports, that mysterious phrase 'invisible exports' arrived to allay any fear that the astonishing prosperity of the country was not as real, as exciting, as stupendous as it seemed. It *was* real; it *was* exciting; it *was* stupendous.

Nevertheless, there was great economic inequality in the new democracy created by franchise reform. These were Labour's hurly-burly days—when troops quelled unemployment riots in the mid-eighties; when trade unions, drawing women into their embrace (one-third of all females over ten were in employment) and reaching their first million pounds in annual subscriptions by 1890, moved upon the tide of prosperity from concern over wages to conditions of employment, arriving with employers at methods of arbitration and conciliation, while their thoughts turned to the Promised Land of Socialism hymned by middle-class prophets; when Socialists were disowning any connection with anarchism which filled the respectable with dread of bombs in every unattended parcel; and when Ruskin and William Morris, extolling the rights of working men above suffocating patronage by the wealthy, were succeeded by the Fabians whose apostle George Bernard Shaw declared that landlord, capitalist and burglar were equally

2

dangerous to the community. The Labour Party as a separate Parliamentary force was being born. Our comfortable Victorian, viewing the scene from the capital and incommoded through he had been by strikes that brought out now the dockers, now the police, the postmen, the cabmen, the bus-drivers—who 'won' a seventy-hour six-day week —little realized how soon Labour would storm the ramparts of power that he himself had lately reached. If a brass band blared the fact as it conducted Keir Hardie to Westminster after the 1892 election, our Victorian noted only the vulgarity of the man in wearing a tweed cap.

Yet the ruling classes were not indifferent to the existence of Disraeli's Two Nations. To bridge the gap between rich and poor a reforming spirit built more zealously than caricatures of our Victorian grinding the faces of the poor might suggest. The problem of poverty beat upon the conscience even of those who found nothing wrong in the terribly long hours worked or the wholesale employment of children aged between ten and fifteen. Education, the abolition of child begging, slum clearance (given the impetus of cheaper mass transport away from congested areas), factory inspection, public health, and the acquisition of utilities for the common weal were all the subjects of unprecedented advance.

The achievement was owed to propaganda from sources as diverse as Nonconformist pulpits, the new popular press, novelists like Walter Besant and Mrs. Humphry Ward, and the London School of Economics (1898); to the legislation of successive Governments; to private visionaries; but above all to the growth of local government.

The period saw substantial completion (the London County Council was first elected in 1891) of the municipal system we know today with all its apparatus of counties and boroughs, popular election, and wide powers of administration financed by rates and public borrowings. Too lacking in drama even for our Victorian who was nothing if not earnest, this development yet represents probably the greatest of all Victorian achievements and an essential part of the ethos which produced the Boer War. Whereas in the U.S.A. civic government often degenerated into corruption, in England it became a remarkable instrument of reform and public service, wielded with brisk honesty and attracting some of the best talents of the middle class. The Socialist Manifesto of 1892, rejecting revolution in favour of working within the framework of constitutional government, has ever since spared

England the bloodiness of the barricades: it derived from confidence in the reforming ability of such institutions as local government.

For our late Victorian, however, prosperity seemed the keynote of his time. It was closely connected with the growth of company formation, in step with vastly increased activity on the Stock Exchange, which the prospering middle class provided with a rich new source of funds. The process first asserted itself fully during the late eighties when a boom in brewery and South African gold shares sparked off investment in undertakings to exploit the new inventions, create amalgamations of existing concerns, or convert private firms into public companies. One by-product was an increasing loss of personal contact between owner and worker, merchant and banker, tradesman and shopper. Thus banks were absorbed in combines; the departmental shop like Whiteley's, Lewis's and the rest grew apace; and workers who had intimately known their master never saw a remote board of directors. The impersonal hugeness of modern commerce had begun. In a single year of the nineties, £25 million could be lost by the speculating public through fraudulent promotors, but without checking investment in limited liability companies whose capital, at £1,000 million in 1895, totalled one and a third times more than that of France and Germany together.

In all this expansion of trade, industry and Stock Exchange activity there was one factor very relevant to our story. By the eighties the expanding economy had caused an acute shortage of gold. Gold was not only the everyday currency but was deemed so fundamental to the whole economy of nations that the want of it had moved a top international conference to consider the alternative use of silver. The gold sovereigns and half-sovereigns which our Victorian exchanged for a new issue in 1891 were rubbed smooth by over-use; and the great bank amalgamations resulted largely from the difficulty of individual houses holding a sufficient reserve of bullion. But these had been merely obvious pointers. Whenever trade sagged, or wages lagged, or any other economic ailment appeared, the cause was traced to the shortage of gold. Production—ran the simple thesis—had increased more than there was gold to pay for it. And at that juncture Providence decreed the discovery of gold in quantities dwarfing all that had ever been found in the history of man. Hardly less miraculous, it lay within Britain's sphere of interest.

The find took place in the late eighties in the Transvaal; specifically, in a ridge of high ground many miles long called the Witwatersrand (the 'Rand').

The Transvaal had been bloodlessly annexed to the Crown in 1877. For over a generation before, white people had been trekking from the Cape into the hinterland, giving and taking terrible blows on encountering the Natives migrating or migrated from further north. The whites were British subjects, since the Cape became a British Colony after Napoleon's defeat, but they were of Dutch, German and French descent. The trekkers, mainly frontiersmen, were called Boers ('farmers'); and their kinsmen who stayed, Cape Dutch—both were to be called Afrikaners, distinguishing them from the colonists of British descent at the Cape and elsewhere in S.A.

The chief impulse behind the Great Trek was a desire to get away from British rule. But inter-tribal 'washing of spears' and warfare between Boer and Native resulted in England extending control over the hinterland to safeguard the Cape. In the process a number of Native quasi-states and three other white-dominated territories were created— Natal, as a British colony where Durban had long been a British settlement; the Orange Free State (O.F.S.) as a Boer republic; and the Transvaal, likewise a republic until the annexation.

That annexation was carried out at a moment when the Boer Government set up at Pretoria, having only the revenue of a thinly scattered rural community, was on the verge of bankruptcy (the Post-master-General was taking his salary in stamps) and threatened with tribal restiveness dangerous to the whole sub-continent. Essentially, the British Government saw annexation as a step towards a federation by which alone S.A.'s search for economic stability and settled relations between whites and non-whites might be ended.

To say that the British took over the Transvaal because it was poor and then would not leave it alone because it was rich, is a tempting aphorism which, however, distorts the truth and ignores the sequence of events. But the opening up of the Witwatersrand gold-fields years after the annexation must in any account of late Victorian England be noted as meaning more to her than a direct new source of wealth: for her national economy it seemed to supply ballast which her wonderful inventive and maritime achievements had only made the more necessary—so necessary that ten years were required before she met the bullion needs of other countries and materially increased her own reserves. That these were years which brought her to the fantastic prosperity of 1899 suggests either causation or coincidence. The point is one for the economists; for the historian who does not believe that any particular factors or individuals brought about the Boer War, the only importance of the association between the discovery of gold and England's prosperity is that the Transvaal registered itself in people's minds as a desirable property. In other words it helped create a predisposition to make war if war came about. But it does not of itself explain why war should have come about, since the situation was not that Britain faced deprivation of the products of the gold-fields (the threat that she might be was there but not close), nor that no other reason existed which could with equal force be argued as having caused the war. For example, Russian expansionism cast a long shadow over the Suez Canal, making more dire the threat we shall see arising from within to Britain's control of the Cape, that vital station on her alternative sea-route to the East: no more than the lust for gold can this be said to have caused the war but, again, merely helped create a predisposition. Nothing is more significant than that when war broke out the nation as a whole did not really know what it was all about— and yet entered upon hostilities with enormous ardour. The explanation is that England was guided into war by many currents and many pilots: in short, by the entire epoch of the late nineteenth century, so that the years must be probed a little deeper than the outline given above of scientific and economic developments.

Suppose, then, that our Victorian, hearing the newsboys' shrill overture to battle in October 1899, reflected upon the course of events which had embroiled the most powerful nation on earth with a handful of farmers in remote S.A.

The annexation of the Transvaal in 1877 made a good starting point, but he would have remembered hardly noticing it at the time, in the last years of Disraeli's Conservative premiership. He had no inkling of the fabulous discovery ahead, and the country was but one of the many fragments of Africa for which European Powers were then or later scrambling. There as elsewhere Britain's off-handed, half-hearted, semi-accidental method of empire-making blinded him for a long time to the swelling of his Imperial patrimony. He was in fact given to understand that the Boers approved the annexation, but across the newly

opened telegraph line to S.A. in 1880 one of the first messages spoke
of opposition, led by a certain Mr. Kruger, and in June *The Times*
declared: 'Englishmen will find it difficult to reconcile themselves to
the forcible occupation of a country whose people declare that they
never have been and do not wish to be Her Majesty's subjects.'
That year the Liberals under Gladstone won the general election.
Their victory owed much to his famous Midlothian campaign in which
he appealed for 'righteousness' in foreign affairs as opposed to the
alleged unrighteousness of Disraeli's Government. Yet he did not
immediately undo the Transvaal annexation: he let go so unpressing
and remote a problem to face a storm nearer home, the Irish Question.
The tormented and enigmatic Parnell arose to lead the Irish Party at
Westminster (southern Ireland being still part of the United Kingdom),
while Ireland itself was plunged into violence and boycotting.

In 1881 Lord Beaconsfield died. Latter years had accentuated his
powerful nose at the cost of his withered cheeks. It imposed upon his
features that Jewishness which his policy had expressed, a world-view
opposed to insularity, so that he had striven to make the sea-lanes
secure for his country's trade. Yet if our Victorian was among those
who attended the sale of effects in Dizzy's Mayfair house—though the
influence of William Morris might have made the wall hangings of
brocade, blue embroidered silk and crimson damask not to his taste—
he could scarcely have thought he was attending the last obsequies
of imperialism: already Gladstone had landed himself in a colonial
war.

The war was in South Africa, for the Boers had struck for their
independence. In this, called either the First Boer War or the Boer Insurrection, their operations culminated in the defeat of an inferior
British force at Majuba Hill near the Natal frontier. To the scene
marched another British force whose commander thirsted for revenge.
But since the Boers had now made abundantly clear that they wanted
independence in spite of the assurances given at the annexation, Britain
agreed to a peace.

A very un-Disraelian what's-the-use-of-an-empire sentiment had
after all set in, and Gladstone gave the Transvaal (entitled the South
African Republic or Z.A.R.) independence in everything except,
mainly, the right to make treaties with any country other than its sister
Boer republic of the O.F.S. This quasi-independence was called a

suzerainty. Some British opinion protested that Majuba had been allowed to betray loyalists in S.A. and invite future Boer intransigence, to which *The Times* retorted: 'The fact is, between England and the Transvaal there is no connection whatever.'

Within a few years connection enough was to be created by the discovery of gold. Meanwhile England was preoccupied by more urgent events. Irish Troubles were again to the fore, kept there by the Phoenix Park murders, by terrorists who exploded dynamite in England—even out-guying Fawkes in the House of Commons—and by Gladstone's fruitless appeal to the Pope to moderate the violence of his flock. At the same time Egypt and the Sudan became news.

Egypt's bankruptcy was followed by insurrection against the established Government which appealed for help. Britain, vitally concerned as a leading creditor and part-owner of the Suez Canal, responded: an expedition under Sir Garnet Wolseley quickly restored order. The troops were poised for withdrawal when lobbying by the Anti-Slavery Society, agitated by slavery in the Sudan, made Gladstone hesitate. (The British stayed around to train the Egyptian Army whose cavalry were the care of a certain young Captain Herbert Kitchener.) Then when the Sudanese dervishes under the fanatical Mahdi overwhelmed an Anglo-Egyptian force, General Gordon was sent out with an expedition but no very clear directive. In the result he was butchered at Khartoum, a relief column arrived too late, England erupted in indignation, and the Queen roundly censured her Cabinet.

An officer killed in the relief attempt was eulogized by *The Times* as 'gallant, frank and sweet-natured', and in the phrase is something of the sentimentality underlying the public's growing passion for British prestige, but Gladstone, taking advantage of a war-scare over Russian designs on Afghanistan, quietly withdrew most of the garrisons in danger of Mahdist attention. The presence among the British forces of a contingent voluntarily sent from Australia (though there were Australians at Majuba) adumbrated a new concept of empire unnoticed in the excitement.

Another general election returned the Liberals to power in 1886 after a brief interregnum by the Conservatives under the Marquis of Salisbury, Disraeli's successor. Gladstone now brought forward his Home Rule Bill proposing semi-independence for Ireland. It aroused such furious controversy that the London Season was ruined, since no society hostess dared invite a guest of opposed views. Gladstone's own party split. A substantial group hived off under the label of Liberal Unionists; their outstanding personality was Joseph Chamberlain.

'Joe the Brummagem screw-maker'—the familiar kind of denigration does little to conjure up the remarkable man it scoffs at. Tall, trim, lacking either the whiskers or the belly of the 'typical Victorian', something of a dandy with his monocle and his orchid buttonhole, he is vividly preserved for us in Sargent's portrait: that thrustful face in which coolness and ardour run close-reined conveys the central fact of the nineteenth century—the arrival of the middle class, first beneficiary of all the scientific advance, Stock Exchange activity, trade expansion, and the enlarged democracy created by electoral reform. A *Punch* of 1880 could depict duke and tailor as ex-Etonian both; and the assault of wealth upon power and privilege gathered strength as the century waned. But this is not to say that men of Chamberlain's type had not a strong sympathy with the working class. He defended trade unions against wealthy legislators 'acred up to the eyes and Consolled up to the chin'. Nevertheless, there were more differences between his radical Liberalism and the growing Left than appeared at the time.

He broke with Gladstone because he believed that municipal government and not separation from England was Ireland's remedy. His own fame derived from his municipal work. At eighteen—being a Unitarian he was barred from the universities—he had gone to Birmingham, leaving a long line of prosperous London shoemakers to partner his uncle in the screw industry. Twenty years later he sold out his interest for over £120,000. By then he was mayor of the city. His first interest had been education, and he played some part in the process by which, through elementary schools, technical schools expanded into secondary, provincial universities, local authority scholarships, University Extension and Settlement schemes, the establishment of an Education Board and finally free schooling, the British working man could presently become the most educated in the world.

To obtain power in the city council Chamberlain tightly organized the local Liberals, introducing the revolutionary technique of the caucus into British politics—and politics into local government. Then he set about a great programme of slum clearance, acquisition of gas and water undertakings, establishment of libraries, art galleries, parks, baths. He transformed the city and in eight years more than halved the death rate of fifty-three per thousand. But he had a caustic tongue and radical views, which ranged from charging Disraeli with telling a lie in every speech, through a cry for 'Free Church, Free Schools, Free Land, and Free Labour', to flirting with republicanism. Consequently he had upset the respectable. At his first attempt to be elected for Parliament, on the Gladstone ticket of abolishing income-tax (then threepence in the pound), he failed; but in 1876 he entered Westminster and only four years later took office as Gladstone's President of the Board of Trade. He did so well that by his resignation over the Irish Question he seemed to be denying himself the ultimate certainty of the premiership.

In the midst of such drama over Mr. Gladstone's abortive Bill the full significance of a minor-seeming event was little appreciated. London had staged its first big 'exhibition' only three years before (the Fisheries Exhibition, followed by the Health Exhibition), and now in 1886 a Colonial Exhibition was held. A bewildering range of products for the first time made palpable to the man in the street his possession of an empire greater than the Romans'. Behind the scenes the Colonial Secretary was 'at home' for discussions with colonial representatives who came to London for the occasion.

Gladstone shelved the Home Rule Bill and soon resigned, causing a second general election within seven months. Back came Salisbury to head a Conservative administration. Randolph Churchill was Chancellor of the Exchequer but when he resigned a Liberal Unionist succeeded him, pointing to an alliance between the two parties despite the fact that the leader of one, Chamberlain, had been called by the leader of the other a Sicilian bandit. Among Salisbury's first actions was putting through the Coercion Bill which signalled a policy of ruthless oppression in Ireland. His legislation also included an awesome expansion of the Navy, the issue over which Gladstone had resigned. The object was to make it stronger than the combined fleets of England's only maritime rivals, France and Russia; and here was another cause for national pride, when the building of ten new battleships could be put in hand at a stroke. No threat as yet came from Germany, but the new young Kaiser Wilhelm II was already showing an ambitiousness displeasing to England even if he was Queen Victoria's grandson.

It was during the years of this Tory Government that the Rand goldfields were proclaimed, the great Stock Exchange booms started, prosperity surged forward, and the Transvaal appeared in an altogether different light.

Johannesburg, City of Gold arising overnight in the centre of the Witwatersrand, became the object of an international rush of people and capital. Thus was joined a classic antagonism. The Boers were people of the Book and the rifle. Faith in the former and mastery of the latter had brought them through the Wilderness. Consequently their puritanism, beside which even the rigid *mores* of the most respectable Victorian reeked of ungodliness, was appalled by the rabble of *uitlanders* ('foreigners') who descended on their republic. Worse, the predominating element was British, creating a fifth column in the heart of the republic. Hostility to ungodliness and British alike was combined in no man more fervently than the President of the Republic himself, Paul Johannes Kruger, whose middle name by an irony of ironies graced the Gomorrah thrust up on the veld only thirty miles south of his capital.

'Mr. Kruger' or 'Oom Paul' (the Boers called their elders, with affectionate respect, 'Uncle') from this time began to carve himself deep into the consciousness of Europe. The boy of ten who went on the Great Trek had grown into a monumentally hideous patriarch who sat, squat and square, on the open veranda of his simple Pretoria house drinking coffee, puffing at his meerschaum, and growling out opinions with papal infallibility in rich Bible-ese for the benefit of humble farmer or polished diplomat, to whom alike he freely gave audience. He was democratically elected by his fellow burghers to preside over their Parliament, the Volksraad, yet so formidable was his presence that he wielded a virtual dictatorship. His courage had been proved by prodigious feats in his youth, his piety by the inflexible 'Dopper' creed of extreme Calvinism, his generalship by success in Native wars, his patriotism by leadership of the revolt against the annexation; and though he lacked both formal schooling and experience of government in a modern state, his political acumen presently became as celebrated to our Victorian (for whom it was variously labelled brilliant astuteness, blind bigotry or peasant cunning) as the old man's frock coat, top-hat, hooded eyes and heavy leaden features with their fringe of beard from ear to ear—a portrait avidly seized on for innumerable cartoons, notably Tenniel's series in *Punch*.

His piety and patriotism accorded with the Victorian's own ideals, not to mention his production—through two wives—of sixteen children; and among South Africans an attitude half admiring and half risible found expression in endless stories, mostly apocryphal. An example: hard on the heels of the Johannesburg fortune-seekers arrived various clergy who applied to him for church building-lots; to each he granted two lots, but to the rabbi only one because 'You only use half the Bible'. Persuaded to perform the opening ceremony when the synagogue was subsequently built, he did so 'in the name of our Lord Jesus Christ. Amen.' These are sidelights more colourful than revealing of a character likened to granite and of whom a later summing-up concluded, 'A ruddy-hewn grandeur belongs to his memory, but he was the father of woe.'[1] *

Whatever the truth of that parentage, the prospects of woe were little heeded by an England still aglow over Victoria's Great or Golden Jubilee. Patriotism had tingled with pride at the homage paid by the crowned heads of Europe, amid scenes of lavish pomp, to the most venerated woman in the world. The Liberals, weakened by the defection of the Unionists, made little impact during the life of this Parliament and the Tories set the pace with social legislation. Out on a limb, Chamberlain the Unionist echoed a little of his old radicalism in making the novel proposal of an old age pension, but he was drawing closer to the Tories than to his former colleagues who loathed him as a renegade.

Under Gladstone the Liberals contrived a precarious come-back at the next general election (1892) even though they now had to depend upon the support of the Irish Party and the new parliamentary force of Labour. Gladstone was eighty-three; not far from him on the Government benches sat a child of twenty-nine, a wild Welsh lawyer named David Lloyd George. Fostered by a cobbler, passionate for the abolition of poverty, no lover of the established Church or of the capitalist, he had in each of these points an affinity with Joseph Chamberlain; but in politics, as is sometimes claimed for marriage, it is opposites who often respect each other most.

Gladstone fought his last battle over Home Rule for Ireland. During scenes of intense emotion he got his new Bill through the Commons, but the Lords threw it out. The middle class, after all, had not wrested the ramparts of power from their betters, only come to share them; and

* A list of the sources quoted from will be found on p. 517.

significantly Joseph Chamberlain was not on the side opposed to their lordships.

The hubbub made grumbles of discontent from the Transvaal scarcely audible. The Uitlanders were complaining that Kruger ruled a corrupt oligarchy which ill-used the mining community and denied them a vote in a State they had salvaged from bankruptcy. For his part, Kruger saw them only as a godless threat to his country's independence who must at all costs be kept down if not altogether out. And he was as obstinate in wanting the Boers' independence as the Lords were in denying the Irish theirs.

Wearied after sixty-one years in the House, Gladstone stepped down —to the unconcealed gratification of Her Majesty who took it upon herself to designate Lord Rosebery as her new Prime Minister. Rosebery's victory in the Derby publicized an interest in the Turf hardly becoming, many thought, to the successor of Gladstone. But jockeying was the order of the day within a party divided over leadership. The disruption of Liberalism from within therefore developed apace, while in Parliament the hostility of the Lords reduced it to impotence. On a night in June, 1895, the Government lost a division on the minor subject of cordite reserves for the Army, and Rosebery resigned.

The general election which followed is crucial to our story. From it grew the crisis of England's conscience and the climax to the nineteenth century—which is to say, Boer War II and the makings of World War I.

For the first time Conservatives and Unionists were in formal coalition. The Liberals opposed them with a programme which included Irish Home Rule, abolition of the Lords, and removal of the Church's privileged position in Wales. The electorate gave a resounding verdict:

Conservative-Unionists   411
Liberals, Irish, Labour   259

Not only was the Liberal Party routed but Labour almost extinguished.

The nation's decision has been well described as 'a return to safe ground'.[2] A glance at the England of that year, 1895, will show clearly enough why our Victorian had come, in the midst of increasing prosperity and power, to feel deep unease. In all essentials the description holds good too for the remainder of the century, and makes explicable many otherwise puzzling aspects of the Boer War.

✳   ✳   ✳   ✳

Our Victorian in the fateful year of 1895 found no clearer or more alarming symptom of decay than in the arts. The belief of Walter Pater that life should be lived at an exquisitely sensitive level had first produced a cult whose clean-shaven but long-haired devotees wore velvet and 'lived beautifully', reading poetry or viewing the work of Millais and Leighton with adoration; whereafter it degenerated into advancing the proposition that the development of a colour sense was more important than a sense of right and wrong. This decadence of the nineties was typified by the exotic flavour of Beardsley's *Yellow Book* drawings, the sensuousness of Swinburne's poems, and the jewelled brilliance of Oscar Wilde's prose. If our Victorian was suspicious of this aspect of the 'aesthetic movement' he was uncomfortable before the maundering unhealthiness of the Pre-Raphaelites: the vogue for their curious evocation of a never-never land of medieval, Renaissance and Biblical subjects had survived the death of Rossetti to bring Burne-Jones a recent knighthood. Finally, while our Victorian might put up with the fashion for applying so-called canons of beauty to everything from industrial goods to wall-paper, even to the extent of reacting against the machine-made to worship the hand-made, he deplored the alliance of artist and Socialist which had been perpetuated by Ruskin, Arnold and Morris after the death of Carlyle. Something of the sort seemed to be debasing the theatre. The recent introduction of Ibsen ventilated subjects smacking of indecency, and though this was the work of the non-commercial Independent Theatre our Victorian, happy with Gilbert and Sullivan or with Irving in *The Bells* or *The Corsican Brothers*, or with fashionable old comedies and perhaps even French farces, noted a distressing tendency for the popular theatre to interest itself in moral and social problems since the wild success of *The Second Mrs. Tanqueray*. Now all these developments, which in their various ways were bringing forward the realism of our age and which had already made for increased personal freedom, less rigid conventions and saner ideas on morality, were suddenly given a sinister twist by the trial and conviction of Oscar Wilde on charges of immorality. Our Victorian's worst suspicions seemed justified; and indeed the immense success that same year among aesthete and low-brow alike of Du Maurier's simple tale *Trilby* seemed to indicate that decadence, at least, was in retreat.

Nowhere did the crash of Wilde's fall reverberate more than in

Society where his wit had made him a prince, and where already there had been the flux of changes unwelcome to our Victorian. The ordered atmosphere of complete house moves to London for the Season had been transformed by fast comfortable trains into constant journeys between town and country, ushering in the era of lavish week-end parties. The aristocracy had entered trade. Conversely, millionaires had invaded the upper strata, giving a new importance to hotel and restaurant where the *maître d'hôtel* could smooth over their deficiencies as hosts. Worst change of all was the mania for money-making which had seized the whole of society. Its one aspect, though shocking enough to our solid Victorian, was not new: outright gambling in games like baccarat which had succeeded whist, drew even the Prince of Wales's name into the pit of scandal; and in 1891 a man broke the bank at Monte Carlo to the delight of London's streets, which echoed with celebratory grindings of the barrel-organs. But the other aspect of the mania was new: the decanting of even larger sums into the Stock Exchange. The huge fortunes made, especially by the gold and diamond magnates who set up palaces in Park Lane, spread a fever of speculation.

> Women who had never seen 'the City' went off in hansoms after breakfast to consult their brokers; gilded youths in clubs of an afternoon turned the evening papers at once to the list of Stock Exchange quotations. Rich men with no other passport into society were asked to dinner on the chance that they might have good speculative tips to give. [3]

But in this very year of 1895 society was suddenly unnerved by a collapse of the gold shares' boom. Though Barney Barnato, one of the most colourful of the 'Randlords', averted disaster by sustained buying, our Victorian had a sharp reminder of the follies of speculation.

His belief in hard work and thrift was equally outraged by tendencies at the other end of the social scale. Not grasping that education had outrun provision for the material welfare of the working class, he grumbled at the use of his rates to educate people who then became discontented, went on strike to the detriment of dividends, or gambled and drank on an unprecedented scale. They smoked too, sharing in the new predilection for cigarettes. The habit had been brought back by soldiers returning from Egypt, then spread by the manufacturers' extensive Press advertising of different brands. Modern advertising itself seemed to our Victorian as vicious a novelty, blaring not only from newspapers but from hoardings and illuminated street signs.

What was happening was a vulgarizing process, a loud, brash, bursting process through all classes of society. The coster songs our Victorian remembered from the eighties ('E's orlright when you know 'im, But you've got to know 'im fust') had given way to coon songs, but neither equalled the altogether shocking *Ta-ra-ra-boom-de-ay* introduced a year or two earlier in a swirl of Lottie Collins's red petticoats at the music-hall. The music-hall, indeed, was getting beyond the pale: concern in the eighties over nude paintings at the Royal Academy was now being echoed in the more insalubrious matter of 'Living Pictures' and similar euphemisms for displays on the public boards. The public was agape for sensation. Cody's Wild West Show and Barnum's Greatest Show on Earth were specimens of one kind, the activities of Jack the Ripper of another; but above all, sport now commanded the enthusiasm of the multitude.

By the early eighties, when lawn tennis was at the height of its first popularity (superseded by golf in the nineties), the middle classes already shared the pleasures of sport with the aristocracy. But in the following years as the new cheap Press blossomed on a huge semi-educated readership, as transport facilities improved, and as 'individualism' faded and the new impersonality of industry and commerce increased so that many people felt the need for extraneous enthusiasms, vast crowds of all classes attended the arenas. They went not to play but to watch. There were 'Ranji' and W. G. Grace to delight the summers, while the month-long fogs of winter were relieved by the new professional soccer teams. Swimming and boxing were popular. Horse-racing, already so widely followed in 1886 that jockey Fred Archer's suicide had caused national sorrow, was even more so, and the introduction by Fred Sloan of the 'American seat' was about to modernize racing technique as much as the new journalism had already popularized betting with the 'starting price' idea and the creation of the whole professional fraternity of book-makers.

The sheer desire for spectacle and a heady partisanship are not to be forgotten when much is made of the love of 'sportsmanship', or when it is asked why the prospect of so deadly a game and terrible a spectacle as war did not appal. The strength of national fervour was shown in the year of the momentous general election recalled by our Victorian, when there was the first instance of sport causing strained international relations. At Henley a misunderstanding over the start of a race between American and British crews, and in U.S. waters congestion of the starting line by sightseeing craft at a challenge for the *America*'s Cup, caused a storm of ill-feeling. It temporarily halted the improvement in Anglo-American relations that had followed Britain's sympathetic response to the attempted assassination of President Garfield in 1881 (in which year too the public had been stirred by news of seven-storey buildings going up in New York).

Avidity for spectacle and sport was part of a general restlessness, as if the seams of the age were bursting. Emigration to America and the colonies, though stimulated by unemployment, resulted from a desire to cross boundaries. The family trek to the seaside for holidays was well established, and the Cockney tourist's excursion across-Channel to 'Boulong' a hardy *Punch* annual. But like nothing else the questing mobility of the time was expressed by the cycling craze.

Never before or since has the whole nation taken to a single activity with such united and spontaneous enthusiasm. In 1895 the craze was at its height. Mayfair forsook horses to cycle in Hyde Park or to pedal to Battersea for picnic breakfasts; on Saturdays the masses swarmed out of towns to discover the delights of the countryside. Everything connected with the bicycle industry boomed. If our Victorian regretted the difficulty of maintaining his dignity on a bicycle he could rejoice in a pursuit so happily combining good fun, good business, and—good health.

For exercise and cleanliness now asserted a novel compulsion. The industrial grime and polluted atmosphere of the cities as much as his fear of disease accounted for our Victorian's idolatry of the wash-bowl. He scrubbed himself as zealously as his local authority pushed forward with sewage schemes and public bath-houses; he got himself vaccinated and muzzled his dog; and looking at less fastidious foreigners he could not help feeling as superior in hygiene as in worldly goods. When he went to war, anxiety to keep his complexion unsullied in comparsion with the 'unwashed Boer' was to be a subject of fully reciprocated amusement.

It was in the interests of health that a serious movement began for rational dress, especially women's. 'A woman can no more be trusted with a corset', cried a prominent reformer, 'than a drunkard with a glass of whisky.' But our Victorian in his unease at prevailing trends was more concerned about the state of ladies' heads than their waists. In the eighties, despite efforts to obtain the franchise—a movement then over twenty years old—and the qualifying of the first woman surgeon, the serious intent of the New Woman did not dismay her parents so much as her riding on top of omnibuses, joining in the banjo-playing that strummed the drawing-rooms, and even learning to fence and box. But the nineties had brought worse—a more insistent demand for political, economic, educational and even moral equality. Plays and books after the production of *The Second Mrs. Tanqueray* dwelt on the theme that women often had a Past, that she was not the docile mother-housekeeper-goddess-silly-little-thing he liked to think her. And there in support of the aggressive raucous spirit of the times she brazenly cycled about without a chaperone, talked slang, smoked.

But still, thank goodness, women whom he could respect were in the vast majority, sugaring idealism with sentimentality. Wives, for example, could be inspired by books of instruction like that of the best-selling American Dr. Emma Drake, who wrote that while separate rooms for husband and wife might seem a cold English custom, 'Is not this better than a freedom which degenerates into licence?'[4] And when the numerous products of such rigidly controlled unions grew to the age of awkward questions, frankness was urged: 'The simplest way is to teach them that the egg from which the little downy chicken came is laid by the mamma.' Nor would adolescence find wise counsel lacking: popular books of instruction like *What a Young Man Ought to Know* had chapter-headings which included: Evil thoughts will enter the purest mind—The sin is harbouring them—The helpful influence of a pure-minded woman—Sleeping on feather beds: feathers too heating—No young man can afford to read fiction before twenty-five years of age.

Sigmund Freud was just at this time embarking on his epochal discoveries, but less well known is the theory put forward by Unwin[5] that a society or class observing strict standards of sexual morality is always an expansionist one. The late Victorians paid such regard to those standards, at least outwardly, that a divorce case could ruin the public careers of a Dilke or Parnell and threaten a Gladstone or Lloyd George. Directly bearing on our story, however, is the fact that the sugary idealism in which the average Victorian female was cocooned prevented women from exerting an effective influence on national affairs. It was the reverse and largely the cause of the 'decadence' of Oscar Wilde, the astringency of the Fabians, the militancy of the New Woman. Its components of decorum, service and moral rectitude were firmly bound together by religious faith, but here too the currents of change had been running deep.

The Church (of England) had managed to emerge intact from radical agitation for removal of its privileged position, but it was assailed from without by rational thinkers and from within by ecclesiastical controversy. The first were inspired by scientists like Darwin and Huxley. Agnosticism had enjoyed a dramatic hour in 1881 when the House of Commons rejected a newly elected member who refused to take the oath; when Darwin died in the following year the volume of foreign tributes surprised a public unaware of his stature; and now in 1895 Huxley also died: the great debate between science and religion, so perturbing our Victorian, was practically over—but the Church would never be the same. Its defensiveness was apparent from fierce quibbles over ritual like the burning of incense, which brought parsons imprisonment for popish misdeeds and filled newspaper columns with letters of learned disputation; while in the reforming movement of the time it had little to do, even the Church Army being but a tardy shadow of the Salvation Army, then only recently free of ten years' persecution by street gangs. Dissenters were making headway, gaining entry at last to Oxford and Cambridge and the right to be buried in parish churchyards. On the further fringe of the attack on traditional faith and custom people were advocating cremation (first recorded in 1882), theosophy or spiritualism, and they were talking about hypnotism and mental telepathy.

*   *   *   *

Such was the England that put into power the Conservative-Unionist Coalition. Labour soon said that Liberalism was defunct, because having achieved the new electoral democracy it had become indistinguishable from Toryism: both regarded social reform as something which might be conferred on the worker rather than recognized as his right. But while our modern Welfare State was to wait on this shift of emphasis, the trends and events so far touched on provide sufficient explanation of the Liberal and Labour defeat in the 1895 election. By voting if not for the Conservatives then for their Unionist ally, our respectable Victorian squared his protest against the rate and nature of change with his desire for temperate reform. His rejection of the Liberal proposals to weaken further the Church and the constituted order echoed the cry of conservatism: *What I have I hold.* It applied not merely to the question of Ireland or to any territorial or material possession, or even to values of character, institutions of society, traditional beliefs; but all of these. In sum, the greatness of England.

His pride in that greatness was shared by every section of society, even by those who satirized it. It transcended boastfulness; it entered into no bigger-and-better argument with Americans. It took for granted that England, by her power, wealth and civilization, stood in the vanguard of human progress. And that being so the possession of an empire was not only right, as both the perquisite and prop of greatness, but an obligation laid upon the superior to help the inferior as surely as a Christian must toil to convert the heathen. Economic pressures and opportunities played their part, but man does not live by Marx alone. The vitality, curiosity, and technocratic passions of the time found the American with ample scope within his own huge country. But the British had to go abroad to build bridges, mark out ranches, mine metals, lay down railways, to explore, shape, dream. Thus pioneer, engineer, missionary, trader, idealist who wished to spread the benefits of British civilization, and the out-and-out Jingo who simply got a kick out of all that red on the map, united behind the flag even if they disagreed among themselves. In this mixture of enterprise, aggrandizement, evangelism and trusteeship lay the new imperialism. Some of the events which had increasingly opened the eyes and hearts of Englishmen to their Empire have been sketched on these pages. By 1895 the process was being accelerated by two remarkable men.

To understand the influence of the one, the money-making mania so alarming to our Victorian must be recalled. In such an atmosphere the public's demigods, the pin-up boys of the time, were financial colossi like J. B. Robinson with his gold, Carnegie with his steel ('When Mr. Carnegie rattled his millions in his pockets all England became one rapacious cringe,' gibed Shaw[6]), Rockefeller with his oil, Pierpont Morgan with his railways; above all—Cecil John Rhodes. Both creature and sponsor of the new imperialism, here was a legendary character, the consumptive son of a Hertford parson who had gone to the Kimberley diamond fields with only Greek classics in his pocket and yet created the fabulous De Beers' monopoly. Then he launched the British South Africa Company which under Royal Charter proceeded to place him among the handful of immortals who have given their names to a country. Endlessly he proclaimed his gospel of spreading the Empire further and further across Africa—with, in particular, the whole of the sub-continent from the Zambezi to the Cape federated under the British flag. Society could be a little bored with that voice, breaking into a squeakiness odd for so lumbering a body, but his Chartered Company's romantic work north of the Transvaal and his own magic touch of success fascinated the general public.

The other man who fostered the new imperialism had also recently come to the fore. Rudyard Kipling burst upon England at the age of twenty-four after some years as a journalist in India. He arrived in a momentary gap between two generations of literary giants. Dickens, Thackeray, Browning, Tennyson, George Eliot, Trollope, Charles Reade, Wilkie Collins were gone: Wells, Shaw, Conrad, Bennett, Galsworthy, Wilde, Shaw, Barrie had not yet arrived. There were, it was true, Henry James, Gissing, Thomas Hardy, R. L. Stevenson and Rider Haggard, but none had the effect of Kipling. Becoming famous overnight he sat unattractive and fecund like a spider upon the world and spun extraordinary stuff for half a century. He remained a bestseller all his life despite the reaction of Art for Art's Sake critics against one who eulogized action before words, as if denying the validity of his own art. His influence was felt not only by the general reading public but—surprising to us—the young intellectuals described by H. G. Wells in one of his novels:

> The prevailing force in my undergraduate days was not Socialism but Kiplingism . . . in the middle nineties this spectacled and moustached little figure with its heavy chin and its general effect of vehement gesticulation, its wild shouts of boyish enthusiasm for effective force, its lyric delight in the sounds and colours, in the very odours of empire, its wonderful discovery of machinery and cotton waste and the under officer and the engineer, and 'shop' as a poetic dialect, became almost a national symbol. He got hold of

us wonderfully, he filled us with tinkling and haunting quotations . . . He helped to broaden my geographical sense immensely,
and he provided phrases for just that desire for discipline and
devotion and organized effort the Socialism of our times failed
to express. [7]

He soon became the unofficial poet laureate, accepting no payment
for *The Times*'s publication of his more solemn pronouncements. It
was with his Indian tales and *The Light that Failed* that he, more than
anyone, introduced into the popular mind a belief in the aptitude
and the glory of Englishmen as colonizers. This belief was reinforced
by constant evidence of colonial achievement in restoring peace among
warring peoples, exorcising corruption, instituting sound administration. It turned easily to contemplate further expansion. Thus, a year
or two before, describing the remarkable work of the Cromer régime,
a book entitled *England in Egypt* called for conquest of the Sudan.
Winston Churchill records that it was regarded as 'more than a book.
The words rang like a trumpet-call which rallies the soldiers after the
parapets are stormed, and summons them to complete the victory.' [8]
The author of the book was a certain Alfred Milner.

Against the tide of pride in imperial achievement the broom of
Liberal 'Little Englander' sentiment plied in vain. It failed for another
reason. England was peculiarly vulnerable. She had entered into no
alliance with any major Power. Between the designs of a jealous
France, Russia or Germany and her possessions strung around the globe
only the Navy interposed. Her army was small, there was no National
Service, no conscription. It is a wonder of history how so unmilitarist a
nation had built the greatest empire ever known. But that was in extent,
not strength. Or even—for the greater part—in the supply of wealth:
no profit and loss account has ever been struck, but significantly the
Little Englanders made much of the costliness of empire. Yet in proportion to the envy roused among foreign nations, and the menace that
this envy brought, Britain clung to her possessions. 'What I have . . .'
The attitude derived from considerations of naval strategy and hence of
trade; from the colonial activity of foreign rivals; and most potent
reason of all, from the fact that for England to give up possessions
would appear an abdication of responsibility, a weakness, which would
put her own survival in jeopardy.

Therefore it seemed to our Victorian all the more important that his Government should be stable, conservative, strong. With their internal dissension and uncertainty in imperial matters the Liberals were none of these. The folly of their ways was never clearer to him than in their handing back the Transvaal to the Boers, who attributing Gladstone's action to military defeat and spinelessness were now making life intolerable for British subjects and pitting the reactionary old warrior Paul Kruger against the visionary Cecil Rhodes. Things had clearly to be ordered differently in the future. And they were. A few years later the Minister in charge of Colonies was to say, 'We are all Imperialists now.' It was the prevailing sentiment. In it all the passions and instincts of the majority, of whatever class, came together to oust Liberalism and all but silence Labour. Their high priest, and the Colonial Minister who triumphantly spoke those words, was Joseph Chamberlain.

CHAPTER II

Outbreak of War

ON Sunday, 23 June 1895, the Marquis of Salisbury received the Queen's Commission to form the new Government. The following noon at his London house in Arlington Street he told Chamberlain that he could have any Cabinet post he chose. The public expected him to be Chancellor of the Exchequer or Foreign Secretary. He astonished them by going to the Colonial Office, a minor-seeming department only set up since the Crimean War.

But with Salisbury (Prime Minister and Foreign Secretary), dexterous wary Salisbury who kept himself so aloof that two members of his Cabinet were uncertain whether he knew them, and with Salisbury's urbane and sociable nephew Arthur Balfour (First Lord and Leader of the House of Commons), Chamberlain proceeded to form a triumvirate of power. And it was the man of the middle class who made the pace, emerging as the dominant personality in England's affairs at a time when questions of empire and of foreign affairs were inextricably related: 'With accentuated competition in armaments afloat and ashore as well as in commerce and territorial aims, the age of Weltpolitik was about to begin its majestic and seismic disturbances.'[1] First he gave the Colonial Office a shake-up to the furthest outpost of empire. Staff who had referred to his predecessor as 'Peter Woggy' spoke of him as 'The Master'. Maps forty years old were thrown out; electricity replaced candles; and merit not patronage henceforward governed appointments to an empire which, even excluding separately administered India, the globe in his tall-windowed office showed strewn across one-sixth or 10,000,000 square miles of the earth's surface—eleven territories with internal self-rule, and innumerable other colonies and protectorates directly governed from London.

24

He tackled their affairs with gusto. As soon as he had dealt with one box of papers he rang his table-bell—like his voice, 'well-toned but peremptory'—and jested, 'The machine is ready to take some more.' A subordinate said of him, 'When he screwed his eye-glass you felt you were going to be sifted to the marrow.' But he was kind, delegated authority to others whom he loyally supported, inspired devotion. With his businessman's acumen and political ambition that could be relentless went sudden nervous headaches, bursts of impetuosity and a disconcerting frankness quite inconsistent, like the facts, with the cold Machiavelli who stalks Liberal memory.

He was fifty-nine. His first two wives had died, one producing a future Chancellor of the Exchequer, the other a future Prime Minister. For eleven years of widowerhood he travelled the valley of private sorrow, then in 1887 he married a third time with lasting happiness. His wife, like Kipling's, was American, the daughter of President Cleveland's Secretary of War. The marriage followed his first visit to the U.S.A. and Canada. He returned transformed. From absorption in Birmingham's civic and England's domestic affairs he turned his eyes upon the Empire and America. Unity—even a federation—of the one, alliance between it and the other: those became his dreams.

Hence his choice of the Colonial Office. He set about promoting trade, mutual defence, interdependence between the Colonies and England. He discouraged Canada from commercial union with the U.S.A., encouraged Australia to federate. Tirelessly he preached to the public a gospel not of imperial expansion, as Rhodes did, but of development, for there were colonies totally neglected for hundreds of years. He pressed for advances in tropical medicine, set himself against flogging and the liquor traffic. He agitated for extended telegraph lines throughout the Empire, faster steamships; and new railways filled him with joy.

Thus he attended a dinner in London to celebrate the opening of the Durban–Pretoria railway in S.A.—destined within a few years to carry history itself along its single track. In his speech he spoke of the Empire being hung together by only a thin thread, but one which might be like the thread which carries a powerful electric current: could not the imperial thread carry 'a force of sentiment and sympathy that will yet be a potent factor in the history of the world'?

But in a speech shortly before, he had used a different metaphor:

'We are landlords of a great estate; it is the duty of a landlord to develop his estate.' He never quite recognized that the 'force of sentiment' implied a relationship between equals, which was very different from the relationship between tenant and even the most enlightened landlord. His ambiguity of outlook owed something to the great differences in civilization between different parts of the Empire. Among the earliest questions to come to him was that of the King of Ashanti in West Africa who had broken his treaty obligations; Chamberlain ordered out an expedition which found his Majesty drunk and abject: 'Prempeh, taking off his crown, put his head between Governor Melville's feet.' There your enlightened landlord calls in his bailiffs, deals promptly with a fractious tenant and follows the action with just and honest management. But he is still landlord, still governor, and more advanced parts of the Empire had men as insistent on being their own freeholders as those building the U.S.A. into a new world Power.

This Chamberlain recognized by scrupulously refraining from trying to impose his will on the self-governing colonies. But it was a recognition limited to those who gave allegiance to the Crown, and here his monocle permitted him to see out of only one eye. Just as he saw with ardour the necessity for social reform in England (soon he would press again for old age pensions and improved workmen's compensation), but based on a form of State philanthropy without clipping the wings of capitalism and therefore seeming to the forces of the Left a mere cosseting of the very system they wished to overthrow, so did his vision of enlightened imperial development stop short of abandoning British paramountcy. Once this is understood, a recital of events culminating in the Boer War need be brief.

Chamberlain's utterances and correspondence, especially in connexion with S.A., have been criticized as devoid of ethical content, in direct contrast with Gladstone's plea for 'righteousness' in foreign affairs. But 'British paramountcy' *was* an ethic. It meant: British Paramountcy is Good, its Overthrow is Bad. And this was so for all concerned. To quote Chamberlain again: 'I believe that the British race is the greatest of governing races that the world has ever seen.'

That this claim should have been made when the maintenance of an empire seemed essential to Britain's trade because of tariff, industrial, strategic and prestige reasons, struck the foreigner as a blatant example of British hypocrisy and British arrogance. It struck Chamberlain as divine providence.

To Cecil Rhodes it was a whole religion.

Soon after Chamberlain's assumption of power the two men were in official communication. They had first met at a dinner-party six years before. On that occasion, when the ladies left the table Rhodes in his unsubtle way said to Chamberlain: 'I am told that you do not like me.'

Chamberlain replied: 'I am not aware that I have given anyone the right to tell you that. But if you put it to me, why should I? I only know three things about you. The first is that you are reported to have said that every man has his price. It is not true, and I do not like the man who says it. The second is that you have talked of "eliminating the Imperial factor" in S.A. The third is that you gave £10,000 to Parnell, and that is not exactly a claim on my gratitude.'

Rhodes had in fact given large donations to the other parties as well as the Irish, using them all as he used Press, Society and the general public to advance the British flag in Africa, and with it railway and telegraph lines—the Victorian's supreme bequest to the twentieth century. His reference to the 'Imperial factor' expressed dislike for obstruction by the Colonial Office. The every-man-has-his-price story is unproven. At all events much had happened since this exchange over port. He was now not only head of the mighty De Beers, of a large Rand gold-mining group and of the romantic Charter Company which had created a country bigger than France and Germany combined, but he was also Prime Minister of the Cape Colony. Hence he and Chamberlain were now obliged to deal with each other by virtue of their respective offices. Both were imperialists, both wanted to see a British federation of all Africa south of the Zambezi; and there all affinity between them ended.

The Cape was a self-governing British colony like Natal, but un-like Natal it had a minority of British settlers. Rhodes had therefore only become Premier with the support of the Cape Dutch. Their political aspirations found expression in a party called the Afrikander Bond, headed by the statesman Jan Hofmeyr, who recognized that racial co-operation between British and 'Dutch' was essential to South African progress. To have won this support counted amongst Rhodes's most notable feats; it was sustained by Afrikaner belief in the sincerity of his expressed desire that both sections of the white population would develop in partnership. The Cape Afrikaner was more liberal and cultured than his kinsman in the Transvaal, both because he drew on a longer experience of settled civilization and because British rule tended to encourage racial equality. Towards Native and half-caste, against whom the original founders of the Cape, the Dutch East India Company, had set up no colour bar, a more liberal attitude therefore prevailed than further north. And no great love was felt for Paul Kruger, recognized as needlessly repressive and narrow in his views.

Possessing such political and financial power, Rhodes at forty-two bestrode the height of his fortunes. His vogue in England exceeded that of the eighteenth-century nabobs and the railway kings like Hudson. Yet none of the crowd who attended the Burlington Hotel to pay court to their large crumple-clothed hero realized the implication of his florid features. The workings of his mind have been the subject of perfervid controversy: but those of his heart, which would serve him only a half-dozen years yet, are also important.

He has been charged with using his propaganda for imperial expansion as a cloak for financial manipulation. All the evidence is that on the contrary he neglected his money affairs. For the incalculable play of individual character upon history, it should be recalled why Rhodes never gained control of the Rand gold-mines when, rich with Kimberley diamonds, he was perfectly situated to do so. He did in fact acquire a string of options which would have given him that control, and his representative in Johannesburg urged him to come up and exercise them. But a young man from Oxford called Pickering, as fair and slender as any youth beloved in Rhodes's Greek classics and with whom he had been sharing his simple Kimberley quarters, lay dying. Rhodes refused to leave his bedside.

The doctor in attendance was also a young man, but small-built. Possessed of a magnetic personality, this doctor—son of a Scots lawyer who had left his practice to be an unsuccessful poet—had given up the post of registrar at University College Hospital to follow the dictates of his restless, nihilistic mind. It had brought him to Kimberley, and to the bedside of the dying Pickering and the stricken Rhodes. So had a friendship sprung up between the two, between the believer in dreams and believer in nothing, between builder and gambler: Cecil John Rhodes and Leander Starr Jameson.

Subsequently Rhodes acquired a lesser stake in the gold-fields, from which his critics deduce that he coveted Kruger's Republic. But his interest was broader-based. He was Prime Minister of the Cape and head of the Chartered Company which controlled Rhodesia. Between the two, from west to east, lay Bechuanaland, the O.F.S., the Transvaal, and Natal. Bechuanaland was part British colony and part British protectorate; Natal was a British colony; the O.F.S. was Boer but amenable to federal progress under the British flag. The Transvaal, and only the Transvaal, expressed in the voice of Paul Kruger unshakeable opposition to the idea of a South African federation under the British flag. Rhodes and Kruger were therefore opposed to each other not so much in practical interest, which can always be compromised, as in passion directed at fundamentally conflicting objectives.

Intent above all things on keeping his people free of British domination—and it should be noted that a majority of the Volksraad were even more inflexible than their President—Kruger had three major difficulties to overcome if Rhodes was to be thwarted.

One was the Transvaal's treaty with Britain which gave the British a suzerainty or control over Boer foreign relations, depriving Kruger of the right to make alliances other than with the O.F.S. He nevertheless sent his chief diplomatic adviser, the smooth and genial Hollander Dr. Leyds, to sound Berlin, and himself made a speech at a Pretoria banquet in honour of the Kaiser's birthday wherein he made clear his desire for an understanding with Germany. Rhodes and observers in England saw now a threat to Britain's position in Southern Africa and the raising of issues crucial to international relationships. From this moment starts the trail of gun-powder.

Kruger's second difficulty was the franchise increasingly demanded by the Uitlanders—

who came from the four corners of the earth to build a huge rambling city at Johannesburg where corrugated iron alternated with stucco and marble facings, and to develop there an industry the like of which the world had never seen, in mines which were owned, for the most part, by overseas shareholders, controlled by European managers and miners, and worked by hordes of black barbarian labourers. And in their wake came the cosmopolitan riff-raff that had corrupted Kimberley.[9]

Although the Uitlanders were doing well enough in the way of money-making, they were denied a vote or representation in the Volksraad, while paying far more tax than the burghers. They wanted the vote, moreover, in order to be protected from the Kruger Government's alleged repression and malpractices. These included the grant of monopolies in explosives and coal transport, both vital to the mining industry, and in liquor which debauched the Native workers; also widespread corruption among the Pretoria officials, including numerous Hollanders brought out by Kruger and of whom it was alleged that they, like the monopoly concessionaires, fleeced the community for private gain. But Kruger, seeing the Uitlanders beginning to outnumber his own burghers, would not let them have a vote which might mean the end of his Boer Republic. In the year before Chamberlain came to the Colonial Office, Kruger sought to put the Uitlanders on the same basis of compulsory wartime service as his burghers but without giving them the vote. To still the intensity of feeling this aroused, the British Government's chief official in S.A., the High Commissioner, went to Pretoria and crowds of Uitlanders swathed Kruger's carriage in a Union Jack, an insult he never forgave. He withdrew his demand for war-service, but his love for the Uitlanders had not been increased.

His third difficulty has already been hinted at, the fact that his country was almost surrounded by British territory, which also meant he controlled no outlet to the sea. With Chamberlain's accession to office this encirclement, which rendered him as vulnerable economically as strategically, took on a more sinister aspect because Rhodes moved closer too. Several years before, an expedition under General Sir Charles Warren had cleared Bechuanaland of Boer infiltration. Now Rhodes's first official communication with Chamberlain asked for cession to the Cape of all Bechuanaland. Chamberlain eventually added only part of the territory to the Cape, making the rest a Native protectorate, though he did cede to Rhodes's Chartered Company a strip of it along the Transvaal's western border. This was for the railway then building from Cape Town via Kimberley with the object of reaching Rhodesia and ultimately Cairo.

In the course of the negotiations Rhodes's representative tried to tell Chamberlain something in confidence. Chamberlain refused to listen to confidences. He therefore did not guess at the importance to Rhodes of that strip along the Transvaal's western border, nor did he guess at the import behind the assembling there near the village of Mafeking of about 500 Chartered Company police under none other than Dr. Jameson.

Rhodes had persuaded his friend to help him in his dreams, and his friend, finding the pursuit of dreams as pointless as any other pursuit, had agreed to forsake medicine, thereafter playing a brave and conspicuous part in Rhodesian development, though always with a shrug of the shoulder. His presence now with a force near Mafeking was for the purpose, Rhodes assured Chamberlain, of protecting railway construction from Native interference. Chamberlain was also mollified by the thought it would be useful if trouble broke out in the Transvaal, since British troops in S.A. were few, their garrisons far.

And trouble loomed close, even before the negotiations over Bechuanaland ended. Kruger had given Hollander interests a concession to build a railway between Pretoria and Portuguese East Africa, where it continued to the port of Lourenço Marques on Delagoa Bay. The Cape line that had hitherto served the Rand was therefore presented with a rival. A freight war ensued, and when the Netherlands Railway Company imposed swingeing charges for its section of the Cape within the Transvaal's border, merchants tried transferring goods to ox-wagons at the Vaal. Kruger, intent upon making himself as economically independent of the British as possible by preserving the access which the new line gave him to Europe and the rest of the world, thereupon closed the fords or *drifts*. The Drifts Crisis raised mutterings of war to talk of war. Chamberlain made a peremptory demand for withdrawal of this embargo which violated treaty provisions. The Cape actually agreed to pay half the cost if war ensued, and the O.F.S. was at that moment scarcely less hostile, since its own economic interests were hard hit too. Kruger gave way.

But already he had placed heavy orders for armaments with European firms and planned a fort to command Johannesburg. This provoked the Uitlanders as surely as Chamberlain's strong reaction to the Drifts Crisis emboldened them. Also, they had recently formally petitioned the Volksraad for the grant of the franchise and had been turned down flat. Hot-heads on either side were breathing fire, a member of the Volksraad declaring himself tired of constant threats from the Uitlanders and challenging them to 'Come on and fight! Come on!' This

31

is exactly what the Uitlanders prepared to do. A body of persons called the 'Reformers' plotted rebellion. It was common gossip all over S.A.

Chamberlain soon heard. Believing the overthrow of Kruger a good thing in everybody's interest he hoped that the rebellion would succeed. But he did nothing to foment or aid it: to have done so, especially in secret, in a foreign country enjoying internal sovereignty, would have cost him his career and dragged his country through the mud. The absurdity of the slander is proof of his enemies' rancour. On the other hand the probability of rebellion obliged him to plan ahead. The High Commissioner suggested that if it broke out he, the Commissioner, should at once go to Pretoria and call a constituent assembly elected by every white male adult. If necessary Jameson's force on the border could be placed under direct British authority and used to secure the peace, as it was closer than any of the regular garrisons.

Chamberlain, anxious that British influence should immediately make itself felt, agreed. Otherwise the Germans might get in first. The Kaiser had declared his flat opposition to South African unity between British and Boer States. He had raved about Britain's alleged policy of 'selfishness and bullying', charged her with wanting to make war 'for the sake of a few square miles full of negroes and palm trees' (an unlikely arboreal feature of the Transvaal), and so encouraged Boer aspirations that Britain protested. Had Kruger seen Germany's State papers he would have been disillusioned by a note in the Kaiser's hand: 'We must make capital vigorously out of this affair for eventual naval increases to protect our growing trade.' Wilhelm II was preparing for the vast naval expansion which presaged World War I.

Chamberlain had a further reason for wanting to exert influence if rebellion broke out. The High Commissioner reported that 'nine out of every ten Englishmen in the Transvaal would prefer an anglicized and liberalized Republic to a British Colony,' since they disliked the attitude of Parliament and of philanthropic societies towards colour questions. While the proposed constituent assembly would not be coerced into making the Transvaal a British colony, official influence would be directed to that end. Otherwise Chamberlain, profoundly mistrusting Rhodes, would prefer Kruger's Republic with all its defects: one 'governed by, or for, the capitalists of the Rand would be very much worse,' Chamberlain declared, 'both for British interests in the Transvaal itself and for British influence in South Africa.'

It was on 6 December, 1895 that Chamberlain notified the High Commissioner of his agreement to the proposed mediation. The rebellion was then imminent, a date secretly fixed, and the smuggling of arms and ammunition into Johannesburg going on apace. Then suddenly on 17 December came a bolt from the blue.

That day, to the public's bewilderment and anger a message was delivered to the U.S. Congress by President Cleveland, threatening to arbitrate with force in a dispute between England and Venezuela over the boundary of British Guiana. The U.S.A. and Great Britain teetered on the edge of war. Energetic action by Chamberlain and good sense on both sides averted disaster but not before the ultimatum had widespread consequences. It—

> exposed the complete nakedness of Britain's isolation in the world. The Turkish Sultan was encouraged to kill more Armenians; the German Emperor exhilarated; President Kruger edified before Providence. The Uitlanders were weakened and divided by the possible jeopardy of Britain's own position and by those amongst them whose natural feelings were predominently pro-American or pro-German. The original dream of revolution was ruined by the disappearance of confident impulse.[1]

What confident impulse remained among the Uitlander leaders was soon further sapped by argument about whether the intended rebels would reform the Republican Government or hoist the Union Jack. Other excuses for postponement were found in the presence of so many Boers at Pretoria for Christmas church-services and the gathering of crowds for a big race-meeting in Johannesburg. To all intents and purposes the revolt was fizzling out before it had started.

So matters seemed to stand on New Year's Day 1896, when extraordinary news burst upon Chamberlain and the British public. Dr. Jameson was riding across the Transvaal to give Johannesburg armed support. His action 'entered into the destiny of continents, dynasties and peoples; and had its share in making more history than mankind has yet finished with'.[1]

What had happened was this. Kruger's courtship of Germany had persuaded Rhodes to accede to requests from the Reformers to support them. Acquisition of the Bechuanaland strip and posting Jameson in it had been part of a deliberate plot. Jameson was to ride to Johannesburg the moment rebellion broke out. But the subsequent hesitancy of the Reformers had tried him sorely. On the one hand his force threatened to disperse and on the other the Reformers clearly needed a stimulant. Moreover, his sport was gambling; a bold throw by him had previously resolved a crisis in Rhodesia; and knowing, as Rhodes's doctor, of his heart condition, it may be that he wanted to make possible before too late the realization at last of his friend's dream of a united British South Africa. He resolved to ride in—not as a result of rebellion but to precipitate it.

The Reformers sent to dissuade him; he would not listen. Rhodes telegraphed him not to move; he cut the wire. He also ordered his troopers to cut the other telegraph line, to Pretoria, but they were so drunk that they cut a farm fence instead. Hence the first man to know of the invasion was Kruger. His commandos under General Piet Cronje gathered to surround the filibusters.

From beginning to end Chamberlain utterly repudiated the Raid as an unwarranted act of war. He tried to stop it before it could either succeed or fail, and he urged all British subjects to abstain from giving Jameson aid. Legend, sniffing sulphur wherever Chamberlain's hand alighted, would have him guilty of collusion in the Raid conspiracy. The facts and probabilities are wholly otherwise. For a time his political career was in peril. The public saw Jameson as a Galahad, a Havelock of Lucknow, another John Brown. His name was cheered in the music-halls and the Poet Laureate extolled him in bad verse, while Chamberlain's repudiation was denounced by Jingo newspapers as truckling to Kruger.

Events followed quickly. On Friday, 3 January, the nation heard that Jameson had been surrounded and had surrendered the previous day. It seemed a humiliating blow and next morning the newspapers carried another shock from a different quarter: the Kaiser had sent Kruger a telegram—'I express to you my sincere congratulations that without calling on the aid of friendly powers you . . . have succeeded in . . . defending the independence of the country against attacks from without. WILHELM IR.'

A gale of anti-German feeling swept England. In the ensuing days the war which eventually came in 1914 seemed likely at any moment. The Kaiser talked wildly of making the Transvaal a German protectorate, and of sending German marines to Pretoria. His Chancellor pointed out that embroilment with Britain would leave Germany exposed to Russia and France, and calmed him down. But from this time German naval expansion forged ahead.

The situation would nowhere be the same after the Raid. Kruger handed over the leaders to Britain for trial. They were brought to England and smuggled up the Thames to prevent public demonstrations. Sympathy for them was so great that at the trial the Lord Chief Justice had practically to order the jury to bring in a conviction for unlawfully fitting out a military expedition against a friendly Government, and the accused were sentenced to short terms of imprisonment. In Pretoria the leading Reformers were also brought to trial, sentenced to much longer terms of imprisonment and heavily fined. Here Kruger missed an opportunity, if he wanted any, of gaining British sympathy by an act of magnanimity, and his method of getting the Reformers in his hands had something of Rhodes's lack of scruple.

But feelings on all sides were now too raw for niceties. In England the Opposition, moved on idealistic grounds but also by their dislike of Chamberlain and the opportunity to embarrass the Government, pressed for an inquiry. In the result Chamberlain's name was cleared. Rhodes, masterfully facing his interrogators on a diet of stout and sandwiches, was cleared too, in so far as the Raid had finally taken place without his authority. But his political career lay in ruins.

He had to resign from the Chartered Company and from the Cape Premiership. Worse: the concept of Anglo-Afrikaner partnership in S.A. which had sustained the Cape Bond's support of him crumbled irreparably away. Afrikaners henceforward identified the British Government and people with the Raid, viewing it as a bungled attempt to 'jump' the Transvaal which would inevitably be repeated in spite of official declarations that Britain had no designs on the internal independence of the Republic. All British concern for the Uitlanders would therefore be viewed as a cloak for aggressive intentions. The Raid injected into race relations more poison than the past sixty years have been able to eliminate, especially as the Boer has an Irishman's memory.

The immediate practical effect was that Kruger acquired massive support among the Cape Dutch, and the O.F.S. drew closer to him too. Not simply Transvaal independence but a Boer hegemony over the

whole of S.A. became, though as yet dimly, a dream to set beside
Rhodes's. A twenty-six-year-old Cape Dutch lawyer, who had returned
from a brilliant career at Cambridge and recently taken up politics on
the side of the Rhodes–Bond alliance, has left an account typical of the
way the Raid worked upon Afrikaner minds.

> How shall I describe the sensations with which I received the news
> on New Year's Day of 1896 of that fatal and perfidious venture?
> ... It became so clear to me that the British connexion was harmful
> to S.A.'s best interests that I feared my future position as a Cape
> politician would be a false one. I therefore left the old Colony for
> good. . . .[11]

The writer, by name Jan Smuts, migrated to the Transvaal and there
presently became Paul Kruger's State Attorney. He was to be heard of.

*   *   *   *

Having repudiated the Raid, Chamberlain braced Salisbury to make
a demonstration of naval strength and otherwise show a bold front to
Germany. He urged on the High Commissioner in S.A. to put firmly
to Kruger that the Raid was but a symptom of trouble which could only
be removed by some redress of Uitlander grievances, and that no
foreign interference in S.A. would be tolerated; characteristically, he
suggested municipal government for Johannesburg. All these moves,
followed by his vindication at the inquiry and two speeches in the
House of Commons, full of fire and unwonted emotion, gave him
new stature in public eyes. He emerged from a critical test with greater
sway over national fortunes than before.

One of his Westminster speeches, made when the atmosphere was
still heavy with crisis some months after the Raid, had the following
passage:

> A war in S.A. would be one of the most serious wars that could
> possibly be waged. It would be in the nature of a civil war. It
> would be a long war, a bitter war, and a costly war . . . it would
> leave behind it the embers of a strife which I believe generations
> would hardly be long enough to extinguish ... to go to war with
> President Kruger in order to force upon him reforms in the in-

ternal affairs of his State . . . would have been a course of action as immoral as it would nave been unwise.[12]

In the same speech Chamberlain generously pleaded for Rhodes, on the ground that his past services to the Empire should not be forgotten. But Rhodes was in eclipse. It is true that he went unarmed to quell a Matabele rising in Rhodesia, thereby making a gesture strangely close to self-atonement; that he recovered his position in the Chartered Company; and that he re-entered Cape politics. But his place as the chief antagonist to Paul Kruger in S.A. was taken within eighteen months of the Raid by a new man—one who had neither pioneered nor suffered nor rejoiced in S.A. Sir Alfred Milner was the last, most ill-starred entrant to the arena.

Despite Chamberlain's prophetic insight into what war would mean, events during those eighteen months prior to Milner's appointment served only to worsen ill-feeling. Immediately after the Raid he hoped for a visit from Kruger. Instead, there was a prolonged 'war of dispatches'. Two Conventions governed the relationship between England and the Transvaal: the latter (Pretoria, 1884) scrubbed all the articles in the former (London, 1881) but said nothing about their preamble which gave England control over the Transvaal's external affairs. The Boers claimed that this suzerainty, which limited their independence, either no longer existed or should be removed if it did. The British, their eyes fixed on Germany, demurred. With relentless gravity the lawyers on either side split hairs and infinitives. But all the time action threatened to overtake argument.

Before the end of 1896 Chamberlain was telling the Cabinet that the Boers had accumulated 45,000 rifles, 30 million rounds of ammunition for them, and 76 assorted guns. He wanted to send out a reinforcement of 10,000 troops as a precaution. The War Office said it could not even scratch up 5,000, and the matter lapsed. Not for long.

In the spring of the following year, mutual distrust precipitated another crisis. Its causes were various. Disputing the suzerainty Kruger had entered into extradition treaties without British approval. Believing the Uitlanders bent on more mischief he passed laws restricting liberty of movement and speech. For defence, as he claimed, and offence, as the British feared, he entered into an alliance with the O.F.S. He began building forts.

Chamberlain protested against the breaches of suzerainty and the anti-Uitlander laws. His protest was backed by a naval squadron sent to Delagoa Bay and a regiment with two batteries sent to reinforce the small S.A. garrisons. Kruger moderated his attitude; the crisis passed. Boer sentiment saw in his attitude a yielding to British bullying for the sake of peace. British sentiment feared that he might only be biding his time.

Against this background came the appointment of Sir Alfred Milner as High Commissioner in S.A. He had emerged from Balliol as, in the words of one authority, 'the finest flower of culture that had been reared in the University of that generation'.[13] After brilliant administrative work in Egypt he had become Chairman of the Inland Revenue in England. This, with his education in Germany, makes the appellation of 'Prussian tax-collector' more tempting than just. Yet no ruthless tax-collector has ever left his Government with fewer bad debts or more bad blood.

However, our story is a true tragedy and therefore needs no villains. It needs only men whose ideals and actions give us the luxury of passing superior judgements at a safe distance.

The public welcomed Milner's appointment. Such a cool and clever man would soon make the troublesome Kruger see reason—secure the Uitlanders their just rights and keep the Germans away. At a banquet in his honour at the Café Monaco one Saturday evening in March 1897, the warm tributes paid him by many different public men expressed the concern everyone felt for an end to the troubles. But the most significant remark was Chamberlain's: the overwhelming necessity in S.A., he said, was that British paramountcy had to be maintained.

With Kruger moderating his attitude so that the latest crisis presently passed off, and with Milner taking up his office as proconsul, South African affairs slid out of public sight for upwards of a year.

The nation turned to the summer joy of saluting Queen Victoria on the Diamond Jubilee of her reign. The Golden Jubilee had been called the Great; this was the Greater. 'It is not easy, perhaps it is not possible, for living recollection to suggest even faintly to a later age what depth of reverential emotion, what breadth of political vision entered into those days of changing pageantry.'[1] Although as before the whole civilized world paid tribute to its most honoured woman, this time the accent was on Empire. Had not Victoria's sixty years' reign seen the emergence of an even bigger empire than that lost by her grandfather?

To the Jubilee came all the premiers of the self-governing colonies. They were present for the military parades and the nightly illuminations, the touching service of thanksgiving for which the old Queen stayed in her carriage at the steps of St Paul's, for the constant singing of *Rule Britannia* and the fantastic display of naval strength at Portsmouth which made the song no hollow boast. On this high noon of the Victorian Age when England's power and plenitude dazzled all beholders, *The Times* published Kipling's *Recessional*, sounding its note of warning against vainglory. But the raucous bursting energy of the multitude was not to be gainsaid. Not Kipling but Chamberlain with his confidence in the imperial future was therefore the chief minister to that hour. Tirelessly he urged on the colonial premiers the vision of an empire so closely knit in trade, defence and sentiment as to constitute the most vital force for peace and civilization the world had ever known.

Ironically, and as though to pronounce upon the wisdom of Kipling's *Recessional*, the aftermath of the Jubilee was filled with danger for England. A nation not called on to fight for her life for nearly a century seemed unlikely to enjoy such immunity in the course of the two years which separate the Jubilee from the outbreak of the Boer War.

Germany's naval expansion, now well under way, expressed a spirit epitomized by the Kaiser's charge to his brother, commanding a squadron of warships, to go as 'the mailed fist' of German authority and, on the pretext of the murder of two missionaries, seize a Chinese port valuable for strategic and commercial purposes. Russia thereupon exacted Port Arthur from China and increased influence over the whole of Manchuria. Japan, closely linked to Britain, with whose help she was about to emerge as a modern Power, watched these moves with alarm and built up armaments which were presently to begin the ruination of Tsardom. For Britain the Russo-German action threatened a partitioning of China where she had a preponderant commercial interest, and before long Germany sought to expand in the South Seas, to the dismay of Australia and the U.S.A. At the same time, French foreign policy become revitalized by a Gallic Rhodes–Chamberlain in the person of M. Hanotaux, dreaming of the Quai d'Orsay ruling an African empire from the Atlantic to the Red Sea and from the Mediterranean to the Congo. Consequent vigorous French penetration jeopardized British interests in Nigeria, and native levies confronted each other under the banners of their rival white captains. Near the opposite coast of Africa events were equally ominous and even more dramatic. The brave and famous Marchand carried the tricolour from the Congo to the White Nile and hoisted it over the village of Fashoda in the Sudan, which the French therefore claimed by the simple law of possession. Now eighteen months before, the Jameson Raid had distracted attention from the British Government's decision to send an Anglo-Egyptian expedition to wrest the Sudan from dervish barbarism: the decision was prompted on the one hand by the start of Marchand's journey, and on the other by a request from the Italian Government for a diversion because Italian territory on the edge of the Sudan was threatened by dervishes after the Italian defeat by Abyssinia at Adowa. The Anglo-Egyptian Army had therefore been on the march. Commanded by Kitchener, now risen to Sirdar, its successive victories culminated in the triumph at Omdurman. Having avenged Gordon, Kitchener continued southwards to Fashoda where Marchand defiantly awaited him. This explosive situation was not the better for a steady deterioration in Anglo-French relations because of the Dreyfus affair. England's partisanship even embraced Dreyfus's imprisoned defender Emile Zola as a martyr, in spite of his writing novels no decent Englishman would permit in his house.

Thus for two years after the Greater Jubilee the country lurched from crisis to crisis with Germany, Russia and France. There were lesser though agitating troubles, ranging from more Turkish atrocities or Belgian misdeeds in the Congo rubber plantations, to Anglo-Indian expeditions on the North-West Frontier; but it was the big crises which held the constant risk of war. It was averted—deferred—by a mixture of firmness and compromise. Chamberlain was the chief negotiator, intent on preserving the Empire by preventing either a hostile coalition or a war which would invite flank attack by an uncommitted rival. A makeshift precarious peace was maintained as the Powers exchanged territories like small boys swopping stamps. And as Cleveland's outburst in the Venezuelan affair showed that Jingoism was not an English monopoly, so now the U.S.A. shared the imperialist impulse of the European Powers. She entered world politics through her interest in Samoa and her annexation of Hawaii and Manila after defeating Spain in defence of the Cuban uprising.* By refusing to join in European hostility to the U.S.A., England at Chamberlain's instigation embarked on a course of Anglo-American friendship which has held fair to this day.

These tangled and perilous events of 1897-9 bore directly or indirectly on the S.A. situation. Two aspects should be noted in particular.

The first is the importance which nations attached to upholding their prestige by the assertion of rights wherever rights were believed to exist, and by never relinquishing even the shadow of a claim without the substance of compensation. This must be remembered when Chamberlain's policy of British paramountcy in S.A. is impeached. An identical outlook animated the political leaders of every country, including the Transvaal where Kruger was determined on Boer paramountcy. 'Paramountcy' in some form or another was everywhere equated with 'survival'. In England the importance of prestige in the darkening international situation raised Kitchener to a national hero because of his decisive victories in the Sudan. He appeared as a new kind of warrior, one who set about his task with marvellous organizational efficiency. His victories served, not least, as a powerful impulse to Jingo bellicosity. At the same time—and this is the other notable aspect of the international situation—war in S.A. was not anything that situation made obvious, easy or desirable for Chamberlain. Therefore he sent Milner out, and constantly reminded him, to be firm and patient, not to provoke war. But firm and patient for British paramountcy.

*   *   *   *

For many months after his arrival in May 1898, Sir Alfred Milner observed the letter and spirit of his brief. He learned Dutch to read the Afrikaner newspapers and worked zealously on every question relating to the Queen's interest in all the vast lands south of the Zambezi. He discovered the depth of Afrikaner distrust left by the Jameson Raid, and the equally deep feeling among British South Africans who considered that the 'surrender' after Majuba, Kruger's exploitation of the

---

* It was at this juncture that Kipling addressed his celebrated sermon to the U.S.A. bidding her take up 'the White Man's burden' for the sole reward of doing her duty, since nothing else would come of colonialism except the 'blame of those ye better' and the 'hate of those ye guard'. He sent a copy to his friend Theodore Roosevelt, who privately described it as 'rather poor poetry, but good sense from the expansionist standpoint'.

Jameson Raid, and the continuing repression of the Uitlanders reflected a betrayal of them by their mother country, exposing them to the derision of Afrikaner people and Press. But he hoped that this racial ill-feeling, so obviously suicidal for white S.A., would disappear with a solution to the Transvaal problem. That solution he saw in hopeful prospect, for moderate and progressive voices were being raised among another generation of Transvaal Boers—and Kruger's term of office was expiring.

The presidential election which duly took place is therefore of the same importance to this story as the 1895 general election which had brought Salisbury and Chamberlain to power; both were expressive of prevailing national mood and outlook.

In the previous presidential election Paul Kruger had won the narrowest of majorities over the moderate General Joubert. In fact there were persistent stories that only corruption among pro-Kruger electoral officials saw Kruger home, General Joubert himself remarking that 'the whole administration is corrupt, and I can tell you, whatever is done, justice will not be done.' [14] Since then five years had passed. A great many self-seeking Hollander officials with whom Kruger had surrounded himself were gone: he had finer men like State Secretary Reitz and young State Attorney Smuts around him, while restraining voices like that of the Transvaal's Chief Justice and the influential moderate Schalk Burger raised hopes that this time the winds of world progress would blow sufficiently hard on the old régime to topple it. But this opinion overlooked how for the Boers 'progress', 'British', and 'wickedness' had become synonymous, how the Jameson Raid had raised an unlayable ghost, and how Kruger in his Joshua-like manifestation of defender and avenger could make an irresistible demand upon the emotion of his people. The outcome, announced in February 1898, was that Oom Paul polled more than twice the combined votes received by his rival candidates, Schalk Burger and General Joubert (who became Vice-President and Commandant-General of the Transvaal respectively).

Thus at this critical time both Boer and British Governments held the same philosophy of the sacredness of national aspiration, and the issue was simply whether they were to insist on it being mutually exclusive. In May Gladstone died. For two days the nation attended his lying in state at Westminster Hall; the Prince of Wales helped carry the coffin to its interment in the Abbey; and many of those who watched could not but wonder if they witnessed the burial of Liberalism itself. Torn by rivalries for leadership, the party had made no recovery since its 1895 defeat. On the contrary, the Transvaal Question tore it further, for against the Little Englander group another believed in imperialism as a duty to the weak or backward; while some were sympathetic towards a small republic standing up to a great empire, others disliked a system which imposed taxes without representation; and while few were not fully Victorian in their dislike of any government thought authoritarian and corrupt, fewer still did not detest Chamberlain. Such disagreement over leaders and policies left them almost as powerless as Labour. And as we have seen, generally neither Church nor women exerted any constructive or far-seeing influence upon affairs.

Kruger's election victory enabled him to be even freer of the embarrassment of opposition. He sacked the Chief Justice, who had tried to stop him overriding the constitution, and growled at the judges, 'if you . . . set aside a decree of the Volksraad, then you adopt this right of criticism from the Devil.' He ignored the report of a commission headed by Schalk Burger which had found adversely on the dynamite concession granted by one intent on keeping all potential munitions away from Johannesburg control. He made clear that he intended not to lessen his despotism or his hostility to the Uitlanders.

Milner's attitude changed abruptly. He saw now only the prospect of diminishing British prestige and a growing Afrikaner alliance. He saw Kruger as a humbug using his simple farmers' reverence for the Bible to gull them into opposing the most civilized race on earth. He saw him as immoral in despising the Uitlanders while taking their gold in order to maintain himself in power; to permit individuals to make corrupt gains; to allow favouritism for his *volk* that in matters like education outweighed considerations of just government; and above all to pile up armaments at the rate of three-quarters of a million pounds per annum, that the Uitlanders themselves might be kept in permanent subjection. He believed that to desert the Uitlanders was inconsistent with Britain's prestige or duty. It smote him to the quick not only that Kruger should deny the British Uitlanders the equality which the British accorded the Cape Dutch, but that the Cape Dutch should sympathize with Kruger and make anti-British propaganda in their newspapers. Soon he gave vent to his indignation in public, using the language of a scolding schoolmaster. He thereby placed himself squarely on the British side against the Afrikaner.

He did not care. His mind was made up. He wrote bluntly to Chamberlain: *There is no way out . . . except reform in the Transvaal or war.* Reform was unlikely while Kruger lived. Therefore—*I should be inclined to work up to a crisis . . . by steadily and inflexibly pressing for the redress of substantial wrongs.* He had no illusions about Kruger's equal determination: *It means that we shall have to fight.*

Chamberlain, full enough of the international troubles previously described, read this private message with alarm. His reply was the final word of wisdom in the whole tragedy: 'The mis-government in the Transvaal will in the long run produce opposition within its borders, and when the present rule of President Kruger comes to an end, as it must do before many years are over, we might confidently look for an improvement in the situation.'

Milner strained at the leash. He was out of patience with democracy. The despotism of a Kruger was precisely what he wished for himself that he might clear the whole matter up by a few brisk strokes of his brilliant administrative pen. Overworked and nerve-strung he applied for leave in order to see Chamberlain personally. He could not go at once because the Cape Ministry patched together after the fall of Rhodes crumbled and itself fell. A general election followed, proving to be one more fatal ingredient in the melting-pot. Risking a Bond victory Milner disregarded Rhodes's suggestions of manipulation, and scrupulously observed the rules. The Bond did win, though by a bare majority, and a Ministry was formed headed by W. P. Schreiner. A Cambridge-trained barrister of forty-one, Schreiner was the son of a German pastor and an Englishwoman; his wife was a sister of Reitz, the Transvaal's State Secretary, and his own sister Olive had written the best-selling *The Story of an African Farm*.

Although his Ministry delicately avoided hostility towards Britain it was deeply sympathetic towards Kruger, and Milner realized that in a war the whole-hearted support of the Cape was unlikely; given time, it might even be persuaded to link up with Kruger. He therefore saw the threat to British paramountcy as greater than ever. Convinced that there had to be a show-down, he sailed for England.

But *tête-à-tête* Chamberlain was no more forthcoming. He refused to precipitate a crisis. Milner must be patient.

Milner went back on board ship with unchanged views, but he confided in a letter on 31 January that it is no use trying to force them upon others at this stage. 'If I can advance matters by my own actions . . . I believe that I shall have support when the time comes.'

Matters, though Milner did not realize it, were already being fatally advanced.

One night just before Christmas 1898, in a Johannesburg apartment block called Florrie's Buildings, four policemen had illegally broken down the door of Tom the boiler-maker who was suspected of assault. The man came at them; he brought his stick down on the head of the leading constable, a Boer named Jones whose father was said to have been one of Queen Victoria's coachmen; and Jones shot Tom the boiler-maker dead.

He was later acquitted of manslaughter by a Boer jury, and a Boer judge commended the verdict. A widow and child were left destitute. But as when a shot rang out at Sarajevo fifteen years later the individuals concerned were of little account beside the enormity of the consequences.

The Uitlanders loathed the police (called 'Zarps' from the initial letters of their Dutch title) who were tough young Boers armed with loaded pistols and an attitude which made them seem 'like a foreign guard amidst a subject population'. Such was the intensity of indignation now evoked that organized Uitlander opinion, stifled by the Jameson Raid, burst out anew in spite of restrictions on speech and meeting. In an increasingly bitter atmosphere of antagonism on both sides, a petition pleading for help was got up and addressed this time not to the Volksraad but to—the Queen of England. In sober language it set out the grievances of a community who formed a majority of the country's population and paid five-sixths of its taxes yet were denied any voice whatever in its government.

The petition reached England in mid-April 1899, when Chamberlain had scarcely finished emphatically telling the House of Commons that no new case existed for intervention in the Transvaal. Now the petition was deliberately brought forward by the Uitlanders to provide just such a new case. Not that its contents were new; and in asking the Queen to help them get the franchise they were asking her to help them divest themselves of allegiance to her. But the fact of an appeal direct to her was new; and the 'ordinary obligations of a civilized Power to protect

its subjects in a foreign country'—this from a Chamberlain dispatch—
were less doubtful in international law then than now, raising vital
issues of prestige and influence.

The petition had either to be accepted or rejected. Rejection might
be construed as impotence which would everywhere be noted to
England's prejudice and her empire's peril. Accepted, and she was
committed to the prospect of war—for though firmness had twice
sufficed to make Kruger climb down, Chamberlain recognized that
firmness on the franchise question, which involved no treaty provisions
and which Kruger regarded as fundamental to the maintenance of
internal independence, might this time lead to war.

His painstaking biographer gives no hint that the dilemma cost him
any anguish. And his critics may say that his tactics of patience and firmness enjoined on Milner were anyway a mere euphemism for, 'I don't
want to fight, but by Jingo if I do . . .' But this is to give an emotional
slant to a maxim questioned by nobody from the President of the
U.S.A. to the President of the Transvaal—Clausewitz's 'War is a continuation of policy by other means'. The legitimacy of that 'other
means' was not in question; when to resort to it was what bothered.

In watching Chamberlain approach that *when*, no study in villainy
is required—but in the character of the whole epoch, with its pressures
and principles this outline has shown at work. They had brought
Chamberlain to office and they bore him along at a pace now suddenly
made faster by the cumulative effect of Milner's urgings and the direct
appeal to his impetuous nature by his countrymen in the Transvaal.

Nevertheless he moved warily, to be sure that if the transition from
peace to war had to be made Kruger should clearly be shown in the
wrong over an issue regarded as vital by a majority of the British public.
In other words they would have to appreciate that the crux was not the
Uitlander question but that of British paramountcy. Again his 'political
astuteness' has cast an odium upon him. But it followed a precisely
similar course to Kruger's. Neither wanted war. What sane man does?
Both were brought irresistibly to accept it through the delicate inter-
play between public opinion or external circumstance on the one hand,
and their own dispositions or their own estimate of duty on the other.

Entirely consistent with his concept of imperialism, Chamberlain
placed before the Cabinet a draft dispatch for Pretoria accepting the
Uitlanders' petition and stating that the Queen could no longer ignore

their grievances. Polite and conciliatory, it was nevertheless at best an essay in 'brinkmanship', at worst an ultimatum of war. The Cabinet hesitated, postponed decision for a week.

During that week a dispatch arrived which is among the most notorious of Victorian political documents. Invited by Chamberlain to set out his views in publishable form, Milner struck with all his might. For the present only the Cabinet read his passionate argument that S.A. could not prosper under two conflicting systems—the British colonies with complete (white) equality, the Transvaal with 'permanent subjection of British to Dutch'—'It is idle to talk of peace and unity in such a state of affairs. . . . The case for intervention is overwhelming. . . . The spectacle of thousands of British subjects kept permanently in the position of helots . . . does steadily undermine the influence and reputation of Great Britain.'

This did it. The Cabinet approved Chamberlain's draft. And then at the eleventh hour Milner cabled a suggestion: if he met Kruger across a table either the old man would moderate his attitude or alienate the Cape Dutch by his obstinacy. Chamberlain seized upon the idea and tacked it on the end of his final dispatch.

So came about the Bloemfontein Conference, held at the invitation of the O.F.S. President, ex-Judge Steyn. He attended it with Kruger, Milner and their respective advisers. Given a free hand by Chamberlain, Milner did not invite Schreiner for he feared a united Afrikaner front against him, although Chamberlain urged an invitation: 'He wants peace and will try for a settlement.' No, Milner would do this in his own way. 'I am not hopeful of the result of the Conference,' he told a confidant—and set out to justify his pessimism. It is said that he refused to shake hands with Kruger.[11] What is certain is the complete lack of sympathy or trust between him and the Boers. Seeing him as the emissary from an avaricious power they distrusted this taut and haughty intellectual, this 'flower' of Oxford beside whom Kruger with his heavy fringed face has been likened to palaeolithic man in a frockcoat. When on a later day Milner quit S.A. he was to write of the next High Commissioner: 'If he does not trust the Boers (which I pray he may not do) he will be better able to pretend to trust them than I am, weary as I feel of their eternal duplicity.'[15]

The conference began on Wednesday, 31 May, and nothing happened to improve matters. Let Milner press for franchise reform and the old man suspects a sinister threat to Transvaal independence ('I am not ready to hand over my country to strangers'). Let he himself propose a limited franchise and Milner suspects a ruse to outwit the Uitlanders. By Sunday Milner is cabling Chamberlain that the conference is likely to fail. But Chamberlain sees hope in Kruger making any franchise proposals at all and cables back: 'I hope you will not break off hastily.' The message arrives in Bloemfontein on Tuesday morning. It is too late. The previous evening Milner has imperiously terminated the conference and curtly said good-bye to Kruger.

> Towards the end of this prologue to tragedy the solemn-minded iron-hearted old man cried, 'It is our country you want,' and his head was bowed for a moment while tears were forced from his eyes. Whatever were his faults, it was for the separate life and law and freedom of his people, the highest cause for him as he saw it, that he was fated to stand. In that sense the hand of the Lord was upon him. [1]

So the conference failed. President Steyn reacted promptly, sending an immediate order to Germany for Mausers and cartridges. Throughout S.A. a war-scare had steadily been spreading. Now belief in the inevitability and imminence of hostilities took frantic hold.

In England where there had been no general consciousness of the pass things had reached, the temperature rose violently on publication of Chamberlain's dispatch accepting the Uitlander petition, and even more so by Milner's passionate 'helot' dispatch which was also released at this moment. It created a furore. While the Jingo section of the Government Coalition bayed for Kruger's blood, sections of the Opposition regarded the publication as needlessly provocative and bayed for Chamberlain's and Milner's. The Liberal Party had lately taken on a new leader in the House of Commons. Sir Henry Campbell-Bannerman owed his appointment, said *The Times*, to the likelihood that he would 'sit on the fence, fully satisfying no section of his followers, but at least vitally offending none'. Nevertheless, he made clear to Chamberlain that the Opposition would not support a war. Nor, at that moment, would a sufficient majority of Englishmen. But during the next two months doubts were silenced as the energy, the vulgarity, the sentimentality and the pride of that epoch were directed to the Transvaal Question.

On 26 June, in his diocese of Birmingham, Chamberlain said that the Government had put its hand to the plough. But sufficient of the public had still to be persuaded that the field should not be left fallow a while longer. Chamberlain himself was not yet certain. He cautioned Milner on 'exhausting moral pressure before proceeding to extremities'. Cape Afrikaners were trying to press a more conciliatory attitude on Kruger. And then on 18 July reports from S.A. announced that the Volksraad had brought in a new franchise Bill substantially meeting Uitlander demands. Chamberlain rejoiced. Milner said it was a trick, the Bill in reality would achieve nothing. Thereupon Chamberlain, with Cabinet support, proposed to the Transvaal Government a Joint Commission to investigate the proposals.

The following day, 28 July, the House of Commons debated the issue in an atmosphere charged with excitement. Chamberlain's many enemies at home and abroad hoped for proof of their belief that he and the Prime Minister were at odds. But Salisbury spoke more strongly than Chamberlain had ever done, hinting that if there were war the Transvaal would not merely be reformed but annexed. Campbell-Bannerman admitted that the Uitlander grievances required ameliora-tion but, like an earlier Chamberlain, urged patience always and war never. Chamberlain spoke for an hour. He referred, as he often had, to the fact that Britain had given back the Transvaal its internal inde-pendence upon the understanding that, in Kruger's own words, 'All strangers have now and will always have equal rights and privileges with the burghers of the Transvaal.' But this was scarcely a fair re-proach, since no one had foreseen the discovery of gold and the influx of Uitlanders. He spoke of the 'humiliating inferiority' of British subjects in the Transvaal, which was more to the point, perhaps the whole point. If the Uitlanders were being repressed it was repression of a very upholstered kind and consisted, apart from their lack of a vote, more of slights to their pride than positive subjugation. However, it was altogether too specious of the pro-Boer to say that the Uitlander should have been content with being allowed to make the money which was the alleged sole object of his presence in the Transvaal.

On this subject prejudice played more often that reason. Hilaire Belloc was to write that the Boer War was 'openly and undeniably pro-voked and promoted by Jewish interests in South Africa';[16] and in a bitter satire (*Verses to a Lord*) castigated German-Jewish Rand financiers for cowardice when it came to actual fighting. Racialism and anti-capitalism thus helped to stir up passions already disposed to warmth at the idea of a small country's independence being menaced either from without or from a Trojan horse within. But many Jews were among the Transvaal's staunchest friends, capitalism was practised and upheld by the Boer Government as keenly as any financier, and the freedom in question was that of the Uitlanders not the Boers.

The fundamental fact was that when Chamberlain pleaded for (white) equality in the Transvaal as in the rest of S.A., he meant equality only under the British flag; and that when Kruger cried out for Transvaal independence he meant independence only for the Boers. That the British flag brought for the individual of whatever race a juster, more democratic and materially better life mattered not when racial pride was aroused. The very achievements of British civilization created a discord of arrogance on one side and resentment on the other. Unhappy the country that at the same time possessed the personification of that arrogance in a Milner and the personification of that resentment in a Kruger!

It is therefore idle to apportion 'war guilt' or to follow in any detail the political and diplomatic intricacies of the remaining two months of peace. As dispatch succeeded dispatch between S.A. and England, hopes dwindled. Many people—Rhodes was one—refused to believe that war would come. It seemed inconceivable that Kruger would take on the whole might of the British Empire. Sympathetic foreign Powers, the Cape Dutch and certain Liberals like Labouchere pressed Kruger to agree to Chamberlain's Joint Commission on the franchise. He made no move. And then belief that he was bluffing seemed justified when young Smuts approached the British Agent at Pretoria with proposals eminently acceptable to Chamberlain—only to be followed by official formulation of quite unacceptable pre-conditions. Chamberlain, fortified by messages of support from the Empire, reacted sharply.

The impetuosity he had long kept in check found public expression in a return to the caustic language of his younger days: 'Mr. Kruger procrastinates. . . . He dribbles out reforms like water from a squeezed sponge.' While this phrase attracted wide adverse publicity, more important was another metaphor he used: 'The sands are running down.'

After further dispatches on either side, a crucial Cabinet meeting was held on 8 September. The German *Official History* estimates that at about this time the Boers had in reserve 80,000 rifles and 80 million cartridges, for their own 50,000 men in the Transvaal and O.F.S. and for the 40,000 Cape Dutch they expected to rise to their aid. The stream of munitions into the Transvaal and O.F.S., a great part of it ironically passing through the British Colony of the Cape because Schreiner would not antagonize his pro-Kruger followers, exerted a potent influence on British thought. And it, rather than any question of Uitlander grievances, the franchise or suzerainty, may be said to have precipitated the war. The Governor of Natal, the colony whose accessibility and possession of a port made it the most vulnerable target if war broke out, let the Colonial Office know of his alarm. Milner saw it as the 'gravest feature' of the whole situation.

The previous June the War Office wanted to take precautionary measures but desisted lest the move provoked what it was intended to forestall, though a group of special officers ('given sums inadequate for the purposes of respectable commercial travellers'[17]) did go out in July for local recruitment and Intelligence, and in August two battalions of infantry were ordered to Natal. The effect was merely to convince the Boers of Britain's aggressive intentions without substantially adding to British preparedness: when the Cabinet met on 8 September, the total of British forces scattered all over S.A. was only 12,000 men. Lord Wolseley, C.-in-C. at the War Office, was therefore authorized to drum up a reinforcement of 10,000 men, mainly from India, for immediate embarkation to S.A. under Sir George White. The decision was taken after Chamberlain had circulated a memorandum stating that at stake was the power and influence of England throughout the world, not merely in S.A. where even the Natives recognized that the gauntlet had been thrown down. The Cabinet agreed a dispatch harder in tone than any before.

Behind the diplomatic exchange on both sides was now the unspoken necessity of gaining time not for peace but for the right moment for war. England's ignorance of the Boers was such that *Punch* could depict them on foot, whereas they were out-and-out horsemen and hence not disposed to ride until the S.A. spring a month hence brought life to the parched veld. For their part the British were desperately anxious lest the overseas reinforcement under Sir George White did not arrive in time. If it did, Wolseley staked his reputation on Britain's defensive position in S.A. being utterly secure.

War fever was spreading as more and more people joined in the Jingo clamour, though the majority of responsible people quietly accepted that war was probable and with it an inescapable call to duty. A wing of the Liberal Party, called the 'Liberal Imperialists' and led by Lord Rosebery, shared this view but radicals and other factions in the party did not, nor did the Irish party. Hence anti-war opinion was voiced with vigour. From Canada where he was visiting at this time the Liberal Lloyd George cabled, 'If I have the courage I shall protest with all the vehemence at my command against this outrage which is perpetrated in the name of human freedom.' Against increasing interruptions, which obliged the police to warn the conveners, Liberals held meetings of protest. In particular a great Liberal rally at Manchester in mid-September declared against war, even though Kruger was urged to grant reforms.

He had little intention of accepting the advice. Only a week before, he declared in the Volksraad that the British had 'asked for his trousers and he had given them; then for his coat, he had given that also; now they wanted his life, and that he could not give.'[17]

What he could have given at any time in these months and so prevented war was the franchise to the Uitlanders, while still entrenching his burghers' parliamentary majority. He would not do so because he regarded any such thing as a British foot in the Transvaal door of independence. Chamberlain could at any time have prevented war by acquiescing in Kruger's attitude. He would not do so because he regarded it as a Boer foot in the British door of paramountcy.

The British miscalculated who thought as Milner did that Kruger would 'bluff up to the cannon's mouth' and would never by himself take on the whole British Empire. He did not reckon he was by himself. He, his people and his God were all one in his mind. In the words of the 83rd Psalm, which he urged his burghers to ponder, he complained aloud to God about British machinations: 'They have taken crafty counsel against thy people . . . they have said, Come and let us cut them off from being a nation. . . . Let them be confounded and troubled for ever; yea let them be put to shame and perish.' God apart, others could be reckoned to stand with him. The O.F.S. was bound by treaty and the Cape Dutch by blood. Germany and France had now sorted out the vexing troubles with England which followed the Jubilee, but let the Boers deal a few hard blows and they would scarcely neglect a chance to dismember the empire they coveted. Foreign intervention might not even be necessary, for the Opposition in England might return to power and, as certain Liberals like Labouchere secretly assured Kruger, accede to Boer demands as Gladstone had done after Majuba. If all else failed, he had his burghers, reared from birth to the endurance and fighting skills required of a pioneer race. And always he had the Lord.

To the Cabinet's dispatch approved on 8 September he therefore returned as hard an answer. The Cabinet rejoindered through Chamberlain that since four months' negotiation on top of five years' agitation had come to nothing it was useless to pursue discussion on previous lines: H.M. Government would make their own proposals shortly. Wits called this Chamberlain's 'pen-ultimatum'. It was in fact to give time for the 10,000 men approaching S.A.'s shores; and orders were given for the mobilization of an army corps under the command of Sir Redvers Buller.

It was also the signal to the Transvaalers to move quickly. Their strategy must be to strike hard, far and fast. On 27 September Kruger telegraphed to his junior partner in the Boer alliance: 'Executive [i.e. the Transvaal Cabinet] unanimous that commando order should be issued today.' The commando was the military unit of the Boers: men of a town or district assembled together under their elected commandant and his subordinate officers the field-cornets, and wearing no uniform but each having his own rifle and horse they could with little preliminary ride to the scene of action. President Steyn hesitated. His attempt to secure American mediation failed but still he strove for peace. He had never shared Kruger's pugnacity, and anyone forgetful of the ironies of history would have prophesied him as the weakest link in the Boer chain. He havered and again Kruger had to urge him before he called out the O.F.S. burghers.

War was now a matter of weeks, days, perhaps hours. *The Times* published Kipling's denunciation of Kruger—'Cruel in the shadow, crafty in the sun', and 'Sloven, sullen, savage, secret, uncontrolled'— and he reminded England of her traditional opposition to tyranny.[18] The British Cabinet met again, this time to agree Chamberlain's draft of a final ultimatum. The Natal Governor had telegraphed that traffic along the Durban–Pretoria railway was closed at the border, the telegraph cut; commandos were assembling beyond Laing's Nek, the pass through the mountains on the border, but still 'I can't think the Boers will be so crack-brained as to strike the first blow at us.' For the moment the British ultimatum was held back.

From Johannesburg and Pretoria these weeks past Uitlanders had been fleeing the country. The exodus became a panic. Trains left crowded; open trucks were hitched on at the rear and were tight-packed—a heavy trial in the heat of day, a kind of comfort in the bitter cold of night. At the same time the great empty spaces of the veld were suddenly delivering up throngs of men, mostly bearded and riding shaggy ponies along every road to Pretoria. They carried rifles; bandoleers were slung across their everyday coats and their saddle-bags were filled with *biltong*—dried meat, traditional rations for trek or campaign. Some had come hundreds of miles. Children and old men arrived in wagons with their families, eager to join despite the age limits (sixteen to sixty). Old rifles exchanged for new Mausers, ammunition issued, and the commandos streamed to the front. Wild excitement in Pretoria accompanied the departure of troop-trains, munitions and horses. The batteries of artillery drawn through the streets amazed British bystanders. Rapidly stores were built up at border towns and the veld was burnt to hasten spring growth.

On 2 October the Volksraad approved war. Hot-heads were present, as thirsty for action as the young men streaming to the fronts. But in the main the members approached decision with anguish. For many it would mean civil war: intermarriage with the British; shared dangers in the past against Native, pestilence and storm; the conviction that, feel against each other what they would, Boer and Briton had a common stake in the future of their great sub-continent—all this weighed heavily. But Oom Paul reassured them with the verdict of the Almighty: 'God hath spoken in His wisdom,' he quoted: 'I will rejoice.'

In England the nation's absorption in the now certain conflict was both reflected and intensified by the Press. The new journalism was preparing to show its paces for the first time in a major war. 'Our Correspondent at the Seat of War' was soon to become the familiar of every newspaper reader, and reporters were in a rush for S.A. They were to include famous men—among them one whom Chamberlain found time on 5 October to commend to Milner:

I am sending a line to anticipate a probable visit from Winston

Churchill, the son of Lord Randolph Churchill who is going out as correspondent for the *Morning Post*. . . . He is a very clever young fellow with many of his father's qualifications. He has the reputation of being bumptious, but I have not myself found him so, and time will no doubt get rid of the defect if he has it. . . . He is a good writer and full of energy. He hopes to be in Parliament, but want of means stands in the way.

A few days later the British reinforcements arrived at Durban. They were in the nick of time. That very day an ultimatum drafted by Jan Smuts called on the British Government to withdraw their troops from the frontiers and send away all the reinforcements.

At 6.15 a.m. on Tuesday, 10 October 1899, Chamberlain was woken and read the ultimatum with amazement. He had never expected the Boers so clearly to accept the onus of aggression and give him a cast-iron case to lay before the public. 'They have done it!' he exclaimed. That evening the British Government cabled the Queen's rejection of the Boer demands.

In Pretoria the Union Jack was hauled down and the British consular officials departed, leaving the U.S.A. Consul to watch their interests. Over all S.A. ran the thrill and dread of a war that some might say was written across the wide heavens since ever Boer and Briton came together in that land. Yet there never was a less necessary war, and nothing is odder about the strange conflict which was to follow than the ignorance on both sides as to what it was all about. A Boer was heard to remark in Pretoria: 'In the future I must either take off my hat to an Englishman, or he must take off his hat to me.'[14] This was equally the crude sentiment of the British colonist.

But the masses in England, moulded by the pressures of that tumultuous epoch, vociferously waved their flags with little sensibility and less responsibility. Kipling wrote *The Absent-minded Beggar* which was recited and sung (to Sir Arthur Sullivan's music) as no verse has ever been—

> When you've shouted 'Rule Britannia', when you've sung
> 'God save the Queen',
> When you've finished killing Kruger with your mouth,
> Will you kindly drop a shilling in my little tambourine
> For a gentleman in khaki ordered South? . . .

Duke's son—cook's son—son of a hundred kings—
  (Fifty thousand horse and foot going to Table Bay!)
Each of 'em doing his country's work
  (and who's to look after their things?)
Pass the hat for your credit's sake, and pay—pay—pay!

A frenzy of fund-raising began for soldiers' dependents and for gifts of clothing, tobacco, cigarettes and 'delicacies' for the men. One of the Queen's sons was photographed at the docks lighting the cigarettes of embarking troops. The Princess of Wales, dubbed the Princess of Pity by a Press hardly able to keep their newsprint unsmudged in an orgy of sentimentality, was head of the Red Cross and helped equip hospitals and hospital-ships. Americans in London, led by the widowed Lady Randolph Churchill, financed the hospital ship *Maine* as a gesture of Atlantic brotherhood.

Offers of help from the Empire poured in, moving audiences at the music-hall to cheer England's 'cubs across the sea'. Soldiers with bushy moustaches and going to a major war in khaki for the first time, gazed out from under their sun helmets at an adoring populace. Ladies pressed sachets of lavender along with Bibles into the kit-bag of that surprised hero of the hour, Tommy Atkins.

Yet the country was not wholly united. The anti-war groups, increasingly jeered at as 'pro-Boer', did not abate their opposition. When Parliament met some days after the war had begun, Rosebery's Liberal Imperialists showed that even if they supported it they were as hostile to Chamberlain personally as were the out-and-out opponents of the war. In the first debate of the session this vendetta found expression in such speeches as that of the aristocratic radical Philip Stanhope, who denounced 'Imperial Joe' for having deliberately conspired with Milner and Rhodes to bring the war about, and of Sir William Harcourt who denounced him for his conduct of negotiations. In a scene the more dramatic for the crowded benches and galleries of the House, Chamberlain rounded white-faced and scornful upon his accusers. Speaking in a low strong voice for nearly three hours he defended himself and the Government, and carried the day by 362 votes to 135. 'Very, very good,' murmured the Queen when the speech was read to her at Balmoral: 'I am delighted with it.'

But already bullets were sounding louder than words.

CHAPTER III

Arms and Armies

WHATEVER doubts our Victorian might have had, the outbreak of war gave him no qualm about the military prospects, for contemplating the range of invention during his lifetime he could find nothing more impressive than the new weapons and ammunition at England's disposal.

When he was a boy, the Army used cannon that had scarcely changed in 500 years. They were loaded down the front of the smooth cast-metal barrel with round iron shot which was fired by a charge of gunpowder. This charge, of haphazard quantity, might blow up gun and gunner in the process. If the shot was not solid but filled with gunpowder and metal fragments—the invention, in our Victorian's grandfather's time, of a Lt. Schrapnel—the same thing might happen. Even if the shot emerged its direction was highly problematical. Yet with such guns had the Army fought from Edward III's siege of Calais in 1347 to the last major war, the Crimean campaign of 1854-6.

In the Crimea the Army for the first time used muskets with grooved or rifled bores which fired further and straighter than the former smooth-bore muskets. This 'rifle' had in fact been tried out by the Life Guards two centuries before but not found acceptance, so that the British smooth-bore 'Brown Besses' were no match for the Colonists' Kentucky rifles in the American War of Independence. Nevertheless the rifle had to wait on the Crimean War to prove itself, and then it made even the smooth-bore cannon look obsolete.

This was serious for a nation so dependent on the firing power of her ships. England was therefore a leading contender in the armaments race with Germany and France. Her foremost individual was a Newcastle-on-Tyne solicitor turned inventor, W. G. (later Lord) Armstrong, who armed the world from the dying empire of Austria to the awakening island of Japan. From the time (1855) that he brought out a rifled gun built up from layers of metal and loaded from the back or breech with an elongated projecile, artillery was revolutionized. The invention of brass cartridge-cases and smokeless powders such as cordite to fire off the shot (now called shell because it was a container with the destructive material within); wholesale improvements to details like quick-firing, fuses for exploding the shell on target, sites, gun-carriages; Nobel's perfection of high explosive—all these combined to produce the artillery two world wars have made familiar enough. By the nineties there were guns able to fire up to twenty miles, but the heavy position pieces usually counted less in land war than the typical horse-drawn field gun that could fire a twelve- or fifteen-pound shell for several miles with great accuracy, or the squat snub-nosed howitzer developed from the old mortar for lobbing explosives at a steep angle. England had latterly concentrated on experiments with explosives—as Germany had on war balloons and France, to Germany's incredulous amusement, on submarines—and our Victorian was told horrific tales about a new explosive called lyddite that would kill a Boer fifty yards from the point of impact.

Small arms had developed with equally startling rapidity. Our Victorian was a child when a Scots Presbyterian Minister called Forsythe received, on the day of his death, a belated payment from the British Government for inventing a chemical detonator to replace the flint-lock which for 300 years had been the means of firing a musket or pistol. This, and rifling, were followed in the sixties by breech-loading, and the process culminated in the eighties and nineties with the advent of copper-enclosed lead bullets plus rimless cartridges, smokeless powder and a magazine for quick-firing. So to the modern rifle. In 1895 the Lee-Enfield was issued: somewhat modified it was the rifle England carried to battle in World War I and much of World War II. With it or the similar Lee-Metford Mark Two an infantryman could pour a rapid succession of bullets accurately on an enemy well over half a mile away, without either betraying his position by a cloud of smoke or having to stop in a stock-still upright position while he re-loaded.

In the nineties too the automatic self-loading pistol was perfected in the wake of the American-invented revolver.

Finally, there were machine-guns. The idea had ancient origin in a

row of muskets bound together like organ pipes and fired off almost
simultaneously, but the modern weapon had its first really reliable
representative in the Maxim, introduced by the eighties. Standing on a
high tripod or a gun-carriage and automatically fed by a belt of cartridges, it fired continuously so long as the trigger was pressed. The
French had used a type of machine-gun in 1870, developing it as their
'secret weapon' to destroy the Prussians; but in so doing they totally
neglected their artillery and consequently suffered a severe defeat which
cast quite illogical doubts on the prospects of the weapon.

Thus in England, though our Victorian had been enthralled to read
about the grisly new toy (as fascinating as the new armoured trains)
when it was used by the Army against the Matabele in 1893 and again,
with telling effect, against the dervishes at Omdurman (1898), the War
Office lords largely wrote it off. Besides, they thought it all very well
for use against savages but hardly in 'civilized' warfare in which it
might confuse artillerymen and infantrymen alike. The Maxim in its
modified form of the Vickers was to be described by Lloyd George as the
most lethal weapon of World War I—had not one the firing power of
fifty riflemen? Yet, though the War Office had this weapon fully
available, only junior officers were trained for its use and comparatively
few were to be sent to S.A.

Our Victorian could however feel satisfied that the Boers would be
dealt with by a deadly variety of weapons, as modern—before Nagasaki
disappeared in a mushroom of radio-active smoke—as the twentieth-
century soldier would know. But only in the nineties did these weapons
reach such refinement. The Boer War would therefore be testing them
fully for the very first time. The question was how exactly they would
be used—what effect they would have on tactics, especially against an
enemy similarly armed and less concerned about doctrine based on the
last war than adapting himself to the new one. But that was a question
which our Victorian, venerating the armed forces only less than his
Queen and his Flag, never dreamt of asking.

He might have been less confident had he known how Chamberlain
feared the War Office more than the Boers, though very few men
realized that the new weapon called for changes in military thought
more far-reaching than any required since the invention of gunpowder.
In this respect as in much else the Boer War provided the great transition from the ways of past centuries to those of our own.

The Crimean War had initiated an era of reform but the diehard royal Duke of Cambridge, recently retired after nearly forty years as Commander-in-Chief, retarded the process. Once—for a hundred years after Edward I—England's small, swift army of bowmen had been part of the national life, with a distinctive character which gave it pre-eminence in Europe. Since the advent of fire-arms in the Wars of the Roses the Army had become a closed corporation wedded to its own traditions and rigid Continental systems. Imperial expansion gave rise to variations between the establishments at home and abroad, as in India and Egypt, adding confusion to inefficiency. Not that the legend of God-given sufficiency had been shaken by a plethora of imperial wars: soldiers of the Queen had been in action somewhere or other in the world for all except seven of the forty-five years since Crimea; victories against 'savages' were cheap.

The wonder is not that England had bad soldiers but that she had any good ones. Although the purchase of commissions had been abolished in 1871, wealth and influence were still passports to promotion. Subalterns complained that their pay was insufficient to cover their mess bills even if they toasted the Queen in water. War was prepared for in an atmosphere best conveyed by a quotation from the memoirs of Field-Marshal Sir Evelyn Wood[19], to whose generation many Boer War brass-hats belonged: describing his reforming zeal while in command of Aldershot, England's chief training base, he triumphantly produces a letter written to him on his departure: 'I thank you for all you have done, which is a very great deal, while at Aldershot for the Fox hounds.'

What time officers were busy being gentlemen in or out of gorgeous dress uniforms, their men's welfare counted for little. Evelyn Wood reports of Southern Command as late as 1902 that commanding officers did not know where their men's privies were, much less their condition, and in the canteens the contractor's agent had to sleep among the groceries, 'his head on a cheese and his feet in a butter bowl'. When it came to actual manœuvres the new weapons were so little regarded that many exercises dated from a *hundred* years earlier. The accent was on solid line formations, mechanical precision, rigid dependence on orders, firing strictly in volleys at a word of command, bayonet charges. My good fellow, had not Napoleon been broken by such methods?

Only two months a year were spent training. For the rest a man was parading ('At 9 o'clock,' Evelyn Wood noted in his diary during the Zululand campaign, 'I had a second inspection of the 90th Light Infantry, looking at every man's boots, which were unsatisfactory; this took me till 11.30.'), mounting guard, pipe-claying or polishing his gear, scrubbing floors, or acting as gardener, cook, valet, porter or clerk.

Between social and sporting activities his seniors fought a spirited battle of form-filling. The Treasury still insisted on arrangements originally devised to stop Kings misusing the Army or diverting funds to their mistresses. Calculating all costs by the day and food by the ration, each company furnished monthly returns to a total of 400 pages.

In the highest realms, those of the central direction of the Army, there was no General Staff to plan and think out fundamental questions of strategy and tactics: time was monopolized by the concocting of more regulations or inventing 'expensive and ridiculous man-millinery'.[17] The Intelligence Division was maintained at a cost of £11,000 per annum, compared with the quarter of a million spent by the German General Staff. Exactly two officers were responsible for the entire Colonial Empire, at a time when the Transvaal Republic was spending £90,000 per annum on Intelligence. The standard of planning and its pre-requisite of accurate information is hit off by a bitter *Punch* jest six months after the war began, defining a map as 'a chart upon which names are sprinkled without any special significance as to exact locality.'

A great number of officers, from Sir Garnet Wolseley down, had served in S.A. in the First Boer War or against Native tribes. But no information had been systematically collated nor any real idea of the Boer formed, aggrieved Uitlander descriptions doing much to foster belief that he was wholly an ignorant peasant. His successes in the First Boer War were put down to opportunist numerical superiority, before Gladstone prevented the Army really going into action.

In particular the Boer military system appeared positively laughable. Except for the German-trained State Artillery and the police the Republican armies were purely citizen forces, without uniform or pay and with no parade-ground training. A burgher learnt only by experience in war or hunting. Whether opposed by man or beast his sole weapon was the rifle with which he grew up, and he preferred to keep his distance, neither using a bayonet nor believing in the heroics of

61

man-to-man struggle. He kept his pony close to the scene of action, usually a hill, so that he could simply run away if things got too hot—and live to fight another day. This to the Victorian was hardly playing fair, but to the Boer absolutely essential on account of his slender man-power. Every man between the age limits, even if he had a wooden leg and a missing arm, was liable to be called up, but the magistrates (*landdrosts*) succeeded only in raising two-thirds of the potential strength when mobilization was ordered. Being dependent on popular vote they were reluctant to enforce penalties. Not only were commandant and field-cornets—commanding officer and warrant-officers of each commando—also elected, but every burgher was their equal, entitled freely to give advice and participate in councils of war. This freedom extended to the individual on the battlefield, where he obeyed orders only for the most part voluntarily and often acted entirely on his own initiative. Accordingly when mobilization brought about 35,000 burghers into the field in the Transvaal and O.F.S., about 35,000 generals were ready—very often with their families who went on their wagons with the supplies, kept as close as possible to the commandos when on the march or parked in a *laager* (encampment) some distance in rear of an action. This identity of a man with his family also applied as between one man and another, because in such a small community intermarriage bound them together in a whole mesh of relationships. The result was a sense of individual responsibility and caution as strong as a sense of being answerable to God whose people they believed themselves to be. Finally, being mostly countrymen and therefore hardy, accustomed to the terrain, and simple in their ways, they reciprocated the contempt of the British, whom they considered effete and incapable of outstaying them in a contest of will or courage. In numerical terms there could also be cause for confidence. Even if their expectation that 40,000 Cape Dutch would come to their help was not realized, and even if those burghers not yet mobilized failed altogether to join up, it would still be necessary for Britain to send abroad the largest army in her history and maintain it at a greater distance per man than in any country's history.

One would not have thought that the Army Corps which the Cabinet had authorized to be raised under General Sir Redvers Buller would have presented any difficulty. But there were not the required 50,000 trained and able-bodied men in the home army. Enough troops had already been drawn from abroad for Sir George White's force just arrived in Natal: memories of the Indian Mutiny did not encourage a further weakening of British garrisons in the Colonies. This consideration would not apply if native troops were called on: there were 170,000 Indians with the colours, hosts of Egyptians, West Indians, West Africans, East Africans, and a great potential pool of Natives in S.A. itself. But considerations of race relations in S.A., added to those of imperial defence, brought a crisp decision: this was to be a white man's war. So for the first time the Native Question in S.A. materially affected matters, having so far been a very minor factor, merely helping to stir up anti-Boer emotion on allegations, mainly by missionaries, of black bondage. Not since Agincourt had Britain sent out an expeditionary force composed exclusively of Britons.

To make up the Army Corps the Reserves started being mobilized on the eve of the Boer ultimatum, adding to the excitement of the ensuing days as crowds followed the men to their depots. Offers of volunteers by the self-governing colonies were welcomed by Chamberlain as proof of empire solidarity but were not seriously regarded by the War Office who liked only regular soldiers. The total from this source was therefore limited to about 2,000 whom Chamberlain was advised to stress should be infantry. Paraphrased as 'unmounted men preferred', the request was to become one of the harshest jokes of the war. The enemy was wholly mounted and yet to counter such mobility only ten per cent of the Army was mounted. These were mainly cavalry, equipped with sabre or lance and—a little-used novelty —a short rifle called a carbine; but there were also a few mounted infantry (M.I.) who like the Boers were riflemen able to ride to a favourable position and fight dismounted, unlike the cavalry who fought on horseback. General military opinion held that the M.I. were a new-fangled absurdity. Things were certainly not as they had been— clearly shown by the discarding of centuries-old scarlet for khaki, first worn by the Army in India (though the word came from Persia, meaning 'dust'). But few realized that an entire age was being bade farewell as streets echoed to the tramp of marching boots and a song—

> Good-bye Dolly I must leave you,
> Though it breaks my heart to go,
> Something tells me I am needed,

At the front to fight the foe,
See, the soldier boys are marching,
And I can no longer stay—
Hark! I hear the bugle calling,
Good-bye Dolly Gray.

To the Admiralty was left the business of arranging transport for the Army Corps. 600,000 tons of shipping were needed for the men, horses, guns, vehicles, ammunition, equipment and medical supplies, besides prodigious quantities of food and forage both for the journey and the campaign. Our Victorian noted with satisfaction the strength of a merchant fleet that could provide so many ships with scarcely a ruffle among freight rates. But with all the efficiency which in this respect at least the war was launched on the British side, the distance to the Cape remained 6,000 miles: no transports could be ready until 20 October, nor begin reaching the Cape before the beginning of November. There even seemed the risk that they might not arrive at all. Wild stories of a Boer privateer upon the high seas had the escorting warships of the Royal Navy fruitlessly chasing an unidentified cruiser near the Canaries; the transports therefore sailed under a blackout and on an altered course that lengthened the voyage.

The Boers were suffering from similar jitters. The belief spread that the British were launching air balloons which would drop explosives. That this specific 'barbarism' had been banned for a period of five years by an international conference in July did not prevent reports flowing into Pretoria from people all over S.A. who had seen whole flotillas of death afloat in the sky. But from first to last this was to be a war not only fought on land but dominated by the sheer expanse of land to be defended or conquered. The potential area of hostilities stretched from the Zambezi to Cape Town, equal to all Europe between Dublin and Vienna.

In the centre stood the two republics, surrounded except for Portuguese East Africa by British territory. Invasion or counter-invasion could be sprung from any point around a vast circumference, but the railways decided strategy. Without them transport of men, supplies, even water was dependent on the slow and vulnerable ox-wagon. The speediest advance, the safest retreat lay in possession of four main tracks, all originating at S.A.'s few ports.

The D.B. Railway from Pretoria to the Portuguese East African port on Delagoa Bay must now, as Kruger had foreseen, be the Transvaal's life-line with the outside world. The Natal railway ran from Durban to Pretoria with a branch into the O.F.S. From the Cape two lines went northward: the Western railway along the western border of both republics to Rhodesia, and the Central railway straight up the centre of the republics from a complex of junctions connected to all the Cape ports—Cape Town, Port Elizabeth, Port Alfred, and East London.

These four trunk lines—the D.B., Natal, Western and Central railways—formed the framework of the ensuing campaign (see end map). The portion of the Cape westward of the Western railway will be referred to as the western Cape; that eastward of the East London branch of the Central railway as the eastern Cape, and that between the two as the Cape Midlands.

The War Office had a plan all ready for Sir Redvers Buller to carry out as soon as he arrived with the Army Corps: he would entrain his men at the Cape ports for the junctions in the Cape Midlands, whence they would strike along the Central railway at the heart of the republics. But since the Army Corps could not start reaching S.A. before November, expiry of the Boer ultimatum at 5 o'clock on the afternoon of 11 October 1899, cast a heavy responsibility on the troops already there to keep the Boers at bay in the meantime.

That night the commandos began crossing borders into British territory, their aim to hit out hard before Buller could affect the situation. By the end of the month their activities would result in the establishment of precise battle-fronts, but much happened first.

*　　*　　*　　*

In the north, along the Limpopo River which divides Rhodesia from the Transvaal, all that stood in the path of the Boers were thirty policemen commanded by Colonel Plumer, a chubby-faced man with an impressive moustache under his pugnacious nose: he had been one of the special officers sent out in July, and had successful campaign experience of the country as well as of colonial irregulars. At first there were minor patrol clashes, but after he had been joined by the Rhodesia Regiment of irregulars whom he had been organizing, there was a skirmish on 31 October severe enough for each side to believe that the other planned an invasion in force. President Kruger rushed up one of his grandsons, Sarel Eloff, with fresh burghers and artillery, but with passing time everybody concerned was relieved by the falsity of their conjectures, and indeed this area was to play a very minor role in the war.

Southwards, the territory west of the Transvaal was that Bechuanaland which Rhodes had tried to get Chamberlain to cede to the Cape after Sir Charles Warren's expedition. In the result the portion north of the Molopo River became a Native protectorate, and the portion south of it incorporated in the Cape Colony—the whole segment between the Molopo and the Orange Rivers is referred to in this narrative as the far north Cape to distinguish it from the western Cape. Now, on the outbreak of war, commandos crossed into the Protectorate to attack Native villages, tear up culverts of the Western railway and skirmish with the patrolling armoured train *Powerful*. At the same time they began to turn their attention to the far north Cape and the town near the southern bank of the Molopo, Mafeking.

The hinterland of S.A. stands on a vast plateau 4,000 feet high, from which the primeval waters of the earth drained so long ago that earliest man could evolve there. The narrow coastal belt varies from Mediterranean-like conditions on the Cape littoral to the tropics of eastern Natal, whereas the plateau is a sea of grass (*veld*—though this means the earth generally) never very green nor high because of the dry climate, with usually only a few thorn trees or sudden low rocky hills (*kopjes*) to break a vista seemingly endless in the wonderfully clear light. But while the plateau rises from the southern and eastern coasts by a series of dramatic geophysical heaves which will play a part in this story, it descends to the Atlantic more gradually, so that from the western Transvaal and O.F.S. it is ever flatter westward to the coast and far drier until the veld becomes first a semi-desert of sparse grass, scrub, thornbush, and then almost totally desert in the Kalahari.

Mafeking stands midway between grassland and desert. It looked like a town in a Western film. The buildings along its couple of dusty streets were all single-storeyed except for a Roman Catholic convent next to the hospital on the outskirts: corrugated iron roofs and wooden verandas were their only features. The town normally had a population of about a thousand and straggled for scarcely half a mile in any direction. Yet in the wide open spaces even an otherwise insignificant place becomes important to trader or hunter if it offers supplies, communication with the outside world, and such features of civilization as government administration and saloon bars. The war gave it added importance. Jameson had started his raid hereabouts and the Boers were not anxious for a repetition of the attempt on a more thorough scale. They wanted, besides, the town's stock of provisions—the leading store alone had £30,000 worth—and above all possession of the biggest railway depot between Kimberley and Bulawayo. It was in particular its position on the railway line which gave it strategic significance, and with unconscious aptness the godson of Robert Stephenson, most famous of railway engineers, happened to be put in charge of defending it.

Robert Stephenson Smyth Baden-Powell was an unknown forty-two-year-old Lt.-Colonel of Dragoons when he was included in the batch of special officers sent out the previous July. He was one of seven children of an Oxford clergyman professor, and a galaxy of the great surrounded his childhood. In knickerbockers and Holland jerkin he watched Ruskin, Jowett and Browning around the parental hearth. Thackeray gave him a shilling which he never spent, being careful with money and keeping a double-entry personal account book from the age of five, a frequent entry being not sweets but 'Orange—£0 0 1'. To the dismay of his prep. school headmaster who wanted him to stay on gratis because of his healthy moral influence he duly went to Charterhouse, where he was called 'old Bathing Towel'. He was a model schoolboy, drew well with his left hand, had the reputation of being a humorist, and played the part of old women in theatricals. He performed on musical instruments, sang pleasantly, kept his distance and made no deep friendships. Something a little priggish and amateur clings to Baden-Powell, but in a sentimental age neither was a bar to the fame which was soon to replace 'old Bathing Towel' with the reverberating consonants of 'B.P.' On service in India and Matabeleland (part of Rhodesia) he had learnt to become a good rider and teacher of men. He had also formed a passion for scouting, which is to say moving unseen through enemy country drawing miraculous deductions from spoor and leaf, and generally carrying on like a Sherlock Holmes in flannel shirt and topee. This accorded well with the prevailing idea in England of war as a splendid game; and more so when *Aids to Scouting*, on the proofs of which Baden-Powell was working at this time, disclosed that here was a man to match against the Boer, to whom the public ascribed an almost supernatural ability in field-craft.

On his arrival in Mafeking the previous month Baden-Powell brought a body of colonial irregulars whom like Plumer he had been training further north. These with the town guard of clerks and shop-keepers totalled 1,200 men. Half a mile outside the town were the round huts of a Native *stad* (city) having a population of 7,000, from which he raised 500 cattle guards and watchmen armed with elephant guns and similar ironmongery for their own defence. His artillery amounted to only half a dozen seven-pound muzzle-loaders besides seven Maxims, and though additional guns were due in from the south on the armoured train *Mosquito* he decided to make his defensive peri-meter nearly eight miles long to keep the Boer guns as distant as possible and to enclose the native stad, grazing ground, and the town's water wells.

A complicated system of trenches, redoubts and forts was ener-getically built, all linked by telephone. Minefields were laid, streets barricaded for house-to-house fighting if the perimeter gave way, sus-pected spies gaoled, and bomb-proof shelters for the town's 650 women and children constructed. Food stocks were organized, being especially plentiful so long as the Natives' cattle could be preserved. Clad with railway sleepers gathered in from up and down the line a train was effectively armoured. Baden-Powell had prepared thoroughly.

Well he might. While the ultimatum was expiring 10,000 Boers massed on the Transvaal border. They were under the command of General Piet Cronje, said to be the only Boer general with military training, and regarded by many of the Boers as their ablest. A British authority[17] describes him as a man of 'truculent and stubborn energy'. He had hammered a British force in the war of 1881 and captured Jameson's force in 1896, but whether he was past his prime remained to be seen. Under this stern-faced, dark grizzle-bearded man were subor-dinate commandants, who included a certain J. P. Snyman and, more important, Koos de la Rey.

Moving across the border the night the ultimatum expired, it was men of Cronje's army who were active in the protectorate north of Mafeking, cutting communications with Rhodesia. Others went to the south of the town, and here they not only tore up the line but presently waylaid the *Mosquito* bringing precious guns to Baden-

Powell. After a brisk engagement they captured it, so drawing first blood in the war.

The commandant responsible was Koos de la Rey. Though for long far less well known to the public than Cronje, we shall see him emerge as perhaps the only man of original genius on either side in a story of many great men. *The Times History* describes him at this time when he was already over fifty years old: 'Dark, with shaggy eyebrows, great aquiline nose—mark of old aristocratic Huguenot or Spanish blood—deeply lined face, and a vast bushy beard fast turning grey, he would have made a striking model for some warrior prophet of the Old Testament.' But there was nothing doom-spelling or aggressive about this chivalrous and acute-minded man. He was a farmer in the Lichtenburg district, a hundred miles west of Johannesburg and Pretoria. Though lacking almost any formal education he had achieved a pre-eminent position in his district because of his character and progressiveness. To his fine farm he brought an English governess for his children, until seeing the inevitability of war he conducted her to Kimberley thinking to get her out of harm's way. A moderate in the Volksraad, he had voted against war, but since it had come it had to be fought out.

Following his capture of the *Mosquito* he began tearing up the line closer to Mafeking. Baden-Powell happened to send out a truck of surplus dynamite which exploded near the Boers and left them with an exaggerated notion of his minefields. De la Rey then appears to have gone on southwards, but the bulk of Cronje's forces closed round the town, now cut off from the world except for occasional Native runners. After preliminary skirmishes in which Baden-Powell took the offensive, the Boers called on him to surrender. The invitation was declined. The Boers formed their laagers on every side and the famous siege had begun.

Having, they said, 'shut up the meercat in his hole', the Boers started a desultory bombardment with their superior artillery which did little harm to the garrison and townsfolk, warned by a system of bells when to take cover. A message was presently got through to England: 'October 21st. All well. Four hours' bombardment. One dog killed.' This threw England into a convulsion of merriment and admiration. Leading articles and verse in the newspapers made 'B.P.' world famous overnight. A large portrait of him worked in silks was among the gifts showered on his mother; gutter-merchants did well out of brooches with his face smiling on the enamel; 'to complete this apotheosis, Mme Tussaud announced in flaming placards that Baden-Powell had been added to the number of her immortals'.[17] Meanwhile the Boers had brought up one of their four huge Creusot guns called Long Toms which could fire ninety-four-pound shells for a distance of six miles. Cronje considerately warned Powell that he would reluctantly have to use this gun, called Big Ben by the garrison, and Powell returned an ironic reply. The gun duly fired, creating a fearful noise and killing one chicken. By the month-end three skirmishes had left the honours with Baden-Powell.

The Boers had not reckoned on such spirit. A serious assault on the place would mean much bloodshed, which seemed to them pointless. So while their newspapers daily forecast the imminent fall of the town, the Boers sat round it and patiently waited for it to be delivered to them.

Their confidence in its easy capture was increased by the speed with which Koos de la Rey and others were acquiring stations and villages all down the line to the Orange River.

Village after village along this 300 miles of the republics' western border surrendered without a struggle. At one, Vryburg, the major in charge of the police post was so distressed by the townsfolk's anxiety to surrender that he shot himself. Here as elsewhere the advancing burghers hoisted their flag and threatened heavy punishment against anyone who harmed them or co-operated with the British. These threats came strangely from people who were themselves trying to subvert subjects of the Queen. But the emotions aroused by war have little to do with political frontiers: the men who gave up their villages or even joined the advancing commandos were Boers by blood, and a long history lay behind this territory which in Boer eyes made much of it morally theirs.

Only one town other than Mafeking did not immediately submit, and it the biggest. Kimberley, with its great workshops and fabulous diamond industry, stood only a few miles from the high wire fence marking the O.F.S. border. To the richness of this prize was added the presence of Cecil Rhodes himself. Reaching the city by one of the last trains to get through from the Cape two days after the war started, he was determined to see out the crisis at the place where he had won the fortune that provided the weft to the warp of his dreams.

Over thirty years before, a visitor's chance glimpse of a brilliant pebble being played with by a farm child had resulted in a low plateau on the flat dry scrub-covered veld attracting a great horde of diggers who presently gouged out the two biggest man-made holes in the world. Around about, embracing more mines, grew a city of over 50,000 people of whom 13,000 were whites. Rhodes and others had beautified it as best they could with trees and gardens, but its most conspicuous features were the scattered 40- to 120-foot-high blue-grey dumps of mine 'tailings' and the De Beers' mine headgear in which, nearly 160 feet up and overlooking many miles of country, a crow's nest had been fashioned as the headquarters of the military commander. His name was R. G. Kekewich, Colonel of the 1st Loyal North Lancashires.

More than half his forty-five years had been spent in the Army; he had fought on the Nile and in Malaya. His thinning hair crowned a round pink face, giving him a high brow, and his thin moustache overhung the corners of his mouth like two drooping feathers: a coolly determined face, perhaps a little supercilious, as of an able man but one unaware of his limitations. He arrived in Kimberley a few weeks before the outbreak of war to find it dangerously unprepared.

Rhodes's De Beers Company which dominated it, and the municipality which administered it, had both long urged the Cape Government to supply armaments for defence. In June, Schreiner, who was then giving passage to supplies for the Boers, replied: 'There is no reason whatever for apprehending that Kimberley is, or in any contemplated event will be, in danger of attack.' Since then some arms had been smuggled in, but by the time Rhodes arrived to throw his weight behind the preparations it was too late to advance them very far. The hastily raised defence force of 3,000 infantry and 850 horsemen, of whom the bulk were townsmen and the rest members of Kekewich's regiment, was short of arms and ammunition. 'It makes one wild,' Rhodes grumbled to the Cape as he strove to help organize the defences, 'to see good men walking about asking for arms.' Counting what was brought in by outlying police whom Kekewich recalled to the city, eleven machine-guns and fourteen seven-pounder cannon were available, the latter not only comparatively feeble but muzzle-loaders at that.

On 14 October Kekewich was talking to Milner by telephone when the conversation was abruptly ended by the appearance of Boers on the horizon. Kekewich proclaimed a state of siege and warned prospective rebels. A fortnight passed before the Boers made their first rush. It was beaten off. But they were bringing up their strength to 5,000 men with superior artillery, and encirclement could only be a matter of days.

*   *   *   *

While these events unfolded through October in the far north Cape, the Midlands bordering the southern O.F.S. held nothing worse for the isolated British garrisons than dust storms and false alarms. The inhabitants were mainly kinsmen of the Boers and they openly talked rebellion. Many rode across the Orange to join the Free Staters, and others urged the commandos to invade, but President Steyn had assured the Cape Premier, Schreiner, that he would not do so. Besides, he was uncertain about the security of his eastern frontier, part of which was overlooked by the mountains of Basutoland, a Native territory under British protection.

He assured the Basutos that he would not harm them if they left him alone. The British too, having decided that it was a white man's war, urged them to keep out. Thus Basutoland was conveniently placed to be the Switzerland of this war in providing a base for spying and intrigue.

The rest of the O.F.S. eastern border ran with Natal, on which the eastern Transvaal also abutted. And it was here, in the north-west corner of Natal, that the opening month of the war saw the first full-scale military operations.

CHAPTER IV

First Battles—Natal: October 1899

FOR weeks before war broke out the main Transvaal army including the State Artillery and Hollander, German and Irish volunteer corps had been concentrating near the Natal frontier under Piet Joubert. The sixty-five-year-old Commandant-General was a lawyer of Huguenot descent who, as leader of the moderates' party, had opposed the war. More cautious than his burly figure and great beard suggested, he had encamped a safe fifteen miles up the line from the border, though two wings were thrown forward to left and right under Generals Erasmus and Kock respectively, while further round to his left waited a force under Lukas Meyer. The Transvaalers totalled 14,000 men; in addition, 6,000 Free Staters under the O.F.S. Chief Commandant M. Prinsloo lay along the Drakensberg (the 'Dragon Mountains') near Van Reenen's Pass.

In Natal the Commander-in-Chief was the newly arrived Sir George White, an Irishman as old as Joubert. He had been in the Army since he was eighteen, fought in the Indian Mutiny, won the V.C., and risen to succeed Roberts as C.-in-C. of India. On expiry of this appointment he had been about to become Governor-General of Gibraltar when the S.A. emergency arose and he brought out the last-minute reinforcements. These, with the original garrison commanded by a General Penn Symons and volunteers being raised in Natal from among colonists and Uitlander refugees, made a sizeable force. But the troops were strung out at various places, notably at Ladysmith, where White had 8,000 men, and Dundee forty miles away, where Penn Symons had 4,000. This splitting of strength was due to political pressure: to have concentrated on Ladysmith would have meant abandoning the whole north-west corner of the colony, which was intolerable to local British pride and considered foolishly alarmist.

On the night following expiry of the ultimatum all the Boer forces were on the march. They rode through the grey mists of dawn; and young hearts, as always at the start of war, beat faster with anticipation. 'As far as the eye could see the plain was alive with horsemen, guns and cattle, all steadily going forward to the frontier. The scene was a stirring one, and I shall never forget riding to war with that great host.' So wrote Deneys Reitz in his reminiscences of the Boer War, *Commando*. He was a youth with General Erasmus's force when he rode that morning towards the wall of mountain along the border.

Advance units crossed into Natal that same day, but Joubert with the main army rested for the night under the looming eminence of Majuba, hill of glowing memory for Boer arms. Then, while he cautiously followed the direct route over Laing's Nek and along the railway line, he sent his left wing under General Erasmus to cross the mountains by a pass further east.

It was the rainy season and they rode in a deluge which made cooking impossible, for their wagons were left behind and they rode light, without tents or overcoats to protect them against the bitter wind sweeping the mountains. Reitz describes how on catching their first glimpse of Natal, 'with one accord the long files of horsemen reined in.' General Erasmus was a tall swarthy man in a top-hat and frock-coat; by conducting a Native war from behind a Maroola tree he had acquired the nickname of 'General Maroola': now 'General Maroola, with a quick eye to the occasion, faced round and made a speech telling us that Natal was a heritage filched from our forefathers, which now must be recovered from the usurper.' Roused to cheers and continuous singing of the Transvaal anthem, the *Volkslied*, they rode on—'into the smiling land of Natal full of hope and courage'.

As they advanced into that beautiful country of green hills, streams and pleasant valleys, they were unopposed. Joubert himself, nosing forward like an uncertain mastiff, could hardly believe that the British should have thrown away the advantage of their mountain barrier and be leaving his men to spread over northern Natal, helping themselves to cattle and the booty of farms deserted by fleeing colonists. But if he suspected a trick he found no evidence of any. A police post surrendered when the astonished occupants learnt for the first time that a war was on. No passes were mined, tunnels blocked or bridges blown up. The railway line was left untouched. Of this neglect *The Times History* comments: 'The least damaging explanation is that Sir George White never realized fully that the Boers were civilized opponents who could make use of a railway for military purposes.'

So Joubert was enabled to bring supplies by rail as fast as he advanced. Within a few days he was at Newcastle. His forward wing under Erasmus moved towards Dundee from the north, establishing contact with Lukas Meyer who was closing on it from the east. His other wing, under General Kock, moved on Ladysmith from the north while the Free Staters steadily approached this town from the west.

White felt increasing unease about dividing his strength between Dundee and Ladysmith. Both were threatened with a concerted move which might cut them off from the rest of Natal—from help or escape. 20,000 Boers were advancing from different directions: only by joining his two forces together and attacking portions of the enemy before they combined could he hope to meet them on at least comparable numerical terms. Above all he had to stop them coming between himself and Symons.

He therefore anxiously asked Symons to fall back and join him in Ladysmith. But the message was hesitant—White was not really sure of the Boers' whereabouts or strength—and Symons was confident that he could deal with the situation. No time was given for further thought: on 19 October, an advance guard of Kock's force pounced on Elandslaagte, capturing a supply train and the little settlement. It only consisted of a railway station and hotel, and a few buildings and mine shafts. But possession of it completely cut rail, telegraphic and direct road communication between Dundee and Ladysmith.

*   *   *   *

Neither this fact nor the direct threat of Erasmus and Lukas Meyer ruffled General Penn Symons. Aged fifty-six he had been fighting Natives, Burmese and Indians for twenty-two years. He had been appointed to the Natal command only recently, upon gaining a knighthood after the latest N.W. Frontier campaign. He was said, somewhat ambiguously, to have only two ideas—his duty, and doing it 'in the spirit of a high-minded, chivalrous gentleman'. His face was rather ferrety, and his wide sweeping moustache had an unsuccessful twirl. Now he called his perturbed officers together. 'I have informed Sir

George White that I feel perfectly safe, and I am dead against retreating.' When reports came in that same day of the enemy's nearness he rejected them as ridiculous.

Dundee was little more than a coal-mining village with a station for the branch line from the Durban–Pretoria railway, a string of tin-roofed buildings along a main street, and an English church. It was in a long shallow valley surrounded by low hills, except flat-topped Impati, which reared up for 1,500 feet on the north side of the town. Though it dominated the valley and contained the town's water-supply General

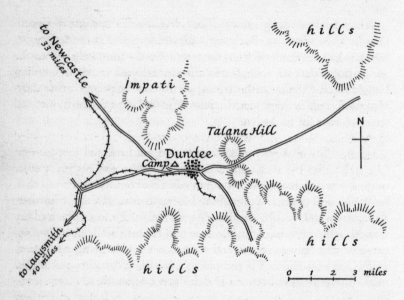

Penn Symons posted no picket on it. Nor did he do so on either of a pair of low hills much closer—two miles east of the town—of which the nearer was called Talana. Any possibility of the Boers occupying such positions, much less hauling up artillery, he entirely discounted. He declared that no number of Boers would dare take on an entire brigade of the British Army.

The town's population was swollen with loyal Afrikaner and British refugees. But loyalties were often as mixed as blood and as difficult to be sure of, so that spies moved freely about. Symons scorned to check them. The Boers could therefore plan with an exact knowledge:

Erasmus would occupy Impati and Meyer would occupy Talana, and Dundee would be in the jaws of a nutcracker.

The evening of 19 October came in heavy rain. Beyond a river east of Dundee 4,000 men under Lukas Meyer—an enormous man with a white beard reaching to his chest—saddled their ponies. The clergy-man attached to each commando urged them to fight manfully, putting their trust in the God who had brought them safely through their wanderings. With heads bared to the downpour they said a prayer. Then they crossed the river and hauled their guns with difficulty down the slushy road to Dundee.

At the same time Erasmus's 4,000 men moved across the quagmire to which the rain had reduced the veld at the approaches to Impati. As was the Boer custom, they left their ponies at the foot and climbed the steep wall of the mountain, fearful that the frequent flashes of lightning would betray them to the strong guard they expected on top. Its desertion came as a complete surprise. They huddled together, wet and cold, to wait for the dawn.

As Lukas Meyer meanwhile advanced towards Talana he stumbled on a British patrol at 2.30 a.m. and a sergeant escaped to carry the alarm. General Penn Symons was not alarmed. It was merely a Boer raid, not worth bothering his senior officers about.

When the camp awoke at daybreak the surrounding hill-tops were obscured in a swirling mist. After 5 a.m. morning parade the artillery horses were led to water a mile away, and the men busied themselves with the usual camp fatigues before breakfast. Suddenly the mist lifted, the whole crest-line of Talana and the adjoining hill was seen crammed with Boers outlined against the pale eastern light. Next moment the Boer gunners, amid cheers and clapping, sent the first shell of the war screeching over the heads of the stupefied troops. The second shell buried itself in the soft earth a few yards from Symons's tent.

He required no such stimulation. Despite the surprise, and the con-fusion caused by the artillery horses dashing back through their lines, the infantry formed up steadily. The guns came quickly into action to rake the top of Talana, and not only were the Boer guns silenced but nearly a thousand men rushed in a panic down the other side of the hill, leapt on their ponies and made off; one prominent Boer did not stop for fifty miles and reported the whole Boer force destroyed. But while a citizen army is strong in its cause its want of trained discipline need not be fatal. Thus, though many ran away, many stayed. Spreading themselves among the rocks they prepared for battle.

Symons immediately ordered a frontal assault on Talana by his infantry and sent his cavalry down the valley between Impati and Talana to cut off any retreat from the latter. He ignored Erasmus's 4,000 men on and about Impati because he declined to believe in their existence. His men hurried through the town to a dried-up water-course about a mile from Talana. Women and children torn between terror and enthusiasm cheered them on. Menfolk of the town guard seized rifle and bandoleer and followed. The town was left defenceless, and Symons's flank totally exposed, against Erasmus poised on Impati.

Beyond the water-course was a plantation of blue-gum extending to a hundred yards from the foot of Talana. Crawling through the plantation under heavy plunging fire which stripped the trees and filled the air with the smell of eucalyptus, the troops wavered before finding protection behind a wall along the end of the plantation. The artillery was brought closer and systematically pounded Talana.

Fortune is apt to favour the foolish as well as the brave. Symons being both, he was abundantly favoured. Firstly, the Boers had not yet learnt how best to position their guns, which were quickly silenced. Secondly, Meyer let the greater part of his forces stay with him on the hill adjoining Talana which was left defended by only four or five hundred men, and he made no attempt to help them by sweeping down on the British flank or the town. Thirdly, Erasmus on Impati was gripped by irresolution, Reitz recording that in the thick mist of day-break when he was asked for orders he merely stood glowering into the fog, and he continued merely glowering.

All the same, the four or five hundred on Talana poured so fierce a fire on the British that they could not advance beyond the wall, a hundred yards from the foot of the hill. General Penn Symons grew impatient. He galloped forward from the water-course, strode though the stripped plantation, and calling up groups of soldiers still huddled there, reached the wall. Disregarding his staff's entreaties he stepped over to view the hill for himself, and here his luck ended. He turned to one of his officers and said calmly, 'I am severely, mortally, wounded in the stomach.' He was helped back to his horse and carried from the battlefield in a dying condition.

His second-in-command, General Yule, was left to launch the assault.

A blaze of fire from Talana above them and the adjoining hill to their right greeted the waves of infantry that tried to cross the level grass to the foot of the slope, and the veld was soon dotted with prostrate khaki figures. Some men succeeded in getting a little way up the hill where another wall sheltered them for two hours while reinforcements gradually arrived and the artillery lobbed shells on to the crest above. It was separated from them by a cliff about fifty yards away across a terrace in the hill-side. The Colonel of the King's Royal Rifles yelled as the artillery stopped: 'Advance!' To their officers' cries of 'Forrard away! Forrard away!' the men, their bayonets gleaming in the drizzly light, staggered blindly across the terrace against a fire the more desperate for the Boers' fear of the bayonet. But somehow enough reached the cliff and hauled themselves on to the crest to send the Boers flying, though the last of them emptied their rifles in the faces of the leading officers, killing the colonel. Another lived to tell the tale:

> The ground in front of me was literally rising in dust from the bullets, and the din seemed to blend with every other sound into a long drawn-out hideous roar. Half-way over the terrace I looked round over my shoulder and the whole ground we had already covered was strewn with bodies, and no more men were coming from over the wall. At that moment I was hit through the knee. I hopped to the foot of the cliff. There I began to pull myself up; bullets from both flanks were flying thick. I was hit a second time by a shot from above; the bullet hit me in the back and came out in front of my thigh. . . . I had crawled on to the crest line when a Boer stood up twenty yards in front of me. He threw up his rifle and covered me and I took a step forward and covered him with my pistol. I forgot my wounded leg, and as I pulled the trigger the leg gave way and I fell. I drew myself back under cover of a rock and raised myself carefully, ready to shoot if I spotted my man again. He was gone, and as I was looking I was hit a third time, along the back, the bullet coming out just by my spine. After a while, hearing W——'s voice I asked if he had any dressings. He brought me one. He was wounded over the eye. The firing was gradually dying down, only to bring to our ears what was infinitely more painful to hear, the moaning of wounded men from the terrace below and the hill-side around us. [21]

Even more painful to hear was the sudden bursting of shrapnel as the gunners below, unaware that the battle was won, opened fire again. The crest was cleared of friend and foe alike except for the wounded frantically searching for shelter. The Boers might have recovered possession had they acted before the mistake was discovered. Instead, they completed their withdrawal and fled from the adjoining hill as well. The British gunners, hauling their guns on to Talana, saw a remarkable sight. Across the valley below them streamed the whole of Meyer's force at point-blank range. But the artillery commander was still unnerved by the mistake of firing on his own men. He hesitated, sent back for orders, and the chance was gone.

Now the cavalry Symons had sent to cut off just such a flight became entangled in the fleeing Boers and split into two. The smaller section eventually returned safely to camp, but the other blundered towards Impati. Erasmus's force at last comes into the story. The sun had broken through the mist and lit patches of the valley below them. Into such a patch they suddenly saw the troop riding, and acting on individual initiative a number of them at once ran it to earth in a farm-house. After a two-hour engagement the British surrendered. It was Reitz's first experience of modern warfare, and he was as disappointed at seeing only an occasional helmet and spurts of dust as he was to discover that the British wore khaki instead of scarlet, which 'seemed to detract from the glamour of war; but worse still was the sight of dead soldiers. . . . I had pictured the dignity of death in battle, but I now saw that it was horrible to look upon.' Having helped themselves to swords, bayonets, horses and other trophies, the triumphant Boers returned to their envious comrades on Impati.

So ended the Battle of Talana (or Dundee). It was represented in England as a glorious victory. True, Dundee had been saved, but its situation was now more critical than ever. The Boers were in possession of Impati and the town's water-supply; they were little discomfited by casualties of about 150 and could attack again at any point, this time with perhaps more unison. The British commander lay dying, his force was depleted by 546 casualties, and direct escape to Ladysmith was impossible since the Boer capture of Elandslaagte the day before.

* * * *

In that place there was no longer a small advance party of Kock's force: Kock himself was in the settlement with upwards of a thousand men. Appealed to by his advance party to reinforce them he had hesitated, for he knew Joubert's wish for caution and being old himself, shared it. Then he reluctantly agreed, and rode all night with most of his force to reach Elandslaagte, where he rested through the day while the battle raged at Dundee—and a new character entered the story.

He was a short powerful man with heavy jowls, a bushy moustache and a bull neck. John Denton Pinkstone French, aged forty-seven, had arrived to take command of the cavalry under White. Son of an Irish sailor he himself started in the Navy at the age of fourteen before joining the Hussars, fought in the Sudan campaign of 1844-5, and since held various posts in England. He was rumoured to have run off with his colonel's wife, consistent with his reputation as a dashing cavalry-man. But his success in handling large bodies of mounted troops on manœuvres could not obscure his lack of battle experience, and his appointment to S.A. caused some controversy. With him as his Chief of Staff was a Major Douglas Haig.

General French arrived at Ladysmith the same day as the Battle of Talana. He promptly captured a Boer patrol who, probably unaware of Kock's arrival, led White to believe that the restoration of communications with Dundee would be simple. French was ordered to recapture Elandslaagte at dawn.

In ignorance of these arrangements Kock's men that evening held a smoking concert in the Elandslaagte hotel. They invited the British captured with the supply train and settlement. Old General Kock had been fighting the British since he was twelve years old but he had a warrior's heart that bore an enemy no malice. With the help of luxuries from the supply train and hotel, a convivial atmosphere was soon established. *God Save the Queen* and the *Volkslied* were sung with vigorous impartiality; and

> Please sell no more drink to my father—
> It makes him so strange and so wild.

was doubtless rendered with the same enthusiasm as the Boer hillbilly ditties.

French's attack at dawn achieved complete surprise. But the Boers were too quick to be caught. They leapt on their ponies and made for the nearby hills where they had two guns in position. It was French's turn to be surprised, by the strength of the Boers and the accuracy of their artillery. Telephoned for instructions, White resolved to strike hard, at once. Guns, horse and infantry were rushed up to French by rail and road. To command the infantry White sent Colonel Ian Hamilton.

Like French and Haig this was destined to be a famous name. He had followed his father into the Gordon Highlanders when he was nineteen and the twenty-seven years since then had brought him much campaigning in the Middle and Far East, besides S.A. where he was severely wounded in the First Boer War. Among his appointments had been that of Military Secretary to White in India after Roberts's retirement. A slender Scot with a thin pale rather pinched face, a thick moustache and a lofty brow, his light-brown hair parted a little off-centre, Ian Standish Hamilton expressed his romantic attachment to war when he wrote of 'the clash of sword and hollow reverberating clang of brazen buckler, the storm and wild joy of battle . . .'[22] and he was the most sensitive and lyrical regular of his time.

The last of the reinforcements reached French by three o'clock that afternoon. Three six-gun batteries began a preparatory bombardment. The force comprised 3,000 infantry (Manchesters, Devons, Gordon Highlanders) and mounted troops (Lancers, Dragoons and Imperial Light Horse). The I.L.H. consisted largely of Johannesburg men, the same Uitlanders whose failure to go to Jameson's aid had earned them accusations of cowardice and their city the name of 'Judasburg'. They had waited a long time to vindicate their honour. The opposing force could scarcely have been more representative: not only were the majority Boers from Johannesburg but present also were detachments of the detested Hollanders and Germans.

The British occupied one arm and the Boers the other of a ridge shaped like a huge horseshoe, the arms being three miles apart across level veld. That occupied by the Boers was a hogsback in outline, the open end clustered about by three kopjes cradling their guns. Before the attack began Hamilton addressed the infantry. He told them that the Devons would attack the hogsback from across the open veld directly before them, while the rest of the infantry would work along the curve of the horseshoe extending from their right front and, reaching the beginning of the hogsback, roll up the whole Boer line. He said he was sure they would shift the Boers by sunset and send the little newsboys crying victory through the streets of London next morning. The troops cheered lustily, waving their helmets and breaking from their ranks crying, 'We'll do it, sir! We'll do it!'

As the attack started an anxious Sir George White arrived to watch from the heights behind the British lines. An immense thunder cloud, edged by the rays of the fast sinking sun, overhung the sky behind the Boers; its blackness made every puff of bursting shrapnel clear. Flashes of lightning revealed the sharp edges of the hogsback occupied by the Boers. Sounds multiplied—rolls of thunder, the screech and crash of

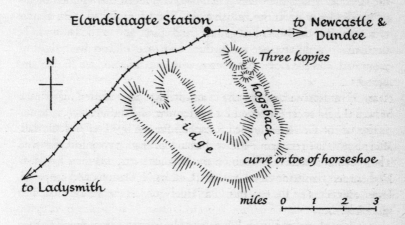

shells, the growing intensity of rifle-fire, the galloping of horses as ammunition wagons were rushed up from the rear.

The Devons advanced across the veld in an open formation never before seen in European warfare. Aldershot's still sacrosanct rules required infantry to advance almost shoulder to shoulder. But Hamilton deployed his men at intervals of nearly a yard, enabling them to advance unscathed, firing in volleys, though presently they had to crawl behind the cover of ant-hills—eighteen-inch-high mounds of hard earth. A quarter of a mile from the enemy they came to a standstill.

The Boer gunners, outgunned eighteen to two, were often silenced but they stuck to their task. The Manchesters, meanwhile, led the flank attack along the curve of the horseshoe. They reached the bottom of the hogsback but could not gain a foothold. Then the great cloud opened and for ten minutes a torrential downpour blotted them from the Boers' view. The Manchesters ran forward to the boulders strewn along the lower slopes. There the I.L.H. dismounted, and the Gordon Highlanders reinforced them. The fury of the Boer fire checked them but they rallied until a barbed-wire fence, put up for farming purposes but now the precursor of World War I terror, again stopped them. As they clustered at the gaps in it batches of them were mown down before the very intensity of the Boer fire cleared a way. At last the defenders were wavering when from a farm-house down the rear side the German detachment which had been concealed there hurled themselves recklessly upon the British right. The I.L.H. killed them almost to a man. But the Boers had gained fresh spirit, and in the fading light the British could advance no further: half their officers were dead or wounded, and the slope was strewn with casualties sodden in rain and blood.

Ian Hamilton dashed into the firing-line having gathered many men who had held back. He ordered a bugler to sound the advance; a drum-major of the Gordons stepped forward into the open to play the call, and rhythmic firing from below meant that the Devons had renewed their frontal assault. The men on the hogsback gripped their bayonets and surged forward, faltered, rallied, and this time carried the crest, even overrunning the still smoking Boer guns as the gunners fired to the end.

Yet it was not the end. There suddenly burst upon the British a violent counter-attack of about fifty Boers concealed in rear of the crest. Old General Kock himself led them, blazing away in his top-hat and frock-coat.

For a hundred yards the British fell back in confusion along the hogsback. Hamilton was in the thick of them, yelling that help was at hand. A lieutenant of the Gordons called on his men to follow as he went forward, only to fall riddled with six bullets. French himself came into the firing-line and everywhere the officers tried to stem the panic. Waving a silk scarf the colonel of the I.L.H., wounded in leg and lung, urged on his men until a bullet pierced his brain, his last words being destined to send a throb through the Empire, 'My fellows are doing well.' The retreat was stopped. The men charged forward again as the

Devons emerged from the plain below. In a wild three minutes the combined assault overwhelmed the defenders. Cease-fire rang out over the battlefield and the pipes of the Highlanders skirled a paean.

Boer survivors made away into the gloom on their ponies. The Lancers and Dragoons lay in wait. Lance levelled and sabre bared they galloped into them. Some Boers tried to bring their rifles to bear; others threw themselves on the ground and begged for mercy; most tried to break away, but their ponies were no match for the big horses of the cavalry who rode through them for a mile and a half, so repeatedly hacking and spearing that one young Boer received sixteen lance wounds, before they wheeled and began to take prisoners. From this incident was born a mortal hatred of the British cavalry, whom the Boers swore to hunt without mercy. But a cavalry charge could not succeed if constantly checked in order for individuals to be given quarter.

It was dark now. The troopers were wet through but as the dead were insufficient to supply cloaks for the Boer wounded they gave their own. On the hills parties of men searched for their wounded by lamplight or blew whistles to attract their attention. Groups of shivering wounded were found mixed up with the dead where the gaps had been in the barbed wire, and again the corpses were stripped to provide additional clothing. Not far from the Boer guns old General Kock was found fatally wounded and carried into Ladysmith.

As was the custom among the Boer generals—and often their men— his wife was quite close at hand. She was seeking news of him among fugitives from the battlefield and trying to arrange to get through the British lines to see him when young Reitz encountered her, 'the memory of her tear-stained face giving me my first hint of what women suffer in time of war'.

The battle caused such grief among Boers and British alike. Death, mutilation, sorrow are poor rewards for courage, yet are the more frequent the greater the courage. The day had shown neither side to have a preserve of courage. The lieutenant of the Gordons who fell in rallying his men and two captains of the I.L.H. gained V.C.s, and French recommended one for Hamilton but the War Office regarded valour as a senior officer's duty. The Boers gave no decorations to men or officers. It was an attitude which at least denied the gloss such trophies give to war.

As Sir George White rode back to Ladysmith in the darkness he could have reflected on the extent of his victory at Elandslaagte: the Boer general lay dying while half his force was killed, wounded or captured; his two guns were lost and so were his laager and all his equipment. Moreover, the enemy thrust between Ladysmith and Dundee was thrown back. The British for their part had sustained but half as many casualties, and they might now draw their own two armies together along the line of communications which their victory had freed.

But these were not Sir George White's thoughts. Riding back in the darkness he was in a mental fog as well. A messenger galloped up with a dispatch from Ladysmith saying that the Free Staters, who he believed were 10,000 strong, were about to pounce on the town. He believed also that Joubert was approaching Elandslaagte with the main Transvaal army. Neither was true, and the Free Staters totalled only 6,000—an important difference when White had 8,000. But on the strength of these three pieces of misinformation he decided there and then to abandon Elandslaagte.

A curse lay on the decision. Battle-fatigue, the mud, the darkness, the lack of preparation and fear of a Boer attack turned the retirement into a rout. Panic-stricken men abandoned their prisoners and quantities of captured arms and equipment. The Battle of Elandslaagte, so hardly won, was made a sheer waste of toil and life.

* * * *

Such were the events of the early hours of Sunday, 22 October. In Dundee, for the second successive day following the Battle of Talana, General Yule nervously marched his men backwards and forwards across the rain-soaked valley sporadically shelled from Impati. He sent to White for help but White replied that none could be sent.

At last he came to a fixed decision. With the direct road to Lady-smith denied him by White's withdrawal he would have to go over sixty-four miles by a bad and roundabout way at the height of the rainy season.

That evening he fell-in his thousands of already exhausted men as silently as possible and leaving all his tents standing marched into a providentially dark night. To avoid spies he had, with a ruthlessness harrowing to the soul of a Victorian officer and gentleman, to abandon the unwarned townsfolk to the enemy, together with his dying general, three months' supplies, and much equipment. The column straggled out for over four miles and men fell asleep in their tracks while it was pulled together. Dawn found them in the hills ten miles south, asleep over their breakfast until roused by Yule to trudge on.

A thick mist blotted out Dundee from the Boers on Impati. When Erasmus, sending down ten men to investigate, found that it had been abandoned his men, says Reitz, went

> whooping through the town and behaving in a very undisciplined manner. Officers tried to stem the rush, but we were not to be denied, and we plundered shops and dwelling-houses. . . . It was not for what we got out of it, for we knew that we could carry little or nothing away with us, but the joy of ransacking other people's property is hard to resist, and we gave way to the impulse.

For days they had been wet and cold in the open, their diet mainly biltong, and the British camp outside the town was a revelation: 'Here were entire streets of tents, and . . . mountains of luxurious foods, comfortable camp-stretchers and sleeping-bags . . . even a gymnasium.'

As Erasmus restored order to the town and organized a pursuit Yule's men were far removed from such comforts. They made their way over the hills fearful of pursuit or ambush. In the plains they met with swollen rivers and almost impassable mud. To distract the Boers reoccupying Elandslaagte away to the right, White on the second day of Yule's march 'demonstrated' against them.* The Boers in pursuit, however, pressed ever closer. By the fourth night they were harrying Yule's rearguard. It was a night so dark in the torrential rain that the men linked hands as they floundered knee-deep in mud and over starved and exhausted oxen and horses that fell down and could not be raised. But day revealed to them, across a short expanse of plain, the blessed sight of Ladysmith. By noon they were safe. The garrison lined the streets to cheer them in, and despite their fatigue they feebly tried to sing. Yule's health was broken.

In Dundee Penn Symons died without knowing if his men were safe. Wrapped in a blanket his body was carried to the graveyard of the English church. The gentle Joubert sent a message of sympathy to his

* Called the Rietfontein Action, mainly an artillery duel. British losses 110, Boer 30.

widow. Then his combined forces moved on Ladysmith, where at last the whole of the Natal Field Force stood together.

*   *   *   *

At the sack of Badajoz a gallant young cavalryman called Harry Smith rescued a beautiful Spanish woman whom later he married. He did much work in S.A. where he was widely admired but his lady could little have guessed how her name, given to a little town in Natal, would one day ring around the world.

Ladysmith derived its importance from being a garrison town and standing at the junction of the Natal–O.F.S. and Natal–Transvaal railway lines. Sited by a stream that meandered through a broad valley it consisted of a few streets with tin-roofed houses and the gardens beloved of English wives. Even in the rainy season the sun shone more often than not, giving it a sleepy atmosphere.

This atmosphere was a little different now as supplies, replacing the losses at Dundee, poured in from the south, the only route still open. Trains, wagons pulled by spans of sixteen oxen, mule trolleys, water carts and pack trains disgorged at the camp or in the town, where White turned schools and churches into warehouses or hospitals in front of which rose pyramids of beef boxes and flour sacks. Then there were refugees or visitors trapped by the turn of events. The most notable was Dr. Jameson, doomed like Rhodes to be an impotent and embarrassing spectator of events he had himself largely precipitated. A town guard of tradesmen and others paraded about manfully in front of their womenfolk; and martial law ruled.

Nevertheless, business went on much as usual and the officers' wives and leading ladies of the town were not to be deflected from their garden parties. None doubted that the Boers would be put to flight. White himself was confident. The Boers had been repulsed at Talana and defeated at Elandslaagte. He now had the whole of his force together, under officers like French and Hamilton, and they were ready to avenge their two ignominious but unjustified retreats.

The Boers approached with equal confidence: 'a fine sight it was,' says Reitz, 'as the masses of horsemen breasted the green slopes towards the final hills from which we could look down on Ladysmith.' On the central and highest, Pepworth Hill due north of the town, they began to emplace one of their fearsome ninety-four-pounder Long Toms.

This was Sunday, 29 October. Their preparations were plainly visible from the town. White had nothing to match the calibre of the big gun. He had sent to the Cape for naval guns which had been successfully tried out on land by an inventive genius, Captain Percy Scott of H.M.S. *Terrible*, but they were still on the way. A cavalry reconnaissance showed that the town would be completely encircled within a few days unless he acted quickly. To assess the situation he sent up a balloon which had the whole town agog.

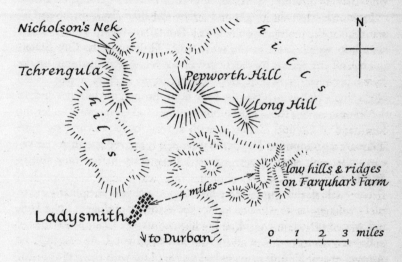

From his dangling basket the observer saw below him a semicircle of hilly country rising from the plain round the north of Ladysmith. In the centre of the semicircle stood Pepworth Hill, from the right of which the broken country swept round—via Long Hill midway—to a series of ridges on Farquhar's Farm four miles east of the town. Left of Pepworth was a valley leading from the plain, then a hill called Tchrengula continued the semicircle round to the west of the town. Somewhere in this western sector the Free Staters were taking up position, but White decided first to attack the Transvaalers who he believed occupied a line from Pepworth to Long Hill.

Young Reitz was near Pepworth that Sunday, when Piet Joubert arrived to give an eve-of-battle address: 'He started by scolding the men for having looted a farm close by, and got so worked up that he forgot to tell us what the real object of his visit had been. We took his wigging in good part, but I am afraid no one treated our commander-in-chief very seriously.' Preparations went forward seriously enough. For the first time the Boers could bring up their full concentration of guns, arranging them on or behind the Pepworth–Long Hill arc.

When night came White made his dispositions for battle. He sent a brigade under the command of Colonel Grimwood to march in the darkness to the ridges on Farquhar's Farm east of the town: his orders were that at daybreak, with the support of French's cavalry, he would swing north from the ridges and attack the Boer flank on Long Hill and thence Pepworth, upon which a frontal assault by a force under Hamilton would burst at the same time. To distract the Free Staters and cut off any retreat by the Transvaalers White sent a column up the valley between Pepworth and Tchrengula to occupy a pass called Nicholson's Nek which was the back door through the hills beyond. In the column were a thousand Dublin Fusiliers and Gloucesters under the command of Colonel Carleton, with a string of mules carrying guns and spare ammunition. The mules were newly arrived and their restive-ness under untrained drivers caused a long delay before they finally set off.

The flank assault force under Grimwood reached Farquhar's Farm safely whereupon he wheeled to face the shadowy outline of Long Hill, and waited for dawn to launch his surprise attack. There were indeed to be several surprises, but all for Colonel Grimwood. At first light he discovered that half his brigade had not kept up with the rest and that French's cavalry were in the wrong position. And then suddenly 4,000 Mausers tore the dawn apart, raking his position with a storm of bullets that came not from the supposed Boer flank on Long Hill ahead of him but from *his* flank. While the bulk of the Transvaalers were around Pepworth, none at all were on Long Hill and those under Lukas Meyer had all the time been skilfully deployed a little back on the same series that Grimwood occupied. Hastily he wheeled his men to the right to answer the Boer fire and French's men dismounted to help them. The artillery also opened up but for a long time pounded the deserted Long Hill.

These first sounds of battle were not all that woke the town. Early risers saw a column of white smoke above Pepworth Hill and then an explosion shook the railway station. The Boer gunners waved their hats in jubilation at Long Tom's first effort. Other guns scattered about the hills opened up. The British artillery covering Hamilton's frontal advance on Pepworth were pushed forward and a sustained gunnery duel ensued. Recalling the din of bursting shells and thousands of rifles Reitz says, 'I was awed rather than frightened.' The new weapons robbed battle of its former theatricality, keeping the combatants at unseen distances apart instead of masses of men locked together in smoke and fury.

The youth was in the vicinity of Pepworth, against which Hamilton's frontal assault soon started. But as it was to combine with Grimwood's would-be flank attack on the right, and as the artillery were distracted by a fight for survival against the Boer guns, it was not pressed far against stiff opposition. So Reitz set off to Pepworth which the British guns had turned into a cloud of smoke and flame, making the ground shudder even where he lay with his commando a mile away. At the back of the hill he found dead and mutilated artillerymen laid out on a square of canvas. An ambulance van had some of its mule team dead in their traces and 'the native drivers were running wildly to the rear. At the guns above twenty or thirty shells were bursting with terrific noise.' He worked his way up to the sand-bagged ramparts. Among more dead and wounded crouched the surviving gunners unable for the moment to use their guns under the storm of shrapnel.

However, the British guns were not able to concentrate on Pepworth. The Boer guns among the other hills were being used with telling accuracy. Concealed and using smokeless powder they could not be located until their recoil on the hard ground—so quickly had the sun burnt out the rain—sent up clouds of dust. Even then they were nimbly moved to new positions.

As the sun rose higher over the battlefield White's anxiety at the progress of his attack was increased by a sinister new factor. Loose mules and straggling gunners began to arrive. Apparently Carleton, fearing his delayed departure would expose him at daybreak in the valley between Pepworth and Tchrengula, decided to spend the night on the latter rather than risk trying to reach Nicholson's Nek; but climbing the slopes the mules stampeded and ran off with the spare ammunition. The noise, increased by panic firing by some of the men, would certainly have brought the Boers swarming to attack. White tried desperately to find out what was happening. An officers' patrol, one of whom gained the V.C., and Native runners all failed to get through. He had heliograph* signals flashed to Tchrengula. No answer came.

Yet he knew Carleton was there, for during lulls on the main battle-field he heard firing. He could not send any of the reinforcements which were arriving by train from the south, for these were immediately flung into support of Grimwood at Farquhar's Farm, where the situation was fast deteriorating.

Troops pinned to the edge of the ridges for hours under the blister-ing sun were utterly unable to advance. The truth was that the Boers' tactics and determination were far superior to anything yet seen. Their commandant was the same Lukas Meyer who had proved his incom-petence at Talana, but he had fallen ill and deputizing for him was a cheerful friendly man called Louis Botha.

At that time a tall handsome bright-eyed farmer of thirty-eight, dark-featured with moustache and small beard, he looked more French than Dutch though the blood of both flowed in his veins. He had been born a British subject in Natal, trekked away at an early age and adventurously intervened, under Lukas Meyer, in a Zulu civil war which resulted in the grant of the Vryheid district to the Transvaal. There he had been farming so progressively that he turned virgin veld into a property worth £30,000. Yet he had scarcely three years' school-ing, although his wife, an Irishwoman descended from Emett the revolutionary, taught him much. Happiest playing the accordion to entertain his family and friends, he had found recent years trying, for like his old chief and neighbour he was a member of the Volksraad and a moderate. Though convinced of the wrongness of England, for whom his wife's ancestry implied no love, and despite the death of his own father in consequence of the First Boer War, he saw war as un-mitigated disaster and he abstained from voting on the issue. But when war came he rode once more under the command of Lukas Meyer, until this unexpected moment of himself assuming command. And such was his instinctive grasp of leadership that his men threatened at any moment to sweep Grimwood clean off the ridges.

So it was reported to White. The situation in the town seemed equally bad. The loose mules and straggling gunners from Carleton's column, the stream of wounded from the front, and the intermittent

* A mirror swivelled on a stand to catch the sun and transmit Morse.

pounding of Long Tom, unnerved the townsfolk. Panic threatened, and the town commander also sent word to White that the Free Staters showed signs of intended attack from the west. White immediately gave the order to all troops: 'Retire as opportunity offers.'

The signal to Carleton on Tchrengula went unanswered. Hamilton's men in front of Pepworth retreated in good order. But as those at Farquhar's Farm rose at last from their ordeal they gave Louis Botha the opportunity to see them off with the full violence of his 4,000 Mausers. They fled in panic. Rushing to the edge of the ridges the Boers had them at their mercy on the open plain before Ladysmith.

But as the infantry ran wildly past, the gunners of two batteries that had been in rear of them stood firm and drew the Boer fire. Then, enveloped in smoke and dust they withdrew in stages, each battery by turn keeping up the bombardment to cover the withdrawal of the other, and though the Boers pressed closer and guns overturned in a tangle of limber* harnesses and stricken horses, they got away. A vital quarter of an hour had been prised from the enemy, allowing the infantry to escape. Even then the Boers could have wrought havoc in pursuit, but Botha was newly and temporarily in command and Joubert's caution prevailed. And at this moment, by a story-book coincidence, the naval guns ordered by White arrived by train: some were rushed into action, further deterring the Boers. (The story made Captain Scott of H.M.S. *Terrible* a newspaper hero of the hour in England.)

In the town all was anxiety and grief. Refugees huddled in their wagons or the already overcrowded railway station. An eye-witness account is eloquent with the sentiment of the age: 'The condition of the women, wan and weary with waiting, was pitiable in the extreme. The barbarity of war was more marked in the horror written on those pale faces . . . than in the mangled frames borne from the battlefield.' Gradually the troops re-formed and some calm descended. But now no sound came from Tchrengula. It was evening before White's uncertainty about Carleton's column was ended. A message from Joubert brought the gist of what had happened.

After the mules stampeded, the column had climbed on to Tchrengula. By dawn the Free Staters, attracted by the noise, were creeping

---

* Detachable part of a gun-carriage. The horses were harnessed to its other end. It carried some ammunition and, on the march, a couple of artillerymen.

up the slopes. Most serious of all, Carleton discovered that he occupied only one of the two portions into which the mile-long crest was divided. A Boer vice-commandant perceived that the unoccupied part being higher was the key to the whole situation. He promptly persuaded enough of his comrades to gallop round to the unoccupied side, dismount, and climb up on to it. His name was Christian de Wet.

Though portraits of De Wet show rather sleepy Oriental eyes and an affable expression, the ubiquitous Reitz, presently encountering him for the first time, is nearer the mark in referring to his 'fierce eyes and keen determined face'. A little unkempt beard, climbing in a fringe along his jaw-bone and joined on either side his mouth by his moustache, adorned a man whose silences and sardonic humour kept him aloof from his fellows and little known to them despite his membership of a leading O.F.S. family and his pre-war occupation of potato-speculator. And if they knew him they did not like him, for all his unquenchable love of country—the one characteristic shared with that other Boer for whom this day first brought distinction, Louis Botha.

Having seized the undefended part of Tchrengula Christian de Wet pressed on. Wounded, he continued to lead a slow determined advance across the crest. It was littered with rocks behind which more and more dead or wounded soldiers were found, many of them Irishmen fighting for the British as zealously as their countrymen in a volunteer force called Blake's Brigade were at this very moment fighting for the Boers in the main battle. Carleton's chief defences were hastily built stone breast-works whose tops the Boers had only to spray systematically. Where his men could raise their heads long enough to fire, Aldershot's rules forbade them to do so except in volleys and then only when an officer gave the command. By the time an officer spotted a Boer, directed his men's aim and gave the order the Boer was safely behind another rock.

For several hours in the blazing heat the British fought back as best they could, but forced ever back, stalked on all sides, lacking ammunition reserves, and finally becoming aware of the main army's retreat into Ladysmith, they were in a hopeless situation. When the Boers began to overrun his part of the crest and men surrendered, Carleton ordered the general cease-fire to be sounded. The bugler was so frightened that he was unable to produce a sound but at last got out a thin quivering note. At the same time a white rag was raised and the men walked towards the Boers with their rifles at the trail. One group, by chance unscathed and unsighted in a fold in the ground, could see no reason for surrender, and officers broke their swords in indignation. To Reitz the inevitability of surrender was plain: 'Dead and wounded lay all around, and the cries and groans of agony and the dreadful sights haunted me for many a day, for though I had seen death by violence of late, there had been nothing to approach the horrors accumulated here.' Over 800 prisoners were taken; the rest were dead or wounded. *The Times History* has recorded:

> In their moment of triumph the Boers behaved with the same un-affected kindheartedness which they had shown at Majuba, and which they displayed after most of their victories. Though exul-tant they were not insulting. They fetched water and blankets for the wounded, and treated prisoners with every consideration.

This should be set alongside the British treatment of Boer wounded after Elandslaagte, because in such matters the respective victors' behaviour is more typical of the war as a whole than the atrocities, alleged from the outset by the journals of each side against the other, would have one believe. No doubt some wounded were killed, Red Cross and white flags abused, brutalities committed, hospitals shelled, etc., etc., but the fact that the men in the field made so little of such allegations justifies reference to the subject only as showing how sedulously propaganda was worked up. A hate campaign against per-sonalities was equally well maintained, from sinister cartoons of Kruger in England to epithets like 'The Franchise Scoundrel!' beneath pictures of Milner in Pretoria.

The message from Joubert which told White of Carleton's sur-render also granted an armistice for the British to bury their dead, bringing to an end the story of the battle variously named Ladysmith, Farquhar's Farm or Mooi River. Its subsidiary action has always been called by the name of the place Carleton never reached, Nicholson's Nek. The British losses totalled over 1,200 men; the Boers' 200.

Considerable though this victory had been, the Boers gathered round their laager fires voiced much criticism of Joubert for not ordering a pursuit of the British flying from Farquhar's Farm. Reitz was with De Wet on Tchrengula when they saw the rout through billows of dust and he heard him mutter, 'Loose your horsemen, loose your horsemen.' It was said that when Joubert was urged to order a pursuit he replied, 'When God holds out a finger, don't take the whole hand'—a Dutch saying which, a Boer commented, might be sound theology but no good in making war.

To the British public the day became known as Mournful Monday. All that they were told at first about the main battle was that there had been 'an armed reconnaissance in force', but the disaster to Carleton's column could not be concealed. An eye-witness recalls:

> The news was published on a grey raw day. In London people bought up the early editions of the evening journals. The placards caused the horse-omnibuses of those days to stop that passengers might buy the papers. There was neither noise nor gesture. The news was read, the journals were not flung down, but folded and kept; few men desired speech with their neighbours. It was certain from then, whatever this war might bring, that national will never would give in.[1]

Ironically, the constant fear of many in authority was that a sharp reverse might mean another 'Majuba'—that the new 'street-bred' democracy which waved flags so vigorously today would as raucously opt for peace tomorrow. But the general feeling was that the Boers by springing an ultimatum had caught Britain momentarily at a disadvantage. The dramatic story of the bluejackets' last-minute arrival at Ladysmith assured everyone that the Boers' surprising (despite all the talk of their armaments) superiority in artillery was being redressed, and the release of White's dispatch in which he accepted all responsibility for Nicholson's Nek disarmed any criticism.

Behind the scenes there was less complacency. Chamberlain angrily wrote to a Cabinet colleague concerning the Secretary of War:

> Do you remember Lansdowne telling us . . . that modern guns required elaborate platforms and mountings which took a year to consolidate? The Boers apparently find no difficulty in working their 'Long Tom', without these elaborate precautions. On the whole I am terribly afraid that our War Office is as inefficient as usual.

But no one grasped the essential lesson of Mournful Monday summed up by *The Times History*: 'The Battle of Ladysmith was the first engagement on a large scale between British troops and Dutch burghers, and the first in which the two military systems were fairly matched against each other. And it showed conclusively that in the open field 12,000 British troops were not a match for an equal number of Boers.'

To the public such a statement would have been absurd and incredible. In any event, the great Army Corps was beginning to arrive under the veteran of many a victory, General Sir Redvers Buller. *Punch* was presently to depict an urchin confiding to a chum: 'The Boers 'll cop it now. Farfer's gone to South Africa, *an' tooken 'is strap!*'

CHAPTER V

Arrival of the Army Corps: November 1899

> There is no stronger commander in the British Army than this remote, almost grimly resolute, completely independent, utterly fearless, steadfast, and always vigorous man. Big-boned, square-jawed, strong-minded, strong-headed . . . Smartness . . . Sagacity . . . Administrative capacity . . . He was born to be a soldier of the very best English type, needless to say the best type of all.

AT THE risk of marring this typical contemporary description of Sir Redvers Buller it should be mentioned that his big bones were particularly well covered, especially in the region of the stomach, and that his square jaw was not specially apparent above a double chin. He had entered the Army with no disadvantages, his mother being a Howard and niece of the Duke of Norfolk, and he was very wealthy, which was fortunate in view of his preference for a diet of ample good food and champagne. But his record was something to conjure with. Since the age of twenty-one he had fought in five campaigns, including the Zululand wars when he was the dashing leader of irregular cavalry. A winner of the V.C. twice over, he had such a reputation that many people thought he and not Wolseley should have been head of the British Army, and there was universal satisfaction over his appointment at the age of sixty to lead the Army Corps in S.A.

When he embarked at Southampton on 14 October he could look forward to assembling the Army Corps as fast as it was delivered by the fleet of ships converging on the Cape ports, and to carrying out promptly the War Office plan of a direct thrust at Bloemfontein and Pretoria from the Cape Midlands which President Steyn had obligingly pledged himself not to attack from across the Orange. Confidence in an early end to the war increased as a passing ship signalled by means of a blackboard hung over the side: BOERS DEFEATED. THREE BATTLES. PENN SYMONS KILLED. These battles (Talana or Dundee, Rietfontein and Elandslaagte) seemed to justify Wolseley's assertion that the Boer invasions to east and west would be held by the forces already in S.A. Only when he reached Table Bay on the last day of the month did Buller have cause to doubt: the first news brought him was of White's defeat at Ladysmith the previous day.

A great crowd turned out to cheer him through the streets of Cape Town. Loyal colonists and refugees did not view the course of events with the same equanimity as their countrymen in England, and at sight of that impassive face they welcomed him as a saviour.

The situation in fact made mock of the comfortable reflections of a fortnight ago. The Boer success was bringing volunteers from Europe at a doubled rate. In the republics themselves General Joubert's victory dispatch from Ladysmith was vividly confirmed by the sight of a thousand British prisoners marching through the streets of Pretoria. Many burghers who had hesitated at taking on the mighty British Empire were saddling their horses for the front. Worse, Cape Dutch were riding across the Orange to throw in their lot with Steyn's commandos strung along the border, restive under his pledge of non-invasion.

On the very next day, 1 November, Steyn renounced his pledge. His commandos began to cross the Orange River into the Cape Midlands. The wonder is that he should have delayed so long when these districts were to be the base for Buller's intended offensive against his country.

The commandos threw back the handfuls of police guarding the bridges. These were left intact and unmined, though one commandant cautiously made the mayor of a village stand in the middle of a bridge while his men crossed over. The invaders advanced into village after village, where they were received with cheers, flowers and recruits. They hoisted the Republican flag, made fiery speeches, and rode on. Local parsons fanned the embers of revolt with exhortations from the pulpit. A theological seminary closed down because the students rushed to join the commandos.

In vain the Cape Government, spurred on by a Milner desperately afraid of a general uprising, pointed out the consequences of treason and imposed martial law in the invaded districts. The sombre fact confronting Buller was the creation of a third front and a direct threat to the spring-board of his own projected invasion—for the main direction of the Free Staters' movement was towards Naauwpoort and Stormberg. These, with vital De Aar on the Western line, were the junctions for all the railways from the Cape ports.

Despite their knowledge of the quantities of men and supplies being disembarked at those ports, the Boers advanced with ultra-caution. Consequently though the British forces covering the key junctions 'were small they were still far from danger. Buller nevertheless ordered their immediate evacuation. And as the situation on this newly opened Central Front deteriorated bad news rained on him from every quarter.

On the Western Front the siege of Mafeking was a fortnight old, and in a few days came news that Kimberley too was besieged following Kekewich's rejection of a Boer invitation to surrender. How long could the two towns hold out? The whole railway line from the Orange River to Rhodesia was in Boer hands. With the British garrisons bottled up, commandos under leaders like the O.F.S. Judge J. B. M. Hertzog were spreading across a vast area from which they might thrust down into the western Cape. Further, direct communications were cut off from Rhodesia whose border with the Transvaal had at best an uneasy equilibrium: early in November Plumer was forced to retire from the Limpopo.

On the Natal Front the position was most critical of all. On 2 November the Boers cut the railway southwards out of Ladysmith. Their encirclement of all White's men, a refugee-swollen populace and huge quantities of stores, was complete. Small British forces which were scattered down the line hastily withdrew as far as Estcourt: they were all that stood between the Boers and the Natal capital, Pietermaritzburg, eighty miles away and only fifty-four miles from Durban. Alarm raced through the colony. Volunteer forces were got together,* some naval guns and bluejackets rushed ashore, and town guards patrolled. These were slender measures against the Boer host drawing their net round Ladysmith, spreading over northern Natal to drum up recruits or exact oaths of non-participation, and bringing down supplies by the

---

* Including in due course: The Imperial Infantry Corps, Murray's Mounted Volunteers, Thorneycroft's M.I., Umvoti Volunteers, Durban Light Infantry.

railway so conveniently left intact. Clearly they would soon either overwhelm Ladysmith or bottle it up while they swept on, and in either event engulf all Natal to the sea.

Buller took a desperate decision. He threw the War Office's plan to the winds for the moment and split the Army Corps into three unequal parts. The larger would relieve Ladysmith, the next Kimberley, while what was left would contain the O.F.S. invasion until he reassembled the Army Corps in the Cape Midlands to carry out the original plan.

Milner, alarmed by the defencelessness of the Cape, protested. But Buller refused to leave the beleaguered towns to their fate: their fall would be an unthinkable blow to British prestige, besides their loss of resources and a corresponding gain by the Boers. For the Cape he insisted for the time being on 'holding' tactics which he entrusted to small forces under two men, one to operate towards Naauwpoort and the other towards Stormberg. The first was French, whom he had summoned immediately he arrived at Cape Town: French left Ladysmith with his Chief of Staff Douglas Haig on the last train to get out, and the two future commanders of the British Army in World War I only escaped with their lives by lying flat on the carriage floor while bullets laced the woodwork around them. The other commander for the Central Front was just arriving with the Army Corps, Lt.-General Sir William Gatacre (pron. gáttakker).

To command that portion of the Army Corps which became known as the Kimberley Relief Force Buller appointed another new arrival, Lord Methuen. His lordship's orders were to assemble his forces at Orange River Station on the Western railway and, relieving Kimberley and Mafeking in turn, reopen communications with Rhodesia. This left unannounced the most important command of all—that for the relief of Ladysmith. But Buller kept his lips sealed.

On 2 November, three days after the first Canadian contingent sailed from Quebec, the Ottawa Government offered a second contingent; the Australians and New Zealanders were also on the way; on 11 November the War Office called out a 5th Division. Meanwhile units of the Army Corps were dispatched up-country as fast as they arrived. Day and night trains, ships, wagons and conveyances of every kind distributed men, animals, supplies from end to end of the war fronts in conformity with Buller's new plan. Much of November was to pass before everything could be got ready, but the three beleaguered towns heard the sounds from afar, and took comfort.

In Kimberley, only seventy miles north of Orange River Station where Methuen was fast organizing his relief column, it was comfort badly needed even though the defences were by now well consolidated. Round a perimeter eventually twenty miles long, materials and labour poured out by the De Beers Company had enabled Kekewich to erect barbed-wire entanglements between a series of redoubts made in the dumps of tailings, the whole connected by telephone to him in his tower. The guns and five searchlights known to the Boers as 'Rhodes's Eyes' were strategically placed, mines real and pretended sown in the outskirts, and while mostly the town volunteers manned the perimeter the regulars and horsemen were kept in reserve at the Botanical Gardens. Food stocks were efficiently controlled and when the Boers cut the river supply of water it was replaced from springs in a mine. To reduce the mouths to be fed—and the risk of insurrection—Rhodes sent away 3,000 Natives; they were turned back by the Boers but later 8,000 got out. Including refugees there were still however nearly 50,000 people and even though Rhodes kept many busy on public works they constituted Kekewich's real problem, more acute than the threat of direct assault by the enemy.

The Boers in fact had little intention of sacrificing their straitened manpower when methods less painful than direct assault could be applied. Upon Kekewich's rejection of their surrender demand they began a daily sporadic shelling with half a dozen guns, doing little damage but rubbing the nerves of the populace raw. Imagination fed on stories of the destructiveness of modern artillery, and to the excitability of the Natives was added the uneasiness of women huddled with their children in the shelters, when every signal of a renewed Boer artillery onslaught caused fearful speculation about their intentions if they broke in. A Boer offer of a free passage south for women and children was misinterpreted and therefore rejected, to the anger of the populace when the story got out. There was mounting agitation as the uncertain days passed, even though the ingenuity of De Beers' chief engineer, an American named Labram, provided the artillery with home-made ammunition to answer the Boer guns. The agitation was championed by Rhodes. He fulminated with fierce impatience against the delay in the dispatch of a relief column which he had urged

on Milner from the outset 'because if Kimberley falls everything
goes'.

Sharing the general misconception of Boer powers, Rhodes saw no
reason why a small column could not march instantly to lift the siege.
That none was sent he ascribed to the bone-headedness of the military.
Kekewich was in the unhappy position of a Lilliputian obliged to sit
on the head of a pinioned Gulliver. There is high comedy in the
spectacle of the colonel and the colossus bound unwillingly together:
the stiff-necked bafflement on one side, the squeaking rage on the other.
But at last relief was in prospect. Whether or not a stream of frantic
messages from Rhodes and other civic leaders about the 'hordes of the
enemy' and the imminence of 'terrible disaster' influenced Buller's
decision to split up the Army Corps, the one thing that mattered to
Kimberley had happened: though Methuen's arrival at Orange River
Station to lead the relief force was kept secret, the sight of parties of
Boers leaving the siege lines for the south on 21 November made clear
that momentous events impended.

A day or two earlier the defenders of Mafeking had noticed a similar
movement in Cronje's lines. The skirmishes of the previous month
continued into early November, with Baden-Powell still giving better
than he received, whereupon Cronje had contented himself with the
desultory bombardment, which was suspended on Sundays. But stung
at last to the necessity of action in view of Methuen's preparations far to
the south, he rode off on 19 November with a large number of his men
to meet this threat. But he left two or three thousand burghers in the
siege lines under the command of Snyman.

Elsewhere too there were Boers who did not watch the massive
British build-up with indifference. In Natal on the morrow of Ladysmith's encirclement, younger men like Louis Botha (now promoted
assistant-general) urged Joubert to make for Durban and the sea rather
than waste time on siege operations. The old general was reluctant. The
small British force down the line at Estcourt seemed full of spirit,
keeping in touch with Ladysmith by heliograph and searchlight, and
daily sending an armoured train to patrol as far as Colenso, fifteen miles
away. Before moving further Joubert wanted to make sure of Ladysmith. But instead of storming the town while the British were still
shaken by defeat he unhurriedly set about squeezing the life out of it.

Sir George White, with over 12,000 men and relatively strong in artillery, gave up any thought of a break-out. He resigned himself to the role of besieged—without evacuating civilians and cavalry horses uselessly consuming food; or sending back guns short of ammunition, together with troops for them, to help the relief force. As at Kimberley and Mafeking a defence ring was erected, here fourteen miles long in a two-mile radius from the town along low hills and expanses of plain between stone-works, fortified posts, and artillery, all linked by telephone. And as at Mafeking and Kimberley a new tight-closed little world was created, where previously unconsidered features of the landscape became monumentally important, a pile of sandbags or a heap of rocks notable additions to geography, and the names bestowed on hillock or fort more significant in one's daily life than all the great names on earth.

About a mile from the British perimeter the Boers occupied the surrounding cordon of hills. The weather was fine, and they lay in the open watching the garrison or took turns to forage for supplies. They severely mauled a cavalry reconnaissance sent out by White on 3 November, but far from showing any offensive activity they themselves were soon hard at work digging in. Though they had 22,000 men they were no more disposed than at Kimberley and Mafeking to embark on storming tactics. They brought up a second Long Tom, setting great store by their artillery which they thought responsible for winkling the British out of Dundee and defeating them at Ladysmith. The daily bombardment soon agitated the townsfolk so much that White got Joubert to allow a daily train from the south to provision the sick, wounded and non-combatants. These were moved to a special camp outside the town. The troops called it 'Funkendorf' because it included quite a few able-bodied men, for White made nothing like full use of the townsmen. Botha and his younger colleagues thought Joubert's courtesy excessive. Train and reception camp saved the defenders food, the depressing effect of sick or terrified people, and the immediate spreading of disease.

The Boer bombardment, against scattered houses and a fourteen-mile perimeter, achieved little. After a week Joubert half-heartedly agreed to a general attack, the main target being a prominence called Observation Hill. But any aggressive spirit was sapped by recent drafts of 'Poor Whites' from the slums of Pretoria, and round much of the siege lines the attack did not even start. This abortive affair of 9 November confirmed Joubert's belief that without his expending irreplaceable lives the British would either sensibly give up soon or wait on the fullness of God's time for fear, starvation, sickness, and cumulative bombardment to decide for them. But, like Cronje outside Mafeking, he could no longer ignore the threat of the fast-arriving Army Corps. He at last yielded to the pleas of his more vigorous commandants. To the most promising of them, Louis Botha, he gave command of an expeditionary force, nearly 4,000 strong—though as an insurance against youthful impetuosity he went along with it, leaving Vice-President Schalk Burger to carry on the siege of Ladysmith with the rest of the army.

Moving south along the railway, the expeditionary force overran Colenso on the bank of Tugela River beyond the hills that bounded the Ladysmith plain. By 14 November advance patrols probed the outskirts of Estcourt. The British there knew that reinforcements were on the way, and stifled their impulse to leave. Next day, despite Botha's proximity, they sent up the armoured train as usual in the direction of Colenso. It had three trucks in front of the locomotive and the rest behind, with sides made of boiler-plates six feet high pierced by loopholes; the last truck carried a naval seven-pounder. On board were 150 soldiers, also six plate-layers to repair any damage to the line, and young Winston Churchill. He was the *Morning Post*'s war correspondent at a record salary of £250 per month plus expenses, but it is doubtful whether he would have been present at an occasion which was to lay the foundation of his fame had he not recently been defeated in a bye-election on his first attempt to enter Parliament.

As the train puffed along the switchback of hills it could plainly be heard for miles. Unobserved an advance Boer patrol allowed it to pass by. Then they packed the bottom of a long incline with boulders, placed their artillery to overlook the scene, and sat smoking their pipes in a downpour of rain. As soon as the train reappeared they opened fire to make the driver accelerate down the incline. The leading trucks hit the boulders at the bottom and capsized, bringing the train to a halt. Within seconds a Boer shell knocked the seven-pounder clean off its truck. A brisk action ensued during which Churchill led a party for an hour under fire to free the locomotive. With the wounded loaded aboard it returned to Estcourt while the rest of the detachment fought on. Churchill helped their officer rally them, but even against Churchillian oratory the odds were too great. The Boers made seventy prisoner, and before packing them all off to Pretoria complimented Churchill on his gallantry, which was widely publicized in the British Press.

The Boer expeditionary force continued their advance towards Estcourt. British reinforcements—the vanguard of the Army Corps—reached it the following day but made no attempt to stop them. Across a great expanse of country they were helping themselves to cattle and the contents of unoccupied farms on a scale described by a German participant as 'a tramps' crusade', and on 20 November were completely encircling the town while their patrols ranged as far as only ten miles from Durban.

*   *   *   *

The date is significant. In England the Kaiser arrived on a State visit, apparently proof of German neutrality in the Boer War. The Prime Minister's wife died that very day, so that Salisbury was temporarily absent and Chamberlain was free to strive to assure neutrality with an alliance which would include the U.S.A. and end England's 'splendid isolation'. He worked hard for it; and the Queen gave a banquet at which she laid out all her gold plate reported to be worth two million; and the public was polite. But no alliance was forthcoming. The English did not really want it and the Germans, deeply anti-British at that time, even less. For both, as for all the leading nations, the struggle on the veld would declare where England stood in power and military strength.

Club, train and home knew scarcely any other subject of conversation. To the maps, 'Notes by Our Military Correspondent', and explanations of how all the new weapons worked, which newspapers had carried since the start of the war, had been added through most of November exciting accounts of the Army Corps' disembarkation and the 'brave defiance' or 'heroic bearing' of the besieged towns. Any day now the army would move, the sieges be raised. In fact on the evening of that same 20 November Methuen's force was fully assembled at Orange River Station. The men sat round camp-fires that blazed by the hundred along the river bank, and they sang until a late hour because they were too excited to sleep: before daybreak they were on the march for Kimberley. In Natal the force to relieve Ladysmith was almost as ready, units of the Army Corps being moved up the line immediately on arrival at Durban, and the sole question was who would be placed in command.

The day after Methuen began his march Buller abruptly quit Cape Town by ship. He left his various commanders—Methuen on the Western Front, French and Gatacre on the Central, Plumer in Rhodesia, those on lines of communication—to carry on as best they could while he deliberately withdrew from overall direction of the war. For when he appeared again a day or two later it was in Natal, his nominee to command on this front at last made clear: General Sir Redvers Buller. He himself would sweep away Joubert and relieve Ladysmith, then returning to Cape Town regroup the Army Corps, and carry out the War Office's original plan. He would be away only a fortnight.

The news awaiting him on his arrival in Natal was that the British commander at Estcourt had attempted to strike at Botha's encircling expeditionary force. During a night of violent rain, lightning and hail-stones as big as eggs, some of his troops crept onto the edge of a hill-top but did not receive any of the reinforcements intended for them and the commander of their artillery had not even been told of the attack. Louis Botha, his horse shot from under him, swept them off the hill with eighty casualties. Following this action, known as the Battle of Willow Grange, the Estcourt commander withdrew all his forces into the town and prepared for a siege although his force was as large as Botha's—and the rest of the Army Corps was preparing only a short distance down the line.

But Joubert intended neither to stay nor allow Botha to go any further. Concerned over Methuen's march, the O.F.S. was calling for some of its commandos from Ladysmith just when Buller's prepara-tions clearly boded an imminent attempt to relieve it. Also the Tugela River was coming down in flood and might cut off the expeditionary force from the main army round the town. These were decisive argu-ments for a cautious old man who was now very ill. He ordered back the expeditionary force across the sodden veld and hills. They drove before them a great herd of captured cattle and hundreds of wagons of loot strung out for ten miles.

About the same time the Free State invaders of the Cape Midlands were becoming aware of French and Gatacre's arrival. For the three weeks since they crossed the Orange they had moved extraordinarily slowly, so that to Milner's relief French was able to reoccupy Naauwpoort which also to some extent lifted the danger to De Aar, essential to Methuen on the Western Front. On the other wing of the Central Front the Boers were a little more vigorous and approaching Stormberg, but Gatacre was moving up the East London line to thwart them.

The whole strategical situation of the war had therefore changed. The first phase was over. Broadly speaking the Boers were halted. They held the border districts of the Cape Midlands, a huge part of the far north Cape, and northern Natal; the prizes of Ladysmith, Mafeking and Kimberley only required a little time to fall into their hands; their own territory was everywhere intact. Now, in face of Buller and the Army Corps, they were as resolved to hold on to their gains as the British were to wrest them away before launching a final crushing counter-invasion.

CHAPTER VI

Buller's Offensive:
November–December 1899

ALTHOUGH Mafeking and Kimberley were besieged, the battles in Natal had made the Western Front a side-show. But with the start of Methuen's march from Orange River Station it provided equal drama for the watching world.

Paul Sanford, Lord Methuen, was a Guardsman of considerable campaign experience but this was his first independent command. His tall bony figure stooped; and his short nose, solid chin, and thick moustache tending to the same reddish colouring as his hair, made his appearance rather less attractive than his nature, which the campaign ahead was to temper and refine in some extraordinary passages of fortune. At the start of his march at 4 a.m. on 21 November 1899, he left his campfires burning but the Boers were not deceived. By the same afternoon their newspapers carried the news that the British were marching to relieve Kimberley.

Although Cronje was already heading south with the greater part of his army from Mafeking, the Western railway was blocked by Kimberley and there was no line from Bloemfontein. Men and wagons had therefore to travel by a long route and supply laagers had to be formed along the O.F.S. border up to the head laager at Jacobsdal, south-east of Kimberley. For the present there were therefore only a couple of thousand Free Staters in Methuen's way. Their leader, Commandant J. Prinsloo (not to be confused with General Marthinus Prinsloo, commanding the Free Staters invading Natal), had orders to delay him until the Boer strength was assembled. Methuen thought there were twice as many Boers who might oppose him, but he was unaware of the reinforcements moving down from Mafeking and Kimberley. Not that he would have minded a full-scale clash. 'My good fellow,' he said to one of his colonels, 'I intend to put the fear of God into these people.' He had already sent a message to Kimberley with the glad tidings that he would be there within a week—by 27 November—unless delayed at the Modder River. This river, the only one of any size between the Orange and the Vaal, flowed westward from beyond Bloemfontein and was crossed by the Western railway twenty-two miles south of Kimberley.

Advancing up the railway he would be kept in supplies and water—all-important in that hot flat land of low scrub and thornbush where he could deploy his forces with the precision of manœuvres on Aldershot plain. Steadily the camp-fires receded as his army marched with a will in the cool crisp air before the heat got up—eventually nearly 12,000 men of the Grenadier, Coldstream and Scots Guards, of famous regiments in Lancashire, Yorkshire and Northumberland. A few hundred troopers rode with them including an advance Australian unit (N.S.W. Lancers); there were droves of transport animals and long lines of guns and wagons; an armoured train ranged ahead. Presently they were joined by a detachment of the Naval Brigade, uneasy in khaki which marked their severance from the sea many hundreds of miles away.

By easy marches they came to the station of Belmont. Nearby was the first of three small clusters of abrupt stony kopjes which were the only possible defensive positions in the eighty miles between the Orange and Kimberley. Breast-works along the crests indicated that Prinsloo was present and Methuen, in order not to leave his line of communications exposed, decided to clear the position. It was quite formidable—steep sides covered sparsely with leafless brush and tufts of grass. Methuen therefore ordered out his Brigade of Guards to lead an attack under cover of darkness. But his maps were faulty, axes had to be used to chop down the railway fence in the absence of wire-cutters, and when dawn came the Guards found themselves still some distance from the nearest kopje. Amidst complete silence from the Boers they advanced, nerve-strung, across the open. Then suddenly, says a witness, 'there ran along the crest of the kopje quick, vivid jets of fire like jewels on a coronet.'[23]

The Guards, applying the lesson of Natal, were in open formation which to some extent protected them from the plunging fire. All engagements so far had exacted heavy casualties among British officers, since in leading their men they were made conspicuous by shiny buttons, gleaming sword hilts and badges of rank. But following a similar heavy loss during a reconnaissance not far from the present scene a fortnight before, officers had begun to cover their buttons and hilts and carry rifles with dulled butts to make themselves look like their men. General Fetherstonhaugh leading the brigade supporting the Guards, however, rode up and down in front of his men. This hampered their firing and announced his importance to the enemy, who promptly shot him down.

The Guards were played into battle by their regimental band. They advanced at a steady double, drew breath on reaching the hill, fixed bayonets, and clambered up on hands and knees. Though the Boers leant over their breast-works to pick out the helmets as they appeared they could not stop the disciplined rush of numbers and fell back to other parts of the kopjes, until finally they took to their ponies and fled.

Even before news of the battle reached London, crowds assembled in a lobby of the War Office on rumours that the Guards were going into action, and anxiously scanned the notice board headed 'South Africa'. The little Aladdin's lamp above it presently revealed over 300 names of dead, wounded and missing. Correspondents' tales uplifted the heart or chilled the spine—about, for example, a chaplain who had stood upright in a storm of bullets administering the sacrament to the dying; or a well-known boxer who was killed while trying to get his bayonet out of a man by throwing him over his shoulder.

Addressing his men back in camp at Belmont, Methuen said: 'Comrades, I congratulate you on the complete success achieved.' Then he wrote a letter of protest to Prinsloo about the Boer use of dum-dum or expanding bullets which inflicted multiple wounds and had been banned at the international conference in July—though Britain had reserved the right to use them against an overwhelming rush of 'savages'. This was the first such allegation, but throughout the war both sides were to accuse the other of using them. There is more substance in the fact that modern magazine or automatic fire could pump more bullets into one man than was generally realized. A correspondent at Belmont wrote of the casualties that their 'khaki was dyed so deeply with crimson that some . . . must have received more than half a dozen shots'. [24]

The Free Staters had less than a hundred casualties but they were not happy. The position seemed strong, yet the British had shown themselves able to storm it. The delay achieved had been trifling and the battle gave scant hope for the future. They largely blamed Prinsloo's leadership. In this low state of morale many hung back from defending the second cluster of kopjes, near the station of Enslin.

The result was that particular importance attached to the arrival, in advance of the rest of Cronje's Transvaalers, of Koos de la Rey. He had reached the hot rocks and scrub at Belmont but too late in the battle to warrant intervention. With the defection now of so many Free Staters his commando brought the total Boer strength to about the 2,000 it had been at Belmont and he virtually assumed command. Infusing fresh spirit into waverers he deployed with care, mainly along a crest-line of kopjes whose ends turned back at right angles to protect his flanks.

Methuen heard from the patrolling armoured train that the position was defended. He rested his troops a day and marched on. Not knowing of De la Rey's arrival he did not expect the Boers to be as numerous as at Belmont after their drubbing there. At first light on 25 November he ordered his cavalry to ride out wide of the kopjes to cut off any attempt at escape, while his infantry and artillery moved along a broad front against vigorous fire. Two hundred and fifty Marines and bluejackets of the Naval Brigade were in the van. Methuen turned them suddenly half-right to make for the dominating end of the front line of kopjes. De la Rey saw at once that Methuen's frontal attack was to cover this oblique move by the Naval Brigade which was the real tactical crux of the battle. He called up his men from all parts of the hills, concentrating them in the centre both to oppose the frontal attack and enfilade the Naval Brigade. Even though the British artillery hammered the crests, the brigade was exposed to a murderous fire. They had started well spaced out but converging on their objective offered a concentrated target to the Boers above.

Their matchless charge was to thrill an England where eyes were moist on reading how a terrier followed a major of the Marines into battle and stood over his dying master; how an officer had his water bottle, revolver, belt, and the magazine of his rifle hit in turn but himself escaped injury; how a midshipman struggled on after being twice wounded to fall dead when hit a third time; and how in the end nearly half the brigade was struck down. Yet their final rush up the slope succeeded, because at the same time the infantry all along the line hurled themselves at the kopjes in a 'soldiers' battle' which threw plans to the wind.

The Boers broke. Running down the further slopes they leapt on to their ponies and made away, leaving some distinguished prisoners in British hands, including Jeppe, a pro-Boer millionaire Uitlander. The troops were so parched, for supplies of all kinds had fallen behind, that they pressed round the locomotive drivers offering a year's pay for a cupful of water; and officers making do on bully beef thought longingly of the delicacies and champagne still stacked down the line at De Aar. But the cavalry pursued—only to be cut up by the Boers' skilful covering tactics which also got their wagons away, to the displeasure of Methuen who sacked his cavalry commander. He was in fact hopelessly short of mounted troops against such a mobile enemy.

But the essential point was that the Boers had again been brushed aside. He might now be a day or two later than 27 November in reaching Kimberley, but as everyone at home could see from their newspaper maps he was already half-way there. The Boers' technical skill and courage, which in his victory address he was the first British general to acknowledge publicly, had not availed in this latest fight, called the Battle of Graspan, and could not be expected to do so at the last defensive position remaining to them—the Magersfontein range of kopjes a mere dozen miles south of Kimberley. It lay beyond the Modder River to which, after a few days' rest, his force resumed the march.

Profound despondency marked Boer discussions at their head laager. They had given better than they received, but Methuen was still advancing and they saw no hope of trying to resist a British infantry charge, however strong the position. There were more defections by Free Staters who had totally lost confidence in Prinsloo.

Koos de la Rey listened to the arguments and then spoke his mind. Where had they gone wrong? They had not failed for want of courage or marksmanship, and their dispositions on the kopjes had been perfect. Those kopjes. Ah! They seem so ideal but look here, consider what happens. You fire down on the advancing British—*down*—so a bullet has only one chance to hit a soldier before it buries itself in the ground. Then when discipline and courage have carried the enemy to the foot of your hill, those steep sides are actually a protection not for you but for him: you have to lean over, exposing yourself to him or his fellows on the plain below, while his artillery pounds you because the crest you occupy makes a clear target against the sky, and next thing Tommy is upon you with his bayonet.

Now, De la Rey said, across the British line of advance flowed the Modder River. Its bed was well below the level of the veld from which the banks fell away steeply to the shore of the stream. By installing themselves against the southern bank with their backs to the river and their rifles at veld level they would be behind cover, the British completely in the open. But above all, the potential destructiveness of their fire would be many times greater since a bullet's flat trajectory ensured

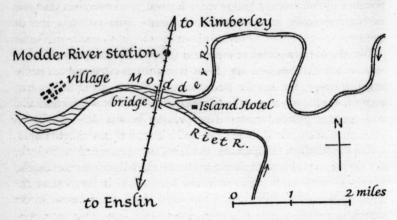

that if it missed one soldier it would travel on and perhaps hit another or another in the ranks behind. Finally, by being below ground level they would give the British gunners no clearly defined target.

That, De la Rey said, was the answer to what had seemed an insoluble problem; and persuaded by such logic and hopefulness the Boers made for the river. Close to and east of the railway bridge, which they had blown up, the Modder was joined by a tributary called the Riet, here-abouts flowing roughly parallel to it and nearer the British. They there-fore dug themselves into the south bank of the Riet and, after it joined the Modder, the south bank of the latter. Above the banks of the two rivers trees and bushes provided perfect concealment. More Free Staters arrived and so did Cronje with a few commandos of his main army, bringing the Boer strength to 3,500. If De la Rey's revolutionary idea startled him he did not try to interfere.

Methuen approached the Modder with about 8,000 men knowing that Boers were about because a reconnaissance had reported them near the railway bridge. It was not a very thorough piece of scouting: the number seen was small, and even convoys of their wagons within ten miles of the British flank moved supplies up unseen. When Methuen went forward to survey the scene for himself the belt of foliage was a pleasant sight after the unending dry scrub. In the distance beyond were the blue hills of Magersfontein just in front of Kimberley itself. If the Boers were going to try one more stand they would surely choose those hills, as reports from Kekewich in Kimberley indicated. The men observed at the wrecked bridge were, he concluded, merely a shadowing party or on the way to join their comrades. If he saw a number of white stones and biscuit tins lying about he was not to realize that these had been carefully placed at measured intervals by the Boer artillerymen to aid their gun-laying. Even when his cavalry and a Native informant reported that the Boers were in greater strength than had been thought he dismissed the information because it was inconsistent with his previous deductions. That evening he was close enough to Kimberley to announce his presence to Kekewich by searchlight signal.

Next morning, 28 November, the camp was roused at four o'clock. No breakfast—they would breakfast at Modder River Station on the other side of the bridge. By seven they breasted the last rise before the river, welcomed by that belt of greenery along the winding banks with here and there the whitewashed walls of a farm-house or cattle-kraal. A step further and they saw beyond the line of trees on the nearer bank a verdant little oasis. This was in fact the tongue of ground between the curving arms of the Riet and the Modder just before their junction, an ideal site for an hotel much frequented by Kimberley businessmen before the war. 'It lay now,' wrote Conan Doyle who carefully got the tale from men who were there—'calm and innocent, with its open windows looking out upon a smiling garden; but death lurked at the windows and death in the garden, and the little dark man who stood by the door, peering through his [field] glasses at the approaching column, was the minister of death, the dangerous Cronje.'[25] It was unknown to the British at that time that the Moriarty in charge of this particular service was Koos de la Rey, although it was Cronje sure enough who had just finished his breakfast and now contemplated the advancing troops.

The Guards strode out slightly in advance of the rest of the force which altogether covered a front of over three miles on either side the railway track to facilitate a rapid fording of the river. The main line of advance was towards the right of the bridge, which De la Rey had anticipated and placed his main strength there, leaving the river left of the bridge to Prinsloo's Free Staters. A spluttering long-range artillery fire was directed on the British from the far right: Methuen at once put this down to the small shadowing party his cavalry had reported, for even through field-glasses he saw no sign of any other Boers.

The Guards were within 1,200 yards of the river. Nestling among eucalyptus trees beyond was the agreeable sight of Modder River Station with its promise not only of a halt and breakfast, but water, since they had only the contents of muddy pools the night before and the sun was already hot. Methuen directed two aides-de-camp to ride forward and requisition a house he pointed out for his headquarters. Glancing again at the peaceful scene before him he murmured to one of his senior officers, as though throwing off a nagging presentiment, 'They're not here.' The officer replied, 'They're sitting uncommonly tight if they are, sir.' The instant echo of his words was a blast of fire from the river bank.

The men in front threw themselves flat, crawling frantically for such cover as scrub or ant-hills could provide, while the bullets came at them 'in solid streaks like telegraph wires'. Their comrades to the right rear thereupon tried to relieve the pressure by outflanking the Boer left. But Methuen was ignorant of the exact course of the Modder and its tributary, nor did his map show how the Riet did a wide loop so that though it flowed from east to west in front of him, it flowed from south to north across his right, and flowed too strongly to be forded, barring his infantry or cavalry from any move to get round the flank of the Boer line.

The Guards repeatedly tried to advance against an enemy they could not see, whose bullets ripped through their ranks from end to end, and whose artillery largely eluded the British artillery by being scattered and unseen while having the range so accurately that it could kill the entire crew of a machine-gun at a stroke, leaving the weapon the only object standing above a plain of supine or crawling men. Although a man was fairly safe while he kept flat, to lift his head was fatal, and the constant storm of bullets and shrapnel overhead, especially the bursting of strings of shells from the automatic one-pound gun which was new to the troops, who called it a pompom, had a nerve-shattering effect. Retreat became as impossible as advance. The temperature rose to 108°. Men had to lie on their rifles to keep them cool enough to use if the chance came. The backs of the Scots Guards' knees were gradually blistered raw and when a momentary breeze ruffled their kilts they betrayed their position to the Boers. From the broken ant-hills the occupants emerged to add to the British discomfiture. As the hours passed, the craving for thirst drove many men to run back to the water carts and die in the attempt. Others were so overcome by hunger and exhaustion that they fell asleep. Spells of complete inaction descended on the battlefield as the Boers, no longer sure of the range, saved their ammunition until at noon a herd of black and white goats roamed across the firing zone, and the Boers used them as range-finders.

Methuen left his headquarters to hustle about trying to get his advance moving again, but he fell wounded. All the time sixteen British guns vainly pounded the river banks with thousands of shells, stripping the trees and leaving no building unshattered; though the Boer gunners and horses suffered severely their riflemen were safe behind the banks.

But at last came a gleam of hope. All morning the brunt of battle had been on the right. The troops on the left were commanded by General Pole-Carew who had succeeded Fetherstonhaugh: he had a handsome friendly face with a modest moustache and grey tawny hair, and friends said that a better soldier than 'Polly' Carew never wore the Guards' bearskin. Early in the afternoon he increased the pressure on his flank far to the left of the bridge and found the weakest point in the defences. The wavering Free Staters began to give way when two guns bombarded them from close range. A trickle of Carew's force reached the river, found it shallow enough here to be crossed, and slithered over rocks to form a bridgehead on the further bank. Close-by stood a village which they captured before swinging to their right, threatening the whole Boer line from flank and rear. But their hold was precarious, the Boers rallied and held them back, and at this moment an additional battery arrived. It was covered by the dust of fifty miles—travelled in twenty-eight hours in response to Methuen's appeal—and though the crews were exhausted from having walked much of the way to spare

E

the horses hauling the limbers, they at once went into action hazardously close to the river in support of the small party on the other side. The result was bathos: their shells fell among their own men and unwittingly helped the defenders stop any further advance.

All along the front the firing grew more desultory as the afternoon wore on. Except for their precarious lodgement across the river the British had not advanced a yard since the battle began. When night came nearly 500 men lay dead or wounded.

In spite of his wound Methuen was determined to resume the offensive. During the night preparations were made to reinforce the bridgehead across the river at dawn. But dawn revealed only dead horses, gutted buildings and shell-pitted earth. The Battle of Modder River was over.

De la Rey had been outvoted at a council of war the previous evening. The defection of many Free Staters and the inevitability of the British bridgehead being reinforced convinced the majority that they should retire into the Magersfontein hills, join the gathering tide of reinforcements, and make a decisive stand before Kimberley. Although —perhaps because—De la Rey had that day seen his eldest son mortally wounded at his side his grief was greater at the decision to pull out.

In Kimberley the day had cast a cloud over expectations because a strong 'demonstration' by Kekewich to distract the surrounding Boers had got out of hand through the impetuosity of one of his leading officers: the affair cost the garrison fifty-five casualties. Gloom was dispelled by Methuen's searchlight, closer now because following the battle he could encamp on the Modder.

But that battle, which for the first time gave the newspaper reader in England pause for thought, brought no immediate relief to the besieged. 'It had been', Methuen wrote in his dispatch, 'one of the hardest and most trying fights in the annals of the British Army.' He little guessed that he had fought the precursor of battles which were to sear millions of lives on another Western Front only fifteen years later. But he might have reflected on something Lord Roberts had recently remarked, that the new conditions of warfare made a frontal attack over open ground impossible, and that a commander's first duty was reconnaissance. At the Battle of Modder River an untutored farmer of genius proved the truth of both principles. For ignoring them Methuen now found himself pulled up sharply in his tracks. Only the Magersfontein hills prevented an actual view of the town, but ten days would be needed before his wounds knit and replacements made good his thousand casualties in the three battles he had fought since leaving Orange River Station.

This delay was the supreme advantage the Boers gained from the Battle of the Modder. They had time for all their reinforcements to arrive, and to patch up quarrels resulting from Free State defections. When Paul Kruger heard of the quarrels he appealed to President Steyn: 'The decisive struggle is fast approaching ... Your Honour must impress upon officers and burghers that they must hold out to the death in the name of the Lord!' Steyn at once publicly reproached those burghers who stayed in their laagers while their brethren fought, and asked them how they expected God to help them if they were not united. Then, as the moment of Methuen's final bid for Kimberley drew near, he set out to exhort his men at the front.

*   *   *   *

The atmosphere of impending climax on the Western Front during the closing days of November was equally marked on the other fronts.

In Natal, the returning Boer expeditionary force came to a stop— but not to rejoin the siege of Ladysmith. As soon as they were over the Tugela River by the village of Colenso they blew up the road and railway bridge and entrenched themselves on the further bank. Added to this event was a momentous change in command. General Joubert's illness obliged him to go to Pretoria, leaving Louis Botha in sole charge on the Tugela. Reinforcements rode out from the Ladysmith siege lines, small locomotives were carted to the railway line south of Ladysmith to keep him supplied, and he established a complete communications' system by field telegraph.

Buller was making his forward base at Frere, only ten miles away, building up the biggest concentration of men, guns, vehicles and animals ever seen in S.A. A five-inch gun or naval 4.7 was called a cow gun because it required a team of oxen to haul it into action, or a steam road locomotive; even the smaller guns had to have six horses each. Besides, apart from military, medical and food supplies for nearly 20,000 men, no officer liked to travel without all necessities at hand, which often included a piano, long-horned gramophone, chest of drawers solid enough for a ship's cabin, and a range of paraphernalia from polo sticks to portable water-purifier. Buller's own requirements are illustrated by the following example of preparations made for him in the field: 'a superb tent, an iron bathroom, and a sumptuous kitchen with a fine battery of culinary accessories'. But the fact remained that he had 20,000 men at his back, and there were White's 12,000 men ready to strike out as he struck in. Perfect co-ordination was possible by means of Native runners or carrier-pigeons which also delivered maps, photographically reduced, of the surrounding countryside. (On 9 November a pigeon was sent out conveying the town's congratulations on the Prince of Wales's birthday.)

From the Central Front the crucial news was that the Boers had occupied Stormberg Junction while Gatacre was still too far down the line to prevent them. With French 190 miles away at Naauwpoort in the west, a great gap invited the invaders to sweep into the heart of the Midlands as well as to deny Buller all chance of using the area for his cherished counter-invasion. A heavy responsibility rested on Gatacre. Hurriedly he prepared to capture the junction and cripple the Boers' further advance. Even as he made his forward base forty miles down the line, they were moving round his right flank to Dordrecht, threatening the whole of the eastern Cape as well.

In England tension was increased by a speech Joseph Chamberlain delivered after the Kaiser's departure, advocating his idea of a triple alliance with Germany and the U.S.A. To the public this smacked of nervousness about the general situation, and of toadying to secure the Kaiser's continued neutrality in the war, so that the Colonial Secretary's stock took a sudden plunge. After all, the war was about to be decisively wrapped up. Troops were still pouring out to make assurance doubly sure—the War Office called up yet another division, the 6th—and interest throughout the Empire was intensified by news that the Canadian and Australian contingents had entrained for the fronts.

December opened with a flurry of minor events. Successful night forays were made on Boer gun emplacements by the Ladysmith garrison, startling the darkness with three cheeers for the Queen. In the Cape Midlands, French actually advanced from Naauwpoort, the Boers falling back and allowing him to take the village of Arundel. And on the Western Front, two Northampton companies thwarted J. Prinsloo when he arrived at Enslin with a thousand Free Staters to disrupt Methuen's line of communication. After six timorous hours he withdrew, to encounter the wrath of Steyn who was bent on sustaining the morale of his men at this critical juncture. He put Prinsloo under arrest for incompetence and cowardice.

Minor though these events were, they gave an auspicious start to the last month of the year as Buller, Gatacre and Methuen each advanced to the attack. The result was to be three successive battles within a week that 'vibrated through the world'.[1]

CHAPTER VII

Black Week: December 1899

In the last Sudan campaign, gaunt William Gatacre had won a knight-hood and promotion to major-general even though, Churchill wrote in *The River War*, his restlessness made him 'the exhausted victim of his own vitality'. He had a mania for imposing physical exertion on others as well as on himself, thinking nothing of a twenty-mile ride before breakfast. 'General Backacher', as his troops called him, planned to send up his force by rail to Molteno, the nearest station to Stormberg Junction, on the afternoon before making a surprise dawn attack directly on the pass through which railway and road entered a ring of kopjes around the junction. To deal with the 2,300 Boers and Cape rebels who guarded the basin under the command of General Olivier, he had 3,000 men available, plus a reserve to guard Molteno.

In his force he proposed to include 400 men from an outlying post, whom he ordered to join him on his intended arrival at Molteno. At midnight on 8/9 December this order to the outlying post was handed in at his base telegraph office, and as no acknowledgement was asked for, the fact that the clerk forgot to send the message went unnoticed. At 4 a.m. the main force was aroused to entrain for Molteno. Teams of mules blocked the line and arrangements generally were bungled, so that the troops stood about in the baking sun for hours; the last of them only reached Molteno at 8.30 that evening.

Hearing that the railway pass was strongly held Gatacre gave up the idea of a direct attack along the main road. The western wall of the basin was a range of kopjes called the Kissieberg, whose end nearer Molteno formed one side of the railway pass: by taking this end of the Kissieberg he would dominate the pass and make his entry into the basin simple. But a detour was involved which meant a longer march, on a secondary track. This at night across rough country unknown to him made skilled guidance essential. He happened to have a captain of Intelligence who knew the terrain thoroughly; but he had been left behind. Gatacre therefore selected guides from the Cape Mounted Police.

At 9.15 p.m. the Irish Rifles and Northumberland Fusiliers led the way out of Molteno along the main road. Having been standing about or travelling since 4 o'clock that morning they were already jaded as well as two hours late in starting. The 400 men of the outlying post had mysteriously failed to materialize but Gatacre determined to push

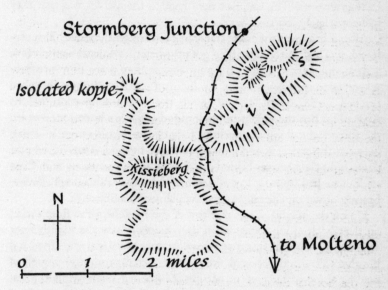

on by the light of a benign full moon. Though not expecting action until dawn, the troops had to fix bayonets. After a while they branched off the main road to take the detour. In their wake came the artillery, the wheels of wagons and guns covered in raw hide to minimize noise.

Some distance behind rode three newspaper correspondents. In ignorance of the changed plans they continued up the main road, until puzzled by not overtaking the artillery they turned back and encountered a medical and supply column, whose commander had not heard of the changed plans either. The newspapermen galloped back to Molteno, but the officer left in charge was equally uninformed and urged them to carry straight on. It was decided to wait until dawn, the newspapermen missing their story but saving the column.

While this little incident was taking place along the main road the assault force was having a bad time in the rough terrain far to the left of them. Tired men were not made fresher by having to carry their rifles in one position because of the fixed bayonets, and the moon went down leaving them to flounder about in seemingly perpetual darkness. To Gatacre's increasingly anxious inquiries the guides returned comforting answers. The one fact they kept to themselves was that they had completely lost their way.

After a brief rest the force tramped on through the night. Twenty-four hours had passed since they got up when they found themselves in a dark and sinister valley. By pure chance they were now precisely where Gatacre wanted to be for his dawn attack, though they had reached it deviously—i.e. alongside the foremost portion of the Kissieberg. But the guides misunderstood Gatacre's intentions and led the force right along the western foot of the whole range to a pass between the end of it and an isolated kopje beyond. Thus in the pre-dawn light Gatacre was behind the hills he was supposed to be in front of. But he had by now lost all sense of direction and thought he was bearing down on the railway pass which was his objective.

Up on the heights at this rear end of the Kissieberg the Boer picket sat sleepily drinking coffee when they suddenly saw the British force winding through the shadows below. At once the alarm was raised and burghers all around opened fire. Gatacre acted promptly enough in sending some of his men to occupy the isolated kopje while the rest threw themselves against the slopes of the Kissieberg without waiting for orders.

Had Gatacre known that the position was defended by merely a token force he could have entered the basin and captured the junction by simply marching on round the hill. Instead, the greater part of his force grappled with the steepest part of the Kissieberg, and though the impetus of their attack carried them well up the slope they were then met by solid cliffs of jutting rock, impossible to scale except at widely separated places. A few men found these and fought desperately for a foothold on the top, from which they were swept off by their own gunners who had laboriously dragged their guns on to suitable positions but had to fire with the rising sun in their eyes.

The attack begun to fail almost as quickly as it had begun. Barred by the cliff, confused and exhausted men began to dribble down to the foot of the slope. The officer commanding the Northumberland Fusiliers took it upon himself to order a retirement. The action was barely half an hour old.

Gatacre, who had gone to the isolated kopje, saw with horror the demoralized infantry streaming back across the valley, but he was powerless to prevent them. The men with him were too few to retrieve the situation, the retiring infantry too exhausted. He began marching them back to Molteno and as he did so a commando came up from the west and for a while the British guns stood trail to trail firing against foes on two sides of them simultaneously. The infantry retreat degenerated into a huge mob of stragglers. Despite a brisk rearguard action by their mounted infantry and artillery, scarcely a man would have escaped had not the Boers shown an ineptitude matching that of the British. So wild was such fire as they did bring to bear that the British sustained only ninety casualties by the time they reached Molteno and safety. Or so it seemed until a check-up revealed that by a mere oversight *six hundred men had been left behind on the slopes of the Kissieberg.*

Unaware of the order to retreat they came down hours after Gatacre's departure and had to give themselves up to the Boers. As the result of a battle that had been no battle at all, the situation in the Cape Midlands was now more critical than ever.

In London it was given out that Gatacre had been treacherously led into an ambush. News of the disaster was published next day, 11 December, a Monday.

*　　*　　*　　*

The day that Gatacre was completing such an original page in the chronicles of war, Methuen set out from the Modder on the last lap of his bid for Kimberley. His wound was healed, and his force not only restored to full strength but increased to 13,000 with the arrival of a brigade of Highlanders. He also had more artillery, including a 4.7 naval gun called 'Joe Chamberlain' by the troops, and a balloon section. The newly arrived Australian and Canadian contingents guarded his communications down to Orange River Station. Strong in arms and preparation, he heliographed to Kimberley that he was on his way.

In Kimberley the past few days had severely strained relations between Kekewich and Rhodes, previously soothed by the approach of Methuen's relief force. The reason was disclosure of a message from Methuen that on reaching the city he would not occupy it in strength but would take off 20,000 white and Native townsfolk, bolster the defences with men and supplies, and then retire to assemble for the counter-invasion from the Cape Midlands as soon as Buller returned from relieving Ladysmith. The citizens had no wish either to be subjected to a continuance of the siege or to become refugees at Cape Town, nor did the De Beers Company want idle mines and unemployed Natives to cope with indefinitely. Rhodes led furious protests at what he called this unjustified 'jumping in and out' by the military. The bantam colonel's handling of him was not helped by Methuen's instructions not to allow Rhodes to interfere, and in fact to include him among the first people to be deported. When Rhodes had simmered down after this to him incredible information he co-operated, even placing at the proposed refugees' disposal the grounds of his great Cape Town estate, Groote Schuur. So on Sunday, 10 December, all was set: trains standing by at the station, the thousands of refugees ready packed, and an air of excitement in which all ruffled feelings were forgotten. Beyond the Magersfontein hills, Methuen was on the march

From the river he had so painfully gained, the veld rose gradually to the Magersfontein hills. There was no treacherous river bed which might trap him on his way: the ground stretched evenly before him with only scrub and thorny but sweet-smelling mimosa bushes sprinkling the sparse grass. The hills were clustered in the shape of a triangle pointing at Kimberley; their base, being roughly parallel to the river, confronted Methuen—though the left-hand corner was further from him than the right, which comprised the hill of Magersfontein itself. It rose to nearly 200 feet, out-topping the other hills and standing stark above the plain like a ship's prow that pointed somewhat past his right. The Boers had been visible for some days entrenching the slopes, and a daily cavalry patrol kept an eye on them.

He could not go round by the waterless tracts westward, and eastward he would again have to force a loop of the Modder. His route lay straight ahead. Given possession of the dominating Magersfontein

Hill he would have a clear passage into Kimberley. He decided to revert to the tactic of a night march followed by a dawn assault. The difficulties of a night march had already been demonstrated at Belmont —besides Carleton's experience in Natal and Gatacre's in the Cape Midlands. But this time there was no hilly terrain to flounder across, no faulty map to mislead. The Magersfontein position lay perfectly clear to him across five miles of flat ground; he had given it many days' study, and in addition to the cavalry patrols a R.A. major called Benson carefully reconnoitred the best route for a night approach. To

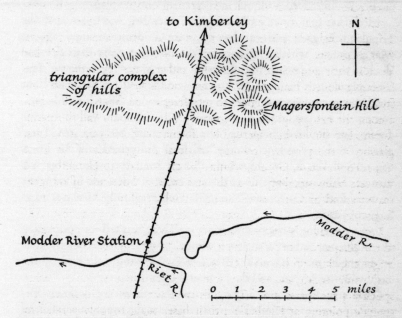

make certain of success he selected for the spearhead of his attack the redoubtable Highlanders, forming what was generally regarded as the finest fighting brigade in the British Army.

It was commanded by Maj.-Gen. A. J. Wauchope, adored throughout Scotland as Andy Wauchope. He had entered the Army thirty-four years before at the age of nineteen: in each of the three colonial wars in which he had fought so far he survived severe wounds, but there were friends who said he believed he would not live through a fourth. As the inheritor of extensive coal-mines he was one of the richest men in the country. Then in Gladstone's famous Midlothian Campaign he had come close to defeating the great man himself at the general election, and again in 1892 been narrowly defeated contesting one of the safest Liberal seats in Britain, because of universal admiration for his character. His clean-shaven bony face with its strong chin and fine eyes gave the impression of a youth prematurely aged, and legend has it that on that Sunday he bore 'the reflection of death'. He did not like the idea of an attack on Magersfontein, believing it to be more strongly held than Methuen supposed. But once he had been persuaded he threw himself with vigour into carrying out the plan.

Methuen's first move on Sunday, 10 December, was to send out the Highland Brigade and cavalry to make a 'demonstration' against Magersfontein, whether to unnerve the Boers or draw their fire and disclose their position is not clear, but either way they made no sign. The brigade was marched back again, and the artillery began an hour and a half's bombardment with everything it had. Watching Magersfontein all but consumed in great spouts of red earth, yellow lyddite fumes, and boulders flung fifty feet into the air, Methuen could feel satisfied that any defence works had been pulverized and the Boers severely shaken if not dispersed—though even the Jingo Press was critical of him on reports that a great number of Boers was killed while at worship, by tacit consent Sunday having previously been treated as a day of peace.

Before evening a heavy drizzle set in. There was talk of postponing the night march but Wauchope wanted to get it over. Shortly after midnight he set out with the Black Watch leading, followed by the Seaforths, the Argylls, and the Highland Light Infantry.

They marched into a driving storm that made the darkness impenetrable except for flashes of lightning—and the faint violet beam of Kimberley's searchlight beckoning them on. Iron-stone boulders and prickly mimosa bush impeded them less than the quagmire which, by one of the swift transitions familiar in S.A., the burning sand of a few hours before had become. But keeping shoulder to shoulder in ninety-six successive lines, making a solid rectangle of 4,000 men shepherded on either side by rope-connected guides, they fell only a little behind schedule. Despite the disturbance to his compass by the lightning, Major Benson led them unerringly. After three hours' march Wauchope dimly perceived the shoulder of Magersfontein in the greying light.

Benson suggested that he now deploy the brigade. But knowing how quickly the S.A. dawn breaks Wauchope wanted to leave the least possible open ground before he was revealed to the enemy. To extend his lines would eat into precious time; and, extended, they would advance slower. He pushed on another several hundred yards and was about to give the order when the foremost men encountered a belt of thick bushes. It could only be penetrated in ones and twos and he had to wait until this had been cleared by about a quarter of a mile in order for the rear ranks to get through as well. Magersfontein seemed now about half a mile ahead. The time was 4 a.m. At last Wauchope gave the order to deploy, and his men began to move away from each other. As they did so, while they were still on the wrong foot and crowded together, the silence and darkness were shattered by an appalling blast of fire that shrivelled them in their tracks.

No one in that demented moment could understand what had happened. They had walked into a terrifying trap. Thousands of rifles were directed on them at point-blank range—not from the slopes of Magersfontein but seemingly from nowhere, from the very feet of the leading Black Watch. In less than a minute hundreds were killed or wounded, the brigade was turned into a panic-stricken mob, and Wauchope himself lay dead.

*　　*　　*　　*

To understand how this devastating stroke came to be delivered by the Boers in the opening second of battle it is necessary to go back some days. Following his appeal to the faint-hearted, President Steyn arrived at the front to find that all the reinforcements from Mafeking, Kimberley and Natal had joined with the force pushed back from the Modder. Arrived too were commandos previously watching the Basutoland border until satisfied that no danger threatened from that quarter. Altogether Cronje had about 8,500 men (British Press reports said 10,000–25,000).

Following his withdrawal from the Modder he ordered the Kimberley side, i.e. the rear, of the triangle of hills in front of Methuen to be fortified. De la Rey had watched this work with increasing unease. Finally he urged Cronje to occupy the foremost part, including Magersfontein Hill from which the British would otherwise dominate the whole situation, and to dig *trenches on the plain below*. This was the logical application of the principle tried out at the Modder. But it was too revolutionary for Cronje: a range of kopjes was available, classic Boer terrain for defence, and he would brook no alternative.

In the midst of the argument President Steyn arrived. He backed De la Rey, and Cronje had to give way. Everyone moved to Magersfontein. A few men were left to position themselves on the slopes of it and the adjoining hills while the majority descended into the plain where they began a series of field-works described by *The Times History* as 'one of the boldest and most original conceptions in the history of war'.

The trenches were dug along a line parallel to the whole length of the triangle of hills on the side facing Methuen, and then from the foot of Magersfontein they continued in a crescent, which should be noted, still further round to the right, almost to the Modder River some distance upstream from Methuen's camp. The whole chain extended over twelve miles with the centre in front of Magersfontein, where the straight line ended and the crescent began.

By burrowing out a line of such length De la Rey prepared against being outflanked and taken in the rear. A feature of the trenches was their narrowness; he correctly deduced that against all except direct hits this gave complete shelter against shrapnel. By digging them 200 yards in the open he aimed not only at springing a surprise: the line of hills behind would act as a constant attraction to the British gunners, tending to make them fire over the trenches. Finally, barbed-wire entanglements were erected and the Boers stuck branches and bush on to the excavated earth, screening themselves to such purpose that reconnaissance at a hundred yards would not have revealed them. In any event these trenches were so novel that no one was looking out for them; and the few Boers left to fortify the slopes of Magersfontein drew all attention.

Since many of the Boer force had retreated from three successive battles against Methuen it speaks much for their courage that they left the protection of the hills, and their faithful ponies waiting close beyond, to immure themselves in trenches from which there would be no escape if the British overran them. Undoubtedly Steyn's presence helped; and by dismissing Prinsloo he removed the chief source of the Free Staters' lack of confidence. With this act the President departed.

Ammunition and supplies were distributed from the head laager at

Jacobsdal and trench-digging vigorously pressed forward. As it was, the work was incomplete, especially the last mile or so of the crescent towards the river, when Methuen opened his attack on the afternoon of 10 December with the Highland Brigade's demonstration and the sustained bombardment.

That bombardment, which Methuen watched with such satisfaction, achieved a sum total of three Boers wounded. The greater part of Cronje's army lay safely in the trenches below, terrifying though the holocaust sounded overhead. Methuen had forgotten 'the mule of Matanzas'—the sole casualty, the Spaniards said, of a sustained American bombardment in the previous year's war over Cuba—and simply alerted the Boers to the imminence of attack. Cronje called a council of war on Magersfontein towards evening and enjoined constant vigilance. Thereupon he lay down in the drizzling rain to rest.

He got up at 1 a.m., and in rain and darkness lost his way. With his six adjutants he was wandering on top of the hills at the same time as Wauchope was having better fortune in being guided across the plain below, little though the British realized that as they began to perceive Magersfontein in the grey darkness so did thousands of Boers, waiting with rifles cocked and straining gaze, perceive the black mass of infantry moving towards the trenches in which they lay totally concealed and totally unexpected. Then came the instant when bullets and fear swept through the Highland Brigade like the wrath of God.

*　　*　　*　　*

The Boer fire was as intense as if delivered by machine-guns, but providentially for the British it was at first rather high, so that while the leading Black Watch suffered severely many survived to complete their extension and lie flat. The ranks behind them, however, panicked and ran back towards the bushes which had caused Wauchope's fatal delay, and running into the Seaforths set up a chain-reaction of terror which turned half the brigade into a wild mob. While all this was happening, during the first few seconds, Wauchope stepped in front of the leading line to discover from the flashes exactly where the Boers were, and he ordered one of his young aides-de-camp—as it happened, a cousin—to have men come round from behind to his immediate right, where there was in fact a gap between the end of the straight line of trenches and the beginning of the crescent. In these moments officer after officer fell dead or wounded—Wauchope and the young aide-de-camp and the officer to whom he carried the order.

But the order remained, and in the semi-darkness groups of men struggled to break out of their nightmare. A handful actually reached the trenches, only to be wiped out. Then about a hundred men found the gap in the Boer line and bursting through to the side of Magersfontein began to climb it. From the crest they would be able to command the Boer rear and with more men about to follow them through the gap turn disaster into triumph.

At this moment Fortune cast her lot. In the greying light Cronje and his six adjutants found themselves, after their hours of fruitless wandering, close to the same point from which they had set out at 1 a.m. Suddenly sighting the climbing British they threw themselves down behind a rock and poured such a hail of bullets into them that not realizing how few opposed them they took cover. The Boers below now hastily sealed the gap, thrusting back the threatened break-through and turning their rifles on the party on the hill-slope. In ignorance of the situation the British artillery also opened up against the slope, raking it with shrapnel. Less than half the party survived, and those who did were taken prisoner. With them all hope for the dawn attack was extinguished.

The sun rose bright and increasingly hot in a sky clear of storm. Beneath it, their gleaming mess-tins and dark kilts conspicuous against the sandy veld, were strewn the kilted figures of the Highlanders who had not run away. They crawled forward against almost point-blank fire. They crawled forward inch by inch, completely wiping out a corps of fifty Scandinavian volunteers in advance of the Boer line, until they got within 150 yards of the main trenches. They could advance no further against fire not only from the trenches in front but from the crescent on their right and the slopes of Magersfontein above. Behind ant-hill and bush they lay as still as if already dead.

Far behind them, beyond the fateful belt of thorn bush, officers rallied the men who had fled. A young lieutenant of the Seaforths led out a machine-gun crew to the left of the prostrate Black Watch, cleared the way through a barbed-wire fence and fought until two wounds and the loss of most of his crew drove him back. To the wailing of the pipes other men were led against the upper part of the crescent on the right of the Black Watch, but desperate attempts—'sublime courage', Cronje's dispatch called it—to rush the trenches all along this section were flattened by concentrated fire that not even sustained pounding by over thirty artillery pieces could reduce: the Boers would not shift from trenches which gave them their only hope of survival.

A war balloon drifted meaninglessly in the sky while higher circled more meaningful vultures. In little groups and straggling lines the Highland Brigade lay along a front of three miles, their faces pressed against the burning sand, the backs of their knees burnt raw, their water bottles emptied or given to wounded comrades out of reach of the medical staff whose courage gained one a V.C. No reinforcements came; only an order from Methuen: 'Hold on until nightfall.' Nightfall was many hours away.

The Boers in the upper part of the crescent on their right now threatened to storm forward and envelop them. Methuen threw in his mounted troops who pushed forward on foot with a field battery; and on their right again the Guards advanced against the centre of the crescent, joining hands with the Yorkshire Light Infantry who followed the Modder towards the lower half of the crescent. Many Boers lay here in unfinished trenches or even on the open veld, needing all their officers' exhortations to keep them, but Methuen would not press his attack on this sector because his fixed idea, from which he could not budge, was that all depended on a break-through by the Highland Brigade in front of Magersfontein. For the same reason he paid even less attention to the sector left of Magersfontein, where there was little advance.

By eleven o'clock the Highlanders reached a state beyond endurance and showed signs of wavering. The Gordons were ordered to charge through them at the trenches. They were flung back and pinned down among their comrades, who nevertheless received some encouragement from the attack and despite a thin trickle of retreating men most hung on. Among the groups nearest the Boers was one in which all but three men were wounded; an unarmed commandant crawled forward to tell them, in admiration for their bravery, that they would not be fired on any more if they themselves stopped firing.

At half past one the pressure long threatening on the right of the Highland Brigade erupted. A commando from the little O.F.S. village of Ficksburg gallantly led an attack which the dismounted Lancers and M.I. could hardly contain. The senior surviving officer appealed for help from the Guards a little distance on his right, but two successive runners failed to survive with the message, and at last the Highland right began to crumble.

The movement communicated itself all down the line. First in tens then in hundreds the Highlanders rose from the ground. The Boers, presented with a better target than ever, fired with the frenzy of men scenting victory. Before them fled their enemy in stark demoralization, and none suffered more severely than those who having advanced furthest had furthest to retreat. Yet it was not all rout and shame. A captain of the Gordons won a V.C. by refusing to leave his mortally wounded commander until help came to carry him off. Other officers strove to stem the rush. Nearly half a mile back they were beginning to succeed when the Boer guns, kept quietly beyond a curve of the Modder while the British artillery had thundered, suddenly opened up. Their first shells fell plumb among the rallying Highlanders, who broke and fled again. They were not re-formed until nightfall. Some men had actually been unable to move from their advanced positions and in the evening the Boers called out to them—so close were they—that all who could walk might go unmolested provided they left their rifles and ammunition.

By this time the firing was everywhere dying away. With nightfall the mounted units and guns were withdrawn a short distance, but the rest of the troops in front of the crescent and left of Magersfontein remained. Water carts and food arrived at last, the medical staff moved more freely—though in parts of the battlefield were wounded who received no attention or food for thirty-six hours—and everywhere men slept the deep sleep of exhaustion.

Night passed without incident. If Methuen hoped that the Boers would retire as they had done from the Modder, dawn disillusioned him. He was now beset by conflicting counsel, whether to retire or renew the battle. Most of his staff were for retiring: gun ammunition was short after a day which had consumed thousands of rounds, water supplies were difficult at such a distance from the river, and a third of his army was shattered. Methuen decided to retreat.

First there was an armistice. Ambulances were brought out and amid complete silence moved about the battlefield; British doctors and stretcher-bearers approaching the Boer lines were guided blindfold in order not to bring away information. A short outbreak of firing occurred through a misunderstanding, then silence descended again while the wounded and the dead were gathered.

Methuen began his retreat at noon. The Boers, cautious as ever in following up an advantage, used only artillery to harass them. At 4 p.m. the troops were back in their camp on the Modder. They had lost upwards of a thousand men killed, wounded, captured and missing. Three-quarters were Highlanders, whose leading companies lost sixty per cent of their officers.

In the circumstances the Boer losses, about a quarter of the British, testified to the intensity of the struggle. Ironically the chief architect of victory was absent on the day of battle. De la Rey had gone to break to his wife the news of their eldest son's death.

Among the British killed were many notables, including the Marquis of Winchester, premier Marquis of England, but none was to arouse such emotion as Wauchope. After the battle Methuen sympathized with the Highland Brigade on their losses, adding that the advance had been perfectly executed: '. . . We were within an ace of carrying the position. . . . Everything depended on one word. That word was "Forward!" ' This was taken as a hint that Methuen felt betrayed by the Highland Brigade. The result was a bitter controversy, for the Highlanders believed that they had been sent to certain death— 'taken into a butcher's shop and left there,' said one—and that Methuen had done nothing to relieve them all day. Wauchope's initial reluctance to attack Magersfontein was blown up into rumours of a dispute between him and Methuen. Scotland mourned him as a national hero.

But this was an aspect for the future. The news of Methuen's defeat was given out in London on the Thursday: Monday's news about Stormberg had been a misfortune, but that 13,000 of her finest troops should now have been defeated in the open field struck England numb. Yet optimism quickly revived. The commander-in-chief himself, with the most formidable army of all at his back, was on the march in Natal.

★　　★　　★　　★

At dawn on the day following Methuen's retreat back to the Modder, Buller's army set out from his advance base at Frere with the intention of crossing the Tugela River and marching through the hills to

Ladysmith. Louis Botha's force totalled 8,000 men lying astride the direct road and rail route which crossed the river by the village of Colenso. Though Buller had 18,000 men he decided against the direct route in favour of by-passing the Boers, since they were entrenched on the further side of the river bank and then along the ridges which rose behind it to the hills around the Ladysmith plain. Further, on Buller's side the open ground sloped gradually down to the river bank, so that he would be exposed to the trenches opposite. The position, he

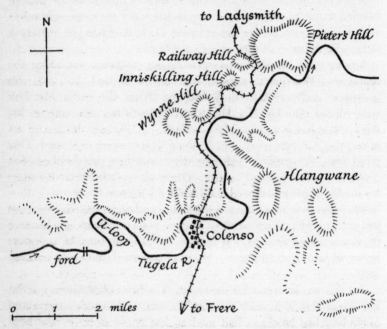

reported to the War Office, was impregnable; therefore he would march upstream around it.

But that same day the news from Magersfontein following the Stormberg disaster shocked him into a conviction that he must restore his guiding hand to headquarters at Cape Town as quickly as possible. He stopped the movement and for the next two days unleashed an intensive long-range bombardment against the Boer position. Then he called in his senior officers to announce his revised plan, expressed in orders issued later that night: '[1] The enemy is entrenched in the kopjes north of Colenso Bridge . . . [2] It is the intention of The General Officer Commanding to force the passage of the Tugela tomorrow.' He would take the direct route after all.

It was precisely in anticipation of this decision that Botha had entrenched himself opposite Colenso, protecting his flanks by extending his line to a total length of ten miles. To thwart Buller's proposed frontal attack with a vastly superior force he placed supreme reliance on keeping his exact dispositions secret, but having skilfully camou- flaged them his difficulty was to hold his force together. The strength of the British army was scarcely more frightening to the burghers than Buller's reputation. How could their own commander, merely a farmer, newly appointed to lead and little tried, compare with the British C.-in-C. himself, proven in a lifetime of professional soldiering? Applications for sick leave poured in, which Botha had to order his doctors to deal with less indulgently, and he had to spend much of his time encouraging his men. His special difficulty was manning his left flank, Hlangwane (pron. shlang-wahn-ee) hill which dominated his whole line but was cut off from the rest of it by a northward twist of the river. As soon as the British started to move, the men rushed back across the river and only a telegraphed admonition from President Kruger persuaded them to draw lots for the hill.

Then came the two-day bombardment. Botha strictly enjoined silence, and a message from Cronje at Magersfontein assuring them of the harmlessness of lyddite if they stayed in their trenches was soon found to be true. At night they repaired any damage. On the evening Buller issued his battle orders the two armies lay four miles apart, every tent on the British side visible to the Boers while Buller, looking at the hill-slopes which he had battered with an even greater weight of explosive than Methuen had used against Magersfontein, saw little indication of any trenches and no signs of life: he wondered if the Boers had not fled.

Having told his senior officer his plans Buller did not let White know. The messages they had been exchanging to co-ordinate their movements had led White to believe that the attack would take place on 17 December, for which date he was in process of preparing a field force drawn from almost the whole garrison to march out simulta- neously with Buller's advance. Now Buller was not only going to attack on the morrow, 15 December, but carefully keeping White ignorant of the fact. White had reported Ladysmith riddled with spies, and it may be that for fear of them Buller decided to forgo the combined attack and rely on his own strength to steam-roller a way through.

It was a very surprised White who woke next morning to the rumble of artillery on the distant Tugela. As messages confirmed that Buller had indeed launched his assault White, caught unprepared, resigned himself anxiously to await the outcome—though in the siege lines at this time were scarcely 6,000 Boers, the remainder having gone to reinforce all the other fronts, including the Tugela, or simply departed on leave—a right on which the individual burgher was very insistent.

The day had dawned without wind or cloud. The sun, soon to be scorchingly hot, rose on Buller's columns moving across the veld to-wards the Tugela. At 5.30 the heavy guns rumbled into position behind the marching men and three miles from the river opened up on the Colenso kopjes in case any Boers were still around. Red clouds of smoke and yellow-green lyddite fumes swallowed the kopjes from view; exploding shells sent up a column of grey smoke hundreds of feet. No response came from the Boers, no movement.

While the heavy guns thundered from far back, horse-teams drew the field guns and oxen the naval guns into position for assault, which was to be by a brigade each against the Boer centre and Boer right until the river had been forced, when the two brigades would link up, the mounted brigade meanwhile seizing Hlangwane to enfilade the Boer line, and two further brigades being kept up in support generally.

For the attack on the Boer centre there were twelve field and six naval guns manned altogether by about five hundred men under the command of Colonel C. J. Long, who had won distinction leading the artillery at Omdurman. Buller had told Long to rely on the long-range naval guns until the infantry brigade assigned to this sector under an able major-general, Sir H. J. T. Hildyard, had advanced—in accordance with orthodox belief that artillery should always be behind the in-fantry. But a theory had arisen that the guns should be pushed right into the face of the enemy to destroy him at short-range. This was Long's own conviction. In spite of the infantry's pleas to slacken pace he forged ahead until he was a full mile in front.

Still the Boers remained silent and invisible. Long's ground scouts, ranging ahead almost as far as the scrub along the nearer bank of the

river, reported no sign of them. The two field batteries were within
two hundred yards of the river and to the right of Colenso village before
Long ordered them to stop for action. As he did so a single shot rang
out from the opposite bank, instantly and violently followed by a
burst of fire that swept through the British gunners.

Once again the British had walked into the arms of Boers they could
not see and whose strength or position was a total mystery to them.
The Guards at the Modder, the Highlanders at Magersfontein, and
now the Royal Artillery at Colenso. And once again the only reply
was the extraordinary courage of ordinary men. While rifle and
machine-gun and, soon, artillery fire swept them they struggled to free
the horses who were led back a quarter of a mile to a *donga*, a shallow
crevice which the slower naval guns had just been crossing when the
blast of fire killed many of the cattle and sent the Native drivers flying.
The bluejackets strove to bring them into action to help the twelve
field guns hopelessly out in the open. The stranded gunners fought
back unflinchingly but futilely against an invisible enemy increasing
the concentration of his fire with every moment. In less than an hour
officers and men lay dead or wounded by the hundred. Long, himself
mortally wounded, was urged to abandon the guns. He shouted above
the roar, 'Abandon be damned! We never abandon guns!' Then he
was carried to a nearby ditch already full of wounded, and in a
delirium kept crying out, 'Ah, my gunners! My gunners are splendid!
Look at them!' The ammunition was almost exhausted, spare ammunition was in wagons still three miles in rear, the position of the survivors
rendered hopeless. At 7 a.m. they were ordered back, leaving the
batteries standing as deserted monuments to Long's stupidity.

Buller was quite unaware of all this and had taken no action to hasten
the infantry attack on the Boer centre. His attention was absorbed by
the move on the left. The brigade assigned to the attack in this sector
was drawn from Irish regiments and led by one Arthur FitzRoy Hart,
a cool-eyed veteran with a moustache extending in waxed points
across the breadth of either cheek. He had come out from a command
at Aldershot, 'a position', according to a contemporary account, 'which
it is simply impossible for a man to hold unless he is a very thorough
and up-to-date soldier.'

It was this up-to-date war-horse's conviction that spacing out men
was a fallacy and that nothing could stop a resolute attack in compact

formation. Cavalry screening his left flank got a clear view of Boer entrenchments across the Tugela directly opposite him, but he dismissed their warning. Having no proper map, despite the fact that a garrison had been posted in the district for two generations, he depended on a Native guide to show the way to a ford by which he intended to make a crossing. The fellow led him wrongly, towards the mouth of a U-shaped loop in the river. As he approached, the Boers all round the loop and on the heights beyond opened fire. The British instinctively began to deploy. Hart peremptorily stopped them and urged them forward. An officer, seeing no ford and finding the Native guide had bolted, turned the brigade away; but Hart bustled up and though he had not studied the map and had no idea of what he was doing he ordered his men directly into the loop. He dashed about spurring them on, then called up reinforcements to add overcrowding to the confusion of men who were already a bloody tight-packed target while themselves unable to see their enemy or any clear objective. Within forty minutes four hundred of them were mown down. They were brave, and would not yield so long as Hart with unquenched ardour kept them there, until mercifully Buller rode down from the high ground where he had been watching and compelled him to withdraw. Battered as they were, the Irishmen pulled out under protest.

This retirement on the British left started almost simultaneously with the abandonment of the guns in the centre, but at the same time the mounted brigade was setting out to attack on the right where possession of the dominating Hlangwane would make the whole Boer position untenable despite Botha's success so far. The brigade was a mixture of cavalry and M.I., including the S.A. Light Horse which faced fire for the first time, and its commander was Douglas Mackinnon Baillie Hamilton, twelfth Earl of Dundonald. A guardsman who had commanded a Camel Corps in the attempt to relieve Gordon, he had lived to carry the dispatches announcing Kitchener's avenge. He was also something of an inventor. With his curly black hair, trim sidewhiskers and pointed moustache he cut a handsome figure as he led his men to the edge of a mealie field, where they dismounted and crept to the slopes of the hill against vigorous fire.

There they clung precariously while reinforcements were sent for from the nearer of the two supporting infantry brigades. Its commander refused. He would not accept responsibility for sending help, preferring to leave the men on the hill-side to survive as best they might, since he had just received orders from Buller not to commit his force.

Buller at this moment was as ignorant of Dundonald's straits as he was of the abandonment of the guns. Knowing only that Hart had been repulsed on the left, he had decided to stake everything on his attack against the Boer centre. Hildyard's brigade, which Long had so disastrously outpaced, was moving into position for this attack when a staff officer galloped up to Buller and reported the fate of the guns. The news seemed even worse because Buller thought the six naval pieces were also out of action. Coming on top of Hart's repulse it was a blow so bitter that he gave up all hope of carrying the Boer defences. At all costs he must get the guns back. They represented nearly half his artillery and without them he had no hope of relieving Ladysmith until replacements arrived from England weeks hence.

Hildyard's role was confined to seizing Colenso village to cover the guns stranded to its right. As Hart's men were now doing nothing more menacing than bathing their exhausted bodies in a distant stream, more Boers could reinforce their centre on the Colenso kopjes. But Hildyard deployed his Devons and Queens with skill. Aided by the naval guns they advanced into the village and had the Boers on the further bank running in the open to trenches higher on the ridges. Three miles back, the muzzles of the heavy guns were trained on the scurrying figures when a cry went up, 'They're our men!'—and the opportunity was lost.

Buller was meanwhile riding through the lines to a point not far behind the deserted guns, and as soon as Hildyard's brigade was covering from Colenso village he ordered the guns to be rescued.

The order was given to his A.D.C., whose call for volunteers was promptly answered. The Boers were intent on preventing so great a prospective prize being denied them. They turned everything they had on the party of men galloping across the open. One of the officers, only son of the famous General Roberts, fell wounded in three places. Another, wounded and unhorsed, crawled to him and with the help of an army doctor who had been tending the wounded in the ditch for the past two hours dragged him away. The rest of the party, under a captain whose clothes were torn by six bullets which yet left him untouched, reached two of the guns and hauled them back. A further attempt, this time with teams of horses, was beaten back with half the men and horses lost.

Buller remained so close to the scene that he himself was under heavy fire. He disregarded it even when his staff surgeon was killed beside him and a fragment of shell severely bruised his side, which he mentioned to no one. He remained apparently unmoved and impassive, eating sandwiches. He watched five V.C.s won, eighteen D.C.M.s, but saw plainly that courage was not enough. In those moments his spirit broke.

To the shock of his wound and his distress at all that had happened during long hours in his saddle under a broiling sun, the heart-breaking gallantry of the rescue attempt came as a final blow. He decided neither to wait for darkness in which to recover the guns, nor to blow them up. He left them there, with their breech-blocks intact, and though half his force had not yet been engaged, though the Boer position had not yet really been attacked, he ordered his whole army to retire.

Included among the medical staff who had been constantly at work on all parts of the battlefield was a small unit of volunteer Indian stretcher-bearers, among them a young lawyer named Gandhi. A half-dozen years before, he had organized the Natal Indian Congress, forerunner to his great Congress Party of India; but essentially his success and fame were to spring from protest against just such violence as he saw that day. With his comrades—'body-snatchers' in troop parlance—he helped carry the wounded to field hospitals, record their injuries and their names from tags sewn into their uniforms, feed them with Bovril, and then from operating tent or dressing-station carry them on to hospital trains for the general hospital pitched at Chieveley, the next siding (where young Roberts was to die next morning). When Buller ordered the retreat towards noon the entire army followed the direction of their wounded, reaching camp at about 2.30 p.m.

Dundonald's Mounted Brigade extricated themselves with extreme difficulty from the slopes of Hlangwane, but many groups in isolated positions elsewhere along the front received no orders and were encountered by the Boers who came over the river to collect the guns at 5 p.m. Some were allowed to go unmolested after animated argument. Others, parched with thirst, were glad to surrender. The Colonel of the Devons declared he would fight it out; a Boer avoided bloodshed by stunning him with his rifle butt.

'Today,' Louis Botha telegraphed the Volksraad, 'the God of our fathers has given us a great victory.' Ten guns had fallen into his hands, with six hundred rounds of ammunition in abandoned wagons. His losses were less than 40 against Buller's 1,127.

Next morning Buller was granted an armistice until midnight to collect his dead and wounded still on the field. Savagely critical of his conduct of the battle, *The Times History* a year or two later commented with a freedom surprising by modern standards: 'Just as in the crisis of the battle he had failed the men whom he led, so now in the hour of trial he was to fail his country which had entrusted the fortune of war into his hands.' For without waiting on an opinion from the War Office or his own senior officers, much less from White himself, he heliographed to Ladysmith:

> As it appears certain that I cannot relieve Ladysmith for another month, and even then only by means of protracted siege opera-tions ... you will burn your ciphers, destroy your guns, fire away your ammunition, and make the best terms possible with the general of the besieging forces, after giving me time to fortify myself on the Tugela.

As soon as the armistice expired at midnight he struck camp in order to avoid being shelled. Hampered by a total eclipse of the moon, his army moved slowly down the line to Chieveley and left Ladysmith to its fate.

*　　*　　*　　*

He had meanwhile telegraphed to the War Office: 'I regret to report serious reverse. . . .' Who would have thought such sober words could unleash such frenzied consequence? The dispatch reached London on Friday night, rounding off the week in reverberating fashion. Britain's greatest and best equipped army ever to leave her shores was dis-astrously checkmated by untutored farmers: the three besieged towns doomed to surrender, the Cape to rise in rebellion, the whole sub-continent wrenched away from England with all that meant in material and strategic loss; but infinitely worse, an exposure of weakness that put her own survival in the balance.

By next morning the news was public property. The whole world seemed to reel. The week was called Black Week, and in its impact upon England there has never been anything like it, before or since.

CHAPTER VIII

Black Week's Aftermath

TOTAL British casualties in Black Week's three battles were 3,000; in World War I Passchendaele alone cost the British a quarter of a million men. After Black Week there was no one immediately able to destroy England; in World War II Dunkirk left England seemingly defenceless against Hitler. Yet neither World War produced the emotion of Black Week.

The uninterrupted span of peace enjoyed by the Victorians; their belief in England's superiority over the rest of mankind; the impunity with which they had enlarged and maintained her Empire; the sentimentality of a people long separated from the realities of suffering; and the feelings entertained for them by the rest of the world—all have their measure in the reaction to Black Week.

In England it was, says one authority, 'a succession of shocks and humiliations. Our national life and thought never were the same again.'[1] Another sums up: 'The knowledge that the whole of our boasted arms were reduced to the pause of defeat, bit as with acid. . . . It was one of the grim signs of that week that women then first began to buy newspapers, as men do, from the sellers in the streets.'[2]

To the newspapers in fact the phenomenon of Black Week owed much. The telegraph enabled them to give news with an immediacy unknown in any major war before. And the education of the masses provided readership on a scale never possible before. Even without the whipping-up of emotion by some of the 'gutter Press' this combination of circumstances would still have brought war home to the majority of Englishmen for the first time. The trifling casualty rate and remoteness of war against 'savages' had not prepared them for such lists of losses in print, or the detailed descriptions still almost reeking with

144

lyddite fumes and quivering from the thud of Mauser bullets. People were made aware not only of war but modern war, here and now, and with this awareness they viewed an international situation more perilous than anyone could remember.

In the Indian Mutiny reinforcements quickly brought a succession of victories; in the Crimean War England had powerful actual and potential allies: here there was a crop of failures unknown since the American War of Independence, and isolation in a world that howled for her destruction like jackals round a stricken lion. And again for many people in authority doubt redoubled over whether the huge new industrialized democracy could exhibit the same temper in adversity as Englishmen of former centuries.

One must bear in mind the England sketched in the opening chapter of this book to understand how Black Week's convulsion of thought and feeling, which still work their influence sixty years afterwards, brought not only intense resolution but its caricature, hysterical 'patriotism'. On one hand the great majority of people felt that ranks must be closed, dangers confidently met: the gravity of the situation, Campbell-Bannerman declared, furnished 'no ground for doubt or despondency . . . our moral and material success is certain'—or as Queen Victoria put it: 'I will tell you one thing. I will have no depression in my house.' On the other hand 'patriotism' gushed as never before. Pictures of war leaders and heroes multiplied in shop windows; schoolboys sprouted badges of their favourites; invalided soldiers were vociferously acclaimed, the most famous incident being that of a fourteen-year-old bugler John Dunne who was wounded at the Battle of Colenso. He was reported to have lost his bugle in the Tugela (pron. tew-gée-le) and after his arrival at Portsmouth where he was met by a vast crowd and chaired through the streets he was taken to Osborne for the Queen to present him with a new bugle, gratifying the entire country except those who wondered what a child was doing on the battlefield, though it was not such a rare event. The incident provided the following specimen, by a canon of Carlisle, of the hilariously dreadful patriotic verse which Press and bookseller poured out for an avid public:

> 'What shall we give, my little Bugelar,
> What for the bugle you lost at Tugelar?'

'Give me another! that I may go
To the front and return them blow for blow.'

With this fever of 'patriotism', and increased hostility towards 'pro-Boers', went as yet little criticism of the conduct of the war, even though there were preliminary rumbles of discontent and the beginning of a more realistic appraisement of the enemy as brave, skilful and chivalrous instead of merely foxy and primitive. But a few people on the fringe of authority had been watching events with unease even before Black Week. The doubts of Chamberlain have been noted, and there were others. It was Lord Roberts's voice, however, which was to have the most immediate practical effect.

He was then C.-in-C. Ireland, a post of semi-retirement. A fortnight before Black Week he had written about the war to Lord Lansdowne, Secretary of War, who had been Viceroy of India during his command there. He wrote of the pessimistic tone of Buller's dispatches and the burden of responsibility on one who like every other general in S.A. had never exercised an independent command before—yet 'the Force now in the field is . . . more than double what Marlborough had . . . or that Wellington had.'[26] The situation in S.A. was deteriorating, Roberts said, and a serious reverse would endanger the Empire. He offered to take over the command himself: 'I shall hope, with God's help, to end the war in a satisfactory manner.'

Lansdowne had discussed the letter with Salisbury, but the Prime Minister doubted Roberts's stamina at the age of sixty-seven and in any event Buller might well 'achieve a brilliant success on the Tugela within the next two or three days.'

The next 'two or three days' brought Black Week, and Buller's 'serious reverse' dispatch with his opinion that Ladysmith must be abandoned. The beginning of a week-end and the approach of Christmas made the moment inconvenient for communication with the British Government. But Lord Lansdowne had stayed in town; and next morning he acted vigorously. Disregarding the War Office's inclination to acquiesce in Buller's conclusion he consulted Balfour and sent an unequivocal order. Buller must persevere, he said, or hand over to a subordinate and return home.

Later that Saturday Lord Salisbury arrived. An informal meeting was held and the unusual course adopted of ignoring Lord Wolseley and the War Office, a course the easier because Wolseley was a Liberal. The politicians took the bit between their own teeth. Salisbury would now agree to Roberts superseding Buller, provided he had as Chief of Staff that younger idol of the public, at the moment consolidating his conquest of the Sudan and eager for more glory, Kitchener: he wired from Khartoum, 'Delighted.' A telegram was sent to Roberts in Dublin. On Sunday morning, meeting the ministers at Downing Street, he accepted the command. In the afternoon Lansdowne took him the news of his only son's death. It was a terrible blow, but he pushed on with his preparations. When he went to the Queen to take leave of her she recorded in her journal: 'He knelt down and kissed my hand. I said how much I felt for him. He could only answer, "I cannot speak of *that*, but I can of anything else. . . ." '

The bereavement lent added emotion to the drama of that Sunday, when in the evening his appointment as C.-in-C. in S.A. was announced to the public. They were told that the situation in Natal required Buller's undivided attention. It was the kind of half-truth used in the game governments play with their people in time of war. But it also gave notice that the Government was resolved to fight the fight out.

They had a limited choice. To the delight of Britain's rival Powers the deficiencies of her military machine had been pitifully exposed. The German Foreign Minister, Count Bülow, wrote: 'The vast majority of German military experts believe that the S.A. war will end with a complete defeat of the English.' Chamberlain's proposal of an alliance was scornfully rejected: the Boer victories were taken by most of the Powers to mean the imminent dissolution of the British Empire. The Press in both Germany and France waged a violent anti-British campaign, and in Russia a war party urged the Tsar to seize the opportunity to strike south into long-coveted India. The mortal threat to England was a maritime combination to challenge her mastery of the sea. For the moment the Royal Navy awed the restive Powers into inaction and the governments of each were further restrained by various considerations such as French dislike for Germany being but second to her Anglophobia, German concentration on building up her fleet, and the Tsar's nervousness about Japan, Britain's only substantial friend if it came to a world war. The whole question was whether that ghastly possibility could be averted when the excitement, the exaltation, which swept the nations of Europe might force their governments' itching hands.

The months after Black Week were a revelation to England of the extent to which she was loathed. Across the Continent raged a storm of hatred for all things English. It was a hatred fed not only by commercial rivalry or envy of England's prosperity and power, but by her 'lording it' both as a nation and through individual tourists, by clerical passions against English liberalism aroused since 1848, by intellectual dislike of what was called the Englishman's 'self sufficiency, phrasemongering, false sentimentality'. All this and ardent partisanship for the Boers as the weaker side, joined poet, scientist and politician in a condemnation that spared not the English Queen, the English soldier or the English people. Lampoons and caricatures of everyone connected with 'Chamberlain's War' were sometimes so obscene that the police had to act, but international scurrility ran unbridled.

Feeling was far less excited in the United States of America. Absorbed in building a strength which had still to be asserted upon the world, she was less interested in events outside her border. There was much 'anti-colonialism' and sympathy for the Boers, especially by the Irish, and there were appeals to President McKinley to intervene. He would not. Britain's refusal to take sides against the U.S.A. in the Cuban affair with Spain was now remembered to her advantage. The influence of Kipling, who was read as widely in the U.S.A. as in England, was one of the reasons for the failure of pro-Boer propaganda. Another was the identity of imperialist impulse behind both the Cuban and Boer Wars which were believed to be crusades against anachronistic tyranny. That this, rather than the parallel which the Boers drew between their struggle and that of the Americans' War of Independence, was the majority view among eminent Americans is reflected by the historian A. T. Mahan, U.S.N., in a letter to Roberts:

> It is a time of deep disappointment and sorrow, not unmingled, I fear, with something of humiliation—of chastening; but I am persuaded that your noble people will come out of it purified and nobler, to resume its beneficent work in the world. With my prayers for the success of yourself and your cause, which I believe the most and best of my countrymen recognize to be that of equal rights and human welfare.[26]

The official policy was neutrality, but there were American volunteers on both sides. Those with the British included many from the Rand and even some Texan cowboys complete with their mounts.

A feature of world reaction to Black Week was that not all of England's nineteenth-century record was recalled to her disadvantage. Though she now looked more vulnerable than anyone had thought possible, it was the smaller nations who rallied to her, except for Holland whose historical and vested interests placed her squarely on the Boer side. Italy remembered the help given to the unification movement and General Riciotti Garibaldi offered his services with volunteers from his country; Scandinavia, Austria, Hungary, Portugal, Servia, Bulgaria, Montenegro were all, at least in their ruling circles, pro-British; Japan was ardently so. Above all, Greece gave passionate voice to her sympathies: at Larissa where a typical memorial service to British casualties in S.A. was held, a cenotaph was inscribed 'in gratitude to the champions of civilization'.

That cenotaph in Larissa caused some Englishmen, reflecting that they were trying to take away the independence of two tiny republics, to hang their heads in shame. For others, it was fresh confirmation of the liberalizing crusade which inspired such idealism as the Victorian Age may boast of. The war, in short, meant a crisis of conscience, made the more vexing by Black Week and amid all the excitement little acknowledged. It is interesting to dip into the diary kept by Beatrice Webb, that chilly if brilliant high priestess of the Fabian Society which has had such a formative effect on twentieth-century British political thought:

> Liberals of all types are depressed and uncertain of themselves. The dismissal of Massingham from the editorship . . . of the *Daily Chronicle* reflects the strong patriotic sentiment of its readers; any criticism of the war at present is hopelessly unpopular. The cleavage of opinion about the war separates persons hitherto united and unites those who by temperament and training have hitherto been divorced. No one knows who is friend and who is enemy. . . . And who can fail to be depressed at the hatred of England on the Continent: it is comforting and easy to put it down to envy and malice, but not convincing. To those who . . . believe the indictment of British policy to be justified, the times look

black. . . . To my mind, given the fact that the Boers were fully armed, confident in their strength, and convinced of our weakness, war was inevitable. Whether this condition of affairs was in itself inevitable, or whether it was brought about by the impossible combination in British policy of Gladstonian sentimental Christianity with the blackguardism of Rhodes and Jameson, is another matter.[27]

But though the mass of people did not give the hour to a Beatrice Webb's soul-searching, there is something more to be said before the subject is left. The British were not a people notable for their humility. Nearly a thousand years' undisturbed and closely-knit occupation of their island, near enough to the Continent for ideas and inspiration but out of reach of swords, brought less humility than great prosperity and great attainments in literature, science and the art of government. But what it had also brought them, even after bestriding the world for the greater part of a century with unexampled confidence, was a quality unique among the makers of empires: possession of a conscience. Its fullest working in the Boer War, which was to provide a striking illustration, had yet to be seen. The immediate issue thrown up by Black Week was whether the country should sue for peace and thereby, as it believed, lose its international position if not its empire; or see out the war at any cost and at the risk of whatever the Continental Powers might conspire. The terse answer was Lansdowne's treatment of Buller's message and the appointment of Roberts and Kitchener. It was supported by calmer spirits and 'patriots' alike.

There was a rush to join the colours. 85,000 men were already in or on their way to S.A., leaving 100,000 theoretically still available from the Reserve, but only twenty per cent were fit and equipped. The War Office was therefore obliged to rely on volunteers. But it believed only in the Regular Army; the fact that a pack of irregulars was giving regulars the fight of their lives in S.A. mattered not: war was for professionals. This opinion it clung to as unshakeably as that which caused the 'mounted troops preferred' absurdity when the Empire had first offered help. Now both notions were painfully revised.

On the same day that Buller sent his gloomy message about Lady-smith he sent another. Defeat, as Dr. Johnson said of hanging, concentrates the mind wonderfully. After the Battle of Colenso Buller saw the virtue of mobility, even if he did not see that it was the supreme factor when the enemy was entirely mobile. He asked for 8,000 mounted men. A tiny light twinkled in the dark dull depths of War Office mentality: it was felt that to meet the request would at the same time provide a partial safety-valve for the embarrassing public enthusiasm. The raising of volunteer forces, both mounted and infantry, was accordingly agreed to—but fenced with rigid rules to ensure that bumbledom would not be bothered while raising reinforcements by the more orthodox means of calling up the whole of the first-class Reserve and inviting the Militia—enthusiasts who did a little peacetime training—to come forward.

Rules for volunteers required them to present themselves already organized and equipped: the Government would only provide arms, pay, and—once they were in S.A.—tents, food and transport to the fronts. A committee of 'influential and patriotic gentlemen' was set up to raise the 8,000 mounted troops which were called Imperial Yeomanry. This committee, constituted by Army Order, functioned like an amateur War Office and soon found themselves competing with the Government in the purchase of horses and equipment. Finally, they found they could not get the men out to S.A. because of a provision in the Merchant Shipping Act. The fantasy of a private army within the public one had to end with the War Office taking over after all. Meanwhile the central recruiting depot at Suffolk Street in the Strand and depots all over the country were besieged by craftsmen, clerks, farmers, and younger sons; many M.P.s and peers joined, including the Duke of Norfolk as an example to his fellow Roman Catholics and in answer to anti-British clerics. Contributing to funds for this and other purposes become a patriotic duty, discharged by one of the finance houses accused of causing the war, Werner, Beit & Co., with £50,000.

Besides men directly raised by the Yeomanry Committee, affiliated companies were raised by individuals. Lord Donoughmore formed the Duke of Cambridge's Own, a highly thoroughbred troop who bore the cost of their own passage and donated their pay to the Widows' and Orphans' Fund. There were Earl Dunraven's Battalion of Sharpshooters, and Paget's Horse, and Lord Lathom's Roughriders, and others. A similar body was Lord Lovat's Scouts raised by Lord Loch from some of the bluest blood in Scotland. The quaintness of a lot of barons setting out with their own little armies in service of the Sovereign went un-

noticed in all the emotion, the men themselves feeling less the sentiment of giving liege than that expressed by a *Punch* character out riding
with his girl friend who murmurs poignantly, 'Isn't it sad to think this
is our last day?' To which he replies: 'Oh, I don't mind so much. You
see, I'm going to take over my gees to S.A. The season is hardly over
there, I believe.'

Of the unmounted volunteers who offered themselves for infantry,
artillery and other duties, the most famous were the City Imperial
Volunteers (C.I.V.) of picked infantry marksmen from London volunteer regiments and commanded by the Earl of Albemarle. £100,000
was promptly subscribed by the public, shipping companies offered
much free transport, the freedom of the city was conferred, and amid
boundless enthusiasm the first 2,000 men were at sea within a month.
Other volunteers made up the strength of regular regiments which
were partly converted to M.I. The Honourable Artillery Company
volunteered, and the Elswick Battery was the donation of Lady Meux.

The rush to join the colours was accompanied by immense public
emotion. Beautiful young society women in their long tailored skirts
and large feathered hats lowered their veils and clasped their muffs
more tightly against their tiny waists, and old women twitched at the
shawls around their shoulders, and men gnawed their moustaches and
lifted topper or high-crowned bowler aloft in the air, and everyone of
every degree was gripped by a tremulous excitement at sight of a man
in uniform. He was admitted free to places of entertainment, led the
choruses of patriotic songs, and for a little day took possession of the
kingdom. After all this it must be recorded that the number of enlist-
ments as permitted by the reluctant authorities seems hardly significant.
Only 20,000 volunteers plus a like number of Militia embarked for S.A.
in the six months or so following Black Week. But the majority came
from the upper classes, which were now involved in war far more
deeply than their connexion with the officer class of the Regular Army
had meant, and the fact that almost every influential family soon came
to have a close relative donning khaki profoundly influenced English
life. Besides this, the atmosphere of shock and crisis may be measured
by the 165,000 men who came forward in the ensuing year for a fortnight's training at emergency camps for home defence.

Black Week had cast a cloud over many reputations. For one man it
brought unexpected reprieve from public displeasure. Chamberlain's

gaffe in suggesting an Anglo–German–American alliance was forgotten. As the Press gradually got round to flaying the War Office for supplying inferior guns and faulty maps and for criminally underestimating the enemy, Chamberlain not only escaped censure as he had nothing to do with the conduct of the war, but he was borne upward to fresh heights of popularity by public clamour to see the war through to victory, and by his part in strengthening the bonds of empire, for nothing was seen as a stronger retort to Continental forecasts of disintegration than the repetition of England's own emotion throughout the Empire.

Australia, whose miners had formed a large proportion of the Uitlanders, headed the list of contributors with an ultimate total of 17,000 men and £1,250,000. New Zealand contributed 6,000 men and £300,000, Canada 8,500 men and nearly £1 million. India, the Malay States, Ceylon and all the other colonies sent contingents of whites while non-whites, barred from joining them, assisted in local drives for funds; and in mosque, temple and church prayed for the success of British arms. The volume of supplication addressed heavenward by either side in the course of the war was only matched by its variety of denominational inspiration.

The Empire's total contribution of manpower was limited in the end to upwards of 40,000 volunteers, which is less significant than that such participation, freely offered, made this the first time the Empire as a whole went to war. Hence it was something of great importance in the evolution of the Commonwealth of Nations.

Yet the Boer War was only partly an imperial war. It was equally a civil war between the whites. The schism found clear expression in Cape politics. Having been elected by the Afrikander Bond precisely to oppose Milner's brand of imperialism, Schreiner knew that the logical outcome, which was at least to declare the Cape neutral and close the ports and railways to British troops, would invite an upheaval by British colonists, a constitutional crisis and even a charge of treason. On the other hand, *Ons Land* which was the leading Afrikaner newspaper, openly preached rebellion, supporting its campaign with the same kind of lies as could be found in much of the British Press: exaggerations of successes, innuendoes against enemy announcements, and atrocity stories were staple diet. Responsible men behind Schreiner, like Jan Hofmeyr, urged him to follow a constant policy of obstruction.

However loyal to his status as a British subject and unwilling to become Kruger's, and though he was deeply affected by Steyn's invasion in betrayal of his pledge, Schreiner's sympathy for his kinsmen and his opposition to imperialism were not to be gainsaid. Between the remorseless demands of Milner and those of his own followers he trod a tortuous path, eyed with suspicion by both. Just as previously he had avoided defensive measures in order, he claimed, not to provoke a Boer invasion, so now in order not to inflame rebellion he only took limited action like imposing martial law in areas actually occupied by the invaders. Afrikaners saw half-measures of this kind as aiding the British. Milner saw them as preventing the Cape from throwing its full weight behind Britain, and he pleaded with Chamberlain to suspend the Cape constitution, but Chamberlain refused to give his critics ammunition by such a repressive action.

Meanwhile the British colonists and refugee Uitlanders were up against the Army's obstinacy over volunteers, especially colonists who were apt not to be gentlemen. The Kaffir Wars had given the country the highest proportion of fighting men in the world; they knew the terrain intimately; the war was as keenly their concern as anybody's. Yet enlistment was hedged about with restrictions, and only the heightened feeling following Black Week permitted additional corps, making an ultimate total of well over 30,000 men of whom a number were loyal Cape Dutch.* A great many more volunteered for stretcher-bearing, town guard and other duties, and the Railway Pioneer Regiment was formed by an American engineer from Uitlander railway experts. Tiny Rhodesia produced 1,500 volunteers to join Plumer or help guard the Limpopo drifts, the Chartered Company now mooting the raising of a large overseas reinforcement.

The disasters which had overtaken the great white Queen's troops were quickly known to the vast audience of Natives. Swaziland, Basutoland and Bechuanaland waited to see which way the wind would finally blow, but some chiefs took the precaution of keeping in touch with Boer agents. Of the leading Native tribes within the three

---

* Names of corps which will stir older memories include, in addition to those listed on page 100, the Imperial Light Horse (I.L.H.), South African Light Horse (S.A.L.H.)—including Warren's, later Roberts's, Horse and Kitchener's Horse—Colonial Scouts, Bethune's M.I. and Brabant's Horse, and Bayly's, Nesbitt's and Orpen's respective Corps. At first the irregulars were tied to regular regiments but later many formed their own Colonial Regiment under Gen. E. Y. Brabant.

British colonies, the Matabele of Rhodesia had too recently (1896) felt the heavy hand of the whites to invite trouble, but the Zulus as well as tribes in the eastern Cape were restive and there was the possibility of Boer incursion. Hence in Zululand Native police and white volunteers patrolled the border; and in Native districts of the eastern Cape where raids on adjoining farms of whites were already taking place, 4,000 Native levies were recruited under white officers to stay within their frontier for police and defence duties.

Not that non-whites had played no part in the operations so far. On both sides were half-caste and Native transport drivers, servants, spies and dispatch runners. The Indian stretcher-bearers at Colenso came from an unpaid volunteer corps of a thousand of the derided 'coolie' immigrants, others of whom assumed responsibility for Indian refugees from the Transvaal and collected money and gifts for hospitals. 'They are sons of the Empire after all!' declared a Natal newspaper magnanimously. [28]

To a detached observer of the time, studying the impact of Black Week on the nations, the reaction of the people who had caused all the commotion must have seemed extraordinary. The Boers were almost entirely unmoved.

The climax of that week, Buller's attempt to force the Tugela at Colenso, happened to occur the day before an anniversary sacred to the Boers. Sixty years before, a tributary of that same river ran with blood when their Trekker fathers avenged a treachery by the Zulu chief Dingaan and broke his power. As the annual celebrations of that event coincided with the morrow of their victory over Buller the following days were set aside for solemn thanksgiving. There was scarcely any jubilation. That God had once more protected his people was a matter for pious reflection, not festivity. They did not share the rest of the world's surprise at their defeat of the British, whom they considered were being destroyed by the judgement of God. Discussing this view with a colleague, a British Baptist minister, allowed to continue living in Pretoria, records: 'Neither of us could believe that what had taken place was any indication of the hand of God at all. It was an unhappy circumstance of which one day . . . we should have an ample explanation.' [14] Throughout the war God hovers upon the scene, his support the object of ceaseless negotiation by either side. 'O Lord,' cried a Boer parson at the burial of some of the Boer killed in the Ladysmith sorties against the siege guns, 'What shall our men think if the enemy is allowed to be victorious?' Threatened, begged or bribed, God kept neutral—although one Pretoria newspaper reported significantly of a recent storm that whereas lightning killed two Boers it killed *four* Englishmen. They had no occasion to exult over beating an enemy with whom they had not gone to war out of hatred: they could even feel sympathy, like the simple *vrou* who lamented that for the poor old Queen defeat must mean that she would now have to do her own laundry. Above all, they were civilians glad that the unpleasant business of fighting, which brought neither glory nor advancement but discomfort and suffering, was over for the present. Perhaps for good. England had tired of war against them before, with less reason than now when added to her defeats was the increasing probability of intervention by other Powers. A minority of Boers looked forward to wiping the British from the whole of S.A., but the leaders repeated after Black Week that they wanted only freedom from interference (plus payment of war expenses), though Kruger himself wanted also a passage to the sea. He dismissed Joubert's suggestion that now was the moment to propose a peace settlement. If the English had not had enough they soon would have.

Yet when the more vigorous Boers urged a follow-up to the successes gained in Natal and the Cape before the new British commander arrived with reinforcements they were turned down by their cautious elders, or found themselves up against their fellow burghers' individualism which became mere indiscipline when no immediate danger threatened. Nevertheless preparations were pushed ahead to meet the fresh threat posed by Roberts and Kitchener after Black Week.

Steyn did not lack vigour in exhorting his burghers, organizing supplies, and inspecting camps. Nor did President Kruger, who had from the outset sent streams of telegrams from Pretoria with advice and instructions to the fronts, couched in pious phrases that recall the Puritans. A crying need was manpower, but raising all 20,000 men who had not responded to the call-up proved beyond the ability of most officials. Depending on votes for their position they disliked imposing penalties, prefering this example of magisterial pronouncement:

Well beloved burghers and friends, I cannot do otherwise than entreat you not to disappoint us further. It is a very hard task for us to threaten our burghers with the law, so I would beg of you all in a friendly manner of one accord to proceed to Ladysmith, without incurring the rigour of the law—Your well-intentioned friend P. M. Bester, Landdrost.

Many who answered such appeals never reached the front because they attached themselves unasked to bridge-guards, supply depots and hospitals. Others got to the front only to stay in their laagers while their comrades fought. Nor did the so-called 'leave-plague' help: no national emergency would make a free burgher forgo his constitutional right to short leave every three months. The generals were besieged by applicants, eventually allowing ten per cent of each commando a fortnight off in rotation.

There were two other sources of manpower. One was the foreign volunteers brought by every ship to Lourenço Marques for months after the outbreak of war, Black Week greatly stimulating the process. They included pensioned-off regulars anxious for a good fight, sincere idealists in the Boer cause, and soldiers of fortune who had fought in the Foreign Legion, the Dutch army in the East Indies, Cuba, or South American revolutions. They flocked into Pretoria in a riot of picturesque uniforms inherited from some foreign army or thought up for the occasion. They were surprised by their reception. Kruger greeted a party of German volunteers thus: 'Thank you for coming. Don't imagine that we had need of you. Transvaal wants no foreign help but as you wish to fight for us you are welcome. I take your coming as a gratifying sign that Europe is gradually beginning to recognize the right of the Afrikander nation.' Many having arrived thinking they would immediately be made commanders-in-chief found themselves asked to join the commandos at the fronts on the same basis as the burghers—horse, saddle and rifle provided but no pay. If they lacked the fare home or were too shamefaced to confront their friends, they joined. More welcome were Dutch, German, French and Russian ambulances whose doctors and nurses did valuable work. Least welcome of all were opportunists out for loot. Not finding any at the fronts they sold their equipment to contractors for sale back to the Government; then they pretended to be new recruits and repeated the trick, or were given supplies and equipment for volunteer corps which subsequent inspection revealed to be non-existent.

The Boers' other source of manpower, by which they set far greater store, was their Cape kinsmen. The critical question for the republics as for the British was how quickly the 40,000 expected rebels would now materialize. The immediate result of Black Week was that women sympathizers in the Cape openly wore Republican colours, and baked cakes or worked favours to welcome the hoped-for commandos to whom their men sent encouragement and information about British troop movements. They were cautious about actually joining their kinsmen in the face of warning proclamations by their own Prime Minister and of British propaganda about imaginary troop dispositions, but numbers of young men slipped away and to Milner it seemed he was sitting on a barrel of gunpowder, which at any moment might explode. The decisive moment after Black Week waited solely on military developments.

Apart from manpower the Boers' problem was supplies. For a people supposed to be backward peasants they did astonishingly. They repaired guns and even made a howitzer at their Pretoria railway workshops, turned out ammunition from the dynamite factory at Johannesburg, set up committees to obtain horses and goods, started a clothing factory in Johannesburg to employ poor women and implement clothing made at home, and organized bakeries. Meat, mealies, oxen, horses were in good supply, but a shortage was starting in such things as coffee, cloth, sugar, even though stock-piling and the Uitlanders' exit left a hump to feed on. Yet the civil administration ensured that burghers were adequately mounted, fed and clothed; it kept ten gold-mines running, directly owning five, to accumulate millions of pounds; and most farms continued to be maintained in their owners' absence. All this was achieved in spite of corrupt contractors and even individual burghers who sold their horses and equipment when on leave. But every article from the outside world had to come to Delagoa Bay and this life-line Britain strove to choke.

She had carelessly failed to ratify an agreement with Portugal twenty years before which would have given military passage and control over Portuguese East Africa. Milner and Buller therefore urged the Government to blockade Delagoa Bay. In the delicate international situation this was refused, but the Navy did search ships and put a stop to obvious war material. European firms grew chary about dispatching munitions to the Boers, and British agents tried to buy up non-warlike goods as fast as they were landed. The colonial Portuguese merchants had a financial picnic, and British firms in the territory were not averse from profitable trade with the Transvaal either, while the Portuguese Government weighed in with a costly passport system for volunteers arriving to join the Boers.

Among the ships stopped and searched by the Navy several were German-owned, further inflaming German hostility, and the threat was made of breaking off diplomatic relations. For the while, however, the Kaiser restrained himself. So long as his neutrality might last Britain gained the further advantage that German South-West Africa, the only other foreign territory adjoining belligerent soil, was denied the Boers both as a refuge for Cape rebels and a jumping-off place for attack, especially on the copper-mines of Namaqualand.

* * * *

All these, then, were the emotions, the dangers actual and illusory but real enough to those who confronted them, the preparations, the ramifications, and the consequences, of the period which arose out of Black Week, mid-December 1899. Some were immediate, some continuing and protracted, but the first event to rivet attention was the departure of Roberts two days before Christmas at a moment when everything was to play for. Attack by Russia, Germany, France; the loss of S.A. in a holocaust of military defeat, Native eruption, Cape uprising; the survival of an empire and the safety of England—all appeared to be in the balance.

He left London from Waterloo, which for a British general was a better omen perhaps than for a foreign. Many in the great crowd of Royalty, cabinet ministers, soldiers and civilians wore some black in sympathy with his loss. Another great crowd saw him on to the *Dunnottar Castle* at Southampton. As the liner cast off into the grey of a winter's day they cheered him. The little old man in deep mourning raised his hat, turned away, and paced the deck.

CHAPTER IX

Christmas 1899–New Year 1900

ROBERTS was due to reach Cape Town on 10 January. In the meantime along the battlefields themselves the tempo of events slackened almost to a halt. It was a curiosity of the war so far how Boer and Briton had become locked in a struggle on the side-lines. Natal and the Western Front had provided most of the drama, when neither matched the strategic or political importance of the Cape.

Buller's gamble in leaving weak forces to defend the Midlands while he divided his strength between the Western and Natal Fronts had abjectly failed. The crucial question was how quickly the invading Boers would press their advantage and spark off the imminent uprising. They could move from Stormberg against a dazed Gatacre, turn on French a hundred miles to the west of him, pour down the gap between, or cross French's front to take De Aar and cut off Methuen from Cape Town: any or all boded disaster. Whether it could be averted depended now primarily on one man, General French.

To the good fortune of his escape from Ladysmith was added the fact that Naauwpoort Junction, unlike Stormberg, had been reoccupied before the invading Boers reached it. For this he had to thank the excessive caution of the Boer commander on this sector, General Schoeman, who had scarcely budged from his base at Colesburg since first crossing the Orange. Although Schoeman's force totalled 4,000 men or twice his own, French set out to prod his forward positions and ceaselessly patrol and reconnoitre. Douglas Haig was with him as Chief of Staff, and another name to be heard more of was E. H. H. Allenby— a handsome Dragoon in his fortieth year, with a straight nose, strong chin, large eyes and fine waxed moustache, he had served in Warren's Bechuanaland expedition and in the Zulu War of '88. French used such men to conduct harassing operations with an enterprise unique among his fellow generals. Providing the only gleam of comfort to British pride at this period, he made his name. His 'hotting up' tactics, supported by British propaganda stories of reinforcements, so mystified Schoeman about his strength and intentions that in spite of information from sympathizers and prospective rebels the Boer general stayed practically moribund. French boldly pushed forward to the Boer advance position at Arundel, half-way to Colesburg, whereupon Schoeman simply fell back and a subsequent belated effort to recover the position was easily beaten off by a force of cavalry.

The result was that Black Week did not bring the immediate disaster it threatened to the Cape. Schoemen's inactivity was no encouragement to Olivier at Stormberg: Gatacre was left unmolested to recover his strength and send out small forces to control the surrounding countryside. The ensuing skirmishes created two new heroes for a public anxious to replace fallen idols. One was Captain the Hon. R. H. L. J. de Montmorency, heir of a popular aristocratic Irish general. The previous year, as adjutant of the famous 21st Lancers in Kitchener's expedition, he had won the V.C. for rescuing a brother officer while surrounded by a horde of dervishes. Now he led a scout corps in a number of dashing exploits to make Olivier chary of leaving the fastness of Stormberg. Another corps leader to achieve distinction was E. H. Dalgety who occupied Dordrecht on the extreme right where the Boers had made their deepest penetration southward.

But no one was under any illusion about the Colony's safety. At any moment the situation might be transformed by the pleas of the younger Boers for a switch of forces from the other fronts to aim a paralysing blow at the heart of it. A clear indication that this was about to happen came with the appointment of Christian de Wet's brother, Piet, to assist and ginger up Schoeman.

Yet in Black Week's black aftermath it was not the danger to the Cape which commanded most attention in Britain, but the besieged towns of Ladysmith, Kimberley and Mafeking. Their names still ring in the ears of older Englishmen because they symbolized England's own danger. The very fact of their being besieged, much less the disastrous failures to relieve them, seemed to shriek her weakness and raised such an ominous question-mark over the intentions of rival Powers. This identity of the three towns' fate with England's was so strong as almost to create the belief that if they fell so might England, and as they stood fast so might she and her empire.

In Ladysmith after Buller's defeat at Colenso, White was little aware of what this crowning disaster of Black Week meant in the world at large. He only knew that the upshot of a nerve-racking day was not relief but the stupefying message from Buller instructing him to burn his papers and surrender. Buller (as he explained in after years when he was publicly castigated for this message) believed that horse sickness and enteric were about to desolate the garrison, that the Boers were poisoning the town's water-supply by putting in dead horses, and that supplies could only last another fortnight. Enteric was indeed exacting an increasing toll—180 soldiers in the past month—and rations for the horses if not the humans were seriously depleted, but by and large the situation was not nearly so desperate as Buller thought.

The fact remained that White had received an order from his C.-in-C.: if he did not obey, and Buller's fears were justified by events, he would bring down his long military career in disgrace. It was a career to which the opening phase of the war had added no lustre; but now he obeyed not Buller but that instinct which has often redeemed the dullest English officer and confounded his enemy. At first he thought Buller's message was a fake perpetrated by the Boers. When he had to take it seriously he tried to cheer Buller up: things, he declared, might not be as bad as they seemed. He urged him to harry the Boers lest they turned their whole strength on the town: 'The loss of 12,000 men here would be a heavy loss to England. We must not think of it.'

He reduced the rations and issued an order to the garrison and towns-folk. The defence would be continued, he announced, *in the same spirited manner as it has hitherto been conducted until the general officer commanding-in-chief in South Africa does relieve it.* He did not however apply his dictum of 'spirited manner' to any attempt at breaking out. Buller, having completed his retreat as far as Chieveley where his force could rest and gather fresh supplies, guns and men, was dazed with defeat. He sent White querulous messages asking what course he should now adopt, to which his subordinate replied urging him to keep active—while not himself making a bold move of any kind.

The 'heroic defenders' of Ladysmith became such a stirring legend that it is a pity to question its validity. But the fact of the matter is that at this stage 13,496 combatants in Ladysmith were being kept there by

a Boer force which 'leave-plague' and the drawing off of men to the
Tugela and other fronts had reduced to less than half that number. A
resolute attempt to break out would have compelled Buller to re-
engage the Tugela force in order to keep it occupied, and the total
Boer army of 14,000 could have been set upon from two directions by
the total British force of well over 30,000. Every day that this course
was not taken added to the list of sick and disabled, further enfeebled
the horses, depressed morale, and generally sapped White's strength.

So the Boers were left undisturbed to impose their policy of trying
to reduce the town by starvation and bombardment. Yet their need for
action was scarcely smaller. The repulse of Buller to a safe distance left
the Tugela force momentarily free to join the besiegers in an all-out
assault before Buller might assert his superior strength or the arrival
of Roberts transformed the situation.

Instead, they waited. It was a very pleasant method of conducting
war. Reitz, one of the Boers on the Ladysmith heights during those
long hot summer days, has left a faithful account:

> Neighbouring farms were laid under tribute and plundered of
> everything that could be turned to account. . . . Our native boy
> Charley also entered an appearance, beaming with delight at
> having tracked us down. He travelled on foot all the way from the
> Transvaal border, and although several times arrested as a spy, he
> had talked and argued his way through until he found us. Needless
> to say, he was received with open arms, as we were once more able
> to turn over to him our duties of cooking, carrying water, horse
> guard, and etc., so my brother and I settled down to a life of ease.
> There were no drills or parades and, except for night picket and an
> occasional fatigue-party to the railway depot to get supplies, there
> were no military duties. Our commando received many fresh
> drafts . . . but discipline was slack, and there was a continual stream
> of burghers going home on self-granted leave, so that we never
> knew from day to day what strength we mustered. . . . [Our
> leaders] lived at the head laager miles away and to all intents and
> purposes we were a law unto ourselves. . . . We settled down to a
> stationary life, and if occasionally time hung heavily on our hands,
> conditions were otherwise comfortable enough. Our boy Charley
> proved a capable freebooter, and thanks to his foraging expeditions

into the hills among the Zulu kraals where he made play with his descent from Chief Moshesh, our larder flourished. . . . After a week or two tents were served out. . . . So quiet were things around Ladysmith, that, as time went on, many burghers had ox-wagons brought down from their farms, and some even had their wives and families with them, which tended further to increase the spirit of inactivity that was gaining on the commandos. . . . We thoroughly enjoyed the business of besieging Ladysmith, sniping at out-posts, riding from camp to camp to pay visits, and making regular excursions to see the guns fired into the town. We went once every week to look up a Norwegian uncle of ours . . . commandeered for service very much against the grain, as he held we were bound to be defeated. I was surprised to see in what good part the burghers took his outspoken comment on their chances, but the real fighting Boer is ever a tolerant, good-natured fellow. . . . The British now and then shelled our camp, upon which we would take cover at the first sign of trouble, and the damage was generally confined to a riddled tent or two, and perhaps a few horses injured. . . . During the day time no guards were set at all, as there were always a sufficient number of men on the hill above amusing themselves with sniping to make sure of an alarm being given in case of need, and at night although we went on outpost so close to the English sentries that we could hear them challenge each other, and sometimes exchanging shouted pleasantries with them, we did not take our watch very seriously. We used to go on foot after dark in parties of 20 or so, and, on reaching neutral ground on the plain . . . two men at a time would walk forward a short distance. Here they stood or sat on sentry-go while the rest of us pulled off our boots, spread our blankets and went to sleep until it was the turn of the reliefs. At daybreak we collected our belongings, and tramped back to camp in time for morning coffee.[29]

Not every Boer even bothered to keep the night watch, Reitz instancing his uncle who rode to sentry-go in a cart, spread his bedding and, tipping one of the younger men half-a-crown to do his duty for him, slept in comfort. For the besiegers life thus became a glorious picnic. A stream of visitors arrived from Pretoria to join in the social life and derive a thrill from watching the guns bombard the town.

An exactly similar situation developed in the Boer lines around Kimberley and at Magersfontein. Whole families joined the burghers, visitors constantly arrived, and a general attitude of slackness inevitably prevailed. Yet the desirability of a prompt follow-up to the successes of Black Week was even greater on this Western Front than in Natal, for here the Boers had no railway to bring up supplies, which were carted seventy miles cross-country from Bloemfontein to the head laager at Jacobsdal. Not enough forage could be brought up for the horses who were undernourished by the feeble grass; soon a third of Cronje's 8,000 men were unmounted. Moreover, his entrenchments were over five miles from the nearest point on the Modder from which he could get water without molestation from the British lines. De la Ray and Christian de Wet—now promoted to fighting-general and in command of the Free Staters under Cronje—appealed for an early assault, if only on Methuen's line of communication, but Cronje would not agree. Nor was much done to stir up rebellion in the surrounding Cape territory, except forming a small rebel band at Sunnyside north-west of Belmont. But preparations were completed for an attack on the isolated little settlement of Kuruman, far to the north-west of Kimberley.

Originally a mission station made famous by Moffat and subsequently by Stanley Livingstone who there met him and married his daughter before setting out to explore the north, it had become an administrative centre for a wide area of farms. The previous month its force of sixty white police and settlers and a like number of Bastards (of whom only fourteen were armed), had beaten off an attack by nearly 700 Boers. Now over a thousand encircled the settlement and added it to the list of besieged towns.

Methuen had to sit helplessly by on the banks of the Modder—a situation from which even *Punch* was unable to extract anything better than, 'Nigger News from Transvaal: De British hab got alongside o' Modder. But they habn't got no Farder.' Immediately after the Magersfontein disaster Buller in fact telegraphed him to retire all the way back to Orange River Station if he did not feel strong enough to attack Cronje again, but in the middle of the night Pole-Carew came to him with an alternative plan that made him hesitate and temporarily postpone the retreat. The following day Milner, convinced that a retreat would precipitate Kimberley's fall and increase the danger of

Cape rebellion, persuaded Buller to let Methuen stay where he was. Next, Methuen's position as commander was put in jeopardy. The 5th Division was beginning to arrive at Cape Town and Wolseley cabled orders for its commander, General Sir Charles Warren, to supersede Methuen. Buller protested at this interference, the order was countermanded, and eventually Warren with the 5th Division joined him in Natal.

These two events, Methuen's retention of his position on the Modder and Warren's posting to Natal, were to bear profoundly on what was to follow. For the present Methuen strengthened his guard on the railway line with 11,000 newly arrived British, Australian and Canadian troops; he brought up supplies, daily bombarded the Boers, and pushed forward his advance posts to within a mile of theirs. But he made no attempt to attack their communications strung out eastwards from Magersfontein at right angles to his own and hence very vulnerable. With his 12,000 men he nightly watched the flickering light which announced that Kimberley still held out, and by day ventured out only against the flies that swarmed upon his bivouac.

Beyond the Magersfontein hills whose great blackened and purple boulders swum in the heat the Boers in the siege lines around the city had been the first to bring news of the battle, signalling exultantly: 'We have smashed up your fine column.' That it was gallingly true, a message from Methuen presently confirmed: and with his message the information that they might have to hold out two, three months longer. At any rate it put an end to arguments about what would happen when the siege was lifted. Kekewich returned to a policy of pin-pricking little sorties against the enemy lines, the populace to dodging the daily aimless bombardment, and all to the tedium of a twilight life on dull rations.

*   *   *   *

Arriving close on the heels of Black Week, Christmas did a little to relieve the general gloom. In England, where the thronged churches were the scene of fervent prayers for peace on earth, goodwill to men, and the triumph of British arms, people found a welcome distraction in disputing whether the end of the month would be the end of the century, the argument being settled by a statement from the Astronomer Royal that the world would have to wait another year, until

1 January 1901, for the twentieth century. But the happiest distraction was provided by Winston Churchill.

The Boers kept their officer prisoners of war in the State Model Schools at Pretoria. Churchill, no very model pupil at even the most august of schools, tried in vain to argue and bribe his way out. Although he was a war correspondent he had been armed with a pistol and taken an active part in the armoured train affair; besides, said the Boers, 'We don't catch the son of a lord every day.' He kept watch from a privy and chose an evening shortly before Christmas to slip over a wall when the guards were not looking. His hair-raising adventures as he made his way to Delagoa Bay, including keeping company with rats down a mine-shaft and lying thirst-racked for fourteen hours in a wood eyed by a vulture 'who manifested an extravagant interest in my condition, and made hideous and ominous gurglings from time to time,' thrilled and delighted half the world. The twenty-five-year-old newspaper correspondent had made a claim on public attention he was never to forgo, and the Providence that looks after these things had kept him ignorant of the fact that the Boer Government had already scheduled his release for the morning following his escape.*

All along the fronts Christmas arrived in a cascade of gifts from home, including lovingly knitted balaclavas for men dripping with the sweat of midsummer. Messrs Lyons sent out 10,000 Christmas puddings, and about this time too every soldier received the Queen's gift of a small tin of chocolates bound in red, white and blue ribbon and bearing her portrait. In the besieged towns the day was marked as festively as supplies allowed. Cecil Rhodes had Christmas puddings distributed among the Kimberley garrison, while at Ladysmith the Boers fired Christmas puddings into the town from their guns. The bluejackets there enlivened the occasion with great effigies of John Bull and Paul Kruger, the latter somewhat battered, and every toy in the town was bought up for 200 children.

Only at Kuruman, the little besieged settlement in the arid plains far to the north-west of Kimberley and south-west of Mafeking, did any fighting disturb the tranquillity of the day. The Boers' usual caution, and the resolute opposition of a force a sixth the size of theirs, brought

---

* He was afterwards accused in England of deserting fellow conspirators and also of breaking parole. He issued a number of writs for libel.

little progress. The Transvaalers chafed, and on Christmas Day wanted to go on fighting, but their O.F.S. comrades did not. The Transvaalers hence kept up the fight on their own sector while the Free Staters fraternized with the British from the opposing trenches and even went swimming with them.

So the year dragged hot and limp to a close, and what major events marked the final week only served to add to British misfortune and turned thoughts hopefully to the little man and the big man pacing the deck of the *Dunnottar Castle*. On the morning after Christmas Baden-Powell had his fingers scorched in trying to seize a Boer outpost called Game Tree Fort, nearly fifty men being killed or wounded in the over-ambitious attempt. A few days later the haunting danger to the Cape startled afresh when Olivier stretched out a tentacle from Stormberg and obliged Dalgety on Gatacre's right to give up Dordrecht and expose all the eastern Cape as far as the vital seaboard. At about the same time a Boer commando invaded the district of Upington, 400 miles away on the Orange and a sally-port for invasion of the western Cape. The extremities of the long thin British defence line in the Cape were clearly as vulnerable as the centre between French and Gatacre. New Year's Eve in Cape Town was a night of alarm, with rumours flying about of a great uprising to be signalled by the kidnapping of Milner, so that he and all vital establishments were heavily guarded.

But New Year's Day brought news that was music to British ears. French had gradually edged forward from Arundel and now, strongly reinforced, was attacking the enemy position upon which any extensive invasion of the Cape depended, Schoeman's stronghold of Colesburg. He had decided to hazard his force and the safety of the Cape on joining battle which the Boers had so far evaded. This time they stood at bay. Schoeman's constant back-pedalling had disheartened them, but Piet de Wet was among them and they too had been reinforced.

*　　*　　*　　*

The town of Colesburg, near which Paul Kruger had spent his boy-hood, lay in the semi-desert of the Karoo. Except for occasional clusters of rocky kopjes it was flat, scrubby country, its red or yellow earth and mauve shale here and there cracked into shallow ravines and gaping holes when sudden storms provided too much water where usually there was too little. Horseman or wagon sent up clouds of red or yellow dust, and at sunset the sky was diffused with a gentle mush-room or heliotrope glow. It was a landscape monotonous and even hideous to the new-comer, but those who knew it loved the clarity of light and the freshness of air beneath an ever blue sky, the sense of boundless space, and the rare glory of wild veld flowers summoned by the rain.

The town was open on the north but the other three sides were protected by hills: those facing French to the south were particularly formidable. He therefore launched his attack from the west, moving up the assault column by night. The situation was ominously like that at Stormberg—the hilly objective, the night march in readiness for a dawn attack from the west. But this time the troops arrived fresh on horseback or wagon. Nor did they blunder about, for careful recon-naissance enabled them to go directly to the point of action. And as they launched their attack at dawn they were supported by strong demonstrations from south and east which fully engaged the enemy and sent the New Zealanders into action for the first time. French was buoyed up by his run of success and he expected to enter the town within hours. The western assault overran hills commanding the Boers' defences on that side and the Suffolks even seized a dominating hill north-west of the town. But the opposition was stern, braced by Piet de Wet's presence and new men, and the attack ground to a stand-still by early afternoon.

Yet the gains were substantial. The Boers were threatened with encirclement and their morale sank even further than Schoeman's leadership had already reduced it. One more push, French believed, and the town would fall. He decided to wait for reinforcements to be brought up. The Boers waited likewise, staying only in expectation of their own reinforcements.

Satisfaction over the first phase of French's bold offensive on the Central Front was tempered by news from the Western. The settlement of Kuruman had surrendered at last in the face of artillery brought up by the Boers, ending an episode of valorous defence and laying open tens of thousands of square miles of the far northern Cape to the roam-ing commandos. It was space cheaply bought but of questionable advantage. Nearer Methuen the rebel commando at Sunnyside north-west of Belmont was engaged by a column he sent out which surprised the Boers and captured their laager, and this was better news than the other was bad, since it discouraged the spread of rebellion across the Orange.

The Sunnyside raid blooded the Australians and Canadians. It also helped sting Cronje into action at last. Responding to Koos de la Rey and Christian de Wet's appeals, he agreed to a limited foray to blow up the railway line behind Methuen and seize a supply train. These two shrewd and daring men riding out with a compact mobile force constituted a powerful combination. Yet the fact is that their guns got lost in the night, they arrived too late for the train, and the men carrying the dynamite precipitously fled. The episode serves to chasten the too-ready critic of British blunders. It ended in mutual recriminations and confirmed the older leaders' belief in the virtue of inertia.

Shortly afterwards De Wet was appointed second in command to Cronje over all forces around Magersfontein, and Koos de la Rey set out for Colesburg to assist the defence against the imminent renewal of French's assault.

Before he reached the town, Piet de Wet had already resolved on a counter-offensive. He took advantage of improved morale brought about by the arrival of Zarps from Natal to make a dawn attack with 700 men on the vital hill to the north-west which the Suffolks had seized. But the Suffolks held firm, and put him to flight with fair loss. French, now fully reinforced, resolved that the moment had come to take the town.

A short distance from the Suffolks a kopje called Grass Hill stood only a mile to the north of Colesburg and completely dominated it. Colonel Watson of the Suffolks begged to be entrusted with a night attack on this key position and though French had first intended a dawn attack he believed with Watson that the hill was scarcely guarded, if at all, and acquiesced. He is a great general who can avoid the snare of success, for the attack was conducted with more optimism than forethought. The men who set out with Watson at midnight, wearing soft shoes and strictly enjoined only to deal out silent death with the bayonet, had climbed 700 yards up the gradual rocky slope when a blast of fire met them out of the darkness. Confusion and panic sent half the men running away, and the rest failed in repeated charges to close with the Boers. By dawn Watson and most of his officers lay dead or wounded. Though the British artillery opened up the remnant of the attacking force had to surrender, making French's total loss in the engagement

161 men. The burial party he sent on to the hill were received with help and sympathy. One old Boer asked if he might speak. Uncovering his grey head he testified in a farmer's simple words to the tragedy of war that sacrificed human life, and he prayed for the time when all men could live in peace. Then with his fellow burghers he sang a hymn.

For French the rebuff was more serious than thwarting his plan to capture the town: it meant the sudden loss of the moral superiority his unbroken run of success had gained. Schoeman's force now totalled over 6,000 and upon De la Rey's arrival at this juncture he immediately made his presence felt by taking up position on the east of the town, where he repelled French's attempt to switch his attack to this side and cut the railway line. French's advance was brought to a final halt.

But neither could the Boers advance. Intended to start a general movement, an attack was launched from De la Rey's sector against a forward hill: overcoming the Yorkshires who held the crest, the Boers were on the verge of success which would have imperilled French's whole forty-mile front when Captain W. N. Maddocks at the head of a small party of New Zealanders repeatedly charged, sometimes single-handed, until the attackers in ignorance of the slender strength left against them abandoned what was thereafter called New Zealand Hill.

Likewise on the other wing of the Central Front the Boers tried in vain to move down from Stormberg against Gatacre, who repulsed them at Cyphergat. Along this whole front, then, a state of deadlock like that on the Western Front was being reached by the time of Roberts's arrival.

The nibbling nature of operations in the Cape Midlands gives them far less drama than exploits on the other fronts, but they were crucial. The deadlock reached here by mid-January was very much to the British advantage. The Boers depended on the progress of their invasion to stir the Cape to rebellion, and now the favourable atmosphere created by Black Week was fading. Of the 40,000 rebels they hoped for only 7,000 had come forward. The measure of Schoeman's timidity and French's enterprise was that the British had staved off the acute danger both of a thrust on De Aar to cut off Methuen and of invasion in depth. Apart from his direct success, he had distracted attention from the yawning gap between himself and Gatacre, given his men invaluable

experience and confidence, resuscitated British morale, and drawn off
Boers from the other fronts to help in the defence of Colesburg.

This drawing-off of men had an important repercussion in Natal.
Before more commandos were sent for from the siege lines around
Ladysmith the younger Boers repeatedly urged the capture of the town
so that men could be released for the inevitable day of reckoning with
Buller. Kruger and Steyn supported them. At a council of war in
Joubert's headquarters on 2 January the old man had to agree at last to
a full scale attempt to storm the town.

It was the moment on which England had been awaiting with
profound apprehension, even while people tried to console themselves
with thinking the Boers would not risk storming tactics.

*   *   *   *

A ridge or plateau of high ground called the Platrand dominated
Ladysmith from the south-east. The crux of the Boer plan was to
capture it in order to have the town at their mercy.

The Platrand was 300 feet high, much of it a quarter of a mile broad
on top, and it extended four miles west and east. It was really a succession of three hills roughly in a straight line and flat-topped. Viewed
from the Boers as they looked at it from the south, the left-hand and
smallest hill was called Wagon Point, but is here referred to as the
Point. It was separated by a gully from the centre called Wagon Hill,
which a slight dip joined to the right-hand hill called Caesar's Camp.
The slopes of the whole Platrand were strewn with bush and rocks.

The Boers planned a simultaneous attack on all three hills with 2,000
men in concert with an artillery barrage from the nearby hills. At the
same time strong demonstrations would be made on the other sectors
round the town by the rest (3,000) of the besiegers, except for a mobile
force that would work round behind the Platrand from the left to cut
off retreat or reinforcements. Botha would bring a force up from the
Tugela to act as a reserve.

It was a situation shaped for the Homeric propensities of Ian Hamilton who held the Platrand with a thousand men. These were not
enough to guard four miles, but he had carefully fortified it under
cover of night to avoid the Boer artillery. This seeming disadvantage
actually meant that the Boers were ignorant of his dispositions on the
crests of the three hills—a row of small forts along the back of Wagon

Hill and Caesar's Camp, with a line of pickets in front of the forts and on the Point.

The timing of the assault was left to Joubert so that no spy could carry word of it to the British. At sunset on 5 January 1900, he called his commandants together, and told them to attack at dawn. While townsfolk and troops slept unaware of what was intended for them, the Boers gathered in position. Young Reitz was among those detailed for the 'demonstration' against the British perimeter, his party's objective being a fort on the other side of the town from the Platrand, and his account illustrates the kind of action fought generally around much of the town while the main struggle developed on the Platrand.

The whistles, he says, blew at 3 a.m. for his commando to assemble, but about half the men were recently recruited 'poor whites' who for the most part stood about wretchedly, refusing to follow. The remaining couple of hundred men advanced towards the fort. They were discovered half-way and stopped by heavy fire as dawn broke. Exhorted by one of Paul Kruger's bodyguard, a tall splendid figure in police uniform, they pressed on. Some reached the shelter of rocks only twenty-five yards from the fort. Then the policeman led about a dozen men in a frantic charge:

> A single volley flamed along the loopholes and before we had time to think the attack had withered away. We saw the men go down in a heap, leaving only . . . [the policeman] erect. . . . Undeterred, he ran up to the fort and tried to scale the wall. Bayonets were thrust at him which he parried with his rifle until a revolver was fired point-blank into him. He sank below the wall where he sat rocking to and fro his head resting on his hand as if in great pain, and then another bullet found him.

The remainder of Reitz's party kept up pressure from behind cover. The sun blazed down and the advancing hours brought racking thirst and the cries of the wounded. Everything hung on the main attack. The whole perimeter of the defences was aflame but only the Platrand mattered.

There, the storming parties had steadily climbed the slopes during the night. As the moment for action drew near many lost heart and fell back but the rest went on steadily. And now chance intervened with the same caprice that sent Cronje wandering about the heights of Magersfontein during Wauchope's advance. Before Buller's repulse from Colenso, White had moved two or three naval guns from the Point to another position to cover Buller's expected advance. That advance not having materialized, White decided to return the guns to the Point and chose of all nights the 5/6. Thus a work party was about and pickets alert on the Point and the adjoining end of Wagon Hill. At 2 a.m. they heard the Boers climbing up the gully between. These were Free Staters commanded by Fighting-General C. J. de Villiers. Three-quarters of an hour later they were dimly discernible to a small party of Imperial Light Horse posted on the Point and the Gordons at the end of Wagon Hill, who all opened fire.

A desperate struggle took place in semi-darkness. The confusion was increased by the Gordons firing on the I.L.H., mistaking their slouch-hats for those of the Boers. Gradually the Boers forced their way on to Wagon Hill, some reaching so close to the walls of the nearest fort that the rifles of attacker and attacked almost crossed. But too few in number to sustain their position, they drew back before point-blank fire, only to cling tenaciously to a line of rocks along the edge of the plateau.

Ian Hamilton's quarters were near the other end of the Platrand on Caesar's Camp. He woke to the sound of firing which was now general on both sides and along the foot of the whole ridge. Finding Caesar's Camp in no immediate danger he ran on to Wagon Hill while bullets whistled round him in the darkness and struck sparks from the boulders. De Villiers's foothold called for immediate action. He telephoned White to send reinforcements.

Unknown to him, even as he left Caesar's Camp about fifty Boers storming from their right reached the edge of its crest. The manifest strength of the forts surprised them and they concentrated on trying to roll up the picket line strung out in front, which would also help their comrades who were now stopped on the front slopes of the ridge by the picket line's intense fire. The nearest pickets were Manchesters. They were pressed back by the sudden flank attack until reinforcements helped them stop the Boer advance and as day broke a shrapnel bombardment followed by a bayonet charge finally broke it. But as the Boers rose they fired into the charging men and ran back only as far as the rocks on the edge of the plateau. Joubert and his wife were watching intently from Bulwana mountain. It was she who pointed out the effectiveness of the British artillery, prompting the Boer guns to be turned on it but skilful placing gave them little chance. However, the Boers could not be dislodged from the position they had now taken up.

The dawn situation, then, was that a party of Boers clung to the right-hand extremity of the plateau on Caesar's Camp, and another did likewise near the left-hand extremity on Wagon Hill. This latter party under De Villiers was now about 250 strong, strung out not only on the edge of Wagon Hill but down the gully and up the slope of the Point where scattered groups of bluejackets, sappers, I.L.H., and Highlanders tried desperately to keep them from advancing higher. The Point's crest itself was deserted except for one of the wagons which had brought the naval guns, and its span of sixteen oxen who munched the grass while bullets and shells streamed around them.

On Wagon Hill a mere hundred yards of flat grass separated the Boers at the plateau edge from a parallel row of rocks close to the nearest fort. Behind these rocks Hamilton drummed up all available men to dislodge De Villiers. He threw charge after charge against the Boer line until so great was the loss of officers as they tried to lead their men against point-blank fire that he had to give up. Boer and Briton lay pinned down behind their respective lines of rocks, exactly as their comrades were at the other end on Caesar's Camp, and the hours crawled on in gruelling heat.

All this time the greater part of the assault force was either immobilized on the front slopes of the Platrand or withdrawn to a safe distance on the plain below, from which they kept up a long-range fire more dangerous to their own men on the heights than the British. Towards noon the firing everywhere slackened off.

De Villiers now saw that possession of the Point would give him command of at least the flank of Wagon Hill. At his orders two field-cornets went down, collected a small band of men, and began to climb the Point from their extreme left. The moment was ripe, for the exhausted defenders were taking advantage of the lull to sleep or look for food. As the Boers approached the top the sudden sight of their bearded faces and slouch-hats struck panic through the British: a rattle of rifle-fire, a cry of, 'Here they come!' and they streamed down the back of the hill.

The luck which goes with successful generalship did not desert Hamilton. At this very moment he himself happened to be behind the Point conferring with his senior officers. Together they stemmed the rush, faced the men about, and led a charge back up the hill. It was a race for the summit. Hamilton and his leading men reached it at the same time as about a dozen Boers, but fire from the nearest fort on Wagon Hill kept back all except three Boers who raced forward for possession of the pits prepared for the naval guns. Two of the Boers made for the higher emplacement but Hamilton reached it first and leaning his arm on the sandbag parapet he fired as the Boers leapt in; simultaneously one of his men fired, and the two Boers fell dead against the wall of the pit. At the same moment a couple of men had reached the lower gun-pit and beating the third Boer to the draw killed him also. The rest of the Boers fled. A few demented moments had restored the hill to the British.

In Ladysmith White waited anxiously as the hours brought no news of the Boers being driven off the Platrand. The dramatic struggle for the Point increased his disquiet. Hamilton wished to wait until night-fall before dislodging the enemy at bayonet point, but now White overruled him, directing both ends of the ridge to be cleared at all costs. He ordered a reinforcement of Devons forward; dismounted Lancers and Hussars were brought round from another part of the Platrand. Flashing heliograms to Buller he stressed that all his reserves were thrown in and the need for a diversion. Black storm-clouds obliterated the sun, so that Buller and London received only the ominous opening words, 'Attack renewed. Very hard pressed.' Tele-grams reaching the newspapers during most of the day filled England with an uncertainty about Ladysmith's fate which this brief message turned to deep gloom.

By Buller's army at Chieveley the sounds of battle had been heard since dawn, but it was afternoon before any attempt was made to demonstrate against the Boers' Tugela line to prevent reinforcements joining the Ladysmith attack. However, this very dilatoriness seems to have kept Botha uncertain of Buller's intentions, so that he delayed taking the promised reserve to the Platrand.

Meanwhile the black clouds which had stopped White's message broke upon the scene with more violence than Reitz says he had ever experienced: the storm 'leapt at us with a roar, and there fell a deluge which in an instant blotted all from view.' He and his comrades on the further side of the perimeter took the opportunity to end their nine hours' vigil in the heat and bolt back, leaving their dead and wounded.

On the Platrand the Boers feared the British might charge through the storm and they added their own violence to the elements, their fire reaching a crescendo on the plateau and from the plain beneath. In the mist the British on the Point again panicked and again were rallied. But at the further edge of Caesar's Camp the reinforced Manchesters renewed their counter-attack and at last made headway: as the rain lifted towards 5.30 they broke the Boers' resistance, sending them head-long down the slopes, many to drown in a flooded rivulet below. It was at this stage that Botha reached the scene, too late.

The Devons sent to reinforce Hamilton had meanwhile arrived at the rear of Wagon Hill. Hamilton went down to them. Charge after charge, he said, had failed against De Villiers. Could they succeed? 'We will try,' said their colonel. He formed up his men with bayonets fixed. As their bugles blew the advance they cheered and climbed the hill and rushed out into the open. The Boers rose to empty their magazine into the advancing line. The Devons fell in droves. Still they charged on, madly cheering and joined now by their comrades who had been pinned down behind cover all about. The Boers fired to the last second. When they broke it was only to take up a new position a little further back. For another half-hour the struggle raged. The Devons suffered severely, one of their young subalterns winning the V.C. for fighting on in spite of six wounds, and then darkness brought release to attacker and attacked. Quietly the Boers made away. C. J. de Villiers, whose courage and resource had sustained them since before dawn, was the last to leave.

So ended the sixteen hours' fight for the Platrand (sometimes referred to by the name of only part of it, Caesar's Camp). It created a legend of the last British soldier being flung into the breach when Ladysmith was on the point of extinction. If this rather magnified the event, drama was certainly not lacking. Yet the losses were com-paratively light: 400 on the British side, about half as many on the Boer. Of the sixteen oxen on the Point, eight were unscathed—such were the chances of surviving unaimed fire.

The result of the battle was that White advised Buller he could no longer co-operate in any renewed attempt at relief. Enteric and dysentry were now rampant in the town where 1,300 hospital cases testified to the physical debility to which people in hot, overcrowded and under-nourished conditions were being reduced, and the battle attenuated still further his available able-bodied strength.

For the Boers it confirmed Joubert once more in the wisdom of caution. The night was a wretched one for his men, whose tents and belongings had been washed away to upwards of a mile. They could not light a fire or dry their clothes, but had only their failure to brood on and the memory of their dead and wounded. These they fetched next day under a flag of truce.

The date was now 7 January. In England news of the Boer repulse was known that morning. 'But, at last, the nervousness had bitten too deeply to be lessened, even by such news, and such heroism. From now onwards the references to Ladysmith always betrayed a gloomy under-current of belief that the town must fall, and that we had better make up our minds to the fact.'[2]

Three days later Roberts arrived at Cape Town. The situation await-ing him was a complete deadlock. A section of the northern Transvaal border where Plumer fenced with a small force of Boers; Mafeking, Kimberley and Magersfontein on the Western Front; Colesburg and Stormberg on the Central; and Ladysmith and the Tugela in Natal, were as scattered islands upon which sixteen groups of Boers and Britons lay in a clinch—hot, sticky and apparently unbreakable.

The Boers had let go the opportunities presented by Black Week. They relied on time to give them victory by delivering up the besieged towns and realizing one of several possibilities: the collapse of British will, either through more losses or a change of government at West-minster, was one; intervention by foreign Powers was another. So they had let go the initiative which it was Roberts's task to seize. Victory swift and unambiguous was England's need before the world. But Buller too had that purpose when he arrived upon the same ship, and with massive reinforcements also, scarcely more than two months before.

CHAPTER X

Spion Kop: 24 January 1900

KITCHENER had been brought by warship to join the *Dunnottar Castle* at Gibraltar. He completed the small staff Roberts had got together hurriedly in London. It included as his military secretary Neville Chamberlain—no relation of Joseph—who had been with him in India and was said to be the inventor of snooker. Of greater importance, the party included Colonel G. F. R. Henderson as Roberts's Chief Intelligence Officer: he was the biographer of 'Stonewall' Jackson and author of *The Science of War* in which he had drawn on the military lessons of the American Civil War. Roberts had admired his writings and his own thinking was greatly influenced by him.

During the weeks of the voyage, perhaps for the first time in British military history something approaching a scientific appraisement of strategy and tactics was made by a group of experts able to put their decisions into practice. With this embryonic General Staff to help him, Roberts felt his way towards a clear-cut plan of campaign.

Buller too had arrived with a plan, the War Office's proposed counter-invasion from the Cape Midlands. It had never been put into operation. And the day Roberts arrived at Cape Town a telegram was handed to him whose outcome might upset all calculations. He had cabled Buller from Southampton, again from Gibraltar, and a third time from Madeira, asking him to stay on the defensive. The telegram waiting from him at Cape Town stated that Buller was nevertheless setting off on a renewed campaign to relieve Ladysmith.

*   *   *   *

At Chieveley and other bases down the line Buller had increased his strength to 30,000 men. These included the 5th Division under General

Sir Charles Warren who had been the subject of his angry protest to the War Office. Torrential rains had held up his renewed effort to pierce the Tugela line, which he now intended to do by outflanking Botha at Colenso, and it was coincidental that he should set out from Chieveley on the very day that Roberts arrived at Cape Town.

He left a garrison behind him and bases along the railway beyond Chieveley while 23,000 men marched with him. With upwards of sixty guns and a vast convoy of wagons they made slowly for a village twenty miles to the north-west. Rain had the veld awash. The force, said a newspaper correspondent,[30] found itself 'wading, sliding, sucking, pumping, gurgling through the mud'. One wagon could not be unstuck by eighty oxen; mules, knotted in their harness, half drowned; and by nightfall men, animals and vehicles were strung out knee- or axle-deep in slush from end to end of the road. Not bothering about the time given to the Boers to prepare, Buller proceeded unhurriedly to establish himself at the village with a fortnight's provisions. 'It is poor economy to let a soldier live well for three days at the price of killing him on the fourth,' wrote Churchill who was soon back on the scene after his escape, receiving an unpaid commission from Buller and combining reporting with serving in the S.A.L.H.

Meanwhile the mounted brigade under Dundonald went on ahead and seized some unoccupied heights called Spearman's on the nearside of the Tugela. Presently Buller himself rode on to Spearman's to survey the scene. Along the horizon far to the left of him and curving round to the north loomed the great pinnacles, serrated ridges and the monstrous fangs of the Drakensberg. From these mountains sprang the stream that ranging through the foothills became the Upper Tugela where Buller now contemplated it below him, and the Lower Tugela by the time it reached Colenso of fateful memory, twenty miles to his right.

Immediately beneath him it was easily fordable. Set back from the other side a range of hills extended away to the right of the ford and another, dominated by a demi-mountain called Spion Kop, to the left; but between them, immediately beyond the ford, were merely low ridges. A flat and open plain behind the ridges reached almost into Ladysmith only twenty miles away—so close, he could see its heliograph flashing in the sun.

He replied with reassuring messages, for here was his obvious route. The Boers were still mustered mainly at Colenso and numbered only

2,000. It was a heaven-sent chance. But the baggage, the endless impedimenta no officer could fight a war without, had all to be brought
to the village Buller intended to be his forward base. Completing the
complicated transport arrangements took four days, by which time the
Boers had doubled their strength across the ford. Buller decided to attack
elsewhere.

Upstream, below the further end of Spion Kop, was another ford
called Trichardt's Drift. Adjoining Spion Kop on the left rose a high
hill called Tabanyama, over the right shoulder of which a road led
from Trichardt's Drift, round the back of Spion Kop, and across the
plain to Ladysmith. This road Buller now resolved to take with the

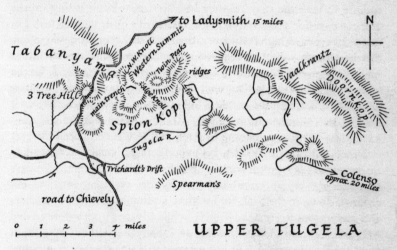

greater part of his army, which he called an expeditionary force, while
the rest remained around Spearman's as a containing force under
General the Hon. N. G. Lyttelton (since leaving Eton this third son of
a baron had nearly thirty-five years in the Army behind him, which
he bore lightly, his features marked by a relaxed detached expression
adorned with greying curly hair).

But instead of Buller himself leading his 'expeditionary force' he
put Warren in charge of it. Warren had the reputation of being a strong
man, difficult to get on with. He was in his sixtieth year, having begun
his military career in the Royal Engineers and made his name in South
African campaigns culminating in his clearance of Bechuanaland. Later

he had command of the Straits Settlements where the civil authorities found that 'the tinge of acerbity in the General's temper was somewhat conspicuously revealed.'

Buller's appointment of him to lead the bulk of his army for him was both comic and extraordinary. Out of pique at the War Office's efforts to push Warren forward, or because his nerve was still shaken, or whatever the motive, he virtually abdicated his authority in favour of a man with only a divisional staff to command a large force and convoy across a difficult river into rugged, hazily reconnoitred country.

On the 16th Warren duly set out for Trichardt's Drift. Lyttelton made a feint across the ford from Spearman's which brought the Boers rushing to man the trenches they had been busy constructing on the other side, and left Warren to reach Trichardt's Drift undisturbed. His troops marched in high confidence, their officers having laid two to one that Ladysmith would be relieved within a week, and this optimism spilt over into dispatches that brightened the gloom in England. Of the scene by night Winston Churchill wrote, 'It was not possible to stand unmoved and watch the ceaseless living stream . . . and before them a guiding star, the red gleam of war.' There were in fact probably not more than 500 Boers opposite Warren but he was convinced the area swarmed with them. Besides, his experience of 'savage' warfare had made him as baggage-conscious as Buller, so that he required two days to build one bridge on trestles and another on pontoons, and cut channels down to the bank for his guns, ammunition carts, ambulances and 500 wagons to cross the Tugela, while advance troops were ferried over and occupied the lower slopes of Tabanyama without opposition from the few Boers about. It was pleasant to watch the twittering tom-tits, the large grey secretary birds, the fluttering of colourful butterflies; but the men wondered why the enemy was being given so much time to prepare.

The Boers had indeed woken to the danger threatening them both from Warren's large-scale crossing of the Tugela and Lyttelton's force nearby at Spearman's. Louis Botha was about to quit the Colenso sector on leave but Kruger telegraphed asking him to take command on the Upper Tugela over the heads of the O.F.S. General A. P. Cronje (not to be confused with Piet Cronje commanding on the Western Front) and the Transvaal Vice-President Schalk Burger. Botha at once rode over and began strengthening the defences.

That same day Dundonald with his mounted troops took a second road from Trichardt's Drift, this one winding round the left of Tabanyama. He found no sign of the enemy and sent to Warren for reinforcements so that he could scale the inviting flank immediately. Warren was furious at his enterprise: he held the orthodox view that mounted troops should be used solely to screen the infantry or to reconnoitre. Giving Dundonald the benefit of his 'tinge of acerbity' he deprived him of some of his brigade and cut him from his councils.

He decided he would make a frontal attack on Tabanyama by moonlight. Then he changed his mind.

Instead, he would feel his way round to the left, along the road around the further end of Tabanyama where Dundonald had reconnoitred. At 2 a.m. on the 19th he ordered his 'expedition' to cross a small tributary of the Tugela which lay across the route of the proposed movement. But when he set off in advance along the road he decided it was too open to attack by Boer long-range guns, and upon hearing from Dundonald that the delay was being used by the Boers at Ladysmith to send out reinforcements which would dominate the road from the hitherto deserted side of Tabanyama, he again changed his mind. The greatest confusion prevailed at the rivulet as the leading wagons turned back into the rest of the convoy.

During these three days of nothing accomplished he was frequently visited by Buller with advice, criticism and comment, but no orders. Buller was restive at the lack of progress but contented himself to being, in the words of *The Times History*, 'umpire at manœuvres'.

At last, on 20 January, Warren geared himself to make a frontal assault on Tabanyama. Early that morning his men began the ascent under cover of an artillery bombardment which shepherded them up in stages. With surprising ease the leaders made up the re-entrants formed by projecting spurs of the hill, and reached the top—only then to discover why they had so far encountered little opposition. What they had thought the top was only the edge of an upward sloping plateau bounded half a mile in front of them by a ridge, along which Botha had posted his men behind stone walls or in breast-high trenches, with enfilading works thrown forward.

They were well protected, even against the sustained bombardment of six batteries which were hauled some distance up the hillside. For four hours the British tried in vain to advance, losing 300 men in the process while scarcely ruffling the Boers. Warren called off the attack until nightfall could give it cover. But at nightfall the men strung out under the edge of the summit were not ordered to attack.

Warren waited until morning, then ordered his troops on the left of the Tabanyama assault line to storm the summit from this flank. They were led by General Sir Francis Clery, sixty-two year-old Irishman, tall and big-boned with a tremendous array of whiskers which crossed the lower half of his cheeks from nose to ears while his chin was clean-shaven. He was the author of a standard work on tactics which had been translated into four languages, and nothing could have presented a greater tactical opportunity than this attack on the Boer flank. For here they were most vulnerable. Lyttelton was making frequent demonstrations from the vicinity of Spearman's, and away down the river at Colenso the garrison from Chieveley also made forays: the Boers' available manpower was less than a third of the British so that they were fully extended along the various points already threatened and at others where they might become so. The extreme end of the line on Tabanyama was hence very weak, and it began to give way before Clery's attack. But on the verge of success he inexplicably called it off with the futile loss of another 170 men.

On the ground below, Buller continued to pester Warren with advice and criticism. Escaping from him Warren went forward to inspect the position and decided to renew the frontal assault on Tabanyama. First however he would flatten the Boer defences with two or three days' bombardment. He sent to Buller's headquarters at Spearman's for powerful howitzers, and Buller in part complied. So the day passed with long-range gun- and rifle-fire, during which the Boers strengthened the weak extremity of their line on Tabanyama.

It was now come to the morning of the 22nd. In nearly a fortnight a British army of over 20,000 had done nothing except drag itself through mud, climb the slope of a hill and come to a full stop, while nearly 500 men had been sacrificed to their superiors' ineptitude. Buller suddenly gave vent to his impatience. If something were not done quickly, he blustered, he would withdraw the whole force across the Tugela! He would have none of Warren's sustained bombardment or frontal assault. Warren must attack again on the left of Tabanyama, this time all-out. But Warren had an irrational fear about that side, or perhaps was sensitive about not seizing it when Dundonald could have

done so without firing a shot. In desperation he suggested, suddenly—
Spion Kop, the looming eminence on the right of Tabanyama. It was
a compromise proposal and Buller accepted it, though later, on
exploring the situation, he was so confirmed in his earlier opinion about
mounting an all-out attack from the left that he actually composed a
letter to Warren setting out a plan of action, but he did not press it.
In this fashion was the die cast for an attack in which neither Buller
nor Warren had their hearts.

And yet the Boer situation was not hopeful. They were so thinly
spread out that only a picket guarded Spion Kop, standing as it did
between Tabanyama to the left and the hills opposite Spearman's to the
right. Their morale, in spite of a flying visit by President Steyn, was low
all along the line. Botha had from the outset urged the men who first
occupied this part of the Upper Tugela to forestall the British seizure
of Spearman's; and since they had not, and the British had crossed the
river, they grumbled now at the incompetence of their leaders. The
demonstrations at Colenso and Spearman's, together with Warren's
manœuvres and attacks on Tabanyama, harassed them with uncertainty
about Buller's intentions. Besides, they were under constant bombardment on a scale they had never experienced; and the shelling increased
as unknown to them the moment for the assault on Spion Kop drew
near.

The spirit on the Boer side is recalled by Reitz, who was among the
reinforcements hastily rushed out from Ladysmith; his figures are an
overestimate but testify to the impression made on him:

> Ever since sunrise there had come the unbroken boom of guns
> and the rattle of small arms. . . . I reached a point where I could see
> the Boer front strung out along the top of the next rise. Black
> mushrooms of earth and smoke hung along the course of the
> positions from the heavy shells flung across the Tugela, and puffs
> of shrapnel flecked the air above. . . . I reached the line in safety. . . .
> Far below on the plain the Tugela wound shining in the sun, and
> the bank beyond was alive with English foot and horse. From the
> wooded hills further back came the flashes of the British guns. . . .
> There were probably 10,000 or 12,000 burghers in all on these
> hills, with the bastion of Spion Kop standing like a pivot in the
> centre. For the most part the men made slight reply to the fire in

order to husband their ammunition, and our artillery kept silent
for the same reason, although it was estimated that there were over
200 guns firing at us, and I have heard that this was the heaviest
concentration of gun-fire that had been seen in any war up to the
present. The casualties were considerable, and I saw some men fear-
fully mutilated. . . . It was a day of strain. Not only was there the
horror of seeing men killed and maimed, but there was the long-
drawn tension and fear of the approaching shells.

On the British side, the troops still lying below the summit of
Tabanyama were baked by the sun, sniped at by the Boers, and perplexed by not knowing what they were there for. Meanwhile Warren
completed his arrangements for the assault on Spion Kop. The summit
was to be seized on the night of 23/24 January by a mixed force of
1,900 men commanded by a general of fifty-five and in bad health, Sir
Edward Woodgate. Arrangements were made for support companies
to follow and dig trenches on the slopes in case of retreat. Orders were
issued for a dressing-station to be set up on the summit and a hospital
at the foot. Water supplies, reserves of food, plans for the engineers to
build a road and gun-slides up the hill—all was prepared.

All was prepared; though none expected a battle as extraordinary as
history has to offer.

★　　★　　★　　★

With an unerring instinct the British were tackling the most formidable hill in the whole line of the Tugela heights. There was something preordained about the attempt: they had toyed with the idea of
attacking to the right of it (opposite Spearman's) and made half-cock
attacks on the left of it (Tabanyama), while all the time it stood aloof
as if reserved for the hour when it alone must provide the climactic
battle to these past three months' struggle across the whole expanse of
country its summit surveyed—from the hills of Ladysmith, across
Elandslaagte to Dundee in the north, to those of Colenso in the east and
Estcourt in the south. Its name meant 'scout peak', after the first Boer
Trekkers who looked down from it upon the verdant land of Natal.

It rose nearly 1,500 feet above the Tugela and was four miles long.
Its shape and certain contiguous features are important to remember.
The right or eastern end near Spearman's consisted of two eminences

186

called the Twin Peaks. From them a long narrow ridge led westwards
to a small rise whose spiky aloes gave it the name of Aloe Knoll. A
slight saddle-shaped dip led on to the main summit on the west. This
fateful western summit which overlooked Trichardt's Drift and
Warren's army was hump-shaped but its exact delineation was unknown to the British, although they could easily have found out by
using their balloon, which could rise to 2,000 feet.

From the summit the sides of the mountain fell away precipitously
except for a spur on the nearer or south-western corner that promised
a reasonable way up for the assault party. There was a second spur from
the further corner on the north-west, from which rose another knoll,
called in this narrative the N.W. Knoll. Close to it, on the right-hand
slopes of Tabanyama before these joined the slopes of Spion Kop,
perched a mound called Three Tree Hill. The humped western summit,
Aloe Knoll to right of it, N.W. Knoll to left rear, and Three Tree Hill
to left of it—these, and the Twin Peaks on the far right, were to be the
inanimate participants in tragedy. In order of appearance the first of
the dramatis personae were Woodgate's assault party made up mostly
from Lancashire regiments with some Royal Engineers and unmounted
M.I. under Colonel A. W. Thorneycroft, a vigorous and bulky man of
forty-one who had not been on campaign since his early youth despite
his efforts to get posted to trouble-spots during the years between. His
chance was now come, and he acted as guide.

They set off from the Tabanyama slopes at 11 p.m. The night was
dark. There was a slight drizzle. The password was Waterloo.

A thick mist blanketed the summit which first light would otherwise
have revealed. After a four-hour haul, during which Woodgate had
to be helped up, an easing of the gradient warned them to fix bayonets.
As a Boer sentry challenged and fired wildly at their cry of 'Waterloo!'
they charged and put the picket to flight. Then, not having brought a
field telegraph and unable to send signals through the mist they gave
three cheers to announce their capture of the mountain to Warren
waiting anxiously below. His artillery at once began dropping shells
over the rear of the mountain and on to the dip between it and Tabanyama to discourage counter-attack.

Woodgate's task was now to make the summit of Spion Kop secure.
That he occupied the whole of the summit he was certain because the
ground sloped away on all sides from the area his men had reached.

Everyone started digging defence works, mainly a 200-yard trench in the shape of a flattened V pointing north. They found the ground too rocky for them to gouge out more than a broad shallow ditch, especially as the engineers had been allowed to discard some of their implements during the wearisome ascent. And by accident they had not brought sandbags, so they had to make do with a bulwark of stones and rubbish eighteen inches high along the front of their shallow trench.

The Boer picket sent flying through the mist spread consternation among the laagers behind the mountain. 'If the hill went,' records Reitz of his reaction at the time, 'the entire Tugela line would go with it, and we could hardly bring ourselves to believe the news.' Many Boers at once began trekking away but the leaders acted promptly. Assisted by Schalk Burger, Louis Botha rallied his men and urged them to climb Spion Kop in spite of the lobbed shells, while signallers were sent up to direct his artillery which he ordered to fresh positions. Reported to by telegraph, Kruger at Pretoria and Joubert at Ladysmith both appealed for the summit to be recaptured at all costs.

At seven o'clock the mist over the summit lifted, very slightly, but enough for Woodgate to make out that he was not quite in possession of the whole summit, because though the ground in front of him sloped down it did so only very slightly before the true end of the summit, which was marked by a fringe of rocks about a hundred yards away. He sent forward a detachment to entrench themselves there in order to dominate the further side of the mountain up which the Boers were already creeping through the mist.

About this time Reitz reached the foot of the mountain below his advancing comrades.

Here stood hundreds of saddled horses in long rows, and we looked up at an arresting sight. . . . Eight or nine hundred riflemen were climbing up the steep side of the hill in face of a close-range fire from the English troops. Many of our men dropped, but already the foremost were within a few yards of the rocky edge which marked the crest, and the soldiers were rising from behind their cover to meet the final rush. For a moment or two there was confused hand to hand fighting, then the combatants surged over the rim on to the plateau beyond where we could no longer see them.

The advanced British detachment fell back only a short distance behind more rocks some way in front of the main trench. Almost at once the mist descended again and no one could see anything.

Woodgate took the opportunity to send a messenger to Warren and Buller; except for asking that Lyttelton support him from Spearman's he reported that his position was quite satisfactory. It was not until after eight o'clock that this illusion was shattered. As the mist lifted, there burst upon the British a storm of fire from no less than three directions at once. The truth about their position was suddenly and appallingly clear. They occupied only a fraction of the western summit, their main trench being in a slight rise across the middle of it, so that their field of fire was limited to the expanse of at most 200 yards between trench and summit edge all around them. Permitted to creep up the slopes unopposed the Boers were by this time not only on the edge beyond but had got on to Three Tree Hill, the N.W. Knoll and Aloe Knoll, from which they now sprayed the totally unexpecting British. In fact, from Aloe Knoll they enfiladed the right of the main trench so directly that afterwards seventy of the killed were found with bullets through the right side of their heads. From this knoll, too, the Boers could accurately direct their artillery which began to play on the crowded western summit with deadly accuracy, while the British signals proved ineffectual in directing their ten times stronger artillery on either the Boer guns or reinforcements being rushed up.

Woodgate went bravely among his men encouraging them and sending forward reinforcements to the detachment among the rocks in front. But nothing could undo his position in a death trap, the middle of a plateau 700 yards wide and 350 yards broad, overlooked by several nearby points which enabled the Boers to sweep him with fire from round an arc of 120°. With every minute the situation grew more desperate. At 8.45 he signalled a message—destined to reach Warren only an hour later—reporting the terrible cross-fire and the need for water and help.

The Boers were pressing closer but were not coming unscathed through the ordeal. Although a few of the British ran forward to surrender, the rest resolutely answered their fire. Reitz says:

> We were sustaining heavy casualties and the men grew restive under the galling point-blank fire, a thing not to be wondered at

for the moral effect of Lee-Metford volleys at 20 yards must be experienced to be appreciated. . . .

Some of the English troops lay so near that one could have tossed a biscuit among them, and whilst the losses they were causing us were only too evident, we on our side did not know we were inflicting even greater damage upon them. Our own casualties lay hideously among us, but theirs were screened from view behind the breast-work.

Woodgate had not the consolation of knowing the toll his men were exacting, for a few minutes after sending his message to Warren for help he was mortally wounded in the eye and dragged away sobbing, 'Let me alone. Let me alone.'

Command passed to the senior surviving officer, Colonel Crofton. His imperative need was reinforcements. Finding the signals officer he instructed him to send an urgent call. The heliograph had disappeared in the confusion and the officer gave the message to the flag-signaller, not obeying regulations by writing it since he had no paper and every second counted. The flag-signaller hence conveyed an even stronger message than Crofton had intended: 'Colonel Crofton to GOC Force. Reinforce at once or all lost. General dead.'

Meanwhile Warren remained ignorant of the shambles on the summit. The first indication that the assurance in Woodgate's earlier message might no longer hold good came only with final dispersal of the mist which hung round the mountain until nine. The realization then smote him that heavy firing was in progress. He ordered up reinforcements of Middlesex and Imperial Light Infantry, a newly raised corps unblooded in battle. A little later, just before ten, Crofton's alarming message reached him. 'Hold on to the last,' he answered: 'No surrender!'

But having started reinforcements on the long climb up the mountains he made no move immediately to relieve pressure by launching a general attack on Tabanyama, which in fact was being stripped of defenders as Botha rushed them over to Spion Kop. So 10,000 soldiers idled while their comrades were being slaughtered on the adjoining summit. Nor was Warren prompted to change this state of affairs by a message from Buller warning against a possible attack against the *British* on Tabanyama! He contented himself with distributing a thousand sandbags among the reinforcements setting off for Spion Kop.

In their wake followed their brigadier. General John Talbot Coke came from one of the oldest Derbyshire families with a beautiful country seat, Debdale Hill, and was Lord of the Manor of Trusley, and against this not unhelpful social background had passed nearly fifty years in the Army, rarely disturbed by the sight of bloodshed. His slender figure and somewhat soft face were given a military air by a fine waxed moustache, but at this moment he did not exactly look, as newspapers were fond of describing soldiers, a true son of Mars, for he was still lame after a broken leg and climbed slowly.

On the far right, Lyttelton had earlier begun a demonstration against the Boers opposite Spearman's until Buller, fearing a flare-up on this flank, stopped him. But when Woodgate's message came with its request for support he decided to storm the Twin Peaks with a battalion of the 60th Rifles.

Behind him, on Spearman's, the sailors manning the naval long-range guns saw through their telescopes the Boers on Aloe Knoll and elsewhere on that side of the western summit. At 10.30 ten guns were authorized to open up but they had hardly begun, with telling effect, when Warren agitatedly sent them word that his men occupied the whole of the summit! He urged them instead to turn on the enemy guns, but later these instructions were altered and re-altered, and in the end the British artillery, unlike the Boers', never succeeded in co-operating with the infantry on top—because Warren had no idea that his men were only on the western end of the summit, and only a line along the middle of the western summit at that.

The battle was already a classic in bungled communications. Few and limited messages were reaching Warren, and then only hours after their dispatch although he was a mere two miles away from the summit. One reason was that messages were relayed to him via Spearman's where Buller saw them first. Thus Buller had not only the whole of the army at his command but the first opportunity of issuing prompt orders. But he gave none, choosing not to interfere beyond inhibiting any action on either of the flanks. When the garbled message from Crofton came through, Buller decided he had lost his nerve and urged Warren to put Thorneycroft in command. Warren at once helio-graphed instructions to the summit, but he did not tell Coke, toiling slowly up the mountain with his lame leg.

The time was now getting on for noon. In the three hours since

Woodgate's death the situation on the summit had increasingly deteriorated for the British. More and more Boers were continuing to arrive, hemming them in. Botha had by now organized his artillery to drop a curtain of shells ranging from one to ninety-four pounds at the rate of over ten per minute, 'blowing human beings into unrecognizable fragments, inflicting the most ghastly wounds, and terrifying those whom they did not slay'. The Boer gunners laid their shells with such accuracy behind the advance detachment that the men in the main trench could not come to their aid, though parties were twice led by Thorneycroft and others in vain attempts to charge. Gradually the whole advance line was beaten back or annihilated. By noon the British were confined almost solely to their main trench.

The sun, little past its midsummer zenith, blazed down on a scene of fantastic carnage. The cries and groans of the wounded and dying, and the exhortations of Boer and Briton to their comrades, and all the sounds of human voices were lost in the din made by gun and rifle, by shattering explosives and bullets ricocheting among the rocks. The main trench was being choked with dead and wounded. Many of the survivors were utterly demoralized and cowered down not daring to raise their heads, while others crawled about in groups through the choking fumes and dust, hopelessly trying to find shelter on the slopes behind the trench as shell-fire incessantly raked them. To agony and terror was added the craving of thirst. No water had reached the firing-line and men cried and screamed for it.

About now, Warren's order placing Thorneycroft in command reached Crofton. The first messenger he sent fell dead at Thorneycroft's feet, and when eventually Thorneycroft assumed command he could do little more than continue moving about in ceaseless effort to prevent the total disintegration of his force. He had twisted his leg in one of the abortive attempts to rescue the forward line but he inspired enough resistance to make the Boers think twice about advancing further.

They too had been suffering severely. Botha had never stopped sending up fresh men wherever he could lay hold of them, repositioning his artillery, invigorating the counter-attack with something of his own tenacious resolution; yet many men began to dribble back down the mountain. Reitz, whose climb to the summit had been saddened by the discovery of every one of his tent-mates killed, was with the burghers at the summit edge in the vicinity of Aloe Knoll: they were mainly from the eastern Transvaal village of Carolina, under Commandant Daniel Opperman who was called 'old Red Daniel' on account of his flaming hair.

> The sun became hotter, and we had neither food nor water. Around us lay scores of dead and wounded . . . and by midday a feeling of discouragement had gained ground and was only kept in check by Commandant Opperman's forceful personality and vigorous language to any man who seemed wavering. Had it not been for him the majority would have gone. . . .

As it was, old Red Daniel now pressed the British with renewed determination. On this side their trench had from the first been most vulnerable because of the merciless enfilading fire from Aloe Knoll only 250 yards away. As Opperman and his men came closer, the soldiers' morale at last gave way. White handkerchiefs were fluttered by some but others continued firing, and for several minutes confusion reigned until all the survivors along this part of the trench, about 150, went out with raised hands.

Up to that moment Thorneycroft had been too hotly engaged further along the trench to see what was happening. No sooner did he hear the news than his burly limping figure was seen rushing along with a handful of men hastily collected. 'I am commandant here,' he yelled at the Boers. 'Take your men back to hell, sir! There's no surrender.'

But the position was hopeless. His men could not rally and more Boers were swarming over the right-hand edge of the summit. Thorneycroft and a few others retreated to some rocks near the summit edge behind the main trench, exchanging fierce point-blank fire with the enemy who before dealing with them paused to assemble their prisoners. At the same time the Boers in front of the main trench launched an attack on the centre, pushing on with such gallantry that panic seized the survivors and they began running for their lives. Crofton at once dashed in from the left, the bugler at his side sounding the advance, but it was a forlorn hope. The centre and right of the British line were crumbling or crumbled and the whole force faced extinction. At this instant came deliverance. The Middlesex and I.L.I. ordered up by Warren three hours before began to reach the summit.

The leading company of Middlesex attacked the Boers on the right and were thrown back. But with succeeding companies coming up, Thorneycroft himself led a charge which swept the Boers and their demoralized prisoners off this end of the summit and away down the side. In the centre the I.L.I. and more Middlesex reinforcements charged through their panic-stricken comrades and reached the main trench in the nick of time to push back the Boers. The Boer artillery, silent during the attempt to storm the trench from front and right, at once laid down a curtain of flame behind which the Boers could rally and once more man the summit edge.

All along the British line the rapidly arriving reinforcements took their place among the remnants of the original defenders. A breathing space had been gained. Thorneycroft used it to send a dispatch to Warren at 2.30: 'Hung on till last extremity with old force. Some of Middlesex here now, and I hear Dorsets coming up, but force really inadequate to hold such a large perimeter. . . . We are badly in need of water. There are many killed and wounded. If you wish to make certainty of hill for night you must send more infantry and attack enemy's guns.'

On his way down, the dispatch runner encountered Coke, still dragging himself upwards. Previous reports filtering down had suggested that the summit was overcrowded, and he had checked further reinforcements from his division—while making no attempt to use them for any kind of flank attack which would enormously have helped the men on top. On reading Thorneycroft's dispatch he immediately ordered up the Scottish Rifles. He did not know that the writer of the dispatch had succeeded to Woodgate's command, because Warren had never informed him. Consequently he had not told his officer who had led the Middlesex and I.L.I. on to the summit. This was a Colonel Hill, who assumed that his seniority gave him over-all command.

The issue was not of immediate moment for with the Boers renewing the offensive more violently than before, Thorneycroft was fully engaged near the centre of the line some distance from Hill who was at the right rear, and though the fighting was within a compass of only about 300 yards its intensity and the unsighting caused by the contours of the ground resulted in each conducting a separate battle on his immediate front, independent and ignorant of the other.

Hill's struggle was to clear the Boers from the right of the summit. The I.L.I. and Middlesex fought for two and a half hours but every attempt to rush the enemy was repulsed. And then the Boers struck back, compelling them to give way until finally the whole of the summit on the British right was abandoned. The Boers followed up with a movement more dangerous than any before. From the right they worked round towards the southern face of the mountain, rapidly reaching a position where only another thirty yards would give them command of the main trench from the rear. As it was, the men there were showing signs of imminent mass surrender as the Boers in front simultaneously advanced on the centre and left. For the second time total disaster was about to overwhelm the British; and for the second time deliverance came in the nick of time. The Scottish Rifles ordered up by Coke burst on the scene. Fixing bayonets, they hurled themselves on the all-but encircling Boers and drove them back to the edges of the summit.

Further than that they could not dislodge them. A half-hour of fruitless charges brought them by 4.30 to a state in which flesh and blood had endured enough. The exhaustion of both sides took possession and the battle became stationary. Churchill climbed up to the summit with other correspondents and met not only streams of wounded but unwounded men reeling about as if drunk and falling on the slopes in a stupor of shock and exhaustion. The newsmen were so appalled by conditions on the summit that they decided to climb down to Warren and inform him that the position was untenable unless proper shelter could be made in the night and artillery dragged up. Meanwhile the trickle of men from the British line was matched by a steady weakening of the Boer perimeter. Botha decided to rely now on his artillery to make the British evacuate at nightfall. With the skilful positioning and accurate marksmanship which had characterized them all day, the Boer gunners pounded the crowded narrow strip along the summit. A thousand men could find some kind of shelter; another thousand had to huddle behind the main trench as best they could. Of the 500 men who were by now dead or wounded, most lay piled in layers along the main trench, exhausted survivors sleeping among them in spite of the incessant blast of artillery.

And still the greater part of Buller's army of 30,000 men stood idly by. The single exception was the battalion of 60th Rifles whom Lyttelton had long since sent to attack the Twin Peaks at the eastern end of Spion Kop. But even as they marched they were called back by

Buller, who feared that the task was too difficult. The major in command ignored the instruction; when it was repeated he again ignored it, and scaling the peaks cleared them at bayonet point before the reinforcements led by Schalk Burger, whom Botha had urged to safeguard the position, could arrive. It was now 5 p.m. and the British were poised to imperil the whole of the Boer defence and turn all their efforts of the day to ashes. But Buller was blinded by fury at his orders being disregarded. Lyttelton had no choice but to order the 'Old Sixtieth' back, guiding them through the darkness by a great bonfire at the ford in front of Spearman's.

The simple fact is that Buller had no idea how critical the position on the western summit had been through most of the day and still was. Nor did Warren, who assumed from the very few messages reaching him that his men were satisfactorily holding their own. Neither general sent up a staff officer to report, much less went up himself. Coke however, on at last reaching the western summit, just about the time that the 60th Rifles were clearing the further end of the mountain at Twin Peaks, made his way to Hill, on the assumption that this officer was in command. He immediately wrote to Warren describing the situation and asking whether he was to withdraw or entrench for the night, hinting at a preference for withdrawal. Without waiting for a reply he began climbing down again.

An hour's confusion followed in the failing light as to who precisely was in command. Communication between parts of the line was bedevilled by the difficulty of identifying officers who had gone from the one extreme of being too conspicuous to the other of wearing no distinguishing marks whatever and lay pressed together with their men. Eventually Thorneycroft decided he was in command. At 6.30 he wrote to Warren about the critical situation of his men and asked for water, stretcher-bearers and instructions.

The Boers were likewise at their last gasp, and as ignorant of the British straits as the British were of theirs. 'We were hungry, thirsty and tired,' says Reitz of his own sector—'around us were the dead men covered with swarms of flies attracted by the smell of blood. . . Batches of men left the line, openly defying Red Daniel who was impotent in the face of this wholesale defection, and when at last the sun set I do not think there were 60 men left on the ledge near Aloe Knoll.' But old Red Daniel was not finished. In the last moments of daylight he led a gallant charge that reached to within a hand's breadth of the British right before he was beaten off.

This show of spirit might have been an essential factor in the decision with which Thorneycroft grappled as darkness closed over the summit but did not silence the maimed and dying. Neither his courage nor resource, which almost alone had sustained the defence of the summit all through the day, were on the rack, but his faith. His men were without food or water, reinforcements had come in mere hundreds while tens of thousands stood idly by; artillery support had been almost nil; and his sense of betrayal was not assuaged when he heard that Coke had been up without even bothering to see him. He asked himself if he could go on sacrificing his men to the incompetence of his generals and the lack of any coherent military plan. What could tomorrow bring but a repetition of today, except total extinction of his force? They had not the strength or means to improve their defence, and many were already creeping away in the darkness. Drained by the exhaustion of one who had been without rest since he started guiding the force up the mountain over twenty hours before, he made his decision to Crofton and the Colonel of the Scottish Rifles. 'Better six battalions off the hill,' he said, 'than a mop-up in the morning.' They agreed with him. At 8.15 p.m. the men were fallen-in. Carrying as many wounded as they could, they began retiring from the summit. Hill protested, but with little vigour. The retreat continued.

But not only by the British. Schalk Burger and many of his men who had tried to thwart the Rifles' capture of the Twin Peaks and were unaware of their incredible withdrawal saw the certainty of defeat over the whole mountain, and they fled. Likewise the Boers on the western summit, unaware of the losses they had inflicted, believed that their efforts to dislodge the British had failed and discretion lay in flight before the enemy poured through. They melted away in the darkness. Even old Red Daniel departed, though not until past ten o'clock after he had lain listening to the stumbling footsteps of the British without realizing what this meant.

> We descended the hill [says Reitz] by the way which we had
> climbed up nearly 16 hours before, our feet striking sickeningly at
> times against the dead bodies in our path. When we reached the
> bottom most of the horses were gone, the men who had retired

having taken their mounts and ridden away, but our own animals and those belonging to the dead and wounded were still standing without food or water where they had been left at daybreak. The first thing to do was to quench our raging thirst and that of our horses at a spring nearby. . . . When we reached the laager we found everything in a state of chaos. The wagons were being hurriedly packed. . . .

Similar confusion prevailed in all the other laagers, many of which were already on trek for Ladysmith and the safety of the Drakensberg.

Thus the summit of Spion Kop was gradually deserted by friend and foe alike; and all that kept company there were corpses and men too injured to crawl away. Either side had only to discover this state of affairs to occupy the place completely and wrest a conclusive victory from seeming defeat.

As Thorneycroft descended the mountain he did not realize that he was passing large supplies of water and sandbags which unknown to him had been accumulated during the afternoon. But presently he encountered a messenger from Warren. He had been galvanized into action by Coke's dispatch written at the summit after his visit to Hill. Food, guns, entrenching tools and men were being promptly ordered up and arrangements made for renewing battle on the morrow. The instructions brought by the messenger now encountered by Thorney-croft urged him to hold on at all costs.

But Thorneycroft was past undoing his decision. He thrust the message aside and continued down the mountain. He did not en-counter Coke, who might possibly have arrested the flight from the summit, because Warren had recalled him for consultation. However, a captain on Coke's staff met the rearguard of the retreating force and halted them while he could signal headquarters for instructions, which would certainly have called for reoccupation of the summit. But the signal was delayed because oil for the lamp had run out. By the time the message could be sent Thorneycroft had reached Warren's tent and Warren decided to acquiesce in the withdrawal, calling down the force of well over a thousand fresh men waiting within striking distance of the summit.

This was happening at a little past 2 a.m. On the other side of the deserted mountain the Boer laagers were continuing to disperse. But one man had not given up. Reitz recounts a scene which was duplicated far and wide among the Boers that night:

> Just as the foremost wagons moved away and the horsemen were getting ready to follow, there came the sound of galloping hooves, and a man rode into our midst who shouted at them to halt. I could not see his face in the dark, but word went round that it was Louis Botha. . . . He addressed the men from the saddle, telling them the shame that would be theirs if they deserted their posts in this hour of danger; and so eloquent was his appeal that in a few minutes the men were filing off into the dark to reoccupy their positions.

So Botha, indefatigable throughout the day in trying to wrest the summit from the British, rode through the night, exhorting and appealing. If he did not stop the flight, at least he raised a semblance of a force which began to ascend the slopes again. And then at 3.30 a.m. a few burghers came running down with extraordinary news. They had ventured on to the summit and found it deserted!

At once Botha sent an appeal for men from his flanks on Tabanyama and opposite Spearman's where the panic had not spread, and he climbed up Spion Kop with the stalwarts he had rallied, and soon they occupied the summit. Far below, Warren had meanwhile heard about the Boer retreat and decided to resume the engagement, but Buller rode over at dawn and would hear of nothing short of a complete retirement across the Tugela. Botha stood on the summit as day broke, looking down in wonderment and wordless gratitude to God at the whole British army preparing to depart, even while on the plain behind him littered debris marked the flight of his own people's wagons.

The spreading light yielded up the macabre reality of British losses on the summit. In the main trench the dead lay in piles sometimes three deep and often horribly mutilated by the shell-fire. The British casualties totalled 1,200, the Boers 300—of whom 55 belonged to Opperman's 88 Carolina burghers who first climbed Aloe Knoll, sustaining a ratio of losses scarcely exceeded by any corps in the war. From an early hour stretcher-bearers came up and were helped by the Boers to sort the wounded. The British dead were buried in the trenches they had died defending. The Boers carried away most of their own dead wrapped in blankets, put them on wagons and with their horses trotting alongside with empty saddles escorted them to Ladysmith, whence they were taken by train to Pretoria. In Pretoria, too, in due course arrived the British prisoners captured at Spion Kop, their guards being fêted as heroes and marched down to shake hands with Paul Kruger—'the nearest approach to battle honours,' Reitz dryly comments, 'that we ever attained.'

Meanwhile, bridges having been built across the Tugela for the retreating British army, the infantry started crossing in pouring rain and by the 27th not a soldier remained in front of Tabanyama, Spion Kop, or the heights before Spearman's. Buller's second great attempt to force the Tugela line had failed.

It had failed for many reasons, and fierce controversy was soon to follow. But when all has been said the core of the matter remains in the fact that Buller's and Warren's wills were unequal to Botha's. There were men on both sides who fought with unbelievable courage, but what told in the end was the quality of a single man, and it was he who won the Battle of Spion Kop.

*　　*　　*　　*

Ladysmith had been in a state of acute suspense ever since Buller reached the Upper Tugela a fortnight before. The meaning of the continuous fighting that preceded the Battle of Spion Kop on 24 January was quite unknown to White who had largely to guess at what was going on. All the same he reconstituted a flying column to co-operate as soon as Buller broke through, and with his garrison counted the hours to that event. Then on the day of the great battle the distant roar of artillery was incessant and the mountain wreathed in a cloud of fumes. That evening a message was received that Buller occupied the crest. Hope rose as high as it. Next morning the weather was too dull for heliographs to operate but white wagons and dark masses of cattle making for the Drakensberg passes confirmed belief in a Boer retreat, as did glimpses through telescopes of figures apparently entrenching the top of Spion Kop. These were in fact British burial parties, and the wagon flight stopped at news of Botha's triumph—though there were Boers who fled as far as Pretoria, where they heard with unbelief the final outcome of the battle. Not for two days was that outcome known in Ladysmith. Though apparently borne with fortitude it was a savage blow at morale, and from this moment the prospect of survival plunged.

CHAPTER XI

Bobs and K: January–February 1900

BEFORE news of the disaster at Spion Kop reached England, Buller's dispatches since the advance from Chieveley had culminated on the morning of 24 January with the thrilling news that the summit of the mountain was in his hands, the army at last in a dominating position astride the Boers' dreaded Tugela line. The news crowned a month of increasing recovery from the trauma of Black Week. Not only had Roberts arrived, but the lavish reinforcements streaming in were bringing the total forces at his command to 180,000, far outnumbering the entire Boer population—man, woman and child.

Humour could blossom on the efforts of many of the raw Yeomanry learning to ride, or scoff at the more blatant examples of Fleet Street hyperbole. To a *Daily Mail* report that 'the Boers anticipate that Kruger will be crowned at Westminster,' *Punch* retorted, 'Everyone agrees that the Boers are extremely ignorant and narrow-minded, but even the *Daily Mail* must admit that they are not all absolute idiots.' The whole phenomenon of 'war news' was something new. On the one hand was constant protest at the military censorship of correspondents' reports; on the other people were more surprised than we would be to read in one paper that 'President Steyn is said to be much depressed', and in a second that 'The President is stated to be in high spirits'; or 'The Boers are running short of supplies and ammunition, and must soon abandon the campaign', contrasted with 'The Boers are stated on good authority to have ammunition and stores for at least two years'.

A by-product of the extensive newspaper coverage was the new 'shop': conversation became peppered with Afrikaans words that gave a particular flavour to the war—*dorp, kop, kopje, nek, donga, spruit, drift, slim** were a few of many. Wags spoke of Kensingdorp or Ludgate

* Village/town; peak; hill; pass; gully; stream; ford; clever/sly.

Kop, while *Punch* showed Mr. Brown throwing down his newspaper in disgust and exclaiming, 'Why the dickens don't these Boers give some sensible names to their towns such as Brixton, Hampstead or Peckham Rye?'

Now came the name Spion Kop to silence wit and sour optimism as the newsvendors shouted 'Speshal edeshun' along the streets: ' 'Orrible slaughter!' 'Desp'rate fighting!' The result was different from the grief and blaring 'patriotism' of Black Week. It was a bitter angry outburst against the Government. The war had been a series of calamitous mistakes, snarled *The Times*; a muddle from first to last, relieved only by the courage of the soldiers. The Government rocked. Intense criticism from its own followers reinforced that of all sections of the Opposition parties, whose avowed out-and-out opponents of the war such as Lloyd George had not stopped protesting at public meetings, while outside party politics others organized themselves into a Stop the War Committee, distributing literature like W. T. Stead's *Shall I Slay My Brother Boer?* Stories became more persistent about doubtful War Office contracts, bad food and forage, defective munitions.

The Cabinet had not in fact been sharing public optimism. A dispatch from Milner in the middle of the month was alarming. He tore Buller to shreds, urged that the Transvaal's life-line through Delagoa Bay must be blocked at all costs, and saw the Bond Ministry as such a danger that it could only be met by suspending the Cape constitution. Then came the final Spion Kop news. For three hours the Defence Committee, formed within the Cabinet to oversee the war, tried to understand Buller's explanation of what Chamberlain termed 'the sickening fiasco'; and he commented, 'it is clear that whatever else our generals can do they cannot write dispatches.'[31] Buller's popular nickname of 'the Bull-dog' was being wryly replaced by the 'Ferryman of the Tugela', but it was the Government alone against whom indignation and invective were directed. Continental diplomats freely prophesied the collapse of the Salisbury–Chamberlain Cabinet.

In this atmosphere the Houses of Parliament assembled on 30 January for the last full session of Queen Victoria's reign. The Opposition tabled a motion aimed straight at bringing down the Government: it deplored 'the want of knowledge, foresight and judgement displayed by Her Majesty's Ministers'.

The debate raged in the Commons for six days.

While much was made of insufficient men, guns, cavalry and other shortcomings of Government planning, the crisis in England's conscience was subtly conveyed by the fact that the debate centred again and again on the one leading Minister who had nothing to do with the military aspect of the war. Joseph Chamberlain had been raised in public favour by Black Week, but now he was put on trial by his peers. As speaker after speaker fumbled in defence of the Government, its fate and his own career depended on his ability to justify his policy. When a member cried, 'Be it for glory or condemnation this is his war!' he exposed that the real fermentation of the great debate, with the war already four months old, was the question simply stated in the title of another of W. T. Stead's pamphlets, *Are We In the Right?*

The principal Opposition arraignment was delivered by Sir William Harcourt, not the new Liberal leader. Campbell-Bannerman was yet to play perhaps the most important part of all in this story, but for the present he was personally embarrassed in any attack on the Government's state of preparedness by the fact that he had been War Secretary in the Liberal administration when it fell over the adequacy of cordite reserves. He had, besides, the breaches within his party to repair, *Punch* commenting of him:

> The state of health in which I am
> Is not precisely rude or hearty;
> I dare not lead, I cannot damn
> The forward motion of my Party;
> I scarcely know which way to go;
> I *wish* they wouldn't shove me so!

So Harcourt it was who led the attack which did not even omit to revive the allegation of Chamberlain's complicity in the Jameson Raid, and this wittiest of society dinner guests laboriously read his speech page by page in an interminable Victorian oration. Chamberlain listened impassively, with pale drawn face and his head leaned back. His turn to speak came on the fifth day. The House was crammed to overflowing as he rose. 'His first low words soon followed by a louder pitch laid on the House a grip unrelaxed for an hour.'

Beatrice Webb, as perplexed by Chamberlain as were most anti-Conservative intellectuals, labels[32] her period as one not of statesmen

but political artists—Gladstone, Disraeli, Randolph Churchill, Rosebery, Chamberlain had, she says, the charm, pliability, quick-wittedness
of actors. Yet elsewhere she acknowledges that Chamberlain had convictions, which he expressed forthrightly and honestly. The fact is that
he was a superb pleader—actors and barristers are brothers under their
wigs—in a cause he believed in. Thus his defence now was a model for
the politician who would control the House of Commons: first, he
roundly justified the principles of his policy—if anything, he said,
'We have been too anxious for peace'; second, he frankly admitted
mistakes in practice, promising that they would be rectified; and third,
he cast his bread upon the waters of his audience's idealism. The
number of colonials now helping the mother country exceeded the
British Army at Waterloo, almost equalled that in the Crimea:

> . . . and these peoples shortly—very shortly as time is measured in
> history—about to become great and populous nations, now for the
> first time claim their share in the duties and responsibilities as well
> as the privileges of Empire. . . . You are the trustees: they look
> to you as holding the leadership of your race. . . . We are finding
> out the weak spots in our armour and trying to remedy them; we
> are finding out the infinite potential resources of the Empire; and
> we are advancing steadily, if slowly, to the realization of that great
> federation of our race which will inevitably make for peace and
> liberty and justice.[33]

His approach to empire on a racial basis was less 'racialist' than the
words suggest; even so, it demonstrates that gap between modern and
Victorian concepts of the Commonwealth which the Boer War was
bridging unperceived in the 'life and death struggle on the veld'. The
speech was a huge success. Mrs. Chamberlain, keeping the inner
councils of the U.S.A. informed through her relatives, could report
the U.S.A. Ambassador (Choate) as saying that it was 'the finest he
had ever heard in England'. A telegram arrived from Osborne: 'I wish
to say how much I admired your fine speech. V.R.I.' *The Times*
adulated. The Government seemed safely home. And then, on the sixth
evening, notably fine for February, Lloyd George got up.

At recent public meetings he had attacked the Rand Jews, the Rand
capitalists and Joseph Chamberlain—one of whose remarks about 'the

Transvaal, the country we created,' drawing the Lloyd Georgian comment, 'In the Beginning, Joseph Chamberlain created Heaven and Earth—including the Transvaal.' Rising to the debate he gave notice that henceforward his quarry would be almost exclusively Joseph Chamberlain, whose footsteps from radical to statesman he was not only following but using to get himself across the wastes of political advancement. The real blunder, he declared, had not been any by the Government, the War Office or the generals, but by Chamberlain alone in starting the war, a war entirely for the Rand mine-owners who would be taxed less by a British Government and enabled to exploit labour more cheaply. 'Look!' he exclaimed. 'It is simply—l.s.d.!' Jibes came easily at the expense of the Uitlanders—now for the most part not fighting in their cause, he said, but lounging in Cape Town bars while English homes were made to mourn—but his most telling passage unknowingly echoed the essential point Chamberlain had himself once made, that given time the burgher moderates would finally have ousted Kruger. Where were those moderates now? 'In the field,' he answered dramatically. 'They are Boer generals now!' Which was true enough—Joubert, Schalk Burger, Lukas Meyer, Louis Botha, De la Rey, even President Steyn.

That evening Lloyd George emerged for the first time as a dynamic force in national life. But he failed to sway the issue. On the division the Government received 352 votes, the Opposition 139. It was a decisive majority. And the Government had need of it. The latest news from S.A. was scarcely reassuring.

*　　*　　*　　*

So deep had consternation struck when Buller retreated from Spion Kop that the War Office fired off wild suggestions about White breaking out of Ladysmith and abandoning the town. The deterioration in the situation there was due to the danger of collapse from within, either slowly through disease or suddenly from a failure of morale, rather than renewed attack by the besiegers, who kept only a scratch force round the town and contented themselves with starting a large project to dam a stream below Ladysmith in order to flood much of the town and surrounding plain. Meanwhile the daily bombardment continued: a bugler, or a Hindu on a pile of sandbags holding a parasol in one hand to ward off the heat and a flag in the other to wave signals, gave warning to the town to take shelter each time the Boer big guns fired, though the gunners worked with a regularity that made warnings almost redundant, taking time off for meals, bad weather and Sundays. But it wore nerves bare, day upon day, and feelings were not soothed by friction between the military and the townspeople. Unlike Mafeking and Kimberley, Ladysmith had the Army present in force to maintain the defence entirely on their own. Though White had by now formed a reserve of townsmen to fight to the last ditch if necessary, there was no Rhodes either to champion them or throw their full weight behind the military's efforts. Jameson appears to have resigned himself to a passive role in the drama he had helped create. He was openly derided for never venturing from his bomb-shelter except when absolutely safe to do so—though why a doctor in urgent demand should have risked bursting explosives is not clear from the satire published in *The Lady-smith Bombshell*. This was a siege journal similar to those got up, on everything from ledger sheets to brown wrapping paper and in print or duplicated handwriting, at the other siege-towns and most P.O.W. camps. But its tone was markedly different from their steady confidence and high spirits. The slightly sardonic twist of its humour is illustrated by a specimen: 'Regret—one of the Naval Brigade was removing a fuse from a live shell, when it exploded, carrying away his left arm. "Well that is too bad" exclaimed he "for it was only yesterday I paid 10/- for having that same arm tattooed." ' To read this journal is to catch something of the hour-by-hour tedium of a little world cut off from the big world: the harassment of constant shelling, the bitterness over women and children being shelled, the rumours upon which fears and hopes fastened, the contempt for the enemy, the food situation, the delay in relief. 'If a Relief Column takes a day and a half to march a yard and a half,' it asked, 'how much longer will the price of eggs be 10/- per dozen?'

The answer was—less long than it took Buller to get through another case of champagne, for the price rose to 48/- per dozen after Spion Kop. Luxuries were almost all gone—gentlemen of the cavalry were smoking the leaves out of the breakfast teapot unless they could find a cigarette at a shilling each—and this added to the psychological factor in disease, never clearer than when the sick-rate shot up each time Buller retreated. Enteric and dysentery now accounted for nearly 2,000 patients in the hospital, which had been organized for 300, and the fatality curve was climbing steeply. The Boers had infected the water-supply but the ingenious construction of a distillation plant kept it pure. The fundamental reason for the spread of disease was under-nourishment, and strenuous efforts were made to ward off starvation. Most of the horses had been let loose for want of forage and those un-captured by the Boers were rounded up to provide horse-meat in various forms including a soup-paste called chevril, sausages, meat-rolls and jellies. In the absence of flour a bread was attempted from maize with the gluten supplied by laundry starch. But all these were at best delaying expedients. The death-rate was rising beyond seventy per week and it was merely the indicator to the enfeeblement rapidly over-taking the whole garrison. White rejected anything so desperate as abandoning the town, as the War Office suggested, but he confronted the future with intense anxiety. Supplies could not hold out beyond six weeks. The situation looked no rosier in the light of a message from Buller saying he would have another 'fair square try' at rescuing him *but doubted his strength to do it.*

Roberts alone refused to be dismayed. He was assembling his forces with a minimum of publicity and when he could be reasonably sure of success he would strike. He braced White's spirits by sending him his warm congratulations upon the 'heroic splendid defence' of Ladysmith, and confidently asserted that his impending campaign would signi-ficantly reduce the enemy strength by the end of February.

He made the same forecast to Buller, whom he urged to stay on the defensive in the meanwhile. But unlike White, Buller was not im-pressed. He signalled to White: 'I doubt Lord Roberts's forecasts com-ing off and think I had better play my hand alone. What do you think?' White was terrified that another failure on Buller's part, fatally post-poning the chances of relief, would seal Ladysmith's doom. He sup-ported Roberts's advice, urging him to keep up a bold front with harassing tactics while remaining on the defensive until Roberts's inter-vention told on the enemy. Buller was still not convinced.

It was as if the town had become an obsession, like an aloof and elusive woman increasing her suitor's ardour with each rebuff. His pride recoiled at the thought of anyone else having to help him gain her hand—and bring honour to a career which had acquired precious little from the past months. Or it may be that hearing Roberts's fore-cast as the hollow echo of his own first optimism he felt himself bound by his proximity to relieve Ladysmith lest it could not hold out even for the limited period White estimated. Whatever the reason, he disregarded Roberts's advice. The day he received it, 28 January, he announced at a church parade that he now really had 'the key to Ladysmith' and would be there within a week.

To reach this renewal of confidence he had shaken off any feeling of defeat after Spion Kop. By stretching a strictly limited truth to its utmost he assured himself and later the public that he had not been present before Spion Kop or witnessed the operations. It was Warren, he reported to Roberts after the battle, who abandoned the mountain; and Warren's men who were consequently in low spirits amid an atmosphere of mutual recrimination. And he added a note blaming the failure on Warren's slowness: 'I will never employ him in an independent command again.'

The key which he now believed he possessed for unlocking the Tugela defences was a break in the hills to the right of the ford in front of Spearman's. The heights along the further bank ended at a kopje called Vaalkrantz (see map on p. 181). Between it and the next series of heights, which started with a hill called Doornkop, was an open space, gateway to the Ladysmith plain itself. He had only to seize Vaalkrantz on the left of this space and Doornkop on the right of it, and he could march safely through.

The week during which he had assured his troops that they would be marching on Ladysmith was spent in postponements and preparations around Spearman's until, stung by rumours of an imminent Boer attack on the town, he launched his offensive early on the morning of 5 February. His men were in high spirits, for victory was at last in sight.

The picture on the Boer side was very different. Since Spion Kop many burghers and leaders—Louis Botha, Schalk Burger and A. P. Cronje—had gone off on leave. The remaining men, totalling about 4,000, were strung out in small pockets along the whole of the Tugela heights from Tabanyama to beyond Colenso. While Buller had over 20,000 men for his proposed offensive on Vaalkrantz and Doornkop, there were 350 Boers on the latter and 1,200 on the former, mainly at the end nearer Spearman's. The men on Vaalkrantz were mostly from Johannesburg and their commandant was Ben Viljoen. He was a young man risen from policeman to editor of a pro-Kruger newspaper, though his own politics were pro-Joubert. Member of the Volksraad for Johannesburg, he was strong, impetuous and violent to political opponents despite a genial nature. He was a considerable orator, said to have originated the supposed Boer battle cry, 'God and the Mauser!' He had a bold good-looking face with a moustache and short pointed beard kept trim from ear to ear. When he saw all the bustle around Spearman's he appealed for help; whereupon what Joubert thought he needed was a little faith, and sent along an elderly burgher to deliver a homily. But later, prodded by Paul Kruger, he telegraphed to Louis Botha who set off from Pretoria for the front on the night of the 4th.

That was the night the British troops were sitting around their camp-fires until a late hour discussing the prospects of victory on the morrow. And the morrow brought immediate success.

The greatest obstacle to the proposed two-pronged attack on Vaal-krantz and Doornkop was the absence of a ford across the river, but an elaborate feint across the ford in front of Spearman's so diverted the Boers' attention that a pontoon bridge was thrown across without difficulty. The troops for Vaalkrantz, which was furthest from the river, were ready under the command of General Lyttelton to cross in advance. But Buller would not let them move until his complicated feinting movement had been completed, long after it had achieved its purpose. By then it was 2 o'clock in the afternoon and Viljoen, suspicious of what was afoot, had brought about a hundred of his men to the threatened end of Vaalkrantz. Assisted by converging fire from Doornkop he was able to give the assault force a fierce reception when, crossing the bridge, they rushed through a mealie field that extended from river bank to Vaalkrantz. The charge failed. It was renewed as more men crossed the bridge and Lyttelton waited expectantly for the converging fire on his men to be stopped by the capture of Doornkop. But this intended second part of the attack never came. Buller had suddenly decided to call the whole thing off. The fire from Doornkop was heavier than he expected and he lost heart. Lyttelton's men could not now retreat without serious loss and he begged to continue the attack on Vaalkrantz at least. Buller reluctantly agreed. He allowed reinforcements to cross and opened up with all sixty-six guns at Spearman's to turn Vaalkrantz into a huge cloud of smoke. A lyddite shell burst above Viljoen's head, stunning him and killing his comrades around him. He had scarcely come-to when the British were charging with fixed bayonets, sweeping up the slopes and for half a mile along the crest. He escaped, dragging away a pompom, but over half his comrades at this end of the hill were wiped out. Then reinforcements and artillery checked the British advance and Buller would do nothing to help. Night came with Lyttelton's men lying among the rocks and wearily entrenching. He pressed Buller to complete the original plan in the morning, for after all they now had the important end of Vaalkrantz and had only to secure Doornkop to have an open road into Ladysmith. Buller postponed decision until the morning.

By then the Boers were reinforced to a total strength of 2,000 on Vaalkrantz. From before dawn Buller sent messages to Lyttelton, proposing first one course and then another. Finally he telegraphed Roberts. To get through the gap he had already all-but forced would cost 2,000–3,000 men, he said: 'Do you think the relief of Ladysmith is worth the risk? It is the only possible way to relieve White.' And he added despairingly: 'If I give up this chance I know no other.' Roberts, having had his previous advice ignored, could not now stomach the idea of an engagement broken off half-way when White had said the fall of Ladysmith would follow another reverse. 'Ladysmith must be relieved,' he replied, 'even at the loss you anticipate. . . . Let your troops know that the Empire is in your hands, and that I have no possible doubt of their being successful.'

Buller did not immediately act on his commanding officer's instructions but pondered this message, and pondered and pondered, while the two sides kept up an artillery duel. At noon Botha arrived to infuse fresh spirit among the Boers. The grass in front of the British advance line on Vaalkrantz was set ablaze by shells at about 3 p.m. and through the smoke the Boers made a charge which nearly overran them, until a half battalion of the 60th Rifles, lying in reserve, sprang forward with fixed bayonets and checked the stampede. Towards sunset fresh troops arrived to strengthen the entrenchments. Still Buller could not make up his mind.

Through the night he continued undecided. All next morning, while the guns thundered, he remained irresolute. At 4 p.m. he called a council of his generals. They decided to pull out. Buller telegraphed Roberts that the present engagement would uselessly waste life, and that he would make another attempt somewhere else.

The following three days were spent marching the troops, the guns, and nearly 600 wagon-loads of stores back to Chieveley. 400 casualties had been incurred in an attempt of astonishing fatuity, the third attempt to force the Tugela heights.

The news fell dully upon English ears. *The Times* spoke testily of 'the irritating and offensive chatter of the House of Commons'. Parliament indeed seemed robbed of effectiveness by the Government's triumphant majority the day before Buller's latest retreat, and there was more vitality in the constant arguments in office and factory between supporters of the war and the passionate minority who damned it.

In explaining his withdrawal Buller did not of course accept responsibility. He declared that White had failed to detain enough Boers round Ladysmith, while he himself had insufficient troops because of diversions to the force being built up by Roberts. The thought that it was now up to Roberts to achieve a success sufficient to avert the fall of Ladysmith put him in a cold sweat. To rely on it, he spluttered in a telegram to Roberts, was such a grave risk that he himself would rather 'be sacrificed' than lose Ladysmith: he wished his views to be placed before the Secretary of State. This emotional outburst he followed with another, entreating Roberts, if he valued Ladysmith, not to order him to remain on the defensive which would allow the Boers to engulf the town.

Poor Buller! How he yearned to win Ladysmith. With what awkward phrases and stumbling movements he wooed her. How his mind painted her straits and his enemy's strength in exaggerated colours. How hope and despair alternatively seized on him. How he sustained himself by blaming others. How he moved through a mist of indecision, knowing only his passion and his need to reach the town, while he could not bear the thought of losses his men might have to suffer. In a strange way his men understood and loved him. They forgave him his incompetence because part of it was his exaggerated concern for them. Let failure succeed failure, loss pile upon loss, they would follow him as doggedly as he would lead them. In this he was *par excellence* an Englishman. He would never let go.

And Joubert, alone among the Boer leaders, knew it. He knew that this time England would not let go. A blunderer and a cautious man himself, he understood that persistence is the one quality to be feared in an enemy. Therefore he urged Kruger to make overtures of peace.

Kruger refused. Large British reinforcements were undoubtedly arriving but wherever he looked he seemed secure—on the Western Front, in the Cape, in Natal. The fall of Ladysmith and Kimberley was now a matter only of weeks, perhaps days. God would surely not desert his people at this juncture, certainly not while they stood astride every railway. Would any British soldier dare advance a yard without a line to bring up the food, ammunition and even water essential to movement across great distances? Buller had just tried a limited movement away from the railway, and that where water was no problem, with salutary results.

It was not to be contemplated that preparations for precisely such a movement on a vastly greater scale were day and night the toil of Roberts and Kitchener. The news that Buller had broken off the engagement at Vaalkrantz, and the emotional messages which followed, reached them at a critical moment.

*   *   *   *

Frederick Sleigh Roberts, son of an Irish general who lived to be ninety, great-nephew of a bold sailor nicknamed 'the White Devil', dressed his little body with care and loathed cats. He was considered the greatest general of his time, yet his diminutive stature and blindness in one eye, the result of brain-fever that nearly killed him as a child, would have barred him from an Army career today. Nor was there much soldierly promise in the heart and digestive trouble which required him to keep a bottle of sherry by his bedside at his military academy.

He joined the Indian Army as an artillery officer and emerged from the Mutiny at the age of twenty-six with seven mentions in dispatches and the V.C. For the next twenty years marriage and staff work in the relatively efficient Indian Army absorbed him, relieved only by bloodless expeditions against the mad King Theodore of Abyssinia and to release the child Mary Winchester from an Assam tribe. When fame came it came in a rush.

Through the Viceroy's chance reading of a routine staff paper, its author was singled out for command of a column on the outbreak of war to frustrate Afghanistan intrigues with Russia. For three successive years Roberts went on marches against Amir and dissident Mullah that spread his name across the North-West Frontier. Finally he was cut off from the world for three weeks while he marched from Kabul to

Kandahar and spectacularly rescued a beleaguered garrison. He returned to England a hero.

The year was 1881. Majuba rang in English ears as a shame to be effaced and Roberts was sent to do it, but before he reached S.A. Gladstone had made peace. He sailed straight home. A provincial command in India followed until an encounter with Randolph Churchill led to his appointment to the princely office of Commander-in-Chief of the Indian Army. Less bloodshed than reform marked his reign. He had seen Army offenders flogged and mutineers shot from the guns, but while he 'placed duty before life he ranked humanity above ambition' and did much for the welfare of soldiers as well as their proficiency with the new weapons. A remarkable bond of affection was created between him and his men, who called him Bobs. He was raised to the peerage as Lord Roberts of Kandahar and on returning to England found himself suddenly a national figure. The new popular Press was partly responsible, and so was Kipling with his doggerel *Bobs* that echoed in the music-hall and streets:

> There's a little red-faced man,
>   Which is Bobs,
> Rides the tallest 'orse 'e can—
>   *Our* Bobs.
> If it bucks or kicks or rears,
> 'E can sit for twenty years
> With a smile round both 'is ears—
>   Can't yer, Bobs?

The horse was an Arab grey, Vonolel, last of famous war-horses and actually given the Afghan War medals by special direction of the Queen. Roberts rode the animal at the head of the colonial contingents at the Jubilee, by which time he was a field-marshal, a freeman of nine towns, the recipient of an honorary degree at Cambridge in company with Tchaikovsky, and author of *41 Years in India* that ran into thirty-five editions.

Anyone wanting to understand the late Victorian Age could almost begin and end with Roberts. The raucous and more vulgar constituents of patriotism and imperialism delighted in his military successes and flair for the heroic or dramatic, but in the moral force of his character the earnest hankerings of the time found a god. When he was thirty-four he wrote in his diary:

> Before a man can be manly the gifts which make him so must be there, collected by him slowly, unconsciously as are his bones, his flesh, his blood. A man cannot become faithful to his friends, unsuspicious before the world, gentle with women, loving with children, considerate to his inferiors, kindly with servants, tenderhearted with all, and at the same time be frank, of open speech with eager energies simply because he desires it.

The result was a man temperate in habit and speech, modest, simple, and secure in a married life completely happy until his only son's death on the last day of Black Week fused the nation's grief with his own. That he should at such a moment in the fortune of England and in spite of his age have set out for S.A. as a saviour explains the intensity of emotion which surrounded his name.

The man towering behind him as they descended the gang-plank at Cape Town docks was as someone from another planet. Horatio Herbert Kitchener's handsome square face, clean-shaven except for a great moustache, is best remembered from the recruiting posters of World War I, when the glittering emotionless stare of his wide-set blue eyes, which had a slight cast in one as the result of a gruelling desert ride, summoned the manhood of England to slaughter in Flanders.

He disliked the Press—'Get out of my way you drunken swabs,' he spat at a group of journalists waiting outside his tent—and objected to young Winston Churchill's insinuation of himself into the Sudan expedition as a Hussar-cum-journalist. They eventually met when Churchill brought him the news during the final march on Omdurman that 60,000 dervishes were drawing up for battle, and he wrote of the 'vivid manifestation upon the senses' Kitchener's appearance made on him. When Kitchener had killed, wounded or captured half that dervish horde at a cost of 500 Anglo-Egyptian casualties, he occupied Khartoum. During a service in memory of Gordon whom he had long ago been sent too late to relieve, the tears rolled down his cheeks. It was not anything anyone had ever seen or would see again: 'he preferred to be misunderstood rather than be suspected of human feeling,' wrote one of his devoted A.D.C.s—for if his friendships were few they were fervent.

He was born and schooled in Ireland but his parents were English. His father, who considered blankets unhealthy and preferred newspapers stitched together to give the exact degree of warmth required, brought the children up as masters in a foreign land. Kitchener adored his mother who died when he was fourteen. He never married, and there is no real evidence that any woman ever claimed his romantic interest.

He entered the Army in the Engineers and before joining Roberts at the age of forty-nine he had spent the whole of his military life in the Middle East—first land-surveying, then helping to train the Egyptian Army, then commanding an outpost where he often dressed as an Arab and went spying alone. He exercised a fascination over high-born women and in correspondence or on leave spent in their stately homes he manipulated them to exert influence in his interest. His rapid promotion to Sirdar of the Egyptian Army after the abortive Gordon relief expedition, his intolerance with officers who had failed through no fault of their own, and his indifference to the corporate life and graces of professional soldiering made him roundly detested in the Army. But upon leading the Sudan expedition he became, through his methodical advance and decisive victories, a new kind of super-efficient hero in the eyes of the public. Indeed he served the tax-payer well, skimping on cost even to the extent of medical care for the wounded. A grateful Parliament gave him £30,000 and he was raised to the peerage as Lord Kitchener of Khartoum and Aspall (his mother's Suffolk home).

England has never known such a general who lusted to close with the enemy, schemed and toiled to close with him, and once upon him rained down blows in a paroxysm of violence. He had no scruple about means, practising oriental barbarities to overawe oriental barbarians, and his harshness towards his own Sudanese army left them in a state of mutiny. Yet his personal life was one of inviolate purity and self-control, with a strict adherence to an exalted moral code. A further contradiction was that while personal comforts were beneath consideration he surrounded himself with choice porcelain and *objets d'art*, and when the cities of England honoured him he expressed a wish for gifts of gold-plate.

Kitchener baffled his contemporaries because they did not realize that an atavistic Saxon, an invert, and a Victorian struggled to exist in the same person. The result was 'this remarkable phenomenon' described by Curzon when Kitchener later became Commander-in-Chief in India: 'He stands aloof and alone, a molten mass of devouring energy and burning ambition, without anybody to control or guide it in the right direction.'

No affectionate sobriquet was attached to him, only the single letter K. Bobs and K, Lords Roberts and Kitchener—a stranger combination never set forth to rescue the name of British arms and save an empire. From the Khyber Pass to the Upper Nile the earth had trembled where they stood: but would the veld?

It was the veld they had to conquer, whose wide expanses made the few railways so apparently the only means of advance that the Boers could hold successive defensive positions of their own choice. Therefore the conversations on the *Dunnottar Castle* revolved round an alternative. The War Office's plan of an invasion from the Cape Midlands was scrapped once and for all, and Roberts arrived with a grand new design.

He would assemble an army on the Western railway at Orange River Station, from which Methuen had hopefully set out to relieve Kimberley. But instead of continuing north along the railway he would strike eastwards for over eighty miles cross-country to the Central railway at a point south of the O.F.S. capital. If he could do this he would compel the Boer invaders to withdraw in defence of their homeland and he would draw off the besiegers from all the beleaguered towns.

He would have overwhelming numbers at his disposal, while the flatness of the terrain would give the Boers no natural defensive positions. But by abandoning the railway at Orange River Station he would need 2,000 supply wagons and 20,000 draft animals, and since Buller's experience had shown that superior numbers of plodding infantry could be useless against an enemy whose mobility enabled him quickly to prepare and reinforce defensive positions, a substantial proportion of the new army had to be mounted. Roberts's task was therefore not only to weld together into an army the assorted reinforcements pouring into the country but to make them mobile.

The precise system of transport and supply had to be worked out, since his men were drawn from the India, Egyptian and home armies which each had different methods. The result was that when Kitchener was put in charge of transport arrangements chaos ensued and as usual he steam-rollered his way through, earning the censure of the War Office because, in his words, 'I do not agree to follow their printed rot.' The problem was how to achieve efficient distribution-on-the-move, keeping the fighting front well supplied but unencumbered. Every regiment would have pack mules and carts for water and ammunition, essential artillery and engineers' vehicles, and a few ambulances. For every two regiments forty-nine mule-wagons would carry the baggage and two days' food and forage. Replenishments would come from a 'supply park' of ox-wagons, themselves kept stocked from the nearest fixed depot on the railway line.

To get as many men as possible on horseback, mounted troops were called in from almost every front, mounted colonial corps raised, unmounted ones converted, and infantry regiments provided recruits for the M.I., their first efforts in the saddle providing universal merriment. Horses were less easy to find. Cape farmers had plenty but were reluctant to part with them and Milner did not want to risk antagonism by commandeering. Eventually 12,000 were got together from England, Australia and the Argentine, involving a long ocean voyage.

While Roberts and Kitchener immersed themselves in the task of organization, Henderson set up his Intelligence Department to which Roberts gave funds, staff and an importance hitherto almost unknown in the British Army. It began preparing detailed maps of the O.F.S., and through spies and scouts gathered what information it could about the enemy.

Roberts was determined to achieve the advantage of surprise. No one knew his plan except a dozen key people. He could not of course conceal the reinforcements pouring in, but by sending many up to French—ready to be switched to Orange River Station at the last moment—he bluffed the Boers into thinking that his counter-offensive would come from the Colesburg area. But although he pushed forward his preparations with all speed, events began to pile up against him.

One of his discoveries since his arrival was the immense prestige value attached to Kimberley by Boer and British South African alike, and reports from the city were ominous. The election of a new commandant in the siege lines, J. S. Ferreira, and no doubt awareness of

Roberts's arrival in S.A., had caused the Boers to intensify their bombardment and on some sectors to move in closer. De Beers' American engineer Labram, without any experience of ordnance manufacture, had a modern twenty-eight-pound gun made in the workshops—as *The Times History* says, 'one of the most remarkable events in the history of beleaguered garrisons'. Named 'Long Cecil' in honour of Rhodes it went into action on 19 January and considerably improved morale. But the health situation caused increasing concern. The meat ration was reduced to four ounces and included horse-flesh which tasted somewhat like beef though browner in colour, and Rhodes helped strenuously to organize a soup-kitchen: the meagre and ill-assorted food and the nervous strain, however, were rapidly increasing the incidence of enteric and dysentery; scurvy broke out, and the infant mortality rate in December alone was about 800 per 1,000 white and Native children.

The outlook for Ladysmith was if anything bleaker. On 25 January came the news of Spion Kop, and the subsequent exchange of messages between Roberts, White and Buller will be recalled, in which Roberts urged Buller to stay on the defensive lest the fall of Ladysmith were precipitated before his own campaign could take effect.

He had to get going quickly. And at this juncture Henderson brought alarming news. The dry conditions in the country through which Roberts proposed to march had been worsened by a three months' drought. The prospect of water was utterly uncertain—and failure to secure it on a single day could have disastrous effects. Roberts reacted with a new plan even bolder than the first. He would stick to his eastward flank march, not however from Orange River Station but from just behind Methuen's position on the Modder River, which he would follow eastwards to strike at Bloemfontein itself, pausing only to outflank Magersfontein with his mounted troops in order to relieve Kimberley.

Additional railways were hastily constructed at the nearest sidings on the Western railway and complicated arrangements undertaken to move an entire army up to various points along the single track behind Methuen on the Modder. Engineers probed with diamond drills for water along the way for the host of transport animals, new camps were erected, and troops quietly moved from the Colesburg and other areas.

The activity could not go unobserved. Cronje decided that another attack was being planned against his Magersfontein defences. Then a fortuitous incident put him right off the scent. The Boers had been renewing their activity to raise rebellion westwards, and to clear the area Methuen sent out the Highland Brigade whose new commander Hector Macdonald was unusual in having started life as a draper's assistant and risen from private to general. News of their march convinced Cronje that Methuen was planning a flank attack on him from the west, and De Wet dashed out with a force to repel it. After a brief clash* the British quietly withdrew, leaving Cronje satisfied that he had dealt with the threatened attack. He had no idea that Roberts was preparing his major blow on this front.

The Boers at Colesburg continued to be convinced that the British preparations were directed at them, for even while the bulk of the forces was being withdrawn the illusion of strength was kept up by a series of stratagems. Rows of dung-fires were lit at non-existent camps, posts were noisily occupied by men who promptly retired secretly to occupy a series of further posts with equal noisiness, and newspaper reports hinted at massive troop concentrations in this area.

So far so good; but Milner viewed the new plan with dismay. Roberts was concentrating his main strength 600 miles away from Cape Town, and then for 100 miles of country at the driest and hottest time of the year he would be cut off from the railway while only a skeleton force remained along the Central Front. There was an ominous parallel here with Buller's gamble in going to Natal. A reprieve had been gained but all might be lost if the gamble were disastrously repeated. At Colesburg were 7,000–8,000 Boers, revitalized by the arrival of De la Rey and Piet de Wet and easily able to seize the railway junctions of Naauwpoort in front of them or De Aar only sixty miles to the south-west, severing Roberts from the Cape which would then be at their mercy. Roberts could not be swayed. He staked everything on his flank march.

On the evening of 6 February he and Kitchener slipped out of Milner's house into a waiting brougham. It took them to the station from which a special train with fifty armed men had already ostentatiously departed. They themselves quietly boarded the ordinary northward mail. Complete secrecy surrounded them lest the train were wrecked. For two days they travelled to the Western Front across an increasingly hot and

* At Koedoesberg Drift.

dusty land. Towards the end, the sea of tents and the concourse of men, animals, vehicles and equipment presented a stirring sight. The task now was to turn this multitude scattered down the line into an organized army. Men who had arrived pell-mell had to be grouped in divisions and brigades. Officers had to be posted. Artillery, M.I. and transport had to be allocated. Horses had to be rested after their long ocean voyage and journey to the front. Roberts's need was time in order to settle all the details for an expedition with the greatest field force he and Kitchener had ever led.

But bad news awaited him, for it was at this moment that Buller reported having broken off his attack on Vaalkrantz after all and, retreating across the Tugela, sent the emotional messages previously described. If Roberts felt exasperation he showed none. He decided to let Buller blunder along as best that extraordinary man might. More than ever he had to hope that his own efforts would transform the whole situation sufficiently to save Ladysmith.

Kimberley too was threatened more acutely than before. Only the previous day the Boers had brought up one of their terrifying Long Toms. Labram the brilliant engineer was one of its victims, and it spread such dismay through the townsfolk whose nerves and health were at breaking-point that Kekewich reported the situation to be serious. Next day, 9 February, Rhodes had a stormy interview with him. He told Kekewich that unless he was given definite information of Roberts's intentions about lifting the siege he would call a public meeting in two days' time to 'consider the situation'. This was followed by a petition signed by the leading citizens stressing their anxiety.

Kekewich jumped to the conclusion that Rhodes intended to advise the townsfolk to surrender. After an exchange of messages with Roberts he saw Rhodes again. Roberts, he said, wished him to make clear 'the disastrous and humiliating effect' of surrender, and that the town would soon be relieved; Roberts had instructed him to prevent public meetings and even to arrest Rhodes if he thought fit. Rhodes retorted that surrender had never been thought of, much less mentioned, and left the meeting with his opinion of the military scarcely enhanced.

Beside this deterioration of the Kimberley and Ladysmith situations, Roberts had to keep an anxious eye over his shoulder at the Cape Midlands where De la Rey's presence at Schoeman's side might any moment spell disaster for his communications. Time was running out which he badly needed to complete his organization and rest his horses, of which only a number sent out by London bus companies were fit for work.

He came to a bold, perhaps a reckless decision. He would complete his organization on the march. This and the condition of the horses were risks to add to those that Milner had already dilated on. But Roberts was wedded to the idea of speed, and determined that if Kimberley or Ladysmith fell it would not be for want of it.

General French, recalled from Colesburg, was in command of the Cavalry Division which Roberts planned should ride in advance to relieve Kimberley by a right hook around Magersfontein. On the evening of 10 February Roberts went to his bivouac near Methuen's camp on the Modder. Calling together the senior officers he said: 'I am going to give you some very hard work to do, but at the same time you are to get the greatest chance cavalry has ever had. . . . You will remember what you are going to do all your lives, and when you have grown to be old men you will tell the story of the relief of Kimberley.'

Their first objective was to seize fords across the Riet and Modder Rivers on Cronje's flank before he could realize what was happening and try to stop the main army, which would at the same time be marching to take over the fords from the cavalry and stand clean across his line of communications to Bloemfontein. What would happen then was uncertain. He could try to fight his way through, or turn north to struggle with French who if all went to plan would by that time have swept on to Kimberley, or trek westward into the wilderness. Seizure of the fords, then, was more important to Roberts's strategy than the relief of Kimberley, for so long as they could be held his infantry would be poised either to deal with Cronje or proceed with their march along the Modder to Bloemfontein.

The prospects of success were great. Cronje suspected nothing, least of all that Roberts intended to stray far from the railway line. Nor had the fighting edge of the commandos been sharpened by their sweltering days in the trenches, the accumulation in the laagers of women and children, the Bank holiday atmosphere and the weakening of the horses grazing off the poor scrub.

A few hours after Roberts's address to the Cavalry Division, as midnight had scarcely sounded, the order was given for the great flank march to begin. The field force consisted of over 25,000 infantry, nearly 8,000 cavalry and M.I., over 100 guns and thousands of wagons. Behind them were to stay another 7,000 men under Methuen to confront the Magersfontein defences and 18,000 to guard the railway down to Orange River Station.

Except for their sentries, the Boers along the Magersfontein trenches, around Kimberley, in their head laager at Jacobsdal, or scattered about in small groups elsewhere east of the railway line, slept through a moonless night.

CHAPTER XII

The Flank March: February 1900

THROUGH the day (11 February 1900) which in England was one of prayer and intercession though none knew what impended, all was astir in the British camps dotted along the Western railway, and between the railway and the first objective. This was the village of Ramdam to the eastward where Roberts's organization would be completed as the scattered forces converged and received their complement of officers, guns and transport en route. Ramdam was chosen because it was the only watering-place before the Riet River, which would have to be crossed in the next leg of the march to the Modder. Gradually the whole force swung into action like a great snake uncoiling.

French left all his tents standing in order to delay Boer discovery of his departure. At Ramdam he completed the organization of his cavalry division except for some M.I. units due from far down the railway. He decided not to wait and next morning pushed on for the Riet.

Cronje had not discovered his departure from his bivouac until midday. This with news of a small Boer force's entanglement with M.I. some distance south (the reason for their delay in reaching French) led him to a totally wrong conclusion. He decided the British were making a strong demonstration towards the important village of Fauresmith in the south-east, and he sent Christian de Wet to check them.

Making his way north-east next morning French thus soon ran into De Wet coming the opposite way, but distracting his attention by a feint he crossed the river upstream of him. This only served to confirm the Boers in their belief that the British objective was Fauresmith, whereupon De Wet went still higher upstream to cover the road leading south to that town.

After their arrival at the Riet in the gruelling heat, French's men were as exhausted as their horses—heavy animals, weighted with all the impedimenta of cavalrymen. They rested, waiting for the main army to come up, and prepared for an early start on the morrow. They would have to cover twenty-five miles of waterless veld to the Modder, crossing Cronje's flank almost under his nose and revealing for the first time the true direction of the British march. Success was vitally necessary, and an early start important to success. But as the foremost supply wagons reached the Riet a pile-up miles long brought chaos until Kitchener diverted some columns to another ford. The result was that supplies reached French too late for the early start he depended on. By the time he set off in the morning (13 February) Roberts had arrived. The delay had materially increased the risks to the opening phase of his campaign, and he watched anxiously as 6,000 horsemen made away across the scrub with their ammunition wagons, medical units, forty-two guns and a cable-cart unwinding telegraph wire as it went.

He was not alone in watching their departure with concern. Unobserved De Wet had come to a nearby hill. When he saw the great array spread across a front of five miles he at once sent word to Cronje by dispatch-rider as his own telegraph wire had been cut by French's patrols. But instead of harrying French until Cronje sent reinforcements, which was exactly the danger the cavalry's late start had exposed them to, he withdrew to his position twenty miles upstream.

French swept forward, brushing off a party of Boers who confused Cronje further by reporting the British objective as Jacobsdal. But in the early afternoon as he neared the Modder his right was harassed by a small Boer force. He executed the classic cavalry manœuvre of turning half right, so that while approaching closer and closer to his intended crossing of the Modder in front, he appeared to be making for a ford far to the right, where the Boers hastily prepared to resist him.

The pace told on man and horse. The animals had no water; and especially those pulling the guns and vehicles suffered greatly. The veld was so dry that it caught fire from a trooper's match, burning the telegraph wire. At last the green banks of the Modder appeared and the whole force wheeled and charged for the crossing. Groups of Boers in the vicinity fled, leaving wagons of welcome food. The British forded the river to occupy some kopjes beyond, securing their bridgehead, then threw themselves down to rest and drink the muddy water. A blinding dust storm descended through which stragglers made their way to camp; there were many, for 500 horses were dead or no longer fit to ride. But French could report success in his vital task, and the vanguard of the main body trudged on towards the position he had gained.

Behind him the whole expedition was now adrift from the railway line. It strung out in a huge procession approaching or crossing the Riet. Great palls of dust hung over the fords as the animals strained to pull wagons axle-deep in sand. The mules could not pull their wagons and had to be replaced for the crossing by the oxen. To haul each of the naval guns across, 400 men were needed in addition to teams of oxen.

Though he was now situated to make a dash for Kimberley, French could not leave the Modder until sufficient of the infantry came up to hold it in strength. The leading division did not reach him for two days despite a forced march of twenty-four miles in as many hours, the last stage of the journey taking place in darkness and a rainstorm.

During these two days the incredible truth dawned on Cronje that despite their distance from the railway not only cavalry but infantry were marching round his flank; and that the enemy were on the Modder not ten miles from his head laager. Once again he made a wrong deduction. He thought the British were trying to draw him eastwards from his Magersfontein defences, which they would then attack from the south and south-east. It was wishful thinking induced by reluctance to abandon defences so laboriously constructed and to move with his great encumbrance of wagons and all the women and children who had flocked to the laagers. Therefore he stayed where he was though he withdrew his head laager a little northwards from Jacobsdal, leaving his own and captured British wounded at the hospital there in the care of mainly German doctors, and sent only 800 men to confront French. These took up position a short distance in front of him.

As soon as the leading infantry division arrived and covered the crossing he had seized, French set out on the ride that he hoped would end twenty miles away in Kimberley. It was 8.30 a.m. on 15 February.

After leaving the river the cavalry were shelled, but the field batteries quickly silenced the two guns Cronje had sent with the 800 men.

225

These were posted along two miles of kopjes around a broad valley which narrowed towards the further end, marked by a low ridge. French decided to ride through the valley: if he succeeded he would have broken clean through the Boer defences and Kimberley would lie almost at his feet.

So was the stage set in front of the infantry for one of the last of the great cavalry charges. The German *Official History* records: 'The spectacle displayed to the eyes of the sixth division was magnificent; every man held his breath; the moment was one of the most extreme tension, for it seemed that the result of the bold attempt must be the utter destruction of the gallant riders.' The 9th and 16th Lancers were first into the valley. As they thundered forward they sent up a huge cloud of dust into which the Boers poured their fire. Wave upon wave of horsemen followed, their pennants flying, lances poised, sabres bare. Behind them the artillery kept up a bombardment until the very last moment. The dust and wide formation of the galloping horses made accurate marksmanship impossible. All the Boers and the watching British soldiers could see was an occasional riderless horse. Only at the end of the valley, as thousands of cavalrymen charged on to the ridge, did the Boers make out their adversaries, and then but fleetingly before they broke and fled from all round the valley, leaving a score captured or speared.

To the terror of the cavalry charge was added the knowledge of what it might mean to the whole Boer position, and the flying burghers carried panic like a contagion wherever they went. French paused only for an hour while his force recovered wind and strength, then he rode on. He was passing close to the head laager Cronje had moved from Jacobsdal: had he known of this and of the panic, he could have seized a rich prize. But his target was Kimberley—and in another hour he could see it in the distance.

Away to his left rear, the Magersfontein range was aflame with a sustained bombardment unleashed by Methuen, fully occupying Cronje's main force. And the Boers besieging the town, their numerical inferiority made worse by the psychological blow of French's tumultuous break-through, were already melting away like mist. But French could not advance. The British in Kimberley would not believe that relief had come at last. Despite a great column of dust which had told them the previous afternoon that an army was on the move, they suspected a hideous trick and took a long time to be persuaded that the horsemen on the horizon were their own.

At last, shortly after 4 o'clock, a patrol of Australian horse rode into the town. People emerged from their shelters, and from the 1,200-foot mine-shafts where Rhodes had provided safety since the Boers' Long Tom opened up, in an intoxication of delight. Towards evening when French rode in, thousands lined the streets to cheer that squat figure whose seat for a cavalryman was remarkably awkward and whose face, in accordance with the military fashion of the day, bore an emotionless expression. The news was flashed to an England for whom it meant the first real success after months of anguish, and totally unexpected: *Kimberley has been relieved.* The four months' siege, the near-strangulation of hope, was over. It had cost over 1,500 deaths among whites and Natives from wounds or disease, and many women were said to have minds permanently impaired by the strain.

But large though Kimberley loomed in the imagination of the watching world, the relief of the town was militarily almost the least important of the crowded day's events.

While French was making his break-through after leaving the advance infantry division posted on the Modder, the long procession of infantry and transport continued far behind. Part of the force wheeled in to Jacobsdal, the C.I.V. going into action for the first time to overcome stern resistance by a small party of burghers, and to occupy the former Boer headquarters for use as Roberts's own headquarters and base. Still further behind, the long haul of the transport columns had been so slow that a convoy consisting of 170 wagons, the leading section of the great 'supply park', was just through the crossing of the Riet—this fifth day since the cavalry first seized it. The oxen were exhausted after doing much of the mules' work as well as their own. As they rested at the river under the surveillance of a small escort Christian de Wet suddenly appeared.

With reinforcements from Fauresmith his strength was now a thousand men. As he advanced, the oxen were driven down to the shelter of the river bank, a laager made of the wagons, and breast-works built of oat-sacks and biscuit-tins. For a time the escort held the Boers off. Then when they tried to get the oxen away, De Wet fired into the animals, making them stampede: the Native drivers bolted, and 1,600 oxen were lost to the British. Reinforcements were sent for from the infantry far ahead, but by nightfall reports reaching Roberts made clear that more men would be needed to save the convoy.

Here was a serious predicament. He wanted every available man well up, for Cronje might at any moment throw himself on one part or another of the long line strung out between the Riet and the Modder. On the other hand, if Bloemfontein were to be reached all transport and supplies possible would be needed. Could he let go 170 wagons packed with food and forage? He consulted his Service Corps commander, who told him that only half-rations would be left. Then pacing up and down for a moment he said, 'I'll do it. I think the men will do it for me.'

The convoy set upon by De Wet was abandoned. Whether the decision would turn out to be rash or wise, it took courage to make and increased the hazards of the future. Other generals than Napoleon have known the nightmare of marching unprovisioned through a hostile land. Immediate action was taken to make good as much of the loss as possible. Refugees arriving from outlying districts had their wagons commandeered, Red Cross vehicles were stripped of their markings, and the hauling of supplies from the nearest point on the railway to Jacobsdal started without delay.

Roberts need not have been anxious about Cronje's hostile intent. Cronje was a broken man. While Methuen's guns roared at him he heard the news of French's break-through to Kimberley and he was gripped by a paralysis of will. He scarcely moved from his tent where he sat in utter dejection while his wife patted his head. Burgher after burgher came to him, imploring him to act before the semicircle of steel closing on him made flight impossible. After many hours he roused himself to thought and action. He could not go north, because French was in Kimberley; nor south, because of Methuen; and the west, though open, offered nothing but an inhospitable waste to which he could not commit his women and children. Eastwards lay his only hope: there seemed no British yet between the advance division waiting at the Modder and French in Kimberley. Before the gap were closed he might hope to slip through. He would thus not only maintain his communication with Bloemfontein, but cover the approaches to the capital if Roberts, contrary to all Boer calculation, marched eastwards against it.

By midnight the Magersfontein defences were abandoned. 5,000 men, many with their families, moved away in a convoy of 400 wagons and several thousand horses. To the distress and anxiety of flight was added grief at leaving their sick and wounded in Jacobsdal. The moon was up, shining all too brightly upon them; their route was only four miles north of the Modder; the British were on both sides of them: they could scarcely hope to escape detection. Slowly, at the nerve-racking slowness of an ox's pace, they made their way eastwards.

As dawn began to break, advance British units were setting off from the Modder to close the gap with French: an infantry division and a brigade of M.I. under O. C. Hannay, with Kitchener himself present to ensure speed. And then in the grey light a huge pall of dust to the north-east announced that it was too late: the Boers were through.

So defective were British scouting methods that not a soul had seen Cronje's flight clean across their line. Even now no one knew whether the convoy was Cronje's or a secondary one while Cronje himself prepared to attack French in the north.

Hannay's M.I. at once rode off in pursuit. Kitchener sent out an order to the infantry, 'Objective changed. Go for convoy.' The M.I. advanced eastward to get between the river and the convoy. An unauthorized order brought them to a halt, offering a sitting target to the Boer rearguard posted on a hill half a mile away. Swept by fire, men and horses plunged down the steep river bank and there was inextricable confusion as they struggled in the water or thick mud. When the division of infantry eventually came up they were held off by skilful Boer rearguard tactics. All this time the convoy was drawing well away.

Roberts was in a quandary. There were no fresh troops near enough to join in the attack. He hesitated to divert any of the troops strung out south of the Modder because the abandonment of Magersfontein was only discovered by Methuen at midday and Roberts was still uncertain of where Cronje himself was. He telegraphed French to send part of his force to head off the convoy, but Cronje had cut the telegraph wire on his way through and the message never arrived.

Thus Cronje and the convoy got away to a distance safe enough for the moment and he formed a laager near the river. The M.I., recovered from their confusion, rode up towards the opposite bank and with a battery of guns tried to harry him but were driven away by a sharp counter-attack.

Meanwhile French, unaware of Cronje's break-out, was intent on trying to round up the Boers who had been besieging Kimberley. One body, under the siege commander, J. S. Ferreira, had already gone north-east; but the main body with their great Long Tom and their loaded wagons were now twenty miles to the north. French went after them. His vanguard reached the sandy dunes where the Boers had posted themselves to protect their convoy. In a hard-hitting action the British gained the advantage but could not exploit it because no water was to be had and their horses were exhausted. The remainder of the force did not come up in support because it was tenaciously detained by less than 200 rebel Boers. French had the galling experience of watching his prize trek away not five miles in front of him as he gave the order to withdraw while his horses still had strength to carry him back to Kimberley. On the way he turned his batteries loose on the rebel Boers who had thwarted him, but a dust storm came swirling across the veld and under cover of it the Boers leapt on their ponies and escaped.

It had been a wretched day for the British. The previous day's relief of Kimberley had been a substantial achievement; but the Boers had not been defeated in battle and were largely intact. Now the besiegers of Kimberley had got clean away, and the main force under Cronje required only a short rest and another march to place them out of reach.

The outlook for Roberts's communications was at this moment forbidding. From the Central Front came news that General R. A. P. Clements, who had replaced French in command before Colesburg, was in difficulties. De la Rey, after his rebuff at New Zealand Hill, had felt out the British strength and persuaded Schoeman to co-operate in an all-out offensive. Delays by Schoeman, and then stout resistance by an Australian contingent and the Wiltshires in particular, made Boer progress slow, but Clements reported that he had retired to Arundel, bringing the capture of Naauwpoort and De Aar in ever closer likelihood.

While this was the situation behind Roberts, in front of him he had the prospect of lengthening lines of communication, short supplies because of De Wet's coup, and a Cronje given time to be reinforced and prepare defences astride the precious water line of the Modder— for by nightfall Roberts knew for certain that the convoy escaping eastwards was indeed Cronje's main force. Roberts staked everything on speed. He issued orders for the whole army to march as fast as possible in pursuit of Cronje's convoy—as the leading infantry and Hannay's M.I. had already started to do. Kitchener flung his energies into hustling men forward all through the night, and a message was at last got through to French at Kimberley telling him to head off the convoy at a point fifteen miles ahead of its present position so that the infantry might have time to catch up.

But the cavalry were in a poor way. The day's futile expedition north of Kimberley had been the sixth day of almost continuous action in midsummer heat since the flank march started. Many of the horses had not had time to be conditioned at the start and men overloaded them through ignorance of horse-mastership. An officer wrote in his diary: 'I had a horse-parade, and there were only 28 horses that could raise a trot. A week ago I commanded the best mounted regiment in the British Army, and now it is absolutely ruined.' The result was that when Roberts's message reached French, only 1,200 sound horses could be mustered to attempt the thirty-mile dash to the point designated.

French allowed a few hours' rest, and then accompanied by two batteries of field-guns the force set out on their forlorn mission. Not only were they hoping to stop a determined body of 5,000 Boers but, unknown to them, J. S. Ferreira's force several hundred stronger than their own was roaming across their path.

At the same time, as a new day stole upon the wide spaces of the veld, Cronje had resumed his progress eastwards. He was in no hurry. Even though he did not know that the British infantry had been making forced marches through the night and were plodding on under the relentless urging of Kitchener, he did know that he had only to keep going to outdistance any pursuit completely.

Just before noon, after passing a hill on the north bank of the Modder called Paardeberg, he prepared to cross the river in order to take the Bloemfontein road. The banks of the river were steep, often like cliffs, before the fringe of sand and rock shelf was reached along the water's edge; but the leading wagons began to descend by a convenient declivity in the nearer bank, while the men lay down in the shade of trees or helped prepare the midday meal. Into this quiet pastoral scene suddenly burst a salvo of shells.

It was a literal bolt from the blue that caught the Boers so unprepared that panic broke out. As hundreds of oxen scattered, men, women and children rushed for the shelter of the bank. None paused to investigate the size of the force attacking them.

French had eluded J. S. Ferreira, or rather startled him to flight like the buck and hares and birds that scattered before his mere appearance on the horizon, and so after a ride of remarkable endurance he arrived unmolested and unseen at a hill a mile and a half north of Cronje. As his guns sprayed the crossing, small groups of Boers presently tried to dislodge him but were dispersed by the unmounted troopers lying among the rocks. The bulk of the Boer force remained in a state of fruitless panic. They could not collect their oxen or get the wagons across under shell-fire which they did nothing to stop.

Yet French was in a position of extreme precariousness, even when some M.I. reinforcements reached him. The Boers on the Modder outnumbered him nearly four to one; he was safe only so long as they did not turn on him, and if Ferreira's force came up in rear of him he might be annihilated. As hour succeeded hour through the hot after-noon he anxiously scanned the western skyline. It seemed a miracle when straining eyes caught a glimpse of an approaching force from the west. Kitchener had driven the infantry on a march of thirty miles in twenty-four hours of mostly scorching heat, and he halted them a mile or two from the Boer outposts. They were exhausted, covered in dust that lined their throats and caked their lips, and they had only their emergency rations. But Cronje was all but cornered.

The day had thus retrieved the misfortune of the previous twenty-four hours. But Roberts was suddenly taken ill at Jacobsdal, and con-fusion resulted as to whether Kitchener's position of Chief of Staff entitled him to command, or the infantry commanders present who were his senior in rank. In the result Kitchener asserted command, one of the commanders—General T. Kelly-Kenny, an Irishman who had been fighting in China while Kitchener was still a child—huffily tele-graphed Roberts: 'This is not a time to enter into personal matters. Till this phase of the operation is completed, I will submit to even humiliation.'

As night closed over the scene, Kitchener and his two aides-de-camp lay down to snatch some rest for the morrow.

In the Boer laager many commandants urged Cronje to break away before the British surrounded him. He rejected their advice. Too large a proportion of his men were unmounted owing to the horses lost through poor feeding. To break away would also mean to abandon the wagons, which were his burghers' private property. He had already sent for reinforcements from Bloemfontein; and he could count on Ferreira with 1,500 men to the north, and on De Wet with a similar force closing in from the south.

He would fight it out.

CHAPTER XIII

Paardeberg: February 1900

18 FEBRUARY: FIRST DAY

Kitchener believed that Cronje had 10,000, not 5,000 men and he knew that other Boer forces in the offing might arrive at any moment. Besides French's force to the north, he himself had 15,000 men whom he was resolved to hurl on Cronje without delay, since the remainder

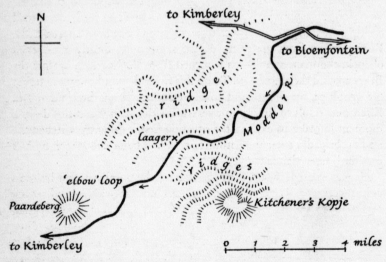

of the British infantry could not be expected before late afternoon, too tired for immediate use.

Dawn broke to reveal the Modder River flowing sinuously from the north-east, cutting its way between high steep banks 200–300 yards apart. The Boer wagons were in a straggling line along the veld above the northern bank, with a concentration about midway to form a

laager. Close to this, oxen and women and children were below the
bank—on the rocks or sand which bordered the water, and to some
extent screened by foliage. In addition to their wagons the burghers had
hasty defences of shallow trenches scratched out of the veld above the
banks on both sides of the river and in the banks themselves. Upstream
and down from their central laager they occupied altogether about
five miles of the river.

The country on either side of the river extended in a gently rising
gradient to a ring of low ridges and kopjes. The river was therefore
like a deep crack across a shallow saucer with the laager in the centre.
On the northern rim was French's force gradually augmented by men
previously left behind in Kimberley. On the western rim, near the
south bank downstream from the laager, was Kitchener's force. The
nearest Boers occupied a part of the river which hereabouts twisted in
an elbow pointing north, whereafter it was comparatively straight.

At dawn units of Hannay's M.I. with infantry support worked their
way along the south bank. They left the bend behind them, continued
well past the laager, then crossed the river and began to approach the
Boer position from upstream. At the same time, shortly after seven
o'clock, the main assault was launched from downstream against the
Boers around the river bend. To do this from the south meant entering
the crook of the elbow and so drawing fire from three sides. But
Kitchener, resolved simply to overwhelm the enemy and not delay a
moment in order to explore the situation first, exultantly watched the
leading brigades enter the battle zone. 'We'll be in the laager by half
past ten!' he exclaimed.

He was excited, inflamed by the sight of the bombardment his guns
unleashed on the laager, blowing up ammunition wagons and setting
others alight, and his killer instinct inflexibly resolved him on storming
tactics which filled the older commanders with foreboding. They
would have preferred to surround the laager and reduce it with a
minimum of loss. They obeyed orders dutifully but it was not with a
will that they sent their men forward against a hail of fire.

An hour's desperate fighting followed before the leading troops,
bayonets fixed, reached most of the bank within their side of the bend.
But they were too exhausted and their losses were too great for them
to attempt a crossing. To Kitchener it was essential to clear the whole of
the bend so that he could advance along both banks into the heart of

the laager. He threw in the Highland Brigade who tried to advance on the left. They too suffered severely. A Cameron piper leapt into the river just below the bend and found a safe crossing for reinforcements of Seaforths and Black Watch. With Canadians and other units joining them, the left arm of the bend was thus under attack from both banks while pressure on the right arm continued from the south bank. Presently troops sent round to the north attacked from that quarter, placing the bend under fire from north, west and south, but the Boers bitterly contested every inch the British tried to advance. For hours the bloody struggle raged and still they clung to the bend. At the same time the combination of Hannay's M.I. and infantry upstream of the laager could not develop their attack because the reinforcements Cronje relied on from Bloemfontein had arrived in rear of them and fully engaged their attention.

Cronje himself was in the river-bed, and in the tempest above and around him he seemed to find a grim consummation. He sat holding his wife's hand, comforting her in the midst of a pandemonium of ammunition wagons blowing up in a fusillade of explosions, rifle-fire, the crash of artillery, the cries of wounded men and frightened children, the bellowing of animals.

But if his men had entrenched themselves hastily they had a genius for concealment and the British artillery found extreme difficulty in locating them. 'Mon,' a Scots gunner said, 'the guns would be better sighted wi' ear trumpets.'

Not being staffed for executive command, Kitchener lacked the means of having tactical details worked out and orders properly disseminated. But even if he had it is unlikely he would have behaved differently. As at Omdurman, he himself galloped all over the field trying to co-ordinate his attack from every direction. In the appalling noise and confusion he gave orders piecemeal to whomever he could lay hold of, whether commanding officer or subordinate. Hence no single-minded purpose animated those carrying out the offensive: 'I was in a complete fog,' records H. Smith-Dorrien, one of his best brigade commanders.[34] Half past ten came and went with little to show for the hours of savage fighting, except mounting losses that sickened the older officers.

But nothing could deflect Kitchener from his consuming purpose. As the attack on the bend began to wither he insisted that Hannay's

M.I. and the infantry upstream disengage themselves from the Bloemfontein force and concentrate everything on attacking the laager by
pushing forward along both banks of the river from that side. This they
attempted to do, but the attack failed to carry to more than a thousand
yards of the laager. Hannay sent back a galloper to Kitchener with a
message that any further advance was out of the question. His men,
like those concentrated about the bend downstream, were utterly
exhausted. They had rested for only a few hours after twenty-four of
continuous marching under gruelling conditions and some had not even
had time to eat before being pitched into the desperate struggle of
the day.

Still Kitchener was not satisfied. He saw the smoking ruins of the
Boer wagons and the carnage wrought by his guns. He knew that his
own losses must in some measure be matched by those of the enemy,
and he had men to expend that they had not. No consideration of flesh
and blood would deter him. He decided now to leave the south bank
almost entirely, and throw everything into attacking from both upstream and down along the northern bank where the laager lay. While
troops were detached from the south bank for this purpose he replied
to Hannay's message: 'The time has now come for a final effort. All
troops have been warned that the laager must be rushed at all costs.
Try and carry [the infantry support] with you, but if they cannot go,
the M.I. should do it. Gallop up if necessary and fire into the laager.'

Hannay was a brave Highlander but to him these were the words of
a madman blinded by blood-lust. The time was after 3 o'clock: for
eight hours attack upon attack had achieved nothing but five miles of
ruin and death to his countrymen and Boers alike. As Thorneycroft
on Spion Kop had experienced, exhaustion and anguish drain away all
faith—but unlike Thorneycroft he had clear orders. And regarding
them as inhuman, he resolved upon a soldier's protest.

He sent away his staff on various pretexts and placed himself at the
head of a small group of his M.I. whom he instructed to advance. He
was complying with his orders. But as the group advanced he galloped
ahead, far outstripping them, and rode full-tilt into the Boer defences.
The Boers hesitated. 'We didn't know what to think of this lone horseman rushing at us,' one of them has related.[35] 'We didn't want to
shoot a man so blatantly inviting death and so defenceless. But we were
afraid that he was running berserk or would suddenly wheel away to

give information about us. We had no choice. We shot him.' He fell riddled with bullets inside the Boer lines. Today his grave is preserved, a lonely monument in the quiet reaches of the veld above the Modder.

The battle raged on. Upstream and down the British strove to advance. It was late in the afternoon when Kitchener launched a frantic last assault from all sides. On the north bank the Cornwalls charged with fixed bayonets against the Boers in the bend downstream, while upstream battalions of Welsh and Essex thrust forward along the route of Hannay's last ride.

At this moment Christian de Wet once again appeared out of nowhere. Without delay he stormed a hill—called Kitchener's Kopje—a mile or two south of the river and directly opposite the laager. Some British were posted on it whom he rapidly killed or captured, then he fired a string of pompom shells westwards, just below the river bend. Some transport had arrived there not long before and in seconds the oxen, officers anxiously watching the last attacks, and wounded in an emergency hospital tent were scattered in all directions. Kitchener— 'swearing violently'[36]—had immediately to divert men and guns to deal with him.

At about the same time, Ferreira, having arrived upstream of the laager, joined hands with the Bloemfontein contingent. Opening up on some of the British batteries pounding the laager, they too caused the attackers to divert men and guns.

Helped by these arrivals and given fresh vigour Cronje's men at the bend threw back the charge of the Cornwalls, who should have been supported by a brigade north of them, but the overcast sky prevented Kitchener's heliogram reaching it. Upstream of the laager the Essex and Welsh were likewise brought to a halt. As night came exhausted men laid down their rifles. Most were desperate for water, which the enemy despite his own straits allowed them to get from the nearest part of the river.

On the British side 1,300 casualties were the cost of Kitchener's day-long efforts to storm the laager, but he was scarcely any closer to success than he had been at dawn. His failure was ironical in stemming from neglect of his own principles of thorough preparation, so that he had attacked the toughest part of the Boer defences and then lacked the means of communicating orders properly. He had never fought white men before and had no acquaintance with the Boers' mercurial

fighting spirit which, sustained by the iron will of Cronje, that day
expressed itself in skill and courage of a very high order.

Nevertheless he had largely destroyed their mobility; and had Buller
and Methuen used as he had the whole of the force to hand, and with
his ferocity, Black Week might never have been. Yet older men
deplored an attitude which strove so ruthlessly for victory. In the controversy that followed the Battle of Paardeberg, Kitchener appeared to
lose no sleep over criticism of his tactics. 'I hope the authorities will
keep their hair on,' he wrote to one of his pedigree lady friends, 'and if
they want a victim to sacrifice I am always at their disposal. War means
risks, and you cannot play the game and always win.' (Not however 'a
game of polo, with intervals for tea', which was his description of his
brother officer's attitude to war. The controversy did not reach the
public's ears because of the strictness of the military censorship. Even a
year later it was generally unknown whether Kitchener or Kelly-
Kenny was in command.)

The Boers' battered laager was not a scene of rejoicing. They were
hardly less exhausted than the British, and their casualties of 300 had
been relatively heavy. All their doctors had been left behind at
Jacobsdal so that the women had to do what they could for the
wounded. The outlook was disagreeable unless help came quickly.
Again Cronje's commandants urged him to break out. Again he
refused. But he shortened his line along the river: the dogged defence
of the bend downstream could not be sustained indefinitely against
enveloping attacks, so the positions there were quietly abandoned
during the night.

19 FEBRUARY: SECOND DAY

Thus in the morning Kitchener found that only two miles of the
river were now occupied. His target had contracted and he was eager
to renew the onslaught, especially as the whole field force was now
present. The other commanders so vigorously demurred that Roberts
was appealed to for a decision. He had been disturbed by reports of the
battle the previous day and, having nearly recovered from his illness,
left Jacobsdal at four in the morning and reached Paardeberg by 10 a.m.

The wagon in which he travelled was his headquarters. To it a messenger came from Cronje requesting a twenty-four-hour armistice for
the dead and wounded to be dealt with. Roberts's humanity tussled with

the tactical necessity of not allowing the Boers time to rest, strengthen their defences or bring up more reinforcements. He rejected the request and called on Cronje to surrender. Cronje answered: 'Since you are so unmerciful as not to accord the time asked for, nothing remains for me to do. You do as you wish.'

This was mistranslated from the Dutch to mean surrender. On the troops moving towards the Boer trenches a hot fire drove them back. Roberts sent to Cronje to ask him what he meant. 'During my life-time,' Cronje replied, 'I will never surrender. If you wish to bombard, fire away. *Dixi*.'

It was a defiant, even an arrogant, exclamation by a man so apparently doomed in the midst of a charred and reeking encampment among the corpses and carcasses strewn along the river. Less than 5,000 men were surrounded by six times their number and almost completely exposed to bombardment by scores of guns. Yet as he rode out to view the scene Roberts could not feel certain of success. None of his senior officers except Kitchener wanted to pay a further instalment on the price of attempting a direct assault, and his hospital service was already over-strained without all the casualties of another attack. The alternative was a siege which would take time, and time was pregnant with danger.

Milner's warnings had acquired a haunting validity ever since the Boers at Colesburg had pushed the British back to Arundel. Though the five days since then had surprisingly not seen a further thrust, the moment must be very near. That it had not come before was in spite of De la Rey's and Piet de Wet's urgings. The inertia bred by Schoeman's previous inactivity and the burghers' insistence on their rights as free men not to be hustled, had resulted in their moving their wagons across the hills with time-consuming slowness. Then the start of Roberts's march had filled President Steyn with such uncertainty that he forbade a further advance. But on the very day Roberts viewed the situation at Paardeberg the Boers decided to launch an offensive within the next twenty-four hours. While Roberts did not have this precise informa-tion, the imminence of attack and of all it might imply for his own situation was clear enough.

The danger closer at hand was even greater. At any moment fresh reinforcements might arrive for Christian de Wet's and Ferreira's commandos. (Ferreira in fact was dead: inspecting his pickets in the night he had prodded a sleeping sentry whose rifle went off with fatal results. Consequently, De Wet assumed command over both forces.) If reinforcements strong enough and quick enough rescued the laager, and if Roberts were harried and delayed in attempting pursuit, he might be stranded in the middle of the veld until, cut off from the Cape, he starved and bled to death. De Wet's coup had already made him short of supplies, while his horses had eaten little for the past couple of days.

In the face of threats so appalling Roberts hesitated, and put off decision for the present. Strenuous efforts were made to bring up supplies, helped by Rhodes who organized small convoys from Kimberley. The only military activity authorized for the moment apart from continued bombardment was an attempt to dislodge De Wet from Kitchener's Kopje. He had hauled up guns in the night to shell the British from an early hour, and now all through the day he beat off infantry attacks while by heliograph he encouraged Cronje with the assurance that help was on the way. Nearly a hundred men were able to dash to him from the laager under cover of his fire.

The Boer Governments were exhorting their people in all the less menaced areas to hurry to Paardeberg. Kruger and Steyn were under intense strain, for as will presently be described events in Natal were also mounting to a climax at this time. Nevertheless, 2,000 men were detached from the Natal Front and were on their way under General A. P. Cronje, while from elsewhere too a spreading tide of reinforcements was beginning to roll in. The main body of Boers who had besieged Kimberley and then eluded French in their northward flight hung back, and temporized with a request for instructions which, as Transvaalers, they sent to their Commander-in-Chief in Natal. Joubert answered:

> How is this possible? Are there not instructions enough from the banks of the Modder River, whence for so many days already General Cronje has been calling in his agony 'Come relieve me'? What other instructions can now be given or demanded than, with one voice and with one mouth, 'Burghers of South Africa, go and help deliver your General from the might of the tyrant'? ... Relieve Cronje, cost what it will ... wavering and doubt, unbelief and mistrust, will not only bring sorrow on our South Africa and the whole Afrikaans people, but destroy our whole

national existence. Therefore trust firmly in God and He shall give you strength. Relieve Cronje.

20 FEBRUARY: THIRD DAY

The relief of Cronje had become the dominating theme in Boer thought and emotion. Operations far from the scene lost vitality even though they might bear directly on the laager's fate.

Thus the attack launched at last on the British at Arundel on Clements's sector of the Central Front was lamely pressed, and weakened by the recall of many burghers that same day to Bloemfontein. De la Rey's shrewdness and zeal availed nothing. Clements beat off the attack with little difficulty, and as the Boers drew away in increasing numbers to deal with Roberts the offensive on this sector passed rapidly from them.

On the other hand Milner sent him anxious messages about two Transvaal commandants, Steenkamp and Liebenberg, who had crossed the Orange below its junction with the Vaal and were drumming up rebels in the wide Prieska–Carnarvon area of the western Cape, from which they might move against De Aar and the Western railway. Roberts at once put in hand arrangements to meet this threat.

He could now feel reasonably comfortable about his lines of communication. He decided definitely not to risk storming Cronje's laager but to reduce it by siege. He positioned his guns to keep up a sustained bombardment. Unable to fire full out because ammunition was short, they were used to prevent the Boers massing for a sortie while the shelters they had made for their food and animals were systematically blasted out. But as his operations drew off, as he had anticipated, Boers from the other fronts he faced the growing risk of help reaching the laager from outside. His first need was to dislodge De Wet before his position became formidable.

21 FEBRUARY: FOURTH DAY

Strong infantry forces were posted between Kitchener's Kopje and the river, while French with the cavalry approached in a wide arc from the south with the idea of driving De Wet into their arms. De Wet was not one to wait while his enemy encircled him. He led his men in a furious gallop down a valley French had left unblocked, and got clean away almost unscathed. This was the birth of his legendary fame as a phantom figure. He rode on to a village called Poplar Grove between Paardeberg and Bloemfontein, where he fell in with the first of the Natal reinforcements under General A. P. Cronje, and the village now became the rallying point for the Boers flocking to rescue Cronje.

Roberts learned for the first time that women and children were in the Boer laager. Cronje declined his offer of a safe-conduct for them. Roberts also offered doctors and medical supplies, but would not accept Cronje's condition that the doctors would have to remain in the laager, presumably to avoid leakage of information. Cronje proposed a neutral hospital but Roberts did not reciprocate Joubert's quixotic gesture at Ladysmith, and refused.

With De Wet out of the way he could concentrate on trying to throttle the life out of the laager. He disposed his troops in two complete rings around it, the further about a mile and a half from the Boers, the closer only three-quarters of a mile. They kept up a relentless pressure. On the west, pushing forward along the north bank from the ill-starred bend, they actually reached to within 600 yards of the Boer trenches. All the time machine-guns and upwards of fifty pieces of artillery, ranging from twelve-pounders to four great naval 4.7s, made all movement within the enemy lines impossible and filled the river bank with a green cloud of lyddite fumes.

Yet a Boer was remarkably safe in the trench he had now perfected. In section it was like a short bottle: a narrow opening, scarcely wide enough for him to stand in with his rifle, descended to a broader hole in which he could lie down. Here, day-long in the heat, he endured flies and unhygienic conditions which added to the stench of rotting carcasses—so great that it could be smelt for miles around, and as carrion also infected the river the latter became known to the British troops as dead-horse soup. Cronje's chief danger was therefore not the fire that pitilessly combed his defences but disease and starvation.

Kitchener's attitude to the slowness of such a method is not recorded, but significantly Roberts this day was relieved of his presence by sending him to organize railway- and bridge-repairs as the Boers drew away from the Colesburg area.

22 FEBRUARY: FIFTH DAY

From a balloon sent up a thousand feet an engineer made sketches of the Boer position. He also signalled the artillery on the accuracy of their aim. The Boers had no respite from shell or bullet. They waited and prayed for help from their countrymen.

Those gathering at Poplar Grove now totalled 4,000. They were not in good heart. The sudden turn of events precipitated by Roberts's flank march had cast them down. But conscious that every minute increased the suffering of the besieged and the possibility of disaster, the leaders determined not to wait for more men but to strike hard before morning. They would thrust away the British south-east of the laager and by keeping clear an arc from Kitchener's Kopje to the river upstream provide an escape corridor for Cronje.

23 FEBRUARY: SIXTH DAY

In the result many burghers skulked behind and only in parts did the attack on Roberts's lines attain any vigour. Cronje did not mount a co-ordinated attack because cloudy weather prevented messages being heliographed to him. The attempt fizzled out. De Wet withdrew to Poplar Grove, the spirit of his men as dampened by the failure as were their bodies by the rain that came pelting down.

The deluge at first brought some relief to the laager, for a great many carcasses were washed away in the rising river. But soon it added to the discomfort of men confined to their narrow trenches. The wounded were particularly wretched. Cronje agreed to release all wounded British prisoners, Roberts allowing an equal number of Boer wounded to leave the laager for the Jacobsdal hospital. But these humane arrangements did not diminish the intensity of the siege.

24 FEBRUARY: SEVENTH DAY

Still it rained, all through the night and all day, warm and flooding rain.

With his colleagues at Poplar Grove De Wet decided that the only course now was to distract the British while Cronje fought his way out. Because of the rain the heliograph was useless. A certain Daniel ('Danie') Theron volunteered to try and get the message through to Cronje.

Theron had formed a corps of scouts that bore his name, but this was a mission for himself alone, which accorded with a character noted as singular before the war when he thrashed a certain Mr. Moneypenny who ran a scandal-sheet in Johannesburg. 'He was a slight, wiry man of about twenty-six, dark-complexioned and short-tempered,' Reitz describes him, adding that 'although I never saw him really affable, his men swore by him for his courage and gift of leadership.'

In the evening he rode through the darkness and the deluge towards the British lines. He crawled through their outposts, then had to swim the river which had become dangerously swollen. But he reached the laager safely and conveyed De Wet's plan to Cronje.

25 FEBRUARY: EIGHTH DAY

Cronje called his commandants together. De Wet's proposal was clearly their only hope and they agreed to attempt the break-out that night. But the continuous rain had risen the river by eight feet and though this had now washed away a thousand of the loathsome carcasses, it created a barrier of swirling water which would have to be crossed before even the British siege lines were reached. The break-out attempt was deferred until after they had built a bridge.

They were close to that limit of endurance where a man loses the will to escape the very cause of his agony. Imprisoned in their narrow water-logged trenches under the constant strain of high explosive and lacerating shrapnel, unable to still the cries of their wounded or properly bury their dead, choked by shell fumes and the stench of putrefaction and excrement, they were prevented from surrendering only by the iron hand of Cronje. He would not yield. Their food was giving out. They were desperately anxious about their women and children. They felt abandoned by their countrymen. But Cronje kept them to the task of holding back the relentless pressure of the encircling British infantrymen.

The latter were also under considerable strain. The stench reached out to them and the muddy infected river was their lot too. They had no cover against the continuous downpour. Their ration was only one and a half biscuits and a lump of trek-ox. Their long forced marches capped by their ordeal in Kitchener's attack on the 18th, and then keeping up an investment while never knowing when a relieving force might fall upon them, had bitten deep into physical strength and morale alike. To Roberts came increasingly serious news of the rebellion in the western Cape, threatening many towns* and an imminent move towards vital De Aar.

* Upington, Caledonia, Carnarvon, Victoria West.

Instinctively aware that the climax to the siege was near, Paul Kruger led his people in an all-night vigil of prayer in the Transvaal churches.

26 FEBRUARY: NINTH DAY

The bridge had been started, but now hardly a voice was raised in favour of the proposed break-out and many officers openly urged surrender. Cronje was immovable, the more so because the next day would be Majuba Day, a sacred anniversary for the Boers because of their victory over the British in the First Boer War. To Cronje it meant that if his countrymen did not come to smite the British, the God who had been the shield and sword of His people surely would. Decision was postponed for two days.

In the afternoon Roberts brought into action several pompoms which in previous actions had been a Boer monopoly, pouring out a stream of one-pound shells notable for their demoralizing effect. Even more serious for the Boers, a siege train of four howitzers arrived and started to drop 120-pound shells: as each exploded a cloud of smoke took shape, an eye-witness said, 'like rows of magic trees springing suddenly into life'. Under this eerie beauty the whole earth shook and soon the bridge which the Boers had painfully advanced was destroyed. At the same time the infantry pressing from the west reached to within only a couple of hundred yards of the trenches.

By evening the opinion was general that the end had come.

27 FEBRUARY: TENTH DAY

Hector Macdonald, wounded on the first day's battle, had vivid memories of Majuba where he had also been wounded and which he longed to avenge. He sent Roberts a message imploring a decisive attack to mark the anniversary. Roberts hesitated, but agreed when the Royal Canadians undertook to lead the action. Commanded by Colonel W. D. Otter, they were made up of 'elegant extracts' from the best-known militia units in the Dominion, including a fine French company, and they occupied the foremost position reached the previous day on the west. In the dark of early morning they advanced to within sixty yards of the trenches before a withering fire compelled them to lie flat, but they kept up the attack for two hours while engineers dug trenches immediately behind them. These the Canadians securely occupied at daybreak.

At this moment Danie Theron slipped away from the laager and once more penetrated the British lines. Making his way back to Poplar Grove he announced that the laager's doom was sealed. President Steyn arrived at the village to hear the news, and departed at once to organize the defence of his capital.

Between 5 and 6 a.m. the Boers raised white flags above their trenches facing the Canadians. Other groups followed suit. Cronje could not stop them. He bowed his head at last and sent a message to Roberts that he surrendered, throwing his burghers on the mercy of Her Britannic Majesty. Roberts at once ordered the cease-fire.

Sending one of his generals to escort Cronje for the formal capitulation, he formed a hollow square of Highlanders opposite his headquarters-wagon in front of which he walked up and down while he waited. He wore his trim khaki uniform without any badge or embellishment except for the jewelled Kandahar sword by his side. Presently Cronje rode in on a grey bony horse, seeming in his old green overcoat, frieze trousers, rough veldschoen boots and slouch-hat even bulkier by contrast with the neat little field-marshal. At the moment Cronje dismounted and Roberts stepped forward a camera clicked, to place a thrilling portrait before England where every detail of the events leading to this climax had been eagerly followed. The sudden right hook round Magersfontein that relieved Kimberley, Cronje's flight, the battle when he stood at bay, and finally the siege, had provided the tensest period of the war.

Roberts stepped forward to shake hands. He said: 'I am glad to see you. You have made a gallant defence, sir.'

Cronje looked from under glowering brows at his conqueror and made no reply.

The two men then breakfasted under a tree and completed the details.

The end was curiously muted. On the river bank, piling their arms in a great stack, 4,000 prisoners assembled. In addition, 150 wounded were found. The casualty rate had been kept remarkably low by the Boers' trench system. This was the first object of scrutiny by staff officers and newspaper correspondents picking their way among the shambles, but more remarkable to them were the Boers themselves. Were these the giants who had trampled on the flower of the Army under Methuen, thrown back Kitchener, endured the terror of these past ten days? As the long line of prisoners trudged off in their begrimed clothes, carrying their belongings in gaudy handkerchiefs, some with bright blankets over their arms and others holding aloft white or coloured umbrellas, they seemed but motley vagrants marching to gaol. Some of the women went with them as far as Cape Town, but those with children were mostly taken to Jacobsdal.

As the procession wound across the veld, a Cape-cart passed. In it were Cronje and his wife whom Roberts had allowed to accompany her husband into captivity. Stern and forbidding despite every respect paid him, he was given the State rooms on a cruiser at Cape Town; but soon, for fear of attempts to rescue him, he was taken to St. Helena. *Punch* duly depicted him saluting the shade of Napoleon: 'Same enemy, sire! Same result!' The comparison reflected England's state of elation, but if Paardeberg was not exactly a Waterloo it was a blow to the Boers far greater than either side had yet suffered, and the more disastrous because it fell on the side least able to bear it.

'The English,' cried Paul Kruger, 'have taken our Majuba Day away from us.' Wherever he looked he saw his cause suddenly and starkly in the descendant.

The Western Front, except for the continuing siege of Mafeking, had utterly collapsed.

The Central Front was fast disintegrating. De la Rey and Schoeman had already left for Bloemfontein with most of their burghers. Even as the surrender at Paardeberg was taking place, the rearguard they had left in the town withdrew in the face of Clements's advance—to the pleasure of loyalists whose places in the local gaol were taken by the rebels who had kept them there. Eastward, Gatacre was preparing to advance on Stormberg after a strong reconnaissance in which the famous Montmorency was killed in an ambush. While Gatacre desired 'to place on record'—his announcement ran—'the full sense of his sorrow' he took comfort from the waning strength of the enemy. On his right flank loyal farmers and empire volunteers in the Colonial Division, set up under General Brabant by Lord Roberts to soothe feelings ruffled by the attitude of the officers of regular regiments to which they had previously been attached, were clearing the country in a wide arc to the north-east. The following week a hard thirty-six-hour fight in the rugged hills was to dislodge the Boers, who at the same time evacuated Stormberg, so that without a shot fired Gatacre was at last to occupy the scene of such unfortunate memory.

The Boers on the run from the Midlands made for Poplar Grove and Bloemfontein while others simply trekked north, their rearguard fighting holding actions as Clements and Gatacre lumbered after them. Although rebellion was still unchecked in the western Cape Milner could at last sleep more easily than had been possible ever since Steyn's burghers first crossed the Orange four months ago.

But it was in Natal, where intensive operations had been going on simultaneously with the siege of Cronje, that the events at Paardeberg were matched by a scarcely less dramatic twist in fortune. Precisely as the cease-fire was sounding out over the Modder, the culminating moment was reached to Buller's efforts at that other river, 300 miles away, which these past months had made so conspicuous in English minds. The Tugela heights guarding the approach to Ladysmith were reverberating with the sounds of battle for the last time.

CHAPTER XIV

Ladysmith—The Final Round:
February 1900

BETWEEN the time he broke off the action at Vaalkrantz on the Upper Tugela and the day Cronje was surrendering at Paardeberg, Buller provided his most remarkable exhibition of the tragi-ridiculous.

After Vaalkrantz he telegraphed Roberts that he would now make a 'desperate dash' for Ladysmith. He signalled White that he would make this bid on 10 February, but merely assembling his force at Chievely took him until the 11th. For the next five days while White waited anxiously for news he marched—five miles. He kept changing his plans or deciding that the weather was too hot.

The direction of his march clearly pointed at the Tugela heights on the eastern side of where the Battle of Colenso had been fought. Given timely notice, the Boers began to reinforce this part of the river to a total strength of 5,000. Botha also came down from the Upper Tugela to take over command from his old chief, Lukas Meyer, but he had no time to impress himself on the situation because Buller at last attacked on the very day of his arrival, the 17th.

It may be remembered from the Battle of Colenso (see map on page 136) that the Tugela did a sudden twist northwards after passing the village, thereby detaching a dominating hill, Hlangwane, from the rest of the Boer line which was along the left bank. Hlangwane was the first of three hills along the right bank (i.e. on Buller's side) manned by only 2,000 of Botha's forces. These had not only been badly positioned by Lukas Meyer but were unnerved by the thought that retreat would not be easy because the river, resuming its eastward course, curled round behind them.

The three hills were Buller's target on the 17th. His attack was notable for the efforts of his men to keep in perfect alignment as they advanced over rough bushy ground, but the S.A.L.H. distinguished themselves by surprising an enemy advance guard on a prominence in front of the further of the three hills. Guns were hauled up in the night and next day Buller's army, for the first time attacking as a whole instead of being sent in piecemeal against portions of the enemy line where the Boers could concentrate their own manpower, stormed the two hills next to Hlangwane in spite of heavy artillery and machine-gun fire. By early afternoon the Boers were streaking back across the Tugela. Buller made no effort to exploit their utter exposure to pursuit, contenting himself with what he had won.

In the night Hlangwane too was evacuated in defiance of Botha's orders and Buller found himself in possession of the whole right bank. For the British the Natal Front therefore provided a little cheer on the day Kitchener was vainly trying to storm Cronje's laager at Paardeberg.

In Botha's laagers all was dismay. Buller could use the commanding hills he had captured to force a crossing of the river below Colenso or he might sweep round to the east and cut off the Transvaalers' line of retreat past Ladysmith. They began inspanning their wagons and trekking away. Botha tried in vain to stop them. The situation appeared so hopeless, in despair he telegraphed Kruger that the Tugela and even Ladysmith should be abandoned.

Buller meanwhile took two days cautiously bringing up his army to the Tugela in the vicinity of the captured hills. No doubt he heard of the Boers' flight with a sigh of satisfaction, for he prepared to march sedately into Ladysmith, informing White on the morning of the 21st that only a rearguard opposed him on the hills across the river and he would be in the town by next evening.

But it was not a rearguard opposing him.

When Kruger received Botha's message, although he was beset by Cronje's tribulation on the Modder, he remained unshakeable. 'It seems to me', he replied, 'as if your faith and that of your burghers has been replaced by unbelief.' And he went on:

The moment you cease to hold firm and fight in the name of the Lord, then you have unbelief in you; and the moment unbelief is present cowardice follows, and the moment that you turn your backs on the enemy then there remains no place for us to see refuge, for in that case we have ceased to trust in the Lord. No, no, my brethren; let it not be so; let it not be so. Has not the Lord hitherto given us double proof that He stands on our side? Wherever our burghers have stood fast, however hard the task, the Lord has beaten back the enemy with a small number of our burghers. My brethren, is it not the same Lord that cleft the Red Sea and routed Pharaoh and all his host, when Moses stood firm in his faith? Is it not, again, the same Lord that caused the stream of water to spring from the rocks whence thousands could drink? Is it not still the same Lord who walked on the sea and rebuked the waves of the sea and the winds, and they obeyed Him? . . . It seems to me from a study of God's word that we live at a point of time spoken of in the Revelation, in which the Beast has received power to persecute the Church of Christ in order to purify her, as gold is purified through fire. . . . This, indeed, is the struggle for the crown, both in a material and a spiritual sense. Read Psalm XXVII, verse 7, where the Lord says, 'Be of good courage, little band of god-fearing ones.' The Lord is faithful, and in your weakness shall He make perfect His strength. Read Psalm XXXIII, verse 7, to the end, where it says that victory is in the hand of the Lord alone, and not with the multitude of horses and chariots. . . . No brethren, let us not bring all our posterity to destruction. Stand fast in faith to fight, and you shall be convinced that the Lord shall arise and shall scatter His enemies (Psalm LXVII). Our faith is now at its utmost test, but the Lord will now shortly prove that He alone lives and reigns. The young men preferred death in the fiery furnace to forsaking their faith. Our ancestors preferred the stake to abandoning their faith, and the Church has been preserved, and all those who have preferred death to forsaking their faith have been as a sacrifice on the altar. Read this out to all officers and burghers, and my faith and prayer lie in my firm confidence that the Lord shall strengthen His people in their faith. Even if they have no earthly rock behind which to seek cover, they shall win on the open plain.

To give support to this message (which characteristically took some liberties with Biblical quotations) Joubert arrived from his headquarters at Ladysmith and similarly urged a stand. Gradually, as Buller was moving so slowly, the burghers were persuaded to rally. On the morning of the 21st it was hence no rearguard but a force of 5,000 men holding the hills opposite Buller.

These hills stood one behind the other beyond Colenso and parallel with the northward bend of the river from which they were separated by a shallow valley, the road from Colenso to Ladysmith. Buller proposed to reach this road by crossing the river westward from the foot of Hlangwane.

He had a bridge made and the leading troops and transport reached the other side without incident. But when they started to advance up the valley the Boers opened up from the flanking hills, and brought them to a stop with a hundred casualties. Buller nevertheless continued to pour men, guns, and baggage across the river all day, all night, and into the next morning. The result was a tremendous pile-up behind the immobilized advance troops.

It now occurred to Buller that something should be done about the situation. He sent a brigade against one of the flanking hills, selecting Wynne Hill to the left front of his advance troops. As he provided no flank support the brigade suffered severely from the Boers on the adjoining hills as well as Wynne Hill itself. By evening the survivors were clinging to the slopes and edge of the crest. Throughout the night they were swept by shell- and rifle-fire, and Boer attempts to push them off were only held at bay by frantic bayonet rushes. Some reinforcements arrived but after another day's hard fighting the casualty list already totalled 500.

That afternoon Buller tried to relieve the pressure on them by sending Hart's Irish Brigade against the next hill, called Inniskilling Hill. Having to pass between Wynne Hill and the river on the way the Irishmen used the cover of the river bank, though one part of it was exposed and they found themselves tramping over dead or wounded comrades in the mud and water. To repeated bugle calls of 'Charge!' and 'Double!' they made for the foot of the hill, cut their way through a barbed-wire fence, and against intense fire from above and from hills on either side, they struggled up to the crest, a stony and thorny plateau defended by only 500 Boers. As they charged across it the Boers met them with a tremendous fire that killed scores and drove the rest back. In the fading light the boom of artillery suddenly stopped, the gunners being unable to distinguish the opposing sides when more men reached the crest and unleashed a final desperate charge. The Boers stood up to club with their rifle butts or pour their magazines into the stumbling ranks. The Irish were thrown back to the edge of the crest, night closing on 500 of them dead or wounded, and the survivors clung on through the darkness exactly like their comrades on Wynne Hill to their left, constantly sniped at and harassed by the cries of the wounded and dying.

Buller had got himself into as fine a jam as he had yet contrived. His 25,000 troops, outnumbering the enemy by five to one, were strung out for miles along the river with no room to concentrate sufficiently on any one point of the Boer defences; their units were inextricably mixed up and the artillery too crowded together to be effective. All next day the droves of men clinging to Wynne and Inniskilling Hills continued to be without water or rest from the continuous fire which kept all help away, their wounded racked by thirst and pain, the air thick with the stench of the dead who lay among them in grotesque poses. Another tormented night; and then some relief came with the dawn of Sunday, 25 February: Botha agreed to a twenty-four-hour armistice for the dead and wounded to be dealt with. Boer and Briton emerged from their forward positions to exchange tobacco and talk about the war. A burgher encountering General Lyttelton remarked, 'We've all been having a rough time.' To which he replied: 'Yes, I suppose so. But for us of course it's nothing. This is what we're paid for. This is the life we lead always—you understand?' 'Great God!' said the Boer.

Botha needed the respite. He could not exploit the vulnerability of the distended British line because his force was tired after a week of battle. Even more wearing than the fighting and bombardment was the panic from which they had rallied—and the knowledge that their line had only to give way at any one point for the huge superiority of the British to overwhelm them. Ever since Buller first came to the Tugela this superiority had been balanced on a razor's edge by Botha's resolution and shrewdness, and his burghers' courage; but above all by Buller's blunders. Buller had but to do things right once, only once, for no shrewdness or courage to stay him. Nor was there any comfort for the Boers in the news from the Modder where Roberts's siege now held little hope for Cronje. Botha was personally embarrassed by his venerated former chief, Lukas Meyer, who despite a diplomatic recall by Joubert insisted on staying to 'help'. With unbounded relief he saw that Buller was using the armistice to withdraw his force back across the river. If the British were once again pulling out he would have time to rest his men, ease out Lukas Meyer, and inject fresh resolution into the defence.

But Buller was only manœuvring for a fresh attack. It took him until the afternoon following the armistice to decide exactly where. Riding with Warren along the Tugela as it left its northward course to turn eastward again behind Hlangwane and the adjoining hills captured on the 18th, he made up his mind. Opposite this eastward turn of the Tugela stood Inniskilling Hill. He would have another crack at it, but instead of repeating the Irish's disastrous approach along the valley on the further side he would build a bridge and mount his attack from directly across the river. At the same time he would attack the two hills to the right of it (Railway and Pieter's), and generally launch an offensive along the whole Boer line with all his men and all seventy of his guns. The gunners, posted in a wide arc, were strictly enjoined not to worry about hitting their own men but to maintain the full weight of their bombardment unless otherwise instructed.

At dawn next day, 27 February, Majuba Day which the Boers round Ladysmith marked with a salute of twenty-one guns, Buller's engineers began the pontoon bridge. It was a hundred yards long, and at 10 a.m. they had finished it with a sign-board marked *To Ladysmith*. As the leading battalions stepped out, the exhilarating news of Cronje's surrender at Paardeberg was passed around. Buller's massed artillery, machine-guns and rifles shook the earth and clouded the sky, while his infantry swarmed along the opposite bank which concealed them from the Boers pinned back by the cascade of bullet and shell. Then the assault began, directed first at the further of the two hills on the right of Inniskilling Hill.

Botha darted quickly enough to the threatened sector and took the conduct of the battle once and for all out of Lukas Meyer's hands. But he was like one trying to preserve a sandcastle against the breakers crashing down on it. Reitz, approaching from the rear of the first of the heights being stormed, saw that under the bombardment the crest was almost invisible under the clouds of flying earth and fumes, while the volume of sound was beyond anything that I have ever heard. At intervals the curtain lifted, letting us catch a glimpse of trenches above, but we could see no sign of movement, nor could we hear if the men up there were still firing, for the din of guns drowned all lesser sounds . . . then, suddenly, the gun-fire ceased and for a space we caught the fierce rattle of Mauser rifles followed by British infantry storming over the skyline, their bayonets flashing in the sun. Shouts and cries reached us, and we could see men desperately thrusting and clubbing. Then a rout of burghers broke back from the hill, streaming towards us in disorderly flight. The soldiers fired into them, bringing many down as they made blindly past us, not looking to right or left.

After months of blunder and disaster, after chance upon chance had been wasted with nothing gained but an increase in the dead and maimed, the offensive unfolded in textbook fashion. For the first time Buller used the whole of his army against the whole of the Boer line. As the attack on one hill got under way the attack on the next began. In such fashion, giving the Boers no chance to reinforce or otherwise help any one position, the waves of khaki swept over their defences. And in a mere six hours Buller found himself master at last of the Tugela heights. At this dazzling moment he could permit himself a meed of elation: 'Everything progressing favourably' was his message to White.

Though he sustained 500 casualties in that final assault it was a victory so sudden, so overwhelming, that it seemed a remarkably tame climax to the months of fighting along the river. Altogether his casualties since he first set out to relieve Ladysmith totalled more than the entire strength of the Boer force opposing him. But Joubert had been right in fearing the man's persistence, for Botha's force was now totally broken.

Botha still hoped to make a stand before Ladysmith but wherever he looked he saw horsemen, wagons and guns in headlong retreat. The steep approaches to the fords of a rivulet across the Transvaalers' escape route south-east of Ladysmith were made chaotic by the struggle to escape. Even the elements had turned against them, night coming on in a storm the like of which one observer had never seen before:

The thunder was terrific, the rain was like an incessant water-spout, and the fearful lightning in its vivid play along the rocks and down the hill-sides revealed thousands of men bedraggled and drenched, rushing as fast as they could, no one seemed to know where. Some were on horseback, some in mule and bullock wagons, and many afoot, all hurrying on, along mountain-sides, over rushing rivers and sluits now turned into raging torrents; cattle and men, in some instances, being caught by the wild waters and hurled down by their fury to destruction; but on and on went the main body pell-mell, nobody apparently pursuing, only the frightful storm fiend and awful panic speeding them; and no human power could stay that rush on that memorable night. [37]

Reaching Joubert's head-laager in the morning Reitz describes spending 'a dismal hour or two watching the tide of defeat roll northward':

We knew that the siege of Ladysmith would have to be raised, and now came the news, while we halted there, that Kimberley had also been relieved, and that General Cronje had been captured at Paardeberg with 4,000 men, so that the whole universe seemed to be toppling about our ears.

They had correctly assessed the position. As soon as the news of Cronje's surrender reached him Joubert, urged though he was by Kruger to make one more attempt to stop Buller, ordered the siege lines to be abandoned and his men to retire on Elandslaagte twenty miles behind. Meanwhile Botha was making for Ladysmith in the hope of rallying sufficient men to form a fighting rearguard to cover the retreat of his men higher up the Tugela line who would have to cross the front of Buller's advance to the town.

But Buller's thoughts were on neither advance nor pursuit. Having made no move to follow up his success of the previous day, he spent the 28th luxuriating in the spectacle of the Boers' flight, contenting himself with a signal to Ladysmith at noon: 'Have thoroughly beaten the enemy. Believe them to be in full retreat. Have sent my cavalry to ascertain which way they have gone.'

Thus a portion of Dundonald's mounted brigade approached Ladysmith late that afternoon. Ian Hamilton with his staff on Caesar's Camp saw the column approaching. 'Who goes there?' challenged the sentry. 'The Ladysmith relief column,' came the reply. Men issued from their shelters with tears streaming down their faces. When the troopers reached the ford at the entrance to the town where the populace had flocked to meet them, there were touching scenes, for the detachment consisted mainly of S.A. volunteers with relatives and friends among the besieged. A sudden silence fell at sight of their healthy faces and plump horses, and then as they rode up the main street, White with his Chief of Staff, General Archibald Hunter, and Ian Hamilton rode forward to greet them. White had all at once grown ten years younger. A great shout of applause broke from the relieving column at sight of him, and town and garrison took up the cheers. Briefly he thanked them. 'I thank God we have kept the flag flying,' he said. Everyone burst into *God Save the Queen*. Then people surged round the troopers to beg a cigarette or bread, and the siege of 118 days was over.

The news of Kimberley could now be topped with unexpected swiftness by a message which rejoiced the heart of England: 'Ladysmith has been relieved.' In London enormous crowds stopped traffic around the Mansion House and in the principal streets. Pall Mall, made brilliant by all the clubs lighting their gas flambeaux, was blocked from end to end by a cheering swirling multitude bearing aloft soldiers and banners and flags. Art students marched from South Kensington to cheer Chamberlain at Prince's Gate.

While the night was being made merry with similar scenes throughout the Empire, Botha struggled to form a rearguard to cover the retreat from around Ladysmith. He could not find enough men. The demoralization was complete. In another black and stormy night, says Reitz, 'we turned our backs on Ladysmith for good and all.' Though the rain stopped, allowing the sun to rise warm with encouragement, and the big guns were got away safely by train, the proposition was seemingly proved that among a civilian army nothing defeats like defeat. The plain beyond Ladysmith during the retreat to Elandslaagte was covered, says Reitz, 'with a multitude of men, wagons and guns ploughing across the sodden veld in the greatest disorder.'

Wherever a *spruit* or mullah barred the way there arose fierce quarrels between the frightened teamsters, each wanting to cross first, with the result that whole parks of vehicles got their wheels so interlocked that at times it seemed as if the bulk of the transport and artillery would have to be abandoned, for the mounted men pressed steadily on without concerning themselves with the convoys. Had the British fired a single gun at this surging mob everything on wheels would have fallen into their hands, but by great good luck there was no pursuit and towards afternoon the tangle gradually straightened itself out.

White had badly wanted to pursue, ordering out everybody able to march. After five miles many could go no further in their feeble condition and the force had to turn back. Buller arrived at Ladysmith in advance of his army and was highly displeased by this attempt. He would brook no pursuit. He returned to his army and spent a day or two about the agreeable business of organizing a formal entry into the town. It took place with due pomp. The mayor delivered an address of welcome; Buller made a speech of thanks to his troops: and so Ladysmith disappeared from history and returned to the obscurity of a small Natal town astride a railway junction.

The Boer retreat had not stopped at Elandslaagte. Botha arrived there with Lukas Meyer and finding Joubert gone they tried to bring some order to the congestion of traffic. In vain they attempted once more to stem the rush, even threatening to shoot the horses of men wanting to accompany the wagons, but the tide swept irresistibly by. Huge quantities of stores which had made Elandslaagte the supply base for the Boers' Natal operations could not be got away and were burnt, making a pyre visible for fifty miles around.

*　　*　　*　　*

For the British it was a bonfire of victory. The change in their fortunes had been dramatic beyond anyone's imagining. Within a mere fortnight both Kimberley and Ladysmith had been relieved; the Boer army in the west captured almost entire, that in Natal shattered beyond hope of mounting an offensive again, and the invaders of the Cape Midlands were likewise in full flight. A fringe of northern Natal, a pocket of rebellion in the western Cape, a tight little circle around Mafeking— scarcely any British territory now lay in thrall to the Boers, while Roberts with his army about to resume the advance towards Bloemfontein stood with a knife at their throats.

He ordered his men to bivouac upstream of the shattered laager, leaving its stench and carrion to the vultures. He needed time before marching against the Boers who barred his path at Poplar Grove. Since he would be cut off from the railway until he could reach the Central line, he got more wagons from Kimberley with Rhodes's help and another hundred were patched up from Cronje's laager, enabling the troops' half-ration to be increased to three-quarters. Roberts's next concern was Mafeking.

Since Baden-Powell's unsuccessful sortie against Game Tree Fort on Boxing Day, he had concentrated on steadily pushing out more trenches, connecting galleries and sapping works. With Native assistance both sides toiled mainly at night, approaching for long periods as close as sixty yards, in the process exchanging conversation as well as shots and forming friendly acquaintances. This ant-like burrowing gradually pushed back the Boers under P. J. Snyman, of whom a German witness wrote, 'with touching patience and a truly classical repose he lay before Mafeking and passively allowed circumstances to occur.' On the other hand Baden-Powell was never idle. He had megaphones made for sending bogus orders, audible to the Boers, about attacks on their trenches, and further drew their fire with dummy forts and dummy armoured trains. He had lances made and paraded men against the skyline to make the Boers think reinforcements of Lancers had arrived. He sent out fake signals at night and delivered grandiloquent manifestoes to the Boers offering a free pardon if they returned home before he counter-invaded. Such measures perplexed the Boers and kept up his men's spirits. *The Mafeking Mail* was regularly published, and entertainments (at which he performed), baby-shows and gymkhanas were held. Idle Natives were employed on public-works, women on making cartridge bags. He issued stamps, paper money and set up a summary court of jurisdiction.

As the story got out to England his fame grew. Many circumstances joined to make Mafeking the constant object of interest and anxiety now that Ladysmith and Kimberley were relieved. One of the Prime Minister's own sons was on Baden-Powell's staff, but above all— 'Because of its farness, loneliness and smallness; because of the humorous ingenuity of the long defence—this beleaguered village in Bechuanaland became the ewe lamb of the Empire.' Roberts considered sending Methuen, now based on Kimberley, with a relieving force; but he could not afford the men. Already he had lost 5,000 in casualties and the inevitable wastage of a long march. He therefore hoped that Baden-Powell would hold out, and he brought up more men from the rear to make up his full strength before resuming his march on Bloemfontein.

He had already issued a proclamation stating that the quarrel of the British nation was with the Boer Governments, not the people; indeed, the British were 'anxious to preserve [the people] from the evils brought upon them by the wrongful action of their Government.' Burghers who returned to their homes would not suffer in any way; goods requisitioned would be paid for immediately at market rates; and soldiers were prohibited from molesting persons or injuring property.

By the blandishment of this offer as much as the impressive array of strength at his back, Roberts hoped that the way would be made easy before him.

CHAPTER XV

Bloemfontein: March–April 1900

WE know war to be either an immorality play or a misadventure, but as an ultimate test of a man's regard for himself it puts on trial his faith in his own rightness—proved not by the outcome of victory or defeat but by the single fact of his staking his life and the well-being of lives important to his own. Because 'confidence' suggests a basis of reasoning it is inadequate; 'faith', with its element of mystery and unreason, better describes why people will wage war even when they cannot sensibly hope for victory. Blindly, like a lover in the full spate of his passion or the devout intent upon expiation, they give themselves over to this faith. It assumes an importance greater than the cause to which it was committed. Usurping logic it will fight unarmed against steel. It may even conquer an enemy abundant in both. But as faith may sustain adversity, so may it be necessary to sustain success: for success can breed its own self-doubts, sap the will to go on, raise barriers of pity, blur the memory of original causes, and blunt the edge of purpose.

The Boer War, embarked upon by both sides with confidence, was now to be maintained by faith; and we shall see also how that faith was expressed, and by whom, and what became of it.

* * * *

Paul Kruger did not stand idly by while his forces disintegrated. He took train to Natal where the flight from Ladysmith was in full flood, sweeping on to Elandslaagte and then further up the line to Glencoe. There Kruger found Joubert sick with illness and defeat, and with him tried to stop the stampede. He entreated and exhorted. He even promised that intervention or arbitration would end the war in a month if only they would stand firm. Many, crying out *'Huis-toe!'* ('We're going home!'), still pushed on as far north as Newcastle before they could be persuaded to return.

Thus he shored up some semblance of morale on this front and departed for even worse-threatened Bloemfontein. He left Joubert with the other leaders to determine their future strategy at a council of war on 5 March. The council decided to send as many men as possible to help oppose Roberts; the rest of the Free Staters in Natal would guard Van Reenen's Pass lest Buller tried to enter their republic by that route, and the rest of the Transvaalers would withdraw to the Biggarsberg, a range straddling Natal about twenty-five miles north of Ladysmith (it was this range Yule had crossed in the retreat from Dundee). There, looking over the wide sweep of country to the south from which they had been driven, the remaining Boers waited for Buller, busy making Ladysmith his new base.

Meanwhile Paul Kruger arrived in Bloemfontein to confer with President Steyn upon the crisis in their fortunes.

The capital was a pretty town, as its name (*bloem*—flower; *fontein*—fountain) suggests. To preserve it against Roberts was essential. Its loss might depress Boer morale beyond hope of recovery; and the longer he could be delayed, cut off from the Central railway and far removed from the Western, the more precarious would his supply position become—whereas if he captured it he would be poised for a northward march to Pretoria, completely bisecting both republics.

The Presidents reckoned up their forces. De la Rey was already outside the town (the Johannesburg Zarps under his command had been ordered out of the town following riotous and mutinous behaviour) and the rest of his men and baggage would soon be up from the Colesburg area. At Poplar Grove Christian de Wet had 6,000 men entrenched on hills along twenty-five miles on either side of the Modder, barring Roberts's approach from Paardeberg.

When the reinforcements from Natal and the Cape arrived, the Presidents hoped to assemble upwards of 12,000 men. They were sure they could continue the fight; at the same time, responsibility demanded that they make a peace overture. To the British Government they addressed a proposal 'in the sight of the Tribune God' that all forces withdraw to behind their own frontiers and the two Republics be accorded full independence. While the British Government considered this message, the Presidents set out to prevent their burghers giving way to any impulse to surrender.

Paul Kruger spoke to a large gathering in the town and to laagers on the way to Poplar Grove, his theme that of the message he had sent to Botha (page 251); and travelling by his four-horse Cape-cart with an escort of mounted police he arrived at Poplar Grove itself early on the morning of 7 March.

Christian de Wet met him and conducted him to his tent. They had no sooner entered than sounds of firing brought De Wet quickly out again to see what was happening. By sheer chance Roberts had chosen this very morning to resume his march. His army was being flung in a huge net around the Boers and, all unknown, around President Kruger himself.

*　　*　　*　　*

Roberts had issued his orders the previous afternoon at his bivouac above Paardeberg. He did not put them in writing but called his commanders together and said:

> I have asked you to meet me here this afternoon in order to communicate to you the proposed plan of operations for to-morrow. The enemy, as you know, occupy a strong but somewhat extended position in our immediate front. The object is, of course, to block the road to Bloemfontein, and as far as the information we can procure goes, it is apparently the only place between here and Bloemfontein where our progress could be checked. It is difficult to calculate the exact strength of the enemy, but allowing that the troops withdrawn from Colesburg, Stormberg and Natal have joined, it seems scarcely possible that it can number more than 14,000, at the outside, with perhaps 20 guns. To meet this number we have 30,000 men and 116 guns.

French with the mounted troops would ride in a wide arc round the right of the Boers and turn to attack from the rear. Meanwhile a division of infantry would follow him up some distance before attacking the Boers from the right, ushering them towards the river: there a second division would attack from the front, while a third division marching along the opposite bank would prevent the trapped burghers escaping to or receiving help from that side.

264

But French was late in starting and rode slowly. Mindful of Cronje's fate the 4,000 Boers south of the river did not wait to be surrounded by 30,000. When De Wet came running out of his tent he saw them inspanning their wagons and trekking away. He was at first unaware of the sound reasons for their behaviour and flew into a rage at what he took to be cowardice. Quickly bundling the President back into his Cape-cart, which raced off in a swirl of dust, he tried to rally his men. All he could form was a rearguard.

Had French ridden hard and the infantry moved smartly, the President and one of the few major forces left to the Boers might have been theirs. But French was having a sluggish day. He waited over-long for the infantry to advance behind him and they themselves marched unduly slowly. His horses were in an increasingly poor condition—but nothing to the condition of his own erratic mood. He was in a huff, brooding on wrongs done him. Roberts, misled by a faulty calculation by his supply officer into thinking the cavalry horses were receiving a bigger ration than he had laid down, had issued a reprimand. This and other rows between French and headquarters, who hinted at bad horsemanship while he asserted that they knew too little about horses and expected too much, accounted for his huff.

Eventually, after he had been further delayed by small parties of Boers skilfully using long grass and rocks for cover, his horses were too done up to ride further. The President, Christian de Wet and his whole force got clean away with their wagons. The infantry were left to plod along as if swotting at a fly that was not there. They marched twenty miles without firing a shot.

A day that might have ended the war produced a lesson which the British did not notice, much less learn. They felt only jubilation at having turned the Boers out of the last strong-point before Bloem-fontein. The fact that turning them out and defeating them were entirely different matters occurred to precisely no one.

*   *   *   *

Though the British did not overtake the Boers retreating from Poplar Grove, panic did. At a farm called Abraham's Kraal, fifteen miles back, Paul Kruger was joined by De la Rey who had been riding from Bloemfontein with a thousand police to help De Wet. Together they were enveloped in a cloud of horses and wagons being driven helter-skelter towards the capital. At once they tried to stop the rout. An eye-witness has recorded of Kruger at this moment—'Despair seemed depicted on his hard leaden features; threateningly he lifted his heavy stick against the fugitives, whom no one seemed able to check; at last he ordered the detachment of Pretoria Police close by to shoot everyone who attempted to pass.'[38] No one was in fact shot and thousands made their way to Bloemfontein before some could be persuaded to stay.

The name Abraham's Kraal had a hopefully Biblical ring not lost on Paul Kruger. Before he left it was decided that De la Rey should attempt a further stand here to gain De Wet and President Steyn time for organizing the defence of Bloemfontein.

Three days later Roberts's army, having paused at Poplar Grove to bring up supplies, advanced in three columns, ten miles apart, with a view to converging on the Central railway well south of Bloemfontein within four days. The northernmost column, commanded by French, soon discovered De la Rey's men at Abraham's Kraal and on Roberts's orders wheeled to by-pass them to the south. But De la Rey had anticipated just this and quietly extended his line. Thus French did not ride out of trouble but into it as he approached a range of kopjes at which De la Rey had arrived before him with a reinforcement of Zarps, bringing his strength to 1,500. This seemed a pitiful opposition against 10,000 men; yet he held French at bay through the entire day. It was 6.30 p.m. before the infantry got close enough under cover of an intensive artillery barrage to charge in overwhelming numbers. The Essex were foremost, one of their lieutenants who had won the V.C. at Paardeberg falling mortally wounded. The Boers emptied their magazines into the charging lines until the last moment, so that many were too late to reach their ponies and their casualty rate of 300 was proportionately higher than French's 400. But their resolution gave new hope to the Boer leaders consolidating a fifteen-mile defence arc outside Bloemfontein.

Next day Roberts continued the three-pronged advance. Then the day after he suddenly changed his plan. Riding out to join French with the advance cavalry his thoughts were clouded by reports of strong Boer reinforcements from the north. His fate hung on the rapid capture of Bloemfontein in order to seize vital provisions and also rolling stock without which the railway would be of little immediate help. Altering his objective from the point previously chosen well south of the city, he ordered French to ride full-tilt for Brand Kop, a dominating hill only four miles south-east of it. Possession of this hill would outflank the Boers' defence arc and place their city at his mercy.

French set out at 1 p.m. on a three-hour ride through intense heat. He reached the railway safely, and cut it to forestall any of the commandos retiring from the Colesburg area; then leaving his weary horse-batteries to crawl after, he approached Brand Kop in waning light. Major E. H. H. Allenby, destined in World War I to lead cavalry in their final triumphs, took possession of a nearby ridge and the attack was joined. On the hill were 400 Boers, but unable to see how many were attacking they took fright and fled.

At the news that their defences had been turned and that the British were in easy shelling distance, panic broke the spirit of the burghers. No attempt was made to recapture Brand Kop. An evening council of war decided on a final stand but no one took any notice, except the townsfolk who were indignant and scared at the thought of the town being bombarded. Roberts sent in a prisoner with a proclamation undertaking to protect the inhabitants if his entry was unopposed, and this made a powerful appeal. Besides, the town contained many English and moderates who had opposed war. The State archives had already been sent to Kroonstad, over a hundred miles to the north, and now arrangements were hurriedly made for transferring the machinery of government there. As thousands of burghers and wagons trekked north that night, President Steyn and other leaders departed by train, leaving a weak rearguard and some of Theron's Scouts in disguise as spies. They got away just in time, for French sent out an adventurous patrol which cut the railway northwards from the city.

Bloemfontein is probably the only capital city ever captured by newspapermen. Three enterprising correspondents rode in next morning unopposed. They found the principal citizens assembled in the local club and prevailed on the mayor and two other prominent men to drive out to Roberts with the keys of the town.

That afternoon, 13 March 1900, Roberts accompanied by his A.D.C.s and foreign attachés made his formal entry at the head of the Cavalry Division. The troops were tattered, hungry and tired, but eyes shone at sight of gardens, and solid buildings, and women, and the promise of all the pleasures of urban life. The streets were decorated; the crowds cheered. It was a surprising reception, accounted for largely by the quasi-civil war nature of the Boer War, such that with the ambiguity of a feud within a family relationships were likely to be as cordial at one extreme as they were bitter at the other.

Lord Roberts halted at the Residency. His wife had worked for him as a parting gift a little silken Union Jack, a shamrock adorning one corner, and now with due ceremony it was run up the flagpole.

*   *   *   *

The capture of Bloemfontein set the seal on the complete reversal of fortune which Roberts's advance had wrought in Britain's favour. First and foremost was the international implication. Over the words 'Who said "Dead"?' a *Punch* cartoon showed the British lion emerging from a cave, putting to flight a donkey labelled 'Continental Press'. '. . . Doubt of our powers had ceased to gnaw us. Confidence was indeed so extraordinarily restored that it became positively volatile; a few weeks after this Lord Milner had to . . . urge the authorities at home to stop a constantly increasing stream of tourists.'[2] (Messrs. Cook's actually advertised tours of the battlefields.) In recent days Queen Victoria had twice driven through the streets of London to give huge crowds an outlet for public emotion. Tumultuous and touching scenes occurred, but none as remarkable as that of both Houses of Parliament drawn up in the courtyard of Buckingham Palace to sing the Anthem in homage to her. Significantly it was Chamberlain who addressed her on their behalf, and his biographer comments: 'The chords were deeper now than in the unawakened time of the Jubilee pageants already so far away, part of a vanished age of illusion.' Yet there was another illusion, that patriotism required almost hysterical mass demonstrations. This new habit, distorting values because importance was attached to an event according to a popular mood of the moment, was clearly seen on 17 March. The Irish were in the news because the Queen in recognition of their valour had agreed to the Household Brigade being joined by Irish Guards, and St. Patrick's Day brought everyone out wearing shamrocks to celebrate *en masse*.

At a more sober level, a £35 million 2¾ per cent War Loan issued at 98½ was oversubscribed eleven times. Though the Budget which followed put fivepence on the income-tax, raising it to one shilling, it was cheerfully accepted as a war tax which would not need repeating. Revenue was in any event buoyant, helped by the estate of 'Chicago Smith', an obscure millionaire, which produced nearly a million in death duties.

In this atmosphere of victory, the peace proposal made by Kruger and Steyn prior to the fall of Bloemfontein had a curt reception. Salisbury cabled back: 'Her Majesty's Government can only answer Your Honours' telegram by saying that they are not prepared to assent to the independence either of the South African Republic or the Orange Free State.' The Queen of Holland entreated the Kaiser to support collective action on behalf of the Boers. But the Kaiser, made more than ever wary by Roberts's advance, replied that unless the U.S.A. took the initiative God's instrument for punishing injustice 'with relentless severity' might well be the great German fleet a-building: 'Till then Silence and Work.'

It was in England itself that the real challenge to imperial policy lay. In a list of 'Don'ts' *Punch* said: 'DON'T make pro-Boer observations in railway carriages or other public places: it is an unhealthy practice, just at present.' The tempers of pro-Boer and anti-Boer alike were rising. In Glasgow the City Hall was the scene of mob violence as Socialist dockers and Tory students clashed when Lloyd George and others held an anti-war meeting. At this, the first of the famous 'Lloyd George Nights', he escaped with only the windows of his carriage smashed, though Keir Hardie was knocked about until police rescued him. Less spectacularly agitation went on by all kinds of other individuals and groups like the League of Liberals Against Aggression and Militarism, and the Peace Society. But at a time of such war psychosis that *Punch* showed a baby saying as his first word, 'Bang!', the majority of the nation felt only satisfaction at the trend of events.

During the days following the fall of Bloemfontein the newspapers could fill their pages with no news that was not good news.

Troops sent down the Central railway joined hands with Clements who had been advancing on the Orange, repairing the railway and bridges as he went. The remnants of the Colesburg commandos were therefore obliged to retreat north-west. They fell in with the commandos of Boers and Cape rebels under Olivier and others flying across the Orange north of Stormberg. The combined Boer force of 6,000–7,000 men, with 800 wagons and 10,000 oxen, formed a convoy twenty-five miles long. They set a course hugging the towering heights of the Basutoland border along the eastern O.F.S. Slowly they trudged northwards, sending up a huge pall of red dust as they strove to get clear of Gatacre and Brabant (commanding the Colonial Division).

At the same time Kitchener, having taken charge of dealing with the rebellion in the western Cape, sent columns on forced marches, with C.I.V. cyclists keeping them in touch with each other, to occupy dissident towns and drive the more determined Boers under Liebenberg and others back over the Orange.

It was the turn of the O.F.S. to feel large-scale invasion. British columns began systematically scouring the whole southern half of the republic. Clements in the south-west and Gatacre with Brabant in the south-east pressed steadily forward. No one opposed them. In a proclamation issued on 15 March Roberts promised that all burghers who laid down their arms and swore to take no further part in the war would be granted immunity and a pass to return to their homes. Eight thousand Free Staters and rebels availed themselves of the offer. They went to the nearest British officer or magistrate and handed over a rifle, took the oath, and went back to their farms. The ultimate fate of Cape rebels, however, had to await the clemency of the British Government.

As district after district came under imperial sway, officers or sometimes the original landdrost assumed the civil administration. In the capital itself a market was opened and a civil service inaugurated; prices were fixed, police organized, treasury and Customs officials set to work. President Steyn's brother accepted a contract for supplying the British Army with wood fuel, and his brother-in-law one for slaughter cattle.

Roberts allowed the great convoy under Olivier and company to pass Bloemfontein close to the Basuto border where it split up into its component commandos. He left it alone because he was confident that once back in their home districts the burghers would surrender like so many of their countrymen. In any event he had to rest and gather his strength to deal with the main body of Boers who had fled headlong to the north.

His single need was to move swiftly in their wake. If he exploited their present confusion and despair by advancing through the rest of the O.F.S. and into the Transvaal, on to Pretoria itself, he could look forward decisively to ending the war. Only one more big push was necessary. But though the end-product of all military training, the object of discipline and the virtue ascribed to tradition, is the creation of a mechanism, the army Roberts led into Bloemfontein consisted of 34,000 tattered, exhausted and hungry human beings. He wanted time to turn them into a mechanism again before he could think of advancing.

They had only five days' food left and scarcely any forage when they entered the city. The Cape ports, to which the British Government had sent a three months' supply of bread-stuffs, tinned meat, groceries and forage, were not only an average distance of 500 miles away, but the railway bridges across the Orange had been blown up by the fleeing burghers. Roberts was only retrieved from possible disaster by the seizure of several weeks' supplies in the town.

In one particular his luck did not hold. The polluted river and unhealthy conditions in the crowded laager at Paardekraal had fostered an outbreak of enteric fever. The disease found an indulgent host in the troops, exhausted as they were by their hardships on half-rations. Upon reaching Bloemfontein they relaxed and the disease ran amok, its virulence encouraged by their lack of tents. Roberts's decision to push on despite De Wet's capture of the wagon train had meant cutting medical equipment to a minimum and this was matched by a shortage of doctors and nurses. Men went down by the thousand. Hospitals had to be improvised in schools and assorted buildings like the Bloemfontein Club, which Dr. Conan Doyle took charge of. It was a fortnight before repairs to the railway bridges enabled trains to bring up medical supplies. But from this time, among Boer and Briton, soldier, burgher and civilian, the disease killed far more people than bullets or shell-fire ever did. Roberts's wife and daughters presently joined him at Bloemfontein—the Boer generals were apparently not such oddities in this respect—and they helped visit the sick who were soon dying at the rate of fifty per day.

Restoration of the railway system did not provide an easy solution to Roberts's problem of quickly building up his strength. The lines from the Cape ports became a single track ninety miles south of Bloemfontein, creating a bottleneck. Only eight trains were available of which two had to keep him in his daily requirements, leaving only six to bring up medical necessities, reserves of food (he wanted a stockpile of at least three months), clothes to replace his men's rags and fit them out for the colder weather ahead, ammunition and equipment of every kind including massive siege guns to reduce the Pretoria forts.

He had also to bring up men. By now the fervour of Black Week had resulted in plentiful replacements and the additional numbers on which, leaving nothing to chance, he insisted before resuming his advance. Soon he had upwards of 200,000 men under his command throughout S.A.

Horses were needed, since French's cavalry reached Bloemfontein with only a third of his horses still in commission. Heavy purchasing was done abroad and from the now more co-operative Basutos. Efficient care of the animals remained a problem. That relic of a by-gone age, the Remount Department, was notoriously incompetent as it provided a sinecure for officers who were no good at anything else, and hence properly qualified officers avoided the stigma of having anything to do with it. Horses from abroad were used before they were acclimatized; worse, to relieve the pressure on the railways mobs of them were driven across the veld from the Orange to Bloemfontein.

All these circumstances, to which others were to be added, protracted Roberts's halt at Bloemfontein far beyond expectation.

*　　*　　*　　*

The fall of the city had a profound effect on the Boers. Fatalism and depression were rampant. Men took themselves off home and others wandered aimlessly up and down the line to Kroonstad, the new seat of government. Here burghers agitated for leave, foreigners and adventurers pressed fanciful schemes for the destruction of Roberts, and friction was rife between Free Staters and Transvaalers.

In Pretoria Chief Justice Gregorowski led a lawyers' deputation to urge Kruger to stop the war. The President replied that Revelation made clear how the Beast (England) would war with the Church (Boers) and seem about to overcome it when God would intercede. The lawyers asked whether recent events did not suggest that God was against them. Kruger ended the interview with the angry retort, 'Your God is not my God'.

Within a fortnight General Joubert's long period of ailing ended with his death. His brand of moderation, which baulked at attempting to do rapidly that which in the long run he believed impossible against overwhelming numbers, did not make him less of a patriot than the more fanatical Kruger; but it had much to do with the present straits of his

1. Uitlander exodus from the Rand

2. Departure of Canadians from Ottawa

3. Gordon Highlanders before their departure for South Africa

4. Burial of Wauchope

5. General Joubert (seated, centre) breakfasting with his staff

6. Queen Victoria visiting war wounded

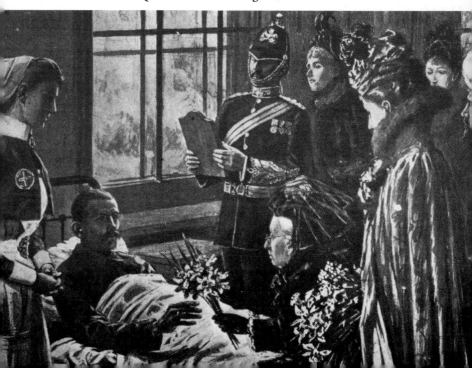

7. The cine-camera on the battlefield for the first time

8. Red Cross wagons after Spion Kop

9. General French meeting Rhodes at Kimberley

10. Meeting of Roberts and Cronje at Paardeberg, 27 February 1900

11. War correspondents, including
    Churchill (middle row, centre)

12. Edgar Wallace, *Daily Mail*

13. Conan Doyle at Bloemfontein

14. Rudyard Kipling and others
    preparing the Bloemfontein *Friend*

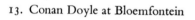

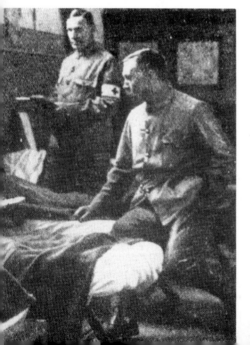

15. British Amazon

16. Boer Amazon

17. Victorian sentiment: 'The Last Embrace'

18. Victorian sentiment: 'Back from the Battlefield': the consolations of being shipped home wounded

19. Sword-sharpening in the field

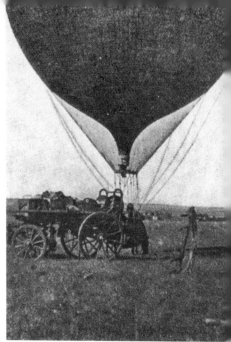

20. Military balloon anchored to a drum on the back of a wagon

21. The cycling craze in war: scouting, dispatch carrying and ambulance work

22. The Boer charge at Bakenlaagte

23. Grenadier Guards at Biddulphsberg

24. 'Mafficking' in Piccadilly Circus

25. Presentation of war medals by Edward VII at the Horse Guards' Parade,
June 1901

26. General and Mrs Louis Botha

27. President Kruger's arrival in Holland

28. British War Cabinet. Sitting: Marquis of Salisbury and A. J. Balfour; standing: G. J. Goschen, Marquis of Lansdowne, Duke of Devonshire

29. President Steyn (middle row, centre) with Commandants; on his left, Olivier and M. Prinsloo

30. Lord Roberts boarding the *Dunnottar Castle* at Southampton

31. Return of the C.I.V.: the scene in London's Strand

32. General Sir Redvers Buller

33. Lord Kitchener

34. General Christia(a)n de Wet

people. However, his virtues far exceeded his failings and the Boers mourned him deeply. He was given a State funeral. His horse followed the gun-carriage bearing the coffin; and Kruger in his magnificent coach, all the consular officials, and a large crowd were in the procession. Roberts sent Kruger his condolences, saying of the dead Commandant-General: 'His personal gallantry was only surpassed by his humane conduct and chivalrous bearing.' Rudyard Kipling wrote a valedictory tribute unique for being to an enemy in time of war:

> Later shall rise a people, sane and great,
> > Forged in strong fires, by equal war made one;
> Telling old battles over without hate—
> Not least his name shall pass from sire to son.

Though the Boers regarded his death as a grievous loss it had advantages. By his own wish command of all Transvaal forces passed to Louis Botha, a younger and greater man. The disappearance of both Cronje and Joubert from the scene meant an infusion of more vigorous blood in Boer leadership. Besides Botha there was Christian de Wet, with a number of others including Judge Hertzog and Jan Smuts coming more prominently to the fore. But matching their vigour were two older men: Koos de la Rey the shrewd warrior, and President Steyn.

It was President Steyn who in these days when his country was being dismembered stood out as the dominant and indomitable spirit. The glowering figure of Kruger begins to recede in the mists of old age and grief. Steyn instead offers the image of a man whose intelligence and resolution illumine the dark hours of his cause. An Australian war correspondent captured by the Boers had an interview with him shortly before the fall of Bloemfontein and describes him as 'a man of notable type':

> He is a big man physically, tall and broad, a man of immense strength, but very gentle in his manner. . . . He has a typical Dutch face, calm, strong, and passionless. A man not easily swayed by outside agencies; one of those persons who think long and earnestly before embarking upon a venture, but, when once started, no human agency would turn him back from the line of conduct he has mapped out for himself. He is no ignorant back-

block politician, but a refined, cultured gentleman, who knows the full strength of the British Empire; and, knowing it, he has defied it in all its might, and will follow his convictions to the bitter end. [30]

At a series of meetings in Kroonstad the Boer leaders agreed on plans to meet the mortal threat of Roberts. They banned convoys of families and goods which had brought paralysis at Paardeberg and debilitation around the besieged towns, and all transport would be reduced to a minimum. The regulations governing leave were tightened, while military courts would impose stricter discipline generally. By these means the manpower still in the field—about 12,500 near Bloemfontein and 15,500 at the other fronts—could be more effectively used. Further, Steyn welcomed foreign volunteers more warmly than Kruger had done. Comte de Villebois-Mareuil, a colourful Frenchman who had been pressing a scheme for Roberts's discomfiture, was put in command of all the foreign corps. The O.F.S. artillery, in disarray through losses at Paardeberg where their commander Albrecht had been captured, were pulled together under Judge Hertzog who also helped Steyn and others of the O.F.S. Executive to reorganize the issue of clothing and field transport.

With these practical and determined measures went much oratory from both Presidents. Spies' reports of the exhausted condition of Roberts's troops and horses were confirmed by the long delay in resuming his march. Gradually the Boers rallied.

The commandos (5,000 men) under Olivier and company east of Bloemfontein did not surrender as Roberts had anticipated. So having secured the city's water-supply which was located in that direction, he sent a mounted column further on to the area around Thaba 'Nchu ('Black Mountain') but they remained obstinately in the hilly country beyond. Then in the closing days of March, deciding to secure an advance base at Karee Siding twenty miles north of Bloemfontein, he found 3,500 Transvaalers astride the railway in equally determined mood under the command of De la Rey. Though outnumbered by nearly three to one, and De la Rey himself happened to be away, they made full use of his skilful positioning along a series of ridges before they withdrew to avoid encirclement by French's cavalry. Their losses were 40, the British 200.

Rudyard Kipling, in Bloemfontein for a week or two helping to run the local paper which the military had taken over, travelled eagerly to the scene to distribute plugs of tobacco and watch the action—his very first experience of battle. One detects his disappointment at the lack of spectacle in his account of how the 'enormous pale landscape swallowed up seven thousand troops without a sign,' leaving him little to do but wait, 'seeing nothing in the emptiness, and hearing only a faint murmur as of wind along gas-jets, running in and out of the unconcerned hills.' (With him on the newspaper was Julian Ralph, famous American correspondent for the London *Daily Mail*. Soon afterwards Harmsworth appointed to his place a young man named Edgar Wallace who had gone out as a private soldier. Kipling warned him that literature was a good mistress but a bad wife.)

The tactics of judicious disengagement applied at Karee Siding were those decided on by the Boer leaders at their Kroonstad meetings. Decisively to stop the overwhelming numbers at Roberts's disposal was impossible. They pinned their hopes on either of two surmises. One was that foreign nations would yet intervene, to which end a three-man mission of prominent Boers* left S.A. via Delagoa Bay to lay their case before Europe and the U.S.A. The other was that Great Britain's will to continue the war would crumble. How much were their thoughts on this issue influenced by the anti-war agitation in England, and how much by their own assessment of British character? The evidence inclines towards the latter, but the former has always attracted more attention. The reason is not only the intensity of political controversy which left no one in England untouched, but the bitterness felt by troops at the front, illustrated by these lines put in Kruger's mouth by a *Punch* parody, *To Certain Members of the Opposition*:

> Doubt not, along your army's fighting lines
> The story, hard to credit, how you strove
> To weaken still the hands, not strong before,
> That held the nations's fate against the world,
> Should do me service breaking sundry hearts.

Until one or other of their two surmises could be realized, the Boer

* C. H. Wessels, A. O. W. Wolmorans, A. Fischer.

leaders resolved to oppose Roberts at every suitable point. More than that, they would carry the war into his own camp whenever and wherever opportunity offered. The newly appointed foreign corps commander, De Villebois-Mareuil, had already gone off on an enterprise north-west of Bloemfontein; and on the very evening before the action at Karee Siding Christian de Wet set out to the north-east with his brother Piet and 2,000 men, none aware of his purpose or destination.

Having thrown any possible spies off the scent he turned south. Another day's ride brought him within a dozen miles of the river that has already figured so prominently in this narrative, the Modder. It passed north of Bloemfontein from the east where the city's water-works were situated twenty miles across the level veld, at a place called Sannah's Post. He halted nearby and gave his men a taste of his discipline so alien to their habits: a commandant named Vilonel persisted in bringing more transport than the recent decree allowed; De Wet reduced him to the ranks.

Next day scouts brought information that the water-works garrison numbered only 200; also that Olivier was about to attack the mounted column Roberts had sent to Thaba 'Nchu and which was now commanded by one of the cavalry brigadiers, General R. G. Broadwood. De Wet quickly called a council of war. He proposed, he said, to capture the water-works, thereby cutting off Bloemfontein's water-supply and standing across Broadwood's line of retreat.

To north and east the area in which the water-works stood was enclosed by a curve of the Modder, on the west by a small tributary or spruit, and on the south by the Bloemfontein–Thaba 'Nchu road along which Broadwood must retreat if Olivier's attack succeeded. Coming from Thaba 'Nchu the road crossed first the river and then the spruit, and parallel with it ran a railway line in process of construction, the half-built station being close to the water-works.

The proximity of Bloemfontein, and a whole British division even nearer at hand, made speed essential. On the night of 30/31 March his men went to their positions. Under his brother Piet 1,600 men approached the Modder from the east, their function being to act as beaters, driving the garrison into the arms of the remaining 400 with whom Christian de Wet hid below the fifteen-foot banks of the spruit and among some nearby farm buildings.

There now enters the story a character called Major F. R. Burnham. He was a Canadian who had learnt scouting from the Red Indians and became famous for various exploits including tracking down a notorious witch doctor called Milimo in the Matabele War. Roberts, as part of his efforts to improve scouting methods, had sent for him from his native land. He had been at Paardeberg and recently began sniffing out the country east of Bloemfontein, happening to reach the same farm buildings near the spruit just as Christian de Wet was coming up. It was a chance in the highest tradition of adventure fiction. Hawk-eye hid himself and waited for dawn.

An hour or so before dawn De Wet learned that Broadwood's whole column together with its supply wagons had already retreated from Thaba 'Nchu and had just reached the water-works garrison. He had to think quickly. With his 400 men barring the path of 2,000 he might himself be enveloped and trapped if his brother, or Olivier following up in pursuit of Broadwood, did not move quickly enough. He decided to take a chance and attempt Broadwood's destruction.

Broadwood's men had thrown themselves down to rest after their long march. Assuming that the garrison commander had reconnoitred, he did not trouble about security. A patrol had in fact gone out to Boesman's Kop, a hill six miles beyond the spruit: running into the Boers, the patrol had retreated to the hill, but its non-return went unnoticed by the garrison. Thus as dawn broke there was only Burnham between Broadwood and complete surprise.

Burnham left his hiding-place and tried to cross the spruit but found it too heavily guarded. He then crept on to a rise and waved a red scarf to attract the attention of Broadwood's men. But the only people to see it were the Boers, who promptly seized him. Exit hawk-eye.

Soon afterwards Piet de Wet went into action beyond the Modder, sending a flurry of shells into the bivouac. Broadwood thought it was Olivier pursuing. His native wagon-drivers, quickly awake, inspanned their wagons and the troopers saddled up as he ordered the column to cross the spruit.

From the spruit itself came no sound. Christian de Wet futher disarmed suspicion by allowing the leading wagons to cross. Then, quietly revealing himself to the drivers and such soldiers as had descended the bank, he terrorized them into lying down on the bed of the spruit: 'Driver to the left, driver to the right,' he said quietly—as methodically, commented a report, as the handing-in of luggage at a cloak-room window. The officers of two batteries following the convoy saw the pile-up in front and thought it was the usual tangle at a river crossing. A couple of them went ahead to sort it out when De Wet suddenly appeared from among the wagons and at gun-point said, 'Dismount. You are prisoners. Go to the wagons.' They did as they were told, and the leading battery descending soon afterwards was similarly captured.

But as this was going on in complete silence one of the captured officers dashed away. He yelled a warning to the other battery, designated 'Q', which at once wheeled about. In the same moment the officer commanding the escort cried out, 'Files about—gallop!' The extraordinary quietness of the spruit was abruptly shattered as De Wet and his men, strictly enjoined to hold their fire as long as he did, opened up on the galloping escort and Q battery, at the same time shooting the horses of the captured battery before they could stampede. One gun was in fact driven away and joined Q battery, which unlimbered in the open veld seventy yards from the station buildings and tried to bombard the Boers. But De Wet was too well protected by the banks of the spruit and the wagons, although he could not himself advance against the fire of the infantry clustered among the station buildings.

It was now about 8 a.m. The gunners were falling fast and Piet de Wet was increasing the pressure from the other side of the Modder. Broadwood ordered some cavalry to work round behind Christian de Wet's position. As they were setting out 600 men arrived at Boes-man's Kop, sent by Roberts to cover Broadwood's return to Bloem-fontein as soon as he heard of his retirement from Thaba 'Nchu. But this forethought came to nothing because the commander of the force split it into two, making its strength ineffectual, and did not at once close with De Wet. In addition the cavalry dithered, and by 10 a.m. Broadwood's position between two fires was becoming critical. Only a handful of his gunners survived, the Boers across the Modder were nearer, and his last cartridge would soon be spent. He determined to break away south of Christian de Wet. First an attempt had to be made to get away the guns of Q battery.

Like the efforts to save the guns at Colenso, the stand of Q battery gave an opportunity for the heroism beloved of Victoria's England. Under concentrated fire volunteers ran out time and time again from the station buildings to drag back the guns and limbers, their coolness exemplified by an officer who had his stick knocked out of his hand by a bullet and stooped to pick it up before continuing on his way. Four men were to win the V.C., and when all that could be saved was brought away the watching troops rose in spite of the bullets and cheered the survivors in.

Covered by successive companies Broadwood finally got away southwards across the spruit. His losses were 600 men, 80 of his 90 wagons, 7 of his 12 guns. Worse for the British was the capture of the water-works. Larger British forces arrived presently, but so did Olivier's 5,000, and there could be no thought of trying to recapture the place for the time being. The loss of Bloemfontein's water-supply brought about an immediate worsening of the enteric epidemic which carried off 2,000 people before the end of April, and the need to bring up water-trains added to the strain on the railways.

Christian de Wet, his classic coup accomplished, left Sannah's Post to his brother and Olivier when he rode southward that evening with a small force. Next day he learnt that forty miles away at the village of Dewetsdorp, named after his own father, were 400 of Gatacre's men. One of the many units bringing the southern O.F.S. under British control, they were now quickly withdrawn by Gatacre on Roberts's orders following the disaster at Sannah's Post. De Wet went after them, joined not only by burghers still on commando but by some who had been allowed to return to their farms upon giving the oath of non-participation. Less than twenty miles from the railway* he overtook and surrounded the retreating men. Gatacre himself was leading a force to the rescue, but when it reached the scene at dawn on 4 April the unit had surrendered only half an hour before after a tame resistance. Nor did Gatacre press a pursuit.

As a result of this affair, to which were added memories of his failure at Stormberg, Gatacre was packed off home and replaced by General H. Chermside. A head certainly had to roll. Roberts was by now almost ready to resume his march and here were the Boers so far from being demoralized that they were rampaging through the country close to his vital line of communications. In a few days they had captured nearly 1,000 soldiers, much booty, and Bloemfontein's chief source of water. Critical voices in England, even on the pro-war side, were less muted

* Mostert's Hoek.

now and from this time comparisons between colonial and home troops were drawn distinctly unfavourable to the latter, Kipling and others being especially pungent about British stupidity and colonial craftiness. But as to De Wet's success, his lightning tactics were scarcely more ominous for the future than the way farmers had broken their oaths and gone back into battle.

It was a finer shade of morality than the Boers appreciated which could expect them to abide by oaths, exacted under the duress of defeat, to acquiesce in the seizure of their country. If they felt bound to respect the price they had undertaken to pay for withdrawing from the war and being allowed to return to their farms and domestic lives, the shackles fell easily before Christian de Wet's grim and coldly impassioned demands on their patriotism. He was the whirlwind that blew their smouldering emotions into flame. If observers wondered where they got the rifles with which they now sallied out, the answer was that the arms they had handed in amid so much rejoicing by the British consisted largely of elephant-guns, flint-locks, blunderbusses, and ancient sporting pieces. They had buried their proper rifles against the day they might have need of them. Even if they never anticipated the call of a De Wet they would have tried every stratagem before parting with weapons that were the extension of their own right arms, kept in constant readiness for wild animal or marauding Native.

While the future was to delve this aspect of the war deeper, De Wet prepared his next move. He could strike south into the Cape or east behind Roberts to delay his projected march indefinitely. But his considerable qualities fell curiously short of greatness.

To the west, against a backdrop of the Basutoland mountains, nestled the village of Wepener. It was occupied by 2,000 troops from Brabant's Colonial Division and commanded by Colonel Dalgety. The force consisted largely of South African volunteers, and more than any military considerations it was the animosity between fellow South Africans which resolved De Wet to attack the 'sweepings', as he called them, who sold their souls for five shillings per day. [40] He prepared thoroughly, waiting some days for his force to be brought up to some 6,000 before he surrounded the village.

During these days interest switched to the Frenchman Comte de Villebois-Mareuil who had gone north-west of Bloemfontein on an enterprise of his own. A former commander of the Foreign Legion, he had retired from the French Army and made a name as a military writer.

Naturally of a quixotic nature, he showed in his life and writings an almost medieval delight in the glory of the soldier's profession. When he came out to the Transvaal he acted even more as a freelance than the other foreigners. He went about from camp to camp criticizing with a good deal of vigour and with no success the dilatory tactics alike of Joubert before Ladysmith, and of Cronje before Kimberley.[17]

Now he had a command of his own, though he set out with only 150 men, mostly French, and a quantity of dynamite. His object was to blow up the repaired bridge across the Modder to embarrass Methuen in Kimberley, but on the way he decided to attack Boshof, a village north-east of the diamond city. However, Methuen was in the vicinity with a large force. Hearing of the Comte's presence on a farm five miles away he advanced with 750 horsemen and a battery, and surrounded the enemy on two kopjes. Most of the Comte's men fled, but for four hours he resisted with a small band that did not surrender until he lay mortally wounded and the British were thirty yards away. So Comte de Villebois-Mareuil died to the sorrow of France, but as he would have wished, and Methuen buried him with full honours, putting up a stone to mark the place.

By now Dalgety, preparing the defences of Wepener against Christian de Wet, had established a strong position in a circle of hills outside the town. Across the border the Native nation of Basutos assembled in great numbers, intent on the spectacle of battle between their white masters and no doubt wondering what the upshot would hold for them. As in a dramatic tableau the tragedy of South Africa was presented at a glance: the two white races at each other's throats while the Native waited, impotent and impassive, on what their fate would mean to his own.

On 9 April bitter fighting started and continued through the ensuing days and even at night, the Boers once storming right up to the British trenches at 2 a.m. to be beaten off at bayonet point. Nor did a four-day downpour of rain stop their persistent attacks under the lash of De Wet who did not hesitate to use his leather thong (*sjambok*) to enforce obedience to his will. The British held firm though they lay in flooded trenches and food could only be brought to them cold each evening when their wounded were taken away. Roberts heliographed his authority for the force to retire into Basutoland, but this was in any event impracticable because most of their horses were shot. They put their trust in the columns marching to their relief.

These were many and large. As soon as De Wet descended on Wepener, Roberts saw his chance to destroy the Boers east of the railway at a single blow so that he could resume his march with his communications unthreatened. He poured troops in from three directions to catch De Wet in a gigantic net. But De Wet was not Cronje. As the columns drew nearer he sent small forces to hold them up while he got his supply wagons away and kept up the attack on Wepener until the last moment. On the morning of 25 April, after sixteen days of siege, the last of his men made away to the north as the first of the relief columns entered the town.

The Boers had again shown themselves unsuccessful siege fighters, and the resolute British defence had tied up commandos De Wet could have used more advantageously elsewhere. On the other hand his tactics might have made the more famous S.A. sieges a different story. As it was he had postponed the resumption of Roberts's march and with skilful rearguard tactics he eluded every strand in the net.

Among his arrangements since the fall of Bloemfontein Roberts had withdrawn Ian Hamilton from Buller's command and placed him under his own. The first task now assigned him was to march from Bloemfontein to Sannah's Post, which he recaptured and so restored the town's water-supply. Then he set off eastwards in the hope of cutting off De Wet, but after desultory fighting he reached Thaba 'Nchu to find the Boer laager already securely positioned at the other end of the mountain. Joined by French he launched an attack round both sides, hoping to take the enemy in a great bear-hug. The opposition was stern and the attack made slow progress. Roberts called it off. Now that the country east of the railway in his rear was cleared he wanted all the troops ready to resume his main march.

He ordered French to the advance base he had seized at Karee Siding; the horses were so ill-conditioned that 200 were lost during his sixty-mile ride to get there. At the same time Hamilton was ordered due north of Thaba 'Nchu to a point about fifty miles east of Karee Siding.

On the way a commando opposed him in hilly country. The engagement was notable for a widely publicized incident on an isolated part of the hills. Under the Russian Colonel Maximoff 150 foreign volunteers surprised a dozen soldiers under the same captain of the Gordons, E. B. Towse, who had stayed with his wounded colonel in the rout at Magersfontein (see page 134). Maximoff called on him to surrender but Towse, quickly ordering his men behind rocks, fired point-blank at him. Maximoff was wounded and so was Towse, who lost his eyesight. (Later Queen Victoria's eyes were moist as she pinned the V.C. on his tunic.) The soldiers held out until help arrived and in due course Hamilton reached his appointed position.

The long halt at Bloemfontein was over. At last Roberts had everything in readiness for his final push. The moment had come for the event which, next to the relief of Mafeking, England awaited in a mood of happy expectancy little jolted by De Wet's successes: the march to Pretoria.

CHAPTER XVI

Mafeking: May 1900

UNDETERRED by the fate of Napoleon's dash for Moscow, Roberts aimed straight at 'old Kruger's lair'. He rejected the alternative of an inch-by-inch conquest. Like every one of his soldiers he believed that the Boers would surrender if they lost Pretoria. Besides, the highly centralized foreign Powers would never regard the Boers as beaten until both capitals were captured. Militarily, he based his decision on a desire to bring them together from every quarter in defence of their citadel, where he intended to impose a final crushing defeat—unless, even before that, demoralization increased to the point of total collapse. He reckoned on this as highly probable when the Boers saw not only Pretoria imperilled but Johannesburg, lying on the route to it and only forty miles away.

Their ambivalent attitude towards Johannesburg—their hate of it and their need of it—made, either way, their possession of it dangerous. It provided them with ammunition and gold, or alternatively they could wreck the mines to the loss of millions in British investments. Therefore when Roberts thought of Pretoria he coupled it with the City of Gold.

Finally, his thinking was influenced by that constant in every S.A. military calculation, the railways. All the trunk lines except the Western radiated from Pretoria, whose capture would enable him to cut off the Boers from outside aid while securing his own means for supply or for any pacification that might still be needed.

In short, he considered that by marching to Pretoria he would destroy the enemy's strength, will to fight, and means of fighting. At this stage the Boers had about 30,000 men,* of whom 17,000 were in

* At Brandfort north of Karee Siding, De la Rey and Tobias Smuts had 2,000 (3 guns); south-east of them Philip Botha had 2,000–3,000, and 1,500 in reserve under Grobler;

the O.F.S. Although they also had a reserve resting on their farms, and no need to expend manpower on guarding lines of communication, their strength was puny compared with Roberts's. In the field he had 170,000 men (theoretically 200,000 but the 'wastage' in such a campaign was great), of whom he proposed to use over 100,000 for his front-line advance from Natal to the Western border and from Bloemfontein to Rhodesia, while the remainder manned garrisons, lines of communication or followed the advance as reserves.

After the relief of Ladysmith Roberts ordered White's Chief of Staff, General Sir Archibald Hunter, to Kimberley with over a division of troops to march in due course up the Western railway. Methuen meanwhile—and this accounted for his presence near Boshof, north-east of the city, which caught the French Comte by surprise—was assembling 10,000 men to cross the north-west corner of the O.F.S. to the Vaal River.

He would provide an additional prong to the spearhead of Roberts's main advance, which would consist of 38,000 men and over a hundred guns in three columns marching roughly parallel with each other straight for Pretoria. One of these columns was under Roberts's direct command and would set out from the advance base he had seized at Karee Siding. On its left front would range the main mounted body under French. On the right the third column, mostly M.I., would be led by Ian Hamilton from the position he had taken up fifty miles east of Karee Siding with a convoy of 500 wagons and 5,000 mules, since, unlike Roberts and French, he would not have the railway to keep him supplied.

While these three columns advanced up the centre of the O.F.S. and Methuen advanced through the country west of the railway, an increasing area east of it would be unsecured. Roberts hoped that his advance would draw off all the Boers in this area, but there was the risk that some might try to slip past Hamilton's right flank and disrupt communications or even invade the Cape again.

Remembering that Buller was at Ladysmith, only twenty miles from the O.F.S.'s eastern border, the reader will be struck by an

round Thaba 'Nchu the two De Wets, Olivier and Lemmer had 6,000; Louis Botha was bringing 3,000 from Natal; Marthinus Prinsloo had 1,500 at Van Reenen's Pass. Snyman had 2,000 round Mafeking. Du Toit and Andries Cronje had 2,000 at Fourteen Streams to the south of it, and there were 1,200 in Griqualand. Lukas Meyer had 8,000 in the Biggarsberg.

obvious solution to Roberts's problem. It was less obvious to Buller.
He had himself long proposed that he invade the north-east O.F.S.,
which would trap the Boers there or at least secure Roberts's flank.
But then he saw difficulties. Roberts wrote of him to Lansdowne at
this time: 'He certainly is an extraordinary man. His first intentions are
generally correct, but his second thoughts invariably lead him astray. I
can never feel sure that he will carry out anything that has been decided
upon.' The result was a flow of telegrams totalling nearly fifty during
March and April as Buller plied excuse upon excuse and Roberts
patiently replied. If Buller had an idea of restoring his glory and
putting Roberts out of countenance by himself marching through the
Transvaal in triumph to Pretoria, he could scarcely have made his
excuse for not going into the O.F.S. less convincing. It would be dangerous to leave the Boers unmolested on the Biggarsberg, he said, misled by Intelligence reports into multiplying their actual strength by
three. He had not enough men, he said. Not enough cavalry, not
enough guns, engineers, boots, clothes, horses. And between excuses
he suggested plans of campaign each cancelling out the last, reaching
the high point of hilarity with a proposal that Roberts should send
cavalry 200 miles away to clear the Drakensberg passes for him. Roberts
gave up. He left Buller to do as he pleased, which was to trundle slowly
towards the Biggarsberg.

He therefore had to safeguard his advance and contain the eastern
O.F.S. by other means. He laid very careful plans, though only time
was to show how effective they would be.

Immediately behind Hamilton, to support him on either flank if
necessary, a division would advance under General Sir Henry Colvile,
who had commanded the Guards Brigade under Methuen. Thirty
years of campaigning had earned him the reputation of being one of
the best Intelligence officers in the Army. A man of ample means, his
keen amused face with its thin moustache was that of a bon viveur, and
he was a writer of some merit, his works including a travel book called
A Ride In Petticoats and Slippers. Behind him an even larger force would
advance under General Sir Leslie Rundle, who had been Kitchener's
Chief of Staff in the Sudan. Rundle's force, almost touching hands
with garrisons from Bloemfontein to Thaba 'Nchu, would form a
barrier from Thaba 'Nchu to the Basutoland border. By pushing the
barrier northwards and keeping the Boers always in front of him,

Rundle's function was to prevent any break-through southwards. But if he failed, the enemy would run into Brabant's Colonial Division and a further barrier formed (under the command of Chermside, Gatacre's successor) along a chain of towns and villages from Bethanie on the Central railway to Wepener on the Basutoland border. Apart from Hamilton's column and the garrisons around Bloemfontein, there would therefore be four successive forces totalling 40,000 men to contain the north-east O.F.S. Every mile of railway line from Kimberley and Bloemfontein to the Cape ports was guarded by garrisons and patrols. Sir Charles Warren, detached from Buller, was sent to clear Boer and rebels from the wilderness south-west of Kimberley.

To the British public, keenly though they awaited the outcome of Roberts's preparations across 1,600 miles from Cape Town to Beira, heart and imagination were still clutched by Mafeking, the more fervently for its continued jeopardy when all other dangers had been swept away. Relief of the village was becoming urgently necessary. For some months a part of Plumer's force of colonial irregulars had been pushing down the Western railway far to the north of Mafeking, and then Plumer left off his running skirmishes with the Boers on the northern Transvaal border and brought most of his men—about 1,500 —down the line. Through March expeditions from this force tried to get to Mafeking and reached within six miles of it, but Snyman, leaving the siege lines, pushed them back, though not further than fifteen miles north of the village. All these operations distracted the besiegers, so that even their bombardment eased off appreciably, but the danger to Baden-Powell was his increasing shortage of supplies. People were eating horses, mules, even locusts (curried). At his advance post Plumer was able to receive over a thousand Natives who escaped from Mafeking and so lightened the demand on Baden-Powell's supplies; but an attempt by Plumer to drive a herd of cattle into the village failed. Baden-Powell had got a message through to Roberts saying that supplies would be finished by 22 May, so that with April slipping away Roberts was resolved on early relief. A flying column detached from Archibald Hunter's force at Kimberley would go on ahead of him up the western border of the Transvaal for this sole purpose.

His plans laid and his troops everywhere in position, Roberts took the train from Bloemfontein at five o'clock on the morning of 3 May 1900. At Karee Siding he assumed command of his column. Intending that he himself would make the first triumphant entry into Pretoria he included in his column men from all over Britain, and from Australia, Burma, Canada, Ceylon, India, New Zealand and S.A. itself, besides blue-jackets on some of the heavy guns to represent the Navy. His head-quarters staff accompanying him numbered seventy. Most of them were useless, many being aristocrats enjoying the privilege of aides-de-camp. Staff organization was not a feature of the time. Roberts kept personal and direct control of every movement across the entire huge arena. Though Chief of Staff, Kitchener did not work out details of plans and transmit them to the commanders concerned. Roberts did this him-self, often without telling Kitchener whom he used to invigorate parti-cular operations. The arrangement had worked so far, but the campaign was now becoming far more complicated and widespread than it had been.

On Roberts's arrival at Karee Siding there rang out for the first time a phrase rich with the undertones of history. Through French's mounted troops posted ahead, through the infantry astride the railway, and through Hamilton's column fifty miles to the right, was heard the refrain: *We are marching to Pretoria!*

* * * *

The Boers were waiting with perhaps 10,000 men in a wide arc from the railway at Brandfort to the Basutoland border eighty miles away. Those at Brandfort, fifteen miles in front of Roberts, were the Trans-vaalers commanded by De la Rey. The billowing clouds of dust and swarming horsemen in front of him announced an end to the weeks of waiting, of rumour and counter-rumour, and sustained attempts to rally his men. But now, numbering only 2,000–3,000, when they saw the tens of thousands of troops coming at them, all the self-confidence so painfully built up since the fall of Bloemfontein began to seep away. There could be no question of making a stand in the open veld where they would quickly be surrounded. De la Rey did the only thing he could, which was to fight a rearguard action while his transport struggled to get away, the tide swollen by civilian refugees similarly intent on evading the British.

So soon, Roberts's expectation of a final demoralization seemed about to be realized. As the avalanche descended, the leaders eastward of De la Rey shared his difficulty in keeping their commandos together.

The numerical superiority of the British was at its most frightening on the rolling plains. Even the rivers were scarcely more than rivulets, but they were the only hope. De la Rey retreated to the Vet River, twenty miles beyond Brandfort, but a mere thousand men stayed with him to face the fresh attack Roberts launched on 5 May.

Young Reitz was present at this engagement, having come on ahead of the reinforcement due to arrive from Natal. He lay with his three brothers, their horses in the river-bed behind them. As the British artillery played up and down the Boer line 'like a piano' the infantry advanced slowly through tall grass until at 3 p.m. they broke into a charge. The Boer dead had been placed in the river-bed, the wounded on their horses to get away as best they could, and now the survivors ran down the river bank, leapt on their horses, scrambled out and galloped for a distant line of hills. Still the British came on. Reaching one end of the hills they began to roll up the whole Boer position.

> We fronted round to meet them but the sinking sun was straight in our eyes . . . another stampede took place . . . by the time I was in the saddle, the nearest infantryman was so close that I could see their faces and the brass buttons on their tunics, but they were blown with running and their aim was poor. . . . My eldest brother's pony was shot through the body from saddle-flap to saddle-flap, but the plucky little animal carried him a thousand yards before he fell dead. Riderless horses were careering all over the place, and by cornering one of these we succeeded in providing my brother with another mount. Bullets and shells were striking everywhere, so we hurriedly transferred his belongings to the new horse and followed the rout now vanishing over the next rise . . . we trekked on till after midnight, our only crumb of comfort being our native boy awaiting us beside the road, his voice quivering with emotion at seeing all four of us still alive.

A squadron of Canadians rode through the retreating Boers to cut the railway further north but the last train had already gone. Away to the right the column under Hamilton kept abreast of Roberts by entering the picturesque old town of Winburg, whose inhabitants the Boer commandant had tried in vain to rally to its defence.

Roberts paused at the Vet for several days. The horses needed resting; and because the railway bridge had been blown up, supplies had tediously to be off-loaded from the trains on to ox-wagons for distribution on the further bank. He took the opportunity to draw Hamilton's column closer in to him because he wished to be well prepared for the next leg of his march. This would be to the Sand River, only forty miles south of Kroonstad and from all accounts the scene of intensive preparations for a stand to save the new capital. A force of Canadians going forward to reconnoitre was beaten back. (Reitz, speaking to two wounded troopers, learnt for the first time that the Empire was taking part: 'as if', he comments, 'the odds against us were not heavy enough already.')

Louis Botha arrived at Sand River with 3,000 burghers from Natal, assuming command of the Transvaalers and releasing De la Rey to go into the western Transvaal and oppose the attempt to relieve Mafeking. He had in fact arrived later than he intended because his men had outstayed their leave on the way from Natal, so that he had to send them stern telegrams and then go on a personal round-up.

He occupied positions along and behind the river. With the Free State commandos on his left, a front of twenty-five miles was manned by perhaps 8,000 burghers. President Steyn came into the fighting line to inspire his people, and on returning to Kroonstad continued drumming up the laggards and faint-hearted. Even as he stood at the station making a speech a train drew out for the front. 'Look, burghers!' he cried——

> There are your brothers going forward to take part in the struggle which you and I have to carry on to its end; and are you going to stand here while they are fighting for their country? . . . We have fought against the hordes of Great Britain for more than seven months; we can fight seven times as long if necessary. Go, then, burghers, in God's name, for the cause of your dear country, for your wives and children. It is better to die on the battlefield than to become slaves of your ancient enemy.

On 10 May Roberts struck. French led a vanguard of 4,000 horsemen round the western flank of the Boer line with a view to cutting in to the railway behind it. Botha at once drew back his centre and wheeled right to fend him off. This highly vulnerable tactical manœuvre, 'forming front to a flank', was successful in compelling French to ride further and further north so that fighting took place all day along a twenty-mile arc from the river, and when night came his horses were too exhausted, after a final successful charge, to reach the railway line. But it also meant that Roberts could advance up the railway without opposition and cross to six miles beyond the river. Hamilton too, after an artillery duel with the Free Staters, was able to advance with little difficulty over a ford carelessly left unguarded, though efforts to cut in to the railway behind the Boers from this flank were as thwarted as those of French on the other.

The Boer attempt to stand at Sand River, which their Presidents had set much store by, made clear that in open country against overwhelming numbers, including a large body of mounted men, the only alternative to encirclement was to fall back—'the long-drawn humiliation of retreat,' Reitz called it: 'All day we were driven relentlessly; the British herded us like sheep to the incessant shriek of shells and the whizzing of bullets, and by evening we were a demoralized rabble fleeing blindly across the veld.'

Next day Roberts advanced to midway between the Sand River and Kroonstad. The shadow of defeat hung dark and hopeless over the town. Steyn stood on a table in the market-place, unbowed before the storm and still exhorting the fleeing burghers to turn back, but they were mainly Transvaalers making shift to return to their own territory, and only a few hundred could be persuaded to stay. As horsemen and wagons streamed through the town Steyn saw the futility of further effort. Declaring Heilbron the new capital he climbed into a Cape-cart and set off for it, sixty miles to the north-east. The railway bridge south of the town was blown up. The stores were opened for everyone to help himself before the remainder went up in smoke. At nightfall all defences were abandoned. The rearguard rode through the darkened streets and for twenty miles beyond before catching up with the fleeing commandos.

Again a British party, this time including Burnham the Canadian scout—who had escaped by a ruse since his capture at Sannah's Post— rode through the retreating columns to cut the railway line, and again the last train had already departed, dropping blasting charges on the track behind it as it went. The following day, 12 May, Roberts marched unopposed into Kroonstad.

He was half-way to Pretoria.

*   *   *   *

In the Transvaal capital itself the Volksraad had just adjourned. As they went their way few members could not have wondered if they would ever meet again as the Government of an independent republic. Beyond the walls of the red-brown building events were piling up to a point where the greater part of the O.F.S. lay conquered and the full weight of British arms threatened the Transvaal from every quarter of the compass.

The Raad's session had opened a few days before, while not only was Roberts marching on Kroonstad, a mere forty miles from the nearest point on the Vaal, but west of him Methuen was approaching Hoopstad, only twenty miles from the frontier; and west of him again General Hunter was actually about to enter the republic from the extreme south-west corner via Fourteen Streams after driving away the commandos posted there to prevent the relief of Mafeking, effectually distracting their attention from the flying column on its way to attempt the relief. At the same time the Rhodesian Field Force had now been raised—it consisted of about 6,000 Yeomanry and Australians under the command of General Carrington—and was arriving by sea at Beira for transit across Rhodesia and a descent on the northern Transvaal. Most menacing of all apart from Roberts, Buller was at last moving from the east: recovered from the suffering and satisfaction of relieving Ladysmith over two months ago, he was advancing towards the Biggarsberg.

The Volksraad therefore met at a moment when Roberts's forces were converging on the republic from all four sides. Most of the surviving members were present, many of them fighting men arrived straight from the fronts. The foreign consuls and attachés attended in full regalia. Lukas Meyer wore the toga of speaker or chairman. President Kruger had his scarf of office and white gloves, a little incongruous on a man for whom finery was an abomination. The chairs of General Joubert and others who had died were left empty, draped with streamers of crape and immortelles. General Piet Cronje, in captivity at St. Helena, was remembered by a *Vierkleur*, the Republican flag, which hung over his chair.

The parson who led the prayers expressed their pride in their dead heroes, and their sorrow. Paul Kruger spoke. He talked of their sister republic's sacrifices, of the goodwill among foreign nations and of the three-man mission which had gone to turn it to practical account. He declared the country's finances to be satisfactory. Then when the president had finished the man spoke his heart, confessing his loneliness since the death of his comrades like Joubert and old Kock who had fought in his top-hat in the gun-pit at Elandslaagte so many months ago.

Arrangements for the conduct of the war were left to the Executive. The Pretoria forts, for the destruction of which the British had only the week before landed great siege guns at Cape Town, were deemed useless since most of their armaments had long been dismantled to serve at the fronts. The decision was therefore taken not to defend Pretoria but to fight the British before they could reach it. Many citizens, unaware of this decision, were agitated by the lack of defensive measures, and to placate them Lukas Meyer was made commandant to organize a show of defence. There were women ardent enough on this question to band themselves into an Amazon Corps to shame their menfolk, though little came of it. More practically, gold and great quantities of supplies were shifted to the village of Machadodorp half-way along the Delagoa Bay railway lest the Transvaal Government had to follow the O.F.S. example and fly the capital.

The atmosphere of doom was intensified by a bitter wrangle on the last full day of debate. Kruger wanted to dispose of certain valuable mining rights for a trifle, but in cash. The moderates opposed the proposal. Kruger delivered a long harangue, 'waving about that thumbless hand, and shaking his forefinger in defiance'. When a member continued to protest at being asked to 'barter away the assets of the country for a pittance at the bid of speculators' instead of grappling with the crisis, Kruger thundered, blew his nose without benefit of handkerchief and finally stormed out of the House, declaring, 'I will do as I like.' [14]

Next day, 10 May, the Volksraad adjourned, its members going back to the task of making war. A day later, at Birmingham in England Mr. Chamberlain announced the British Government's war aims. A South African Conciliation Committee had been formed by eminent people anxious to end the war: it proposed a peace settlement by which the Boers would surrender their arms, control of foreign relations, and the Rand. The idea was fastened on by those Liberal newspapers whose attitude to the war was bringing a disastrous drop in circulation. In fact the only papers able to pursue a consistently anti-war policy were

The Manchester Guardian, The Morning Leader and *The Star*.* The first
survived because of its commercial service, businessmen in Lancashire
ostentatiously crumpling up their copies as soon as they had read the
cotton news; the other two because the working class regarded them as
its own papers, even though it was for the most part so in favour of the
war—despite Radical denunciations of a capitalist war shedding men's
blood for the sake of Rand mine-owners—that at the next Trades
Union Congress the Jingoism of workmen was bitterly denounced.
That Jingoism was now satisfied, and the Conciliation Committee
snubbed, by Chamberlain's declaration. Addressing a packed Town
Hall while a crowd of 60,000 jammed all approaches, he said that both
republics 'must and shall be fully incorporated in Her Majesty's
Dominions': 'That is not a bad fate for them. They will not be worse
off than the people of Canada or the people of Australia. . . . There is
only one cure for racial antagonism and that is a reign of justice and
equality.' This last sentence expressed an eternal verity, but the examples
of Canada, where the French were a minority territorially detached,
and of Australia, which was exclusively British, lacked force. Blood is
thicker than government, however honest. Any prospect of a nego-
tiated peace now vanished. It was to be a fight to the finish. For the
Boers, it was a question of survival as an independent race. For the
British, too much blood had been shed, too much money spent, too
much prestige lost, for them to turn back.

Even as Chamberlain was speaking, the papers carried lists of war
losses as distressing as the previous lists of casualties after battle, for they
were from disease, and there was growing criticism of the medical
services. While most people approved the war, criticism of its conduct
was now taking firm hold and increasing. Buller's Spion Kop dispatches were published with the revelation that the Secretary of War
had asked him to rewrite them because of the blame attached to
Warren and of evidence pointing to disharmony. The public wondered
what else was going on behind the scenes and pounced more readily on
anything suspicious. But on the question of medical services the
Government could produce two eminent doctors who had investigated, reporting that despite 'a plague of flies and a plague of women'—

---

* Prominent anti-war journals that should also be mentioned were W. T. Stead's
Review of Reviews and the *Westminster Gazette*, the latter notable for the flaying of the
Government by 'Saki' (H. H. Munro).

the last, often half-trained enthusiasts who had enrolled with hospital volunteer corps—the standard was excellent.* In any event criticism was easily stilled for the moment by stirring events. White, 'hero of Ladysmith', arrived home to be received by the Queen, though he modestly kept out of the way of the public—who vented their emotion on the returning naval unit drawing their Ladysmith guns through London's streets amid ecstatic crowds. But this was as a gentle breeze compared with the tempest which news from the front was soon to unleash.

Roberts's entry into Kroonstad was immediately followed by Buller's successful assault on the Biggarsberg. He did it by a flanking movement round Helpmekaar and deployed the whole of his force without a hitch, sending the Boers flying from their last stronghold in Natal. He was fortunate in finding the enemy depleted in numbers and their morale not improved by Lukas Meyer's presence as commander. With scarcely a fight they quit Natal to take up position in the Drakensberg passes to the O.F.S. and the Transvaal, leaving Buller to reclaim towns like Dundee and to collect surrenders from Boer farmers in the countryside round about. But chastened by all that had happened to him, and as though scarcely able to credit his good fortune, he advanced with extreme deliberation to the Drakensberg.

Meanwhile Roberts's entry into Kroonstad coincided, more spectacularly, with the last act in the drama of Mafeking.

The flying column from Archibald Hunter's force had set out on its journey of 250 miles from the vicinity of Kimberley on 4 May. It was commanded by Colonel B. T. Mahon, an Irish Hussar who had distinguished himself at Omdurman, and it consisted mainly of S.A. volunteers. A week later, helped by Hunter's distraction of the Boers down the line, it was at Vryburg a hundred miles south of Mafeking. One of Baden-Powell's officers arrived about now, having slipped through the siege lines and brought details of a proposed link-up between Mahon and Plumer. Powell asked for details of Mahon's strength, and in the absence of a cipher the reply was couched as follows: 'Our numbers are the Naval and Military Club multiplied by ten [94 (Piccadilly) × 10]; our guns, the number of sons in the Ward

---

* Of the many who gave their lives tending the sick of both sides, one of the most notable was the great and idiosyncratic explorer Charles Kingsley's niece Mary, who died of fever while nursing Boer patients at Simonstown.

family [6]; our supplies, the O.C. 9th Lancers [Little].' The Mafeking garrison hearing of Mahon's approach and seeing many Boers leaving, prepared at last for the moment of release. But suddenly in the early hours of 12 May that happy expectation was rudely shattered. A party of Boers pierced the outer perimeter of the defences by approaching along the banks of the Molopo, set fire to the huts of the Native *stad* and swept on to capture a fort commanded by Colonel Hore only a quarter of a mile from the town.

The Boers were led by Field-Cornet Sarel Eloff, grandson of Paul Kruger from whom he had just returned on a visit with strict instructions to capture the place at all costs. But Snyman was no keener than his burghers, only a hundred of whom helped Eloff capture the fort. There, having locked Hore and the other surrendered defenders in a room, he prepared to hold out until Snyman sent promised support. By now the whole town, roused by the shots and burning *stad*, stood at arms—including the prisoners in gaol who were released for the purpose. Powell repulsed Snyman's feeble efforts to give support and laid siege to Eloff. One of the foreigners with Eloff, a Frenchman, climbed on the roof of the fort with a bottle of Burgundy and shouted a toast, 'Fashoda is revenged!' before he was shot down. Eloff hung on all day with great bravery until evening when he surrendered to his own prisoners. Baden-Powell arrived to invite him to dinner, and the Boers were saluted by the garrison as they were marched off under guard.

Next day Mahon's flying column for the first time encountered a commando—led by Liebenberg whom Kitchener had ejected from the western Cape—but beat it back. In the morning he joined hands with Plumer who had marched to the Molopo twenty miles from Mafeking, having just received a reinforcement of Royal Canadian Artillery rushed from Beira by mule and stage-coach across Rhodesia. They were in the nick of time, for Koos de la Rey had just arrived post-haste under orders from Louis Botha in the midst of trying to hold back Roberts. With 2,000 men from the siege lines De la Rey took up position astride the Molopo at a place called Israel's Farm eight miles upstream from Mafeking. A stiff five-hour fight resulted early on 16 May. Part of the Boer line gave way and the rest fled. A carrier-pigeon from Plumer bore the news to the garrison that the two columns were on their way.

In the afternoon the garrison and townsfolk, eager at every look-out, saw shells exploding in the distance; and presently a dark mass of horsemen appeared, a heliograph twinkling in their midst: 'From Colonel Mahon's force—How are you getting on?'

Baden-Powell answered simply: 'Welcome.'

Ten men of the I.L.H. rode in at 7 p.m. led by Major Karri Davis, one of the two Uitlanders who had refused Kruger's terms of amnesty to the Reform leaders imprisoned after the Jameson Raid. They were met with frenzied delight, and in the early hours of the following morning Mahon and Plumer entered without any opposition from the Boers, who simply disappeared. The seven months' siege was over.

At a cost of 160 casualties (half the Boers') it had kept Cronje and 10,000 men immobilized in the critical opening months of the war and continued since then to keep Snyman's force idle. But the loss or survival of a one-eyed village in the blue had little real bearing on the war, and the Boers showed to the full their inadequacy as siege fighters, since only one determined push in the wake of a Sarel Eloff must have sufficed to overwhelm Baden-Powell, who did not have to meet a single full-blooded assault. Yet even if allowance is made for the belief in England that 'the pluck and wits of a British handful had won against the odds', this does not explain why England on hearing of the relief reacted as if to news that Paradise had been regained. Given that 'the fundamental grit of the breed'—in the hyperbole of *The Times*— was displayed at Mafeking, with 'the common man of the Empire . . . at the long last coming out, proud, tenacious, unconquered and unconquerable', it still does not explain the phenomenon of Mafeking Night.

There were in fact two Mafeking Nights and a Mafeking Day.

At about 9.30 p.m. on Friday, 18 May 1900, a Reuter message reached London. An excited footman at the Mansion House was supposed to have been the first to catapult the news through the streets. What is certain is that the window blinds were raised to reveal a blaze of light, that a placard was hung out bearing the words MAFEKING IS RELIEVED, that a large sketch of Baden-Powell was hung close by, and that within half an hour the space in front of the building was jammed solid with people.

At the same time the news spread across the capital like flames before a wind. In the House of Commons Arthur Balfour suavely declared that the news was unconfirmed: 'This does not mean that Mafeking has been relieved or that it has not been relieved.' The War Office put up a notice: NO NEWS. It made no difference. Reuter's message was daubed on large boards in Fleet Street. It was printed in special editions which newsboys raced about flinging into gentlemen's hansom cabs without payment. It was announced in music-hall and theatre. At the Lyceum even Madame Duse was interrupted and *God Save the Queen* spontaneously sung. At Covent Garden Opera House, where the Prince of Wales and the King of Sweden were in the audience, someone shouted from the gallery as the curtain went down on the second act of *Lohengrin*: three cheers rang out and when everyone burst into song the Prince beat time on the ledge of his box. All the while the streets were filling with a torrent of people that sprang out of the darkness, out of the paving stones, out of nowhere. From the Mansion House, via Ludgate Circus, Fleet Street, the Strand, Whitehall, Pall Mall, Piccadilly, Regent Street, and Oxford Street to Park Lane this fantastic assembly cheered themselves hoarse, waved flags and banners, embraced, laughed, wept, and raised the roof of the sky with *Rule Britannia*, *Soldiers of the Queen*, *The Absent-minded Beggar* and the Anthem.

> That night the labyrinth of London seemed to give up its millions to view . . . they packed the streets with huge humanity, cheering and singing. Sometimes under opposite pressures immense multitudes found themselves unable to move an inch. Again, they surged this way and that by slow degrees, contrary currents working through each other and roaring like a storm.[1]

From the centre, great waves radiated outwards. Men returning to the suburbs left train for cab and shouted the news to astonished villas. In the provinces—

> Liverpool was alive with parading crowds; Newcastle was startled by the explosion and flare of rockets; Birmingham spread the news like wildfire from its theatres; the brass band of the volunteers roused the streets of York; Glasgow illuminated its Municipal buildings; Leicester and Brighton swarmed with madly cheering people; the Yorkshire dales reverberated with the sound of strangely blown mill and factory sirens.[1]

All commentators agree on the magical way crowds appeared as if at the touch of a conjurer's wand, and on the complete spontaneity of the nation's unprecedented outburst.

The 'mafficking' did not cease with the night. Saturday was at least a half working day for most people, but no one set out to do any work except pickpockets and pedlars. Suburban houses had their awnings out and flags and bunting. People with red, white and blue in their buttonholes sang as they travelled up, ostensibly to work, in trains gaily decorated and letting out festive blasts on their fog-horns. Again London's principal streets became clogged with crowds carrying flags and portraits of favourite generals. Art students devised patriotic tableaux, bands played, and soon traffic was brought to a complete standstill. A coarser mood developed with the day. Drunks multiplied; there was anger at the absence of decoration in Whitehall. Street hawkers kept up an endless supply of toy trumpets or squeakers that were blown incessantly, and of peacocks' feathers and switches called 'Kruger's whiskers' that were provocatively brushed against the faces of either sex by the other as hooliganism spread. The staid were bustled into their clubs and policemen were mobbed, though not always without affection—a much kissed constable at Aldgate declaring, 'I wouldn't go through that kissing again for something. Right in the public street it was.' Towards evening coloured fires burnt along the streets, flares were lit, buildings illuminated, and with singing and dancing the second Mafeking Night was celebrated as vociferously as the first. The comparative calm of Sunday descended, but several evenings were required before the mood finally worked itself out.

The occasion added the verb 'maffick' to the language, which the O.E.D. defines as 'exult riotously'. There was in fact no rioting in the full sense of eighteenth-century mob violence, but the aftermath was a serious misgiving among thoughtful people. Many saw Mafeking Night as indicative of national degeneracy and opponents of the war regarded it as confirmation of their belief that hostilities had been begun recklessly and irresponsibly. Imperialists, sensitive to the shocked derision with which foreign nations reacted, asked whether a people so lacking in self-control could seek to be masters of others.

Efforts to explain it all have reached comical depths. A leading authority gravely puts the whole affair down to the activity of the street hawkers.[1] But the reader who has made his way through the opening chapter of this book and the course of public emotions since the outbreak of war will understand Mafeking Night as the inevitable climax of the late Victorian Age. In a single orgiastic moment the Age was upheaved—and fell back limp.

CHAPTER XVII

Roberts—Climax: May–June 1900

By contrast with the agitated reaction in Pretoria to Roberts's capture of Kroonstad only ten days after leaving Bloemfontein, Johannesburg presented an aspect of indifference. Having played such a conspicuous part in the events leading to the outbreak of war, it had since fallen into the background even though it remained important to the Boers as a supplier of gold and ammunition. The reason was that most of the Uitlanders, half its population, had departed. All the bars were closed, many shops shuttered, the cabs and trams immobilized for want of horses which had been requisitioned. At night the remaining townspeople stayed indoors by decree of martial law. Around the outskirts stood the great dumps of sifted yellow-white mine-sand like spectral hills in a landscape of the Inferno. Along the deserted streets grass was growing and the cold wind seemed a restless ghost of the rumbustious past.

Some mines continued working, several operated directly by the Government. So did Begbie's engineering works. Under the Belgian, Leon (who was injured in the Kimberley siege like his opposite number Labram, though not fatally), and then under two Frenchmen, this factory turned out thousands of rounds for the Boers' Krupp, Armstrong and Maxim-Nordenfeldt guns. But on the afternoon of 24 April it was shattered by an explosion which sent up a mile-high column of smoke and caused widespread damage to the houses of poor burghers nearby. Allegations of treachery were bandied about and excited foreign workmen attended public meetings, resulting in a special guard being formed under the Italian volunteer Ricchiardi.

Some British had evaded the expulsion decree or were permitted to remain as representatives of firms. But most of the population now consisted of people 'either very poor or very rascally'. With the regular police away at the fronts a scratch force was got together; a more efficient body was formed by the mine-owners to protect their property, and looting was kept to a minimum. Far more disturbing to the British was how to prevent an organized wholesale destruction of the mines if the Kruger Government itself determined on such a step. The prospect was not only harrowing to the soul of our Victorian: *Punch* depicted two of the considerable number of Continental shareholders in conversation—

French Rand Shareholder: 'Is he not a Boer and a brother?'
German Rand Shareholder: 'Yes! But if he wrecks our mines?'
1st Shareholder: 'A-A-A-AH!'

Information now reached Roberts that at least a section of prominent Boers were intent on destruction.

He had therefore an added reason for wanting to advance swiftly. But Theron's Scouts posted on the hills beyond Kroonstad saw no sign among the host of tents around the town that he was resuming the march. He was being compelled to mark time.

The railway behind him had been blown up in seventeen places for distances of up to half a mile and twenty-seven bridges were wrecked. Ox-wagons had slowly to bridge the gaps in order that supplies could be distributed while the construction train which had followed him from Karee Siding carried out repairs with the help of gangs of soldiers and Natives. Food and forage became short and among both men and horses disability increased sharply, accelerated by the reaction which a break in the march always caused and the fact that many men had left Bloemfontein before they were fit. Some of the sick were sent back down the line; for those who remained there was a shortage of bedding, necessaries, staff.

Roberts had also to pause while he made sure of his flanks. He sent a mounted force west of the railway to scour the country stretching hot and featureless to Methuen's column. The farmers were found peacefully at work and no future danger threatened. But east of the railway things were very different. As he advanced, so had the Free Staters sidestepped to the right. It was to his right front that they had established their new capital at Heilbron, though they made him think it was at

Lindley due east of Kroonstad. He therefore sent Ian Hamilton to capture Lindley, which emerged in the news for the first but not the last time.

As Hamilton marched he carried Roberts's proclamation offering immunity to burghers who returned peacefully to their farms. Once again an impressive assortment of decrepit fire-arms was deposited with the British, and the Boers kept their lethal weapons intact to await further developments. On Roberts's orders Hamilton took no more than he needed of the standing crops, which were thus left to provision commandos who hovered about and harassed his rearguard. A brief skirmish gave him Lindley, the Boers merely getting out of the way; and as soon as he left the town they reoccupied it. Like the steady dispersal of Boers without being brought to decisive battle, this was an omen no one as yet read.

Hamilton's column now made northward for Heilbron. The O.F.S. Government once again fled. Abandoning his third capital Steyn departed eastward with the State papers. He declared Frankfort, thirty miles away, the new capital. Christian de Wet followed with a large convoy. Marthinus Prinsloo had arrived in the vicinity with the commando released from guarding Van Reenen's Pass by Buller's advance past it. With the other commandos which had drawn aside as Roberts advanced a formidable build-up of Boer strength was taking place in this, the north-east quarter of the O.F.S.—the 'Top Right-hand Corner' as Churchill called it.

The territory extended from the Central railway to Natal, and from Basutoland in the south to the Transvaal in the north. It was very fertile, the granary of S.A.; and instead of the flat plains elsewhere, it thrust up barriers of hill and mountain twined about by valleys. It was not lush like Natal: much of it had an almost barren appearance that seemed to deny its richness. The lonely crooked peaks and isolated kopjes which studded broad bowl-like valleys gave it a haunting and brooding quality, making strangers of all who were not its own people. These ranked among the most redoubtable of the Boer race.

They constituted a potential danger which Roberts had been uneasy about from the first, and De Wet's exploits had not made him feel easier. Despite the series of columns and garrisons he had organized behind Hamilton he regretted showing such forbearance to Buller, and he again asked him to co-operate. Again Buller, who was now only ten miles from the border, put up a barrage of excuses and again Roberts gave up. The dilemma then was whether to postpone his cherished march to Pretoria while he himself invaded the menacing territory, or to by-pass it in the hope that the successive forces under Colvile, Rundle, Chermside and Brabant posted behind Hamilton would contain it until he captured Pretoria and ended the war.

He therefore considered his campaign as a whole. Released by the relief of Mafeking, Baden-Powell and Plumer were together preparing to invade the Transvaal from the west, and so was Archibald Hunter immediately he had repaired the Western railway along the Transvaal border. Carrington was assembling his Rhodesia Field Force as it arrived at Beira for an invasion of the northern Transvaal; Buller was moving on to the eastern border. Thus with Methuen's approach to the Vaal from the south-west, and his own and Hamilton's from the south, he was throwing a huge net around the Transvaal. He resolved to stick to his plan of driving straight on to deliver the *coup de grâce* by capturing Johannesburg and Pretoria.

But this would mean leaving the railway behind him exposed as he advanced, and in view of the possible threat from the north-eastern O.F.S. if the commandos recovered from the confusion of flight, he ordered Methuen in due course to turn eastwards from Hoopstad on to the railway. Another important decision was to order Colvile, who had been trailing Hamilton, to take the latter's place on the right flank while Hamilton switched over to Roberts's left in support of French—lest the Boers made a stand when he approached Johannesburg, lying west of the railway to Pretoria.

*　　*　　*　　*

The delay in Kroonstad lasted ten days. On 22 May the sight of slowly rising pillars of dust, and of troops striding out along every road, announced to Theron's Scouts that Roberts was on the move again. They dug their heels in their ponies and carried the news to Botha, who was striving to keep a sufficient force in being to thwart the final phase of Roberts's great march.

Once again French's cavalry ranged ahead. For the infantry plodding behind, little relieved the monotony of the dry and boundless plains. They marched on and on in pursuit of nothing but the horizon under the endless blue sky—and the boots of the men in front:

303

Don't—don't—don't—don't—look at what's in front of you.
(Boots—boots—boots—boots—movin' up an' down again);
Men—men—men—men—men go mad with watchin' 'em,
An' there's no discharge in the war! [41]

Far outstripping the infantry, French met no opposition as he crossed the last river in the O.F.S. before the Vaal, for Botha did not know of Hamilton's switch to Roberts's left in support of French and feared a pincer movement. French swept on. By 24 May he was looking down on the Vaal itself. Botha had sent back all rolling stock and blown up the main bridge which crossed the river to Vereeniging; but he was denied any chance to defend the crossing by French's swiftness in seizing fords at Parys and elsewhere west of the town.

That day Roberts announced the annexation of the O.F.S. to the Crown. With his flair for the dramatic he made it seem as if he were giving the Queen a spacious gift, for it was her official birthday.

That occasion was marked rather more movingly in the British prisoner of war camp some distance outside Pretoria. The rank and file, numbering over 4,000, were incarcerated at a place called Waterval. They occupied long hot sheds of galvanized iron along the slope of a hill and though they were humanely looked after they were in much discomfort. Drainage of rain-water was bad, sanitation and rubbish disposal were primitive; blankets on cold nights were few, their clothes were in tatters; and one in four men became infected with enteric, dysentery or malaria. Hospital facilities had been inadequate but a committee of people in Pretoria helped make these good. There was a store in the camp to supplement rations, though soldiers could seldom afford the prices. Rumours were circulated of a fund being raised in England to donate five pounds to every prisoner; the gift was so long in coming that it was called the Phantom Fiver. A private gift of £500 did, however, relieve the situation. Morale was generally high, reflected in the tone of a journal called *The Waterval Wag*, hand-written and illustrated on pages from a penny exercise-book. A number of escapes had been made and, foreshadowing adventures which were to entrance generations after the World Wars, an escape tunnel was being constructed from one of the sheds to beyond the barbed wire for a mass break-out. Loyalists permitted to remain in Pretoria knew of this and were alarmed by the dangers while Roberts was still far away on the

Vaal. The conspirators were dissuaded by a colonial lieutenant who had elected to stay with the rank and file prisoners. Addressing them on the Queen's birthday he asked them to do nothing rash. Three cheers were called for, and *God Save the Queen* rose from thousands of throats in a diapason of profound feeling.

The officer P.O.W.s had been moved from the Model Schools, where Churchill made his escape, to a camp just outside Pretoria which they called the Bird Cage. There, as became gentlemen, they played baccarat, poker, roulette, whist and chess. The previous Sunday at church-service they had sung a hymn which shows the 'chosen race' conviction not confined to the Boers:

> As Thy nation deign to own us,
> Merciful and strong and free;
> Endless praising
> To Thee raising
> Ever Thine may England be.

The Baptist minister who delivered the sermon was prohibited by the conditions of his entry from anything beyond his religious offices; but he conveyed a hint of Roberts's approach by taking as his text Proverbs XXV.25: 'As cold waters to a thirsty soul, so is good news from a far country.'

The news in fact was daily better. In French's wake Roberts brought his whole army, brushing aside Botha's rearguards, across the Vaal and marched on. He proclaimed 'personal safety and freedom from molestation' of non-combatants and repeated his offer of immunity to burghers who gave up their arms.

Botha sent away the Free Staters with him to join their countrymen in the vicinity of their new capital at Frankfort. At the same time Transvaalers rallied around him from far and near to stand at bay in defence of Johannesburg and Pretoria. The hopeless retreat ever since that fateful 27 February, when Cronje was broken on the Modder and the Tugela ramparts were pierced, seemed at last at an end. But his difficulty was that the speed of the British advance gave him little time.

Hastily he began preparing a defence line south of Johannesburg, as Roberts continued marching up the railway while French on the left raced up the main road towards the city. The cavalry were only fifteen miles to the south-west on the afternoon of 27 May. A thirty-mile ride

brought French that day to the Gatsrand range of hills where Botha
had a strong rearguard intent on gaining precious hours for his preparations further back. A stern fight ended with French's exhausted
troopers clearing the position by midnight. Next morning Roberts's
whole army was well up. The scene was set for the battle for Johannesburg.

Six thousand men were supposed to be with Botha, but Roberts's
speed and the psychological effect of constantly giving way before him
had so unnerved them that half were absent. These either drew northwards, pausing to join in the looting which had now broken out in
Johannesburg, or skulked in the city on the pretext of getting supplies.
A mere 3,000 men therefore waited on the kopjes overlooking the
Klip River a few miles south of the city to oppose Roberts.

The British occupied a front twenty miles from west to south-east
along the south bank of the river. French on the left was at the junction
of a small tributary with the river at a picnic place called Van Wyk's
Rust; Roberts himself straddled the railway with his right to the east of
it. Botha, correctly guessing that he would repeat his usual tactics of a
powerful left flanking movement, placed the smallest part of his small
force in front of Roberts's centre and right, concentrating on the sector
in front of French. The veld, from kopjes to river bank, had been burnt
so that the British khaki would be conspicuous against the blackened
earth.

French launched his first assault across the river by a ford to the
right of Van Wyk's Rust. The troops made the other side but were
brought to a standstill by the Johannesburg Commando under Ben
Viljoen. Reinforcements crossed by another ford away to the left; after
negotiating swampy ground around the tributary they joined hands
with the first assault force but still no advance could be made. To
French's right another thrust across the river* also failed. Night came
with Roberts's progress checked for the first time.

But in Johannesburg there were no illusions about the outcome. If
ever the gold-mines were to be blown up the moment had arrived.
Botha was passionately opposed to such a course. He threatened to lay
down his command if any attempt were made. Elaborate precautions
were taken and the police tried to get all armed men out of the city
into the fighting line. But at the Grand Hotel that night a secret

* At Jackson's Drift.

306

meeting was held, mainly by Germans, and Judge Kock declared that he had the Government's authority to blow up the mines. This Judge Kock was the son of the general mortally wounded at Elandslaagte, where he was himself captured but given parole to take his father's body to Pretoria. Plans were laid at the meeting and next morning a group of men took a wagon of dynamite to the biggest mine, the Robinson. There they hesitated, and as they did so the German Commandant Runck arrived and stopped them. This little drama, the outcome of which was that the richest mines in the world were preserved intact, took place to the accompaniment of the distant boom of guns as the battle for the city continued.

Under cover of night French had withdrawn most of his troops from the north bank at Van Wyk's Rust and at daylight set out to turn the extreme end of the Boer line by crossing the river further to the left and attacking Doornkop, some kopjes north-west of Botha's main position. But De la Rey, back from Mafeking, commanded this sector and made things so hot for him that again he could not advance. At this juncture Hamilton came up, his long march to switch over to French's rear completed.

He offered to split the Boer defences by attacking a line of ridges which connected Doornkop with Botha's main position. French was not keen, giving way only because Hamilton's men were weary and short of supplies so that he was anxious to get to the Rand towns without delay. The ensuing attack proved to be the climax of the battle for Johannesburg—in the very vicinity where Jameson's Raid had met its end.

As French renewed his frontal attack on Doornkop, Hamilton's Gordon Highlanders advanced eastwards towards the ridges at a slow swaggering pace for a mile and a half. Then they came under fierce short-range fire and broke into a run. By short rushes they stormed forward with fixed bayonets. In the most violent and sustained charge of the war they shot and hacked their way forward against no less resolute a defence, until the Boers were beaten down: their whole flank collapsed and both French and Hamilton burst through to the west of Johannesburg. At the same time Roberts marched up the railway line with little opposition to the rail junction* east of the city.

Next morning, 30 May, Hamilton was at Florida Lake and alleviated

* Germiston.

his supply position by capturing a laden train en route for Potchef-stroom. French, circling round to the north of Johannesburg, achieved the rare feat of snapping up a Boer convoy: it was making for Pretoria under Commandant Runck who 'had lost his habitual smartness as the result of a convivial meeting in Johannesburg'.[17] By evening he was close to a cavalry brigade sent round from the east. The city was all but surrounded.

Roberts had already sent in a major of the Grenadier Guards to the town commandant, Dr. Krause, with a demand for surrender. Accompanied by a member of the Volksraad the doctor rode out to see Roberts. He pleaded that if the city were stormed while burghers still occupied it there might be street fighting with dangerous consequences to women, children and property. And these commodities were held in such respect by our grandfathers that Roberts agreed to postpone his entry until next day so that the burghers might have *time to escape*, provided that Krause actually *hastened them on their way* and protected the mines.

That night Winston Churchill, anxious to cable his paper, volunteered to carry dispatches to headquarters from Ian Hamilton's column which he had been acompanying. He rode through the dark and silent city to a little house at the railway junction where Roberts had halted.

> The room was small and meanly furnished, and he and his staff, who had just finished dinner, sat round a large table which occupied the greater part of the floor. . . . The Field-Marshal rose from his place, shook hands, and bade us in the most ceremonious fashion to be seated. . . . I have never seen a man with such extraordinary eyes. . . . The face remains perfectly motionless but the eyes convey the strongest emotion. [42]

The last day of May 1900 saw Roberts's occupation of Johannesburg. The thousands who marched with him were to have no memories of the gold with which legend paved the streets: only of indifferent foreigners and Natives who lounged in motley array along the barred and shuttered buildings. At the court-house the Vierkleur was hauled down and Lady Roberts's silken Union Jack run up. The troops marched past. Three cheers rang out for Queen Victoria.

In London the newspaper placards that evening were about the races at Epsom. The war, it seemed, was all but over. It was almost as if

Mafeking Night had burst the boil of war-fever, and people turned with relief to the enthusiasms of peace.

But for the Boers these were desperate days. As Roberts was occupying Johannesburg Paul Kruger fled his capital—no longer the capital since he had called an emergency meeting of the Executive Council at his house the previous afternoon and decided to move sixty miles along the Delagoa Bay railway to Middelburg. With him Kruger took a number of his Executive and officials, and young State Attorney Smuts raided the Mint to send him all the gold not already removed. But the President left his wife behind, because none knew what vicissitudes lay ahead, and he believed her safe in a town which it had already been agreed not to defend. Word was left for Botha, drawing his men clear of the British forces surrounding Johannesburg, to delay Roberts as long as possible without committing the Boer forces. The remaining armaments at the forts were dismantled, and the burgomaster ordered to preserve life and property and to hand over the city intact to the enemy.

Roberts had no idea of these decisions. While he had so far been comparatively feebly opposed he could not dismiss the possibility of the Boers making a last-ditch stand in defence of their capital. That was indeed the military calculation he had made and the reason for the massive siege howitzers following him into Johannesburg. What he had not reckoned on was the news which now reached him. Even as he set up his Johannesburg headquarters in the suburb of Orange Grove he was forced to consider whether he dare embark at once on an attempt to reach Pretoria.

The news came from that same quarter of the O.F.S., the northeast, which had persistently nagged at him. While he had been marching from Kroonstad with such spectacular and comparatively effortless success, his preparations to hem in the area were being severely tested. The garrisons and columns strung out successively eastward of the railway line had been maintaining or pushing steadily northward the barrier he desired, but against increasing opposition from the commandos his own advance had pushed aside.* These hovered on their flanks, constantly harassing, sniping, or snapping up detachments temporarily isolated on the march, and if they gave way before, it was

---

* Boer leaders active in these activities were Piet de Wet, M. Prinsloo, Olivier, Steenkamp, Froneman, Du Plooy, Nel, Fourie.

only to close in behind. Many skirmishes were fought and the tales brought home of stalking death and sudden disaster among the kopjes were to be legion.

By 27 May, when he himself was closing in on Johannesburg, the northernmost column in the north-east Orange Free State, Colvile's, had reached Lindley and was setting out for Heilbron to take Hamilton's place in view of the latter's switch to Roberts's left flank. The column was to have been reinforced some days before from Kroonstad by 500 men, the 13th Battalion Yeomanry, but the battalion was late for the rendezvous and Colvile pushed on without it.

It was no ordinary battalion, having basked in much publicity because of its abnormally high incidence of blue blood. Commanded by a Colonel Spragge, one of its units was the Duke of Cambridge's Own which consisted largely of aristocrats who had sprung forward after Black Week. They had travelled out at their own expense, donated their pay to charity, and made their first tedious post somewhere in the Karoo tolerable by a dazzling display of luxuries. The rest of the battalion was made up of three Irish companies, also inexperienced, since British policy in Ireland had not previously allowed volunteers or yeomanry.

They were hurrying towards Lindley to overtake Colvile when they met some Boers who told them that he was indeed in the town. Gladdened by the information they merely disarmed the Boers, who made off ostensibly to their farms but in fact to report to their comrades waiting round the town for Colvile's departure. As soon as he set out for Heilbron the Boers prepared to receive the unsuspecting Yeomanry.

Early next morning Colvile was woken by a messenger from Colonel Spragge: 'I want help to get out without great loss.'

Colvile felt sure from the Boers' constant harrying of him that they were mostly around him and that the Yeomanry battalion was well able to fight its own way out. Also he believed that his rapid arrival in Heilbron, already made difficult by Boer activity, was essential to Roberts's strategy. By three different messengers he returned a negative to Spragge's appeal. Then all day he was absorbed in fending off attacks by Marthinus Prinsloo and Piet de Wet. The Boers fought with a tenacity inspired by their fathers' victory over the Matabele in this same vicinity.* By nightfall he had marched only four miles, still

* Vechtkop.

310

sixteen short of Heilbron; ammunition and supplies were parlously low and there could be no thought of helping Spragge, whom all three messengers had by now failed to reach.

That same morning Spragge had also sent an SOS to the next nearest British column, Rundle's. As harassed by the Boers as Colvile, he had reached Senekal—even further south of Lindley than Colvile was north of it. He did not feel able to march forty miles to the Yeomanry's rescue, and Brabant's Colonial Division was still further out of reach near Ficksburg on the Basutoland border. Rundle telegraphed Brabant news of the Yeomanry's plight, adding that he would attempt to draw off the Boers by advancing towards Bethlehem, an important centre north-east of Senekal. The Boers tapped the wires and read the telegram.

They waited for Rundle in a carefully chosen position in some hills* commanding the Bethlehem road and here hammered him. The losses inflicted by their own shooting were increased when the long dry grass through which the Grenadier Guards advanced to the attack was set alight by a stray match and incinerated the wounded along with the dead. Rundle fell back with 180 casualties, to the Boers' 40 (including their commandant who was brought mortally wounded to a British hospital). Rundle too was now powerless to help the Yeomanry.

Unaware that help was not to be forthcoming from either north or south and making no attempt at a dash for Colvile or Kroonstad, Spragge prepared for a short siege on some high ground as the Boers surrounded him. They were in no great strength, but next day more came down after their fight with Colvile and increased the besiegers to 2,000 under the command of Marthinus Prinsloo. They displayed their usual caution in such situations, however, and Spragge eked out his rations while keeping them at bay. On the third day Methuen, who had just arrived at Kroonstad to fill the vacuum left by Roberts's departure, set out to the rescue. The Boers intensified their efforts. Bringing up three guns in the night, they concentrated on a dominating kopje held by the Duke of Cambridge's Own, and then they charged it. A panic-stricken corporal held up a white flag. Although he was immediately shot by his comrades, the lieutenant in charge of this sector felt himself bound in honour by the corporal's action and surrendered. With the Boers in possession of the key position, Spragge

* Biddulphsberg and Tafelberg.

surrendered too. Twenty-five of his men were dead and everyone else was taken prisoner. Methuen's advance guard actually overtook the convoy with the prisoners, but was too weak to do anything. At a stroke the Boers had inflicted more losses on Roberts than they themselves had suffered during the whole of his march from Bloemfontein to Johannesburg, which he had that day entered.

The disaster cast a shadow over the success of his advance and momentarily shook complacency in England. The public reaction was as great as the pedigree of the defeated battalion was long. A head had to roll, and soon afterwards Roberts told Colvile, in the decorous words of the period, that he 'might go home'. Furthermore, he uttered a dire warning to the Free Staters. Since the annexation of this territory to the Crown they were inhabitants of a British colony and anyone found bearing arms would be dealt with 'in person and property' as a rebel.

The threat fell on men whose morale was far lower than their successes would indicate. Since Roberts's massive procession northwards now threatened Pretoria itself, they recognized that these could hardly affect the issue. No help was forthcoming from the rest of the O.F.S. where the farmers were pacifically back at work on their farms. And to the relentless pressure of the British columns fencing them in the north-east, developments in Natal brought a threat of invasion from that direction also. Since sending the Boers flying from the Biggarsberg, Buller's advance was marked by little incident and much caution. Approaching Laing's Nek and Botha's Pass, the Drakensberg passes into the Transvaal and O.F.S. respectively, he found them held by the remnant of Boer forces after so many had gone—ostensibly or in fact— to help Louis Botha oppose Roberts. Temporarily in command was Louis Botha's brother, and on 29 May Buller wrote him a letter urging him to surrender in order to avoid further bloodshed. A meeting between the two men followed. They agreed on a three-day truce while higher authority on either side considered possible terms.

Weighing all this up in Johannesburg on the morrow of the disaster to the 13th Yeomanry, Roberts found further encouragement in news from the western Transvaal. Baden-Powell and Plumer were meeting no opposition as they advanced eastwards via Zeerust towards Rustenburg; and south of them Sir Archibald Hunter was advancing from Vryburg via Lichtenburg to Ventersdorp and the Pretoria–Klerksdorp railway with a similar lack of opposition. Only in one detail were his plans not going like clockwork. Assembly of Carrington's Rhodesian Field Force was being held up by difficulties of transport from Beira to Salisbury, and around tropical fever-infested stations like Bamboo Creek and Twenty-Three Mile Peg men, horses and stores were jumbled up in time-wasting confusion. But this was a minor factor in the scale of things. What mattered was the general advance and the universal evidence of Boer demoralization. For Roberts this was the decisive argument. He would push on forthwith to Pretoria.

Besides, the 5,000 prisoners of war in the vicinity of the city not only tugged at British hearts but promised a useful source of additional man-power. Voices were raised among his generals warning against the vulnerability of his thousand-mile life-line to the Cape, and especially the several hundred miles to Bloemfontein which were only thinly guarded; but he was not to be deflected.

Pretoria was so close—a mere forty miles. The crown and diadem of his 300-mile march! More—the last redoubt of the Boers. With it taken from them the war would be over, as neat a rounding-off of his strategy as a soldier could wish. In consequence, exactly as he had previously chosen not to be deflected from his march by the situation in the north-east O.F.S., so now he ignored the danger of leaving the Delagoa Bay railway intact. So long as the Boers held it they might easily retreat eastwards in large numbers and with large supplies, and then use the line to get more; and much of the surrounding country was eminently suitable for defence. Weeks ago he had thought of sending Hamilton to enter the Transvaal and cut the Delagoa Bay line, but abandoned the idea in favour of switching him on to his left flank to help capture Johannesburg. Now that he was in Johannesburg he sent a mere 200 troopers round the east of Pretoria to cut the line and when they were thrown back he did nothing more. All thought and strength were concentrated on the grand finale of his march.

On 3 June, leaving a garrison of 3,000 men behind him in Johannes-burg, he set out over the rolling brown hills towards Pretoria.

French rode ahead, ordered to sweep round Pretoria from the west and cut the continuation of the Central railway northwards beyond the city. But a commando drew his horses on over rough country to exhaust them, ambushed his patrols before the Crocodile River, and so skilfully frustrated him that by nightfall he was still almost as distant from the city as the infantry who reached the half-way mark from

Johannesburg. Reports reached Roberts clearly showing a mass exodus of Boers eastward from Pretoria as fast as trains could carry them, but still he did nothing about it.

For several days there had been chaos in the city. Fears alternated with hope as wild rumours went about that French was dead, Roberts captured, Kroonstad retaken. Looting of government stores broke out, and the streets were full of people with hand-carts, wheelbarrows and cabs laden with provisions. When the retreating burghers arrived, says Jan Smuts, they had to pass 'with sad hearts and empty stomachs through the ungrateful capital'. Botha arrived to receive the Executive's order to hold up Roberts for as long as possible. It was easier said than done. His entire army was now reduced to 2,000. He left Koos de la Rey with a rearguard in front of the city while he went in to muster what men he could and speed the evacuation. Ever since he had come from Natal to try stopping Roberts he had been striving to shore up the tottering edifice of Boer defence, only for it to crumble in his hands as Roberts never gave him time to consolidate. He had not been helped either by the fact that the Hollander railway employees who had shown such skill in breaking up the railway line through the O.F.S. left their own sector of the line in the Transvaal untouched, to the bitterness of the Free Staters who saw nothing but mercenary self-interest in this omission.

Roberts resumed his advance on the 4th, rapidly reaching the defence line commanded by De la Rey along the Quaggapoort hills. Though he stood here with slender strength the British infantry could make little headway against a position which Roberts saw was as formidable as he could expect such an adversary to select. It was only when Hamilton arrived at 2 p.m. with a large body of mounted troops that he could force the engagement to a conclusion—and then, un-wittingly, and though the result would in any event have been the same, by a trick. Outflanking the Quaggapoort range a force of M.I. reached a hill two miles west of the town: a lieutenant of the New South Wales Mounted Rifles boldly rode in under a flag of truce to demand surrender and gave Botha the impression that Roberts's whole army was at hand. Botha tried to play for time, but Roberts demanded un-conditional surrender, and Botha left the city to his mercy. He had also, like Kruger, to make the anguished decision to leave his wife behind as he made away into an unknown future.

CHAPTER XVIII

After Pretoria: June 1900

ROBERTS entered Pretoria on 5 June 1900.

The previous night, as Botha and his remaining men fled eastwards, troops began moving in to seize the principal buildings. At the officers' P.O.W. camp the commandant told them at midnight to be ready to leave in an hour with the escort waiting outside; he was promptly himself made prisoner and compelled to send the escort away, after which he was amicably entertained until morning, when the camp guards were also overpowered. The Duke of Marlborough and Winston Churchill galloped in with the news of Pretoria's surrender and everyone made for the city.

There in the square before the Government Buildings a great throng assembled. In it were S.A. colonial soldiers and officials who had been kept in the common gaol and had similarly broken out; and loyalists whom the Boers had allowed to stay on; and townsfolk, some of them sporting British colours in their buttonholes. Gradually Roberts's army arrived and formed up in ordered ranks. Into their midst galloped a corps of scouts with skull and crossbones on the ribbons of their slouch-hats. At 2.15 p.m. Lords Roberts and Kitchener arrived amid thunderous cheers. They halted at the Government Buildings and Lady Roberts's Union Jack completed its much travelled course up a flagstaff. Among those who watched were men who twenty years before, after Majuba and the grant of independence, had helped in a moment of patriotic frustration to bury the Union Jack, replaced by the Vierkleur: twenty years that had shown the lengths to which men go in order to keep aloft or tear down a fragment of coloured cloth.

A two-hour march-past by the troops followed. To the little man

315

who received the homage of the bronzed thousands striding past him, this was a moment of triumph remarked throughout the world.

His march from Bloemfontein to Pretoria has a high place among history's great marches. It was also one of the last, for seldom again would massive troop movements depend on the legs of man and beast alone. Scattering the enemy before him, he had come 300 miles from Bloemfontein in thirty-four days, of which half had been spent at the halt—partly to co-ordinate it with other operations over a vast terrain. He had travelled hostile country, obliging him to bring up every mouthful of food, every bandage and bullet, when a long march with a large body of troops is a notoriously difficult military operation at the best of times. Napoleon marched his Grand Army from the Channel to the Rhine in thirty-four days along good roads with prepared food depots. In a nine-day march during the Franco-Prussian War 200,000 Germans often did twenty-four miles a day, but at the cost of one-third of their infantry. Roberts's own famous march to Kandahar—300 miles in twenty-four days—was with a hand-picked flying column of 10,000 men.

Of the 38,000 men who set out from Bloemfontein a quarter did not reach Johannesburg or Pretoria because of disease, casualties, loss of horses and inevitable campaign 'wastage' from a hundred causes. The loss of horses had been particularly heavy, leaving quantities of cavalry-men kicking their spurred heels all down the line. The actual number of killed, wounded and captured over the whole of S.A. during this period amounted to 3,500.

The Boer losses during that period totalled 500, excluding burghers who had ostensibly handed in their arms.

In other words their manpower was still substantially intact. Time was to show the significance of this fact, compared with Roberts's spectacular achievement of reaching Pretoria so rapidly. But as he took the salute and stood in the eyes of the world as an all-conquering hero, the jubilation of the hour permitted no misgivings. That day, it is true, the Boers negotiating with Buller at the Drakensberg passes rejected the demand for unconditional surrender which, though he himself advised more generous terms, the British Government insisted upon; but he must surely force a passage against ever-weakening opposition before very long. He would then be able to invade from the east as Hunter, Baden-Powell and Plumer were doing from the west. The

Boers were in a hopeless situation. They had lost almost all their principal towns, their railways and supply centres. Their armies were scattered, their Governments fugitive. Above all their demoralization was so deep that at the very moment Roberts stood in Pretoria reviewing his triumphant army a group of their leading generals was discussing surrender.

The scene of their meeting was a whisky distillery a few miles from the city. It was part of a model farm owned by Samuel ('Sammy') Marks, a Russian-Jewish Rand millionaire and friend of Paul Kruger. He was one of those highly individual characters thrown up by the pioneering days of the Transvaal, when luck, shrewdness, resilience and a not too refined sense of honesty bred both wealth and an expansive outlook. Throughout the war he had given to the sick and needy on both sides with impartial generosity, and he was convinced now of the futility of continuing the struggle. In this he reflected what was probably the majority of Boer opinion, and in Pretoria itself a party of surrendered officers was urging their countrymen in the field to make peace.

To the meeting came many leading generals and commandants, including prominent public men like Vice-President Schalk Burger and Lukas Meyer. Sombrely they awaited the arrival of the Transvaal Commandant-General. Botha is said to have entered the room with 'a heavy shadow on his usually confident and open countenance'. In other circumstances the setting of a whisky distillery might have appealed to the men's sense of humour as they opened proceedings with a prayer.

De la Rey took the lead in denouncing the Republican Government's recent behaviour. They had withdrawn to safety down the Delagoa Bay line with millions in gold, while his burghers had no means to buy supplies and were generally unsupported. Other leaders echoed his indignation. Then he went further, threatening to set up an independent republic in the western Transvaal if the Government did not improve. Botha listened in despair. When generals of such proven capacity talked like this, he said, the only course left was to surrender. That was a decision towards which almost everyone present saw himself driven by the inexorable logic of the facts. But they could not, there and then, bring themselves to it. Tomorrow, somehow, the unexpected—even God himself—might magically transform the situation. Schalk Burger and one or two others seized upon this forlorn hope and pleaded for delay. It was agreed to postpone decision for two days while Botha sounded Roberts on what kind of terms could be expected, and while events generally unfolded.

They were to prove a fateful two days.

The meeting adjourned; the leaders parted to continue the fight. De la Rey's destination was a range of hills overlooking the open plain in front of the rank and file P.O.W. camp at Waterval, twelve miles north of Pretoria. Whether there were to be peace negotiations or a prolongation of the war, the most immediate need was to keep all the prisoners out of Roberts's reach. A thousand had already been entrained eastward, leaving 3,000–4,000 still in the camp.

Early next morning a squadron of Greys rode from Pretoria to release the prisoners. As they breasted a rise at the approach to the plain the glint of their steel was glimpsed by the Tommies eagerly looking out from the roofs of their sheds. A great yell went up. Grabbing whatever he valued in a bundle every man dashed out, thrust aside the guards, cut through the barbed-wire enclosure, and streamed towards the cavalry. For a while a dip in the plain hid them from De la Rey, but as they emerged he turned his guns on them. They were utterly caught in the open. It was an extraordinary opportunity for him to inflict the greatest single disaster of the war on the British. By the rules of war he was entitled, and by his duty as a general bound, to mow down the mob scattering wildly below him. But it was not butchery he cared for, and he was spared it by a misconception, for at the same moment the Greys, now reinforced, threw themselves at him. He thought the whole British cavalry were attacking. And while his attention was distracted the prisoners rushed madly to a train waiting to whisk them into Pretoria before he discovered his mistake.

For Roberts this welcome news was followed by the even more encouraging information, brought by Sammy Marks's manager, that Botha wanted to talk peace. To get confirmation, Roberts chose the curious method of sending Mrs. Botha through his lines to make contact with her husband. When she returned from this singular husband-and-wife meeting Roberts at once wrote to Botha proposing a meeting at Sammy Marks's house outside the city.

Before such a meeting could take place, the adjourned Boer council of war met again. It was now that the interval proved to have been crucial, for the council came together aglow with news from the south. Again it was events in the eastern O.F.S. which had upset all calculations.

At dawn on 7 June Christian de Wet suddenly burst into the news with devastating effect. Splitting into three* his force covering Steyn's new capital at Frankfort he simultaneously attacked garrisons along the railway north of Kroonstad. He achieved complete success. His forces killed, wounded or captured over 700 British, and looted or destroyed great quantities of stores—at one place alone to the value of over £100,000. He wrecked an important bridge which had been laboriously rebuilt, and destroyed the track for several miles. Roberts's communications with Bloemfontein were completely sundered.

Kelly-Kenny (in command at Bloemfontein) and Kitchener, promptly sent southward by Roberts, set about strenuously trying to seal the gaps and restore the vital artery upon which his existence depended. But in other respects the situation was altered beyond their power to repair it. De Wet had kindled afresh the waning fire of his countrymen's resistance and the following weeks were to see action erupting all along and east of the railway line. Most important of all, the Transvaal leaders at their resumed council of war no longer talked of surrender.

This may be singled out as a critical point in the crowded and complex events of the war. Black Week had quashed British hopes of quick victory and given the Boers hopes for which they had little reason before. The period which followed had been completely wasted by the Boers and they paid the price at Paardeberg, a blow since proved to have all but destroyed their ability to stand as an organized army. Thereafter their leaders' resolutions and plans to fight had come to little: they were dispersed and hunted and their cities taken from them. But now, as though emerging from the long dark of despair, they were revivified by De Wet's success.

It is hard to say why. They could not hope to keep Roberts's communications cut long enough to force his retreat or subjection. Furthermore, not only were the columns which had invaded the western Transvaal pressing steadily forward but Buller was drawing closer from the east. On 8 May he forced his way through Botha's Pass into the extreme north-east O.F.S., then marched round to the hills guarding

* The officers were himself, Froneman, Du Plooy, Nel, Steenkamp.

the rear of Laing's Nek, and at Alleman's Nek he won a crisp victory which compelled the Transvaalers at Laing's Nek to abandon that last redoubt against the invader. The area of hostilities had thus contracted to a slab of the O.F.S. and Transvaal between the Central railway and the Natal border. Inevitably the British forces on either side of this slab would move inwards, crushing the life that remained like two fingers squashing a beetle.

De Wet's exploit would obviously not have meant so much unless it had come as the confirmation of something already there. In England critics of the Government blamed the demand for unconditional surrender but it is doubtful if any alternative settlement could have been found acceptable to the Boers. They had taken a deep breath of faith, that mysterious essence which there is no explaining, and they talked no more of surrender. Only time could answer whether the preservation of independent republics, or simply a continuation of bloodshed and misery, would result. At that moment the mood of the resumed council of war was set by a young officer named Hendrik Beyers who fiercely accused his elders of cowardice. They rejected the charge— but bent themselves to fighting on with the same determination that was reported of President Steyn and Christian de Wet. They resolved to scrap future councils of war and entrust all authority to the Commandant-General. A heavy responsibility henceforward rested on Louis Botha. He seems at this juncture to have gazed at the realities of the situation with a level eye and yet resigned himself to the demands of faith. He declared his intention to give Roberts battle on the spot.

And though for a while longer some kind of negotiations were kept up with Roberts, that was what he prepared to do. Roberts found that instead of the anticipated Boer capitulation on the fall of Pretoria, he was for the first time opposed by a strength and leadership which might fairly test his quality.

* * * *

Roberts's strength was reduced by losses on the march and the necessity to guard places along the way, to 14,000 men and seventy guns. With the help of De la Rey and others Botha rallied 6,000 Boers from their eastward flight and skilfully grouped them with twenty-two guns along a range of hills thirty miles long a short distance east of Pretoria. All Roberts's tactics had so far turned on the same outflanking movement followed by a thrust against the Boer centre, which had then to give way for fear of being encircled. Against overwhelming numbers the Boers had never been able to form a defensive line, as at Magersfontein, long enough to frustrate this manœuvre. But now a smaller disparity in numbers and a favourable defensive position gave Botha hope not only of thwarting any outflanking attempt, but of crumpling *Roberts's* flanks and falling on his centre. Boer morale was high under inspired leadership.

Kitchener having gone south to try to restore communications with Bloemfontein, Roberts was on his own. On 11 June he left Pretoria and established his headquarters on high ground about ten miles east of the city. The impending battle was of vital importance to him. He was confronted by the only major Transvaal force left in being, and if he could destroy it he must end the war there and then. But if he could not, Boer resistance might receive an incalculable impetus, Pretoria would be threatened, and his own position made critical because of his severance from Bloemfontein.

His battle headquarters gave him a view south-east down a long valley about five miles broad, through which flowed the Pienaar's River. The northern side of the valley was the succession of hills occupied by Botha astride the railway line to Delagoa Bay; a prominent feature in it was Diamond Hill, which was to give its name to the battle and stood about ten miles down the valley from Roberts's H.Q. He proposed to launch his attack from the south against Botha's position along this northern range by, as usual, turning his flanks—Hamilton on the right and French on the left—then throwing forward his centre under Pole-Carew, who had been detached from Methuen's command and marched with him from Bloemfontein.

Immediately battle was joined and the hills reverberated with the opposing cannonades Hamilton, emerging into the valley through the hills bordering it on the south, the Tigerpoort Range, found that he was in for no picnic. Botha had promptly extended his line along some ridges that joined the northern range to the Tigerpoort range, providing a curved barrier across the end of the valley. Hamilton's advancing horsemen ran into this curve exactly as Botha anticipated. The result was a series of hard-fought encounters at one point after another all round an arc of fifteen miles. In one of these the distinguished cavalryman Lord Airlie was killed leading his Lancers back from a fruitless charge; in another, a brave advance group of the Boksburg Commando was routed; and so it went on with fortunes fluctuating with the hour. Only on the arrival of the infantry did any crack in the defence seem likely, for they stormed a kopje in front of Diamond Hill. The Boers on the kopje fell back to Diamond Hill in such confusion that Hamilton wanted to follow up with a charge that might have burst open their line, but Roberts insisted on more troops being brought up, and then the Boers recovered and it was too late. By nightfall Botha's whole position was still intact, with its curved end surrounding Hamilton on three sides.

On the other flank French, with a much smaller force, had run into a similar but worse situation. He advanced into a nest of hills from which De la Rey all but surrounded him. The bulk of his men were forced to dismount and fight from cover. He sent a captain of the Life Guards with an escort to carry the news to Roberts. The Boers, already beginning to creep round French's rear, shot the escort down and the captain got through with great difficulty.

It was a harassed Roberts who returned to base at Pretoria that evening to review his situation. His two flanks, far from turning those of the enemy, were themselves almost enveloped. The course remaining to him was a frontal attack by his centre but he feared heavy losses. All the time he was distracted by the knowledge that he was cut off from Bloemfontein and that the Free Staters were in full cry north and south of Kroonstad. But that evening Methuen reported having encountered Christian de Wet and driven him off westward of the railway, so that time was being gained to restore communications. Roberts could address himself with a freer mind to the problem of the battle.

At past three in the morning he settled his plans. He would try to break through the Boer line by sending Hamilton, reinforced from the centre, to capture Diamond Hill. This was substantially a steep-faced plateau about six miles long, but it was the first four miles that formed the target of Hamilton's intended attack, the remainder being taken up by an almost detached prominence which a few M.I. were only to 'demonstrate' against.

The kopje seized in front of Diamond Hill the previous day was part of a system of ridges, an undulation of the valley, and during the morning the assault troops assembled behind them. At noon they advanced into the open in widely extended formation—Derbys, C.I.V. and the Sussex, with the Coldstream Guards in support. They gradually stormed the hill against stiff opposition, Hamilton at one stage having a field battery dragged up a track on the hill-side to pound the enemy at close quarters, and after four hours they shot and charged their way on to the summit. Yet the Boers' position was only dented, for they retired to ridges beyond while their line on either side remained firm, hemming Hamilton in.

The day's fighting had so far brought little change on French's sector, but De la Rey had been drawing in men and guns from less active parts of the front and now sent to Botha for a few more men that he might overwhelm French, then chop up the British centre which had been weakened by the units detached to help Hamilton. Since Botha's whole tactical scheme had been precisely to pin down the British wings and fall upon their centre, he immediately ordered a force to join De la Rey. But the men were in the act of leaving when a message reaching Botha made him call them back. The British had captured the detached prominence at the end of Diamond Hill and therefore now had possession of all six miles of the plateau.

The message was in fact premature, for the M.I. posted in front of the prominence simply to keep its defenders busy during Hamilton's main attack had so far only gained a footing. Had Botha known the true situation, the defenders required very little help from him to keep off a mere 350 New South Wales Mounted Rifles. These, leaving their horses, had advanced in so wide a formation that the defenders thought them more numerous than they were, and at the threat of a bayonet charge retired for nearly a mile in the closing moments of the day.

All the same, this was small comfort to Roberts. The Boers had simply been pushed back in one sector but they were quite unbeaten. Returning to Pretoria again in the evening, he felt unable to defeat them with his present strength, especially as the evacuation of Laing's Nek compelled by Buller might soon bring more aid to Botha. He ordered a force from the Pretoria garrison to be in readiness to cover French's retreat which seemed inevitable. At the same time he reinforced Hamilton and even wired for troops from the O.F.S. He ordered Hamilton meanwhile to renew the offensive next day by nosing cautiously forward.

But next day the British moved forward against ridges and hills that stood strangely silent. The Boers had gone.

Botha's decision to pull out had been dictated by the Australian capture of the remaining part of Diamond Hill. With the whole plateau in British hands he feared the hauling up of heavy guns that would pulverize all the surrounding Boer positions and, his thoughts being dominated by preserving the slender fighting strength which was all he had between Roberts and Paul Kruger at Machadodorp, he decided to retire further down the line while the going was good. During the night his men withdrew their wagons, their guns and themselves with such quietness that they were beyond pursuit by the time Roberts woke to their departure.

The battle was one of the last major pitched actions of the war. It had lasted for two days across more than thirty miles of country. Yet of the 20,000 men engaged, the British losses were only 200 and the Boers' probably a few dozen. Roberts had issued strict instructions to his commanders to avoid incurring casualties, as was of course the consistent policy of the Boers in the straitened circumstances of their manpower. The battle was consequently very like a game of chess, in which tactics were directed less at removing the opposing pieces than at getting into a winning position. Both sides claimed a victory. It is truer to say that neither was defeated—and for the Boers this was more important than for the British. Though Roberts could feel that Pretoria was now secure as a result of the battle, when the Boers had gone so had his hope of an immediate end to hostilities.

However, no one doubted that merely a rapid mopping-up operation would cure the Boers of their obstinacy. In England a certain weariness of the war was detectable in the slackening of public interest (though the Boxer Rebellion at this time diverted attention), and this was shown by an attitude almost of irritation towards De Wet's outburst in the O.F.S. Criticism of the Government suddenly gained impetus from a series of revelations in *The Times* about deficiencies in the Army Medical Corps. The sick and wounded in hospitals at Bloemfontein and elsewhere were lying on the floor without mattresses or pillows. There were not enough nurses, and doctors had over a hundred patients each. There was not enough staff to ensure provision for elementary sanitation in the field. The Medical Corps was out of touch with modern hospital and sanitation techniques.

A Victorian of course had only to be told that sanitation was bad to react like a parson told the devil was under his bed; but the situation was in fact appalling, as the spread of typhus and other diseases indicated. A Select Committee was appointed, and meanwhile Roberts tried to explain that 900 miles of railway track, much of it single and with many bridges destroyed, made a full supply of necessities impossible.

The real need, upon which everything else largely depended, was a speedy end to the war. He proposed to do this by two swift and simultaneous expeditions—against Botha and the Kruger Government in the eastern Transvaal, and against De Wet and the Steyn Government in the north-eastern O.F.S., since these represented the only concentration of Boer forces left in the field, all the rest having for the most part scattered to their farms, with or without the preliminary of surrendering, handing over a weapon, and taking the oath. A day or two after the Battle of Diamond Hill, Kitchener and company restored communications with the south, and before himself setting out against Botha Roberts made preparations for an expedition to the north-east O.F.S., where one of the great dramas of the war was now to take place.

CHAPTER XIX

The Brandwater Basin: July 1900

ALL through the remainder of June troops, guns, animals, wagons and supplies were involved in an intricate pattern of movement north of Bloemfontein, along the railway line in the sprawling territory east of it and in the southern Transvaal. Almost every day that passed emphasized Roberts's needs to get quickly at grips with the Free Staters.

Christian de Wet, having been driven westward by Methuen from the vicinity of the railway north of Kroonstad, recrossed in a few days. He attacked a construction train on the way, unaware that much finer game was to be had in the person of Lord Kitchener encamped nearby.

South of Kroonstad his successes prompted farmers to take their rifles out of hiding and harass passing trains or convoys from railway to garrisons east of it. For example, on 14 June a commando descended from the hills half-way to Senekal and attacked a garrison of 800 at a siding;* a captain named Pine-Coffin had befriended a Boer who forewarned him and the attack was beaten off after a hard fight in which a pioneering American mining-engineer from the Rand, Seymour, was killed. The commando continued to hover about to the menace of passing convoys, and lives were fruitlessly expended in trying to round it up.

Roberts was stung into issuing a proclamation: attacks on the railways could only be made with the connivance of people round about, who in future would be made prisoners of war and have their houses burnt. This threat he followed with another, that residents of districts through which the railway passed might be carried as hostages to ensure the safety of the trains. Both edicts were based on similar Ger-

* Virginia.

man action in 1871 and achieved as little as his previous proclamation turning all Free Staters who resisted into rebels. The threat to carry hostages was in fact soon withdrawn because of an outcry in England.

On 19 June Christian de Wet was again in action, north of Kroonstad. If he was in a bitter mood he cannot be blamed, for on Roberts's orders Methuen had burnt down his farm. He swooped down on a convoy to Heilbron, but was beaten back and thereupon organized another triple attack against the railway three days later. At two places he was successful and once more disrupted communications; at the third his force was held off by a garrison reinforced by 400 released P.O.W.s who happened to be passing through from Pretoria and threw themselves into the fight with what arms lay to hand.

But though the vicinity of the railway line was the scene of all this Boer activity, the core of Roberts's problem lay eastward of it—beyond the arc of towns (Heilbron–Lindley–Senekal–Ficksburg) which were the bases of the containing columns sent out during his march to Pretoria. Here the writ of the O.F.S. Republic ran unchallenged in spite of Roberts's 'annexation'. The proximity of the eastern Transvaal enabled it to get supplies from Kruger's stores and to send up captured British. Burghers could slip through the gaps in the confining arc to pounce on the railway or convoys travelling between, and they constantly threatened to push back the troops holding the arc itself.

Thus General Rundle was holding his part of the arc, a line from Senekal to Ficksburg, under arduous conditions. Continually engaged in exhausting and dangerous pursuit of commandos who threw themselves at him and then disappeared into a smoke screen provided by the veld they set ablaze, he was poorly supplied with food, his men were in rags, and he had to fend as best he could off the country. But he kept the Boers from infiltrating south of him.

North of him a force left to occupy Lindley after Methuen's attempt to save the 13th Yeomanry Battalion was in its turn soon besieged. (In the fortnight between Hamilton's first occupation of it and Methuen's arrival the town had changed hands seven times.) The siege brought together many commandos hitherto scattered, and eventually a large proportion of the Free State forces was concentrated round the town. This fact was to prove highly important. An incidental consequence was that it caused ill-feeling between leaders of equal rank, in this instance Piet de Wet and Marthinus Prinsloo. Their quarrel did not improve the Boers' habitual inadequacy at siege warfare and for three weeks they made no impression on the defences. On 26 June the famous Transvaal scout-corps leader Danie Theron tried to instil some zeal into a general assault. It failed, and next day the town was relieved.

Soon afterwards Piet de Wet voluntarily surrendered—a seemingly major crack in Boer resistance though Christian de Wet reacted with characteristic defiance, vowing that if ever he encountered his brother he would shoot him down like a dog.

The Boers drew off eastward from Lindley. At the same time Buller's army, since forcing the passes on the Transvaal frontier, was advancing up the Natal railway towards Standerton and would be well placed to prevent any northward flight by the Free Staters from the territory within the confining arc of towns. Roberts's plan was to contract the arc by means of three columns which would shepherd the Boers together and then destroy them.

Rundle would swing in from the south-west. Clements, having brought a column from the Central railway and absorbed the force just relieved at Lindley, would advance eastwards. And from the north a column would advance under General Sir Archibald Hunter: the column was actually Ian Hamilton's, but Hamilton had broken his collar-bone in a fall from his horse. To Hunter, too, Roberts entrusted overall command of the operation.

Hunter was a Scot, very earnest about his profession in which he had achieved a meteoric rise. Four years previously he had been promoted major-general at the age of only forty. Before the Boer War all his campaign experience had been in North Africa. As Kitchener's second in command he was the chief executive officer in the battles before Khartoum, earning himself a knighthood and the thanks of both Houses of Parliament. Then he had come to S.A. as Buller's Chief of Staff but been caught up by the siege of Ladysmith. Now, having completed the task of marching through the western Transvaal parallel with Baden-Powell and Plumer, he set off from outside Johannesburg for the O.F.S. with Hamilton's column.

As he bore down on Frankfort, Steyn once again fled. The President went south to the town of Bethlehem under cover of Christian de Wet. Henceforward the Free State Republicans were to have no capital except wherever Steyn's horse might halt on the veld or in the hills.

Hunter occupied Frankfort and marched on, being reinforced by

Hector Macdonald who had succeeded to the command of Colvile's force. Roberts's plan worked to perfection. The Free Staters everywhere fell back to join Steyn and Christian de Wet at Bethlehem, a typical dusty *dorp* dominated by the steeple of the stone *kerk* and consisting of a few streets with a general store or two, a hostelry, and single-storeyed houses, all with corrugated iron roofs and open verandas. An occasional whitewashed wall, a few trees and gardens, a rivulet—but by and large the S.A. dorp lacks charm, and the glory of Cape Dutch architecture is confined to a narrow region around Cape Town.

Clements reached the town first, on 6 July. De Wet had organized a strong defensive phalanx, but an apathy seized his men and after a day or two's aggression Clements put them to flight. They retreated into the mountains to the south, where Steyn with the women and children had already gone for safety. Soon Hunter also reached the town and Rundle closed in to the south-west.

From Ficksburg to Bethlehem were now gathered 16,000 British troops, a semicircle of steel penning the Boers in the mountains. Except for commandos totalling about 1,500 men who were on their way from the Drakensberg passes on the Natal border, the entire fighting strength of the O.F.S. was here, upwards of 9,000 men with all their guns and their leaders—Steyn, Christian de Wet, Olivier, M. Prinsloo and the rest. Mostly the men came from the surrounding region, but some were the staunchest of the western Free Staters, and the Transvaal was represented by Theron's Corps of scouts, which included many foreigners.

The mountains in which lay such a glittering challenge to British arms are called the Wittebergen and the Roodebergen (White Mountains and Red Mountains). In plan they conform roughly to the shape of a horseshoe which points towards Bethlehem and has its two ends against the Caledon River, flowing along the foot of the Drakensberg on the border of Basutoland. Southwards there was hence no retreat. And the horseshoe itself, seventy-five miles long from end to end, had only four main passes and a few difficult minor exits from its interior. The British had simply to bottle up these passes to seal the Boers from all hope of escape.

But the Boers had not come here to be trapped. They had come as to a haven: those same passes by which the British troops hoped to keep them in could be used to keep the British out. Of all South Africa the region enclosed by the horseshoe is the most fascinating. Against the southern backdrop of the stupendous Drakensberg, now capped with snow, the encircling mountains are themselves often steep and jagged, with great buttresses and foothills rising from wide basins, valleys, gorges and chasms. In the valleys are lesser hills with lesser valleys between so that the traveller has the impression of a land once caught by some elemental upheaval, though by now the sun and the streams flowing down from the heights had robbed it of any aspect of violence and given it rich crops and abundant pasturage. But it is not green. It seems ancient and withdrawn; lonely; indifferent to the passer-by; the twitter of birds sounds remote in a great silence. But to the Boers who came there in the winter of 1900 it was a welcoming refuge from the unyielding pressure of war, a place to rest in and feel themselves free of British domination. They called the interior of the mountains the Brandwater Basin, from the name of the stream which flowed through its broadest valley to the Caledon.

Hunter made no immediate move to block the passes. He stayed at Bethlehem in order to prepare, especially in the matter of supplies, for he was eighty miles from the railway. He had enough supplies for the immediate future and some of his officers suggested that while waiting their troops could as well consume these near the passes as in Bethlehem, the nearest passes being only fifteen miles away. Hunter insisted on waiting. His maps prepared by the War Office were so faulty (for example, they showed a certain pass as a broad passage whereas it was scarcely a vent in the mountain face) that he did not feel safe to move without further information.

And while he waited the Boers had second thoughts. Disputes about seniority which had started during the Lindley siege increased, and there was ill-feeling between the Boers and the foreigners in Theron's Corps. All this bred misgivings which questioned the wisdom of the retreat into the Brandwater Basin.

They asked themselves whether they were not simply cooping themselves up in a place that denied them their traditional mobility of tactics and whose steep hills provided dead ground favourable to an attacker. Had they not been beguiled by the promise of peace and plenty? To wait in the Basin indefinitely would be to call down all Roberts's strength on them, and meanwhile they would be doing nothing to further their cause. They held a council of war presided over by Steyn and debated the issue.

They decided to quit the Basin.

They would split into four parts. The largest, with President Steyn, would leave under Christian de Wet on the night of 15 July; two more would go the following day; the fourth would remain behind under Marthinus Prinsloo to hold the passes. The commandos on their way from the Drakensberg would link up with one of the parties scheduled to leave the Basin on the 16th.

Why did De Wet choose to leave first instead of waiting to ensure that the rest of his forces got safely away? The answer, bedded deep in the character of that extraordinary man, can be left until later.

It chanced that on the very day De Wet prepared to leave in the evening, Hunter began to make his dispositions to bottle up the exits. A column moved down towards one of the main passes, Slabbert's Nek, none other than the one De Wet intended to use for his exodus. The British saw some activity at the pass but, neither investigating nor posting pickets, camped about ten miles away. Their camp-fires were flickering in the dusk as the Boer convoy began to move out: 2,600 horsemen, 5 guns, 400 wagons and carts, the whole spread out over three miles. De Wet imposed his merciless discipline upon them and they moved with precision—so quietly that they passed within a mile of the British camp without a soul knowing.

In the morning the convoy's passage north-westwards towards Lindley was discovered, though Roberts was informed that De Wet had only 300 men with him. Immediately two mounted columns went in pursuit. The chase became a saga on its own, while that of the Brandwater Basin unfolded.

The two parties which were to have followed De Wet did not leave the night after as scheduled. The commandos coming from the Natal border to link up with them had still not arrived; and with De Wet gone the Boers suffered acutely from indecisive leadership. By 20 July, when Hunter finalized his plans, they had still not left.

That day his forces began to move towards the four main passes. These were Slabbert's and Retief's Neks which were quite close together and, being on the curve of the horseshoe, nearest Bethlehem; Commando Nek in the south-west near Ficksburg; Naauwpoort Nek in the north-east. Where the minor passes were not near enough to be covered by his proposed attack he detached contingents to plug them. The single exit left unguarded for the moment was a minor one, the very grandeur of its setting, which gave it the name of the Golden Gate, making access to it difficult from the Basin; and standing at the eastern end it was furthest from both the British and most of the Boers.

Hunter's plan was for his own and Clements's columns respectively to seize the two main passes nearest Bethlehem while the third force (Rundle's) kept up a show of strength in front of Commando Nek and elsewhere; then he would be able to invade the Basin itself. On the eve of his attack a gale and a violent downpour of rain and snow provided a fitting overture to battle. Next morning, 23 July, the British troops set out for Slabbert's and Retief's Neks from camping grounds turned into a sea of mud. The mighty clefts in the mountain barrier looked impregnable. Through one the road twisted at right-angles, appearing to end in a solid wall of rock, while cliffs sometimes 2,000 feet high rose up on either side to merge into precipitous plateaux and ridges which in one direction presently fell away in a great drop to the other pass, similarly flanked by forbidding heights whose crevices and caves gave the Boers perfect cover. They were well prepared with artillery and they manned the lower slopes as well as trenches across the passes.

Events followed in unrehearsed unison. The British massed their guns about two miles away and pounded the Boer centre at each pass while the troops attempted to get on to either flank. But the day's fighting brought little progress. The Boers might have held firm indefinitely had they not that night fallen victim to a fatal flaw in their own military habits. Under cover of darkness three of Lovat's Scouts at one pass and some scouts of Brabant's Horse at the other scaled outlying heights which, if seized in strength, would largely dominate the defenders. They found the Boers' posts on these important situations withdrawn for the night, such was the Boers' scorn—largely justified until now—for their enemy's enterprise. Troops were immediately guided up by the scouts and in the morning the Boers found their impregnability from the front rendered useless by their self-made vulnerability from the side. At Slabbert's they broke by eleven o'clock, precipitating a similar retreat from Retief's, and down the broad valley of the Brandwater River they fled towards the town of Fouriesburg in the centre of the Basin.

Their comrades at Commando Nek made shift to join them lest Hunter came down and took them in rear. Rundle therefore crossed the pass without opposition and galloped on to Fouriesburg itself. He found the Boers gone not many hours before, leaving behind President Steyn's wife and 115 British P.O.W.s while they made into the maze of hill and valley extending across the eastern side of the Basin to Naauwpoort Nek and the Golden Gate.

The former was the nearer and more accessible of these last remaining exits. Here Hunter had already posted a small force, and immediately on forcing the northern passes he detached the Highlanders under Hector Macdonald to reinforce it. At this juncture the commandos which had been so slow in coming from the Natal border arrived on the scene. Under General C. J. de Villiers, of Platrand (Caesar's Camp) fame, they fought outside Naauwpoort Nek to keep it open until their fleeing countrymen could reach it. They failed. After a day-long struggle the Highlanders effectively sealed the pass.

The only exit left to the main body of Boers by nightfall on the 26th was therefore the Golden Gate—twenty miles away from their laager in the heights outside Fouriesburg, across a bad and tortuous track among canyons and gorges. But it was their last hope; and realizing this, De Villiers slipped away in the darkness from Naauwpoort Nek to hold on to it in the hope that they could reach it quickly enough.

But morning rose on 6,000 Boers who were all but doomed. Indecisive leadership had already delayed their departure from the Basin when they should have followed De Wet out. Now the need for leadership was even more vital—that, and cool heads. Instead, the flight and a sense of being trapped bred chaos which no leader could dispel, because none was in overall command. The two senior officers were both chief commandants, thrown together by their retreat from the respective passes they had tried to defend. The Boer system placed no officer above another of the same rank; and as crucial hours wore on, disorganization rooted them to the spot while Hector Macdonald, failing immediately to follow up De Villiers, presented them with a last chance to escape through the Golden Gate. Eventually, that evening they met to elect a supreme commander.

Despite their desperate situation and the imperative need for action, they argued all night. One burgher sat silent. He was that Commandant Vilonel who was reduced to the ranks for his too spirited defiance of De Wet before the capture of the Sannah's Post water-works: never forgiving De Wet he later surrendered to the British, then tried to persuade others to do the same, whereupon they had arrested him and sentenced him to five years' hard labour for treason. It was not a sentence they could impose beyond dragging him about with them.

The two chief-commandants round whom the heated debate revolved were Paul Roux and Marthinus Prinsloo. Paul Roux was a parson. Much criticism has been levelled at Boer parsons, not only for delivering propaganda sermons from the pulpit, but—like Roux and others—actually leading men into battle. Yet priests on either side constantly pleaded for God's partisanship which would clearly have conferred an overwhelming advantage on the side of the successful applicant; and for any of them to have added his own mortal strength to his cause was not only consistent with this plea but seems rather more manly than uttering pieties from a safe distance (or writing bad verse—see page 145). Roux was a brave man, a good organizer during the Natal campaign, devoted to the wounded, and an able general though he was said never himself to have carried arms. Prinsloo's full white beard proclaimed him a much older man: he was a prosperous farmer and an elder in the church; he had commanded the Free Staters in Natal, then retired to his farm after the siege of Ladysmith because he was past the fighting age, until the recent siege of Lindley called him forth again.

It was probably the Boers' veneration of age that finally, towards dawn, swung the vote in Prinsloo's favour. But later the commandos with C. J. de Villiers outside the Golden Gate sent in their votes which would have given Roux a majority, and the uncertainty was not resolved.

That morning Hunter came after them from Fouriesburg. At a break in the hills where the road from the village forked to Naauwpoort Nek and the Golden Gate, Prinsloo persuaded enough men to stand with him while the convoy could go along the difficult track to the Golden Gate. It was a strong position and the British were held off until nightfall. Another day and the Boers might hope to get out after all. But some confusion of orders caused the key Boer position to be abandoned, and in the darkness the Scots Guards took possession of it.

To the Boers the biting cold darkness and the no less bitter dawn seemed alive with English starting up everywhere from grass and rock.

Their demoralization was complete. Those left with the power of movement tried frenziedly to get away, only to find their wagons and their guns and their animals and themselves jamming the defiles, all order thrown to the wind. Some sustained themselves with wild rumours—Roberts had been flung from the Transvaal, De Wet was about to rescue them. Brave men wept with impotent rage. There was now about no hope.

Prinsloo sent an emissary to Hunter to ask for a four-day armistice. The emissary he sent was Vilonel—a convict sent to plead for his gaolers. The plea failed. Lord Roberts telegraphed instructions from Pretoria : immediate surrender of every burgher with his horse, rifle, wagons, guns, and livestock. Prinsloo submitted. He saw the alternative as the murder of his men, but critics were to charge him with treachery, because that evening Roux went to Hunter declaring that the surrender had been without authority, though finally he agreed to be bound by it. In the darkness attempts were made by some burghers to escape nonetheless. They headed for the Golden Gate, rolling their guns bound in logs down parts of the track too steep for the guncarriages, and on reaching their comrades beyond the pass they found their spirits shattered no less than those of the men they had left behind. But with most of the O.F.S. leaders* 1,500 men escaped, leaving nearly 4,500 in the Basin.

At a spot which chance had named Verliesfontein (*verlies* means loss or bereavement) these formally surrendered on the morning of 30 July 1900.

It had been a frosty night, and through the pellucid air the sun flooded the bolder ranges round about with gold and dug deep blue shadows between. Against the white-peaked immensity of the Basuto mountains, in that place they had come to for a haven, they went up—men in their prime, boys, grandfathers—between the silent but sympathetic lines of British soldiers, and handed over their arms. They were to spend their captivity in as lofty but a warmer setting, Diyatalowa or Happy Valley, 5,000 feet above sea-level in the mountains of central Ceylon.

During the following weeks Hunter's troops seized nearly 3,000 cattle, 4,000 sheep, 6,000 good horses. They destroyed two million

* Van Hattingh, Haasbroek, Olivier, Kolbe, Froneman, Visser, Von Tonder, Truter, P. Fourie, C. J. de Villiers.

rounds of ammunition, and legend holds that where this was done the grass has never grown again.

*   *   *   *

The basic cause of the Boer disaster in the Brandwater Basin was Christian de Wet's departure. Had he stayed to make sure of the others first and if necessary fought at the passes, things might have turned out differently. He took with him not only President Steyn but most of the flower of his fighting men, and so can be said to have been intent on preserving the O.F.S. Republic, however peripatetic or nebulous in form, to continue the struggle. Even so, his failure to leave a deputy with proper authority was a crass blunder. The result was that the Boers lost more men and supplies than at Paardeberg. But whether it would prove as catastrophic a blow or affect the course of the war depended on De Wet's survival. If he were now captured into the bargain the British success would be complete; if not, it might largely be wasted.

Included in the 2,600 men who had got out with Steyn and himself were two corps of highly able scouts. One was commanded by Scheepers, a Cape rebel though he now claimed O.F.S. citizenship. The other was Danie Theron's Corps of 200 hand-picked men—Boers, Hollanders, Germans, Russians, Frenchmen, a Bulgar, a Greek, a Levantine, a Turk, and an Algerian Arab—a tough and daring lot whose joviality could not be repressed even by Theron's discipline, which matched that of De Wet's. With men like these and helped by friendly farmers, De Wet hoped to keep tab on the British forces that were everywhere around him. But a three-mile convoy, always betraying itself by the dust it sent up into the clear light, was not something which could be tucked out of sight for long. His chances of escape were therefore slender.

His object, apart from avoiding capture, was to get President Steyn to Paul Kruger who had by now fled from Middelburg further along the Delagoa Bay railway to the vicinity of Machadodorp. After feinting due north, De Wet decided upon a wide detour round to the west of the Central railway.

The British columns, alerted to his escape on the morning of 15 July, soon caught up with him. He rounded on them with a rearguard while sending on his convoy towards Lindley. All day he held them off, then slipped away at nightfall to rejoin the convoy. Such tactics were invariably successful. It never occurred to the British to keep the Boer rearguard busy while they darted smartly around to pounce on the plodding convoy.

To General Broadwood, keen on settling accounts with De Wet since the ambush at the Sannah's Post water-works, Roberts entrusted the chief task of pursuit. Hunter sent him reinforcements, and though the convoy's course was known they did not try to head it off while he came up but made straight for him. In his turn he waited for them, so lost touch with his quarry and spent a day and a half riding in wrong directions. A second column was sent to help him corner De Wet north of Lindley. As 3,000 mounted troops converged, De Wet quickly attacked the second column to prevent a link-up with Broadwood, whom Theron kept from the convoy in an eight-mile running fight.

By such tactics, superb handling of the wagons and constant vigilance, De Wet continued to do the impossible and elude the British. They doggedly stuck to their task. Men were killed, men were wounded, and all who went on were exhausted. The two columns moved parallel to each other only fifteen miles apart, yet so faulty was their scouting that though both were receiving instructions from Roberts in Pretoria neither was in touch with the other. Their unco-ordinated pursuit enabled De Wet to shrug off their patrols and in spite of the heavy guard along the railway he got across it in the vicinity of Kroonstad two days later. Theron took the opportunity to stop a passing train, capture the men aboard, and grab useful food and ammunition, though chance deprived them of £100,000 in specie—carried by a coach uncoupled at the previous station because of an overheated axle.

On they pushed, and the panting British soldiery tracked them across the plains to the hills by the Vaal in the vicinity of Reitzburg. There, after a sharp exchange on 24 July when some of his wagons were cut off, De Wet halted. He selected a circle of hills strong enough to be held indefinitely against his pursuers, who had to draw off and watch from a distance. In nine days he had brought his President and the convoy 150 miles to a secure position where he could rest and gather supplies from the surrounding countryside; and many farmers, who had appeared so pacific when Methuen marched across the north-west O.F.S. during Roberts's advance to Pretoria, took up arms to join him.

As though to flaunt the immunity he had gained he sent Theron south-east in two more attacks on the railway.

So far at least, then, he had made good his escape, and while his countrymen were surrendering in the Brandwater Basin his survival substantially minimized the disaster. But even his survival would mean little if the Boers were compelled to sue for a general peace settlement. All depended on Roberts' own operations which, simultaneously with the drive on the Brandwater Basin and the pursuit of De Wet, he had launched against the Transvaal forces east of Pretoria.

CHAPTER XX

Roberts's Eastern Offensive: July 1900

IN preparing to advance eastward from Pretoria as soon as he had Hunter's expedition to the O.F.S. under way, Roberts felt he could forget about the western half of the Transvaal, since Hunter and Baden-Powell had marched through it with scarcely a shot fired. The uninviting bushveld north of Pretoria similarly offered no menace. It was the east he had to deal with—the region pierced by the Delagoa Bay railway, the Boers' life-line to the outside world.

Ever since the outbreak of war the question of blocking or cutting that life-line had exercised Milner and the authorities in England, besides the military. The Royal Navy's patrol of Delagoa Bay had not been wholly successful in stopping the arrival of war material. For some time pressure had been applied on the Portuguese to comply with treaty obligations and stop railing such goods. Also, British agents outbid Boer agents for the purchase of other supplies. This naturally endeared them to the local merchants, and with Roberts's successes caused a reversal of the previously pro-Boer attitude of the Portuguese colony. A foreign officer sent by Botha after Diamond Hill to collect supplies at Lourenço Marques found the atmosphere very changed since he had passed through on his way from Europe three months before. He had to bribe heavily to avert official gazes from a consignment of biscuit-tins and sacks bursting with war contraband. All the same, by such means, or even smuggling in volunteers and goods ostensibly for Red Cross service, the British blockade was to some extent nullified.

Sporadic small-scale attempts, one of which was the work of the subsequently notorious Roger Casement, had been made to cut the railway at Komati Poort on the border between Portuguese East

Africa and the Transvaal, without success.* Roberts himself had missed his chance of cutting it well east of Pretoria—he might have trapped the Boer forces and Government before they escaped even further east.

Now not only the consideration of cutting off supplies but every other military reasoning came back to the railway line, spine of the whole region. It meant Balmoral, which Botha had made his headquarters after Diamond Hill with the bulk of the Boer army who must inevitably stand at bay in defence of all that lay beyond. It meant Machadodorp, where Paul Kruger sheltered with his officials and millions in gold. It meant stations further along and the towns of Lydenburg and Barberton in striking distance on either side, at which great stores had been accumulated. It meant the concentration of rolling stock withdrawn to deprive Roberts of badly needed transport for troops and supplies all over S.A. It meant Komati Poort, which was the vital point of entry at the frontier.

That shelter captured, that army smashed, that railway seized—surely nothing on earth could then save the Boers from total collapse. Even Hunter's operation in the O.F.S. was incidental to the larger issue of conquering the eastern Transvaal, because here were the O.F.S.'s larder and arsenal: with supplies and the railway, which might bring in more, both cut off, any burghers escaping Hunter must be as doomed as their comrades across the Vaal.

The railway extended for about 250 miles from Pretoria to the frontier at Komati Poort. For about half this distance it passed through scenery typical of much of the southern Transvaal and O.F.S.: undulating treeless veld with few scattered ranges of bare kopjes and rivers of uncertain water-supply. But then, beyond Belfast, it entered a sixty-mile complex of mountains, though the track of course wound through the shortest and least formidable part, before the final stage of bush country to the border.

Roberts proposed to send his main army along the line from the

* First, the previous December, by the English colony at Lourenço Marques, who had been discovered and prevented at the last moment. Roger Casement was in the town at about this time on secret service for the Foreign Office. As the result of a scheme prepared by him, a force which he accompanied was sent in April from Cape Town, the Navy taking it to the Zululand coast preparatory to a cross-country march to Komati Poort, but it turned back on hearing that the Boers were forewarned. Finally, in the middle of June, a party of colonial scouts from Buller's army made a hazardous six-week journey through Swaziland and succeeded in damaging the line without permanently disrupting traffic.

vicinity of Pretoria while mobile columns, like giant grappling-hooks, would be thrown ahead and on either side. Buller's advance in the opposite direction, along the railway from Natal, would drive a barrier between escaping Transvaalers and Free Staters alike, besides providing a much needed second line of communications to Pretoria from the coast. Through June Roberts waited. He had to bring up supplies and make good the column which had gone to the O.F.S. with Hunter. Early in July, at the time Hunter was shepherding the Free Staters into the Brandwater Basin, he was ready.

Botha knew exactly what the British intended. His scouts, mainly foreign volunteers, penetrated their lines with ease. And Roberts's indulgence in allowing Boer wives and even surrendered fighters to continue living in freedom at Pretoria provided him with a further means of information.

He used the lull in Roberts's activities to re-deploy his forces. A new scheme worked out at his Balmoral headquarters and taken by Jan Smuts to the old President for his approval, which it received—to bear profoundly on all that followed—was put into effect. Botha broke up his army by grouping commandos as near their own districts as possible, which gave them the opportunity to rest and reprovision, and checked demoralization. Quite unknown to Roberts, commandos from north of Pretoria went back there; those from west of Pretoria and Johannesburg returned to that region under the command of Koos de la Rey; the remainder, who were in the majority, were scattered along the eastern side of Pretoria and Johannesburg to cover the region against which Roberts now launched his offensive.

As a first move he ordered the hills south of the Tigerpoort Range to be cleared of commandos posted by Botha to worry the right flank of his projected advance. They proved unexpectedly stubborn. Seven thousand troops under French were eventually required in an operation which started on 7 July with the British advance guard, the I.L.H., being severely mauled in a trap. Confused fighting only ended four days later after Botha had quietly withdrawn most of his men to avoid suffering any damage. This evidence of Boer spiritedness was disturbing enough, but nothing to the news which suddenly made Roberts cancel his main advance and urgently summon French back to Pretoria. A totally unexpected emergency had arisen. The western Transvaal, which Roberts had dismissed from his mind, was aflame.

He had thought that the only Boers in the region were a few near Rustenburg where Baden-Powell was now based. The quiet transfer of commandos from the east had been unknown to him; so too a steady flow of farmers from tilling their soil to riding on commando at the call of De la Rey. The Boers had in fact gathered about 7,000 in fighting trim, with many able leaders, including young State Attorney Jan Smuts who now forsook politics for the battlefield little dreaming of a day when he would hold the baton of a field-marshal in the British Army. The region in which he was now to be schooled by De la Rey will recur on these pages to the end. It was dominated by the Magaliesberg range extending for a hundred miles west of Pretoria, and drawing from Smuts in recollection the following vivid description:

It is impossible to contemplate this bleak and uninviting and apparently insignificant mountain range, the silent and grim spectator of so much in the history of Southern Africa, without melancholy emotion.

Rising like a bastion on the lower slopes of the Highveld, it looks on the South at the smiling grassy plains and uplands of the Highveld and on the North at the endless dreary prospect of the lowveld bush. And with the same cold callous look which it wears to-day it has regarded the beautiful valleys North and South along its slopes occupied and cultivated by successive races of men. It saw the nation of the Magatese grow up here in comparative peace until it was the greatest Bantu people in the Transvaal and it took its name from Mamagali, Great Chief of this people. It saw the Magatese power broken and annihilated by the Zulu armies under Moselekatze who cleared the whole country North of the Orange River in order to found on its ruins a kingdom of his own. And where the Magatese bones were bleaching in the sun it saw an endless chain of Zulu kraals and fortifications arising, stretching from a point North of Pretoria to the confines of the Kalahari desert, which can still be seen to-day. It saw in turn the Zulu power smashed in 1837 by the Emigrant Boers in the great actions at Mosega and Maricospoort and this Attila of Central South Africa flee for refuge Northward to the territory of the former glorious kingdom of Monomotapa, where a renewed career of conquest was only to lead to the melancholy fate of his people under his son and successor Lobengula. It saw the country all around converted into one of the most beautiful and fertile parts of South Africa, and Boer and Magatese enjoying the fruits of peace in a land of plenty for more than 80 years. And now it was to see the curtain rise on the most tragic spectacle of all, and a fresh tide of racial war sweep over these fair regions and convert them into ruin and desolation such as even the ruthless barbarians of Moselekatze had failed to effect.[11]

That curtain rose on 11 July. De la Rey's commandos simultaneously struck at three British forces within a thirty-mile radius of Pretoria, on and north of the Magaliesberg. They achieved substantial success. De la Rey himself led the operation in the Magaliesberg, compelling the surrender of almost an entire outpost of 240 men at one of its four passes called Zilikats, a corruption of the Moselekatze mentioned in Smuts's description.

Staff H.Q. at Pretoria had received last-minute warning of something afoot and done little about it. Roberts himself heard too late. Now he found himself confronted by a series of explosions in the western Transvaal such as De Wet had sparked off the previous month in the O.F.S.

From this moment the war began to take on a grimmer aspect. Up to his recent proclamations Roberts had sought to reconcile the Boers by as scrupulous consideration of their persons, feelings, and property as war allowed. But the transition from the nineteenth century to the twentieth was for Britain a painful lesson in the fact that the imposition of imperial power requires the use of ever more force. It was a lesson which the American War of Independence should have taught but did not. It was not learnt in wars against 'savages' because white men universally deemed with impunity that the colour of their skin was an open licence for the game season. Nor was any lesson to be learnt from the Irish, since the issue was domestic rather than imperial. It was learnt, therefore, in the war against the Boers, the more effectively because the Boers were in many respects like themselves, which is to say brave, obstinate, self-righteous, proud, suspicious of theory or innovation, very ready to take life easy yet capable of sustained and astonishing vigour, essentially humourless yet able to joke in adversity, and underneath their violence animated by a genuine charity which mitigated the crudities and unreason in which some of their other qualities trapped them. These remarks apply, of course, to the British and Boers of 1900; the sixty years between have moved fast and trampled much underfoot.

Bolstered by international rivalries and perils, the prevailing concept of imperialism demanded victory; and victory, whether it would bring benefit or evil to the conquered, demanded measures which acutely discomfited all that was generous, just and kind in the British people. This was the lesson, though until it could write itself upon the soul of the nation only a minority read it, and in any event it was a lesson on the inadvisability of going to war, not on conducting one already embarked upon. *That*—if it was to be continued—demanded increasingly severe measures precisely by reason of the obstinacy and courage which both sides had in common.

Until now, life in Pretoria and Johannesburg under Roberts's occupation had been groping towards normalcy. He himself had taken up residence in a baronial Pretoria mansion built by a gentleman who had made a fortune running coaches between the two cities before the railway was built. He had paid a courtesy call on Mrs. Kruger, a kindly, unobtrusive, round black-bonneted lady affectionately known as Tant (Aunt) Sannie; and permitting her to stay in the Presidency, mounted a ceremonial guard in front of the sculptures of two very British-looking lions which Barney Barnato had given Oom Paul to adorn his veranda. Relations between Afrikaner residents and the British were markedly cordial. Boer girls nursed in the hospitals; Mrs. Louis Botha joined in at officers' concerts. Now came a change of spirit. Roberts's immediate fears were for the safety of Pretoria and Johannesburg. The dangers of allowing so many non-British to stay inside, and of the proximity of Botha's and De la Rey's forces outside, were dramatically illustrated by the discovery of two plots.

One was in Johannesburg where a large number of people, mostly foreigners ('socialists and anarchists' said the Jingo Press), conspired to seize the garrison's officers at a race-meeting announced for Bastille Day and hand them over to a commando in the vicinity; the secret was said to have been betrayed by the girl friend of one of the conspirators. The other plot was also betrayed, to the British in Pretoria: a large number of people were arrested here too, the principal being Hans Cordau, a surrendered German who had taken the oath of allegiance.

At his trial before a military court it was disclosed that houses in Pretoria were to have been set alight, creating a distraction under cover of which leading officers were to have been assassinated and Roberts kidnapped. Documents found on Cordau proved his guilt and he was condemned to death. He walked calmly to a chair placed before the firing squad, declined to be tied to it but asked to be blindfolded, and died leaving a letter admitting his guilt. But mainly both plots caused the expulsion from either city of a large number of foreigners, mostly the Hollanders: they refused to work the railways, which was a becoming gesture to their former employers, but the Boers were not sorry to see them go who had waxed fat while despising the source of their prosperity.

But Roberts's action in sending, during this month and the next, some thousands of Boer women and children trekking back to the Boer lines was less welcome. Botha protested vigorously. The refugees would be exposed not only to the dangers of war but of marauding Natives. Roberts's justification was that they kept the enemy supplied with information, and consumed supplies which he needed for his own army when food was plentiful among the Boers, who were busy wrecking trains carrying provisions for his men. But he overlooked two points. He was giving some basis to a bitter legend which still works poison among the Boers' descendants, of British inhumanity against women and children. And he was giving the enemy an added incitement because the Boer women were far more irreconcilable than their menfolk.

The direct military measures he took following De la Rey's bombshells were to reinforce his positions all round the railway between the Vaal and Pretoria. Being especially concerned about the west he deployed more troops and commanders to deal with that region, including Methuen who was sent for from the O.F.S. to confront his old adversary in the march to relieve Kimberley.

Botha assumed Roberts would take some such steps to quell De la Rey. To distract him he launched simultaneous attacks along his eastern front on 16 July. North of Diamond Hill* he achieved no success, his force being swept away by French and Ian Hamilton (now recovered and furnished with a new column). But a bruising engagement was fought with great tenacity by the Boers in the vicinity of the

* Edendale.

Tigerpoort positions from which they had been pushed away only five days before. The commander on the spot was Ben Viljoen, having his first taste of independent command, and he used his force of 2,000 men with skill against 4,000 British in a series of simultaneous dawn attacks; the hardest fight was a six-hour engagement* only ended by strong British reinforcements, the Canadian Mounted Rifles making a brilliant charge in which the son of Canada's Minister of Defence was killed.

De la Rey did not avail himself of these diversionary actions east of Pretoria immediately to follow up his own successes, but first scattered his commandos in the Magaliesberg districts and southwards close to the Klerksdorp–Johannesburg railway. These then proceeded to launch attacks on isolated British forces whenever opportunity offered. At the same time train-wrecking operations were undertaken, and in fact on 25 July the railhead town of Klerksdorp was to surrender to them without a shot.

Nevertheless Roberts felt that Johannesburg and Pretoria were now secure enough for him to get on with his eastern offensive. But again he was stopped, this time by news of De Wet's escape from the Brandwater Basin, which raised fears of a direct northerly ascent on the Transvaal. Not until De Wet's trek westward near Kroonstad dispelled this idea did Roberts at last begin his eastern offensive towards the end of July.

The first phase was to be the occupation of Middelburg, about sixty miles along the Delagoa Bay line. He himself set out along the line with Pole-Carew; Hamilton advanced on his left front, and French set out on the right front with the idea of sweeping round behind Botha's forces and cutting them off by reaching the railway beyond Middelburg. French's Chief of Staff, Douglas Haig, issued precise instructions for the swift accomplishment of this manœuvre. Botha was very vulnerable because the thousands of women and children thrust on him hampered his movements. But no sooner had French started than Roberts in an access of caution restricted him to remaining with the general advance, which once again merely served to push the Boers before him. Fighting delaying actions Botha enabled the long line of wagons and fugitives to withdraw steadily along the line.

While Roberts moved eastwards in their wake, Buller's army followed a parallel course a hundred miles to the south but in the

* Witpoort.

opposite direction, along the Natal railway. Few of Buller's accomplishments quite match the slowness he had been able to achieve since rousing himself from his long hibernation at Ladysmith. During Roberts's 300-mile march to Pretoria he had marched half that distance to reach the Transvaal border town of Volksrust. Jan Smuts has left an account of his countrymen's reaction.

> To the Boers the inactivity of Buller in the North of Natal seemed inexplicable except on the theory, at that time generally believed by the Boers, that owing to jealousy between the two principal officers in the British army, Buller's advance had been artificially stayed in order to give his rival a chance of first entry into the Transvaal. This belief, if unfounded, was due to the fact that the dawdling and sulking of Buller after the capture of Ladysmith could not be explained on any other ground known to the Boers.[11]

With Natal behind him, Buller had set off at a no less leisurely pace to close the 120-mile gap to the outskirts to Johannesburg.

He went so slowly because he was convinced that he had too few men, with the incidental result that he constantly baulked at suggestions from Roberts to detach troops to help in operations elsewhere. He left a needlessly large part of his forces to guard Natal but he still had ample to hold the few commandos who hovered about and sometimes cut the railway or telegraph lines. As he advanced he used up more and more men to guard his lines of communication, so that his army grew smaller and smaller and he became more and more timid. His slowness also owed something to the vast baggage he insisted on trailing along with him. Alone among the troops in S.A. his did not bivouac in the open but always brought along their full equipment of tents. But at last, six weeks after leaving Volksrust, he closed the gap with Roberts's forces outside Johannesburg, and the whole of the Durban–Pretoria railway was open to give Roberts a second line of supply. A day or two later, Roberts himself reached Middelburg as Botha's forces withdrew to the vicinity of Belfast, forty miles down the line. So ended the first phase of Roberts's eastern offensive.

* * * *

This brief account of events in the Transvaal to the end of July 1900 brings us abreast of those in the O.F.S. described in the previous chapter. The overall picture, then, was this: Roberts's army stood poised at Middelburg to complete the subjugation of the eastern Transvaal, just as Hunter had purged the north-eastern O.F.S. in his campaign culminating in the Brandwater Basin. On the other hand, Steyn and De Wet had safely reached the banks of the Vaal and were in touch with De la Rey who had plunged the western Transvaal in ferment, their proximity posing a serious threat of combined action.

The offensive in the eastern Transvaal, with its manifold objects of the Delagoa Bay line, Botha's forces and the Kruger Government, remained Roberts's chief concern, in accordance with his belief that its success must achieve what the fall of Pretoria two months ago had so distressingly failed to achieve, an immediate end to the war. But before going on from Middelburg he decided to make his situation in the western Transvaal more secure. He ordered the evacuation of isolated garrisons in that region which were vulnerable to De la Rey's attacks and he made preparations to corner Christian de Wet once and for all.

CHAPTER XXI

Kruger's Departure: September 1900

AUGUST opened with troops pouring into the north-western O.F.S. to hunt De Wet. At first, however, it was De la Rey who held the stage.

The garrisons whose evacuation Roberts had ordered in the western Transvaal were those stationed by Hunter and Baden-Powell at places along the route of their marches from the western border. But the process of abandoning isolated posts in hostile country is apt to be as dangerous as trying to maintain them.

One of the garrisons west of Rustenburg, which Baden-Powell himself was about to evacuate, had a strength of 500 Australian (Imperial Bushmen) and Rhodesian volunteers under Colonel Hore, who had spent such an uncomfortable day as the prisoner of Sarel Eloff in the latter's attack in the closing days of the Mafeking siege. They were half a mile from the Elands River at a place called Brakfontein, and were guarding not only a large quantity of stores but a number of refugee women and children, when the order came to retire under cover of a force due to be sent from Mafeking. This was Carrington's contingent which had at last come down from Rhodesia. But before Carrington could arrive, De la Rey struck. At his approach on 5 August the garrison hastily erected a bulwark of stores, ox-wagons, biscuit-tins and flour-bags on the rocky kopje where their camp lay.

De la Rey had perhaps three times more men than they and he was also stronger in artillery. On the first day his guns killed most of the thousands of horses and oxen in the British camp, creating a stench which added to the dire straits of the men. On the following day Carrington reached within two miles of the camp, but one of the Boer commandos set upon him and he ignominiously back-pedalled as far as Zeerust, and even gave up that town to get back to Mafeking. The garrison saw Carrington's retreat with dismay, but there remained a distinct hope of relief, for in order to cover Baden-Powell's withdrawal Ian Hamilton had been switched from the east and had just arrived at Rustenburg. There the sounds of battle were distinctly heard from Brakfontein on the first day, so next morning Baden-Powell set out to the rescue with a big mounted column. He got half-way when he heard the firing receding in a westerly direction. This was owing to Carrington's retirement: but Baden-Powell, without sending out a reconnaissance, jumped to the conclusion that Carrington had reached Hore and was taking him off to safety. He therefore returned to Rustenburg. Roberts had a report from Carrington the following day, yet instead of sending Hamilton and Baden-Powell to Hore's rescue he was so fearful of hazarding them that he ordered them back towards Pretoria, abandoning the garrison to its fate.

De la Rey could now give the siege his undivided attention. He began to batter the British not only by day but also by night when they had to send parties of men to fetch water from the Elands River. The colonials scorned suggestions of surrender and grimly stood their ground, even though there was now no British column anywhere near which might bring relief. The Boers adopted their traditional tactics of waiting, content to let each day bring inevitable surrender closer.

These same days were to see the fate of Colonel Hore's garrison and that of Christian de Wet in unintended conjunction, for the morning after De la Rey's siege began on 5 August, so did the hunt for De Wet, eighty miles to the south-east on the Vaal.

*   *   *   *

Roberts had prepared with great thoroughness. His troops who had been pouring into the north-west O.F.S. were drawn in a semi-circle around De Wet's laager near Reitzburg south of the Vaal, leaving his only escape route across the river. There, to receive him, Roberts posted Methuen. And behind Methuen, along the Klerksdorp railway, was General H. L. Smith-Dorrien, an officer of the Derbyshires who had been serving with unobtrusive distinction in various parts of the field since his arrival with Buller's Army Corps; and behind him, in front of the Magaliesberg south-east of Rustenburg, were Hamilton and Baden-Powell. Altogether 26,000 troops were directly concerned in the impending operation, not counting the many thousand more along the Central railway or with Carrington in the north-west. To make assurance doubly sure, Roberts sent Kitchener to direct the hunt.

The quarry, it will be recalled, was De Wet's force which had escaped from the Brandwater Basin: 2,500 men with a three-mile convoy of wagons, guns and, most precious of all to them, President Steyn. As the British net closed round from the south, its strands only fifteen miles away and pinning him to the Vaal, the prospect before De Wet was bleak in the extreme. There was no tropical jungle at hand into which he might disappear: the winter-brown veld offered no concealment except temporarily behind an occasional low hill; and if the only hope lay in movement, every movement raised its tell-tale clouds of dust. The forces closing round him were many times larger than those he had eluded in reaching the Vaal from the Brandwater Basin; and sufficient of them were mounted to place his wagon oxen at a hopeless disadvantage.

By 6 August he knew that time was running out. He determined to make a dash northwards over the Vaal. His Free Staters were reluctant to leave their country, whereupon he sent on their baggage, which obliged them to follow. He headed straight for the nearest and most obvious ford across the river. Methuen's patrols saw the movement, but Kitchener had sent him to concentrate at a crossing lower down. By the time he came hurrying back the next day De Wet was over and kept him at bay while the convoy wound among the hills along the north bank.

Kitchener thought it was making for another crossing well upstream with a view to outflanking the British net and cutting back into the O.F.S., so he sent troops rushing along the south bank to this ford instead of straight across the river to head the convoy off. For a day Methuen entirely lost touch with it before coming up with a portion of De Wet's rearguard. But De Wet had split his convoy into two, and the other half pretended to make for the upstream ford, whereupon the British were confirmed in their supposition of an intended recrossing and rushed more troops there. De Wet never arrived: suddenly changing direction he took his convoy north while the British, floundering up and down the banks of the river, once more lost touch. Already the hunt had a quality of spook-hunting in a graveyard. When they saw De Wet again he appeared to be heading north-east, but it was a feint. His true direction lay due north. Twenty miles clear of the river, he reached the Gatsrand range of hills just before the Klerksdorp railway.

To keep the British along the line busy a commando under Liebenberg, now on his home ground after his long and daring incursion into the western Cape, had daily been making lightning raids and compelled the evacuation of Potchefstroom like Klerksdorp before it. But higher up the line Smith-Dorrien was waiting for De Wet; only, instead of being allowed to extend his position to envelop the convoy as it descended from the Gatsrand he was obliged on Roberts's categorical orders to concentrate at one spot, which allowed De Wet simply to side-step him. Marching through the night the Boers crossed the railway at dawn on the 11th and headed due east towards Ventersdorp.

De Wet was now well and truly at large. But for all his desperate attempts to elude them, the British went after him with unrelenting persistence even though many were in rags, their boots worn through, their heads reeling from exhaustion and lack of sleep. Watering places were few, food often little and late in being brought up to them. They marched and rode themselves into the ground but never gave up, some men marching over a hundred miles in five days, others riding over eighty miles in half that time. Curiously enough it was not Kitchener but Methuen, working out a soldier's penance for his deeply felt failure to relieve Kimberley, who was the soul of the pursuit. It was he who stuck closest to the Boers as they made towards Ventersdorp. He overtook their rearguard, this time shelling it and pressing so close that De Wet had to abandon some wagons and prisoners before night released him. In the morning Methuen clung to his trail but again De Wet held him off and then suddenly swung north in the direction of a pass in the Magaliesberg called Olifant's Nek, the gateway to Rustenburg.

But the Boers were exhausted. They had not wanted for supplies from a friendly countryside, but they had scarcely ever had a chance to rest. An hour or two in the temporary haven of a farm and then the cry, 'Opzaal (saddle-up), opzaal, Khaki's coming!' would send them trudging forward, urging on their horses and their oxen or turning to fend off their nearest persecutors. So it had been for day upon day, night upon night, until they were too tired to do anything but resign themselves to the implacable demands of their leader's will. And Methuen saw how they could finally be trapped.

When he saw them heading for Olifant's Nek he desired nothing better. He knew that Hamilton was moving along the foot of the Magaliesberg from the east with instructions to have a detachment block this very pass, while south of it other troops were advancing under Kitchener. This left only the west open, and determined on a supreme effort Methuen set out at one in the morning of the 14th to ride in a wide loop to close the gap. Covering twenty-seven miles nonstop he reached the Magaliesberg west of Olifant's Nek with the satisfying knowledge that De Wet was now pushed up against a blocked pass by a semicircle of forces in overwhelming strength at little more than ten miles' distance.

But even as Methuen reached his destination, a Native came rushing into the camp with incredible news. The Boers had got through Olifant's Nek after all and were safely across the Magaliesberg.

The pass in fact had not been blocked. Hamilton, misled by messages from Pretoria H.Q. staff, who were frequently a day behind in plotting De Wet's movements, had come on too slowly to block it. Hence while the whole pursuing army were concentrating on one side of the range De Wet got scot-free to the other. The barrier of mountain which had seemed a prison wall was now a bulwark against pursuit.

He trekked eastwards along the further side and coming to a pass held by Baden-Powell invited him, with sardonic humour, to surrender. Then he turned away north, presently to disperse his commandos. He had already left Danie Theron near the Klerksdorp railway line (in the vicinity of which he pulled off several daring coups before losing his life in a skirmish the following month); now President Steyn with a small escort set off on a perilous journey around the far north of Pretoria in an attempt to reach Paul Kruger in the eastern Transvaal; the largest number of burghers set out due north in the hope of eventually doubling back to the O.F.S., while De Wet with a small commando immediately turned back on his tracks.

Eluding further attempts to catch him he climbed a precipitous path over the Magaliesberg and rode southwards, until eventually towards the end of August he reached the Vaal again and the position he had quit when the hunt started. By then he had trekked over 500 miles in the six weeks since he left the Brandwater Basin, and been pursued in the final hunt by upwards of 30,000 troops under some of the ablest generals of the day. By his insight into men, his daring, and his iron discipline, he had asserted before friend and foe alike how the individual will can transcend overwhelming odds.

For the British his escape was another unlearnt lesson on the necessity of thorough scouting and efficient staff work. It showed also the effect of a non-cooperative—if not hostile—countryside, prompting Roberts to issue a proclamation on the day De Wet slipped through the pass Hamilton was to have bottled up. 'It is manifest that the leniency which has been extended to the burghers of the South African Republic is not appreciated by them, but, on the contrary, is being used as a cloak to continue the resistance against the forces of H.M. the Queen.' Farmers failing to report the presence of the enemy would be punished; buildings harbouring scouts or snipers would be razed to the ground; burghers who had not taken the oath would be dealt with as prisoners of war, and oath-breakers would be liable to the death penalty. But proclamations could not make good the flaws in training and method which committed his troops to barren feats of endurance and left them with the chagrin of men grasping at a phantom.

They had one comfort. By leading his pursuers to the vicinity of Rustenburg De Wet brought them within range of Brakfontein, whence came news that Colonel Hore's garrison amazingly still held out against De la Rey. Kitchener set off to the relief. De la Rey did not wait but quietly withdrew on 16 August, eleven days after the siege began. The colonials had done wonderfully well, their survival doing a little to raise British spirits and dampen Boer jubilation over De Wet's escape and Roberts's abandonment of towns in the western Transvaal.

*　　*　　*　　*

Tidings of all this filtered through to an old man in a railway carriage 200 miles away in the eastern Transvaal. The capital of the South African Republic had been reduced to this carriage, and the Government of the South African Republic to Paul Kruger who stayed on it with a few officials. It had stood for some time at Machadodorp and then been moved to the warmer climate of Waterval Onder, ten miles further on. An appreciable difference in climate over so short a distance was due to the character of the region which was all the old man now held sway over.

The gigantic buttresses along S.A.'s coastal belt, shoring up the plateau of the interior, appear in the eastern Transvaal as the far northern

Drakensberg and a whole complex of sister mountains, spurs and foot-hills, together extending across an area roughly sixty miles square. The scenery is superb: mountain streams race down beautiful sudden ravines, and steep passes or jutting shelves of rock command immense vistas of sky, distant peaks and deep lush valleys.

Here gold was first discovered in the Transvaal, bringing a mad rush of fortune-seekers who little guessed how the ore they worked in the mountains was a trifle beside that which lay beneath the unploughed veld of the Rand 200 miles westward. So the region had a tale to tell before the Delagoa Bay railway was built, and war brought the President and the remains of his army for a final stand against the British.

Parts of it have names like Pilgrim's Rest and Devil's Knuckles, which illustrate its two-fold qualities of serenity and turbulence. But neither this nor its colourful history match the drama of its eastern limits: along an irregular line from north to south the earth drops almost sheer for 1,000 feet, 2,000 feet, and more; and there, below whomever comes to that edge, lies a totally different kind of country—endless flat bushveld, which by further contrast with the bracing high-lands above stretches in torrid fever-infested aridity to the Portuguese border eighty miles away.

To the old man in his railway carriage, the crucial sector in this whole region was that through which the track coiled, in particular the sixty miles between Belfast and Nooitgedagt. The bushveld below offered only disease and thirst to any defender: if the life-line to the outside world was to be preserved it had to be up here. Besides, at Lydenburg forty miles northward and Barberton thirty miles south-eastwards were accumulated most of his stores apart from those along the railway itself, and he knew very well that Roberts, however dis-tracted for the moment by events in the western Transvaal, must inevitably return to the main business of dealing with him in this final redoubt.

Thus it was that Botha, on retreating eastward in the face of Roberts's initial offensive, positioned his forces along the edge of the hilly country beyond Belfast where they might cover the approaches to the crucial sector of the railway in the centre and to Lydenburg and Barberton, respectively north and south of it. He had only 5,000 men thinly spread around an arc of fifty miles.

While Roberts had interrupted his eastern offensive to hunt De Wet the Boers entrenched themselves in this position, bringing together for the first time all four of their Long Toms. The trenches were thoroughly prepared, even if some of them—supervised by Lukas Meyer, that Buller of the Boers—were found by Botha to command no field of fire and had to be rebuilt. Morale was improved but unsteady. After every retreat the Boers first became demoralized, until remembering that they had not actually been defeated they responded to the exhortations of their leaders. Botha issued a proclamation: upon their efforts depended whether they would preserve the independence for which their fathers had left England's dominions. He threatened to surrender if they deserted their positions.

On the British side the wheels of the resumed offensive ground slowly into action. Roberts had left French to hold an advance position beyond Middelburg, and from here he had pushed outposts towards the Boer lines and by constant patrol activity gained much information. His vigour not only discouraged the Boers from descending on the railway line behind him, which was being repaired to bring up supplies and troops (and also more Boer women and children to be thrust on Botha), but begun to prey on their nerves, especially as the weeks passed without a definite move by Roberts. Botha wanted to attack French's camp, but his comrades refused to leave the safety of their trenches; and the penalty he had to pay for a citizen army was that he could not compel them in their present precarious state of morale.

At the same time Buller was at last preparing to co-operate directly with his commander-in-chief, who wanted him to clear the country between the Natal and Delagoa Bay lines and then form the right flank of the resumed offensive. On 6 August he left the Natal railway about mid-way between Volksrust and Standerton and headed north. He had 9,000 men; and, only less concerned about their stomachs than his own, he saw to it that they had upwards of a fortnight's supply of groceries, biscuits and meat, which were conveyed with the baggage in 761 ox- and mule-wagons. Forty-two guns were brought, but this time no tents. On the first day commandos which had been making scattered attacks on the Natal railway offered some opposition* before setting the veld alight and disappearing. Buller marched through Ermelo and without further incident, except for a skirmish off the line

* In the Rooikopjes south of Amersfoort.

356

of march at Carolina, he made contact with French's outposts some miles west of this town, eight days and eighty miles after leaving the Natal railway.

Within the following week the hunt for De Wet ended and Roberts could free troops and his mind for the eastern offensive. For this climax to his campaign he had about 20,000 men within about twenty miles of the Boer centre beyond Belfast. On the line was Pole-Carew; to his right, French; and to French's right, due south of the line, Buller. French wanted to make a wide flank attack by way of Barberton, but Roberts telegraphed from Pretoria restricting him to a flank movement on to the railway at Nooitgedagt while Buller would go directly north-east to cut the railway behind Botha at Machadodorp.

But by the time the offensive was due to be resumed Buller had decided he did not like the thought of fighting his way through the Boer left flank and across hills and swampy ground to Machadodorp; he would continue northwards and he would keep with him his mounted troops which were to have gone with French in the flanking movement. The result was that once again any chance of enveloping the Boers was given up, and French instead also advanced towards the Boer centre, getting steadily squeezed between Buller's advance and Pole-Carew's.

Operations began on 21 August while Roberts was still at Pretoria. There was some hard skirmishing involving Buller's force whose northward movement brought it across the front of Botha's left flank; but it was not until 23 August, as the British converged closer on Botha's centre, that the opposition stiffened. Reaching a farm called Geluk ('Joy') Buller came under fire from ridges north-east of it, and stiff fighting resulted. A brief violent artillery duel silenced the Boer guns, a famous volunteer named Van Dalwig being crippled while helping to man them. Then in the course of the advance some companies of the Liverpool Regiment went too far ahead and were furiously set upon. The hilly ground unsighted them from their comrades, who could not hear the firing on account of the wind. Ammunition ran low as the Boers moved closer; an attempt to get more failed, but by ransacking the dead and wounded the survivors held on until dusk, when they escaped.

24 August was spent by Buller and French preparing for the next push, Botha's centre being now almost within sight. That day Pole-

Carew entered the picture by advancing on Belfast: the Guards swept away a German contingent and he occupied the town.

Roberts now arrived from Pretoria to assume direct control. His whole army, confronting Botha's line of fifty miles, was bunched up in the twelve miles between Belfast and Geluk south of it, French being too squeezed in by Buller to manoeuvre. Roberts therefore ordered a new plan. French would ride round north of the railway, supported by Pole-Carew; Buller, after moving in a little closer to the railway from the south, would turn east: then together they would cut through the Boer flanks and execute a pincer movement on Machadodorp well to the rear of Botha's centre.

On 26 August the offensive entered its decisive phase with the start of these movements. Pole-Carew ran into trouble but French, sweeping around still further north, cleared strong positions with scarcely any loss. Meanwhile Buller closed in on the railway from Geluk. The Boers harassed him and it was with some loss that he got into position to turn east. The Boers' centre were formidably placed opposite him and one of their Long Toms, far behind them, had his range. Buller thought again. From an incorrect reconnaissance report he believed that the Boer line ended on the farm Bergendal, north-east of him and still on his side of the railway. In fact this was merely a small gap in the Boer positions, but labouring under the illusion as he did, he thought that by going for the gap he would turn the whole Boer line. He therefore took it upon himself to abandon his commander-in-chief's plan and march not east but north-east to Bergendal.

In the morning he went on to some ridges which commanded a view across a valley. The end—as he thought—of the Boer line was perfectly clear two miles away, a small square kopje 'of immense stones' (his dispatch said) on the other side of the valley, close to the railway. By 11 a.m. he had 8,000 troops and thirty-eight guns in position. He unleashed a bombardment unknown since the Tugela battles against the same Louis Botha, though under Botha's overall command Ben Viljoen had charge of this sector. The rocky entrenched platform which was Buller's target was actually an outpost thrown forward of the gap in the Boer line. It was held by only seventy-four Johannesburg Zarps supported by about a thousand men to their left rear and on either side of the railway line to their right rear.

For three hours the guns blasted the outpost at the rate of four to five

per minute, including fifty-pound lyddite shells, turning it into a cloud
of splintered rock and fumes, while shrapnel sprayed the hill-sides all
around. A huge pall of smoke spread against the sky in the shape of
brown Prince of Wales feathers. The Boer gunners were powerless.
They had lost Van Dalwig; their commander Wolmaraans was busy
against French and Pole-Carew five miles to the north; and the Hollander railwaymen had mistakenly sent away badly needed ammunition. Yet despite the effect of an almost volcanic eruption, the Zarps
clung to their trenches.

The bombardment so clearly presaged attack that Botha ordered a
commando lying north of the railway to reinforce the outpost. And
now was exposed a fatal mistake in his dispositions. Anticipating
Roberts's usual flank attack, and having a position fifty miles long to
man with inadequate numbers, he had arranged his slenderest strength
in the centre, relying on his men's usual alacrity at reinforcing a
threatened position. But this time they could not reach the Zarps because the latter were ringed by the impenetrable bombardment and
their trenches were not connected. Each commando had carefully
entrenched itself without regard to its fellows on either side. Whether
Botha had been disobeyed or failed to make sure of this vital detail is
not known. What mattered was that the commando he ordered to help
the Zarps refused to invite extinction by trying to cross the open. Thus
not only was Buller's force of 8,000 opposed by a mere 1,000 along the
Boer centre, but at the specific point he had selected for attack he was
opposed by what was left of the seventy-four Zarps, whose only
possible source of help was a foreign contingent just across the railway: and it consisted of a mere forty men (their commander rejoiced
in the name of Baron Goldegg).

Roberts rode across the ridges and joined Buller to watch the
infantry attack launched. Under cover of the continuing barrage the
Rifle Brigade and the Inniskilling Fusiliers advanced into a furious fire
from rifles, a pompom and a maxim, the last soon being blown to bits
by shell. Under their commandant, P. Oosthuizen, the Zarps fought
against odds of more than twenty to one with the courage for which
they were renowned; and the British, advancing against a gale that
whipped away the orders from their officers' mouths, had their own
courage equally tried. Baron Goldegg's existence had not been
suspected until he suddenly let loose, but Buller turned additional

359

troops on him while the main attack continued. With artillery blazing until the last moment, the Rifles and Inniskillings made over the broken ground through a hail of fire that brought down over eighty of them, including the colonel of the Rifles, before their bayonets gleamed at the throats of the enemy. Then the Zarps broke, many dashing for their horses and away, but some remained to the last, and as the British stormed over the entrenchments they took prisoner the brave Commandant Oosthuizen who was severely wounded. The scene amid the yellow-stained granite deeply moved one of the British newspaper correspondents:

> [I saw] one boulder as tall as a man heaved out of its place, great splinters lying wherever the spinning shell had flung them, and over all the majesty and the horror of death. The [Boer] dead lay where they had fallen, alone in their schanzes. . . . The blood lay at the mouths of their wounds like frozen port. Not one ill-featured face was there; no man could be ill-featured who had the heart to hold his post against that hurricane of death. The faces were yellowed, and a powder of dust lay over them. One man, handsomely bearded with curly hair, lay with his hand thrown back to the nape of his neck, like a sleeping god. No old man was there, and none, I think, less than thirty. They were massive in their repose, those dead Vulcans. . . . Peace, unbroken peace to their souls, for they were brave men. [43]

Buller, by a combination of disregarded plans, misinformation and Botha's blunder, had punched a hole clean through the Boer line. Though this could not be accounted as productive as Roberts's pincer plan would have been if succeeded in, and though the affair can hardly be termed a battle (it is called the Battle of Bergendal or Dalmanutha), it achieved the effect of a major victory. The moment word of the break-through reached them, all the commandos along Botha's fifty-mile front melted away so fast that pursuit, in any event feebly pressed, achieved nothing.

Roberts had again 'won'—and the Boers were again unscathed. A month before, his spy organization at Delagoa Bay had accurately told him the Boers' plan if they were ousted from their present positions. But he took no heed and pressed on along the railway for several days as if all the Boers were concentrated along it, whereas Botha drew off the larger part northwards to cover Lydenburg and other commandos were in the south to cover Barberton, leaving only a remnant of the centre under Viljoen as a screen protecting the withdrawal of the presidential train.

In it was now not only Paul Kruger but President Steyn. His long odyssey since leaving the Brandwater Basin had come to a momentary halt two days before Bergendal, when he reached his brother president. Together they now travelled thirty or forty miles eastward to Nelspruit.

Accordingly, when the advancing British columns reached Waterval Onder they found them gone. Riding on beyond it towards Nooitgedagt, Buller had his attention suddenly drawn to an extraordinary sight in the railway valley below. A great mob of men struggled up the slopes. They were found to be 2,000 hungry and tattered British soldiers from a prisoner of war camp. When the Presidents had passed through Nooitgedagt shortly before, Viljoen had asked what was to be done with these men, who were mostly the prisoners hurriedly removed from Pretoria as Roberts was closing in and who consequently suffered dreadfully in makeshift conditions. Kruger ordered their release. Viljoen's geniality was unruffled by the eclipse of his country's fortunes, and after cheerfully greeting the prisoners he told them they were free to go. Hence the unexpected and joyful reception which Buller's advancing troops received in that remote place.

Roberts at length realized his mistake in exclusively chasing eastwards. He sent parts of his army north and south as well, fanning out from the railway in an endeavour to envelop the mountains and the Boers from Lydenburg to Barberton. But in truth he regarded the issue as already decided by Bergendal, and the South African Republic as no longer in existence. On 1 September 1900 he proclaimed the Transvaal annexed to the Queen's dominions.

It seemed a somewhat bombastic flourish while, apart from De la Rey's commandos in the west and any in the unpenetrated region north of Pretoria, Botha's 5,000 were intact in their mountain fastnesses. The British forces, reinforced to 26,500 for their enveloping move, found that the wild magnificence of the scenery meant a hell of tortuous roads and precipitous passes sometimes 6,000 feet above sealevel. Physical hardship and the acute difficulty of maintaining supplies were only a lesser problem than fighting the Boers, who drew off through a labyrinth of mountain peaks, plateaux, ravines, valleys, and defiles, exploiting alike the terrain, rearguard tactics and the mists. But scenting absolute victory at last, the troops used not only their weight of numbers but a fine perseverance to press forward even when they had to lead their horses or haul up their guns by hand. In less than a fortnight they achieved the seemingly impossible task of reaching both Lydenburg and Barberton and points further eastward. The Boers' doom was all but sealed as they were shepherded back towards the railway line, losing great quantities of stores at the places they abandoned.

Thus in a mine east of Lydenburg Buller seized a hoard of munitions. At Barberton the booty was still greater. This town was taken by French. Sweeping round from Carolina he fought his way to the top of a pass near Devil's Knuckles; three days were needed to bring up all the baggage, each gun having to be hauled by sixteen horses up the last half-mile: but not waiting, he led his cavalry along a goat track that twisted down for 3,000 feet to the Barberton valley about fifteen miles away. The single line of struggling horsemen offered an easy target for an ambush, but the Boers were completely surprised. French galloped into the town to find 2,500 refugees, nearly a hundred locomotives, a prodigous quantity of stores—and an official trying to make off with £10,000.

As the Boers fell back on the railway line in the vicinity of the two presidents at Nelspruit, confusion and despair seized them. The three-pronged British drive threatened to sweep them away across the seventy miles of country which was all that was left to them before the Portuguese border. Louis Botha was stricken by quinsy and invalided further back along the line. In his absence the whole system of leadership broke down. Men wandered about aimlessly, many without horses, and defeat laid its icy hand upon them all.

Not quite all. President Steyn went passionately up and down the line. 'If you give up now,' he cried, 'what answer can you give to your children when they ask what you have done with the independence you have inherited?' He challenged them, encouraged them, cajoled them. 'One thing I can promise you—I will personally attend to it—at the end you'll each get a beautiful wife.'

Then he helped the other leaders concert measures for the future—if there was to be a future. Much depended on securing the escape of the best fighting men. An even more immediate need was ensuring that the aged Paul Kruger did not fall into British hands, which would count as a mortal blow to the Boer cause. The solution was for him to go to Europe where he would be safe, and perhaps bring the sympathetic Powers to his aid at this eleventh hour.

He bowed to the decision as to the sentence of God, who yet would save His people as now He scourged them. On 11 September he said good-bye to his friends at Nelspruit. Though he was only ostensibly taking leave of absence for six months, few could not have wondered if they would ever see him again. Then he entrained for Delagoa Bay, and while the Portuguese Government received him with all honours he waited for transport to Europe, the last unhappy trek of one of the last survivors of his people's Great Trek. His world seemed lost in a dream, less substantial than the smoke curling up from his meerschaum. Yet now, in what he called his 'night of affliction', he was himself a dream, as of a graven image upon the altar of the past.

At about the same time President Steyn also left Nelspruit. His flight was not away from but back into battle. Rejecting the direct route back to the O.F.S. because of French's proximity in the south-west, he headed north along the bushveld skirting the mountains. He took with him an escort of 250 men, a light baggage train, spare horses, and half a million in gold.

All the remaining Boer forces retired further along the railway to within twenty miles of Komati Poort on the border. Here the best men, numbering 2,000, were divided into two parties under Louis Botha and Ben Viljoen, and for them were picked out one Long Tom, a few field guns, and the best wagons, horses, and stores. The remaining guns were blown up and sunk in the Komati River; the remaining stores were mostly set alight. And the remaining 3,000 men, who were the faint-hearted, the mediocre, or simply those beyond caring, were sent on to Komati Poort with little hope of escaping the British or being interned by the Portuguese. As at the Brandwater Basin the leading Boers were prepared to turn the lesser to the wolves, as if giving them a last opportunity to serve the cause by acting as a bait.

On 13 September Roberts issued another of his proclamations, but this had the style of victory. He announced Kruger's flight, declared that the war was now degenerated into guerilla warfare which could only mean useless misery for the Boer people, and he called on the commandos to surrender. But for the present at least Botha and Viljoen led their men northwards from the railway. Their imperative need was to reach the highveld, leaving the bushveld with its waterless tracts, tsetse fly and fever as quickly as possible. Roberts was forewarned by his Delagoa Bay Intelligence of the Boers' escape plans, but again he paid no heed and concentrated largely on the railway in pursuit of the 3,000 men whom the leading Boers had written off.

Assembled on the Portuguese border these were an embarrassment to the Portuguese authorities, who did not want the international complication of a retreat into their territory with British troops in pursuit. They also feared that the railway bridge would be blown up, to the detriment of trade. This second problem they neatly solved by working on Paul Kruger as he waited for his ship, and it is not the least pathetic incident of the closing chapter in the old man's life that in his gratitude for the hospitality showered on him by the Portuguese he wrote to the commandants at Komati Poort and ordered them not to touch the bridge. The other difficulty was met by Portuguese emissaries crossing the flag-lined frontier to tell the Boers that all who crossed and quietly surrendered would be well treated; the hint was also given that otherwise Roberts would have permission to land troops in their rear at Delagoa Bay. All but 300 men took advantage of the offer. The 300 showed sterner mettle, and slipped away to follow in the northward wake of Steyn, Botha and Viljoen.

When the British reached the end of the railway trail at Komati Poort they therefore found it all but deserted, though smouldering stores and 1,500 trucks loaded with ammuntion showed the haste of the Boers' departure.

By now the leaders' hazardous flight northward was in full cry. Because of Roberts's indifference to the warnings from Delagoa Bay, Buller was slow in spreading his line further north along the mountains to prevent the fugitives trying to cut back through them instead of having to continue right around along the treacherous bushveld. As a result Steyn got through the mountains without difficulty. He was followed at a distance by Botha, leading a small party to protect a coach bearing the State funds, as well as government officials who included Schalk Burger, appointed to act as President in Kruger's absence: he got through just in time to offer Buller a distant view of his dust. But

Viljoen was barred, and to him fell the task of guiding the rest of the Boer force on the long journey around the mountains.

So a week or two short of a year since the war began, there was apparently no longer any Boer army or Boer State. Roberts declared the war over in all essentials: he informed the British Government that many of his troops could now go home, since only police action remained to mop up a few dissident commandos. And to bring these to heel the quicker, he issued a proclamation declaring that burghers surrendering would not be sent out of South Africa—the eventuality they most feared. With this blandishment he coupled a warning that stock and supplies found on farms belonging to men who stayed on commando or who broke their neutrality oath would be seized or even burnt.

But as the groups of Boers in the eastern Transvaal made their desperate bid for freedom, and the future frowned ominously upon all those others scattered through the two new colonies—such as De la Rey in the west, or the Free Staters with De Wet and the commandants who had fled through the Golden Gate from the Brandwater Basin— there remained some hope of help from the outside world, and in particular from the most potent source of all, England herself. The Opposition's sympathy for their cause was squarely placed before the nation by the Queen's proclamation, signed at Balmoral on 17 September 1900, dissolving Parliament.

Early the following month the electorate went to the polls to cast its votes in the 'Khaki Election', one of the oddest and most venomous ever fought in Britain.

CHAPTER XXII

The Khaki Election: October 1900

SALISBURY could go to the country with an impressive case. 'Lord Roberts telegraphs that the war is over,' Chamberlain wrote to his wife; 'he wants to come home.' That was the nub of the matter. Scattered bands of men might still be at large in S.A., fugitives in their own country, but by every criterion of war the Boers were defeated. In the public mind Paul Kruger's exit, following the capture of his capital and the dispersal of his burghers, was conclusive. The Government could claim that it had added 185,000 square miles—an area the size of France —to the British Empire, silenced the crowing of Powers who had threatened her destruction, and successfully concluded the greatest military operation ever undertaken by Great Britain.

Already measures of peace were being applied. In the O.F.S. and Transvaal the efforts of recently appointed District Commissioners and of military governors in the cities were directed to reviving civil life. Natal, untouched by rebellion, was fast returning to normal. In the Cape, the suppression of rebellion had brought no further sign of trouble; on the contrary, political developments had turned in Milner's favour.

His febrile anxiety to suspend the Cape constitution because of Schreiner and the Afrikander Bond's obstructionism may be recalled, as also Chamberlain's refusal to interfere with a self-governing colony. One of the principal questions at issue was how rebels were to be treated. To Chamberlain's insistence on clemency as part of a healing peace he bitterly retorted: 'I am all for a policy of conciliation when war is over, for letting bygones be bygones, for treating Dutch like British, forgetting that nine-tenths of them have been our open enemies at a most critical time'—*but* there must be at least disfranchisement

366

not only of rebels but of Members of Parliament whose constituents had rebelled: 'Are they to be allowed to help in voting down the loyalist minority?' Finally, on this question and on what attitude to adopt towards Roberts's annexations the Bond Ministry foundered. Schreiner resigned. A loyalist Ministry was formed by Sir Gordon Sprigge who by a narrow majority got through a Bill, approved by Chamberlain, disfranchising actual rebels only, and then for merely five years, though leaders would be severely punished if found guilty by special courts. The Cape Parliament was then prorogued—as it turned out, until after the war—and Milner, swallowing the pill, turned to larger matters. He wanted to move to Pretoria, from which to administer reconstruction and reform throughout S.A. Chamberlain agreed, enlarging Milner's High Commissionership and easing his personal financial losses in public service by raising his salary to £11,000 p.a.

All this bore directly on dissolution of the British Parliament and the general election which came about at Chamberlain's behest. Apart from the basic motive of wishing to continue in power, he wanted a mandate to continue his policies. He wanted to be in charge of the peace. The end he had in view was Rhodes's ideal of a S.A. federation within the British Empire. He was stimulated by the fact that he had recently helped hammer out with delegates from the Australian colonies a Bill for Australian federation, which received the Queen's assent in July. This achievement, creating a great new nation of untold potential, was made easier by the emotions bred of common sacrifices in the Boer War. Chamberlain hoped that if his Government were returned to power, the same atmosphere of imperial consciousness and unity would help promote a S.A. federation. He wanted to ensure that the Liberals did not get in and make a peace which would allow Krugerism to survive. He wanted to induce the Boers to co-operate in the knowledge that their hopes of a change in British policy were futile, a subject upon which he was very sensitive: 'If we could have had the warm authoritative support of the Opposition,' he declared in a July debate on Cape rebels, '. . . I firmly believe, as I am standing here, that the war would have been brought to a conclusion before now.' Similarly he wanted to complete the restoration of British prestige in the eyes of the world, removing all risk of foreign opportunism.

The risk had in fact receded with every yard of Roberts's march to Pretoria.

The Boers' three-man mission, on which they set such store, had been going from capital to capital during the five months since their departure from S.A. on the day Roberts entered Bloemfontein, and they had been experiencing that polite but chilly reception well known to the penniless in search of an overdraft. The Queen of Holland received them cordially; so did the President of France; the American President's reception was marked by a rather more rigid formality, while in Berlin and St. Petersburg they were denied even an official reception; and from each and all no help of any substance was to be gleaned. Kruger himself was to fare no better even though emotional crowds attended his passage to final exile in Switzerland: the Kaiser, whose attitude had seemed to promise the Boers so much, refused to see him. If some descendants of the Boers have since displayed a propensity for 'going it' alone in complete indifference to world opinion, the reason need not be searched for further than these depressing pilgrimages which acquainted their representatives with the cynical worst of international politics. It may be noted that at the International Peace Conference held at the beginning of October a resolution was passed condemning the annexation of the republics, but one proposed by certain delegates condemning England's conduct of the war as inhumane was rejected. These certain delegates were of course from England, who has ever provided her own fiercest critics.

Chamberlain's motives for wanting an election to retain the Unionist-Conservative coalition in office for another five years were less appreciated by Salisbury, who feared a revulsion against exploitation of the favourable turn of events for political gain. But Chamberlain had his way precisely because that favourable turn, coupled with Opposition disunity, created a chance which might not recur.

As it was 'Chamberlain's War' so now the outraged Liberals cried 'Chamberlain's Election'. In being fought on a single issue, the South African War, the election campaign from the end of September to early October was not unique. But it revolved less around a single issue than a single man, and he not Prime Minister: in this respect it was and is unique. It was also dirty. 'Former abuse,' says Chamberlain's biographer, 'he might liken to a hot blast from the desert. Now his ordeal was an avalanche of mud.'[1]

368

An election had been in the wind for some months, making Parliament practically moribund while Members' hearts were 'partly at the front and partly in their constituencies'. Chamberlain hoped for a July election but the Boxer Rebellion had momentarily turned attention to China. Now that the moment had come he threw himself into it with 'the force and subtlety,' said an American journalist, 'the command, the finesse and the resources by which he keeps rising and gaining in power.'

In defence or attack he dominated the campaign. Popular belief exonerated him alone from blame for the Government's alleged bungling of the war. In three weeks he made twelve major speeches, sent out a stream of telegrams and messages to help other candidates, and once travelled from his Birmingham stamping-ground to support young Winston Churchill, renewing his attempt—this time successfully—to enter Parliament for Oldham. On the eve of the election Chamberlain published a call to the nation: 'Patriotism before politics. May the union between the Colonies and the Motherland, now cemented by their blood, be for ever maintained.' But the nation was far more stirred by the outburst which followed a passage in one of his speeches quoting a remark by the Mayor of Mafeking that 'a seat lost to the Government is a seat gained by the Boers,' which the Post Office mis-transmitted as 'a seat *sold* to the Boers'. Post Office apologies did not prevent the political temperature rising to white heat.

Liberal loathing for him went to extreme lengths. It was the one thing upon which they could agree. He taunted them with having as many opinions as a caterpillar has legs. There were at any rate three main divisions, and their relative strength was brought out in the July debate on S.A. when thirty-one Liberals—Rosebery's Liberal Imperialists—voted with the Government; thirty-five—Campbell-Bannerman's 'intermediates'—abstained; and forty out-and-out opponents of the war voted against. Of all these, the Liberal Imperialists who supported the war but not its conduct or Joseph Chamberlain, were singled out for his most blistering electoral campaign attacks. Yet it was the Radicals—Henry Labouchere, S. Evans, D. Thomas and others, but above all David Lloyd George—who assailed him.

Labouchere's battle cry was 'Go for Joe!' but Lloyd George had been going for him for months. The first Lloyd George Night at Glasgow in March had even more violent successors. During April he arrived for a meeting in his own constituency spattered with earth from a thrown clod, and while he was constantly interrupted inside the hall a large crowd outside flung stones and cries of 'Pro-Boer!' through the windows and bellowed *Soldiers of the Queen*. In the course of his speech he said: 'Mr. Chamberlain cannot understand Irish nationality, or indeed any other man's nationality than his own. He prefers the patriotism which gives a position of £5,000 a year—and ensures a dividend from the Small Arms Factory in which his relatives are interested.' The first sentence went to the root of Chamberlain's tragedy, and corroded the whole basis of the imperialism he represented. The second was an unsavoury piece of Lloyd George buccaneering.

Leaving the meeting he was hit over the head and staggered into a café from which the police kept a howling mob until he could escape. At his next meeting, in July, pandemonium prevented him from speaking at all: the crowd surged round the platform, cheered Tommy Atkins, booed 'Kroojer', sang the Anthem and *Rule Britannia*, and chaired soldiers round the hall until the police cleared it. But he did not drop his charge of corruption against Chamberlain. He alleged a War Office contract with the Birmingham firm of Kynoch's whose tender had not been the lowest but whose shareholders were members of the Chamberlain family. By letter Chamberlain denied any personal interest as he had sold out his shares on entering public life. Lloyd George thereupon raked up Hoskin & Son, contractors to the Admiralty: the shareholders were exclusively Chamberlains, including Joseph's sons, one of whom held a ministerial post connected with the Admiralty. As company registers were combed to provide a spate of such charges during the election campaign Chamberlain bided his time, and while keeping up his castigation of the Liberals largely ignored Lloyd George.

But Lloyd George never let him go. The risk of physical injury, the steady dwindling of his legal practice, even the necessity of removing his elder son from school to spare him the insults of his fellows, did not deter him. Lives, he declared, were being 'senselessly, needlessly, callously sacrificed on the altar of one man's selfish ambition.' At a crucial meeting in the most hostile borough of his constituency he accused that One Man of protracting the war by insisting on unconditional surrender by the Boers: 'I say it is time to stay the slaughter in the African sand of brave soldiers on either side.' That night and at subsequent meetings he swung his audience round completely. Remarkably and brilliantly his oratory took hold of people and he began to move among cheering crowds who previously had threatened to lynch him.

It was not to be expected that so singular an event as the Khaki Election would find Bernard Shaw silent. Beatrice Webb's diary shows how social democrats were as riven by the issues of war and imperialism as the rest of the country. That richly germinative group, the Fabian Society, was split. A narrow majority had declared against coming to any decision the previous February, with the result that some prominent members like Ramsay MacDonald and Mrs. Pankhurst had resigned—'the Boer trek', wits called it. Now the election demanded a decision. Shaw agreed to draft an election manifesto. With his gift for running with the hare and hunting with the hounds he came down on the side of—Kipling. 'It is a masterpiece,' he wrote with Shavian modesty to a fellow Fabian, '. . . so extra-ultra-hyper-imperialist that you will turn the colour of this paper and fall down in convulsions. . . I am convinced that the Liberal agitation against the Government is greatly strengthening it, because nobody will dare vote for a merely negative and impossible policy in the middle of a war. . . . We have got to teach both Kruger and Chamberlain that countries are not bits of private property to be fought for by dynasties, or races, or nations.' What he proposed—and despite further resignations a large majority of the Fabians supported him—was that in the absence of a world government the British Empire, as the nearest approach to one, should govern a backward community, but in the interests of civilization and by not 'leaving the power of gold in the hands of a small irresponsible community'.[49] His conversion to imperialism—of a kind—he explains thus:

During the war a curious thing happened in Norway. There, as in Germany, everyone took it for granted that the right side was the anti-English side. Suddenly Ibsen asked in his grim manner, 'Are we really on the side of Kruger and his Old Testament?' The effect was electrical. Norway shut up. I felt like Ibsen. I was, of course, not in the least taken in by *The Times* campaign, though I defended *The Times* against the accusation of bribery on the ground that it was not necessary to pay *The Times* to do what it

was only too ready to do for nothing. But I saw that Kruger
meant the seventeenth century and the Scottish seventeenth at
that; and to my great embarrassment I found myself on the side
of the mob. . . . It is astonishing what bad company advanced
views may get one into.

The election was spread over six weeks. When all who were qualified and willing to go to the polls had done so, this was the result:

Unionist-Conservatives	402
Liberals	186
Irish Nationalists	82

The Government majority of 134 compared with 128 at the dissolution
and 152 at the 1895 election. This absence of overall change did not
reflect changes in detail. Scotland, more impressed than elsewhere by
the evidence of Liberal disunity in the July debate, rejected Liberalism
for the first time in eighty years. The towns of England, which had
mostly known the vociferous demonstrations of 'patriotism', voted
solidly against the Liberals. But the country districts were Liberal,
and the party made substantial headway in Wales, owing to Lloyd
George who had, says his biographer, his greatest hour 'until that
November afternoon eighteen years hence when, as Prime Minister of
Britain in the most terrible of all her wars, he would [lead the Commons to the Abbey] to give thanks to God for deliverance.'[44]

A corollary of the fact that this was a One Man election was that
most people detested the Government. They blamed it for the early
humiliations in the field, for faulty medical services, for trying to
tamper with dispatches, and so forth. But a belief that the divided
Liberals would bring a political defeat in S.A. ruled them out as an
alternative. There was hence the anomaly of many people voting for a
Government which they vowed never to support again.

The Government was somewhat reshuffled. While Chamberlain
now enjoyed undisputed dominance he remained Colonial Secretary
to continue a policy regarded as the nation's chief concern. He was in
any event quite unacceptable to a large body of Conservatives as Prime
Minister. Salisbury continued in this office but gave the Foreign Affairs
portfolio to Lansdowne, St. John Brodrick succeeding him as Secretary
for War. Salisbury increased what critics called the 'Hotel Cecil' of

politics by bringing the number of his relatives in or near the Cabinet to six.

The picture which the Government had presented to the electorate of peace drawing gentle wings over the turmoil of S.A. had been given additional authenticity by the appointment, on the eve of the election, of Lord Roberts as C.-in-C. at the War Office in succession to Wolseley. The appointment somewhat mollified the Queen, who had wanted it to go to her son the Duke of Connaught, and altogether delighted the nation. Roberts arranged to give Kitchener the command in S.A. and to leave S.A. in October, but he was to be delayed by the illness of his eldest daughter with enteric, the death from the same disease of one of Queen Victoria's grandsons who was on his staff, and a fall from a horse. Meanwhile there were other distinguished departures.

With the imminent return of many troops Buller's army, the 'Natal Field Force', was broken up and he himself set out for England. He took leave of his men on 6 October: they crowded along the route as he and his staff passed slowly along and they cheered him so warmly that for the first time since his arrival in S.A. nearly a year before, so full of hope and destined to endure so many rebuffs of fortune, his impassive face showed emotion.

On 19 October Paul Kruger left Delagoa Bay on the cruiser *Gelderland* placed at his disposal by the Queen of Holland. It took him to Europe and exile.

In October the C.I.V. returned to London, and the freshened war spirit engendered by the election was now taking an uglier course, expressed by the violence of the crowds who greeted them in London. The police could hardly exercise control and people were crushed to death. That month and also in November first drafts of cavalry and other units, including Imperial Yeomanry, returned too. While they were departing Roberts busied himself with forming the South African Constabulary (S.A.C.) to pacify the country, since he considered only police action was now necessary. Baden-Powell was selected to command the S.A.C. and sent to England to raise recruits.

Not until the end of November did Roberts lay down his command in favour of Lord Kitchener and after a tumultuous reception at Cape Town depart for England, Ian Hamilton going with him as Military Secretary. Immediately he landed the Queen summoned him to Osborne where she made him a Knight of the Garter, an honour not granted a victorious general since Wellington, and also bestowed an earldom on him. On the morning he arrived at Paddington Station it was decorated with flowers and bunting. A stand for 300 distinguished people had been erected on Platform 9. As they descended with the Prince of Wales at their head to greet Roberts a band struck up *See the Conquering Hero Comes*. Something like a State procession followed the Prince's and Roberts's drive to Buckingham Palace for lunch. Fourteen thousand troops lined the route which was thronged six deep with spectators, above whom banners from building to building bore slogans like 'Bravo, Bobs' and 'To Bobs, the kindest of the kind and the bravest of the brave'. Presently Parliament voted him £100,000. Thus did Queen, Government and people show their gratitude. They poured their favours and their acclamations on him. They fêted him, lauded him, named their children and their streets and their pets after him. No returning Caesar ever met with a greater triumph.

And no general has ever been so overrated in England's history, or any country so gulled.

He had gone out to end the war 'in a satisfactory manner'. His achievement was exactly the opposite. He protracted it in a most unsatisfactory manner. If he was not wholly responsible, at best he did not prevent the start of an entirely new war, bringing devastation and misery on an unparalleled scale, the wastage of thousands of lives, the loss of millions of pounds, and an incalculable impetus to Afrikaner nationalism. Since this was what the future was to show—though to the present day the legend of his supposed greatness has not been challenged—it is worth looking at his conduct of the war a little more closely.

Only once did he defeat the enemy—at Paardeberg where Kitchener's ferocity, French's dash, Cronje's pig-headedness and a river in flood brought the Boers to bay; and even then his preference for siege methods instead of a renewal of Kitchener's pitched battle gave the Boers in the Cape Midlands time to escape, promoted the spread of enteric, and caused the long delay at Bloemfontein which enabled De Wet to discover a method of resistance destined to make the new war possible. For the rest he was content to push back the Boers like water before the bows of a ship, under the happy delusion that he was defeating them. At Poplar Grove before Bloemfontein his flaccid commands as much as French's huff enabled the enemy to avoid a catastrophic defeat. Subsequently, when Hamilton's enterprise in the Battle of Johannesburg placed the city at his mercy he deliberately gave the enemy time to escape. At Diamond Hill, which was the only time he was in direct command over the whole battlefield against the Boers reasonably strong in numbers, position and leadership, he fluffed decision and reconnaissance; and again, as at every engagement right up to Komati Poort, merely pushed the Boers back. All this was hidden from view by his apparently triumphant advance, but that advance was a calamitous idea altogether.

He assumed that when the Boers lost their main railways and towns they would be incapable of further resistance. But neither meant much to people who were mostly farmers and accustomed to ox-wagons. Above all, he assumed that the capture of Pretoria would end the war; when events showed the assumption to have been false, his whole strategy collapsed. His single imaginative strategic move was the flank march at the start, though anxiety to rescue Rhodes and the existence at Orange River Station of the only sound bridge across the Orange in British possession, and the strength (afterwards confirmed by De Wet) of Boer defences along the rest of the river, made this approach fairly obvious—even Buller suggested something of the sort. After that start his boldness ebbed, and it is significant that sickness removed Henderson, on whose ideas he leant heavily, from S.A. six weeks after his arrival.

His mistakes arose from several causes. To begin with, he insisted on running everything himself. The sheer magnitude of keeping in harness an army ten times bigger than he had ever handled before, across a huge expanse of territory, at a time when the military concepts of hundreds of years were in a state of flux, against a foe far superior to any he had fought before, and in the midst of acute political complexities, fully absorbed him. It was remarkable, but a pity, that he should have made the attempt at the age of sixty-seven.

His experience in Afghanistan misled him into making a blunder even worse than botched strategy and staff work. In that country troublesome tribesmen would be dealt with by a column which marched out to defeat them, then imposed a fine and burnt down their huts to make them mend their ways. When the Boers failed to respond to his early conciliatory proclamations, he thought he could deal with them by exactly the same method. The devastation of farms, carried out by his troops sporadically from June onwards, made him the author of a 'scorched earth' policy perfectly disastrous from every point of view. Among other consequences it has inflamed anti-British sentiment from that day to this. If some of the Boers' descendants are reproached for remembering bitterness too long, the fact must be noted that the tolerance with which Britain forgives her enemies their trespasses owes something both to the sophistication acquired at the centre of world affairs and to her self-interest as a trading nation, which the Afrikaners are not.

Roberts's proclamations had precisely the opposite effect to that intended. Some Boers read one, some another, many none at all. One moment they found themselves being asked to return in peace to their farms, and the next being harried by their own commandants to go back on commando when no protection was given by the British—who then came up and burnt their farms, creating an unfortunate impression of British bad faith.

On the ground that he was making clear the British Government's resolve to see the business through and to hold out no false hope to the Boers that they would preserve their independence, he has been defended for annexing countries without securing the surrender or consent of their people, armies or governments. But it remains a ridiculous notion that one can annex countries simply by declaring them annexed, and then tell the uncooperative inhabitants that they are rebels.

The solemn running-up of silken Union Jacks worked by his wife, or well-reported dramatic or romantic touches like his 'You have made a gallant defence, sir,' to Cronje, can raise a smile; but not the lives lost by his utter inability to assert authority over Buller. Not sacking him after Spion Kop at latest, he permitted him to blunder on, instead of installing somebody else who might have materially shortened the war. Roberts's declared excuse was that nobody else was available. As Kitchener was merely used as a dormitory prefect after the first day at Paardeberg the excuse does not convince. The suggestion has been made that in his heart he blamed Buller for his son's death at Colenso and was therefore 'all the more anxious not to risk being personally unfair to the man'.[26]

That he possessed great kindliness and consideration cannot be questioned. A member of his staff noted in his diary that when Roberts

entered Kroonstad and found the parson and his wife sitting discon-
solately on the steps of the vicarage which had been requisitioned for
him, 'he, of course, refused to occupy the house; and we are out in the
open again.'[45] But his kindliness, his personal charm, his elevated
moral character, a soldier's courage, and a measure of chivalry are
splendid qualities which do not mean much in assessing generalship.
He was admired for his solicitude for his men, but bad organization
often failed to get them the supplies sent out in such quantity by the
home Government, and slack regard for hygiene brought the huge
losses from disease. Ruthless efficiency and disciplinarianism are not
attributes we are very fond of, but for want of them in our leaders men
and women have had to pay heavily in the long run. Roberts's disin-
clination to risk incurring casualties is a conspicuous example of his
virtues as a man being weaknesses in a general. His defence was that
the British Government kept stressing how dangerously denuded of
trained troops England was, but the result of his policy was a greater
dimunition of strength than a few decisive if bloody battles would have
caused. When Roberts sailed for England no one noticed that a full
year's continuous fighting across thousands of miles had left the greater
and better part of the Boer forces still intact.

In declaring that the war was over, Roberts may have failed in that
very modesty for which he was universally admired. The call of duty
may explain his own request for the S.A. command. The hasty collection of an inexperienced army may explain his single-handed exercise
of that command. But it is difficult not to see in his too-ready belief
that only police action remained in S.A. a desire to get the vacant post
at the War Office before the chance passed him by. To him the war
might have seemed over. To many South Africans, to Britain, the
Empire, and the world at large it seemed over. The only people who
did not think it was over were the Boers.

This was the core of Roberts's failure. He had no idea what he was
fighting. He thought he was fighting first an army and then some
rebels. But his opponents were neither: they were a nation. The past
year, especially the past few months, had refined among the Boers a
consciousness of their national identity which hitherto had lacked
coherence or passion. Now it had both, generating a force like that
behind the holy wars of old. This force of nationalism, embodied in a
small group of leaders, has again and again proved able to wage

resistance against an external Power out of all proportion to their strength, by drawing on the hidden support of their countrymen on the one hand and the overt energies of idealist or adventurer on the other.

The instrument of resistance was to be guerilla tactics—threats of which, said *The Times* a few months earlier, 'need not be taken seriously'. That this meant not mere police action but a whole new war, took Britain a little time to realize, Roberts's insistence that the Boers were beaten being supported by the Government's tendency to make light of the situation. The start of the new war has therefore come to be associated with the start of Kitchener's command. But Roberts only left the scene at the beginning of December when the guerilla campaign had started months before.

Although the activities of De la Rey's commandos in the western Transvaal during July and August, and of De Wet's in the eastern O.F.S. even earlier—during Roberts's halt at Bloemfontein—were essentially guerilla in form, complete Boer dedication to the new war dates from the dispersal of Botha's army in the eastern Transvaal at the end of September 1900.

The Boer leaders had foreseen that if they were to go on fighting it could only be by waging the kind of war which came more naturally to them than orthodox warfare with its demand of discipline among large bodies of troops. Besides, their men were always restless and uneasy away from their home districts. There they could operate indefinitely if left to keep in touch with their families, to recuperate as opportunity offered, or merely to enjoy the security of local knowledge. For this reason Botha had already on the morrow of Diamond Hill carried out the plan agreed with Paul Kruger of grouping the Transvaal commandos as far as possible in their own districts, though some concentration of men from further afield was required to oppose Roberts's advance along the Delagoa Bay railway. And as soon as De Wet returned to the banks of the Vaal after the hunt for him had failed he made similar regional arrangements for the O.F.S., so that while Botha's forces were being pushed back to Komati Poort and then dispersed, the new war was fully launched from the very country of which Roberts had written to the Queen after his entry into Bloemfontein six months earlier: 'It seems unlikely that this state will give much more trouble.'

From De Wet's laager emissaries went all over the colony (as the British declared it) carrying tidings of the new war and rousing burghers to the imminent arrival of the vice-commandants-in-chief whom he appointed to the various regions. These leaders, who included 'Oom' Piet Fourie, C. C. Badenhorst, and 'the Judge'—Judge Hertzog—raised fresh commandos in addition to those still in being. So little did Roberts comprehend the situation that early in September he had telegraphed his generals, 'The numbers of the enemy now in the field are steadily decreasing, especially in the Orange River Colony. He estimated the total of fighting Boers at a mere 3,000, yet before the month was out, up to 8,000 were reported in one district alone.

Through September Boer recruitment in the O.F.S. went quietly forward, but signs of the conflagration to come were already plain. For the purpose of raids on the Central railway, most vital of all the British arteries, De Wet paid a flying visit across the Vaal to secure a quantity of dynamite at Potschefstroom. There a photograph was taken of him with the two-hundredth weapon which had been surrendered to the British for burning and then been quietly salvaged and repaired by the Boers. He appointed the scout corps leader and Cape rebel Scheepers to take charge of the raids—to such effect that in the course of the month the railway was blown up in about forty places. The British had to stop all night traffic and allocate ever more men to guard-duty, reducing their effectiveness elsewhere.

To carry out, as he believed, mere police action, Roberts had divided the country into areas of command, with garrisons in various towns and villages. To put down the increasing insurgence of the countryside he relied on flying columns. But the commandos daily multiplied and were scarcely ever glimpsed by the columns for whom 'flying' was a comic misnomer. They consisted mainly of infantry encumbered with all the accessories of a miniature army, including artillery, hospital vehicles, and overloaded ox-wagons inefficiently driven, while what mounted troops accompanied them lacked striking power because the horses were badly managed and overweighted with equipment (the average load borne by the Yeomanry horses weighed over twenty stone). These columns flew round the countryside at a rate of precisely fifteen miles per day. The Boers, acquainted with their every move, disappeared at their approach and then reoccupied village or district on their departure.

As yet Boer tactics were mainly dispersal and evasion, but an increasing note of exasperation crept into Roberts's orders. At the end of September he reorganized bases and columns to subdue the north-eastern O.F.S. in which he imagined the Brandwater Basin débâcle had extinguished resistance: 'Clear the whole of supplies,' he cried, 'and impress on the burghers that if they choose to listen to De Wet and carry on a guerilla warfare against us, they and their families will be starved.'

The burghers nevertheless rose up in thousands, and October saw the flame of the new war race across the O.F.S.—licking at the heels of every column and supply convoy, around every garrison, along the length of the Central railway. It was a flame carried not only by commandos but by handfuls of men, laying aside their ploughs for the moment to take their rifles out of hiding and try a shot at the nearest British. Troops being sent home in accordance with Roberts's assurance that the war was over found it an odd kind of victory: they could not travel by night, frequently had to leave their trains to fight off enemy attacks, and in some instances had their sailing orders cancelled.

Having thus spurred his lieutenants to action all over the O.F.S. De Wet himself crossed the Vaal with a small force and linked up with Liebenburg to attack a British column at Frederikstad on the Klerksdorp railway. He fared badly. After five days of desultory fighting culminating in an abortive night charge he drew off with heavy losses. He just avoided a column, made up of mounted detachments scratched together from wherever possible, sent to the relief by Roberts. The mobility of this column was therefore an exception, and its commander too was an exception, for despite a fine waxed moustache and a weakness for cigars he displayed the vigour which, alone, might hope to corner the fantastic De Wet. His name was General Charles Knox, and he had been with French in overtaking and stopping Cronje at Paardeberg.

Now he hung on De Wet's trail. After two days he caught up with him at a ford across the Vaal near Parys. An Australian troop cut through his rearguard, and the main body was all but surrounded and in great confusion when darkness fell to the accompaniment of a violent storm which enabled the convoy to escape, though much battered. De Wet thereupon sent on the bulk of his force in a south-westerly direction while he himself slipped back into the Transvaal with a small escort. He was due in Ventersdorp on 31 October to keep a dramatic assignation.

At this point we must go back to find what happened to the Transvaal leaders who fled in the last days of September when Roberts completed his capture of the Delagoa Bay railway. On making his way through the mountains in the vicinity of Lydenburg Steyn reached the railhead town of Pietersburg north of Pretoria. Botha too, with Acting-President Schalk Burger and his government colleagues (who included Lukas Meyer and State Secretary Reitz, Deneys's father), made good their narrow escape from Buller and joined Steyn at Pietersburg. There, on 19 October, Ben Viljoen arrived with the bulk of the men picked out before the final retreat to Komati Poort, having safely marched right round the northern Drakensberg. Ardent young leaders like Beyers and Kemp who had been coming to the fore also arrived at the town, while Koos de la Rey was in easy reach in the west. Since Roberts had not penetrated any distance north of Pretoria a huge crescent of the Transvaal from the far west to the north-east was clear of British troops. Much of it was inhospitable bushveld but gave a safe haven for the fighting Boers as well as many of their families and stock. At Pietersburg the leaders and their men rested, completed all arrangements for the new war already launched in the O.F.S., and from Steyn caught something of his own unflagging spirit.

Roberts's advance to Komati Poort had disrupted their plan of deploying commandos in their regions of origin wherever possible. Through the remainder of October and November the burghers therefore rested and regrouped. Decisions taken at Pietersburg about regional command were also put into effect. Botha, while retaining overall command, assumed local command in the south-east Transvaal; Ben Viljoen went to the north-east; the west was under De la Rey; from the north Beyers was to co-operate with De la Rey, linking the western and eastern commandos. They all made, and continued to make, strenuous efforts to keep their men in the field, recruit others, and prevent surrender. 'I will be compelled,' Botha wrote to one of his commandants, 'if they do not listen to this, to confiscate everything movable or immovable and also to burn their houses.' Meanwhile, all decisions of the new war having been taken at Pietersburg, Steyn departed from that town. He added a fresh chapter to his tale of adventure by eluding the numerous British forces north and south of the

Magaliesburg who tried to snap him up. Thus it was he who had the assignation with Christian de Wet at Ventersdrop on 31 October.

Steyn told him of the Pietersburg decisions and of one in particular. It was no less than a renewed invasion of the Cape. The moment was opportune, for the Afrikander Bond was opposed to Roberts's annexations and since the resignation of the Bond Ministry anti-British propaganda was being made with unremitting violence. An invasion might, even yet, provoke the wholesale rebellion for which the Boers had always prayed. Besides, it would invigorate the awakening in the Transvaal, harness the scattered energies of some of the O.F.S. commandos, and distract the British.

Together the two O.F.S. leaders travelled south and overtook De Wet's convoy. It had reached the vicinity of the ruined village of Bothaville, north-west of Kroonstad. But Knox had been sticking to the pursuit.

At dawn on 6 November his small advance guard found the picket asleep and immediately attacked the Boers, who were laagered on a farm. Caught utterly by surprise, they rushed in panic for their horses. De Wet and Steyn led them away at a gallop leaving behind 130 men whose horses had stampeded. These men took cover in the farm buildings and orchard, and fought to save themselves, all De Wet's wagons and his eight guns. With equal resolution the British advance guard repeatedly tried to rush them in a bitter four-hour struggle. It was itself threatened with extinction when De Wet rallied his men and counterattacked. But more of Knox's column arrived in the nick of time, threw back De Wet, and concentrated such a volume of artillery and rifle fire on the defenders that they surrendered. With the capture of all De Wet's wagons and guns was included a quantity of harnesses, saddlery, ammunition and clothing.

It was a notable feat, though of little account so long as De Wet and Steyn were at large. A mere fortnight later they burst into the news again. Having sent away their men to recuperate after Bothaville they crossed eastward of the railway line, gathered equipment and a fresh force of 1,500 men, and rode south intent on their invasion plan. The secret of their mobility, painfully to be learnt by the British, was lightly loaded wagons, spare horses, accurate scouting, and an almost total absence of artillery.

Their route lay through the hills around Thaba 'Nchu. By now the measures Roberts took during his march to Pretoria to contain the Boers in the north-east O.F.S. had been consolidated by the establishment of a line of fortified posts from Bloemfontein to the Basutoland border via Thaba 'Nchu. These posts, each garrisoned by about fifty men, were spaced less than two miles apart, but by using small detachments to keep two adjoining posts busy De Wet brought his convoy safely between and approached the village of Dewetsdorp. A garrison of 500 held it—mostly Gloucesters and Highland Light Infantry. At first light on 21 November he attacked from three directions.

He attempted no rushes across open ground except at night; during daytime his men, exploiting their marksmanship to the utmost, crept forward with consummate field-craft. By 4 p.m. on the third day the defenders had been crowded together in one sector of their trenches, with no water and scarcely any ammunition. An infantry subaltern hoisted a white flag over one of the gun-pits. It was at once ordered down, but an hour later, upon fanciful rumours that the Boers were killing the wounded, the garrison surrendered. Every survivor was taken prisoner and obliged to march on foot through all that ensued, the officers refusing the offer of wagon transport so that they might share the hardships of their men.

Within a twenty-five to fifty-mile radius of Dewetsdorp were no less than five British forces at the time, yet no relief column arrived until the day after the surrender. De Wet simply drew away and continued southwards with his haul. Again Charles Knox was summoned. By train and horse he arrived from the Transvaal with remarkable speed, and picked up his quarry's scent. One morning he surprised Steyn and De Wet as they breakfasted on a farm but they shook him off and undetected reached the vicinity of Bethulie near the Orange River. Here they made final preparations for the invasion. Fresh commandos brought his strength up to 3,000 men whom the surrounding farmers provided with two to five remounts each. Judge Hertzog also arrived in the last days of November and it was agreed that De Wet and he would simultaneously invade from east and west of Bethulie respectively.

*   *   *   *

While this account of the new war in the O.F.S. up to the end of November 1900 has concentrated mainly on De Wet—since a guerilla struggle turns on the survival of a few outstanding leaders—it should be remembered that at the same time siege and skirmish across a great breadth of country were almost daily adding to the toll of death and misery endured by both sides.

November too saw the full-scale entry of the Transvaal into the guerilla war. As in the O.F.S. the Boers started with a policy of evasion and dispersal. And as in the O.F.S. Roberts totally misunderstood the strength being gathered and used totally inadequate means to cope with it. He had seven groupings of command, exercised through garrisons in the chief towns and flying columns which made solemn but ineffectual processions across the countryside. Thus, French undertook a 170-mile march from Machadodorp to the outskirts of Johannesburg with a view to clearing the country between the two railway lines. His cavalry, in any event overburdening their horses and using outmoded weapons, were denied mobility by a convoy of wagons and guns nearly five miles long. Harried every yard of the way, he reached his destination with a hundred casualties and the loss of a third of his wagons, 1,200 oxen and over 300 horses.

This example indicates how events in the Transvaal followed the pattern of those in the O.F.S. The courage and endurance of the British soldier shine through the depressing annals of that period when raid, siege and harassment made the placid veld a nightmare of sudden danger. But the Boers enjoyed no picnic either. The British seized their stock, destroyed crops, broke dams, and frequently burnt down houses, so outraging consciences in England that Roberts, shortly before his departure, issued a directive that no farm was to be burnt except for treachery; or when used by guerillas for firing on troops or making raids; or as a punishment for breaks to nearby railway and telegraph lines. A commanding officer's written consent had to be given in every instance, and the absence of a burgher on commando was not of itself to justify the burning of his house, but all cattle, wagons and foodstuffs were to be removed or destroyed whether the owner was present or not.

However this directive may have been framed to modify the 'scorched earth' policy which Roberts had initiated, it remained severe enough. Yet no self-respecting Boer allowed himself, any more than an Englishman would have in like circumstances, to be daunted by the increasing prospect of the new war bearing more harshly on himself and his family than the old.

Thus when Roberts laid down his command in favour of Kitchener at midnight on 28/29 November 1900, and told rapturous crowds that the war was over, the Boers had actually reached a level which, in terms of real fighting strength of seasoned men, tactics and leadership, was higher than ever before. Not only had they thrust his army everywhere in the Transvaal and O.F.S. on the defensive but they were actually poised to invade the Cape from two directions.

That their republics had disappeared was an illusion. Though their commandos were scattered, though they lacked a fixed seat of government, though they had lost railways, chief towns and all the other appurtenances of statehood, they nevertheless were all in touch with each other, acting upon a common plan, led by acknowledged leaders, and keeping in being their own civil power in the persons of Steyn and the officials with him in the O.F.S., and Schalk Burger and the officials with him in the Transvaal.

An army scattered but coherent, a Government peripatetic but functioning, a people united behind both—that was their situation. And every blade of grass, every brown iron-stone boulder or shelf of purple shale, every contour of the illimitable veld, and every corner of every kopje, was their ally. What Roberts had won was a shadow. He left Kitchener to grapple with reality.

CHAPTER XXIII

Kitchener Takes Over: December 1900

THE greatest Navy in the world could safely bring Kitchener all the supplies he needed from the richest country in the world. He still had a more complex task than any British general before him.

At first glance it looked simple enough. He had 210,000 troops to deal with at most 60,000 Boers (including foreigners and rebels), of whom only a quarter were in the field at any given moment.* But half his men were guarding lines of communication, thousands more were on garrison duty or required to march hither and thither to help threatened garrisons, and innumerable others had become scattered about during the marches, sometimes to be lost track of for months. There was the constant wastage inherent in such campaigns, as Napoleon found when he crossed the Niemen with 360,000 men and reached Moscow with 95,000. Above all, there was a dearth of men who really mattered in a guerilla war—mounted troops and commanders able to keep long hours in the saddle, sleep rough, live on bully beef and biscuit, endure extremes of climate.

The emergence of the M.I. and various mounted irregulars was revolutionary in the development of warfare, for it rang the death knell of cavalry. The shock tactics of the *arme blanche*, like volley firing by massed infantry, had very limited chances against modern rifles. Though controversy was to make the death throes protracted the lance was already being discarded and instruction given in the rifle. Ironically, the dash and verve associated with the famous 'cavalry spirit' was shown far more by all the other mounted men than the cavalry. But these men were now in desperately short supply.

The last of the infantry reserves had gone to S.A. months before,

* To date about 5,000 had been killed or interned in Portuguese territory. 15,000 were prisoners of war.

leaving only raw recruits behind, and the regiments in the field were stubborn about parting with men for the M.I. At the same time many of the Yeomanry and colonials had begun returning home after a year's service. The War Office had rejected an offer to keep up a flow of fresh Yeomanry drafts from the recruiting organization set up during the crisis of Black Week, so that the organization had become defunct. The Government was actually in process of reducing the Army, and to cap everything, Roberts's assurances had prompted the Remount Department to recall its buying agents from abroad, creating as great a shortage of horses as of men to sit them.

The new war therefore caught Britain as unprepared as the old. Defeat or foreign intervention were now very remote possibilities, but victory was scarcely closer than it had been during Black Week. The situation was comparable with that time. Though lacking the drama and taking longer to penetrate the public consciousness it caused a similar disquiet and made a similar demand on patriotism. But with these emotions went, this time, a critical attitude of increasing bitterness towards the way the war was being conducted—though Roberts was not the object of this criticism, since in England nothing is harder to lose than a reputation.

Kitchener addressed himself to the immediate problem of manpower and presently was to appeal to Britain and the Empire for 30,000 mounted troops. On 11 December the new Secretary for War, Mr. Brodrick, asked Parliament for more money, justifying the mounting war expenditure by citing the case of Napoleon who had to employ 400,000 men to cope with the (inefficient) Spanish, of the Cuban rising in which 40,000 islanders kept 250,000 Spaniards at bay for two years, and of America which sent 100,000 men to quell the Philippines rebellion. More M.I. were put under training and the Yeomanry organization was resuscitated, recruits lining up at fifty-one depots all over the country on the offer of 5s. per day (compared with the regulars' 1s. 3d.). At the same time Baden-Powell was raising the South African Constabulary. Again the colonies came forward—not Canada for some time owing to a political controversy (though many Canadians joined the S.A. Constabulary)—Australia being foremost. However, all these developments would take many months to find expression in the field. Meanwhile Kitchener sought to make better use of material near at hand.

In person or through assistants he descended on hotels, clubs, restaurants, railway stations in the principal centres and sent packing the hordes of officers and hangers-on lounging there. He had villages, farms, rest-camps scoured for soldiers who had taken to a life of ease as servants, cooks, gardeners or merely loafers. He called for more infantrymen to train for the M.I. He withdrew garrisons which Roberts in rash over-confidence had plastered across the countryside as sitting targets for the Boer commandos. He encouraged new recruitment in S.A. besides the re-enlistment of disbanded volunteer corps, and to meet the invasion threat to the Cape he caused town guards and other forces to be raised locally.

But it was a measure of Roberts's failure that the machinery of war, having been allowed to wind down without achieving victory, could never again be wound up to quite the same pitch. The Remount Department hastily started buying again as Kitchener asked for 8,000 horses and 2,000 mules per month—a demand later increased—but the leeway could never be made up. It has been remarked that for every single article required by the troops in the field the War Office kept a pattern which could quickly be copied for mass-production: the only pattern it could not keep was that of a man or a horse. The new men from Britain, the colonies and S.A. were to prove inferior to the old; seasoned troops were allowed to go and the gap was filled by men attracted by the high rate of pay and who were then put into the field half-trained.

The seriousness for Britain of the military situation had its corollary in the political, both domestically and in S.A. On 3 December the House of Commons met for the first time since the election against a background of rising public discontent. Chamberlain was charged with having defrauded the public by pretending that the war was over when apparently it was far from over, and certainly his instinct had been sound in pressing for an election in the nick of time. But first Lloyd George confronted him face to face with the accusation—not direct but by adroit implication—of personal profit from the war. Chamberlain had long wanted to end the smear campaign by suing his persecutors, including *Punch* for its classic, 'The more the Empire expands the more the Chamberlains contract', but had been dissuaded by his legal advisers. Now he rose to protest against having to explain after twenty-five years' public service 'that I am not a thief and a scoundrel'. He had sold out his business interests on entering public life, and that at a loss, he said; he was not responsible for his relations, who in any event had a tradition of two centuries' unblemished business conduct. His defence was delivered with emotion. More effective was Balfour's smooth retort to the Opposition: 'Wanted, a man to serve Her Majesty, with no money, no relations.' Lloyd George's reproof was rejected by 141 votes.

Of more moment, the next Opposition amendment to the Address challenged the Government's war policy, and here Chamberlain surprised his critics by declaring that when peace was made the Boers would be given self-government after an interval to ensure equality (presumably between whites) in law and liberty. No vindictiveness was felt towards the Boers, he said: 'They are brave foes and should be treated as brave foes; and it is in that spirit that we shall approach them.'

Alas for that spirit, Milner's enlarged High Commissionership, involving his transfer to Pretoria as Governor of the two new colonies, was the height of provocation. When Milner confided to an intimate some months before, 'I have saved British interests in South Africa,' he revealed his mind and his hand. The Boers detested no man more, and if his administrative brilliance was to confer some enduring blessings on S.A. his name remains a synonym for that cold arrogance which gave so unfortunate an impression of the English character. Kitchener was at least a soldier, and one innocent of any part in bringing about the war, whereas the Boers saw Milner as a man who had never hazarded his own life in a war for which he was largely blamed. He was now flung in their teeth as so-called Governor. In England he became the target of Opposition attacks, whereupon Chamberlain pointedly had the Grand Cross of the Bath bestowed on him as confirmation of the Government's confidence.

It is significant that Kitchener was prepared to settle for something less than the unconditional surrender which Milner supported the Government in demanding from the Boers. An additional strain was therefore imposed on the delicate relationship war always creates between the civil and military authorities. Such a difference of outlook reflected a temperamental difference between two very different kinds of men. But more important it shattered the hopes anyone might have had of a generous act of conciliation to bring the protagonists together instead of deepening their enmity.

This was quickly proved. Among the captured or surrendered Boers were influential men convinced of the folly of continuing the war. They formed themselves into the Burgher Peace Committee which held a conference at Pretoria on 21 December. Addressing the members Kitchener did his best to soften the demand for unconditional surrender by a genuinely sympathetic approach, promising to give the fighting Boers every chance to surrender in order to end the war and usher in an era of just and progressive government. At the same time, largely on the advice of the committee, he issued a proclamation to the Boers in the field promising that those voluntarily surrendering would be allowed to live with their families in government camps until the war permitted a safe return to their homes, all stock they brought with them being meanwhile looked after unless bought at market values. This proclamation and Kitchener's speech were immediately distributed far and wide, and to speed the gospel by personal contact leading members of the committee rode into the laagers of their countrymen in the field.

Their reception was severe. They were regarded by the commandos as traitors and cowards, and those who did not manage to get back to the British lines were sentenced by courts martial to fines, imprisonment, or worse. In the Transvaal the president of the committee reached Ben Viljoen's laager in the north-east where he was tried and executed for high treason. In the O.F.S. two other members of the committee were court-martialled at De Wet's laager and sentenced to death—a sentence at first held in abeyance through protests by the rank and file Boers until, it is said (though unsubstantiated), one of the two men was flogged and shot by Commandant Froneman in a fit of temper while De Wet looked on.

Before Kitchener saw that the efforts of the Burgher Peace Committee were to come to nothing, he accepted some further advice from them and so made one of the most calamitous decisions of the war.

An enemy's sources of supply are an essential and legitimate target in military operations. His towns and bases having been captured, the Boer looked to his own farm and farm-house, which therefore inevitably became the object of British attention, especially as they were often used to harbour commandos and even as temporary shelters for attack. The 'scorched earth' policy sporadically started by Roberts six months before to meet this situation caused, however, profound misgivings on the ground of sentiment, and even some questioning of its military value. Chamberlain himself suggested to Cabinet colleagues that the shooting or capturing of the Boers' horses would be more effective than farm-burning. Nevertheless, Kitchener decided to continue it. So far the amount of devastation had been slight, but one of its incidental results had been that women and children on devastated farms faced starvation or molestation by marauding Natives. Together with ordinary refugees swept along by the tides of war, they were therefore brought by the British columns to informal extensions of their own camps along lines of communication. The motive was purely humane.

But now Kitchener decided to turn an unofficial refugee policy into an official internment policy. Although, given the devastation policy, this was its humane corollary, he intended the rounding up of women and children as a calculated method of war. He made his reason clear in a memorandum to his leading officers on 21 December:

> This course has been pointed out by surrendered Burghers, who are anxious to finish the war, as the most effective method of limiting the endurance of the Guerillas, as the men and women left on farms, if disloyal, willingly supply Burghers, if loyal, dare not refuse to do so.

Hence was started a systematic policy not only of devastating farms but of interning all women and children whose menfolk were on commando. No careful thought was given to the implications. Elementary considerations like the suitability of camps which had been set up solely for military reasons, or the availability of doctors and sanitary staff, were passed over. While orders were issued for Natives working on the farms to be brought in as well, no regard was paid to the impossibility of preventing large numbers of them being loosed, workless and rootless, on the already troubled scene. These aspects apart, Kitchener was committing his army to a task far bigger and costlier than he remotely foresaw, distracting them from their main task of defeating the Boers while not only releasing the Boers themselves from the burden of caring for their families but increasing their implacable temper.

The camps were in part refugee camps and in part internment camps, but since they concentrated together families from distant farms and villages they were generally called concentration camps. In intention, they bore no resemblance to the Nazi torture and death camps of the same name; in practice, circumstances were to create a tragic connexion.*

★ ★ ★ ★

Even if Kitchener was encouraged by the attitude of the surrendered burghers, the revised policy did not seem to him unreasonable. He was particularly anxious to round up women because he believed that they were more bitter than the men and were mainly responsible for keeping the war going. He subsequently wrote to Brodrick in the course of describing the Boers, other than the leaders and townspeople, as 'uncivilized Afrikander savages with a thin white veneer': 'The Boer woman in the refugee camps who slaps her great protruding belly at you, and shouts, "When all our men are gone these little khakis will fight you," is a type of the savage produced by generations of wild lonely life.' Later he even proposed to sift the irreconcilable women from the rest and send them overseas, but the Cabinet would not let him. Letter and proposal are characteristic of the sudden rush of blood from which Kitchener was apt to suffer in a frustrating situation, so that his brain momentarily became as empurpled as his face. They provide material for a biographer intent on drawing the portrait of some kind of monster, whereas in the Boer War Kitchener, having served under Roberts with soldierly fidelity, showed in turn a soldierly regard for his enemy that made him far more respected than, for example, Milner, and admired more than Roberts. The steely judgement of Jan Smuts, implied in his son's biography of him, was that Kitchener was a *kindly* man.

The fact remains that a concatenation of factors misled Kitchener into a decision which under different auspices might have been given deeper thought. A policy already initiated by his senior was easier to extend than reverse; he had the assurance of burghers themselves that it would hasten the end of the war; above all, the military situation was so pressing that between trying to keep the Boers off on the one hand and to build up his strength on the other, he tended to skate over anything less

---

* The British Ambassador in Berlin before World War II protested against the Nazi camps to Goering, who thereupon without a word produced the German Encyclopedia. The entry 'concentration camps' read: 'First used by the British in S.A.' (Neville Henderson, *Failure of a Mission*).

urgent. And the seriousness of the military situation became worse with every day that followed his assumption of command.

The most menacing aspect was De Wet's presence near Bethulie close to the Orange River (President Steyn having meanwhile returned to the north-east). But it was a menace which could also be an opportunity, if it were used to corner De Wet. Kitchener therefore called in columns from far and wide to converge on the area in support of Knox. By sending troops along the south bank of the Orange, and strengthening both the guard on the railway between the Orange and Bloemfontein and the posts around Thaba 'Nchu, he placed his troops in a huge semicircle into some part or other of which Knox must inevitably drive De Wet.

In pelting rain about 2 December, De Wet and Hertzog parted company in the neighbourhood of Bethulie to carry out their invasion to south-east and west respectively. De Wet disclosed his whereabouts by making an unsuccessful attack on one of the pursuing detachments, then for twenty-seven hours marched non-stop to the east while his pursuers thought he was going north. The rain-swollen Caledon, flowing down from the Brandwater Basin to the Orange, lay across his path. He got over with difficulty, and rode for the ford by which he intended to cross the Orange itself. There he looked down on waters risen almost impossibly high—and the Coldstream Guards were waiting for him on the other side.

He was left with no choice than to turn back north with his horses and wagons. But he left behind two daring commandants with a small force to carry out the invasion when opportunity offered. One was Scheepers, the other, also a Cape rebel, was Kritzinger, an equally bold and stalwart man with a strong face and gleaming eyes. As De Wet himself made away, the cordon closed round him. Though delayed by a brave handful of Highland Light Infantry at the Caledon he struggled across safely, only to find when he tried to break out westward that the railway bristled with troops. Then twisting and turning, doubling back on his tracks, feinting in this direction and that, he made his way northwards for a week. Kitchener viewed this with confidence because of the reinforcements sent to the line of fortified posts around Thaba 'Nchu. The great thing was to drive De Wet on to them. Though scarcely ever seeing him the British stuck grimly to the pursuit. On their endless march they found in the hundreds of exhausted horses abandoned by the Boers some indication that the hunt was telling as savagely on their enemy as themselves. Relentlessly Knox shepherded him towards Thaba 'Nchu where the reinforcements waited tensely for the kill. As dawn broke on 14 December they saw, coming through a passage* between the low hills in front of them, the glad sight of De Wet's great convoy.

They watched it head straight for their line of fortified posts. Then they let loose a sudden storm of artillery fire that drove the Boers back in wild confusion. From the top of Thaba 'Nchu a helio flashed the news to Knox's columns far behind; at once, the prospect of success at last seeming certain, they spurred on their weary horses. Even as they did so a Boer advance guard was engaging part of the British line. General Piet Fourie seized the chance offered by this distraction. Placing himself at the head of the Boers (De Wet was bringing up the rear-guard), and perceiving a slight gap in the British line where a minor post chanced to be unoccupied, he led forward the thousands of men, animals and wagons in a tumultuous gallop while shells and bullets ripped through and through them from either side. They got clean away. Reaching the scene, Knox's men were at their last gasp and incapable of further pursuit. As they watched the clouds of dust settle over the horizon they knew that the Second Hunt for De Wet had failed.

De Wet himself had failed to the extent of not personally carrying out his plan of invasion. But by drawing all British attention to himself he enabled his lieutenants to cross the Orange. Kritzinger, cutting up a troop of Brabant's Horse who tried to stop him, entered the Cape on 16 December with 700 burghers and rebels. On the same date Hertzog did likewise further to the west with 1,000 well equipped men. These forces struck rapidly into the Colony, and half-forgotten names of vital railway junctions like De Aar and Naauwpoort were once more in the news as the call to rebellion again rang through the Cape Midlands. Hastily troops were diverted to try to stop them and to guard the railways. Town militia were assembled, martial law imposed in fourteen districts, and Kitchener himself came hurrying down to organize defence and offence. The Boers' kinsmen were less ready than before to consider active revolt, but almost every farm was a refuge and source of supply or even of young recruits, and the kopjes glowed with bonfires

* Springhaan's Nek.

that warned of British troops in the vicinity. Choosing their moment when to pounce on isolated units or when to run, the commandos steadily advanced—Hertzog south-west beyond De Aar and Kritzinger southwards beyond Naauwpoort.

*   *   *   *

These jarring events in the O.F.S. and Cape during the first month of Kitchener's command were echoed in the Transvaal, where the Boers were striking their first major blows.

In the western Transvaal, De la Rey on 3 December attacked a convoy approaching Rustenburg from the east. He inflicted 115 casualties and captured 1,800 oxen, none of which was as important to him as the contents of 138 loaded wagons. About a week later he was joined by Beyers from the north. Native spies reported his approach but Roberts had bequeathed an Intelligence organization so badly managed that General Clements, commanding the British column nearest to this combination of Boer forces totalling 3,000 men, was told nothing. He was camped at the southern foot of a steep bridle-path which ascended the thousand-foot-high wall of the Magaliesberg about midway* between Rustenburg and Pretoria. Here he was caught completely by surprise early on 13 December. De la Rey attacked from the west, while Beyers with sustained ferocity came over the pass itself, charging between huge boulders on the upper slopes without regard to loss. Six hundred and thirty-seven casualties were inflicted on Clements, and the greater part of his camp was looted by the Boers who entered it singing hymns, before he could withdraw to safety.

After this disaster French was put in command of four columns to retaliate against De la Rey, but parting company from Beyers and drawing away westwards to the vicinity of Ventersdorp he eluded pursuit. His successes brought out so many fresh burghers that he decided on the formation of a separate commando. To its command he appointed young Smuts who, like Judge Hertzog in the south, was now to prove himself in a sterner setting than the court-house.

In the eastern Transvaal, garrisons near the Natal border east of Volksrust were constantly harassed under Louis Botha's direction— Vryheid being the target of a major attack on 11/12 December—as

* At Nooitgedagt.

well as points along the Natal railway as far west as the vicinity of Johannesburg. Then Botha swung north to concert measures with Ben Viljoen for a massive scheme he had in mind. Viljoen, in accordance with the Pietersburg decisions, had taken up command in the north-east Transvaal where Schalk Burger and other officials of the Republican Government had established themselves in the mountains west of Lydenburg since leaving Pietersburg. Now Viljoen moved down to meet Botha. On the way he slipped among a line of fortified posts which Buller had left between Machadodorp on the Delagoa Bay line and Lydenburg, and on the night of 28/29 December overwhelmed one of the garrisons* manned by 200 men and burnt the contents of the camp.

*   *   *   *

Such was the succession of disasters which marked the second Christmas of the war and the last days of the nineteenth century. It seemed a situation so appallingly like that of a whole year before that a detached observer could well wonder what precisely the expenditure of thousands of casualties and millions in money had achieved. The guerilla war had so far exacted scarcely less casualties than the battles of Black Week the previous December; the Cape was again under invasion and the threat of rebellion; the Transvaal and the O.F.S. were more controlled by the Boers than the British. That the enemy was as far off as ever from being crushed was rapidly shown in the New Year.

The continuing fourfold drive by French on De la Rey took a calamitous turn on 5 January when a troop of I.L.H. north of Ventersdorp were deceived by an enemy feint into riding on to an innocent-looking kopje whose long grass concealed a Boer ambush. De la Rey went on to harass convoys south of Rustenburg while Beyers rode eastwards and actually attacked stations along the heavily guarded thirty-mile stretch of railway between Johannesburg and Pretoria before safely making his way beyond the line. Soon afterwards Jan Smuts emerged into the news with his newly formed commando. Reinforced by Liebenberg and others to a strength of 1,500 he overwhelmed a garrison just outside Johannesburg,† then beat back a relief column of almost double his strength.

On the other side of the Transvaal, action was on a more massive

---

* At Helvetia.
† At Modderfontein.

scale as the plan took effect which had prompted Louis Botha's north-ward move on the Delagoa Bay line to join hands with Ben Viljoen. Promptly at midnight on 7 January, in swirling mist and pitch darkness, Botha's men from the south and Viljoen's men from the north simulta-neously swept down on no less than seven British garrisons stationed along forty miles of the line from Machadodorp westward. The most important post was at Belfast, held by 1,700 men. Viljoen had a redoubt-able lieutenant named Muller, who was in the forefront as Viljoen's force got through the barbed wire around an outlying fort on a domi-nating hill, scaled the walls and overwhelmed the British who fought to the end with rifle butts and fists. But the fog made co-ordination among the Boers impossible; they fired on each other, and here as at every other post, the garrison survived the night. Though the Boers withdrew, the extent and organization of their assault boded ill.

To the south, in the O.F.S., the month started with a commando wiping out the Commander-in-Chief's Bodyguard, a picked corps of about 150 men. But the most important development was the gather-ing of O.F.S. leaders in the hills east of Senekal. Applying their democratic habits as best circumstances allowed, they nominated an Executive Council and re-elected Steyn whose term of office as President had expired—'an election', declared the Jingo Press, 'which was irregular and furtive.' Then they organized a large convoy and with over 2,000 men De Wet led the way southwards on 27 January. His destination was once again—the Cape.

There Hertzog and Kritzinger were pushing their invasion steadily deeper in spite of every attempt to stop them. While Hertzog rode west beyond De Aar, Kritzinger penetrated southwards into the Midlands further than any commando before him. French's Chief of Staff was seconded to round him up. Douglas Haig was about forty years old. Son of the Scots distiller whose name was known wherever whisky was drunk he had moved in the choicest company at Oxford before joining the cavalry. This was his passion and seemingly excluded any other for the present.* Since arriving in S.A. with his chief he had moved under his shadow. Now, given command of four columns, he

---

* And for some years. Then in 1905 he was the Monarch's guest at Windsor Castle for the Ascot races. He met one of the maids of honour on a Thursday when he partnered her in a golf foursome, played golf with her alone on Friday, and on Saturday morning when they met on the golf-course again he successfully proposed to her at the first tee.

seized his chance to shine. But for the moment at least he failed to catch Kritzinger who reached Willowmore, less than fifty miles from the sea and almost within reach of the Cape ports.

Apart from the direct threat posed by the invaders they decoyed almost all the troops in the Colony, and increased British fears of rebellion—the prospects of which Hertzog in particular stressed very strongly in the reports sent back to De Wet.

It was a time rich with promise for the Boers. Information reached them of a ship on its way from Europe with munitions and mercenaries, and Hertzog's march westward through the Cape was calculated to bring him to meet this ship at Lambert's Bay on the Atlantic only 120 miles north of Cape Town. At the same time Kritzinger was perfectly situated to foment rebellion in the Midlands. De Wet's new move southwards was directed to an invasion in force to exploit these advantages: he would join Hertzog at De Aar and march on Cape Town. De la Rey would wait upon a favourable chance to support him or to draw off opposition to Louis Botha, who prepared to invade Natal with 5,000 men from the eastern Transvaal and descend on Durban.

Such was the coherence of the Boers and the confidence gained from their successes in the new war that here was an overall strategy aimed at nothing less than dislodging the tenuous British hold on the entire sub-continent.

In England it was a doleful start to the new century. At Osborne on 21 January Queen Victoria anxiously asked her daughter Princess Beatrice, 'What news is there from Lord Kitchener? What has been happening in South Africa these last days?' She was hardly conscious as she spoke, for these were her own last days. At 6.30 next evening she died. No one in the civilized world did not mark that hour, and vivid memories light the passing of a miraculous reign. Across the water the Queen of the High and Narrow Seas was brought upon a small royal yacht towered over by escorting battleships of the nations. On a grey winter's day the funeral procession wound through a London shrouded in purple and laurel. Band after band took up the dead-marches as huge crowds and an endless cordon of troops looked on. The crown, the orb and the sceptre glistened on the silken pall borne by a gun-carriage; behind walked four kings and eight crown princes. The Imperial Age did not depart without reluctance: at Windsor the horses of the gun-carriage bucked, and bluejackets had to haul it up to the castle. In St. George's Chapel a herald cried out across the open vault: *Forasmuch as it hath pleased Almighty God to take out of this transitory life to His divine mercy the most high, most mighty, and most excellent Monarch...*

Presently her son was crowned His Most Excellent Majesty Edward VII By the Grace of God, of the United Kingdom of Great Britain and Ireland, and of the British Dominions beyond the Seas, King; Defender of the Faith; Emperor of India. For the first time the phrase 'Dominion beyond the Seas' was used, in recognition of the enhanced status achieved by the colonies through their participation in the war. And with these resounding titles Queen Victoria's rotund and pleasure-loving son launched the twentieth century upon its riotous journey into tumult. But the country's first task in the new century was the last of the old, to finish the war in S.A. that was supposed to have ended months ago and now raged more extensively and expensively than ever before. Industry was hit by the drainage of man-power. There was a trade depression. And financial scandals involving Whittaker Wright were rocking the City. On 14 February Edward's first act of public ceremonial was to open a Parliament assembling in restive mood. Milner had written to Chamberlain saying that he feared a 'wobble' in British opinion; and Chamberlain replied with frankness:

> As regards the military situation I admit to having been more depressed the last week or two than ever before. . . . No one here dares any longer to fix a limit to the war and its expenditure which is going on at the rate of at least a million a week. The country is denuded of troops—fortunately we can count upon the Navy, for if an invasion were possible I do not see how humanly speaking we could resist it. Nevertheless in view of the staleness of the troops and the necessity of the war, a new effort has been resolved upon and 30,000 more mounted men are to be sent to the seat of war.
>
> But if some progress is not made before long I think public dissatisfaction may become serious and threaten the existence of the Government in spite of the enormous majority.

Now in the debate on the Address, the Opposition sought to intensify if not exploit that public dissatisfaction Chamberlain feared. Campbell-

Bannerman urged withdrawal of the demand for unconditional surrender. Lloyd George denounced farm-burning, named British commanders for alleged cruelty, urged self-government for the Boers immediately peace was declared. Chamberlain repeated that self-government would be granted but only after an interval for reconstruction and achievement of 'the objects with which the war has been undertaken'. But there was no division and Chamberlain emerged unscathed. And at this moment the Boers' invasion scheme was unfolding; and with it an unexpected chance of peace at last.

CHAPTER XXIV

The Great Hunt and the 'Drive':
January–March 1901

RUMOURS of the grandiose Boer design had reached Kitchener. His preparations for fighting the new war were incomplete but he could no longer stand on the defensive. He would strike at the eastern Transvaal where Botha was massing his commandos for the invasion of Natal. He threw his volcanic energies into mounting a major offensive unlike any other so far seen in the war, while skeleton forces were deputed in the hope of distracting De la Rey in the west. Operations began in the closing days of January 1901, just when De Wet was leaving the vicinity of Senekal in the O.F.S. to move down on the Cape, whereupon Kitchener resolved on an offensive against him also.

Three campaigns were thus undertaken at the same time, across an area half the size of Europe. He appointed French and Lyttelton to command the offensive against Botha and De Wet respectively, while Methuen exercised command in the western Transvaal.

The Boers had an early set-back though it was of little real importance. Traversing the 300 miles between De Aar and the Atlantic, Judge Hertzog sent on a detachment to scan the sea from the bluffs of Lambert's Bay for the promised ship with munitions and men. A ship indeed waited for them. But it flew the White Ensign and greeted them with a salvo of shell. A new corps of irregulars, Kitchener's Fighting Scouts commanded by a famous hunter called Johannes Collenbrander, then drove the whole force away; but they hovered near Carnarvon, westward of De Aar, waiting for De Wet to keep his rendezvous. Kritzinger also fell back, and eastward of Naauwpoort waited on developments. With the start of Kitchener's operations against De Wet, developments were rapid.

This third attempt to settle with De Wet became known as the Great De Wet Hunt. It started with deceptively little incident. Eluding early attempts to stop him he slipped through the line of fortified posts around Thaba 'Nchu, and marched south through an extraordinarily quiet countryside that gave no sign of pursuit or garrison. Kitchener had deliberately withdrawn all his troops in the eastern O.F.S. to concentrate them south of the Orange, rushing them there by train from all over the country until Lyttelton had over a dozen columns ready.

Near the river De Wet turned westward across the Central railway, taking the opportunity to fill his bandoleers and flour-sacks from a captured train. Then by an elaborate feint and false rumour-mongering he so foxed his opponents that he was able to cross the Orange* north of Colesburg on 10 February. But already he found the going hard. Eight hundred of his burghers refused to leave the O.F.S. Heavy rains were exhausting his transport animals as they struggled through mud or the torrents that suddenly flooded eroded channels. And the British were beginning to cluster around him.

Through all that follows it should be remembered that though a particular column might at a given moment occupy the forefront of the hunt, thousands of men were constantly on the move within a wide radius of their quarry—heading him off, or following up possible scents, or making for the nearest base to fill up with supplies. Of these swarming columns the closest on De Wet's heels after he had crossed the Orange was one commanded by Plumer. He gave the Boers no time to rest or recruit rebels, and chasing them south-westward along a trail littered with hundreds of exhausted horses he caught them up within a couple of days. But two violent storms within a few hours of each other enabled De Wet to get away, his struggle to do so marked by a great litter of derelict vehicles. Under cover of darkness he crossed the Western railway only twenty-five miles north of De Aar; the rains had turned the area into a swamp in which he had to abandon all the rest of his wagons for fear of Plumer catching him there in daylight.

He was now only a hundred miles from Hertzog waiting for him to the west, but the past week had reduced him to a serious plight. His convoy was gone, hundreds of his burghers were without horses, everyone was exhausted by the British pursuit under Kitchener's merciless goad. Worst of all for him, the hopes Hertzog had aroused of

* At Sand Drift.

massive rebel recruitment were not being realized. Yet De Wet's will was not shaken. He drove on, making a detour north-west, with a fury which prompted a war correspondent to cable about this time, 'De Wet is reported to be demented.'

More troops were called up and Kitchener himself went down to the Cape to organize the next phase. He placed fifteen columns, totalling about 15,000 men, along 160 miles of the Western railway from Orange River Station southward. Plumer was to continue in direct pursuit; the others—in turn, so that each would be fresh—were to strike westward from the railway to bar De Wet if, as Kitchener correctly surmised, he intended to march south and link-up with Hertzog. Using the railways for his troop distribution and the telegraph for intercommunication, he devised the most scientific approach anyone had so far tried.

But De Wet made no immediate move south, continuing to swing away to the north-west. The semi-desert, sucking up the rains, presented an arid tract across which Plumer's men followed the scent, until exhausted and famished after nine successive days they could ride no more. Charles Knox, commanding the next nearest column, took up the hunt. But De Wet could snatch a brief rest, and west of Orange River Station he gathered some horses from surrounding farms. Nevertheless, hundreds of his men were still unmounted, and reaching the vicinity of Prieska he found his further progress west or south barred by the swollen waters of a tributary of the Orange.

His position was now almost hopeless. The rebel uprising had proved a false hope; he had lost his wagons; his men were done in. News that another British force was closing in made up his mind. He abandoned his invasion plan. Sending messengers to Hertzog with this decision and an appeal for help, he began riding back north-east to the Orange on 19 February in the hope that it would not be too flooded to prevent his crossing to safety.

Knox, expecting a southward move, was put momentarily off the scent. A couple of days later two ragged and starving Australians overtook him. They had been in a small party Plumer had left to shadow the Boers and it was this which, mistaken by De Wet for a large force, had clinched his abandonment of the invasion. The news the Australians brought was that De Wet was making for the Orange and Knox at once took up the chase again. De Wet was meanwhile circling the

Orange downstream from Orange River Station, trying to find a crossing, but every ford he came to had been made impassable by the floods.

At last he found a small boat and began ferrying his men over. He had got only 300 across when Plumer's column, now somewhat recovered, approached again and from downstream of De Wet began driving him along the south bank towards Orange River Station. They got close on his heels. The leading troopers, reduced by the fury of the pace to a mere three Australians and a Guards' officer, snapped up his remaining two guns which could not keep up with him. Having covered forty-four miles that day the rest of Plumer's advance guard had ridden itself to a standstill, but there was still hope of penning De Wet against the flooded river: Knox was approaching from the south, and in front of the Boers a column from Orange River Station rode out to bar their way with a chain of pickets, each link a makeshift blockhouse consisting of a wagon covered with sacks of meal. But De Wet concealed his unmounted men against the river bank, and slipped through with the rest so quietly during the night that the column next morning collided with Plumer's, and a vigorous half-hour duel was fought by mistake. By then De Wet was on his way across the railway near Orange River Station. However, he was still not over the Orange.

Meanwhile Hertzog had received his message. Splitting his force into two he made shift to join him. In a desperate ride dogged by British columns which were closing round thick and fast, both parts managed to cross the railway north of De Aar.

All the Boers were now in a quadrilateral about fifty miles by seventy, bounded by the Orange in the north, and on the other three sides by railways—De Aar–Orange River Station, De Aar–Naauwpoort, and Naauwpoort to north of Colesburg. Staking everything on the Orange offering no ford by which the Boers could cross, Lyttelton packed the railways lines and sent in columns to bring the hunt to a decisive conclusion. For several days the Boer commandos were hounded as they tried in vain to find a shallow enough crossing of the river, and in the small hours of 27 February they all came together north of Colesburg to attempt the same ford by which De Wet had begun his invasion. At this moment there were no less than thirteen British columns at various points in the quadrilateral—some almost

within firing distance and the rest straining the railway system almost
to breaking point to gather round the Boer position at the ford.

If salvation was to come to De Wet, then, it could come only from
the river. But in the last nine days he had tried thirteen fords in vain.
What could he hope for from the fourteenth? Two young burghers
stripped naked and urged their horses into the river to test its depth.
They scarcely reached the other side alive. This ford was as hopeless as
all the others had been.

*   *   *   *

Between De Wet's confident departure from the north-west O.F.S.
and this climax on the banks of the Orange a whole month had passed.
During the same period Kitchener's other offensive, that in the eastern
Transvaal, raged in a very different form. But since De la Rey was a
factor liable at any moment to upset his calculations, events in the west
require mention first.

With inadequate forces operating within the limited range of a few
bases Kitchener could only hope that they would succeed in keeping
De la Rey quiet. But De la Rey was waiting to hear from the Cape
whether he should reinforce De Wet's invasion, and this inactivity
conduced to a loss of enthusiasm among his followers. Their stirring
memories of their December successes began to fade before the comfort
of a life little disturbed by the British. Besides, he was short of horses.

At his headquarters in the bushy hills west of Rustenburg he had to
content himself with keeping a small commando of picked men and
horses ready to go wherever needed. It was in action west of Klerksdorp on 18 February, when Methuen, who had been patrolling in the
far south-west Transvaal, attacked a superior group of commandos and
in a hard-fought action scattered them. But in the main, while Smuts,
Liebenberg and his other lieutenants remained in the field, numbers of
burghers dispersed to their homes. The vicinity of Johannesburg and
Pretoria was actually clear enough of guerillas for some progress to be
made in the revival of civil life.

With the fading of Boer hopes in the Cape and De la Rey's passivity
in the western Transvaal, we come to the campaign in the east. In
selecting this region for his major offensive Kitchener was playing for
a rich prize. Except along the Delagoa Bay and Natal railway lines,
war had little touched it. And here in readiness to invade Natal gathered

the tough commandos for which it was famed, under the man whose office of Transvaal Commandant-General made him the most important Boer in the field.

To this office, which virtually made him the executive government as well as Kitchener's opposite number, Louis Botha brought a character very different from the whip-lash De Wet, the astute De la Rey, or the undaunted Steyn, for often he lacked ruthlessness, frequently he lacked subtlety, and on occasion the optimism that shone from his intensely blue eyes gave way to despair. Yet his sturdy figure, so compact of man's frail and fallible grandeur, stands out even in the remarkable group that included people like Jan Smuts who was to be accounted great in any company. Every Boer leader was conscious of a terrible responsibility, for each day that the struggle continued laid a greater load of misery on their people and continued the imprisonment of their captured comrades. This imprisonment seemed the worse to them because much of it was far from S.A.—Bermuda, St. Helena and Ceylon. Although the captives were well looked after in their physical needs, and whiled away the time with sport, handicrafts (the museums in S.A. have a remarkable array of ingenious products whittled in some remote prison hutment), producing journals, and the other activities noted at most P.O.W. camps in S.A., they remained in the leaders' minds as unhappy exiles who looked to them for early repatriation.

Such considerations probably weighed even more heavily with Botha than the other leaders. With his deep emotion and wide vision he felt keenly within himself the struggle between the ideal of liberty for his people and the reality of their condition. He had now to watch Kitchener's offensive roll eastward against him on an unprecedented scale of severity.

General French, as commander of the operation, had at his disposal 21,000 men, of whom one-third were in the engineering, medical and other subsidiary services. The force was divided into seven columns. Five were placed at intervals along a front just eastward of the Johannesburg–Pretoria railway. They were to push this front eastwards between the Delagoa Bay and Natal railways, keeping in continuous contact by heliograph and lamp in order to form an impenetrable barrier. As the railways diverged and the area between widened, the remaining two columns would move southwards from the Delagoa

Bay line, extending the barrier in a curve to enclose the environs of Ermelo, where Botha's force would either be destroyed or pushed back to surrender against the borders of Swaziland and Zululand.

The operation was destined to be the prototype of what was called a 'drive'. French's target was not only the enemy commandos. Strict instructions were issued that every farm was to be visited and all women, children and their Native employees sent to the nearest railway depot for subsequent internment. All crops, stocks and wagons were to be seized or burnt and all bakeries and mills destroyed. In short, the army was to fall like a plague of locusts upon a territory of over 10,000 square miles and leave it not only uninhabited but uninhabitable.

The advance started in sweltering heat on 28 January. Soon hundreds of old men, women and children, piling what possessions they could on to wagons and driving great herds of cattle and sheep, fled before the columns whom Boer rearguards tried sporadically to hold off. Across the undulating grassland of the highveld the troops moved with a slowness imposed on them by their gigantic task of devastation.

The difficulty of trying to keep in continuous contact along a front of thirty miles was quickly demonstrated when Beyers, whose ride eastward after leaving De la Rey may be recalled, found a gap in the barrier and slipped back into the western Transvaal and then to his own district north of Pretoria. But Botha's eastern commandos remained in the vicinity of Ermelo. Upon this town the British columns converged and by 5 February were in an arc about ten miles away.

Botha had no desire to be trapped. As the refugees and their wagons and herds streamed through the town, he deputed a force of about 1,500 men to cover their flight into the bush and mountain of the wild lowveld wedged between the Zulu, Swazi and Natal borders. But the greater and better part of his force, totalling about 2,500, rode with him that night upon a secret enterprise.

The extreme northern end of the British curve enveloping Ermelo comprised a column of 3,300 men under Smith-Dorrien. It had reached a small plateau which rose from a shore of Lake Chrissie north-east of Ermelo. The transport, horse-lines and artillery were in the middle of the plateau, the troops around the edge of it, and pickets on the slopes. Smith-Dorrien had no reason to expect attack, since the great Boer exodus was flowing away to the south-east of him. But in the early hours of 6 February a sudden fury of rifle-fire burst upon the sleeping camp through the mist and pitch darkness, followed by the pounding of hooves as the horses stampeded. Botha had achieved complete surprise. He turned back the stampeding British horses into the congested camp and his men charged forward with them to overwhelm the pickets. But Smith-Dorrien had imposed a vigilance and steadiness upon his troops that served them well. In particular the West Yorks and Suffolks rallied with a determination that robbed the Boers of the advantage of surprise. Thereupon they withdrew—having sustained about eighty casualties, about the same as the British. Daybreak brought a thick fog which baffled pursuit, which in any event Smith-Dorrien was too crippled to press hard, and Botha achieved his prime purpose of getting his force around the British cordon and escaping westward behind it.

That day the cordon overran Ermelo, finding it deserted as the bulk of fugitives fled south-west towards Piet Retief. A crossing of the Upper Vaal delayed the mass of humanity and animals; but the leading British column, commanded by Allenby, was skilfully held off by the force Botha had left to cover the retreat. French then called a halt to any further advance for several days in order to complete the devastation of the surrounding territory, to organize future supplies now that difficult country far from the railways was to be entered, and to prepare the next advance to the Swazi border.

The fugitive Boers used the interval to trek further ahead, but whatever their fate the drive had thrust upon a great slab of country a full consciousness of the terror of war. It had also disrupted Botha's plan for the invasion of Natal at a time when De Wet's invasion of the Cape was dwindling into a frantic attempt to escape. And at this juncture, on 13 February, Botha received a message through his wife that Kitchener was prepared to meet him to discuss terms of peace.

Kitchener had timed the moment shrewdly. The terror campaign of devastation and internment had already profoundly affected the Transvaalers. The grandiose offensive plan had foundered. De Wet was not only in peril of his life but far removed from the more pliable Botha whom Kitchener might hope to persuade.

Botha accepted the offer of a conference. Under protection of a safe conduct, he met Kitchener at Middelburg on the Delagoa Bay line on 28 February.

*   *   *   *

There was to be no talk of the Boers preserving their independence, but Botha raised the question immediately the two men sat down to confer. Kitchener, the servant of a Government resolved on annexation, had to decline discussion on the point. But within that policy he wished to make as lenient a peace as possible. His latest biographer suggests that his attitude was dictated solely by a burning desire to leave S.A. in order to become Commander-in-Chief in India.[36] This over-simplifies. Convinced that a continuation of the war would do nobody any good and that with give and take peace could be made, he was naturally impatient to move on. That is far from unwillingness to see a job through or readiness to make a settlement prejudicial to his country for the sake of personal ambition. He showed consistently not only a soldierly respect for the qualities of his opponents but an un-soldierly insight into the challenge to statesmanship which Boer nationalism presented. He knew that if Botha could not be persuaded, the guerilla war would be protracted to the increasing loss of everyone concerned. But Botha was suspicious, especially of any influence that Milner might exert over the negotiations, calling the High Commis-sioner 'the tool of alien financial vultures'. The absence of Milner doubtless helped Kitchener reassure Botha, whom he found friendly and reasonable. Encouraged, Kitchener made a series of proposals.

These were: a general amnesty for Boers and rebels alike except for temporary disfranchisement of the latter; the speedy return of all prisoners of war from abroad; self-government as soon as possible; a £1m. payment of debts incurred by the Boer Governments towards their own people for commandeered goods; assistance to farmers who had suffered war losses; no taxes to pay the cost of the war; the teaching of both languages in schools. His proposal as to what the position of non-whites would be was a vague understanding that if they were to get the limited franchise they enjoyed in the Cape, this would not be accorded before the grant of representative government to the whites.

The two men then parted upon Kitchener's promise to set out the proposals formally in a letter confirmed by his Government.

As soon as a draft of the proposed letter was submitted to Milner and Chamberlain they began whittling away its more generous aspects. They betrayed their mental cast by their offer of 'the privilege' of self-government in a vaguer future than Kitchener promised, and by their description of the million pounds payment of debts as 'an act of grace'

—which they hedged about with qualifications. They insisted on adhering to the Cape's decision on the rebel question (i.e. courts martial for the leaders). The assistance to farmers would only be a loan which would have to be repaid, and then subject to oaths of allegiance to the Queen. The teaching of both languages in schools was consented to only if parents wanted this—an apparently liberal provision but in fact lacking the grasp of future needs which Kitchener and Botha clearly possessed in agreeing that schools should be dual medium without any qualifications; also, to a people grown mistrustful of British intentions the qualification raised fears of a stratagem to deprive the burghers' children of their own language. The same mistrust was invited by revision of the proposal on non-white rights, which hinted at a possibility that they might be granted before the grant of representative government—even if they were to be 'so limited as to secure the just predominance of the white race'.

Yet there did not seem so much real difference between these amendments and Kitchener's proposals. Hopes of peace ran high as Kitchener forwarded his letter with the revised terms to Botha and awaited the fateful Boer decision.

In the agony of mind imposed upon a patriot who had either to sign away his people's independence or commit them to continued suffering without any assurance of preserving their independence anyway, Botha took counsel with his Government and sent word to such leaders in the field as he could reach. At such a moment faith hung precariously upon the actual course of events. And these, as Botha gradually learnt, had taken a scarcely predictable turn in the couple of weeks since the first British peace overture.

The story of the Great De Wet Hunt was broken off in the critical hours of 27 February, when the Boers stood thwarted by the flooded waters of the Orange and the British columns were closing in. Despair and exhaustion rooted the burghers to the river bank for many hours. The nearest British column, making contact with them from the southwest, shook them to action. Instinctively but without hope they saddled up and rode on along the bank. A rearguard action helped them get further along under cover of night, but they were heading for the railway north of Colesburg and the certainty that trains must be rushing up ever more men to block their way.

So the trains were, in order to plant five columns in front of De Wet in addition to those behind and south of him. But so far only 200 men had reached their allotted position, and riding through the night he brushed them aside. With dawn came an outside chance, for he reached another ford just before the railway line. But the British would be on top of him in a matter of hours, and as he sent a few of his young men to ride into the river he could not but feel, after all their previous soundings of its depth, that these were his last moments of freedom. Sure enough, the water ran so deep that men and beasts were compelled almost to swim. And then, as if by the personal intervention of God, the horses were seen rising clear—the water scarcely reached above their fetlocks. With great shouts of joy the watchers on the bank swarmed into the water, through to the other side, and greeted the open plains before them with a vow never to return across the accursed river at their backs.

That day some British columns, principally Plumer's, tried to go after them; but the hunt was over. Its scope and intensity are clearly indicated by the fact that De Wet had lost his wagons and his guns; he had attacked no British forces; and beating such a hazardous retreat without having succeeded in stirring the invaded districts to rebellion robbed him of much prestige. But he was safe—presently to reach Senekal again, forty-three days and 800 miles since leaving it—and this was the critical news carried to Botha: De Wet and Steyn were safely together, and as inflexibly as ever intent upon continuing the struggle.

As for French's great 'drive' in the eastern Transvaal, it too proved in these weeks to be more bruising to the Boers than fatal. Botha himself with the greater part of his fighting force had already dodged back to the wasteland in French's wake. They dug up supplies hidden before the flight, and now rested in anticipation of fighting anew. At the same time the rearguard commandos and the fugitives trekked into the depths of the wedge between Swaziland and Natal: for the British the difficulty of penetrating this country of mountain and thorn-bush was made worse when the sultry weather erupted into the heavy continuous downpour that nearly brought De Wet to his doom in the distant Cape.

The seven columns, advancing on to the Swaziland border and southwards beyond Piet Retief, had to bridge flooded rivers and toil up muddy mountain roads, and whenever they got close to a Boer convoy the rearguard harried them. But just when it seemed that they might envelop their quarry entire—burghers, families, wagons and herds—their supply arrangements, made increasingly difficult as the railways receded, collapsed. Though they did chase one commando into Swaziland and make a number of hauls by way of surrendered or abandoned Boers and possessions, they were substantially brought to a standstill. Food convoys ordered up from Newcastle were bogged down in sodden precipitous roads that had not been investigated in advance. When supreme exertions got some wagons going again im-passable rivers stopped them, calling for frantic efforts to get supplies over by the use of wire ropes, pontoons and rafts. Compelled to live off country which their own actions had largely emptied of food stocks, those troops which could not bribe Natives to dig up hidden caches of meal were nearly to starve before the supply position could be restored.

Meanwhile, on 2 March, De la Rey broke his period of inactivity by an attack, with Smuts and other of his commandos, on his home town of Lichtenburg. It was defended by a British force half the strength of his own. Despite the surprise and an assault maintained for two nights and a day which took some of the attackers into the pretty tree- and runnel-lined streets, De la Rey was beaten off by the sheer courage of the garrison, the Northumberland Fusiliers being con-spicuous. Nevertheless, the very fact that the Boers were still aggressive was significant.

The position, then, as Botha brooded on Kitchener's letter was not turning out as badly as had looked likely. The burghers who were voluntarily surrendering were not much use to his cause anyway. If farms were being devastated and cattle captured the families that relied on these were being removed to the safety of British camps, relieving him of responsibility for them. When he saw that among the members of his Government and of leaders in the field like De la Rey there was no desire to surrender, and knowing that Steyn and De Wet would certainly be opposed to it, he assessed the consequences of fighting on. His conclusions he set forth in a communication to his burghers: 'The cause is not yet lost, and since nothing worse than this can befall us, it is well worth while to fight on.'

In short, the future held the faint hope of an England sufficiently tired of the war to make gentler terms, or of a resurgence of Liberal senti-ment, or even still of foreign intervention; and if none of these hopes was realized, he believed that at least the terms of peace could not be so much worse than those now proposed. On 16 March he wrote to Kitchener breaking off negotiations without giving any reasons.

In England the breakdown caused deep disappointment. The bad economic start to the year was not improved by yet another (the third) War Budget which added twopence to the income-tax besides fresh duties; another, cheaper, War Loan had to be issued, and the Chancellor was also raising money privately in the City. But this was comparatively unimportant. The troubled conscience of the nation had seized with fervour on the hope that a people for whom, despite the inevitable war propaganda, they had come in the past eighteen months to have considerable respect, might enter the Empire on honourable terms and without further bloodshed. In and out of Parliament there was fierce controversy over the Government's handling of the matter. Kitchener was always to believe that given greater latitude by his Government, especially in the matter of the Cape rebels for whom the Boers naturally felt a keen responsibility, he would have secured peace at the Middelburg Conference. He expressed himself bitterly to Brodrick:

> I did all in my power to urge Milner to change his views, which . . . may be strictly just, but to my mind they are vindictive, and I do not know of a case in history where, under similar circumstances, an amnesty has not been granted. We are now carrying on the war to be able to put 2 or 300 [Cape] Dutchmen in prison at the end of it. It seems to me absurd, and I wonder the Chancellor of the Exchequer did not have a fit.

Lloyd George cried: 'There was a soldier, who knew what war meant; he strove to make peace. There was another man, who strolled among his orchids, 6,000 miles away from the deadly bark of the Mauser rifle. He stopped Kitchener's Peace!'

The question remains whether the Boers would have agreed to any peace settlement short of their independence. 'What is the use of examining all the points,' De Wet said when later he became aware of the proposals, 'as the only object for which we are fighting is the independence of our republics . . .?' Chamberlain was against granting an amnesty in advance, lest this merely encouraged rebellion. Also, he and Milner wished to avoid vagueness which might cause later misunderstanding. Eighteen months' gruelling war had been fought and they felt there were limits to magnanimity. Their revision of the proposals nevertheless rubbed off the glow of generosity Kitchener had given, creating the effect of concessions which sounded grudging, gestures which appeared condescending, offers which seemed influenced by niggardliness.

When all is said, the one solid fact was that the war had to continue, unrelenting and unforgiving, to heap more ashes on the heads of future generations.

CHAPTER XXV

A War Against Space

FRENCH's drive in the eastern Transvaal, resumed when the supply problem had to some extent been overcome, dragged on well into April. It lost much of its impetus as lack of supplies hampered mobility, or horses terribly weakened by the wet and lack of forage could not cope with the rugged sodden terrain. Though pursuit and devastation continued to the Zululand border, some of the ablest burghers had used the delay to slip back through the cordon into mountain fastnesses; others, often including their families, disappeared into wild and inaccessible lairs. The drive simply petered out when the process of beating the empty air exhausted itself and troops were required elsewhere.

The results on paper of this, the first great drive of the war, looked impressive—nearly 400 Boers put out of action by death or wounds, nearly 1,000 captured (mostly through voluntary surrender), guns galore, thousands of vehicles, rounds of ammunition by the hundred thousand, 8,000 horses and mules, and so many cattle and sheep that most escaped owing to the impossibility of killing or keeping them all; and hundreds of families sent back for internment. In reality the reduction of Boer fighting strength was trifling because the surrenders were mostly by people outside the age limits or with no fighting spirit; the guns were useless to the Boers without ammunition; the wagons and cattle were of no immediate military value and even if most of the cattle had not escaped the need for them was largely reduced by the internment of so many families. The net gain by 21,000 soldiers, slogging it out for ten exhausting weeks, was scarcely inspiring. Yet it was accounted so—and the pattern set for similar drives elsewhere.

Even before French's drive ended Kitchener set in motion another. North of a line drawn from west to east along the Magaliesberg range and the Delagoa Bay railway lay a huge expanse of the Transvaal, much of it marked 'unsurveyed' on maps, which the British had so far scarcely penetrated. Most of the Central railway north of Pretoria to the railhead at Pietersburg remained an exception to the otherwise total British possession of the S.A. railway system, and Pietersburg it-self was the only town of any importance under undisputed Boer con-trol, where they could run printing-presses, mills, stock-depots and a centre for general distribution of supplies. Kitchener now directed his aim at both the Pretoria–Pietersburg railway and the whole of the territory eastwards to the Lydenburg–Machadodorp line of fortified posts.

Beyond the unhealthy bush were thousands of square miles enclosed by the mountains on the east, the Delagoa Bay railway on the south, and the Olifant's River on the other two sides, with fertile valleys unscourged by the war, a fruitful and restful region for the com-mandos of Ben Viljoen and the Transvaal Boer Government.

The wanderings of that Government have briefly been touched on: how on Kruger's departure for Europe Botha escorted a caretaker Government with Schalk Burger as Acting-President from the vicinity of Komati Poort to Pietersburg; and how, after the deliberations with Steyn and other leaders there, they had gone into the mountains west of Lydenburg where they now reposed on a farm called Paardeplaats. From this remote eyrie they conducted the business of government across a country of mountains, wild bush, and giant baobab trees which were sometimes a hundred feet in girth; here roamed giraffes, lions, buck and other wild animals that had all but disappeared from more settled regions. They issued paper-money, maintained a postal service to Pietersburg, and appointed magistrates; correspondence even filtered through from Europe, and they kept in touch with all the commandos. Although the subject of much satirical comment, they constituted a living force in the Boer firmament, and while such a Government existed the Boers could claim that their republic was still a reality.

It was therefore one prime objective of Kitchener's new drive. Another was Ben Viljoen's forces which, though largely inactive since the combined attacks with Botha on 7 January, continually blew up the Delagoa Bay railway, and a small expedition to dislodge them had failed. A third purpose was continuation of the 'scorched earth' policy across territory which had so far been untouched by war.

On 26 March Plumer's column, returned from the Great De Wet Hunt, started from Pretoria in secrecy. Riding hard it outsmarted Beyers, the commandant of all the region north of Pretoria, to reach Pietersburg within a fortnight with very few casualties. From here, having wrought destruction, he crossed a range of granite hills and dropped down into the warm sandy valley of the Olifant's River to block the fords. South and east of him the drive proper was launched under the command of a new arrival from India. General Sir Bindon Blood had a fine head of silver white hair and a moustache to match. He had not served outside India for twenty years, and although he shared with Kitchener the unusual distinction of having risen to high command from the Royal Engineers, he soon chafed under the younger but senior man's imperious sway. He had six columns of about 11,000 men under him, and these set out northward from Middelburg and Belfast on the Delagoa Bay railway and westward from Lydenburg.

They were too late to catch the Boer Government. Plumer's advance had already startled it into slipping south over the railway to join Botha in the Ermelo district. However, there were still Viljoen's forces, and as the British closed in from two directions and Plumer guarded a third, Viljoen exhibited a strange uncertainty. His single clear escape route was due north but the Sekukuni Natives, ferocious and hostile, barred even that. After a collision with one of the British columns he rode hither and thither before his pursuers. He was compelled to burn his wagons, many of his men deserted, others were on the point of mutiny. And then, on 20 April, just when four of the British columns were within a dozen miles of him about thirty miles north of Belfast, he made a sudden dash for freedom. Ably guided he led his men on a three-day ride westward up steep bridle-paths, through clawing bush, and in a final non-stop burst of nineteen hours crossed the Olifant's at a shallow part so steeply banked that the British were not guarding it. In this way he reached comparative safety beyond the far-flung British cordon. Thereafter he circled round the Delagoa Bay railway which he crossed near Balmoral Station, going on to join Botha in the Ermelo district early in May. While two of Kitchener's objectives were thus missed with the departure of both Viljoen and the Transvaal Government, the third was vigorously pursued. Once again families, surrendered burghers, and great quantities of stock and supplies were gathered in, and much burning and devastation done, so that the operation as a whole gave a misleading impression of success.

Blood's drive and the final phase of French's did not mean that the guerilla war was elsewhere dormant as summer drew to a close. After De la Rey's abortive attack on Lichtenburg in the western Transvaal, two British columns went after him south-west of Ventersdorp. There was the usual toil expended on feints and false scents, and then 400 of De la Rey's men fell on two squadrons of I.L.H. who were reconnoitring. This small incident was made significant by a revolutionary tactic. De la Rey's men, instead of dismounting behind cover for the attack, charged on horseback, firing from the saddle. Pregnant in its consequences, the episode went unnoticed.

The pursuing columns achieved some success. With squadrons of Australians in the vanguard they caught De la Rey by surprise twenty miles west of Ventersdorp on 24 March, compelling him to abandon his wagons, guns and a great quantity of ammunition. In another kind of war this might have crippled him. But as De Wet and Viljoen had already shown, the Boers were as prepared to abandon their convoys as they had been to abandon towns and fixed bases, so long as they could preserve their core of fighting men. In guerilla war this was all that mattered. So long as they survived they might hope to replenish themselves from the enemy's supplies, and so fight on indefinitely.

De la Rey simply dispersed his men into small groups while the heat was on. Commandos under Smuts and others hovered about garrison towns and convoys, and skirmishes and raids were frequent. The chief area of turbulence was the open country between Lichtenburg, Ventersdorp, and Klerksdorp. In the first week of May Kitchener made a determined attempt to round up the guerillas in this area by sending in five columns, the chief commander being Methuen. Boer scouts were everywhere, British messages were intercepted, a ceaseless flow of false rumours was poured out for British consumption: in such circumstances the slow-moving columns marched hither and thither in vain, achieving more success in destroying stock than in catching men who simply evaporated at their approach.

It was much the same in the O.F.S., although fewer clashes on any significant scale took place. De Wet's tormenting experience in the Great Hunt convinced him that any major adventure by his commandos was to be avoided. Refining his system of district command he divided the O.F.S. into seven regions. Each was placed under an acting commandant-general and in turn further subdivided under commandants. Their writ still ran wide despite the British occupation. Thus Hertzog, in charge of the south-west O.F.S., maintained a semblance of government which exacted taxes from Natives and burghers still on their farms, and paid commandants twenty-five pounds per month. In the military sphere the order was dispersal and evasion. When the British columns, operating under a similar system of district organization, made a series of drives across the greater part of the country they successfully denuded the farms, but in dealing with the commandos they were like a man trying to clutch smoke. For example, Rundle, believing that commandos were again forgathering in the Brandwater Basin, entered it with 2,500 men on 29 April and when he emerged from it about a month later he had seized or destroyed considerable supplies, wagons, mills—but captured exactly one burgher and caused the death of a few others.

In the Cape, De Wet's departure released an increasing number of troops to go after Kritzinger. Douglas Haig's appointment to oversee this operation proved a thankless assignment. With Scheepers and other resourceful leaders Kritzinger operated mainly in the mountainous districts up to a hundred miles south of Naauwpoort. Acting sometimes in concert, sometimes individually, they harried British columns and trains, recruited adventurous youths, terrorized loyalists, destroyed property, and kept resistance aflame deep in the Cape Midlands. It could not easily be suppressed. Martial law was applied with little severity; the Cape Government tardily accepted the expense of self-help; and though anyone openly rebelling was liable to be shot, the farmers continued to give secret support. While there was not the wholesale rebellion for which the Boers constantly hoped, the invaders and rebels constituted a running sore in Kitchener's side.

*   *   *   *

With the close of summer, as May drew the first cold winds across the veld, Kitchener had been in command for upwards of six months. His first need of a sufficient mounted force had gradually been met, until now one third of his army of 240,000 men was mounted* of

* 12,000 M.I., 14,000 cavalry, 7,500 S.A.C.—Canadians, Scots and other irregulars— 17,000 2nd Contingent Yeomanry, 5,000 Australian and New Zealand replacements, 24,000 irregulars raised in South Africa.

whom nearly half were colonials. But these mounted troops were only half-trained, and since Kitchener threw them into action with little preliminary their standards of performance were far below the Boers'. The remount situation was a constant problem. Horses now arrived at the rate of 10,000 per month; another 5,000 per month were commandeered, and many were caught on the veld: but half-trained riders on unacclimatized mounts, and badly organized depots, caused a fantastic wastage of horse-flesh in the arduous campaign conditions.

The Boers' manpower was reduced to about 45,000 men and youths, of whom only about 13,000 were in fighting trim at any one time. The war either hardened the individual's will to fight or impelled his surrender. Around the hard core of fighters was hence a fringe of men either drawing closer to that core or drifting into surrender. Some who gave themselves up began actively helping the British as spies and in other ways. These were mostly men of the impoverished *bywoner* class, except for members of the Burgher Police Force which had been newly formed to help secure the environs of Bloemfontein.

The stress of war upon the minds of a people engaged in a seemingly hopeless struggle for their freedom would provide a fascinating study outside the scope of this book. But a little space must be occupied by a related theme, the relationship between Boer and Native.

The Boer regarded the Natives as his inferior. His attitude went deeper than that of Christian to pagans. In the barbarities he had experienced at their hands he found nothing but confirmation of his profound religious belief based on the Old Testament that the blacks were the sons of Ham, cursed of God. Living in an isolation which largely cut him off from formal education and surrounded him with a black sea, he was governed by severely practical considerations of death or survival. But uncouth as he sometimes was by the sophisticated standards of the urban European, and narrow though his views might be in conformity with his Calvinism—that same Calvinism which he believed had brought him safely through incredible hardships during the pioneering era which was only a generation away—he was no more cruel than he believed the circumstances made necessary.

In a country of violent storms, wild animals and hordes of savages, he himself was remarkably unviolent, unwild and unsavage. The lengths to which he had already gone in the war proved his toughness, but it is notable that feeling for his cause as deeply as he did he exhibited none of the brutality towards his enemy which has been a feature of almost every armed nationalist upsurge on record. Instead, his acts of kindness to that enemy were legion, and the cause of lasting friendships between fighting men on both sides which make political and propaganda vapourings to the contrary look silly. He had a code of honour that appealed to the same strong vein of feudal chivalry which, as the success of Walter Scott's books had shown, appealed so strongly to the British.

All this, when it came to defining his attitude towards the Native, resulted in a policy of paternalism. Miscegenation was illicit and shameful. He insisted on keeping the Natives in a subordinate situation but generally did not ill-use them. Cattle-raids and hut-burning that had been undertaken sporadically since the start of the war were partly the acts of uncontrolled individuals, partly military necessity, partly to terrorize tribes into not exploiting the situation. There were atrocities, as there are to the present day throughout Africa wherever a white individual gives way to a viciousness born of fear or stupidity, and they are exceptions. By and large the Boer policy of paternalism was in practice identical with British policy at that time, but there was an important difference of degree.

The British were more prepared than the Boers to see the Natives as children who might be brought up to adulthood in some vague future which offered no immediate challenge to white supremacy. The startling idea that the Natives might come to feel the very nationalism which the two white races felt, and to wish for that very liberty and respect for which the Boers were now fighting, was only to emerge in later years when the simple racial considerations of 1901 were to be made vastly more complex by the march of events and ideas.

For the present it was enough that the two white races should regard themselves as sole arbiters of the country's future. It followed that the Native should not be armed. This attitude was supported by the danger of releasing upon the scene a flood of armed Natives who might thereafter turn their rifles on their white masters, pursue their favourite activity of intertribal warfare, or menace law and order after the war. Besides, to have used Natives to kill whites would have been to stir up racialism to all its most rabid and irrational depths, and this was not a complication either side wanted.

Hence had arisen the phenomenon, so singular and astonishing, of a war fought across the breadth of a vast region the majority of whose inhabitants were mere spectators. At least, that was the intention. It was to have been a white man's war. But war is a cynical disturber of pretence and a relentless burster of weak seams. The Native had in fact come to play a role of increasing importance.

As labourer, wagon teamster, groom, cook-boy, manservant, he had helped the Boers from the outset; he had his uses also as a spy. Extracts from Reitz's *Commando* in this book have shown how the Native often served his master with touching fidelity, sharing his hardships and his hopes; to prevent molestation by Native marauders and generally to protect the families who escaped internment by constant trekking, the Boers often relied on their faithful Native retainers; and when families were sent to concentration camps their servants were likewise interned. Where the master and servant relationship could be maintained, traditional attitudes prevailed: the Native was kept 'in his place' with good-humoured authority. But the guerilla war aroused strong emotions when commandos on the run found themselves near hostile tribes, or when food shortage compelled them to approach tribesmen more humbly than they cared for, or when—and this was something for which they never forgave the British—they found themselves confronting armed Natives.

The dividing line between combatant and non-combatant is always a source of feverish debate in wartime. But in 1901 the prevailing code, upon whose humanity both sides congratulated themselves, defined a combatant as someone who carried a rifle; and a non-combatant was someone who did not—however much his activities might conduce to the destruction of an opponent as surely as a well-aimed bullet. Under this code the British, like the Boers, from the outset employed Natives in all manner of circumstances short of actually bearing arms. Though armed Native levies were raised in predominantly tribal districts they were solely for police work or self-defence against Boer cattle- and supply-raids, and though there is evidence that some of these levies sometimes strayed beyond their boundaries and clashed with commandos, until latterly the British had fully observed the code in the spirit at least. They too had not wished Natives to be armed, having had sufficient of a bruising from armed Zulus only ten years before.

But without official formulation a policy had been growing up of using Native scouts who accompanied the columns in detachments and, being liable to be shot by the Boers if caught, they were armed. Similarly, Native night-watchmen were used at fortified posts, and for their protection they too were armed. This action, which for many Boers justified their deep mistrust of British integrity, was an unconscious tribute to the success of their own resistance. Because the British, unlike the Boers, received no help from the countryside, they were compelled to rely increasingly on Native spies; because a quarter of a million troops was not enough to deal with guerillas who were able to disappear in the vastness of the veld, recourse was had to additional manpower by way of Native sentries.

The Boers had not in the past been above arming Natives. A notable instance was when they broke the power of the Zulus, in a bloody battle on a tributary of the Tugela, with the aid of a large Native contingent fighting shoulder to shoulder with them. But they regarded this as something to be resorted to in extreme need, which was an excuse the most powerful nation on earth could hardly plead. Today the spectre of armed Natives still affrights the imagination of white South Africa, but the whole subject of the Native in the Boer War deserves more detailed examination than can be given here. Britain, from a safe distance and with a vague and as yet largely sentimental idea of all the inhabitants one day sharing the fruits of their bountiful country, saw at most a political blunder but certainly nothing immoral about arming the Native. The Boer, for his part, had been far removed from the security which permits a view of the Native as a white child with a black face. He had survived in the wilderness by the application of a Bible-inspired hierarchical scale, namely, elder–father–son–women–children–Natives. He saw the British action as a wicked incitement both for the overthrow of the precious values in this scale, and for massive recruitment against him when the odds were already enormous.* His fear of the Native being thus intensified, he began to shoot him even on suspicion of betrayal, but at the same time he had of necessity to come to terms with hostile tribes or to act the supplicant for supplies. Finally, the Native himself—still almost entirely a naked savage in the eyes of the European—obeyed either his white master or his despotic chief, and the latter observed a cautious detachment or served whichever side expediency required: in short, the Native had

---

* Not recognizing the annexations he also, of course, considered the Native still a subject of the Republican Governments and hence a traitor if disloyal.

not reached the political consciousness and unity which would have enabled him to wring any lasting benefit for himself from the situation.

So we come to the ultimate strangeness of this war, that as it went on it did nothing to solve, and much to complicate, the real problem, which was not whether Boer or Briton should rule South Africa but how white and non-white might live together in harmony. At the time the fact was little recognized. It was obscured by the stresses and strains in other directions.

Especially was a great cloud of bitter controversy thrown up by the question of the concentration camps, whose origin was described in the previous chapter. So far (May 1901) 77,000 whites and 21,000 non-whites had been immured in the camps, representing a task of removal and administration so burdensome that the civil government had begun taking them over from the military. But it was only in June that the British public became aware of something appallingly wrong about these camps. Bluntly, of every five white people who entered them one would be dead within a year, and the rate was rising. The tragedy was greater because the vast majority of deaths occurred among children, mainly from measles.

The Opposition was incensed. Campbell-Bannerman talked of Kitchener's 'methods of barbarism', which Asquith, Haldane, Edward Grey, and other members of the Liberal Imperialist wing of the party thought was going too far, the heated discussions over Liberal dinner-tables inviting the description of 'the war to the knife and fork'. Lloyd George, drawing a parallel with Herod who had also 'tried to crush a little race by killing its young sons and daughters', uttered a prophecy: 'A barrier of dead children's bodies will rise up between the British and the Boer races in South Africa.'

Widespread concern, stirred in particular by the agitation of Emily Hobhouse, a Quaker spinster who had worked in the camps, was shared by many Conservatives and resulted in the Government's appointment of a Committee of Ladies who set out from England to investigate and report on conditions in the camps. Meanwhile Continental pro-Boer propagandists were quick to seize on the subject and inflate it to fantastic proportions. The Boers in the field were torn between anxiety for their families and relief at not being responsible for them. Without anticipating the facts the Committee was to reveal, the point must here be made that Kitchener had embarked on a course which, viewed solely from a military standpoint, was of questionable value: to an extent never anticipated it distracted the troops from their real job of defeating the guerillas.

The same is true of the associated policy of devastation. So far in the Transvaal and O.F.S. drives, tens of thousands of cattle and sheep had been captured, mountains of grain seized or destroyed, miles of standing crops, mills, farm-buildings set ablaze. Again this had meant, continued to mean, an enormous labour on its own quite divorced from the primary task of fighting. And to what effect? So vast a country would take a long time to be ravaged effectively and the Boers were no strangers to making do in a barren waste.

Though the commandos and those of their families trekking in constant flight could hope for luxuries only by captures from the British, they had enough meat, and also mealies which they ground in portable mills. They made ersatz coffee from dried peaches, sweet potatoes, tree-roots and other ingredients; they found salt in natural deposits; they traded with the Natives. For clothing, women revived the art of wool-spinning on wheels adapted from old sewing machines and fruit peelers; sheepskins were turned into jackets; leather was used until all tanning apparatus had gone; and uniforms were even stripped from captured soldiers.

This last resort violated the 'rules of war'—and exposed their essential absurdity. Since war is itself a violation of a primary ethical rule among men, the notion of rules for conduct in the event of rules being broken represents a wistful desire to salvage a semblance of morality from an immoral situation. However, unlike Shylock, Mars is inescapably bound to exact his pound of flesh. A Roberts might try to avoid casualties, only to pile up excessive losses in the long run. If you go to war, the bond must be paid, and under such a compulsion all rules, laws, ethical considerations fare badly. The British Press carried constant reports, in great and indignant detail supported sometimes by photographs but more often by highly realistic drawings, of Boers murdering wounded men or loyalist civilians, of brutal treatment of individual soldiers, Native and half-caste scouts, and even their own countrymen who having surrendered tried to persuade others to do likewise. The Boer Press had of course disappeared but the Afrikaner Press in the Cape kept up its anti-British propaganda unceasingly, as did the Continental Press with even more vitriol. Opposing commanders from time to time also exchanged formal recriminations. The war had in fact entered a far harsher and more bitter phase, but both sides, in spite of all the propagandist charges and counter-charges of inhumanity, strove to fight 'cleanly' and a comical by-product of the war was the amount of energy expended upon arguing over their degree of success or failure in doing so. By Kitchener's own policy the Boers had either to go naked or sometimes use British uniforms and break the rules, so Kitchener turned a blind eye on the breach except to mete out capital punishment for infringements in the Cape (where clothes were readily procurable) or for deliberate deception; besides, his own troops extensively adopted the slouch-hat which was the one feature of a Boer distinguishable from a distance.

The Boers were untroubled by the loss of artillery, which was an encumbrance and useless without repair facilities. On the other hand, the caches of bullets which they had buried for use in their Mausers were proving unequal to the demand. But every captured British soldier provided a splendid Lee-Metford and also a quantity of ammunition, which could be supplemented by gleanings from British bivouacs where bullets were carelessly left lying about. The result was that the commandos were in process of being completely rearmed with Lee-Metfords at the expense of the British tax-payer.

Here was another instance of the benefits the Boers reaped from the existence of so many half-trained men in Kitchener's army. It was clear now that in encouraging the Government to release seasoned colonials and Yeomanry after a year's service, Roberts had committed a blunder on a par with his other major mistakes. A subtler mistake was that when he said the war was over honours had been lavishly distributed; consequently commanders in the field were not keen to lose their reputation in the painful and unrewarding business of trying to round up guerillas, especially with highly vulnerable half-trained troops, whereas the piling up of impressive returns of captured people and materials was so much more tangible, so that enterprise was at a premium and excessive caution the common currency.

Kitchener's methods strongly contributed to this tendency. His juggernaut personality stamped above all else on the situation his belief in organization. His Pretoria headquarters staff, carefully fashioned like so many cogs—one for troop distribution, another for remounts, another for supplies, and so on—meticulously turned this belief into a stream of precise orders. The drives were designed to work like great machines operating to a blue-print prepared by him in consultation with the small H.Q. staff and in particular with his Intelligence. Considerable strides forward had been taken to gather information through Native scouts and surrendered Boer spies, to sift it, and get it rapidly to everyone concerned. But though French and Methuen might enjoy a measure of autonomy, all the other generals were integral parts of a highly centralized system, regarding themselves as dependent on Pretoria H.Q. for orders and information alike, to the detriment of their own aggressiveness and scouting.

Every circumstance was therefore making the war not one of direct assault on the enemy forces—though this, as we have seen, was being tirelessly attempted—but of indirect methods, by attrition. Kitchener's army was a giant mechanical scraper to bare the countryside of population, supplies, habitation, and only to an infinite degree of guerillas.

The problem before him, even after he had revivified and strengthened the moribund army he had inherited, was prodigious.

In part it was psychological. Roberts had let the Boers learn that by guerilla tactics they might prolong the war indefinitely, and they were animated by a passionate belief in their cause. On the other hand, the British were not fighting a war of hate which might have spurred on every soldier to bring down his enemy at all costs. They had half forgotten the political issues which had sparked off the war; the Boer leaders at the start had mostly gone; the glory of empire was a softer spur than the passion for independence; above all, the more the two sides became acquainted the less reason they found for disliking each other.

In its military aspects the problem depended on mobility. But since every column operating away from the railways was tied to ox-wagons for supplies—especially, and ironically, as the countryside was being denuded by the army's own exertions—none could move rapidly for any distance, or stay in the hunt very long. Also, a convoy had only to move out along a particular road for watching scouts to know the whereabouts and probable destination of its accompanying column: the news, carried by dispatch-rider or heliograph across the countryside, immediately alerted the local commandos, which could pounce when they chose or disperse into small groups, which the British could not do.

A Boer, however, could range far from his wagons by living for extraordinarily long periods with only a hunk of dried meat in his saddle-bag; his wagons could be concealed at a distance from his overt activity or even screened by sham demonstrations. He had no communications, installations or much else beyond his own person to guard. Schooled by generations' hard experience he could ride huge distances on hardy ponies he knew how to get the best from, and he could exploit his knowledge of a terrain upon which he had been born and bred. Add to these advantages the seasoning of nearly eighteen months' campaigning; give him resolute leaders but at the same time a personal initiative which was encouraged by his military system as much as the British soldiers were discouraged by theirs; and the result, with his independence at stake, was the most formidable fighting man in the world.

In trying to solve the problem by a process of attrition Kitchener essentially relied upon time. But the problem belonged to another dimension altogether—space. It was space which allowed the Boer to exploit his superior mobility, greater initiative, resourcefulness at survival, while it encumbered the British with supply convoys that reduced their mobility as greatly as it increased their vulnerability. It was space which the guerilla war brought fully into its own as the Boers' one, tremendous, unfailing ally, while reducing the British forces, which looked so overwhelming compared with theirs, to the size of an ant on a vast map.

This, then, was the crux of the whole military situation. It took a while for Kitchener to realize it. His gradual discovery that he was trying to match time against space, and how he groped towards a different solution, provide one of the most fascinating aspects of his command.

The first clue was the railways. When he assumed command they were guarded at intervals by open trenches with mounted patrols between. The method was wasteful in manpower and did not prevent raids by rail-wreckers. As the Boers' artillery got less the trenches gave way to enclosed works above-ground commanding a wider field of fire, some being substantial stone forts but most consisting of clumsy octagonal structures made from double walls of corrugated iron let into a solid foundation, with gravel filling the walls except for massive iron loopholes. But since March the Boers had begun to see structures that looked like large water tanks. They were in fact the invention of a major in the Royal Engineers who hit on the corrugated iron cylinder used throughout S.A. for water storage as suggesting the ideal design. Two cylinders of different diameters placed one within the other, the gap being filled with shingle; simplified iron loopholes; an overhanging pitch roof with hatches in the eaves for ventilation; no foundation except level earth—such a blockhouse could be produced by mass-production for about sixty pounds each, transported to position, put up by unskilled labour, and manned by seven infantrymen and three or four Native night sentries.

Already in May these new blockhouses were reducing raids on the railways, which had been cut thirty times a month through the summer, almost to nil. They gave rise to a more revolutionary idea—to use them so effectively that the railways would act as barriers against commandos trying to cross from one district to another. At first placed at strategic parts of the railways, they were now being put down every mile and a half along the whole length in the two new colonies. Rock or earth was often piled up against the walls; entanglements surrounded them, with barbed wire between; the whole system was connected by telephone, and every garrison did its own patrolling to release mounted men. Though these seven-man garrisons were too weak to stop a commando determined to cross the line, at least wagon convoys could not usually cross.

If perfected such a system had immense possibilities. This was hinted at by the existence of the line of fortified posts, which were in fact small entrenched forts with fifty men in each, strung away from the railway at Bloemfontein eastward via Thaba 'Nchu to the Basutoland border. Now came the notion of a similar cross-country fortified line to the west. Kitchener, first creating an encircling 25-mile zone around Bloemfontein policed by the Burgher Police to permit the resumption of civil life, decided to create a further line of fortified posts westward as far as the Western railway. He manned it with Baden-Powell's newly arrived South African Constabulary and ordered them to clear successive belts of country north of it.

There was no real thought about where all this might lead—namely, to the systematic division of the whole land mass into fixed, manageable units in which the commandos might be pinned and so extinguished piecemeal. But though the thought had not asserted itself the tendency was there. And this, more than drives or devastation, was the most significant development of the months since Kitchener assumed command.

★   ★   ★   ★

Such was the situation by May 1901, when the first winds blew heralding the South African winter. For the British they were winds of optimism. It was true that French and Blood's drives in the eastern Transvaal had failed to bring Botha and Viljoen to heel; that De la Rey survived in the west despite some reverses; that De Wet continued at large after the Great Hunt; that the invasion of the Cape, while prevented from assuming major proportions, still continued under Kritzinger, Scheepers and their colleagues. But they had lost the initiative they held when Roberts departed. In some degree at least the scorching of the earth around them, the absence of many of their families, concern for their comrades imprisoned overseas, the hopelessness of the ultimate outlook—all this inexorably sapped will and strength. But more terrifying and immediate was the fact that now the hostility of nature was to be added to that of man. They confronted not only the relentless pressure of a huge army well armed, fed, clothed and sheltered, but the harshness of a winter in which they would have to sleep unprotected and scavenge food for themselves and their animals on the shrivelled veld.

The British might well feel hopeful. Kitchener even corresponded with his Government on the possibility of reducing his forces. And Milner could take a brief holiday in England. Chamberlain cabled that he was going to be given a Roman triumph on arrival, which Milner thought was a hoax, but sure enough at Waterloo he was met by the chief Ministers of the Crown, including Salisbury.

At Chamberlain's prompting Salisbury had suggested that the King send a royal carriage for Milner, but the King had suggested that Salisbury send his own carriage; to Salisbury the thought of sending his carriage *empty* seemed 'with all deference to H.M. . . . a bit of bad manners on my part', so that despite his dislike of ceremonies there he was at Waterloo. He whisked Milner off to Marlborough House for the King to raise him to the peerage as Viscount Milner. He was made a Privy Councillor and a freeman of the City, and given a public banquet. In this way the legend of his public service was sedulously fostered. Whether he served

430

Britain's long-term interests is a question upon which there may be reservations. Between receiving honours he discussed with Chamberlain the tasks of reconstruction. These were already in hand despite the fact that the greater part of S.A. was a huge armed camp, with all the towns and most villages under military occupation. Thus, though Johannesburg still had the gloomy appearance of a beleaguered city the first Uitlanders were returning to it as the first mines reopened, and in both the Transvaal and O.F.S. civil administration was beginning to replace military.

As encouraging for the British was the prospect depressing for the Boers. Many of the leaders met south of Ermelo on 10 May and found little to comfort them. The acting Government and Ben Viljoen, alike just escaped the tentacles of Blood's drive, were there with Louis Botha; so were Jan Smuts from the western Transvaal and officers from other areas. On their minds was the unspoken word, *surrender*. But in common with their absent colleagues they looked on their position as trustees of their people's independence. To this charge they brought an almost religious fervour—anything less would scarcely have sustained them so far in the struggle—and each was loath to accept responsibility for uttering that fateful word. They therefore agreed to ask Kitchener for permission to send an emissary to sound Paul Kruger in Europe. Sensitive to possible reaction by their O.F.S. colleagues, they decided to approach Kitchener without first consulting them: but at the same time President Steyn would be informed of the decision and the suggestion made that in the event of Kitchener refusing permission the British should be asked for an armistice while future policy could be decided.

Kitchener did refuse permission. But he agreed to grant facilities for a private cable to be sent to Kruger and for Kruger to reply. Smuts entered Standerton under a flag of truce and the cable was dispatched through the Dutch Consul at Pretoria.

Steyn responded with vehemence to the Transvaalers' communication. Not waiting to see De Wet he bitterly denounced their decisions. The Free Staters, he declared, were suffering as severely as they but were unshaken; his republic had staked its existence on fidelity to their alliance, and for the Transvaal to weaken now was a betrayal of the Free Staters and Cape rebels alike. At the same time he tried to encourage the Transvaalers by expressing the belief that England would soon come up against international difficulties, and he quoted a Natal newspaper reporting the 'pro-Boer' agitation in England which he believed would make her increasingly anxious to come to terms.

The upshot was agreement to hold a solemn joint council of war near Standerton in the eastern Transvaal, to be attended by the principals of both republics. But to decide on such a meeting was one thing— to hold it, quite another. No armistice was asked of the British. As winter closed in the leaders set about trying to come together secretly in the midst of Kitchener's swarming and interminable columns.

CHAPTER XXVI

Winter 1901

KITCHENER was aware of the Transvaalers' depression. Resolved to add the severities of war to those of winter, he launched drive upon drive across both former republics. Against this continuous pattern of activity, and often entangled in it, the outstanding events of the winter of 1901 took place. Above was the winter sky, unflecked blue by day, a black jewelled brilliance by night. On the yellow-brown veld below were endless mounted columns, infantry trudging with mule- or ox-wagon convoys or patrolling between blockhouses strung along the shimmering railway lines, untold miles of ravaged fields and smouldering farm-buildings; while weaving among all this rode keen-eyed and resolute men. In particular, the efforts of the Boer leaders to meet for their proposed joint council of war spun a thread by which the developments of early winter may be traced.

De la Rey, wishing to accompany Steyn and De Wet, boldly took the most dangerous route. As he made his way southward through the western Transvaal a number of columns advanced upon his hunting grounds. Thereupon one of his lieutenants, the impetuous Kemp, singled out a column south of the Magaliesberg* on 29 May: setting the veld alight by a trail of gunpowder his men charged through the smoke, firing from the saddle or as they ran leading their horses, and exacted 166 casualties before a counter-attack drove them off. After this highly successful exploitation of the new technique of firing from the saddle, Kemp eluded concerted measures to round him up all through June.

Reaching the north-west O.F.S. meanwhile, De la Rey heard that a great drive was turning the south-west into a wilderness. Seven columns drove north towards the line of S.A. posts between Bloem-

* At Vlakfontein.

433

fontein and Kimberley, with 'stop' columns on either side; but for all
its precise organization the drive produced few fighting Boers among
its captures.

Safely joining Steyn and De Wet in the north-east O.F.S. De la Rey
was quickly made aware of a massive drive in this area too, between the
Central railway and Natal. He sat at breakfast with the two O.F.S.
leaders and their bodyguard* on a farm near Reitz—it was the morning
of 6 June—when a burgher galloped up with news that a small advanced detachment of British had captured a convoy of Boer women
near a Native kraal five miles away.†

The bodyguard immediately rode to the rescue. Thinking they were
the reinforcements which had been sent for, one of the British detachment, a lieutenant of the Gordon Highlanders, went forward to greet
them. They promptly stripped him of everything except his shirt. Thus
attired he ran six miles to encounter the actual reinforcements and
guide them to the huts of the Native kraal where an intense four-hour
fight had meanwhile been raging. The Boers withdrew with but little
of their lost convoy salvaged. The affair created typical examples of
atrocity stories. The German Press reported, with illustrative sketches,
that the British made the Boer women and children stand in front of
them and fired from under their arms, infuriating the Boers who ran
forward and clubbed the British. The British Press claimed that not
only was this not true but that the Boers advanced in British khaki
uniforms, shot men who surrendered and encouraged their womenfolk
to do the same. But to return to undisputed facts: while the British
drive across the O.F.S. between the Natal border and Central railway
continued, the Boer leaders slipped between the columns in their
northward ride to the meeting.

Kitchener was intent on preventing it. Besides launching a fresh
sweep in the eastern Transvaal with no less than eleven columns between the Natal and Delagoa Bay railways, he had a special section of
his Intelligence devoted to tailing the Boer Government—derisively
termed the Cape-cart Government as it led a nightmare existence dodging pursuit east of Ermelo. Botha made its survival his special business.
His own accurate Intelligence enabled it time and again to elude cer-

* Also General Piet Fourie who had been relieved of his command because of com-
promising correspondence with the British.

† At Graspan.

tain-seeming capture—sometimes only by minutes and at the loss of its heavy baggage. Thus distracted, he left the task of harassing the British to Ben Viljoen and his lieutenant Muller.

Accordingly on 25 May Viljoen pounced on a convoy carrying sick, prisoners and Boer families north of Standerton;* helped by an improvised squad of cooks and invalids the escort held him off in a running fight typical of many involving British convoys at that time. Muller fared better. On the night of 12 June he took advantage of careless picketing to rout 350 Victorians (Australians) on the Middelburg–Ermelo road† and looted their camp. After this 'mishap' as the newspapers described it, he made off, shedding his prisoners.

The affair had a sequel. These Victorians, like most colonial irregulars at this stage of the war, were not up to the standard of the earlier contingents. Besides, they were apt to have an I'm-as-good-as-you-are attitude in reaction to what they regarded as stiff-necked superiority on the part of the home-born Englishman. The result had been friction with the commander of the column to which they had been attached, a General Beatson, who tried to turn their easy-going scorn of drill and smartness into the rigid discipline of 'a crack cavalry regiment'. They detested and mistrusted him. As soon as he heard of the disaster to the men attacked by Muller he made for the scene with his whole column. Then he mustered the Australians and told them they were 'a lot of wasters, and white-livered curs' and—seeing an Australian officer jotting the speech down—'You can add "dogs" too,' throwing in the further observation that all Australians were alike. An oration of this kind would have rolled off the backs of old regulars; the Australians mutinied and refused to march under him. He had three of the leaders arrested. They were court-martialled and sentenced to death. When Lord Kitchener heard, he commuted the sentence to three years' imprisonment, and when the Australian Government made representations to the British Government a complete pardon was granted. The affair was the subject of a debate in the Australian Parliament very embarrassing to the British, against whom much feeling was aroused. Ironically, the colonial volunteers, of whom the Australians were foremost, were popular heroes in England, and the Antipodes were never higher in the country's affection.

* At Mooifontein.
† At Wilmansrust.

The news of Muller's success against the Victorians reached the Transvaal Government as they doubled back west of Ermelo to meet De la Rey and the O.F.S. leaders who had now reached the border. As so often before, Boer morale reacted sharply to even the smallest sign of fortune's favour. With Kemp's success in the western Transvaal and Viljoen's less successful but vigorous onslaught on the convoy, it was the third action in a fortnight which, seeming so paltry in the scale of things, brought about a change of Boer feeling destined to add vastly to the long catalogue of loss by both sides, besides materially increasing Britain's national debt. For when the leaders met together at the farm Waterval near the railway line at Standerton on 20 June there was no talk of surrender. Besides, Kruger's reply had arrived and it amounted to an exhortation to fight on.

This they resolved to do. That they should be able to meet at all, when tens of thousands of troops were within easy distance by horse or train, had an eloquent hopefulness of its own. They could survive indefinitely; and survive, which was to say to fight, they would. Winter rendered operations on any scale in the Transvaal or O.F.S. impossible, but the Cape's lack of devastation and the continued activity of Kritzinger and his comrades made it an obvious target. The leaders decided that this time the Transvaalers would invade—western Transvaalers, under young Jan Smuts. Strengthened in their resolution they then set off on the hazardous business of getting back to their respective areas.

Again their experiences also provide a résumé of British activity.

Viljoen, returning to the north-east Transvaal, felt the effects of the new blockhouse system when he made a night attack on two blockhouses on the Delagoa Bay railway with a view to crossing between: he was badly mauled not only by the small garrisons but by an armoured train that played its searchlight on him and belched shrapnel and machine-gun bullets through the night. The Transvaal Government continued to be harried ceaselessly in the vicinity of Ermelo for two months, until it found a temporary haven on the border of Swaziland at the end of August.

Their brother Free Staters returned across the Vaal. At the time, the north-east O.F.S. was the object of yet another British drive, which had just overrun the town of Reitz. From a captured document in the town the British were reminded of the enemy's policy of reoccupying

436

a town as soon as they had left it. They marched away, apparently as usual, but that night—10 July—Broadwood of Sannah's Post fame rode back with 400 men. A prize beyond their wildest expectations awaited the end of their cold and frosty ride. All unsuspecting, Steyn was asleep in the town, together with members of his Executive Council and government officials, though De Wet chanced to be at a farm some distance away. In the middle of the night the British troopers burst into the town, capturing the whole government staff* and much of the President's bodyguard, including its doughty commander. A sergeant of the 7th Dragoon Guards saw a figure galloping down the street— night-capped and coatless, with only the halter for a bridle—and raced after him firing as he went, but the fresh Boer pony outdistanced his tired charger. So escaped President Steyn himself, awakened by his faithful Native cook. In his tent he left all his papers and his treasury of £11,500 in notes. Undaunted, he soon formed another staff and Executive, and resumed his odyssey. Characteristic of public discontent in England, the Jingo Press, which assailed the Government no less heatedly for its alleged tenderness towards the Boers than the Opposition complained about its alleged severity, blamed Steyn's escape on the freezing of the breech-action in the sergeant's carbine owing to the inferior oil supplied by the Government!

De la Rey and Smuts returned without incident to the western Transvaal, where they set about organizing the expedition to invade the Cape. It consisted of only 350 men, but hand-picked and well equipped. On 15 July they set out in groups to rendezvous beyond the Vaal. Kitchener got wind of the scheme and tried to nip it in the bud by trapping Smuts near the Klerksdorp railway. He got away and reached the rest of his force beyond the Vaal—only to discover himself in the midst of armies that seemed to be springing up on every hand. Chance had brought him into the thick of the greatest drive Kitchener had so far launched.

By a series of far-flung troop movements, 15,000 men were assembled in the north-west O.F.S. For a fortnight at the beginning of August some columns, starting at the Vaal, drove southwards towards the S.A.C. line of fortified posts between Bloemfontein and Kimberley, while simultaneously other columns advanced from the blockhouse-

* Including Generals A. P. Cronje and J. B. Wessels (first commander of the Boers at the siege of Kimberley).

lined Central and Western railways on either side. But the fighting Boers slipped between the advancing columns by night, and Kitchener's mechanical precision was spent on turning the countryside into a wilderness. Smuts himself darted among the British in a desperate ride that involved four running fights before he arrived near the Orange in the south-east O.F.S. on 27 August, six weeks since starting out and minus nearly a third of his expedition.

It was hardly a propitious start. Besides, in common with the other Boer leaders he now faced a drastic risk if he persisted. For on 7 August Kitchener issued a proclamation far more threatening than any which had preceded it.

Since the failure of the Middelburg Conference his attitude towards the Boers had become increasingly severe. He presented the picture of a man emotionally immature and violently frustrated by the stubbornness of the enemy. It will not do to make too much of this, since he was also a man carrying the burden of a huge campaign which kept him at work every day from 6 a.m. to late at night with scarcely any recreation and no leave. His words are hence more petulant (e.g. he admired Louis Botha yet once gave him 'the mind of an unscrupulous pettifogging attorney') and more blood-curdling than his deeds. Among his more hysterical outbursts was the letter to the Secretary for War partly quoted on page 392 and in which he also said: 'We have now got more than half the Boer population either as prisoners of war, or in our refugee camps. I would advise that they should not be allowed to return. I think we should start a scheme for settling them elsewhere, and S.A. will then be safe, and there will be room for the British to colonize.' Failing this he suggested whipping up hatred between surrendered Boers and those still fighting, so that they would in future hate each other more than the British, who would the more easily rule a divided nation. He also asked for authority to shoot all rebels out of hand and fulminated against the Cape Government's reluctance to declare martial law (he eventually got his way despite Chamberlain's grumble that he would do better to get on with catching Botha and De Wet). The proclamation of 7 August therefore reflected a shift in policy to the greater severity Kitchener had been urging, but it came about in fact at the request of the Natal Prime Minister (an Irish ex-officer named Hine) and with the approval of the British Government. The proclamation was to the effect that all Boers who did not surrender by 15 September would be punished—the burghers by a charge on their property to pay the cost of their families' keep in the British camps, and the leaders by *perpetual banishment* from South Africa.

Some of the Boer leaders sent defiant replies, others an equally defiant silence. For the moment they did not back defiance with action but lay low in readiness for spring. Smuts was an exception. On his arrival near the Orange on 27 July Kritzinger joined him. He was able to report fully on the situation in the Cape.

It will be recalled that Douglas Haig had been sent down to deal with the bands of invaders and rebels. Operating across a hundred miles of country southward from Naauwpoort and fifty miles on each side— 10,000 square miles of mostly mountainous country—they were constantly helped by farmers prepared to ride fifty miles to warn them of Haig's columns. In June Kitchener had therefore appointed French in military command of the entire Cape, giving him nearly 6,000 men and putting in hand a massive extension of the blockhouse system along much of the Cape railways; blockhouses were also a sudden new feature in the middle of many a dusty dorp. After a series of desultory skirmishes in which honours were divided, French launched full-scale drives with the co-operation of the blockhouse garrisons and armoured trains. The results disappointed. From the boulder-strewn Desolation Valley* inhabited only by baboons, Scheepers rode hundreds of miles south-west to within striking distance of Cape Town itself, reaching Willowmore where the town guard beat him off. He went on northwards to a village where he set light to loyalist houses, looted the stores, and beat up the manager of the Standard Bank who refused to hand over government funds. Other commandos were dispersed in less dangerous directions but they soon filtered back, and one of the rebel commanders, Lotter, was caught with most of his commando, with consequences that added to the brimming cup of bitterness both in S.A. and England.

Two of Lotter's lieutenants were executed and many rank and file sentenced to penal servitude. Lotter himself was put on trial. His claim to O.F.S. citizenship conferred on him since the war began was not accepted. He was found guilty of murdering two half-caste scouts, treason, lashing British subjects and wrecking trains. He was taken to Graaff Reinet where the leading residents, Dutch and British, were

* Near Graaff Reinet.

ordered to appear while the death sentence was read out. Next day he was executed on a kopje outside the town. Counting this and other occasions, the public was forced to attend about half a dozen executions, as a warning that contrary to general belief the British were in earnest; the practice was then stopped.

Kritzinger himself, as the result of French's drive, crossed the Orange and so joined Smuts for the new invasion. Kitchener at once tried to surround Smuts, but the Orange was no longer flooded and he got over easily enough on 3 September. His arrival reinvigorated men harassed by French's drives, and soon thousands more troops were pouring in to reinforce French, the position at the close of winter being even worse than it had been at the beginning. The prevailing panic in the Cape was expressed by an observer at the time:

> The bandit forces of Boer and Colonial rebels are scouring the country from every direction, robbing, looting and house-burning—brutally assaulting defenceless Colonists, and plying the sjambok whenever their demands are not immediately complied with. . . . It is little wonder that the inhabitants of the numerous dorps and villages scattered over the present area of operations are bitterly complaining of the incapacity of the military. . . . From the Transkeian border on the east to the confines of the Kalahari on the north-west, the country is overrun by small bands of rebels who are absolutely reckless of their lives and equally indifferent to the ordinary requirements of civilized warfare. [46]

For the rest of the country the remainder of winter was largely a period of stagnation, but significant developments were taking shape.

In the O.F.S., while drives and patrols continued across the desolate plains, a lightning raid on Hertzog's laager in the south-west on 25 August indicated new methods. Kitchener ordered every column to organize a group of picked men, lightly equipped, who could strike quickly and far. In addition, he began to form special mobile columns of such men to operate in individual 'raids' as opposed to co-operation in 'drives'. Escaping his iron direction in every detail they were able to assert a dash, skill and hardihood which compared with that of their opponents. Their exploits created a new series of household names in England. Such men were Rimington, Benson, Garratt, Sir John

Dartnell, Damant. Thus in the O.F.S. Major M. F. Rimington tire-lessly raided the Lindley–Heilbron area in pursuit of De Wet and Steyn. A cavalryman, aged forty-three, long in face, forehead and nose but with a cheerful twirling moustache, he was one of the special officers sent out before the war when he organized a corp of scouts in Natal.

In the Transvaal, a significant development was the extension of the blockhouse system away from the railways. Milner wanted a protective zone around Johannesburg and Pretoria as had already been created around Bloemfontein, to facilitate the resumption of civil life. Kitchener therefore built a line of blockhouses cross-country forty miles to the west. It started on the Magaliesberg, went south across the Vaal and ended on the Central railway north of Kroonstad, a distance of 150 miles. The Boers failed to appreciate the implications—how such a system could assail their indispensable ally, space—so they did not interfere with this work, nor with the establishment of a similar line twenty miles east of Johannesburg and Pretoria, in this instance not blockhouses but fortified posts manned by the Constabulary. By this means an enclave of peace was formed, though it was not without eruptions from within.

Late in August over fifty arrests were made in Pretoria and Johan-nesburg of alleged members of the Boer spy system, most being Boers who had given their parole, taken the oath of neutrality or even been employed in offices under the British. A number of trials followed. The most celebrated was that of Broeksma, an ex-public prosecutor in Kruger's Government who was arraigned in Johannesburg on 12 Sep-tember for breaking his oath of neutrality, and high treason. Cor-respondence found in his house included letters to Europe containing anti-British propaganda and to Boer generals in the field with lists of burghers serving the British, whom Broeksma urged should be executed and even buried alive. Of those tried he was the only one shot. A fund was started in Holland for his wife and children; for this purpose a post-card was circulated bearing a photograph of him and his family with the inscription: 'Cornelius Broeksma, hero and martyr in pity's cause. Shot by the English on 30th September, 1901, because he refused to be silent about the cruel suffering in the women's camps.'

Outside the protected zone the Boers lay low, dispersing at the approach of columns. But British commanders were slowly learning. In the western Transvaal, a column near Klerksdorp sent its convoy in one direction as a feint while itself riding in another, and so snapped up a Boer convoy at the end of August. Against this, when Kitchener launched a new drive early the following month in the hope of catching Kemp, De la Rey's lieutenant not only escaped but inflicted forty casualties on Methuen by a surprise attack in thick bush along a river valley* near Zeerust. In the far north Beyers continued at large but was constantly harried in country cleared as far as Louis Trichard. In the north-east, Viljoen returned from the council of war to find his hunting grounds west of Lydenburg sorely bespoiled and he too was constantly harassed, with the result that he crossed the Olifant's to re-organize. He left behind Muller with a small force about forty miles north of Middelburg: in two successive fights he also was forced across the Olifant's, though during later operations to round him up he ambushed the 19th Hussars before making good his escape. At the same time a man called Jack Hinton acquired a reputation for skilful train-wrecking along the Delagoa Bay railway, arousing the extreme anti-Boer Press to frenzy: 'It is to be hoped that the time will soon come when Hinton, who adds to his guilt the crime of treason, will expiate his sin upon a gallows. . . . The railway men of the military railways have vowed that when they catch him he shall be flung into the firebox of the nearest engine.' It was, however, to the south-east Transvaal that most interest attached in the last weeks of winter.

Here, for want of troops deployed in the drives elsewhere, no great drives took place; indeed Blood was packed off to India, glad to be released from Kitchener's masterful sway. But one of the new raiding columns achieved much success between the Delagoa Bay railway and Carolina. It was commanded by Colonel G. E. Benson, who has appeared earlier in this story for his skilful guiding of Wauchope before the Battle of Magersfontein. Now aged forty, with a square good-humoured face, short nose and bushy moustache, his large lethargic eyes gave little hint of his dynamic energy. The technique he was perfecting was new; called the night raid, it was actually a night ride followed by a dawn attack on an enemy laager. While a Boer was in the saddle he felt himself a match for any soldier, but surprised in his laager at the moment of waking he was very vulnerable. By riding sometimes thirty or forty miles through the darkness, Benson made half a dozen highly successful dawn raids during August and early

* Marico.

442

September—ironical in the light of Wolseley's furious disapproval of training in night raids at Aldershot before the war because it tired the horses.[19] In proving himself as daring and brilliant a guerilla as the Boers, Benson was helped by the Uitlander Woolls-Sampson who was one of the two Reform leaders who had been in prison for years through refusing Kruger's amnesty after being sentenced as a result of the Jameson Raid. He took charge of Benson's Intelligence, knowing Boer, Native and the terrain intimately.

But the district stalked by Benson was only part of a great region, and in a distant part Botha was left unmolested. Quietly he prepared to strike a major blow as soon as spring gave life to the grass for his ponies.

So 15 September came and went with Kitchener's threat of perpetual banishment ineffectual and with the Boer leaders everywhere inviolate. The British were tougher and smarter now, raw troops seasoned by a winter's campaigning. But though the Boers had lost 9,000 men these past few months, it remained to be seen whether this and the winter had materially damaged their real fighting strength or purpose.

In England the winter—summer there—had swept the country with depression over the course of the war. Kitchener's method of attrition, expressed in the weekly 'bag' of captures and confiscations reported to the War Office, and the evolving blockhouse system made no appeal to popular imagination which was far more affected by the commandos' lightning blows. The war was costing £1½ m. per week. Casualties increased daily, and national pride found no pleasure in the spectacle of trouserless soldiers cast upon the veld by the Boers, who had no means of keeping prisoners. The concentration camps and farm devastation troubled all classes of opinion. The result was a bitterness never known before. The squabble within the Opposition was almost rivalled by that within the Government camp.

The ravings of the Jingo Press against the Government have been touched on. A fruitful cause for anger was the resettlement of Johannesburg for which, ran the complaint, refugee Uitlanders were being excluded in favour of surrendered Boers. The Government was accused of threatening Edgar Wallace of the *Daily Mail* with punishment for publishing anti-Boer atrocity stories, which continued to keep pace with anti-British atrocity stories published mainly abroad but not lacking in England either. It is not proposed in this book to keep up with the spate of such stories, but the derailment of a train by Boers north of Pretoria at this period may be mentioned as an example of how an atrocity story—'the guard was ordered to alight, when these fiends . . . blew off his head with a Mauser'—could also be used for a tilt at the Government: 'all this blood was sacrificed to pander to British Pro-Boers', since the Government had overruled the conveyance of hostages on trains 'in response to the factious outcry raised by the friends of the enemy in England'.

Those 'friends of the enemy' were fighting the 'war to the knife and fork' to new heights of acrimony. The splits in the Liberal party were widened by the radical wing's association with the Irish Party. All through the Parliamentary session that summer the Irish filibustered and obstructed to an extent unknown since the Home Rule convulsion. They outdid Lloyd George and the other radicals, making even 'pro-Boers' blanch as they denounced the British Army, called on God to strengthen the Boers, and prayed that S.A. would one day take vengeance by separating from the Empire. Night after night such outbursts raised political furies to a new pitch, and often kept the House up until 3 a.m. The Government arranged a great counter-demonstration of solidarity at Blenheim on 10 August, but throughout the country there was no solidarity. The Unionist-Conservative Coalition was reeling, the Liberal Party had reached its 'last hour of humiliation' in the words of one of its own members, and the nation bickered and fumed. If a meeting in the Queen's Hall called for cheers for De Wet, another at the Guildhall as passionately inveighed against criticism of the war. So autumn descended with its chilly mists upon the scene; but in S.A. it was spring.

CHAPTER XXVII

Spring 1901

THE rains came in the second week of September, and the annual miracle that turns the dry stubble of the South African veld into grazing lands sent a similar throb of vitality through the ranks of the Boers. Released from the stinging thongs of winter they rose up and marched. Their grand plan eight months before of a simultaneous descent upon the Cape and Natal had not been forgotten. Smuts was already riding to the Cape; on 7 September Botha set out for Natal.

He started with a thousand tough fighters who had quietly been concentrating near Ermelo; others were to join him en route. To keep the British distracted he left men behind on the highveld under the overall command of Ben Viljoen. The appointment was surprising because Viljoen had quarrelled with Muller, incurred Botha's displeasure for corresponding with the British, and was losing influence among his burghers. But Botha was ever an indulgent man, though not long before he had suspended one of his principal lieutenants for burning Bremersdorp, the capital of Swaziland, contrary to his instructions to avoid destruction. Prior to this, the lieutenant concerned had stirred up the Swazis and supported them in attacking a post at Bremersdorp held by a British force who had been untactful in their dealings with the Swazis.

It was ironical that Natal, whose Government had urged the minatory proclamation of 7 August on Kitchener, should be Botha's target. Rumours of the projected invasion had long been current, and as Botha marched five columns were sent to overtake or intercept him. But in the mental climate created by Kitchener's machine-like drives and the slow process of attrition, they moved at the pace of their ox-wagons; and being largely ignorant of Botha's whereabouts they were soon out of the hunt.

The rain fell with a vengeance, sapping the strength of Botha's horses as he advanced south-east towards Piet Retief and then south. He reached the neighbourhood of Vryheid on 17 September, his force risen to 2,000, including a commando waiting ahead of him to lead an attack on his first objective in Natal—Dundee.

Though he passed close to British garrisons in the towns, they continued to be thoroughly uncertain of his route or destination. Riding out from Dundee to cover the return of an empty convoy from Vryheid, a small column of M.I. under Captain H. De la P. Gough of the Lancers chanced upon the Boer advance commando grazing their horses near the mouth of a gorge.* It was not a chance to be missed by a young and impetuous cavalryman. He unleashed nearly 300 men in a furious mile-long gallop—the first charge the British had made with rifle blazing from the saddle.

They raced down on the enemy and success appeared certain, when from the gorge on their left thundered 500 Boer horsemen who crossed their front, wheeled, and falling upon the opposite flank dismounted to rush forward and roll up the M.I.'s entire line. In ten minutes the Boers killed, wounded or captured 285 M.I. and seized their two guns. Gough's failure to scout the situation had been turned into disaster by the unlucky fact that Botha's main force had been about to join the advance commando.

The change that had come over the struggle is perfectly brought out by the difference between this clash of galloping horsemen and the Battle of Talana (Dundee) fought by infantrymen and entrenched Boers only a few miles away almost exactly two years before. British complacency then was supplanted now by profound alarm at the vision of a return to those unhappy days when Penn-Symons lay dying and Yule trudged desperately to Ladysmith, itself to be besieged and cut off from help by the battles on the Tugela. Reinforcements were rushed in from all over the Transvaal and O.F.S.: 16,000 troops were gathered, plus the Natal garrison and volunteers, and the Zulu impis were called out to guard their frontier. Yet if tactics and the mood had changed, British chronic unpreparedness in a new situation had not. The railway was choked and transport so slow that columns sometimes had weeks to wait for supplies, while local Intelligence was almost useless. On the other hand, these were not the Boers who rode singing

* Blood River Poort.

and expectant into the promised land of Natal in 1899. Winter on the ravaged veld had weakened their ponies now struggling through mud and rain; and the river before Dundee was impassable.

Turning along the Zulu frontier, sometimes within it and sometimes without, Botha reached the extreme south-east of the Transvaal aware that the swollen Tugela stood across his path once he cut through Zululand; that he had only 2,000 men to fend for themselves in a hostile country; that his return route might soon be imperilled. For the moment he temporized by deciding to attack two fortified posts on the frontier, at Prospect and Mount Itala, about ten miles apart. On the evening of 25 September he sent his brother, Christian, with 1,400 men against the latter, and his brother-in-law Cherry Emmett with 400 men against the former.

Itala was manned by 300 M.I. under a young major of the Royal Dublin Fusiliers, A. J. Chapman. Established only a month, the post was in a weak position on a ridge at the foot of the mountain and protected merely by a circle of trenches. Chapman, forewarned by his Zulu scouts of the intended assault, sent eighty men on to the mountain peak to surprise the Boers. But when Christian Botha's force arrived at midnight it was in too great strength and overcame them, a lieutenant of the South Lancashires dying with a cry of 'No surrender!' At 2 a.m. the camp itself was attacked. A violent struggle raged for two hours in bright moonlight, the Boers sometimes coming right up to the trenches before the stubborn British fire blew them back. At dawn Christian Botha renewed the attack. For thirteen hours men of Lancashire, Middlesex, Dorset and Ireland—so mixed had regiments become in the M.I. and other columns—held at bay a vastly superior body of eastern Transvaalers, themselves unsurpassed in courage. Then in the evening Chapman, wounded but unbowed, called together his Zulu scouts. His ammunition was almost spent; he had lost over a quarter of his men and the remainder were utterly exhausted: he told the scouts to go before the Boers killed them all. But the Zulus chose to share their masters' fate.

In the result there was no annihilation. The Boers themselves had endured enough. A hundred of their best fighters were wounded or dead and much precious ammunition had already been expended. They therefore quietly withdrew so that when Chapman did likewise at midnight, leaving an unarmed party to tend the wounded, he was unmolested.

The other target singled out by Botha, Fort Prospect, was a proper redoubt with walls impervious to rifle-fire. The Boer force approached through thick mist, pierced the barbed-wire entanglement, and twenty yards from the advance trenches made a demand for surrender. A miner in the Durham Militia shouted back: 'Surrender be damned! I'm a pitman at home and I've been in deeper holes than this before.' Thereupon the defenders, assisted by a machine-gun and a party of barefoot Zulu police, drove off the Boers with forty casualties to their own nine.

These two failures clinched Louis Botha's half-formed resolution to turn back. But he had come into a cul-de-sac: the open end, a hundred miles away and only thirty miles wide, was being sealed by the British. In addition they were clustering about him.

At first they moved uncertainly—and wretchedly, on half-rations and in cold wet weather—until after a week they marked him down in front of the mountains east of Vryheid. He was trapped. Only two passes provided a passage out of the cul-de-sac. One was already blocked by troops, and three brigades were within ten to forty-five miles of him. The open pass gave on to a gorge through the mountains twenty miles long between huge crags. Astride the road at the end of the gorge waited a column of 3,400 men ready to make a killing the moment news came that Botha's convoy was on the move through the gorge.

What they had not anticipated was that the Boers would simply abandon their wagons, enabling them suddenly to dash through the gorge by night at a speed which alerted the waiting column too late. The troops moved into the end of the gorge only to be held up by a strongly placed rearguard while Botha slipped out over bridle-paths in a district he knew intimately—his own farm lay near by, turned by the British into a charred ruin—and got clean away.

Though his failure to invade Natal for a second time caused profound relief, his escape was an adverse event of greater importance. With his spectacular victory over Gough's M.I. it was an added spur to the Boers' spring revival. Further, the British found that the task of finding and destroying his abandoned convoy, and of clearing the country round about, meant weeks of toil in swamp, mountain, cave and forest, prolonging the dislocation of Kitchener's troop arrangements. This was Botha's most important achievement. The areas from which troops had been drawn off to stop his threatened invasion were left with isolated columns which offered immediate prey for the guerillas.

*   *   *   *

Botha himself, rejoining his Government in hiding between Piet Retief and Ermelo on 11 October, soon grasped the opportunity. He learnt that in his absence Viljoen had done little, the British much. But 'British' meant only the column led by Colonel Benson, who had continued his brilliant night raids southwards of Carolina with un-diminished success, becoming to the Boers a scourge they could only avoid by never laagering two nights in succession at the same place and always saddling-up by 3 a.m. They longed to destroy him. There were no other troops in the region. For a while Rimington's and another column came up from the O.F.S.—and one dawn, following their capture of a dispatch disclosing Botha's whereabouts, they so nearly cornered him that he barely escaped with his son and a few followers, leaving behind his hat and a bag of correspondence. But on the departure of these two columns there was solely Benson. The commandos gathered around him and waited their moment.

About the middle of October he had refitted on the Natal railway and then ranged abroad with 800 horsemen while 600 infantrymen guarded his convoy of 350 vehicles. By the month-end, when he was near Bethal, supplies were running low and at 4.30 a.m. on 30 October the whole column struck across the shallow undulations of the highveld in the direction of Balmoral on the Delagoa Bay railway. From that moment, as they pushed along a muddy road against rain and wind, they were harried by the enemy. At 1 p.m. the convoy was out-spanned and camp formed; but shortly before, the column having become strung out for two miles by the exigencies of the march, the rearguard realized that in the mist the clustering enemy had increased. In fact, Louis Botha was on the scene with formidable reinforcements, having ridden at one stretch the last thirty miles of a seventy-mile journey. Such was his speed, secrecy and timing that Woolls-Samp-son's spies failed to report him, and until Colonel Benson himself joined the rearguard towards two o'clock the British were unaware of the extent of their danger.

The colonel at once ordered the rearguard to retreat to rising ground half-way to the camp. The rise was called Gun Hill, two guns being placed there. With groups of men scattered on either flank it formed part of a wide but discontinuous defence arc between camp and enemy.

Benson and his rearguard were falling back on Gun Hill when Botha's men, over 800 strong in this quarter of the field, galloped out of the mists. Skilfully using inequalities in the ground they charged from several directions, swallowing up detachments of the Buffs, Scottish Rifles and M.I. as they converged for the most part on the dead ground below Gun Hill. Throwing themselves off their spent ponies they clambered forward, firing and shouting in the terror and exultation of battle. Thirty yards from them, across open veld dotted with ant-hills, was Benson with only 178 men, beset from his front and both sides.

The brief and murderous fight that followed was to take its name from a nearby farm, Bakenlaagte. In minutes the gun-crews were wiped out; likewise the drivers and limber teams who came forward to the rescue. As officer after officer fell about him Benson, himself wounded in the knee and refusing to be carried away, crawled among the ant-hills encouraging his men. One of his young staff officers galloped from the camp to be with him as an act of devotion, threw his reins to a trooper—who was killed instantly with the horse—and walked erect and unarmed towards his chief, to fall mortally wounded a few paces from him. A quartermaster-sergeant, twenty-one years with the Scottish Borderers, came out of the camp to help bring up ammunition, then seized a dead man's rifle and picked off Boer after Boer until he fell riddled with three bullets. All around, the scattered detachments were either hotly engaged or decimated in attempting to relieve Benson. He was wounded a second time less than twenty minutes since action had been joined, but though those minutes left few with him who could still fight he had no idea of surrendering. A trooper volunteered to take a message to the camp forbidding the ambulances to come out lest the Boers used the mules to remove the guns: as he rose a bullet struck him in the foot and ricocheted to wound Benson fatally. A few minutes later the Boers stormed forward four or five deep and overran the position. They turned the guns on the camp but had already lost a hundred brave men and were content with their revenge. Of the 178 men with Benson, 161 were dead or wounded; and he lay dying.

At nightfall the Boers removed the guns, the British their wounded. Benson, brought into camp at 9 p.m., refused help from the doctors until they were less busy. He conferred command on Woolls-Sampson, gave him instructions for the defence of the camp, and died early next morning, saying to the officer who bent over him to catch the words: 'We shall do no more night marching; it is all day now. Good-bye. God bless you.' Altogether the day had cost the British 358 casualties, crippling the column to an extent that paralysed it until relief arrived.

The wrongness and tragic absurdity of war were never clearer than when courage, displayed upon the rack of Bakenlaagte, shone with such splendour but in a cause no loftier than a racial quarrel of two houses. In their hearts both sides were utterly sick of the business, but the bond had still not been fully paid: the struggle ground on. Sixty-four British columns endlessly carried on the process of attrition all over S.A., garrisons stood guard along uncounted miles of railway track, towns or fortified line, and the Boers endlessly hovered to strike.

In the western Transvaal, De la Rey seized the opportunity offered by the withdrawal of troops even before the return from Natal of Botha who had occasioned it. The dislocation had left a column in some isolation and depleted strength near Rustenburg. It had been helping comb the Magaliesberg in whose caves and ravines scattered families of women and children had found refuge. The commander was Colonel Kekewich, the defender of Kimberley, whose duties in the field during the eighteen months since the siege had returned him to obscurity until he emerged now to grapple with the man who had so prolonged the relief.

De la Rey's favourite region west and south-west of the Magaliesberg had been likened to the haunted forests of fairyland because in that wild country of bush, hill and sunken river, the Boers could concentrate in sudden strength as if by magic and by the same process vanish. On the afternoon of 29 September Kekewich's column, about 1,000 strong, pitched camp* on the Rustenburg-Zeerust road about ten miles from the Magaliesberg. He had no inkling of any Boers in the vicinity; and a nearby winding river, sometimes fifty feet below the level of the broken ground above, seemed to give sure protection from surprise on two sides. But the Boers had been stalking him for a week, and having whistled up a thousand men under Kemp and other

* On the farm Moedwil by the Selons River.

451

formidable lieutenants, De la Rey that night sent the greater part of his force into the river-bed to lie concealed among the rocks and bush of the bank nearer the British camp.

The war's three most famous sieges, Ladysmith, Mafeking and Kimberley, had also made famous the respective siege commanders— White, Baden-Powell and Kekewich. These men acquired grossly inflated reputations by reason of the Boers' inadequacy as siege fighters. White had gone off to be Governor-General of Gibraltar; but Baden-Powell and Kekewich, remaining in the field after the sieges, were exposed to a more searching test. Baden-Powell had failed to distinguish himself in the western Transvaal after the dispersal of the commandos in the era following the battle of Diamond Hill, culminating in his culpable failure to exercise elementary boy-scout care to help Colonel Hore on the Elands. But for his recall to form the S.A. Constabulary he might have learnt better in the hard school of guerilla warfare. Kekewich had. He was cool-headed and vigilant and he imposed these qualities on his men.

A pre-dawn patrol discovered the Boers in the river at 4.45 a.m., precipitating the assault and plunging the camp into a sudden mad confusion of flying bullets and stampeding horses. But the British— Derbys, Scottish Horse, Yeomanry—declined to panic. For an hour and a half both sides fought hard. A private called Bees won the V.C. for fetching water from the river to cool the Maxim in defiance of the intense fire that swept the camp and caused severe losses—Kekewich twice hit, outlying pickets annihilated, gun-crews mown down with hundreds of horses and mules. Yet though the commandant who had been responsible for stalking Kekewich for the past week gallantly entered the camp with a few scouts to meet death at the bayonet point, the Boers failed to envelop the camp. Then a major of the Derbys led forward a scratch party of cooks and orderlies, beginning a movement on the river beyond the Boer flank; and at this threat to their whole line the Boers steadily withdrew.

Honours were even. De la Rey had failed to sack the camp or get ammunition he much needed, and his casualties totalled sixty. On the other hand, his stealthy concentration and skilful attack had killed or wounded over 200 of Kekewich's column, besides three times that number of animals, effectively crippling him for the time being.

A fortnight later when Kekewich had recovered from his wounds he and Methuen co-operated in trying to pin down De la Rey. He was about but invisible and the columns parted empty-handed. On 24 October part of Methuen's force, 1,000 strong, was returning to Zeerust along a bad road. From the wooded heights which fringed it* 500 men of De la Rey's commandos under Kemp and others charged down on the rearguard, cutting it to pieces before removing twelve wagons with the supplies and ammunition denied them in the attack on Kekewich.

*   *   *   *

While the main engagements of the spring were fought in the eastern and western Transvaal, the daily toll of death and destruction was everywhere increased by the scouring columns and sudden clashes between forces of varying strength. Thus, in the O.F.S. 200 men clearing a farm near Sannah's Post outside Bloemfontein on 19 September were surprised by a commando and overwhelmed after a feeble resistance. The very next day, far to the south where Kritzinger was preparing to follow Smuts across the Orange into the Cape, he charged down a hundred Lovat's Scouts asleep in their camp, killing or wounding half of them as they struggled out of their blankets. Thorneycroft, of Spion Kop fame, led his mounted troop in hot pursuit and scorched Kritzinger but did not catch him. Except once to use the new charging tactics on a raiding column, De Wet himself kept notably quiet, prompting wishful rumours that he was mad, wounded or dead.

And in the Cape, as spring translated Smuts's threatened invasion into action, every effort to catch him failed. He had crossed the Orange east of Aliwal North on 3 September. A fortnight later he was west of Queenstown. As successive detachments had not overtaken him, Douglas Haig sent the 17th Lancers along a river barring his progress west. But tipped off by a farmer and cloaked in the misty weather, he overwhelmed one of their squadrons which had just off-saddled for its midday meal among the ravines and gorges. He helped himself to its rifles, ammunition, remounts and stores; then he crossed the breadth of the Midlands before swinging south in order to link up with Scheepers. Since French's drives had driven him marauding a hundred miles north-east of Cape Town this bold young guerilla had for ten weeks been

* At Kleinfontein.

453

roaming the districts on the Indian Ocean, bringing upon them the rigours of martial law. But just before he could join Smuts the columns who hunted him found him ill on a farm, unable to move because of appendicitis. He was charged before a military court with seven murders of loyalists or Natives, arson, train-wrecking, ill-treatment of wounded and prisoners, and other offences. He denied responsibility, but two of his own men gave evidence against him. He was publicly shot, to the intense indignation and bitterness of the Boers.

His commando meanwhile reached Smuts and helped him in a succession of skirmishes that took him, after a journey of over a thousand miles, into districts little more than fifty miles north of Cape Town by the end of October. From this region as far north as the environs of Kimberley there were constant reports of rebel activity—the murder and flogging of Natives, rough-handling of loyalists, damage to fences which let loose ostriches (often necessitating their destruction by soldiers whom they attacked), looting and arson. Here, as elsewhere in the Cape where bands of rebels were active, their survival was made easier by the scarcely concealed alacrity with which local militia often yielded up supplies and horses.

*　　*　　*　　*

It seemed, as the third year of the war began, a depressing picture. Huge areas of the country lay silent and fruitless like the desert, and still not a fold of the veld but defied the British. Even in the protected zone of Johannesburg–Pretoria the British had constantly to be on the alert. In Johannesburg another large-scale conspiracy was discovered, this time to assassinate Kitchener and Milner who would be visiting the city on zero day, and to admit a commando under Kemp. Waiting for a rain-storm to ensure that the ringleaders would be indoors, police swooped on them. A series of deportations followed and one man was shot at the fort. The Jingo Press declared that the affair was the result of the Government's alleged preference for Boers, 'socialists' and 'anarchists' in resettling the city: 'Nothing quite so diabolical as this scheme has been devised since the days of the Sicilian Vespers and the massacre of St. Bartholomew.'

The spring drives had produced 4,000 more captives—a Boer per column per day, or per miles marched, or toil expended, an even more paltry result—without more than singeing the real Boer strength.

While their two Republican Governments roamed the field in constant but unchecked flight, their three foremost generals—Botha, De la Rey and De Wet—were as unscathed as their subordinate generals, from Hertzog in the south-west O.F.S. to Viljoen in the north-east Transvaal, while Smuts and others had the Cape smouldering with the constant threat of a general conflagration. The nine varying kinds of engagement described in this chapter cost the British 1,360 men, the Boers 430; and in countless minor skirmishes the same Boer ascendancy prevailed.

The gloom in England could do nothing but deepen. There was anger in the belief that the Boers were committing terrible atrocities almost with impunity. Horror over the tragedy of the concentration camps was complicated by resentment at having to support the Boers' women and children in the camps, as well as surrendered men who betrayed their oaths of neutrality or abused the protection of the camps by treasonable activity. The tax-payer was in fact bearing the entire cost of the war for both sides. Dissatisfaction with the War Office, rising steadily ever since the aftermath of Black Week, reached a crescendo. *The Times* led a revolt by the pro-Government Press, indicting it for inefficiency—'efficiency' in all aspects of national life was a new catchword. Public dismay gained no comfort from the knowledge that Kitchener was saying that many of the mounted reinforcements sent out from England could not ride or shoot, and that officers could not hope to catch the guerillas when they marched loaded with 'kitchen ranges, pianos and harmoniums'.

It was become a never-ending war, causing that very 'wobble' of public opinion which Chamberlain and Milner feared more than anything else. Parliament had been prorogued until after the New Year but mounting expenditure, if not public agitation, might require a dangerous session in December. Meanwhile even pro-Government M.P.s were uttering ominous words. Churchill spoke publicly of the 'disquieting' situation, 'as momentous as it was two years ago'.

There was talk of a new Ministry, a government-of-all-the-talents, with a soldier and a sailor as the political heads of the Services and Cromer recalled from Cairo to be Foreign Secretary. Who would lead it? The single candidate in popular estimation was Lord Rosebery. Imperialism was the dominant political theme of the period, and he was as strong a champion of it as Chamberlain. This rivalry between the two men had in fact underlain much of Chamberlain's election tirades against the Liberal Imperialists.

As winter came on rumours multiplied that Rosebery intended a full return to political life, and with the possibility in mind of a new Government the public gaze was riveted on Chesterfield where he announced he would speak early in December. But except for one phrase destined to have important repercussions, the speech turned out to be so much beautifully delivered hot air. For the present at least the Government stood firm.

As much as anything was its survival owed to the sustained support of the war by the Empire—which seemed a moral vindication of government policy—and to the 'pro-Boers' themselves. The latter urged their case with such vigour that they aroused a counter-blast of fury which distracted attention from the Government. Individuals who talked of making peace on any terms were set upon; the Conciliation Committee was jeered at as the stop-the-war party; meetings were broken up, and Lloyd George in particular found himself as much in personal danger as ever. He never stopped berating a Government which he said would not make peace and could not wage war, but still his chief target was Chamberlain whom he accused of political swindling. He spoke from the pithead to the Cambridge Union, from Edinburgh to London, and when he went—courageously or rashly—to Birmingham's Town Hall in December he caused a riot.

This was the most famous Lloyd George Night of all. He gathered to himself all the animosity excited by the 'pro-Boer'; more, Chamberlain's diocese took the opportunity to avenge the attacks on their hero's personal honour. On arrival Lloyd George made his way unrecognized through a huge mob outside the hall, while four brass bands played patriotic airs and merchants sold half-bricks at 'three a penny, to throw at Lloyd George'. He had scarcely appeared on the platform when the avalanche descended. The mob broke 1,200 windows, battered down the doors, swept aside the police, surged into the hall; and to cries of 'Pro-Boer! Traitor! Kill him!', the blowing of police whistles, the screams of women, and the crash of falling masonry and broken furniture, Lloyd George only escaped with his life by slipping away disguised as a policeman.

Chamberlain, aware that he could not survive an indefinite prolongation of the war, had already been stung into making his first and last sally into the military sphere. Among many letters of discontent reaching him was one in mid-October in which Winston Churchill for the first but not the last time offered advice on how military operations should be conducted. He said that Kitchener was exhausted and should have his activities limited; superior soldiers were being diluted by inferior, mobility restricted by the slowest horseman, and as a preliminary to selecting a striking force of only the best men the whole army, which was being 'bucketed to pieces by constant trekking', should be rested; Remount and Intelligence should be reorganized; and, finally, 'some sort of peace' made. Though favourable to the *corps d'élite* proposal Chamberlain had other ideas. He wanted a great extension of the protected zones in which resettlement and reconstruction could go ahead. Outside these he wanted the Boer leaders hunted. The columns under Rimington and others largely devoted to this task were not enough. He wanted the whole army to concentrate on it to the exclusion of all else: picked columns, 1,000–2,000 strong with Native scouts and the help of information for which large rewards were to be offered, should concentrate first on Steyn or Botha then the others, since 'the war will never end till the leaders are captured'. In addition to circulating the Cabinet with these ideas he sent them to Milner. Milner replied with a corker.

He had himself proposed the large-scale protected zones mentioned by Chamberlain, but Kitchener was proving less co-operative than Milner liked, and Milner's dictatorial temperament seethed at Kitchener's dictatorial temperament. He echoed Churchill's judgement that Kitchener's volcanic energy was being misdirected. He suggested that Kitchener be sacked, and that General Lyttelton should replace him, even though Kitchener himself had made clear that he 'does not want to go until he has "finished the war" '.* This little idea Salisbury killed stone dead with brief, gentle but surgical irony.

The discontent in every quarter did not go unheard by Kitchener. He offered to resign. The offer was not accepted; and indeed, though no one realized it, he had entered the last round.

* Cf. p. 409 and the suggestion that Kitchener wanted at all costs to get to India.

CHAPTER XXVIII

Summer 1901–2

THE story of Kitchener's final struggle with the Boers concerns essentially his attempt to conquer the veld. At last his organizational genius turned to an all-out assault upon that ally of the enemy which had been the chief means of their almost miraculous survival. In the end, imperialism or its little mother nationalism, faith and ideals, political passion or soldierly ardour, the glories of battle or the dreams of history, were less important than an iron cylinder with a projecting A-shaped roof sheltering seven bored men. Placed each within sight of another along an unending fence, the blockhouses parcelled out the whole land in lots too small for a people accustomed to a day's ride between the boundaries of a single farm.

Though Kitchener's policy of attrition and other circumstances all combined to produce the final result, the decisive factor was embodied in our seven bored friends. We may picture them, 70,000 in sevens, through the remaining events of the war. They have helped erect the blockhouse they occupy, and now when the protecting column has marched away they may wonder at a fate which has brought them thousands of miles across the sea, after tearful but proud farewells of their loved ones, to be broiled day after day in their over-size iron pots looking out across lifeless plains. They banter with the Natives who keep watch at night, play with the dog they might keep for the same purpose; the telephone or a walk along the barbed-wire fence half-way to the next blockhouse gives them a momentary companionship with others, and if they are on the railway a train stops every other day to supply coffee, tea, sugar, meat and bread, delivering water through a hose-pipe to the small tank looking like the blockhouse's offspring beside it; but for the rest they are prisoners in a cause they scarcely understand. Night comes and with it sudden alarms that rend sleep. If Native or dog has not already alerted them, a carefully placed spring-gun fires, or dangling biscuit-tins rattle, or some other contraption warns that the wire fence is being tampered with. At once they jump to their rifles laid on prepared rests for accurate fire along the fence in the darkness, the fence being at an obtuse angle between each blockhouse to avoid the risk of hitting the ones on either side. If they see that the enemy is in force they fire a rocket for help from the nearest columns or armoured train. A determined body of Boers can still break through on a dark night, even if failure to cut the specially made wire means that the fence has to be uprooted bodily, but the cumulative effect on the enemy is suffocating and remorseless, and the seven bored men eventually return home knowing at last what the chronicles of war seldom say, that above all things it can be duller than death and more monotonous than hell.

Away from the blockhouses, even in the smaller towns and occupied villages, garrisons were at least big enough in numbers to relieve tedium with gymkhanas, polo, rugby or cricket; tug-of-war contests were popular and so were mule-races. Columns on the march had the diversion of being visited at their bivouacs by Natives in colourful tribal costume: they romped with the children or stood earnestly watched as they shaved, washed or laundered, using a horse's nose-bag or a biscuit-tin as a basin, and a heliograph as a mirror. Water was always a problem, making the discovery of a stream a joyful occasion to strip-off and bathe, though suspect water provided the convalescents with the chore of filtering it through mobile plants before it could be drunk. There were the pleasures of riding through the crisp morning air, the sudden delight of mails descending from home, the camp-fire sing-song. And there was the sadness, after a brush with 'Brother Boer', of auctioning a dead comrade's kit; or the discomfiture, if one had been captured, of trudging half-naked for many miles to the nearest post.

But for our seven bored friends in their blockhouse there was little movement, little change from one day's end to the other. The Boers had no effective answer to their iron cylinder, having lost all their artillery and the hand-grenade having temporarily fallen into disuse among international armaments. Mile by mile the work of building the blockhouses continued. Eventually about 10,000 were strung across nearly 5,000 miles. The evolution of the idea had been slow, but presently a great arabesque of blockhouse lines was being patterned out. The main north–south lines lay along the Western and Central railways; further lines bisected the country between, or were flung out into the eastern O.F.S., eastern Transvaal, western Cape and northern Natal.

The scheme received its chief impetus from Kitchener's decision at the beginning of the S.A. summer to extend the protected zone around Johannesburg to an eventual area of 120 miles by 60. Despite his complaints about Kitchener, Milner was able within this zone, as elsewhere in areas more or less secure, to apply his talents to the one sphere where they had an unqualified beneficence—administration. By December the mines were turning out 53,000 ounces of gold per month and the Uitlanders were returning in droves. Besides mines he reorganized the civil departments of law, finance, education, railways, agriculture, Native affairs. Slowly the City of Gold began to glitter once more.

Outside the protected zones war continued with unrelaxed vigour. Kitchener received a steady stream of reinforcements from England, Australia, New Zealand, Canada and the Empire generally, adding 20,000 men to his May strength of 240,000. Ian Hamilton returned to S.A. to be his Chief of Staff, lightening his huge burden of work. A further and stranger accretion of strength came from the Boers themselves.

The Burgher Peace Committee's efforts having had such a calamitous outcome, the influential survivors now proposed to raise a force among captured or surrendered countrymen to fight on the British side. They believed that their country was conquered, and the prolongation of war a futile tragedy. The corps they raised were called the National Scouts in the Transvaal and the Orange River Colony Volunteers in the O.F.S. Prominent in these were General A. P. Cronje, captured at Reitz the night Steyn narrowly escaped, and Piet de Wet, Christian's despised brother. Payment was at first by the unsavoury method of loot and presents from headquarters, later by regular pay plus gifts for special services; another inducement was privileged treatment of recruits' families in the concentration camps.

The anguished decision of people under enemy occupation is a recurring theme among the tragedies of war. Aside from the rank opportunist or coward, one man sees 'collaboration' as his highest duty towards his own people as sincerely as another believes in dogged opposition at any cost. The fact remains that 'collaboration' enjoys little esteem. Those Boers who favoured it found difficulty in raising the proposed corps, which totalled no more than a couple of thousand before the war's end, and their intervention was militarily useless.

Yet their advantage to the British was that their propaganda encouraged men to drop out of the guerilla commandos even if only to stay passive. The solidarity of the Boers was thereby shaken, the end hastened. But this advantage has been more than outweighed by the bitterness caused among the guerillas, giving to the whole idea of co-operation between Boer and Briton a taint which has discoloured political relationships in S.A. ever since. The guerilla leaders threatened severe penalties against men joining the new corps, a threat sneered at by the Jingo Press who contrasted it with Boer denunciations of British policy towards the Cape rebels.

The National Scouts and O.R.C. Volunteers were recruited mainly in the concentration camps, the conditions in which were now frankly revealed to the world by the Committee of Ladies on completion of their four months' tour of inspection. By the end of October the death-rate had risen to 344 per 1,000—in some of the camps to nearly twice this average. The causes were many. They ranged from the original thoughtless choice of sites to the incompetance of individuals, and from insufficient staff to inadequate regard for hygiene. This last was not confined to the concentration camps. Nearly two-thirds of the British Army's fatalities in S.A. were the result of disease. The Australian war correspondent A. G. Hales wrote of many of these:

> They were due to death through criminal neglect of the most simple laws of sanitation. Men were huddled together in camp after camp; they were allowed to turn the surrounding veldt and adjacent kopjes into cesspools. . . . In some camps no latrines were dug, no supervision was exercised. The so-called Medical Staff looked on, and puffed their cigarettes and talked under their eye-glasses.

Such lack of care, not harmful when applied to simple farming folk whose habits in the wide spaces of the veld had offered no threat of contagion, became lethal in the confinement of camps badly sited. Even when strenuous efforts were made to change these habits it was no easy task among the more ignorant of the inmates. Ignorance had another bad effect. Belief in home cures and primitive quack remedies in preference to consulting the doctors added to the trouble, Kitchener exasperatedly declaring, 'It is impossible to fight the criminal neglect of the mothers. . . . I am considering whether some of the worst cases may not be tried for manslaughter.'*

The Committee proposed a number of reforms and from this time there were drastic improvements, especially as the civil authorities were now in sole charge. Doctors and nurses were sent out from England in quantity, many camps were moved to better sites and the number was increased to reduce the average size. By February the death-rate among the 117,000 people living in altogether forty-six camps was to fall to 69 per 1,000.

The story is not all tragedy. Milner introduced an extensive system of education, and two out of three children as well as many adults attended school, a facility never enjoyed on the same scale before the war. In fact the camps became highly desirable places to the families who still trekked helplessly about, a constant source of anxiety to the guerillas. At long last Kitchener realized that the policy of maintaining the camps directly helped the guerillas. He issued orders (in December) that only families in immediate danger of starvation or those of National Scouts were to be brought in. Louis Botha was presently to give the final lie to stories, spread with such persistence, of British inhumanity: 'We are only too glad to know,' he said, 'that our women and children are under British protection.'

Kitchener, who himself never inspected a concentration camp, regarded agitation on the subject as defeatist propaganda. When Emily Hobhouse—'that bloody woman' as he called her—attempted to revisit S.A. without his permission, he had her forcibly deported after a violent dockside struggle.†

*　　　*　　　*　　　*

All these were the continuing events during what was to be the long last summer of the war. And if they rather than the clashes on the field were to prove decisive, it was the latter, with their tales of courage and spectacular unexpected moments, which constantly absorbed attention.

---

* See also A. C. Martin: *The Concentration Camps*, a recent study.

† In World War I she became as warmly sympathetic towards the Germans as she had previously been to the Boers.

This was particularly so because military operations usually centred on the three highly gifted and colourful Boer generals who had become, either as heroes or ogres, legendary characters in popular imagination and upon whose survival Boer resistance depended. Although Chamberlain's idea of a single-minded man-hunt was not adopted, it was nevertheless against Botha, De la Rey and De Wet that Kitchener exerted all his genius, giving the techniques of anti-guerilla war their final refinement.

The protected zone around Johannesburg cut off De la Rey from the others. Kitchener grasped the opportunity to leave the western Transvaal alone for the present and concentrate on Botha and De Wet, adjoining each other in the eastern Transvaal and north-eastern O.F.S.

He determined to use simultaneously the two distinct techniques so far employed—the multi-column drive and the single-column raid, the former in the main against De Wet and the latter against Botha. But this time both methods would be applied in areas ever diminished by the spreading lines of blockhouses. By early November he had a striking force of 30,000 men ready, well-mounted and equipped, and he split them in half for the two campaigns.

*　*　*　*

In the eastern Transvaal the Constabulary line which marked the eastern limit of the protected zone was pushed still further east. By 16 November it extended from beyond Balmoral on the Delagoa Bay railway cross-country to near Standerton on the Natal railway. With the blockhouses along the railways themselves, and from Volksrust to Piet Retief in the far south-east, a barrier was thus created around the whole highveld west of Swaziland. Then on 3 December a general advance overran the key centre of Ermelo, and a further line of blockhouses was constructed between it and Standerton, the line being rapidly continued northwards towards Carolina and the Delagoa Bay railway, cutting the highveld into two.

To Botha, his Government and commandos, the ominous intent of these moves was clear enough even without reports of innumerable columns preparing to scour the spaces so confined. With a small escort he hurried the Government north-eastward to Carolina. The northernmost of the advancing columns were close and before him stood the blockhouses along the railway, but skilfully feinting he cut the wire entanglements at an unexpected point and the party dashed through under fierce cross-fire at 1.30 a.m. on 3 December. Thereupon the Republican Government again made for the mountains east of Lydenburg while he hustled back to the vicinity of Ermelo. That was the day the British occupied the town, but not before he had sent one group of commandos under Piet Viljoen (not to be confused with General Ben Viljoen, commanding north of the Delagoa Bay railway) to break through to the Bethal district while he led another to the south of it.

Now for two months Boer and Briton played a frantic game of hide-and-seek, mainly between the meridian of Ermelo and the Swazi border. Compared with their situation during the first great drive under French nearly a year before, the Boers had the advantage of being uncluttered with refugees; but many had no horses and the land was impoverished. Besides, the British troops were more seasoned; they drew on endless reserves of fresh men and horses; and the blockhouses had a secondary but valuable function of protecting supply lines, so that the columns were not encumbered with wagons that had brought Benson to his death at Bakenlaagte.

Benson nevertheless lived again in those months, for his energetic night raid tactics were perpetuated. His Intelligence officer, Woolls-Sampson, was attached to the general leading the main raiding columns. Sampson's head man was a surrendered Boer controlling a number of skilful Boer guides and a Native spy in every kraal. Each evening several tried Native scouts rode out on the best horses to visit kraals. They reported to Sampson by morning, when a target for attack was chosen. Upwards of two thousand of the freshest troops secretly gathered in the evening. With the guns in the centre to muffle the sound of their wheels, and with Native scouts ranging wide on the flanks to bring in hourly reports, the columns rode up to forty miles in a night to arrive at the target at dawn and thrust home the attack. Through December and January fourteen such raids, each a little saga of its own, were successful. Even though increasing Boer wariness and dispersion prevented wholesale destruction, 700 of their best fighters and much vital war material were accounted for.

By contrast, combined daytime operations were less directly successful and enabled the Boers to strike back. They adopted the stratagem of sending a small detachment to decoy the British who would then be set upon by commandos waiting in concealment, sometimes wittingly or unwittingly deceiving them by the use of khaki uniforms. An M.I. force lost 135 men in mid-December south of Ermelo. South-east of it a party of New Zealanders was snapped up a fortnight later. On 4 January a British charge on fifty Boers in the hills east of the town was suddenly turned into a counter-charge by 500 Boers, who exacted over 130 casualties in a bitter twenty-minute fight.

By mid-February the campaign reached stalemate. Neither night raids nor daylight sweeps could winkle out an enemy reduced to small widely scattered bands. But hunted by night and day, his own survival constantly balanced on a razor's edge, Louis Botha knew that on the highveld the game was up for the time being at least. Daily pleas from his burghers to give a good reason for continuing the war reached him. He could no longer get them to concentrate in effective strength, and the restricted areas of barren sun-baked veld made the support of any concentration very doubtful anyway. Finally, completion of the blockhouse system made communication with the rest of his command precarious.

He therefore decided to quit the highveld. Gathering 500 men around him he rode into Swaziland and then southwards, outflanking the Volksrust–Piet Retief line of blockhouses to reach the mountains around Vryheid. He wanted time to recuperate. He did not despair. Though he had lost many of his staunchest men, like Commandant Opperman (cf. Spion Kop) and Major Wolmarans of the State Artillery, he relied on the events unfolding in the O.F.S. to sustain resistance until he could re-enter the fray.

With his departure the eastern Transvaal largely disappears from the story. But the fortunes of two groups who hived off in the early days of the summer campaign—Piet Viljoen's commandos to the Bethal district, and the Government to north of the Delagoa Bay railway— should briefly be traced.

Piet Viljoen managed to break through the line of Constabulary posts and penetrate the protected zone. In scattered bands his men roamed as far as the outskirts of Pretoria. At first Kitchener sent a column in pursuit, but after a squadron of Scots Greys had been cut up by the decoy method near Johannesburg* on 18 February he left them

* At Heidelburg.

to roam unmolested for a month while he used his men on more pressing business elsewhere.

Pursuit of the Boer Government was also attempted, but genial Ben Viljoen's lieutenant, Muller, with whom he had quarrelled and who was operating east of Lydenburg, covered it. The vitality of the once energetic Viljoen seemed drained by war weariness and he had taken up his headquarters in the beautiful mountain hamlet of Pilgrim's Rest north-east of Lydenburg. It was a verdant oasis amid the devastation of most of the eastern Transvaal, and having increasingly lost influence among his followers he was content to stay there with about a thousand men still loyal to him. He was so remote and passive that Kitchener left him alone, attention being focused on the struggle with Botha and De Wet. Consequently Pilgrim's Rest led an almost dreamlike existence: women and children lived there with their menfolk, corn was ground in mills, gold mined nearby: and births, deaths and marriages were attended with the ceremony of normal times. Viljoen thought his Government would be happier in this Arcady than in the wild mountains to the west and he set out to prevail on them to join him. They would not be tempted, and on his way back he was surprised one night near Lydenburg and captured, proving his Government's sound instinct for self-preservation. At an earlier time the loss of Ben Viljoen would have been a severe blow to the Boers, but his effectiveness had waned.

*　　*　　*　　*

As soon as he had started his summer campaign against Botha Kitchener set about the destruction of De Wet. The 15,000 men allocated to the purpose were divided into fourteen columns and posted around an area extending for 175 miles south of the Vaal and 100 miles east of the Central railway. They were ordered to converge on a central point south of Frankfort, shepherding the Boers together in an inescapable trap. Elaborate feints, complete secrecy and meticulously timed marches were the features of an operation that went like clockwork for five days, and on the sixth culminated in the troops' arrival at their destination to find not a single Boer in the vicinity.

Every move had been watched by unseen eyes and reported by heliograph from hill to hill, enabling the Boers to slip through the gaps between the columns by night. President Steyn and De Wet could even meet with impunity at a council of war between Lindley and Reitz. There they laid plans for a counter-offensive. A letter from Botha scouting the possibility of peace overtures stung De Wet into action, or rather the reaction which was probably what Botha wanted, for De Wet had scarcely taken the field since his nightmare escape from the Cape eight months before. Steyn was undaunted in spite of failing health caused by interminable flight: he had always to sleep in the open, never rested in one place for two successive nights, and every morning saddled up by two o'clock. He answered Botha's letter with a characteristic defiant exhortation; and De Wet gathered together 700 picked men.

Though columns returning from the abortive drive passed close by all unawares, Rimington—recalled to the O.F.S. after his near-capture of Botha to resume his flying raids and pursuit of Steyn—discovered the secret from a captured Boer. He at once rode to the attack. But De Wet fell upon him with such vigour* that he withdrew to await a renewed drive ordered by Kitchener early in December. For this the rapidly progressing lines of blockhouses were used as 'backstops' against escaping Boers, but to no avail to catch De Wet who had already spirited himself away from the area.

Thereupon Rimington went after a commando under one of De Wet's ablest lieutenants, Wessel Wessels, who had been harassing blockhouse building east of Frankfort. With Rimington was another notable raiding-column leader, F. H. Damant. He was a young man, six feet four inches tall, with side-whiskers down to the jowls of his grim and powerful face. Born at Kimberley of Flemish stock, his name had become a byword for bravery since he left his business to volunteer at the start of the war. Now, like Benson at Bakenlaagte, he was to be fully tested. The ride had distended the two columns. This, and a ruse by the Boers—they got in close unscathed by adopting the Yeomanry's riding formation, besides the alleged use of some khaki uniforms—isolated Damant with ninety men and three guns half-way to Vrede.† The attack was pressed hard against ferocious resistance, and the British were only overwhelmed when the gunners fell in heaps, a mere dozen men were not dead or wounded, and Damant himself lay on the ground with four bullets in him. The Boers pillaged all they could and the affair prompted even more atrocity allegations than usual

* At Spytfontein.
† At Tafelkop.

—explosive bullets, shooting of Red Cross personnel, and the braining of a Native scout as 'a saturnalia of savagery reigned on this ridge.'

This was on 20 December. Meanwhile De Wet himself with the main force was reported between Lindley and Bethlehem, and Kitchener with unquenched zeal had already launched a third all-out drive against him within a month. Once again the toiling columns converged on the target area to find it deserted. Many had now been marching incessantly for six weeks. As one of them returned along the road to Harrismith on the morning of 18 December De Wet sprang an ambush with 900 men.* For once he was discomfited. He expected a fat convoy but confronted instead a column of I.L.H. and Yeomanry under General Dartnell. This was a considerable character. A Canadian aged sixty-three, he had served with the 'County Downs' in the Indian Mutiny, been head of the Natal Mounted Police for thirty years, trudged with Yule from Dundee, and led one of the new raiding columns formed the previous autumn. Heavily built, with a mane of white hair and side-whiskers, moustache and trim pointed beard to match, he had irrepressible ebullience. But on this occasion, though he gave the disillusioned Boers a drubbing, he was shaken enough to ask Kitchener for reinforcements and, being refused, resigned his commission.

A shattering climax to this series of operations against De Wet came on Christmas Day. Near the scene of the unsuccessful ambush a line of blockhouses was being built westward from Harrismith. Among the forces which Rundle, the district commander, had in the neighbourhood to protect the works was a battalion of Kent and Middlesex Yeomanry who manned a hill† near the main road from Bethlehem. On the morning of 22 December De Wet and his staff approached the hill to reconnoitre. Two of his officers, riding closer, seized a Native driving some horses and shot him. The indignant garrison fired their guns, thereby exposing their position, which was the information De Wet sought. He retired to a nearby hill from where he presently watched the pickets take up position for the night, their bayonets outlined against the sky. Now fully acquainted with the lay-out of the camp, he waited until the garrison settled down to sleep through Christmas Eve. Then he rode with a thousand men—Rundle's In-

---

* At Tigerkloof Sprint.
† Groenkop.

telligence had reported only seventy in the vicinity—and under a misty scudding moon reached a side of the hill considered by the British too steep to warrant special precautions.

On stockinged feet the burghers climbed up. Many of the pickets were asleep, a breach of duty for which most paid with their lives. Worse followed. As the Boer fire greeted the first hours of Christmas Day, a full third of the garrison fled from their camp on the slopes below. ('Yet the troops rallied well and there was not the slightest disposition to surrender,' reported the Jingo Press.) The remainder strove to efface this disgrace but their position was hopeless. The Boers swept down through tents, horse-lines, transport; and the night was made unforgettably hideous by their shouts, the terror of stampeding horses, and the cries of men offered a last instant of life between sleeping and waking. In an hour 348 Yeomanry were killed or captured. The entire camp was looted, from plum puddings to clothes and ammunition. Twenty-five Natives were killed, many without mercy; yet De Wet, laying about him with his sjambok, insisted on nothing but tender solicitude towards the British.

Informed of the action—variously called Groenkop and Twee-fontein—Rundle immediately wired his nearest force. The corporal at the receiving office neglected to take any notice of the message, and De Wet made away unscathed.

The festivities of Christmas Day helped shrug off the blow. Wherever British soldiers were gathered they had Queen Alexandra's present of a tin of chocolates in the late Queen's style, and the Field Force Canteen —yesterday's N.A.A.F.I.—arranged for each man to have a plum pudding and beer, with a pipe of tobacco to follow. The stones piled against blockhouse bases were whitewashed, *A Merry Christmas To All*, or notices erected on the fencing conveyed *Compliments of the Season* to passing convoys and commandos alike.

Subsequent attempts to overtake De Wet failed. Making his way northward towards Reitz he dismissed his prisoners, many to endure much hardship before rejoining their comrades, and the year ended with his dispersal of his men to their districts.

It was De Wet and the Free Staters' last campaign in such strength. It was also the last time Kitchener used the drive system on the pattern which had become familiar. The past two months of adversity endured by his troops were final testimonies to its failure: better-trained troops, improved Intelligence, freedom from the distractions of the scorched earth policy, secrecy, the dawning use of blockhouse lines, cunning feints—all had availed nothing. They had not availed simply because the gaps between the advancing columns allowed the Boers to slip through at night. Kitchener now realized this, but also he believed he was not asserting sufficient control, surprising though this might have sounded to field commanders unaccustomed to raising a finger without his express orders. He made up his mind to revolutionize the drive system. The result, known as the 'new model drive', was to be a marvel of military drill and staff organization.

Herodotus tells us that when Darius the Persian conquered the islands of Chios, Lesbos and Tenedos his men used the method of a drag-net: 'Taking one another by the hand and forming a line from the north side to the south side, they march over the island hunting out the inhabitants.' Just so would Kitchener hunt out De Wet, Steyn and their fighting men in the north-east O.F.S. Under a centralized control even more rigid than before, plans would be drawn up in the last detail—complete with routes for every man; times and places to halt, water, provision, received reinforcements. Every man, every horse, every bullet, every bale of forage or roll of bandage would be part of a net so close-meshed that, drawn across each yard of country between blockhouse line and blockhouse line, no living creature without wings could possibly escape. Through the rest of January, while these plans were being prepared—so different in principle from the night raids in full swing against Botha in the eastern Transvaal at this time—fresh troops were brought from north and south by rail; food depots were prepared; and above all, the blockhouse lines were hurried to completion.

'We are much more optimistic here,' Chamberlain wrote to Milner; '. . . the representatives of the Boers in this country and in Holland are almost in despair.' His tone reflected the mood of the country. As the year had turned so, it seemed, had the tide. Edward would soon be formally crowned to confirm the hopes and exhilaration of the new reign. To start a busy year, Parliament met early, on 9 January, but it was far from the crisis session Chamberlain had feared might have had to be called in December. For the first time in many sessions thoughts could be turned to important domestic legislation, including a complete reconstruction of the education system. The main amendment to the Address was still, however, devoted to the war. Once again the fragmentation of the Opposition prevented an effective challenge to the Government. With the radicals and Irish scornfully abstaining Chamberlain won his biggest majority—333 to 123—in rejecting Campbell-Bannerman's charge that the attitude of the Government was preventing peace. The House accepted that by 'unconditional surrender' Chamberlain meant only an undisputed victory to assure a solid peace, and that magnanimity would be the keynote of any settlement. The following month when he drove to the Guildhall the crowds cheered him, and an atmosphere of imminent victory warmed the wintry sky.

In the heat of the S.A. summer Kitchener's new model drive had waited on completion of the blockhouse lines in the north-east O.F.S. There were two east-to-west lines: a northern, from the branch railhead at Heilbron via Frankfort to Botha's Pass on the Drakensberg, and a southern from Kroonstad via Lindley and Bethlehem to Van Reenen's Pass. With the other passes on the Drakensberg fortified, and the Central railway blockhoused, a rectangle 65 miles by 140 was enclosed.

By the beginning of February, De Wet, high on a hill between Heilbron and Reitz, realized something was afoot. He summoned the nearest commando. On the way to join him it was badly mauled,* becoming entangled in the troop movements for Kitchener's first new model drive, for the area he had selected was the western third of the enclosed rectangle. Steyn and half the north-eastern O.F.S. fighters were outside the area but De Wet and 1,800 burghers were in it, and that was enough for the present.

At nightfall on 5 February Kitchener had 9,000 men drawn up in a *continuous cordon fifty-four miles long* between the northern and southern blockhouse lines (i.e. Frankfort to a point west of Bethlehem)—one man per twelve yards. Starting on the morrow it was to move westward at the rate of twenty miles per day, with an unbroken screen of scouts preceding by a mile the main body, transport and guns, until it reached the Central railway in two days and three nights.

The orders issued by Rimington, who commanded one of the units in the driving force and was an originator of the new system, typify the meticulous arrangements for keeping the cordon continuous by night:

* Roodekraal, 3 February.

1. Every man from the Brigadier to the last native to be on duty and to act as sentry for one-third of the night.

2. *Front Line*—Each squadron to be allotted a length of front, to be covered by intrenched pickets of six men, 50 to 100 yards apart; two men to constitute a double sentry; four to sleep close beside them. Guns loaded with case to be posted in front line. . . . Transport, artillery vehicles and all horses to be in small laagers, handy to their units.

3. *Rear Line*—A thin line of rear pickets, each of six men, 500 yards in rear of front line; two pickets to a mile. If attacked, to fall back on the laagers.

4. *Sham Front Line*—A sham line of pickets to be taken up by daylight, a mile or two in front of the real line, and evacuated after dark; fires to be burning along it. The two real lines to be selected by daylight but on no account to be occupied till after dark.

5. *Cover and Obstacles*—Advantage to be taken of natural cover and obstacles, such as dongas, spruits and wire fences. Wire entanglements to be used where feasible.

6. *Lights*—After dark no fires or smoking and only whispered talking. Cooking to be done only at midday halt, and as much sleep as possible to be taken then too.

7. *Subterfuges*—Tricks of every sort to deceive enemy as to strength and position of real front line. E.g. [a] supports to be loudly called for when a picket is attacked; [b] gaps to be left in the smouldering fires of sham front line, opposite strong-points in real front line.

There never was such a fantastic exercise as Kitchener's attempt to dress 9,000 men in perfect alignment across fifty-four miles of country; but he did it. Yard by yard the cordon advanced, while another 8,000 men stood along the blockhouse lines and railway, which seven armoured trains ceaselessly patrolled. As the circle around him tightened from the east, De Wet called to his commandos in the area and rode south. Little more than one-third of the 1,800 burghers concerned heard the summons or obeyed if they did. With these, accompanied by a huge herd of cattle they insisted on taking, he approached the southern line of blockhouses between Kroonstad and Lindley.

And now asserted itself that one factor which Kitchener had striven to eliminate—human fallibility. Our seven bored friends in the block-houses on either side of the point De Wet approached in the dark mid-night of 6/7 February were unvigilant. He slipped through without their firing a shot or alerting reinforcements waiting nearby. Later the great herd of cattle drove down the fencing by brute strength and joined him.

Of the commandos who did not go with him, one group escaped with a scorching through the northern blockhouse line, but the remainder rode up and down in front of the advancing cordon, vainly trying to find a gap as it relentlessly pushed them against the railway. The last hours of the drive had a tingling excitement. Under a pitch-dark sky the earth was as black—the difference, Edgar Wallace wrote, 'between a soot-bag and a velvet pall'. Nobody slept. Machine-gun, pompom and rifle-fire was almost continuous as the fugitives, out-numbered forty or fifty to one, their silhouettes revealed against the raking searchlights of the armoured trains, strove frantically to find a means of escape before dawn should betray them. 'Some few cut their way to safety; some were shot like game; the greater part fell back, stunned and bewildered, into the interior of the trap, their horses foundered, their bandoleers empty, their bodies worn-out, to await capture.'[17]

In all, 300 men were lost to De Wet. If it seemed a result dispropor-tionate to the effort, here in fact was attrition in the one mortal sense of the word—the whittling away of his real fighting strength. And it betokened a final phase of hostilities which gave him no glimmer of hope.

Resting his troops for scarcely three days, Kitchener set them in motion again to bare all the north-eastern O.F.S. omitted in the first new model drive. One cordon of columns started near the Central railway on either side of the Vaal. It swept eastward between the northern blockhouse line and the Natal railway; beyond Frankfort it pivoted southwards towards the Bethlehem–Van Reenen's Pass block-house line, its left skirting the fortified passes of the Drakensberg, its right the Wilge River. To guard this river and seal the area thus bounded, a second cordon approached from the vicinity of Kroonstad.

It was a huge undertaking, too huge, since the first cordon was dis-tended across sixty miles of hilly, river-gashed country. Yet seemingly fate dealt the cards in Kitchener's favour. After the initial new model drive De Wet had slipped back and joined his President near Reitz, for the air was thick with crisis. Now, at the approach of the cordon from the west, they fled across the Wilge, thereby standing square in the path of the other cordon coming down from the north—and with no escape route in any direction.

Scattered about the enveloped area were 3,000 fighting men. Besides these was a mass of civilian refugees who attached themselves to Steyn and De Wet as they turned north, straight towards the advancing cordon. De Wet resolved to force a breach in it. He summoned all the commandos in the area but by sunset on 3 March when a clash was imminent only about 1,200 men had reached him.

From his scouts' information he selected his point of attack,* twenty miles south of Vrede. The horsemen, the terrified women and children refugees, the great ruck of vehicles, the yelling Natives driving a herd of cattle spread across six miles of veld, all moved forward under thick clouds that sporadically parted to admit the flooding beams of a full moon. De Wet's fierce discipline was fully exerted to impose some order. Even so, the picked force of burghers whom he sent into the attack at about 11 p.m. had to shake themselves free of the refugees who swirled among them. The portion of the British cordon immediately in front consisted of New Zealanders and Australians spread down a hill-side, and upon these the Boer advance force hurled itself.

Never did a fitful moon reveal a scene more bizarre. The Boers tore a hole in the New Zealand line, wheeled, and mowed it down through half a mile of blood. Offered this clear but narrow passage the refugee horde was demoralized and confused. De Wet stormed, exhorted, lashed about him. At length 600 fighting men and a remnant of the refugees got through with Steyn and his officials in their midst. Most of the refugees and thousands of cattle, horses and wagons, besides the men who had quailed before that perilous rush, were rounded up, and one complete commando (including one of De Wet's sons) fell back southward to be caught between the jaws of cordon and blockhouse line. But the commandos who had not joined De Wet broke through westward across the Wilge, for here as with the cordon De Wet had pierced, Kitchener's insistence on covering every yard of veld stretched the cordon too thinly at any selected point.

* Langverwagt.

Kitchener was in the area to see the conclusion of the drive, and a message from him on Majuba Day—still evocative of deep partisan emotion—was cheered in the House of Commons. The magical name of De Wet, even if it was only a son of the Phantom, was noted with particular satisfaction in the tally of captives—800 finally—the biggest success in the guerilla war to date. Loud cheering burst out anew when tribute was paid to the gallantry of the New Zealanders.

If De Wet had again escaped, the prospect of further severe losses from the throttling blockhouse lines and of a renewal of the new model drive hit him so hard that he looked about desperately for relief. Steyn proposed a remedy. If he—Steyn—and his officials quit the north-east O.F.S., Kitchener might turn his attention from that unhappy quarter to pursue him. He proposed to get through to the comparatively quiet region of the north-west O.F.S., and he persuaded De Wet, reluctant to leave his burghers but who alone might be relied on to conduct him unerringly, to go with him. They set out near Reitz at sunset on 5 March, spurred by the news that Kitchener had begun yet another drive across the north-east after again allowing his troops only three days' rest.

They pierced the northern blockhouse line, swung north-west, pierced the blockhouse line along the railway, swung south-west, pierced the Kroonstad–Vaal blockhouse line near Bothaville, and having ridden 200 miles and dared the bullets and entanglements of three blockhouse lines in ten days, arrived on the banks of the Vaal. Behind them the renewed drive this time displayed qualities more human than mechanical: troops already exhausted were taxed beyond endurance, gaps appeared in the advancing cordon, and the commandos who had survived continued to do so by slipping through the gaps, or taking to holes in the ground, or even riding full-tilt through the British lines.

But plainly Boer resistance was tottering before Kitchener's hammer blows. As Botha had quit the highveld of the eastern Transvaal the previous month, so now De Wet had quit the north-eastern O.F.S. He did not linger in the north-west, but from the banks of the Vaal rode on. Steyn was tormented by an eye malady and anxious to get treatment from De la Rey's doctor. De Wet therefore led the party into the western Transvaal.

There destiny staged the last great dramas of the war.

CHAPTER XXIX

The Last Stages

KITCHENER's campaigns against Botha and De Wet had left De la Rey comparatively unmolested, yet this would not have happened, nor the climactic battles of the war reserved for the western Transvaal, had not British manpower also been drained by the Cape.

When Jan Smuts broke through the Midlands in October and reached the western districts north of Cape Town with his commando augmented by Scheepers's men, he found that a well-equipped body of rebels, 600 strong, had been organized in the vast tract, sparse in people and vegetation, extending for 250 miles south of the Orange. It was the work of a young corporal called Salomon Maritz, who had started recruitment after De Wet and Hertzog's expulsion in the Great De Wet Hunt of February 1901, earning Smuts's conferment on him of the rank of general. Smuts, as commander of all Boer operations in the Cape, also had nominal direction over several small bands of invaders and rebels operating to the north of the eastern Cape; but it was essentially the combination, about a thousand strong, of his and Maritz's forces that formed the backbone of Boer activity, which hence occurred in the western districts.

The Boer leaders, especially Steyn and De Wet, never gave up the hope of a general uprising by their kinsmen. On a deputation of their clergymen petitioning Steyn to withdraw the invading commandos so that the land could live at peace, he retorted that it would live at peace quick enough if the colonists rebelled *en masse*. They never did. Smuts found the task of organization and recruitment slow going although the farmers maintained an open attitude of hostility to the British and despite the severities of martial law gave secret help to their kinsmen whenever they could. With difficulty he gradually multiplied the bands of guerillas almost threefold.

In November, a hundred Free Staters at De Wet's instigation joined him after breaking through the blockhouse lines along the Orange River and the De Aar railway. The following month Kritzinger with a similar force left the south-east O.F.S. to join him too, but this time the British were more alert. The 5th Lancers pursued across eighty miles in the blazing sun, compelling Kritzinger to shed 110 exhausted ponies before his commando desperately flung itself across the block-housed De Aar–Naauwpoort stretch of railway and got away—but without him. Returning three times through the blockhouse line to rescue wounded comrades, he was himself severely wounded and captured. (As soon as he recovered he was put on trial for offences against the laws of war, and honourably acquitted.)

This capture was almost French's only crumb of comfort in the summer's thankless campaign. The guerilla bands operated in the main 150 miles and more north of Cape Town, along a broad belt of country extending from about Beaufort West on the Western railway to the Atlantic Ocean at Lambert's Bay. In November they hotly attacked a column at one point, a fortified post at another; in December they twice engaged a convoy. These were petty events but they created a climate of restiveness and if allowed to increase in scope threatened a general uprising even at this late hour. In consequence French's numbers swelled to 9,000 men. He divided them into sixteen mobile columns, but the absence of railways meant a slow crawl with wagon convoys, each column a Lilliputian army complete with staff, Intelligence, police, signallers, hospital, guns. He was short of transport and dis-tracted by a gigantic undertaking begun in December, to build a line of blockhouses from Beaufort West to Lambert's Bay 300 miles away. As this line progressed it was manned by Cape half-castes of such doubtful quality that several blockhouses, tested by members of the Intelligence masquerading as Boers, were effortlessly 'captured' while the garrisons were busy playing cards.

Through most of January there was a lull as Smuts built up a granary of supplies in secret places. Towards the end of the month, French started a drive which served only to scatter the bands. One promptly aggravated his transport difficulties by seizing a donkey convoy of 150 wagons on 4 February near Beaufort West, and next day another destroyed a second convoy a few miles away and mauled its escort. Douglas Haig had some success against a Boer laager on the 13th, but on the 29th a police post was snapped up. Again French launched a combined movement—only to scatter some of the bands into the Midlands, into which the guerillas from the north-east also made an incursion, so that these districts once more teetered on the edge of rebellion and the situation was as bad as it had ever been. Thereupon French concentrated on applying steady pressure in a northerly direction to drive Smuts clear of the new blockhouse line. Smuts obliged by withdrawing the greater part of his strength across the wastes of the far north-west, so desert-like that camels were used for carrying the mails. But he had a purpose: here thrived the rich copper-mining industry of Namaqualand. He overwhelmed several mining centres and then laid siege to the most important, O'Okiep, on 12 April. It was stoutly defended by white and half-caste miners besides troops, about 900 in all. In the midst of the siege a fortnight later, a message reached him out of the blue. It contained urgent tidings. So urgent that he immediately quit the scene with a staff of two, leaving the town un-captured—it was relieved on 3 May by an expedition sent by sea to Port Nolleth.

As Smuts made the long journey on which he was now bound he could reflect that he had brought his forces up to about 3,000, of whom all but a seventh were rebels, without ever having been beaten by British forces totalling three times that number. This was his real achievement, the tying up of troops whom Kitchener would sorely have liked to use against De la Rey in the months when Botha and De Wet absorbed the rest of his striking power.

*   *   *   *

A portrait of De la Rey is worth looking at. Every feature is big—ears, nose, eyes, forehead, even his grizzled square beard—and yet the impression it gives is not of a massive man but a fine-drawn one. Boldness and wariness, shrewdness and generosity, gentleness and tenacity, passion and reflectiveness, seem to combine in a knightly figure more Arthurian than the Biblical patriarch suggested by a leading authority (page 69). In the bitter feelings aroused by the guerilla war many villagers refused to bury British dead in their cemeteries; but before the British occupied his home town of Lichtenburg De la Rey marked out a portion of the local cemetery and left strict in-structions that any British dead were to be buried there with full respect: today they lie beneath their rows of metal crosses and the sculpted likeness of De la Rey is turned towards them. In action he was as able as his theories proved sound. At Magersfontein he had adumbrated the fateful idea of trench and barbed wire which underlay the strategy of World War I, as the subsequent innovation under his command of mobile forces firing on the move found a baleful echo in the tactics of World War II. Though the leading Powers had their military attachés present to watch developments on the battlefield so that these passed into the fabric of world military knowledge, it cannot of course be said that any single individual fathered the methods used in the Twentieth Century Tragedy. A notable place in military history nevertheless belongs to this remarkable man, who had no military education and little of any other kind, and whose wise and chivalrous spirit found no satisfaction in the thought of war.

It was apt that he should now play a leading part in the climax of the Boer War, since he had fought its first engagement when he captured the armoured train heading for Mafeking on 12 October 1899. Equally apt, his final opponent was Lord Methuen. Since the battles between them during the first attempt to relieve Kimberley, Methuen had been half forgotten except momentarily when he was foremost in the First De Wet Hunt. Exercising area command in the western Transvaal he had been pitted against De la Rey almost since the start of the guerilla war but the circumstances militated against direct clashes. With few troops to enforce his military administration over a huge expanse of sparsely occupied country Methuen's task had been toiling and so far unrewarding, while De la Rey and his lieutenants, who were fully informed by a network of scouts using heliographs, were able to sally out at will to pluck off a convoy here, an isolated detachment there. The blockhouse lines were still incomplete, leaving wide reaches which the few columns in the region could only traverse if encumbered with a supply convoy. But though he was half forgotten, Methuen occupied that special place in English minds reserved for men who did not give way to adversity—the chief reason for the national desire for magnanimity towards the Boers in spite of their alleged atrocities. Of Methuen a contemporary observed:

> He was the senior of the British Generals in the field, senior even to Lord Kitchener . . . of all those who went out in higher com-

mand, he alone remained to the last, refusing to come home before the war was over, and striving manfully to retrieve the discredit which he thought that the sad reverse of Magersfontein had brought upon his name. Younger men were placed above him; his command was reduced at times to a single weak column; yet he continued to serve his country with unabated constancy and zeal. His chivalrous spirit was proof against all slights and discouragements.[47]

Kitchener, absorbed in the simultaneous campaigns against Botha and De Wet, and gnawed at by Smuts in the Cape, hoped that the limited forces with Methuen, Kekewich and others might keep De la Rey quiet. From November to February the hope was justified. Except for minor operations* De la Rey lay low. The reason was his acute shortage of ammunition and horses, but in February the tide was running so strongly against Botha and De Wet that they appealed to him to act. Towards the end of the month his opportunity came.

Earlier Methuen had been recalled to Vryburg for administrative work. The column he personally had been commanding was quartered, contrary to practice, on Wolmaransstad which was not along the blockhouse lines. The result was that convoys had to travel across open country to Klerksdorp for supplies. One such, empty except for three all-important ammunition carts, left its last staging camp before Klerksdorp at 4.30 a.m. on 25 February, escorted by 700 men. It had been carefully watched by Liebenberg. In a winking De la Rey whistled up 1,200 burghers—quite unknown to the escort, the garrisons at Wolmaransstad or Klerksdorp, or two nearby British columns.

He concealed his force in thick scrub by the roadside.† As the British drew abreast through the darkness the scrub seemed to burst into flame. De la Rey's lieutenants, Liebenberg, Celliers and Kemp, respectively bore down on their van, rear and centre. Despite the surprise they rallied, the Royal Artillery in particular repeating the steadiness which they displayed more consistently throughout the war than any other arm. But the commander of the convoy made the

---

* These revolved round certain of De la Rey's lieutenants. In December and February Methuen successfully attacked Potgieter near Wolmaransstad, but a detachment of his Yeomanry was cut up by Celliers near Lichtenburg in the latter month, when too Kekewich's and another column rounded up Alberts with many of his commando.

† Close to a stream called Yzer Spruit.

mistake of ordering it to push on. Terrified Native drivers lashed their animals wildly, a wagon stuck, the following vehicles piled up, and De la Rey precisely gauged his moment to unleash an all-out charge with fire from the saddle. The escort was ridden down in a tumultuous gallop. Dawn broke on a scene of unmitigated disaster. 178 British were dead or wounded, another 500 captured, and horses and mules in plenty seized along with half a million rounds of ammunition.

The largest 'bag' of prisoners that had fallen to either side since Gatacre accidentally left 800 men behind at Stormberg, raised the often-repeated problem in the guerilla war of what was to be done with them. The Boers' privations, and the knowledge that if themselves captured they would be sent overseas, prompted violent thoughts. De la Rey would have none of it. Having had some of his own men flogged for mishandling prisoners, he released all 500 prisoners the following day to march to the nearest British post. Then, eluding immediate attempts at pursuit, he drew away northwards.

As soon as he heard news of the disaster Methuen determined to avenge it. There and then at Vryburg he could only form a column of poor quality—1,300 mainly raw troops or surrendered Boers, Cape half-castes and other colonials who were better as scouts than as disciplined soldiers. But he did not hesitate. Asking Kekewich to send 1,200 mounted men from Klerksdorp to join him a short distance south of Lichtenburg on 7 March, he set out from Vryheid ninety-five miles away with his scratch column, six guns, and a convoy of eighty wagons of which half were pulled by oxen and half by mules. He started on 2 March. His route across empty dry undulating country was dictated by such watering places as could be found. He fell behind schedule. On the night of 6 March he was still twenty-five miles south-west of his rendezvous with the mounted column, itself moving up rapidly thirty-five miles east of him. Between the two, unknown to either, was De la Rey with over a thousand men.

If the British knew nothing about him, he knew everything about them. He could retreat before the intended junction took place. Or he could attack either the mounted column, or Methuen's column cluttered with its convoy. He did not hesitate over his choice.

At 4.30 next morning Methuen's column broke the night's camp. The ox-convoy advanced a mile ahead of the mule-convoy, and each had three guns and a screen of troops. They had plodded along for half an hour when De la Rey made his presence known by a preliminary attack on the rearguard. Half an hour later he pushed a second wave of burghers forward on the British flank. Methuen, who was in front with the ox-convoy, decided to close up the two convoys, and indeed ox-wagons were already coming to a halt because the Native drivers cowered under them. At six o'clock, before the convoy could close up, De la Rey attacked again from the right, his burghers galloping up close before jumping from their ponies and pressing forward in disregard of the British shells and of rifle-fire whose wildness testified to much indiscipline and confusion. De la Rey chose his moment with deadly precision. His veterans, firing from the saddle, flung themselves on the crumbling screen of troops around the mule-convoy, whereupon the mounted troops fled for three miles before they drew rein, though a handful later rallied in a Native kraal until the Boers blew it to pieces with the guns captured in the previous ambush. Meanwhile the mule-convoy was enveloped; the regulars fought to the bitter end, the artillery commander being the last to survive and, refusing to surrender, the last to die. Then De la Rey summoned all his strength to deal with the ox-convoy and Methuen.

The convoy stood in a hollow near a dried stream. Around it, braced by the nobleman who had long won their devotion and who now refused to take cover, stood a thin line of infantry. They were enfiladed from the river, overlooked by the higher ground, beset on three sides by superior numbers. Within seconds they were suffering severely. Methuen himself fell badly wounded in side and thigh; and his horse, shot beside him, rolled over and crushed his leg; a doctor going to dress his wounds was also shot. The hopelessness of the position allowed of nothing but surrender.

At this, the engagement at Tweebosch, the British sustained the worst defeat of the whole guerilla war. Nearly 200 men were dead or wounded, 600 others made captive. While his burghers collected booty and helped with the wounded, De la Rey found Methuen in a tent. So the two men met face to face at last in the most poignant encounter of the war.

Again there was the question of the prisoners. De la Rey issued them with rations and sent them to the nearest British post. Many of his burghers clamoured for at least so valuable a hostage as the British general to be kept, or at any rate exchanged for a Boer prisoner of similar rank. But De la Rey, out of consideration for his wounds, insisted on seeing that he was taken to the nearest British hospital. He also sent a messenger under a flag of truce to the British lines to arrange for a telegram to Lady Methuen, expressing his concern at the gravity of her husband's wounds (from which he ultimately recovered).

For many decades now a fine hospital named after De la Rey has served his home district of Lichtenburg: Lord Methuen, with Kitchener and other British generals, was among the first to contribute to its foundation. But this is to anticipate the years. De la Rey left the battlefield to meet Steyn and De Wet on their arrival from the O.F.S. He could do something, with news of his spectacular successes, to lift their spirits depressed by Kitchener's new model drives from which they had fled. Steyn stayed with De la Rey but De Wet immediately returned to the O.F.S.

Meanwhile on the British side the immediate sequel of the battle was that Kitchener collapsed when he heard the news. The fact testifies to the intensity of the strain which he had undergone. He remained in bed without food for thirty-six hours, telling his most trusted A.D.C. that his nerves had 'gone all to pieces', after which he ate a gargantuan meal and recovered his poise.

In England the news distressed a public which had wished no man a victory more than Methuen. It shattered the confident expectation of an early peace which had been felt on every hand. 'I see nothing for it,' a deeply disappointed Chamberlain wrote to a Milner equally disappointed, though from a longing to see the back of Kitchener's military dictatorship, 'but patience and a stiff upper lip.' In the House he tried to allay anxiety by pointing to the number of surrendered Boers joining the National Scouts. The raising of this corps had infuriated the radicals and Irish. A famous exchange took place with Dillon, the Irish Nationalist, when Chamberlain spoke of a communication addressed by Vilonel (see page 333), now a commander of the Scouts, to the fighting Boers in which he said that 'the enemies of the country are those who are continuing a hopeless struggle'. Then, records *Hansard*—

MR. DILLON: Yes, but he is a traitor. (*Cheers.*)

MR. CHAMBERLAIN: No. The hon. gentleman is a good judge of traitors. (*Loud cheers.*)

MR. DILLON (*rising amid loud Nationalist cheers*): I want to know, Sir, whether that is a parliamentary expression.

THE SPEAKER: The hon. member himself interrupted the right hon. gentleman by crying out that the soldiers who were serving under the British Crown were traitors. (*Ministerial cheers.*) I deprecate interruptions: I deprecate retorts. If the hon. gentleman will not interrupt he will not be subjected to retorts.'[48]

MR. DILLON: Then I desire to say that the right hon. gentleman is a damned liar.'[48]

Dillon was suspended from the House amid an uproar. As it faded Chamberlain's cool voice was heard: 'I was commenting when I was interrupted . . .' But that same evening Lloyd George raised another hubbub. 'Make peace now!' was his theme: justice demanded it and so did common sense—otherwise an embittered Boer nation would seize their chance as soon as Britain became involved in a foreign war. Though this last argument was not lost on a country very aware of its isolation, there was no general inclination to throw in the sponge, especially as the Empire yet again offered contingents. But already Lloyd George's appeal had been outpaced by events, though these were still hidden deep from public view.

The very day of Methuen's defeat at Tweebosch was marked by an event of much greater ultimate significance: a message from Kitchener reached the camp of the Transvaal Government, then in the bushveld about forty miles north of Balmoral on the Delagoa Bay railway.

Seldom in history has a government carried on an existence so peripatetic as that of Acting-President Schalk Burger with State Secretary Reitz, Lukas Meyer and other officials. Since Kruger's departure and their flight under Botha's protection from the Delagoa Bay railway near Komati Poort in September 1900, they had fled hither and thither across 25,000 square miles of the eastern Transvaal. Identifying their own survival with that of their country's independence, they clung to it as if to the Ark of the Covenant, and by a process of almost perpetual motion eluded all British attempts to capture them these past eighteen months. A list of their temporary 'capitals'—farm-house, mountain-top, clearing in the bush—runs to sixty-six place-names, an average of almost one per week.

At first sight there seemed little about Kitchener's message to suggest that their wanderings might nearly be over. It was an odd kind of communication. Kitchener himself said nothing; the contents were copies of correspondence between the Governments of Great Britain and Holland. From this the Boers gathered the following story.

On 25 January Holland's Prime Minister had made to the British Government a proposal of mediation. (He had in fact been prompted by a passage in Lord Rosebery's Chesterfield speech to the effect that a first step to peace might be 'an apparently casual meeting of two travellers in a neutral inn', consequently sounding Kruger and the Boer delegates in Europe and receiving encouragement.) Lord Lansdowne turned the offer down flat—but added: 'The quickest and most satisfactory means of arranging a settlement would be by direct communication between the leaders of the Boer Forces in South Africa and the Commander-in-Chief of His Majesty's Forces.'

The correspondence was all Kitchener sent. Yet though he himself made no comment whatever, the Boers read into the transaction what they were intended to read. Firstly, the proclamation of the previous 7 August which made outlaws of them was forgotten: they, and not the surrendered Boers—the 'hands-uppers' as the guerillas contemptuously called them—were recognized as the custodians of their people's political destiny. Secondly, nothing was said about their having to lose their independence, yet there was an unspoken invitation to talk things over with Kitchener.

In this manner the two nations contrived to wriggle off the stake on which pride had impaled them, and to take the first steps towards trying to end a struggle both were utterly sick of. Schalk Burger applied for a safe conduct for the Boer leaders to meet so that they might agree proposals for peace. Kitchener readily granted the request. On 22 March Burger and his colleagues entered the British lines at Balmoral and reached Kroonstad next day. The immediate need was to bring together the other leaders from their widely scattered spheres of operation. The strange phenomenon occurred of the British co-operating with the Boers to find and bring together under safe conduct a group of the enemy in the midst of military operations, which continued with unabated vigour. Far from receding into the background, these operations now assumed an even greater importance for the effect they might have on Boer counsels.

Already Kitchener was increasing his striking power in the western Transvaal to 16,000 men, resolved on a supreme effort to settle with De la Rey.

The commandos were reported west of the Klerksdorp–Ventersdorp line of blockhouses (which went on to the Magaliesberg in the north and the Vaal in the south). The area around them—bounded on the other three sides by the Vaal, the Western railway, and a blockhouse line from Mafeking via Lichtenberg to south of Ventersdorp—was too big for a drive on the 'new model' pattern. Kitchener therefore applied a startling adaptation.

On the night of 23 March he drew up 11,000 horsemen, without artillery or transport, along the Klerksdorp–Ventersdorp line. They shot off into the veld and rode westwards through the darkness for forty miles, passing among the commandos who were perplexed by the manœuvre until dawn made its purpose clear. The troops about-turned, extended themselves along an arc of ninety miles and rode back with the object of driving the Boers on to the blockhouse line. But once again, skilfully though most of the movement was carried out and with an audacity which deserved success, Kitchener was let down by man and horse's insistence on falling short of perfection. The pace and scope of the ride opened up gaps through which De la Rey, Steyn and all the leading commanders slipped away with most of their men, though not without confusion and hairbreadth escapes—Liebenberg, for example, lost all his wagons.

It was plain to De la Rey that Kitchener's full fury was directed at him. To meet the challenge he called together almost all his staunchest men—over 2,500, the largest and freshest Boer force anywhere in S.A. for more than a year. They were assembled far to the south-west of Lichtenburg by 27 March. On that day news of the proposed talks reached Steyn. A messenger entered De la Rey's laager bringing word from Schalk Burger at Kroonstad that the Transvaal Government wanted a meeting to discuss peace. Steyn agreed to the meeting and suggested a venue for it.

While these messages were being exchanged, Kitchener sent his 16,000 men, divided into four groups, westward to feel out De la Rey's whereabouts. Starting between Lichtenburg and Wolmaransstad they fumbled about uncertainly for some days until, on the last morning of March, contact was made with the outer fringe of the Boer concentration sixty miles west of Klerksdorp.* It was made by a Colonel Cookson, leading a reconnaissance force of 1,800 men, including a contingent of untried Canadians. De la Rey chanced to be momentarily away. In his absence Kemp early that afternoon attacked the British who had taken up position by the brackish pools of a semi-dry water course. The Boers succeeded in driving in Cookson's outer defence line, but time had been gained by the main body to make themselves secure in a ring of shallow trenches and two farm-houses. Trying to advance over open ground Kemp was rudely checked. When De la Rey arrived late on the scene he would not permit his guerillas to waste lives and ammunition on a well defended position: the moment for attack had been before the British could consolidate. He therefore broke off the action, in which Cookson lost about 178 men, the Boers 67.

Cookson's Native servants had meanwhile fled in panic, carrying reports of his destruction. The nearest columns soon discovered the truth, but only after a breakdown in communications with Kitchener at Pretoria and the first report went uncorrected for forty hours. Under this shock and the realization that the four groups stalking De la Rey urgently needed a commander on the spot to co-ordinate them, Kitchener asked Ian Hamilton to leave his desk and return to the field after an absence of fifteen months. Hamilton suddenly found himself commanding a force which illustrated the Army's adaptation to the novel requirements of the Boer War. It included units from all over the Empire; townsmen in the guise of Yeomanry were on horseback for the first time in their lives, as were infantrymen seconded to the M.I.; and more artillerymen were armed with rifles than with guns, whose limited value in guerilla warfare the Boers had amply demonstrated.

At this juncture Steyn received the Transvaal Government's agreement to a venue for the proposed discussion. It was to be at Klerksdorp. He at once set out for it with De la Rey. Ironically the town was at the same time made Hamilton's base for his first operations which he was already launching against the western commandos now deprived of De la Rey's leadership—for which that of the impetuous Kemp was substituted.

At the moment, however, a hush fell upon a world whose attention was directed at neither of these developments in the western Transvaal but at a sombre procession a little further to the west. Along the

* At Boschbult.

Western railway travelled a train *de luxe* in whose design Cecil Rhodes had taken a hand, as a crowning adornment of the railway which was largely his creation and which he hoped would yet reach Cairo. The train was to have made its maiden journey as soon as war ended. It travelled now to carry his own corpse. He had told Lord Rosebery, 'Everything in the world is too short. Life and fame and achievement . . .' and had died on 26 March because air itself was too short for him who struggled for more, though they cut a hole out of the roof of his cottage outside Cape Town. As the *de luxe* train draped with emblems of mourning bore him north to the Motoppos an armoured train went ahead to sweep the veld with a searchlight; sentries along the route presented arms; and remnants of Methuen's last column, straggling into Vryburg, clashed with Boer snipers who delayed the train for a night. Next day it continued, past the place where Jameson had started the Raid that was Rhodes's real death, and reached Bulawayo on 9 April.

That same day the Boer leaders converged on Klerksdorp. In a large tent erected for them by the British they opened their deliberations without delay. Present, with De la Rey and the Transvaal Government, was Louis Botha, ceaselessly but in vain hunted by the British in the far south-east Transvaal since he quit the highveld, his exact whereabouts unknown to the British until he emerged to confer with his colleagues. (The message that was to recall Smuts from the siege of remote O'Okiep was still on the way.) The O.F.S. leaders present included Steyn, De Wet, Hertzog and Olivier.

They began with a prayer. Then Schalk Burger called in turn upon Botha, De Wet and De la Rey to describe conditions in their respective parts of the country. After this they adjourned to ponder on what had been said. Next day came a crucial decision. They agreed to negotiate— but on terms which they asked leave to lay before Kitchener. That night they entrained for Pretoria, where Kitchener received them with full honours and warm hospitality.

The issue of peace or continued war gave in these hours a supreme importance to events on the battlefield. Repeatedly the Boers had been on the brink of surrender when a success in battle had braced them to fight on. Even as the leaders were enjoying the long-unaccustomed luxury of the railway journey to Pretoria, and rumours of peace excited England, Kemp was deploying to strike at Ian Hamilton.

CHAPTER XXX

Vereeniging: May 1902

ON assuming command Hamilton had formed up his troops in their four groups about thirty-five miles south of Lichtenburg. He had then started them on a great sweep designed to whirl like a scythe through a distance of 140 miles—first south-west, then south, finally south-east to the Vaal and Klerksdorp. The movement was well under way by late afternoon on 10 April when his army was facing south along a front of twenty-seven miles in the vicinity of Kemp's abortive attack on Cookson's reconnaissance force. Kemp in fact was close at hand, ardent for action, with the commandos of Liebenberg and Celliers under him as well as his own burghers, temporarily led by F. J. Potgieter: in all, 2,600 men.

For a moment he showed himself that afternoon, on the British left. From this obvious feint Hamilton correctly deduced that action impended on the right. By chance the British front was not fully extended: a lost staff message brought Kekewich, who commanded the group intended to form the right, behind the centre. Hamilton therefore ordered him to make good the deficiency under cover of night.

Kemp had no idea of this. Next morning he thought Kekewich was still where his scouts had reported him the previous evening, so that when he saw an advance party of M.I. on the British right he did not realize that Kekewich's columns were just over the rise behind it.* With an impulsiveness De la Rey would never have permitted without further investigation he ordered a charge, engulfing some of the M.I. and driving back the rest, and only on topping the rise perceived that the British were in strength a mere mile and a half away. Then occurred

* On the farm Roodewal.

one of the most memorable spectacles of the war. Eight hundred of the Boers continued to advance. They were not galloping but simply moving forward at the characteristic 'trippling' pace of their ponies. Led by Potgieter, conspicuous in a blue shirt, they approached the astonished British across a level plain in broad daylight.

At first, their compact formation and unhurried advance led Kekewich to think them one of the other columns. But once the truth was grasped he acted promptly. His front-line troops hastily deployed to lie among mealie fields—1,500 men at this point, with six guns. Still the Boers came on, riding knee to knee and three or four deep. At 600 yards the British spat a stream of bullets and shell at them, and still they came, shouting and firing from the saddle. There had been nothing so reckless since the charge of the dervishes at Omdurman, but it was less explicable. Perhaps the Boers felt an intoxication in throwing off their native caution, an ecstatic moment of freedom from the eternal vigilance of guerilla warfare. They came within 500 yards—400—300. Then at last they faltered and began to draw grudgingly back, except for Potgieter and a handful about him who did not flinch but rode on until a bullet found his head only seventy yards from the British bayonets.

The strangest part of all is that instead of being annihilated, the retreating Boers left only eighty dead or wounded, which was hardly more than the British lost. The shock of their charge and the confusing effect of their fire had caused some wildness in the troops' aim, gaining them comparative immunity.

Hamilton ordered immediate pursuit. But it took time to get the columns away; the country was bushy and largely unmapped, and a swarm of locusts caused an exhausting distraction by seeming like the dust of a fleeing commando. Yet, apparently barren of result, the vigour of the chase coming hard on the repulse of Kemp's charge cast a deep gloom over Boer hopes. It was to be at a critical moment that the news reached the leaders in Pretoria, where the question of their country's future now tested mind and heart more than the perils of war ever had.

★　　★　　★　　★

We must glance at the military situation in the whole 'theatre of war' as it was known or became known to the Boer leaders when they assembled in a room at Kitchener's Pretoria house to lay their proposals before him on the morning of 12 April.

Operations in the Cape had reached stalemate. 3,000 invaders and rebels were at large, but no general uprising was in prospect.

The O.F.S. was much of it a blackened waste. The south presented the passivity of death to the ceaselessly patrolling British columns. But in the north, despite great areas of devastation, there was still life enough to discomfit the British. Only a few days before, the commandant in the north-west, spurred on by Steyn and De Wet on their way to the Transvaal, overwhelmed a detachment of 200 soldiers. And in the north-east, heart of the Free Staters' resistance, sufficient commandos survived to bring upon them yet another new model drive, which almost came to grief in heavy rains that turned parched riverbeds into roaring floods, breaking the cohesion of the columns and helping the commandos, grown ever more adroit at combating the new methods, still to survive. All together, something like 7,000 fighting men remained at large in the O.F.S.

In the eastern Transvaal, it will be recalled that Kitchener had earlier given up trying to deal with Piet Viljoen, who had broken into the Johannesburg–Pretoria protected zone, rather than permit a further drain on manpower. Viljoen had used the time to increase his strength, and 300 Bays who tried a night raid on him on 1 April were severely cut up.* The protected zone having become singularly unprotected, it was now an object of concern. Kitchener drummed up troops from the O.F.S. and elsewhere and on the morning the Boer delegates sat down with him at Pretoria 15,000 men started out on a drive only a few miles to the east of them. Further afield, Louis Botha had left staunch commandos behind him in the far south-east. North of this, across the Delagoa Bay railway, Muller and other local leaders had 2,000 men ranging the bushveld and the mountains. East of them again, Beyers was vigorously operating around Louis Trichardt far to the north of Pretoria. Though he had some loss in eluding efforts to capture him, only the previous day he routed a party of Kitchener's Fighting Scouts. Finally, De la Rey had left over 5,000 burghers scattered about in the western Transvaal, where Ian Hamilton was preparing a renewed offensive following the repulse of Kemp. Altogether, 12,000 Transvaalers were still in the field.

* Boschman's Kop.

The grand total of the Boers' fighting strength was therefore something over 22,000. British Intelligence estimated only half as many. It overlooked the numbers of Boers who were only drawn into action from time to time and for the rest lagged behind. Compared with the total of a year ago, and despite their spectacular successes, they had lost half their fighting strength. For this, Kitchener's wonderfully organized summer campaign based on the blockhouse system was largely responsible. But except for some notable lesser lights who had been extinguished, the Boer leaders were intact and so were the best of their commandos.

In short, it could not be said at this moment that the Boers were conclusively defeated. Sitting down with Kitchener at Pretoria on 12 April their Governments certainly did not make their Klerksdorp proposals on any such assumption. As first spokesman, Schalk Burger offered a commercial union with the adjoining British territories, votes for the Uitlanders, equal language rights in the schools, and a mutual amnesty. He proposed the settlement of future differences by arbitration, and an 'enduring treaty of friendship'.

President Steyn spoke after Burger. When he declared that their purpose in coming to the meeting was to achieve the objects for which they had fought, Kitchener interrupted with a gesture of astonishment. 'Must I understand from what you say that you wish to retain your independence?'

'Yes,' Steyn answered, 'the people must not lose their self-respect.'

That was the nub of the thing. Self-respect was now to be as tenaciously fought for in the council chamber as it had been on the battlefield. Though nationalism, unleashed like a second Flood upon our age, is invariably used to float individuals to power, it can only do so because of a universal assumption that a man of one race can have no self-respect if he is ruled by a man of another. The difficulty was that England felt her self-respect at stake too. Although an acceptance of the Boer offer, followed by a judicious immigration policy, might well have brought her everything she hoped for from victory, it was necessary to make the victory manifest by waving the Union Jack over the two republics, and it was precisely in this particular that the Boers felt their self-respect denied them.

Kitchener knew that the British Government would reject the proposals, which the Jingo Press called comic and *The Times History* describes as delivered with magnificent audacity. However, since a deadlock threatened and Kitchener was resolved on exploring all possibilities of peace, he agreed to transmit the proposals to his Government. Two days later the Boer leaders met again to be confronted by a flat rejection from the British Government—i.e. Chamberlain. They were also confronted by Lord Milner—'fortunately,' said the Jingo Press, since in him 'the nation had on the spot a negotiator who could be trusted to secure a settlement which should imperil no British interest'. By this time the repulse and pursuit of Kemp were known, depressing to Boer hopes, and neither the rejection of their Klerksdorp proposals nor Milner's presence served to break down the negotiations; and this was a good omen even though the delegates merely said they had no constitutional authority to negotiate on the basis of surrendering their independence, and they invited the British Government to make proposals. At first the request was refused. Again a deadlock seemed certain, and again Kitchener broke it by doing what the Boers asked: he cabled home for instructions. After two successive Cabinet meetings Chamberlain's draft dispatch, which was watered-down Milner, was approved and transmitted to Kitchener through the Secretary for War.

On 17 April it was revealed to the Boer leaders. Chamberlain, with undiminished hauteur, expressed his Government's surprise at the Boer attitude. He referred them to the Middelburg proposals of a year ago: the further losses suffered by the British since then justified them, he declared, in demanding 'more onerous terms'—the phrase was Milner's—but they were still prepared to stand by the Middelburg offer.

The Boers replied with two requests. They asked that one of their representatives in Europe might be allowed to join them; this was refused. But their request for an armistice to enable them to consult with their burghers was granted—or rather Kitchener agreed to what he called a 'go slow'. The Boer Governments and thirty delegates from each of the two former republics would hold a convention on 15 May at Vereeniging, on the Transvaal side of the Vaal, to decide for peace or war. Meanwhile the leaders would have free railway and telegraph facilities so that they could move about the country addressing the commandos, which would also be given facilities for holding meetings to elect the sixty delegates. The war would nevertheless go on, but for four days before the convention no commando whose commander was a delegate would be attacked. Upon this understanding the Boer leaders left Pretoria. But not before Milner delivered a typical lecture to the effect that the way to peace did not lie through procrastination, for he profoundly suspected the Boers of playing a tricky game. Kitchener met them in private and by his tact removed much of the effect of Milner's provocative influence.

The month that followed was unique. The war raged on—with particular vigour in the eastern and western Transvaal where renewed drives were made on a massive scale—but into it were dovetailed moments of peace. With the co-operation, not to say hospitality, of the British, the Boer leaders moved freely among them, though now and then junior officers experienced a delectable moment upon 'capturing' some redoubtable guerilla until disillusioned by Kitchener's free pass: De Wet himself is said to have given a subaltern such a glimpse of glory.

These were weeks when thoughts ranged far and deep. Rumours of peace excited an England the keener to have everything settled in time for Edward's coronation. But inner councils were divided. Milner, confident that the Boers were hopelessly beaten and that winter, now close at hand, would complete the conquest, wanted to give no concessions. These would enable the guerilla leaders to emerge with their moral position unimpaired among their own people, whereas he wanted those Boers who had surrendered and were prepared to work with the British to receive more importance. He wanted to build up an administration based immovably on British domination, because he believed that any compromise would only make for more trouble in the future, since he blamed the war itself on past appeasement. The British domination he sought would mean domination *by him*. This would both satisfy his despotic temperament and enable him to create unhindered a model of clean, just and able government, which was the mainspring of his imperialist idealism.

Kitchener disagreed with his assumptions. Time and again the Boers had been adjudged beaten, and time and again proved the opposite. They could still retreat into the undevastated Cape or the wild unconquered reaches of the northern Transvaal. He wanted a crisp end, now, not a costly prolonged petering out of hostilities to reach a settlement in which he had no faith. Politically his own views were reflected and enlarged by a large section of English opinion. Lord

Rosebery spoke not only for most of the Opposition but for many Unionist–Conservatives who wished to avoid a war fought to an end so bitter that future co-operation between the two white races in South Africa would be impossible. He wanted terms which would encourage the Boers to come willingly into the Empire and to work with their English-speaking fellows for the reconstruction and development of their country.

The Boers were equally divided. Schalk Burger and Botha had long thought that surrender was inevitable. They saw that increasingly their burghers would join the 'hands-uppers', until a time came when more co-operated with the British than with themselves, so that guerillas who remained in the field would be regarded by their own people as little more than bandits. Therefore they wanted peace in order to preserve their own moral position and political future as well as to save their race from irreparable ruin. But Steyn would not budge from his passionate belief in the Boer ideal of independence, even if every Boer had to be sacrificed to it. He did not believe they were beaten, would not believe it. But this belief whose passion had made him magnificent in adversity and had been the mainstay of his people's resistance was all that physical and mental suffering had left him with. As a man pressed beyond the limit of endurance will cry out for his mother or for God, he cried out for independence. It was mother, God, and his staff of life. Because of what he had been and meant he commanded among his close followers unswerving devotion. For lesser men an uncompromising principle becomes a light in the darkness of indecision, and they follow. It is here that nationalism will not yield to reason but even in defeat is kept alive to wait its hour.

So ill that he retired to a farm, he left it to his subordinates to keep their troth with him as they travelled about to arrange the election of delegates for the convention. In particular Christian De Wet addressed commandos from end to end of the O.F.S., and from each extracted a pledge that its delegates would not agree to surrender independence. In England wishful reports said he was warmly advocating peace.

At this time Jan Smuts returned to the Transvaal. With the urgent message which reached him as he besieged O'Okiep in the north-west Cape was enclosed a safe conduct signed by Douglas Haig. The staff of two he took with him included young Deneys Reitz who had accompanied him on his great ride to the Cape and who now went with his chief—himself scarcely turned thirty—to Port Nolleth on the Atlantic. They travelled by troop-ship to Cape Town and thence by rail. Not only did hot baths, soft beds and proper fare seem almost like a dream, but their journey was made as undepressing as possible: 'The British,' says Reitz, 'with all their faults, are a generous nation . . . throughout the time that we were amongst them, there was no word said that could hurt our feelings or offend our pride, although they knew that we were on an errand of defeat.' During the train journey, 'General French came to see us, a squat ill-tempered man, whom we did not like, although he tried to be friendly.' At Kroonstad, Kitchener called: 'He rode up to the station on a magnificent black charger, followed by a numerous suite, including turbaned Pathans, in Eastern costume with gold-mounted scimitars.' Smuts went on to confer with Botha who was busy addressing the eastern Transvaal commandos—'Starving, ragged men, clad in skins or sacking, their bodies covered with sores, from lack of salt and food, and their appearance was a great shock to us, who came from the better-conditioned forces in the Cape.'

In due course all sixty delegates from the Transvaal and O.F.S. converged on Vereeniging. There, with their Governments, they met on 15 May. A tent had been pitched for each country, and a large marquee for their plenary sessions. It was cold and misty weather. When formal business was over, including the appointment of General Beyers as chairman, Schalk Burger addressed the conference. He wished to make clear that the British Government would negotiate on no basis except surrender of independence, and he guardedly recommended submission. A letter from the Boers' representatives in Europe was read out; it was vaguely optimistic about foreign intervention, but since it had been written five months previously, such optimism seemed scarcely to have been justified. Burger declared that if submission was agreed upon it must be unanimous, and when Botha was called on to speak he at once grappled with this difficulty, for there could be no unanimity if the O.F.S. delegates regarded themselves as bound by their pledge to their commandos not to surrender. Judge Hertzog thereupon delivered a legal opinion which Smuts confirmed. It was a principle of law, they said, that delegates were not mere mouthpieces but must vote as their individual judgement disposed them. With their reverence for the law the Free Staters accepted this ruling, but the moral effect of their pledge remained.

Botha proceeded to give an account of conditions in the eastern Transvaal. In all the hundred miles between Vereeniging and Ermelo there were only thirty-six goats, no cattle whatever, and burghers who still had horses reported them almost too enfeebled to move. Women still trekking about were in a pitiable condition, and the Natives were so hostile that at Vryheid recently they had committed a terrible massacre of Boer families. De Wet made a shorter speech. He said they were as well able to fight now as they were a year ago and the Natives in his region—the Basutos—were friendly. He hinted that De la Rey shared his view that the struggle could well be maintained. De la Rey himself did not speak. Other delegates followed, each reporting on his own district. The picture that emerged was one of a land close to total ruin, but in which the attitude of burghers varied according to their hope of wringing food either from the scorched earth or Native kraals. Smuts reported well of his men in the Cape but warned the assembly that no general uprising could be expected.

So the debate swayed between the extremes of pessimism and optimism. An incidental result of communication having been prevented by the blockhouse system was that delegates from better-off areas were shocked to hear of the situation elsewhere, and hitherto unshakeable opinions were shaken. For the first time, the Natives emerged as a major factor. News of the Vryheid massacre made a profound impression and speaker after speaker reported that even Natives who were still helping them out with supplies were increasingly restive.

Next day the anguished debate continued. Submission was inevitable: it was palpable in the tattered clothes of many delegates, in the absence of Steyn who was too sick to appear publicly, in the vivid recollection of ruin from end to end of the country. Yet still men rose and gave voice to an emotion that would not recognize facts. 'As far as I am concerned,' Kemp declared, 'I will fight on till I die.' In vain some commandants urged that if they did not surrender, their burghers would instantly hand in their arms to the nearest British post, for other speakers were at hand to echo the cry of no surrender. The debate became so emotional that calm agreement seemed an impossibility. Then State Secretary Reitz proposed a compromise. Why not hand over the Rand to the British, and forfeit the Transvaal's nominal share in the government of Swaziland, and even let them have control of foreign relations, if they would leave them in peace to rule themselves? It was a practical idea which distracted emotions. The lawyers Hertzog and Smuts were deputed to draft it out. Meanwhile the debate continued in a calmer atmosphere and late that evening the three foremost generals were called for.

Botha summed up the case for submission. It seemed unanswerable. The blockhouses were an intolerable obstruction, food supplies were scarce, horses equally so and weak, and the women's sufferings acute, especially now that they were no longer being admitted to the concentration camps; there was hope neither of Cape rebellion nor foreign intervention; the burghers' abandonment of many areas meant that the enemy could concentrate in ever-increasing number on those still occupied; above all, they might never have another chance to save their language, customs and ideals.

One man, Koos de la Rey, the old lion of the west, had so far said nothing. He had the largest number of burghers; he could draw on plentiful supplies from Native kraals; he had bellicose lieutenants like Kemp. If anyone could go on fighting it was he—and he knew that his voice might be decisive. At last he spoke. In quiet grave tones he cast his vote for peace. It was not a question of fighting to the bitter end, he said: the bitter end had come. And the chance to negotiate might never recur.

The effect on most of his audience was profound. Yet it seemed merely to inflame De Wet. He declared that even the compromise proposal on which Smuts and Hertzog were working was unacceptable. Reason itself was unacceptable to one who saw the miseries of their people as the will of God—'He is minded by this war to form us into a nation worthy of the name. . . . This is a war of religion.'

His ringing words followed the delegates out into the night. Next morning Smuts and Hertzog produced their draft of the proposal to cede the Rand and Swaziland, give up foreign relations and embassies, and enter into a defensive alliance with Great Britain. It seemed a bargain that drew together hope and reality. The convention authorized a commission consisting of Botha, De la Rey and De Wet, together with the lawyers Smuts and Hertzog, to negotiate upon it with the British. But the commission were given an additional mandate of great significance, which was that if the British turned them down on this proposal they could negotiate on any other they thought fit.

On 19 May the scene moved back to Pretoria and Kitchener's house again. The Boer commission laid their new proposal before him and Milner at ten o'clock that morning.

It received short shrift. 'Grant it,' Kitchener said, 'and before a year is over we shall be at war again.' They wanted a definite answer to Chamberlain's insistence upon the Middelburg proposals, which was to say the surrender of independence. The commission, especially Smuts and Hertzog, bent their considerable powers of argument and legal disputation to trying to talk Kitchener and Milner round, but without success.

The meeting adjourned for lunch, and during the break Smuts had an informal talk with the British to open the way to negotiation on some other basis as authorized by the Vereeniging convention. As a result, Kitchener and Milner came to the resumed meeting with a draft document setting out a declaration of surrender by the Boers on terms to be detailed in an annexure. This blunt statement was too much for the commission whose entire energies were devoted to avoiding the dreaded word 'surrender'. Once again deadlock threatened, and with it a continuation of war. That risk Kitchener, who throughout showed himself a diplomatist of the highest order, knew could only be averted if everybody were kept round the council table. He suggested that the British and Boer lawyers should at any rate try to draft out together the terms of peace if surrender were by any chance agreed to.

For two days Milner and his legal adviser on the one side, and Smuts and Hertzog on the other, tussled with each other. Very little could be dragged from Milner. On 21 May the results were read out at a full meeting of the negotiators. A preamble declared that this was an agreement between the Governments of Great Britain, the O.F.S and the Transvaal. Though it went on to make clear that the Boers were in fact surrendering, cast in the form of a treaty it seemed to soften that harsh reality. Botha, with his keen practical sense, was mostly concerned with the financial clauses. The Middelburg proposals, now repeated, provided for total compensation of a million pounds for burghers whose property had been commandeered by their Governments for the war effort. The Boers wanted full payment because many of the promissory notes they had given their followers would otherwise be dishonoured. They proposed a figure of three million pounds and Kitchener was not disposed to argue on such a question when the war cost as much every fortnight. But Milner stood firm at the million already stipulated (and that against his wishes). Anything more should be given as a free gift at Britain's discretion, not on the principle of compensating the republics for having waged war against her. The issue perfectly illustrates how Milner's impeccable logic was vitiated by his lack of human understanding. If a million were agreed to, but were far from enough, the gesture savoured of haggling over money when lives were at stake. He complained to Chamberlain about the Boers' 'preposterous' terms and about Kitchener disagreeing with him even in front of them. But Chamberlain and the Cabinet sided with Kitchener on the point, substantially meeting the Boers' request.

The Boer commission were also greatly concerned by the fate intended for their rebel kinsmen, mainly in the Cape, though a few had come over from Natal. The Middelburg proposals had merely left the matter to the Governments of these two colonies. Milner did not wish to go further, and again Kitchener disagreed with him. Eventually a statement was issued by the Cape Government that rebels would be disfranchised for life (later reduced to five years) and though leaders would be court-martialled none would be executed.

Altogether nine days were spent in negotiation at Pretoria, the exchange of messages with London, and consultations among the Cabinet. The Boer commission, having done all they could, met Kitchener and Milner on 28 May to receive the final draft agreed to by the British Government. Milner said that it was absolutely final. The commission neither accepted nor rejected it. The question had to be decided by the convention at Vereeniging. Milner agreed that they should have until midnight on 31 May to obtain a definite answer, yes or no.

The document which the commission took away consisted essentially of the Middelburg proposals of over a year ago—a costly year for either side to have achieved so little from it, but one which has made itself felt in all the years since. There were ten articles:

1. The Boers to lay down arms and acknowledge the King as their lawful sovereign.
2. All prisoners and internees to be returned on making the same acknowledgement.
3. Burghers surrendering not to lose personal liberty or property.

4. No legal prosecution of burghers except for war crimes.

5. Dutch to be [a] taught in schools where parents so wished; [b] admitted in law courts.

6. Rifles to be permitted for personal protection.

7. Military administration to be followed by civil, and subsequently by self-government 'as soon as circumstances permit it.'

8. Question of Native franchise not to be decided before grant of self-government.

9. No war tax.

10. District commissions to be set up to assist resettlement, provide necessities lost in the war, and honour Republican bank or promissory notes; for this purposes a free gift of three million pounds to be provided by the U.K., also loans on liberal terms.

The undertaking to grant self-government, which was inevitable, is less significant than the provision about the Native franchise. After much anti-Boer propaganda on the Native question and repeated assertions that one of England's war aims was to safeguard the Natives' political future, her shelving of the matter is noteworthy. While it may be thought to invite doubts of her sincerity, it seemed at that juncture the only practical way of securing an immediate peaceful period of reconstruction which might give birth to a revised policy. A further point of interest is that in accepting the guerilla representatives as spokesmen of the Boers, the British were abandoning those surrendered Boers who had co-operated with them and whose political and social future at the hands of their countrymen would therefore be parlous. Here too a breach of faith has sometimes been alleged, which worried Milner more than Kitchener, but if the hopes of immediate peace were to have been fulfilled there seemed no practical alternative.

The future was to have its say on both these questions. But the first question was whether the convention at Vereeniging would agree to the surrender document in its final form. The commission returned on the evening of 28 May. Before the full convention assembled next morning the leaders met Steyn in his tent and showed him the document. He vehemently denounced it as a gross betrayal of the Boer cause. He denounced it utterly, resigned his office as President, and was taken away to a British hospital. When the terms were announced to the assembled convention they were received in complete silence. Then questions were asked. There was an atmosphere of waiting, of giving time an opportunity to let the fact of surrender seep into their minds. For two days men stood up to voice the old arguments, for and against. De Wet, now Steyn's successor as President of the O.F.S., remained inflexible. It was a question of faith in God, a sacred war, in which they still had ammunition enough to participate, still had hope that pro-Boer sentiment in England would prevail. He even suggested —the final word on alleged British brutality in the concentration camps —that women still at large should try to gain admission to the camps by taking along a proportion of the men with them. Schalk Burger retorted that it had been a war of miscalculation: 'We had confidence in our own weapons; we underestimated the enemy; the fighting spirit had seized upon our people; and the thought of victory had banished that of the possibility of defeat.'

The morning of 31 May came with a seemingly unbridgeable gulf between the two schools of opinion. By midnight they were bound to make a decision. A delegate moved rejection of the British terms; another moved their acceptance. At this critical point De Wet interposed.

That morning Botha and De la Rey had privately addressed a strong appeal to him to throw in his weight on the side of peace. Perhaps it was the one moment in that curious and contradictory life that the long view prevailed upon him. He changed his mind as suddenly as if at a nod from God and urged his followers to declare in favour of the British proposals. The day was finally won by production of a statement drawn up by Hertzog and Smuts. It read as follows:

> We, the national representatives of both the South African Republic and the Orange Free State, at the meeting held at Vereeniging from the 15th of May till the 31st of May, 1902, have with grief considered the proposal made by His Majety's Government in connexion with the conclusion of the existing hostilities, and their communication that this proposal had to be accepted, or rejected, unaltered. We are sorry that His Majesty's Government has absolutely declined to negotiate with the Government of the Republics on the basis of their independence,

or to allow our Government to enter into communication with our deputation in Europe. Our people, however, have always been under the impression that not only on the grounds of justice, but also taking into consideration the great material and personal sacrifices made for their independence, that they had a well-founded claim for that independence.

We have gravely considered the future of our country, and have specially observed the following facts:

Firstly, that the military policy pursued by the British military authorities has led to the general devastation of the territory of both Republics by the burning down of farms and towns, by the destruction of all means of existence, and by the exhausting of all resources required for the maintenance of our families, the existence of our armies, and the continuation of the war.

Secondly, that the placing of our families in the concentration camps has brought on an unheard-of condition of suffering and sickness, so that in a comparatively short time about twenty thousand of our beloved ones have died there, and that the horrid probability has arisen that, by continuing the war, our whole nation may die out in this way.

Thirdly, that the Kaffir tribes within and without the frontiers of the territory of the two Republics, are mostly armed and are taking part in the war against us, and through the committing of murders and all sorts of cruelties have caused an unbearable condition of affairs in many districts of both Republics. An instance of this happened not long ago in the district of Vryheid, where fifty-six burghers on one occasion were murdered and mutilated in a fearful manner.

Fourthly, that by the proclamations of the enemy the burghers still fighting are threatened with the loss of all their movable and landed property—and thus with utter ruin—which proclamations have already been enforced.

Fifthly, that it has already, through the circumstances of the war, become quite impossible for us to keep the many thousand prisoners of war taken by our forces, and that we have thus been unable to inflict much damage on the British forces (whereas the burghers who are taken prisoners by the British armies are sent out of the country), and that, after war has raged for nearly three years, there only remains an insignificant part of the fighting forces with which we began.

Sixthly, that this fighting remainder, which is only a small minority of our whole nation, has to fight against an overpowering force of the enemy, and besides is reduced to a condition of starvation, and is destitute of all necessaries, and that notwithstanding our utmost efforts, and the sacrifices of everything that is dear and precious to us, we cannot foresee an eventual Victory.

We are therefore of opinion that there is no justifiable ground for expecting that by continuing the war the nation will retain its independence, and that, under these circumstances, the nation is not justified in continuing the war, because this can only lead to social and material ruin, not for us alone, but also for our posterity. Compelled by the above-named circumstances and motives, we commission both Governments to accept the proposal of His Majesty's Government, and to sign it in the name of the people of both Republics.

We, the representative delegates, express our confidence that the present circumstances will, by our accepting the proposal of His Majesty's Government, be speedily ameliorated in such a way that our nation will be placed in a position to enjoy the privileges to which they think they have a just claim, on the ground not only of their past sacrifices, but also of those made in this war.

We have with great satisfaction taken note of the decision of His Majesty's Government to grant a large measure of amnesty to the British subjects who have taken up arms on our behalf, and to whom we are united by bonds of love and honour; and express our wish that it may please His Majesty to still further extend this amnesty.

This document is of course a piece of special pleading. It exaggerated, for example, the extent to which the Natives were armed and the extent of atrocities committed so far—which the Natives could with some justice claim to have been but a small return for those perpetrated against themselves. The reference to concentration camps may also be contrasted with De Wet's own suggestion that Boer women still outside the camps should force themselves into them. But stripped of protestations like these, which were made in the bitter hour of defeat and which were designed to make surrender more palatable to the commandos whom the delegates had left behind them in the field, it remains a fair summary of the case for surrender.

By a vote of fifty-four to six, the delegates agreed to the British terms.

In Pretoria that night, Saturday, 31 May 1902, nearly two years and eight months after the war began, the treaty was signed at fifty-five minutes short of midnight.

Kitchener shook hands with the Boer leaders. 'We are good friends now,' he said.

In England weeks of rumour and expectancy were rewarded by a streamer strung between the pillars of the Mansion House at six o'clock next evening: PEACE IS PROCLAIMED.* Although it was Sunday, crowds had lately been gathering on the off-chance of just such a moment and suddenly the capital leapt into festivity. Along thoroughfares made darker by the absence of weekday lighting of shops and theatres swarmed a multitude unknown since Mafeking Night, but they mafficked with rather more cause. And next day began the long Indian summer that ended in 1914.

There were some who did not receive the news with pleasure. Kipling's Aunt Georgie, widow of the painter Burne-Jones, hung a black banner from her window, with a notice: 'We have killed and taken possession.' An angry crowd was prevented from setting fire to her hedge by Kipling's energetic intervention. But she was in a minority. The majority would have echoed the sentiment of John Hay, U.S. Secretary of State, who wrote to Chamberlain: 'Great Britain has once more wrought a great work for the world—and she is too wise to complain of blindness and ingratitude. . . . I shall always be glad to remember—during what remains to me of life—that some of the men who did the work were my friends.'

In South Africa Kitchener joined the Boer leaders at Vereeniging and addressed the delegates. He said that no disgrace attached to a

---

* The Press had been excluded from the Vereeniging deliberations. Edgar Wallace, however, kept passing by train, having arranged with one of the soldiers guarding the camp to signal by a system of coloured handkerchiefs. When Wallace saw the man blow his nose with a white handkerchief he promptly cabled the *Mail*, 'Have bought you 1,000 Rand Collieries,' so dodging the censorship and getting the news to London even before the Government had it. But he was robbed of a world scoop by the fact that his paper did not come out on Sundays.

defeat inflicted by overwhelming forces. If he had been one of them he would have been proud to have done as well as they. He asked them now to co-operate in bringing about a reconciliation for, the welfare of their country. Botha and Schalk Burger then thanked the Transvaalers for their heroic sacrifices in the cause of freedom and urged them to give the new Government the same obedience as the old.

The delegates, and the leaders in particular, dispersed upon the bitter errand of breaking the news to their men that it was all over. Most accepted the announcement with resignation; others destroyed their rifles rather than add them to the heaps accumulated under British surveillance. With a few individual exceptions, who were deported, the commandos assented to the oath administered by British officers: 'I now call upon you formally to testify your allegiance to King Edward VII, his heirs and successors. Burghers! You here in the presence of our God acknowledge King Edward to be your liege Sovereign, and that you will henceforth maintain his authority throughout the land. So help you God.'

CHAPTER XXXI

Postscript

THE Boer War was fought because each half of the white community in the Transvaal wanted to dominate. Hostilities broke out upon expiry of a Boer ultimatum which narrowly preceded one already prepared by the British.

The Boers said the war was for liberty. The British said it was for equality. The majority of the inhabitants, who were not white at all, gained neither liberty nor equality.

The war was fought with great incompetence by either side. For a number of reasons unconnected with nationality this is inevitable in every war. Men have never yet devised a more wasteful method of settling their differences.

Both sides considered that the war would be over in three months. It lasted nearly ten times as long. The Chancellor of the Exchequer said it would cost ten million pounds. It cost more than twenty times as much. The War Office thought that 75,000 troops would be sufficient; the German General Staff reckoned 150,000. From first to last 450,000 were needed. The British lost 22,000 men, of whom two-thirds died not from bullets but germs. The Boer death-roll totalled 24,000 of whom 20,000 were women and children in camps far from the battle-field. The financial cost to the republics is as unknown as the fate of the legendary 'Kruger Millions' with which Oom Paul was reported to have fled.

These statistics mean little to the twentieth century, in which World War I alone gobbled up eight million soldiers' lives and cost Britain, who had ten million men engaged, £4,000 million. But they meant much to the nineteenth: the nation employed 750,000 troops, mostly foreign, in the Napoleonic Wars spread over twelve years; and 100,000, also including mercenaries, in the Crimea (cost, £75 million).

Who won the war? The Boers submitted to the sovereignty of the British Crown. But within half a century their descendants control, absolutely, not only their former two republics but the Cape, Natal and South-West Africa as well.

Of the two chief political protagonists who started the war, Paul Kruger died in exile on the shores of Lake Geneva in 1904, and Chamberlain not only failed to attain the Premiership when Salisbury resigned a few months after the end of the war, but following his own subsequent resignation over tariff reform never regained office.

Let us see what happened to some of the other leading characters in this story.

During July Kitchener returned to England on his way to become Commander-in-Chief in India. He was rewarded with a viscountcy and £50,000; but he had to be stopped from shipping off, for the stately home he planned, the statues of Boer dignitaries he had looted from public squares. He was one of the stars at Edward's coronation in August. By contrast, Buller was a very fallen star. Having resumed his Aldershot command, he had made a sensational speech in reply to public criticism of his conduct in South Africa. He said that his message to White telling him to surrender Ladysmith (see page 143) was intended to assist White by accepting responsibility if *White* wished to surrender. The idea of a general assisting a subordinate to surrender resulted in his dismissal.

Two notable soldiers ended their lives by suicide. Hector Macdonald, survivor of Majuba and Wauchope's successor at the head of the Highlanders, took his life in 1903 when faced with an inquiry into allegations of homosexuality. Kekewich, defender of Kimberley, shot himself when ill-health ended his military career in 1914. On the other hand his fellow siege commander Baden-Powell, having founded the Boy Scout movement in 1908, died replete with age and honours in 1941.

Milner stayed on to continue the task of reconstruction. He was helped by brilliant young men—the 'Milner Kindergarten'—whom he gathered around him: Geoffrey Dawson, future editor of *The Times*; John Buchan, novelist and future Governor-General of Canada; Philip Kerr, British Ambassador to the U.S.A. in World War I; Patrick Duncan, future Governor-General of South Africa; F. B. Smith, agricultural expert who became a Nobel Prizewinner; and R. H. Brand, economist. But his work was cut short when he quit after finally quarrelling with Chamberlain over the old question of suspending the Cape constitution. The great achievements of British colonial administrators all over the world have usually stemmed from their love of the country and people they administered. When Milner wrote from South Africa, 'I have always been unfortunate in disliking my life and surroundings here,' he laid bare a fundamental disqualification for his job.

Regarded by the Boers as the quintessence of an Englishman, he was far from that. As Santayana says, 'English genius is anti-professional; its affinities are with amateurs.' Milner was supremely professional. But upon him lay a blight not rare among brilliant men of his kind, that what he toiled to achieve he was fated to destroy. He went to South Africa to keep the peace and war resulted; when it was over, his determined efforts to anglicize South Africa strengthened Afrikaner nationalism; and in the end by importing Chinese labour for the mines to help finance reconstruction he unwittingly helped bring down the Government with which his ambitions were bound up.

For the outcry in England against 'slave labour' turned post-war revulsion against the Unionist-Conservatives into a landslide at the election of 1906. Up to this time political observers everywhere had been astonished that England had continued to be governed by a land-owning oligarchy despite the creation of a popular democracy. The 1906 election marked the beginning of the profound change our century has witnessed. Many of the reasons may be traced to the Boer War. For one thing, the war had severely shaken people's confidence in the ruling caste, especially as represented by its military officers. Ironically it was Rudyard Kipling who led the shake-up.

The minstrel of the Boer War has left in his lays a remarkable evocation of the conflict, but it is worth looking a little beyond this to his underlying adoration of action, of men of action. He moved of course in a man's world, where the Pall Mall club was a national symbol and women's plea for the vote a national joke. Too vague to be termed a cult there was yet, in the air, a reverence for 'mannishness', making acceptable between men a relationship in which emotion, as opposed simply to mental affinity or admiration, often ran deep. Towards the end of his life Kipling was discussing with Hugh Walpole the banning of *Well of Loneliness* and remarked, in Walpole's précis, that there was 'too much of the abnormal in all of us to play about with it. Hates opening up reserves. All the same he'd had friends once and again he'd done more for than any woman.' The subject makes Walpole an unreliable witness, but in any event a fine discretion is needed to interpret this remark by one, himself a husband and father, talking of a period which saw the trial of Oscar Wilde and the partnership in celibacy of Rhodes and Jameson, the worship of virtue and the monasticism of Kitchener. No interpretation is necessary here, but on some aspects of the mystique of mannishness in vogue and of its influence upon history judgement is easier.

The vogue was not wholly a perpetuation of public schoolboy values, since the ideal was a sensitive masculinity midway between the effeminate and the 'muddied oaf at the goals'. A man of action who needed something more than brawn to reach 'beyond the skyline where the strange roads go down' was such a mean. The quotation is from Kipling, expressing the yearning of a generation whose restlessness has been mentioned earlier in this book and was one of the mainsprings of imperialism. Mannishness and imperialism were therefore beats of the same pulse. Their personification was Cecil Rhodes. Kipling was drawn irresistibly to him and, after he had written his epitaph in praise of him who had 'bred cities in place of speech,' to Jameson, model and inspiration of *If——*.

An ascendant England, proud and powerful, became more than ever in his eyes the object for which every Englishman should strive, but the ruling caste which was most readily prepared to follow that particular imperialist vision was barred from doing so by the 1906 election, and he was partly the unwitting cause by his wartime thrusts at British stupidity (contrasted with colonial shrewdness) and his postwar attack on 'flannelled fools at the wicket'. He called on England to learn the lesson of the war; if she did, it was not in the way he expected.

At a crucial moment in the peace negotiations at Pretoria Kitchener privately told Smuts that in his opinion a Liberal Ministry would rule in two years and grant the Transvaal self-government. It had seemed against all the odds, but he was not far wrong.

The new Prime Minister, Campbell-Bannerman, duly granted self-government. Though some British saw this as a foolhardy trust in Afrikaner avowals of loyalty, most have always regarded it as an unprecedented act of magnanimity towards a defeated foe. And it was so regarded by most Afrikaners; but another and unexpressed view was to prove more potent in the long run, that a robber who returns your property after knocking you down to grab it may be a penitent but scarcely a benefactor. At the time, however, the great majority on both sides believed that Campbell-Bannerman's grant placed an eternal seal upon their brotherhood.

With this conviction Louis Botha, who along with other leading Boer generals had been rapturously welcomed by London crowds after the war, became the first Prime Minister of the Transvaal and, in 1910, of the Union of South Africa. Bringing together the Cape, O.F.S., Transvaal and Natal in fulfilment of Rhodes's dream was the work of many hands, including that of Dr. Jameson, turned by a remarkable metamorphosis of fortune into Prime Minister of the Cape. Another hand was ex-President Steyn's.

Confident expectations of a united Anglo-Afrikaner nation building a great new country soon began to quiver as General Hertzog led an assertion of Afrikaner nationalism, incorrigibly suspicious of the 'Imperial factor' championed by local Jingoism. In World War I Botha carried the majority in declaring for Britain and taking the field against Germany's African colonies. But he and Smuts had also the anguish of putting down an armed rebellion by De Wet, Beyers, Kemp, Maritz and other Boer War leaders. De la Rey, muddled in his old age, might possibly have sided with the rebels, but before he showed his hand either way he was accidentally shot dead.

That war, in which Lloyd George became England's Prime Minister and headed a Cabinet that included Milner, brought many names back in the news. Though singular in foreseeing the magnitude of the struggle, Kitchener was an unhappy Secretary for War until he drowned at sea, the one element able to extinguish that molten spirit. French led the Old Contemptibles into France. The British had learnt from the Boer War the value of accurate rifle-fire and of taking cover. The Germans had learnt less well, regarded taking cover as degenerate, and had to bring up five times as many men as the British to hold them. But the lesson of Magersfontein, that barbed wire and trenches too long to be outflanked must force a stalemate, went unlearnt by both, so that until the advent of the tank the only solution attempted was the sacrifice of millions of lives. French was succeeded by Douglas Haig, whose record in the guerilla war had been uninspiring. Lesser lights shone brighter: William Robertson and Henry Wilson, successive

Chiefs of the Imperial General Staff; and Smith-Dorrien, Viscount Byng of Vimy, A. Hunter-Weston and Hubert Gough, among the senior commanders in France, were all schooled by the Boer War. Ian Hamilton was land commander in Churchill's ill-fated Gallipoli adventure, while Allenby gained a rather more secure claim to fame as the conqueror of Palestine (and incidentally as the commander in S.A. of a young officer who died in 1912 on Scott's last expedition to the Antarctic—that 'very gallant gentleman', Captain Oates).

Just before the Dublin Rising of Easter 1916 a German submarine put ashore on the Irish coast three British subjects who included Roger Casement. As his scheme to land an expedition to cut the Delagoa Bay railway in 1900 had failed, so now his efforts for Irish independence came to nothing. He was taken to the Tower, arraigned for high treason, and hanged (despite a vigorous campaign for his reprieve led by the U.S. Congress, Bernard Shaw, Conan Doyle and others) for attempting to suborn Irish P.O.W.s in Germany. It was an idea which was the ironic echo of his own indignant report to the Foreign Office, while he was serving it in S.A., that the Boers were trying to induce Irish P.O.W.s 'loyal to their Queen to be false to their own allegiance, and to be false to themselves'.[50]

In the year war broke out Joseph Chamberlain died. Roberts survived him by not many months. Botha followed soon after the war, but Jan Smuts, man of grey steel who had been his right-hand man and cried out at the grave-side, 'He was the cleanest, sweetest soul of all the land —of all my days,' was to live on until after World War II. He narrowly survived General Hertzog with whom he had alternated in the South African premiership during the years between.

Except for the diurnal Churchill they are all gone now, those famous names woven into this story—from Gandhi to Kipling, and the little boy who lost his bugle in the Tugela. A street here, an old second-hand book there, and vague memories are sometimes kindled by a name; but a generation grew up more personally tied to the past, as a young lady in the twenties, Victoria Pretoria Mafeking May, protested. Her embarrassment is immortalized by a once popular music-hall chorus concerning the Blobbs's infant:

> The baby's name is Kitchener Carrington
> Methuen Kekewich White

POSTSCRIPT

Cronje Plumer Powell Majuba
Gatacre Warren Colenso Kruger
Capetown Mafeking French
Kimberley Ladysmith Bobs
Union Jack Fighting Mac
Lyddite Pretoria BLOBBS.

*   *   *   *

For a decade Afrikaner nationalism has ruled South Africa with little challenge, drawing its strength from the desire for race-preservation. The ultimate victor of the Boer War would therefore seem to be Krugerism. But Africa is astir with a contrary idea, as impassioned as Kruger's, and the real struggle still lies ahead unless averted by majestic statesmanship.

No great nation can advance down the long corridor of history without sometimes opening a wrong door, and Britain has much about the Boer War to regret. But much was gained. The reforms it initiated spared her the disastrous consequences of entering World War I equipped with a Crimea mentality. The Boer War saved the British Empire—a paradoxical accomplishment by the rugged warriors of the veld. But perhaps more important it saved England from herself. It substantially put an end to old-style imperialism, not only opening up the twentieth-century prospect of Commonwealth partnership instead of anyone's 'paramountcy', but enabling mankind at large to look to her still as a champion of liberty, even now that the Pax Britannica has been replaced by the Pax Atomica.

GLOSSARY

of Dutch/Afrikaans words and abbreviations

Bywoner	squatter, white farm labourer.
C.I.V.	City Imperial Volunteers.
Dorp	town, village.
I.L.H.	Imperial Light Horse.
I.L.I.	Imperial Light Infantry.
Kraal	Native settlement or stock enclosure.
Laager	encampment.
Landdrost	magistrate.
M.I.	Mounted Infantry.
Nek	mountain pass or break in hills.
R.A.	Royal Artillery.
S.A.C.	South African Constabulary.
S.A.L.H.	S.A. Light Horse.
Spruit	stream, rivulet.
Veld	the earth, countryside.
Vrou	wife, woman.
Zarps	Transvaal Republican police.

BIBLIOGRAPHY AND NOTES

1. J. L. Garvin (Vols. I–III) and Julian Amery: *The Life of Joseph Chamberlain*.
2. R. H. Gretton, *A Modern History of the English People*, 1880–1922.
3. Mrs. Earb, *The Well-dressed Woman*.
4. Emma Drake, *What a Young Wife Ought to Know*.
5. J. D. Unwin, *Hopousia*.
6. Bernard Shaw, Preface to *Man and Superman*.
7. H. G. Wells, *The New Machiavelli*.
8. Winston Churchill, *The River War*.
9. Eric A. Walker, *A History of South Africa*.
10. *Die Grosse Politik*, Vol. XI, p. 12.
11. J. C. Smuts, *Jan Christian Smuts*.
12. *Hansard*, 8 May 1896. Fourth Series, Vol. XI, cols. 914–5.
13. Dean Church, quoted by Garvin, op. cit. III, 144.
14. H. J. Batts, *Pretoria from Within*.
15. Milner to Chamberlain, 6 Sept. 1902.
16. H. Belloc, *The Jews*.
17. L. S. Amery (ed.), *The Times History of The War in South Africa*. Vols. I–V.
18. 'The Old Issue'.
19. Evelyn Wood, *From Midshipman to Field-Marshal*.
20. H. Begbie, *The Story of Baden-Powell*.
21. Anon: quoted from *The Times History*.
22. Ian Hamilton, Introduction to *War Songs*, selected by C. Stone.
23. Julian Ralph, *Towards Pretoria*.
24. Central News correspondent, Kinnear.
25. Sir A. Conan Doyle, *The Great Boer War*.
26. David James, *Lord Roberts*.
27. Beatrice Webb, *Our Partnership*.
28. *Natal Advertiser*.
29. Deneys Reitz, *Commando*.
30. J. B. Atkins in the *Manchester Guardian*.
31. Garvin, op. cit. (Chamberlain Papers).

32. Beatrice Webb, op. cit. pp. 143, 191.
33. *Hansard*, 5 Feb. 1900. Fourth Series, Vol. LXVIII, cols. 609–24.
34. H. Smith-Dorrien, *Memories of Forty-Eight Years' Service*.
35. To the author, at the site of the battle, December 1957.
36. Philip Magnus, *Kitchener*.
37. Anon: quoted by Batts, op. cit.
38. O. von Lossberg, *Mit Santa Barbara in Sudafrika*.
39. A. G. Hales, *Campaign Pictures of the War in South Africa*.
40. C. R. de Wet, *Three Years' War*.
41. R. Kipling, 'Boots'.
42. Winston Churchill, *Ian Hamilton's March*.
43. Stuart in the *Morning Post*.
44. Frank Owen, *Tempestuous Journey*.
45. Gen. Lord Rawlinson; quoted by his biographer F. Maurice.
46. Quoted by H. W. Wilson, *With the Flag to Pretoria*.
47. H. W. Wilson, op. cit.
48. *Hansard*, 20 March 1902. Fourth Series, Vol. CV. cols. 577–95.
49. Hesketh Pearson, *Bernard Shaw*.
50. René Maccoll, *Roger Casement*.

*　　*　　*　　*

In addition to the authorities listed above, others mentioned in the text, newspapers of the period including siege and P.O.W. journals, encyclopaedias and the like, I have been assisted by the following works:

H. C. Armstrong, *Grey Steel; J. C. Smuts*.
C. Carrington, *Rudyard Kipling*.
Ian Colvin, *A Life of Jameson*.
Duff Cooper, *Haig*.
Virginia Cowles, *Winston Churchill*.
Mrs. De la Rey, *A Woman's Wanderings in the Boer War*.
Charles Eade (ed.), *Churchill by his Contemporaries*.
D. L. Hobman, *Olive Schreiner*.
Holbrook Jackson, *The Eighteen Nineties*.
S. J. P. Kruger, *The Memoirs of Paul Kruger*.
Gordon Le Soeur, *Cecil Rhodes*.
E. W. Lloyd and A. G. Hadcock, *Artillery*.

S. G. Millin, *The South Africans*

—— *Rhodes*

—— *General Smuts*

André Maurois, *A History of England.*

R. J. Mitchell and M. D. R. Leys, *A History of the English People.*

Charles Petrie, *Joseph Chamberlain.*

Mrs. Lionel Phillips, *South African Recollections.*

Harold Scott, *English Song Book.*

G. M. Theal, *South Africa.*

G. M. Trevelyan, *History of England.*

—— *English Social History.*

'Vindex', *Cecil Rhodes; His Political Life and Speeches.*

Basil Williams, *Cecil Rhodes.*

INDEX

(N.B. The following contractions are used: Cape for Cape Province, O.F.S. for Orange Free State, and Tr. for Transvaal)

74–5; and the Battle of Ladysmith, 89–90, 93, 95; besieges Ladysmith, 103–5; illness, 119; suggests peace settlement, 156, 211; and the attack on Ladysmith, 173, 174, 178; and Spion Kop, 188; instruction to Kimberley besiegers regarding Kronje, 241–2 urges Botha to stand at Hlangwane heights, 252–3; recalls Lukas Meyer, 255; orders Ladysmith siege lines to be abandoned, 257; illness, 262; death of, 272–3

Kaffir Wars, 154
Kaiser. *See* Wilhelm II
Karee Siding (O.F.S.): De la Rey's force attacked at, 274; seized by Roberts, 282; Roberts takes command of his column at, 287–8
Kekewich, Colonel R. G., 480–1; character and career, 71; prepares defence of Kimberley, 71–2; besieged in Kimberley, 100, 103, 115, 166; strained relations with Rhodes, 126, 220; clash with De la Rey on the Rustenburg–Zeerust road, 451–452; joins Methuen, 453; supports Hamilton in repelling Kemp's charge, 489–90; commits suicide, 508
Kell-Kenny, General T., 232, 239, 319
Kemp, Lt., 381, 480; leads successful raids in western Transvaal, 433, 436; escapes Kitchener's drive, and attacks Methuen, 442; hunts for Kekewich, 451; cuts down part of Methuen's force, 453; leads De la Rey's force, 487–8; his charge repelled by Hamilton, 489–90; attends Vereeniging convention, 497; in armed rebellion, 511
Kerr, Philip, 508
Khartoum, death of Gordon at, 8
Kimberley (Cape): in danger of attack, 70–2; siege of, 100–3, 126, 220: defences consolidated, 102; relief of, 226–7; escape of the besiegers, 230
Kimberley Relief Force, 101
Kingsley, Mary, 295*n.*
Kipling, Rudyard, 21–2, 39, 41*n.*, 53, 55, 148, 213, 273, 280, 371, 505, 509–10, 512; visits Bloemfontein, 275
Kissieburg pass (Cape), Gatacre ambushed in, 122–5
Kitchener, Lord, 8, 224, 247, 251, 296, 319, 326, 374, 376, 389, 445; victories in the Sudan, 40–1; Chief of Staff to Roberts, 147; career and character, 214–16; in charge of transport arrangements, 217; leaves Cape Town with Roberts, 219; and the pursuit of Cronje's convoy,

231–2; takes command at Paardeberg, 232, 234–9; organizes railway and bridge repairs, 243; deals with rebellion in western Cape, 270; in march to Pretoria, 288, 315; restores communications in the south, 321, 325; directs hunt for De Wet, 351–3; sets off to relieve Brakfontein, 354; becomes Commander in S. Africa, 373, 385; his problems, 386; appeals for 30,000 mounted troops, 387; his tightening-up measures, 387–8; and unconditional surrender, 389–90; and the Burgher Peace Committee, 390; continues farm-burning, 390–1; sets up concentration camps, 391, 392, 424; hopes of capturing De Wet, 393; and the invasion of the Cape, 394; organizes the Great De Wet Hunt, 401–3; his offensive in eastern Transvaal, 405; confers with Botha at Middelburg, 408–9; disappointment over peace proposals, 413; launches offensive on unsurveyed area of Transvaal, 415–18; attempts to round up guerillas in Lichtenburg, Ventersburg and Klerksdorp area, 418; his mounted requirements met, 419–20; and Boer use of British uniforms, 426; his war organization, 426–30; suggests reduction of forces, 430; refuses Transvaal Government's armistice request, 431; launches drive against Transvaal and O.F.S., 433; fresh drive in eastern Transvaal, 435; and Gen. Beatson's trouble with the Australians, 435; launches great drive in O.F.S., 437–8; threatens severity towards Boers, 438–9, 443; his mobile columns, 440–1; extends blockhouses, 441; attempts to capture Kemp, 442; conspiracy against his life, 454; on poor quality of reinforcements, 455; criticized by Churchill and Milner, 457; offers to resign, 457; extends protective zone round Jo'burg, 460; humanizes the concentration camps, 462; his single-column raid against Botha, 463, 465–6; multi-column drive against De Wet, 466–9; his 'new model drive' to capture De Wet, 470–5; and De la Rey, 476, 480; collapses on news of Tweebosch disaster, 438; sends official Anglo-Dutch correspondence to Transvaal Government, 484–5; final effort to round up De la Rey, 486; discusses peace with Boer leaders, 488, 492–4, 498–505; signs peace treaty, and addresses Vereeniging convention, 505–6; becomes Commander-in-Chief, India, 508; forecasts self-